WITHDRAWN
HILLSBORO PUBLIC LIBRARIES
Hillsboro, OR
Member of Washington County
COOPERATIVE LIBRARY SERVICES

All the Odes

Translators

ANGEL FLORES

EDWARD HIRSCH

JANE HIRSHFIELD

KEN KRABBENHOFT

PHILIP LEVINE

CARLOS LOZANO

W. S. MERWIN

STEPHEN MITCHELL

PAUL MULDOON

MARGARET SAYERS PEDEN

RICHARD SCHAAF

GEORGE D. SCHADE

JACK SCHMITT

ILAN STAVANS

MARK STRAND

NATHANIEL TARN

DONALD D. WALSH

WILLIAM CARLOS WILLIAMS

Pablo

NERUDA

All the Odes

Edited by Ilan Stavans

5254 0778
10/13

Farrar Straus Giroux

New York

HILLSBORO PUBLIC LIBRARIES
Hillsboro, OR
Member of Washington County
COOPERATIVE LIBRARY SERVICES

Farrar, Straus and Giroux
18 West 18th Street, New York 10011

Copyright © 2013 by Pablo Neruda and Fundación Pablo Neruda
Introduction copyright © 2013 by Ilan Stavans
All rights reserved
Printed in the United States of America
First edition, 2013

This work contains poems from the following original volumes by Pablo Neruda: *Residencia en la tierra* (1933), *Tercera residencia* (1947), *Canto general* (1950), *Los versos del Capitán* (1952), *Odas elementales* (1954), *Nuevas odas elementales* (1956), *Tercer libro de las odas* (1957), *Navegaciones y regresos* (1959), *Plenos poderes* (1962).

Owing to limitations of space, all acknowledgments for permission to reprint previously published material can be found on pages 859–861.

Library of Congress Cataloging-in-Publication Data
Neruda, Pablo, 1904–1973.
[Poems. English & Spanish. Selections]
All the odes / Pablo Neruda ; edited by Ilan Stavans. — 1st ed., A bilingual ed.
p. cm.
Includes index.
Text in English and Spanish.
ISBN 978-0-374-11528-9 (hardback)
1. Neruda, Pablo, 1904–1973—Translations into English. I. Stavans, Ilan. II. Title.

PQ8097.N4 A2 2013
861'.64—dc23

2013009146

52540778

Designed by Quemadura

10/13

Farrar, Straus and Giroux books may be purchased for educational, business, or promotional use. For information on bulk purchases, please contact the Macmillan Corporate and Premium Sales Department at 1-800-221-7945, extension 5442, or write to specialmarkets@macmillan.com.

www.fsgbooks.com
www.twitter.com/fsgbooks
www.facebook.com/fsgbooks

1 3 5 7 9 10 8 6 4 2

Whence Nature all creates, and multiplies
And fosters all, and whither she resolves
Each in the end when each is overthrown.
This ultimate stock we have devised to name
Procreant atoms, matter, seeds of things,
Or primal bodies, as primal to the world.

—LUCRETIUS,
De rerum natura
(translated by
William Ellery Leonard)

Contents

Introduction: Poetry and Simplicity

Pablo Neruda wrote a total of 225 odes. The number stands as a pledge of alliance with a lyrical form he adored. He was also fond of other poetic forms (the sonnet, for instance), but as a practitioner of *verso libre*, unrhymed poetry, the ode was unquestionably the closest to his heart. He discovered it in his youth, becoming hypnotized by its fresh, elastic, invigorating freedom. His early readings of Horace, Pindar, Ovid, and Catullus left a deep impression on him. And he admired the way Romantics such as John Keats not only addressed universal themes in their odes but humanized those themes by turning them—Love and Psyche, for instance—into interlocutors. Neruda's odes are his direct, uncensored dialogues with nature. And they are politically charged.

The classical ode was designed to be sung to music, often the lyre. Depending on the poet, it had three sections (in Pindar's case), or four (in Horace's case). The English odes produced not only by Keats but also by Dryden, Coleridge, and Shelley streamlined the structure, making it less formal. Neruda took that simplicity even further. He democratized the ode by using it to celebrate the mundane. His topics are a veritable catalogue of the quotidian: a chair, an onion, a pair of shoes, a train station, the dictionary, a village theater, a lover's hands . . . In other words, he championed the significance of insignificance.

"In my work," he stated in *Confieso que he vivido* (*Memoirs*), published in 1974, the year after his death at the age of sixty-nine, "I have tried to prove that the poet can write about any given subject, about something needed by a community as a whole." He added: "Almost all the great works of antiquity were done strictly on request. The *Georgics* are propaganda for the farming of the Roman countryside. A poet can write for a university or a labor union, for skilled workers and professionals. Freedom was never lost simply because of this. Magical inspiration and the poet's communication with God are inventions dictated by self-interest. At the moments of greatest creative intensity, the product can be partially someone else's, influenced by readings and external pressures."

While Neruda's early odes appeared in *Residencia en la tierra* (*Residence on Earth*), a volume he composed, and kept adding to, between 1925 and 1945 (it was published in 1947), it was only as he approached fifty that he devoted a most generous amount of energy to writing odes, and it is in this period that the vast majority were crafted. At the beginning of 1952, already an international figure, his Communist sympathies widely known, he became persona non grata in certain parts of Europe. In Italy, where he found himself at midyear, the government wanted him expelled. An Italian millionaire offered Neruda his home on the island of Capri, where the Chilean and his then lover, Matilde Urrutia, who would become his third wife, were able to take refuge while the political quagmire was sorted out. (The film *Il postino* takes place during this period.)

The time on Capri, Neruda wrote later, "was fruitful, amorous, and perfumed by the sweetness of the Mediterranean." In his poem "El hombre invisible" (The Invisible Man), which he eventually used as the introduction to his yet-to-be-written *Odas elementales* (Elemental Odes, 1954), the first of three major collections of odes, he rejected his past as a writer by announcing that a new poetic identity had been granted to him. He describes himself as being endowed with a type of cosmic knowledge that becomes a responsibility. He is now a conduit for people's suffering. That suffering is transformed into passionate words. Paying tribute to his predecessors, the Pindars and Ovids of antiquity, he profiles himself as a link between life as we see it on the surface and the undercurrent pathos only he is allowed to grasp. "Give me the sorrow / of the entire world," Neruda writes, and "I will turn it into hope." Symmetrically, in "La casa de las odas" (The House of Odes), serving as the prologue to *Nuevas odas elementales* (New Elemental Odes, 1956), a return of sorts to *Odas elementales*, or perhaps a continuation, he emphasizes: "I know what I am / and where my song goes."

He and Matilde Urrutia returned to Chile from Europe by boat. Their journey was via Uruguay. The political conditions were precarious and they ended up in Argentina for a while before returning to his homeland. In Chile they lived in Isla Negra, his house on the Pacific coast, not far from Valparaíso and Viña del Mar. Neruda's politics weren't the only challenge he faced, though. He was in the midst of domestic upheaval as well. His second wife, Delia del Carril, lived in one of his houses in Santiago, La Michoacana, on Avenida Lynch in the neighborhood Los Guindos, while Matilde was in La Chascona, which was still under construction at the bottom of the hill known as San Cristóbal.

The house in Isla Negra was an oasis where he and Matilde were able to connect. It was there that Neruda explored through simple, unadorned odes his lifelong passions: aside from love, nature in all its magisterial splendor. In the odes, he repeatedly sang to water, flowers, birds, and the inhabitants of the surrounding area. The primary motifs of this cycle of poems are the inevitability of being, the urgency of language to capture events that are elusive by definition, and the arbitrariness of fate.

Neruda had just gone through a period of extraordinary productivity. After his bestselling, intimate *Veinte poemas de amor y una canción desesperada* (Twenty Love Poems and a Song of Despair, 1924), which he wrote in his late teens, he produced the epic *Canto general* (1950), an astonishing attempt, written between 1938 and 1949, to recount everything meaningful about Latin America, its history, its religious fervor, its treacherous ideological dreams, its scrumptious cuisine, its struggle for self-recognition, in an omniscient poetry that illuminated everything it touched. Neruda then returned to the personal mode in *Los versos del capitán* (The Captain's Verses, 1952), with its songs about mature relationships. The odes were therefore a reinvention of his poetic drive. In that sense Neruda was eager to reinvent himself: he sought a strategy to survey simultaneously through words the inner and outer, the domestic and public realms.

A change of guard was taking place in the Chilean government at the time. Out was the right-winger Gabriel González Videla, who started his career by aligning himself with the left, even with Neruda, yet soon betrayed those allies he had carefully nurtured. What the poet might have disliked the most was the politician's convoluted language. In came the populist Carlos Ibáñez del Campo. Neruda was full of hope. In his eyes, the age of political treason was over in his country. He rejoiced by endorsing what was an intrinsically democratic form. He was convinced that in his hands the ode would demonstrate the poet's desire to belong to the people. That is because as a poetic form the ode, in Neruda's definition, needed to be accessible in order to be truthful, and vice versa. He was allergic to snobbery. He wanted the odes to be simple yet not simplistic, an antidote to the corrupt, obfuscated lexicon of González Videla's rhetorical treason. Neruda made an agreement with the Venezuelan newspaper *El Nacional*, under the editorship of his friend Miguel Otero Silva, to publish an ode a week. The pace promised to be grueling, but he was prepared. He endorsed the agreement on one condition: that his odes appear not in the Arts and Letters section but in the section chronicling the daily news. When time came to collect them in a volume, Neruda chose an alphabetical order. *Odas elementales* was published in Buenos Aires, the same place all his other collections of odes were released. He followed *Nuevas odas elementales* with two more collections, *Tercer libro de las odas* (Third Book of Odes, 1957) and *Navegaciones y regresos* (Voyages and Homecomings, 1959). But he wasn't altogether finished. He composed a couple more odes, sprinkling *Plenos poderos* (Fully Empowered, 1962) with them. A decade later, in 1972, Neruda published, also in Buenos Aires, the *Libro de las odas* (Book of Odes), in which he gathered many of his odes, though not all.

Needless to say, amid such abundant production (the arc of his career is made of approximately 2,500 poems), it isn't strange that not all are of uniform quality. At his best, as in "Oda al otoño" (Ode to Autumn), "Oda a los calcetines" (Ode to a Pair of Socks), and "Oda a su aroma" (Ode to Her Scent), Neruda uses a loose, jazzy rhythm to describe, often in ecstatic ways, the power of an apparently uninteresting item. In his stanzas, he portrays himself as a troubadour in a state of constant communion with nature, a mystic in love with all things in his environment, seeking to articulate that love and often realizing that words alone are fatuous, inadequate, limited.

He perceives himself as an alchemist making lists, chaotic lists, lists filled with repetition, nonsequential lists, an engineer exploring the workings of the world, not only for his own sake but for the sake of the rest of us, in particular the peoples of Latin America, the continent he championed and sought to represent throughout his life, while encouraging it to find courage, to define a vision for its future. As much a poet as he was a prophet, Neruda conceived his most dazzling odes as hymns to our humanity. Curiously, his *ars poetica* might be said to have been included in a political speech known as "Yo acuso" (I Accuse), which he delivered to Chile's Senate on January 6, 1948: "Here I am. I promised to be loyal to your life of pain. I promised to defend you with my intellect and with my life if that was necessary. Tell me if I have fulfilled my promise, and either condemn me, or grant me the only mandate I need in order to live with honor—that of your confidence, of your hope, of your love."

Neruda also produced odes that seem underdeveloped, mere stylistic exercises, even sheer propaganda. Indeed, a handful have a pamphleteering quality to them. Some were written for ceremonial occasions, yet this doesn't redeem them from their pamphleteering tone. Others were shaped as visitations with an idol and, honestly, Neruda's ideological idols often left much to be desired. The "Oda a Lenin" (Ode to Lenin) not only feels flat but is repulsive in its submissive political fervor ("Thank you, Lenin, / for the air and the bread and the hope"). The same might be said about the overly long ode to Leningrad. The "Oda a un millonario muerto" (Ode to the Dead Millionaire) is a crude, ridiculous, cartoonlike depiction of wealth, just as the "Oda a un tren en China" (Ode to a Train in China) is kitsch plain and simple. These poems aren't built to move but to tilt persuasions. Of course, we read these odes today with the hindsight of how twentieth-century history frequently turned itself on its head: a figure at one point considered heroic was seen a short while later for his true worth. The truth is, time hasn't been generous to Neruda's political loyalties. While his deep sympathies are venerable, he also sympathized with governments (the USSR, Cuba, etc.) that in the best case curtailed individual freedom and in the worst engaged in systematic killings of its own citizens and neighbors. (In 1953, Neruda was awarded the Stalin Peace Prize.) In short, just as Neruda reaches inspired heights in the Keats-like "Oda al picaflor" (Ode to the Hummingbird) and, with similar plentitude, in the partially self-referential "Oda a Juan Tarrea" (Ode to Juan Tarrea), recalling Catullus, or in the superb "Oda al diccionario" (Ode to the Dictionary), in other places he stumbles, at times miserably, making the reader feel he writes on automatic pilot. One such example is "Oda a la claridad" (Ode to Clarity), which is anything but clear.

Neruda's complete odes have never appeared in a single book in Spanish, not to say any other language. The first English translations of the earlier ones date back to 1946. The poet's enormous popularity—he is, arguably, the all-time bestselling foreign-language poet in the United States—explains why a handful of the odes ("Oda a la sandía" [Ode to the Watermelon], for instance) are available in half a dozen renditions. Yet scores of others—close to seventy—have remained untranslated until now. In this volume I have followed Neruda's request to arrange the odes in alphabetical order, in this case by their English titles. The back matter includes a critical apparatus with basic information about each of the poems along with appropriate historical, literary, or biographical facts, as well as an alphabetical index of Spanish titles.

Eighteen translators are at work here. In the case of a bountiful poet like Neruda, this variety is a welcome approach, encouraging a multiplicity of readings. Not unexpectedly, translation strategies vary dramatically from one translator to another. Some believe the purpose is to create an entirely new poem in the target language while others, myself included, seek a balance between accuracy and creativity. In other words, a translation might not be literal but should unquestionably be loyal. I, for one, am a purist in this regard. It isn't the duty of the translator to improve on the original. Translators often rely on each other, as it should be. If and when available, previous translations may help to enlighten a line, or even to find *le mot juste*. I'm a conservative when it comes to syntax. This means that even changes in punctuation should be implemented only when strictly necessary.

Fortunately, having the Spanish and English face-to-face is like being handcuffed. This double vision makes the reader a witness to the translator's every false step, every subterfuge, every reinvention. It is also an invitation to understand how translation is born, making every reader a critic as well as a co-conspirator. The experience is thrilling because in the odes Neruda's Spanish is uninhibitedly plastic. While playing almost allegorically with a handful of key terms (sea, night, yellow), he orchestrates a syntactic rhythm, along with emblematic twists ("the soft softness of chairs," for instance), that insinuates a certain awkwardness, yet this awkwardness is enormously satisfying. Rendering the odes into English shouldn't deprive them of their awkwardness. The translator must find a way to make the awkwardness travel across languages.

One more word about Neruda's plasticity. Simultaneously luscious and lustrous, the odes are a treat to the senses, invoking a wide assortment of smells, tastes, and images. But they normally resist a coherent, linear narrative. Instead, they feel as if the poet were slowly editing a dreamlike, surrealistic movie about a world in constant chaos. If forced to explain how they work, I would say that Neruda's odes are like a beatnik's stream of consciousness, which explains the ardent devotion he constantly awakens among young people. The majority are made up of only a handful of sentences, cut into smaller parts by a melodious, idiosyncratic use of colons and commas. The poet keeps almost completely away from other types of punctuation. Only on rare occasion does a question mark show up and even less frequently an exclamation point.

In short, Neruda isn't a minimalist as much as he is an essentialist. What he wants most is to be natural, confessional, and pleasurable. Indeed, a rediscovery of the pleasures of life via an authoritative, semidivine "I" takes place in this poetic cycle in a way that seems alien to previous cycles in his oeuvre, such as *España en el corazón* (Spain in the Heart) or *Alturas de Macchu Picchu* (The Heights of Macchu Picchu). Neruda's aesthetics are never buried in the odes. He manifests them unabashedly while shying away from pyrotechnics.

It is therefore unsurprising to discover that Neruda didn't quite believe in originality. "It is just one more fetish made up in our time, which is speeding dizzily to its collapse," he wrote in his *Memoirs*. "I believe in personality reached through any language, any form, any creative means used by the artist." He trusted that poetry, all types of poetry, and especially his own, had no owner. It was centrifugal and enduring, earthly and eternal. And it belongs to everyone.

—ILAN STAVANS

All the Odes

PROLOGUE: THE INVISIBLE MAN

Prólogo: El hombre invisible

TRANSLATED BY ILAN STAVANS

Yo me río,	I laugh,
me sonrío	I smile
de los viejos poetas,	at the old poets,
yo adoro toda	I adore all
la poesía escrita,	written poetry,
todo el rocío,	all the dew,
luna, diamante, gota	moon, diamond, drop
de plata sumergida	of submerged silver
que fue mi antiguo hermano	by which my bygone brother
agregando a la rosa,	decorated the rose,
pero	but
me sonrío,	I smile,
siempre dicen «yo»,	they always say "I,"
a cada paso	each time
les sucede algo,	something happens to them,
es siempre «yo»,	it is always "I,"
por las calles	through the streets
sólo ellos andan	only they walk
o la dulce que aman,	and the sweetheart they love,
nadie más,	no one else,
no pasan pescadores,	fishermen don't pass by,
ni libreros,	nor do booksellers,
no pasan albañiles,	brickmakers don't pass by,
nadie se cae	no one falls
de un andamio,	from a scaffold,
nadie sufre,	no one suffers,
nadie ama,	no one loves,

sólo mi pobre hermano,
el poeta,
a él le pasan
todas las cosas
y a su dulce querida,
nadie vive
sino él solo,
nadie llora de hambre
o de ira,
nadie sufre en sus versos
porque no puede
pagar el alquiler,
a nadie en poesía
echan a la calle
con camas y con sillas
y en las fábricas
tampoco pasa nada,
no pasa nada,
se hacen paraguas, copas,
armas, locomotoras,
se extraen minerales
rascando el infierno,
hay huelga,
vienen soldados,
disparan,
disparan contra el pueblo,
es decir,
contra la poesía,
y mi hermano
el poeta
estaba enamorado,
o sufría
porque sus sentimientos
son marinos,
ama los puertos
remotos, por sus nombres,

except my poor brother,
the poet,
he feels the weight
of everything,
and of his sweetheart,
no one is alive
except him alone,
no one cries of hunger
or ire,
no one suffers in his verses
because he can't
pay the rent,
in poetry
no one is thrown into the street
with beds and with chairs
and in factories
nothing happens either,
nothing happens,
umbrellas are manufactured, goblets,
weapons, locomotives,
minerals are extracted
by digging in hell,
there's a strike,
soldiers come,
fire,
shoot against the people,
that is,
against poetry,
and my brother
the poet
was in love,
or suffered
because his feelings
belong to the sea,
he loves remote
ports, for their names,

y escribe sobre océanos	and writes about oceans
que no conoce,	he doesn't know,
junto a la vida, repleta	next to life, full
como el maíz de granos,	of an ear of corn,
él pasa sin saber	he passes by without knowing
desgranarla,	how to harvest it,
él sube y baja	goes up and down
sin tocar la tierra,	without ever touching land,
o a veces	or sometimes
se siente profundísimo	he experiences profound emotions
y tenebroso,	and darkness,
él es tan grande	he is too big
que no cabe en sí mismo,	doesn't fit in himself,
se enreda y desenreda,	gets tangled and disentangled,
se declara maldito,	declares himself damned,
lleva con gran dificultad la cruz	carries with great difficulty the cross
de las tinieblas,	of darkness,
piensa que es diferente	thinks he is different
a todo el mundo,	from everyone else,
todos los días come pan	every day eats bread
pero no ha visto nunca	but has never seen
un panadero	a baker,
ni ha entrado a un sindicato	nor has he gone to a meeting
de panificadores,	of the bakers' union,
y así mi pobre hermano	and so my poor brother
se hace oscuro,	becomes darkened,
se tuerce y se retuerce	twists and writhes,
y se halla	and finds himself
interesante,	interesting,
interesante,	interesting,
ésta es la palabra,	that's the word,
yo no soy superior	I'm not superior
a mi hermano	to my brother
pero sonrío,	but I smile,
porque voy por las calles	because I walk on the streets
y sólo yo no existo,	and only I don't exist,

la vida corre
como todos los ríos,
yo soy el único
invisible,
no hay misteriosas sombras,
no hay tinieblas,
todo el mundo me habla,
me quieren contar cosas,
me hablan de sus parientes,
de sus miserias
y de sus alegrías,
todos pasan y todos
me dicen algo,
y cuántas cosas hacen!
cortan maderas,
suben hilos eléctricos,
amasan hasta tarde en la noche
el pan de cada día,
con una lanza de hierro
perforan las entrañas
de la tierra
y convierten el hierro
en cerraduras,
suben al cielo y llevan
cartas, sollozos, besos,
en cada puerta
hay alguien,
nace alguno,
o me espera la que amo,
y yo paso y las cosas
me piden que las cante,
yo no tengo tiempo,
debo pensar en todo
debo volver a casa,
pasar al Partido,
qué puedo hacer,

life goes on
like all the rivers,
I'm the only one
who is invisible,
no mysterious shadows,
no darkness,
everyone talks to me,
wants to tell me things,
talks about their relatives,
of their miseries
and happiness,
everyone passes by and everyone
tells me something,
and the many things they do!
They cut wood,
haul electrical wire,
bake the bread
of every day, till late at night
with an iron spear
they pierce the guts
of the earth
and turn iron
into locks,
they reach the sky and take
letters, sobs, kisses,
in each door
someone is standing,
someone is born
or the one I love is waiting for me,
and I go by and things
ask me to sing to them,
I have no time,
I must think of everything,
I must return home,
stop by the Party office,
what can I do,

todo me pide
que hable,
todo me pide
que cante y cante siempre,
todo está lleno
de sueños y sonidos,
la vida es una caja
llena de cantos, se abre
y vuela y viene
una bandada
de pájaros
que quieren contarme algo
descansando en mis hombros,
la vida es una lucha
como un río que avanza
y los hombres
quieren decirme,
decirte,
por qué luchan,
si mueren,
por qué mueren,
y yo paso y no tengo
tiempo para tantas vidas,
yo quiero
que todos vivan
en mi vida
y canten en mi canto,
yo no tengo importancia,
no tengo tiempo
para mis asuntos,
de noche y de día
debo anotar lo que pasa,
y no olvidar a nadie.
Es verdad que de pronto
me fatigo
y miro las estrellas,

everything asks me
to talk,
everything asks me
to sing and always sing,
everything is full
of dreams and sounds,
life is a box
full of songs, it opens
and a flock
of birds
flies out and wants
to tell me something
resting over my shoulders,
life is a struggle
like an advancing river
and men
want to tell me,
tell you,
why they fight,
if they die,
why they die,
and I walk by and have no
time for so many lives,
I want
everyone to live
through my life
and sing through my song,
I have no importance,
I have no time
for my own affairs,
night and day
I must annotate what's happening,
and not forget anyone.
It's true that suddenly
I'm exhausted
and look at the stars,

me tiendo en el pasto, pasa
un insecto color de violín,
pongo el brazo
sobre un pequeño seno
o bajo la cintura
de la dulce que amo,
y miro el terciopelo
duro
de la noche que tiembla
con sus constelaciones congeladas,
entonces
siento subir a mi alma
la ola de los misterios,
la infancia,
el llanto en los rincones,
la adolescencia triste,
y me de sueño,
y duermo
como un manzano,
me quedo dormido
de inmediato
con las estrellas o sin las estrellas,
con mi amor o sin ella,
y cuando me levanto
se fue la noche,
la calle ha despertado antes que yo,
a su trabajo
van las muchachas pobres,
los pescadores vuelven
del océano,
los mineros
van con zapatos nuevos
entrando en la mina,
todo vive,
todos pasan,
andan apresurados,
y yo tengo apenas tiempo

I lie down in the grass, an insect
the color of a violin goes by,
I place my arm
on a small breast
or under the waist
of the woman I love,
and I look at the hard
velvet
of the trembling night
with its frozen constellations,
then
I feel the wave of mysteries
rising in my soul,
childhood,
the cry of corners,
sad adolescence,
and I feel sleepy,
and sleep
like an apple tree,
I fall asleep
immediately
with stars or without them,
with my love or without her,
and when I wake up
the night is gone,
the street has awakened before me,
the poor women go
to work,
the fishermen return
from the ocean,
the miners
enter the mine
with new shoes,
everything is alive,
everyone passes,
they're in a rush,
and I barely have time

para vestirme,
yo tengo que correr:
ninguno puede
pasar sin que yo sepa
adónde va, qué cosa
le ha sucedido.
No puedo
sin la vida vivir,
sin el hombre ser hombre
y corro y veo y oigo
y canto,
las estrellas no tienen
nada que ver conmigo,
la soledad no tiene
flor ni fruto.
Dadme para mi vida
todas las vidas,
dadme todo el dolor
de todo el mundo,
yo voy a transformarlo
en esperanza.
Dadme
todas las alegrías,
aun las más secretas,
porque si así no fuera,
cómo van a saberse?
Yo tengo que contarlas,
dadme
las luchas
de cada día
porque ellas son mi canto,
y así andaremos juntos,
codo a codo,
todos los hombres,
mi canto los reúne:
el canto del hombre invisible
que canta con todos los hombres.

to get dressed,
I have to run:
no one can stop
without my knowing
where he goes, what
happens to him.
I can't live
without life,
without the man being a man
and I run and see and listen
and sing,
the stars have nothing
to do with me,
solitude has neither
fruit nor flower.
Give me every life
for my life,
give me the sorrow
of the entire world,
I will turn it
into hope.
Give me
all the joys,
even the most secret,
because otherwise
how will they be known?
I must tell about them,
give me
the struggles
of every day
because they are my song,
and so we'll walk together,
elbow to elbow,
all the men,
my song unites them:
the song of the invisible man
who sings with all men.

1 / ODE TO AN ABANDONED HOUSE

Oda a la casa abandonada

TRANSLATED BY MARGARET SAYERS PEDEN

Casa, hasta luego!	Good-bye for now,
No	house!
puedo decirte	I can't say
cuándo	when
volveremos:	we'll be back:
mañana o no mañana,	tomorrow or another day,
tarde o mucho más tarde.	later or perhaps much later.
Un viaje más, pero	Another journey, but
esta vez	this time
yo quiero	I must
decirte	tell you
cuánto	how much
amamos	we've loved
tu corazón de piedra:	your heart of stone:
qué generosa eres	how generous you are
con tu fuego	with the warmth
ferviente	of your kitchen
en la cocina	fire,
y tu techo	your roof
en que cae	where
desgranada	raindrops
la lluvia	fall like tiny grapes,
como si resbalara	the slippery music
la música del cielo!	of the sky!
Ahora	Now
cerramos	we close

tus ventanas
y una opresiva
noche prematura
dejamos instalada
en las habitaciones.

Oscurecida
te quedas viviendo,
mientras
el tiempo te recorre
y la humedad gasta poco a poco tu alma.

A veces una
rata
roe, levantan los papeles
un
murmullo
ahogado,
un insecto
perdido
se golpea,
ciego, contra los muros,
y cuando
llueve en la soledad
tal vez
una gotera
suena
con voz humana,
como si allí estuviera
alguien llorando.

Sólo la sombra
sabe
los secretos
de las casas cerradas,
sólo

your windows
and an oppressive
premature night
takes possession
of every room.

Darkened,
you stay alive,
though
time hovers over you and
dampness slowly consumes your soul.

At times
a rat
gnaws, papers rustle,
a
muffled
murmur,
a strayed
insect
flails
blindly against a wall,
and when it rains
in this loneliness,
the leak
in the roof
sometimes sounds
like a human voice,
as if someone
is weeping.

Only the shadows
know
the secrets
of locked houses,
only

el viento rechazado	the thwarted wind
y en el techo la luna que florece.	and, on the roof, the blossoming moon.
Ahora,	And so, good-bye
hasta luego, ventana,	for now, window,
puerta, fuego,	door, fire,
agua que hierve, muro!	boiling water, wall!
Hasta luego, hasta luego,	Good-bye, good-bye,
cocina,	kitchen,
hasta cuando	until
volvamos	we return
y el reloj	and the great old heart
sobre la puerta	of the clock
otra vez continúe palpitando	above the door
con su viejo	begins to beat again,
corazón y sus dos	reviving the
flechas inútiles	useless arrows
clavadas	fixed
en el tiempo.	in time.

2 / ODE TO ACARIO COTAPOS

Oda a Acario Cotapos

TRANSLATED BY ILAN STAVANS

De algún total sonoro	Out of some sonorous whole,
llegó al mundo Cotapos,	Cotapos came into the world,
llegó con su planeta,	he landed with his planet,
con su trueno,	with his thunder,
y se puso a pasear por las ciudades	and began walking through the cities
desenrollando el árbol de la música,	unrolling the music tree,
abriendo las bodegas del sonido.	opening warehouses of sound.
Silencio! Caerá la ciudadela	Silence! The citadel will fall
porque de su insurrecta artillería	because, from its mutinous artillery,
cuando menos se piensa y no se sabe	when least expected, while no one knows it,
vuela el silencio súbito del cisne	the swan's sudden silence takes wing
y es tal el resplandor	and with such brightness
que a su medida	all the water awakens
toda el agua despierta,	in its measure,
todo rumor se ha convertido en ola,	every rumor has become a wave,
todo salió a sonar con el rocío.	everything rises up to mumble with the dew.
Pero, cuidad, cuidemos	But, city, let us safeguard
el orden de esta oda	the order of this ode
porque no sólo el aire se decide	because not only does the air decide
a acompañar el peso de su canto	to accompany the rhythm of his song
y no sólo las aves victoriosas	and not only did triumphant birds
levantaron su vuelo en el estuario,	take flight over the estuary,
sino que entró y salió de las bodegas,	but it entered and exited the warehouses,
asimiló motores,	absorbed engines,
de la electricidad sacó la aurora	from electricity it stole the dawn,

y la vistió de pompa y poderío.
Y aún más, de la tiniebla primordial
el músico regresa
con el lobo y el pasto pastoril,
con la sangre morada del centauro,
con el primer tambor de los combates
y la gravitación de las campanas.

Llega y sopla en su cuerno
y nos congrega,
nos cuenta,
nos inventa,
nos miente,
nos revela,
nos ata a un hilo sabio, a la sorpresa
de su certera lengua fabulosa,
nos equivoca y cuando
se va a apagar levanta
la mano y cae y sigue
la catarata insigne de su cuento.

Conocí de su boca
la historia natural de los enigmas,
el ave corolario,
el secreto teléfono
de los gatos, el viejo río
Mississipi con naves de madera,
el verdugo de Iván el Terrible,
la voz ancha de Boris Godunov,
las ceremonias de los ornitólogos,
cuando lo condecoran en París,
el sagrado terror al hombre flaco,
el húmedo micrófono del perro,
la invocación nefasta
del señor Puga Borne,
el fox hunting *en el condado*

dressed it with pomp and power.
And, furthermore, out of the primordial dark
the musician returns
with the wolf and the pastoral grass,
with the centaur's purple blood,
with the first drum of combat
and the gravitation of bells.

He arrives and blows his horn,
brings us together,
telling us stories,
inventing us,
lying to us,
revealing us,
tying us to a wise thread, to the surprise
of his fabulously accurate tongue,
he mistakes us and, about
to burn out, he raises
his hand and continues
the illustrious waterfall of his tale.

From his mouth I became familiar
with enigma's natural history,
the resulting bird,
the secret telephone
of cats, the old
Mississippi River and its wooden boats,
Ivan the Terrible's executioner,
Boris Godunov's broad voice,
the ornithologists' ceremonies
—after he was honored in Paris,
the thin man's sacred horror,
the dog's wet microphone,
the nefarious invocation
of Señor Puga Borne,
the *fox hunting* in the county,

con chaquetilla roja y cup of tea,
el pavo que viajó a Leningrado
en brazos del benigno don Gregorio,
el desfile de los bolivianitos,
Ramón con su profundo calamar
y, sobre todo, la fatal historia
que Federico amaba
del Jabalí Cornúpeto
cuando
resoplando y roncando
creció y creció la bestia fabulosa
hasta que su irascible corpulencia
sobrepasó los límites de Europa
e inflada como inmenso Zeppelín
viajó al Brasil, en donde
agrimensores, ingenieros,
con peligro evidente de sus vidas,
la descendieron junto al Amazonas.

Cotapos, en tu música
se recompuso la naturaleza,
las aguas naturales,
la impaciencia del trueno,
y vi y toqué la luz en tus preludios
como si fueran hijos
de un cometa escarlata,
y en esa conmoción de tus campanas,
en esas fugas de tormenta y faro
los elementos hallan su medida
fraguando los metales de la música.

Pero hallé en tu palabra
la invicta alevosía
del destructor de mitos y de platos,
la inesperada asociación que encuentra
en su camino el zorro hacia las uvas

with pink jacket and *cup of tea*,
the turkey traveling to Leningrad
in gentle Don Gregorio's arms,
a parade of diminutive Bolivians,
Ramón with his serious squid,
and, especially, the terrible history
which Federico loved
of Jabalí Cornúpeto,
when,
puffing and snoring,
the fabulous beast grew and grew
until its irascible corpulence
overflowed Europe's borders
and, blown up like an immense Zeppelin,
traveled to Brazil, where,
with evident risk to their lives,
surveyors, engineers
brought it down near the Amazon River.

Cotapos, in your music
Nature itself was re-created—
the natural waters,
the thunder's impatience
and I saw and touched light in your preludes
as if they were children
of a scarlet comet,
and in that disturbance of bells,
in those fugues of storm and lighthouse,
the elements found their own measure,
alloying the metals of music.

I also found in your word
the unvanquished perfidy
of the basher of myths and dishes,
the unexpected link the fox
discovers on his path to the grapes,

cuando huele aire verde o pluma
errante,
y no sólo
eso, sino
más:
la sinalefa eléctrica que muda
toda visión y cambian las palomas.

Tú, poeta sin libros,
juntaste en vida el canto irrespetuoso,
la palabra que salta de su cueva
donde yació sin sueño
y transformaste para mí el idioma
en un derrumbe de cristalerías.

Maestro, compañero,
me has enseñado tantas cosas claras
que donde estoy me das tu
claridad.

Ahora,
escribo un libro de lo que yo soy
y en este soy, Acario, eres conmigo.

when he smells the green air or a
wandering feather;
and not only
that, but
also:
the electrical elision that charges
all vision, transformed by doves.

You, poet without books,
in life you connected the disrespectful song,
the word that jumped out of its cave
where it lay empty of dream;
and for me you turned language
into a collision of glass.

Teacher, compañero,
you have taught me so many clear things;
wherever I find myself, you grant me your
clearness.

Now
I write a book of what I am,
and in what I am, Acario, you are with me.

3 / ODE TO AGE

Oda a la edad

TRANSLATED BY ILAN STAVANS

Yo no creo en la edad.	I don't believe in age.
Todos los viejos	All old people
llevan	have in
en los ojos	their eyes
un niño,	a child,
y los niños	and children
a veces	sometimes
nos observan	look at us with
como ancianos profundos.	the eyes of wise old people.
Mediremos	Shall we measure
la vida	life
por metros o kilómetros	in meters or kilometers
o meses?	or months?
Tanto desde que naces?	In length since birth?
Cuánto	How much
debes andar	do you need to walk
hasta que	until,
como todos	like everyone,
en vez de caminarla por encima	instead of walking on the surface,
descansemos, debajo de la tierra?	we rest under the earth?
Al hombre, a la mujer	To the man, the woman
que consumaron	who performed
acciones, bondad, fuerza,	acts, goodness, strength,

cólera, amor, ternura,
a los que verdaderamente
vivos
florecieron
y en su naturaleza maduraron,
no acerquemos nosotros
la medida
del tiempo
que tal vez
es otra cosa, un manto
mineral, un ave
planetaria, una flor,
otra cosa tal vez,
pero no una medida.

Tiempo, metal
o pájaro, flor
de largo pecíolo,
extiéndete
a lo largo
de los hombres,
florécelos
y lávalos
con
agua
abierta
o con sol escondido.
Te proclamo
camino
y no mortaja,
escala
pura
con peldaños
de aire,
traje sinceramente

cholera, love, tenderness,
to those who truly
flourished
alive
and matured in their nature,
let us not apply to them
the measure
of time
that perhaps is
something else, a mineral
mantle, a planetary
bird, a flower,
something else perhaps,
but not a measure.

Time, metal
or bird, large-stalk
flower,
stretch
widely
through men's lives,
flower them
and wash them
with
bright
water
or with hidden sun.
I proclaim you
path
and not shroud,
pristine
staircase
with steps
of air,
suit humbly

renovado
por longitudinales
primaveras.

Ahora,
tiempo, te enrollo,
te deposito en mi
caja silvestre
y me voy a pescar
con tu hilo largo
los peces de la aurora!

renewed
with longitudinal
springs.

Now,
time, I roll you up,
I deposit you in my
rustic box
and I leave off to fish
with your long thread
the fish of dawn!

4 / ODE TO AN AGED POET

Oda al viejo poeta

TRANSLATED BY MARGARET SAYERS PEDEN

Me dio la mano	He offered me his hand
como si un árbol viejo	the way an old tree might
alargara un gancho	extend a broken branch
sin	stripped
hojas y sin frutos.	of leaves and fruit.
Su	The
mano	hand
que escribió desenlazando	that once wrote, spinning
los hilos y las hebras	the thread and strands
del	of
destino	destiny,
ahora estaba	now was
minuciosamente	intricately
rayada	scored
por los días, los meses y los años.	by days, months, and years.
Seca en su rostro	Sere on his face
era	was
la escritura	the writing
del tiempo,	of time,
diminuta	minute
y errante	and meandering
como	as if
si allí estuvieran	the lines
dispuestos	and signs
las líneas y los signos	had been ordained
desde su nacimiento	at birth
y poco a poco	and little by little

el aire
los hubiera erigido.

Largas líneas profundas,
capítulos cortados
por la edad en su cara,
signos interrogantes,
fábulas misteriosas,
asteriscos,
todo lo que olvidaron las sirenas
en la extendida
soledad de su alma,
lo que cayó del
estrellado cielo,
allí estaba en su rostro
dibujado.
Nunca el antiguo
bardo
recogió
con pluma y papel duro
el río derramado
de la vida
o el dios desconocido
que cortejó su verso,
y ahora,
en sus mejillas,
todo
el misterio
diseñó
con frío
el álgebra
de sus revelaciones
y las pequeñas,
invariables
cosas
menospreciadas

air
had etched them.

Long deep lines,
chapters carved
in his face by age,
question marks,
mysterious tales,
asterisks,
all that the sirens had forgot
in the far-reaching
solitude of his soul,
all that fell from the
starry sky,
was traced in his
face.
Never had the ancient
bard
captured
with pen and unyielding paper
the overflowing river
of life
or the unidentified god
that flirted with his verse,
and now,
on his cheeks,
all that
mystery
coldly
drafted
the algebra
of its revelations,
and the humble,
unchanging
things
he had scorned

dejaron	imprinted
en su frente	on his brow
profundísimas	their most profound
páginas	pages,
y	and
hasta	even
en su	on his
nariz	nose
delgada,	thin
como pico	as the beak
de cormorán errante,	of the errant cormorant,
los viajes y las olas	voyages and waves
depositaron	had sketched
su letra	their ultramarine
ultramarina.	scrawl.
Sólo	Two
dos piedrecitas	unfriendly
intratables,	pebbles,
dos ágatas	two
marinas	ocean agates
en aquel	in that
combate,	combat,
eran	were
sus ojos	his eyes,
y sólo a través de ellos	and only through them
vi la apagada	did I see the extinguished
hoguera,	fire,
una rosa	a rose
en las manos	in the poet's
del poeta.	hands.
Ahora	Now
el traje	his suit
le quedaba grande	was much too large,
como si ya viviera	as if he were already living
en una	in an

casa
vacía,
y los huesos
de todo
su cuerpo se acercaban
a la piel
levantándola
y era
de hueso,
de hueso que advertía
y enseñaba,
un pequeño
árbol, al fin, de hueso,
era el poeta
apagado
por la caligrafía
de la lluvia,
por los inagotables
manantiales del tiempo.

Allí le dejé andando
presuroso a su muerte
como
si lo esperara
también casi desnuda
en un parque sombrío
y de la mano
fueran
hasta
un desmantelado dormitorio
y en él durmieran
como dormiremos
todos
los hombres:
con
una rosa

empty
house,
and all
the bones
of his body were visible
beneath his skin,
skin draped on bone,
he was nothing but
bone,
alert and instructive
bone,
a tiny
tree, finally, of bone,
was the poet
quenched
by the calligraphy
of the rain,
by the inexhaustible
springs of time.

There I left him
hurrying toward death
as if
death awaited,
she too, almost naked,
in a somber park,
and hand in hand
they would make
their way to
a decaying resting place
where they would sleep
as every man
of us
will sleep:
with
a dry

seca	rose
en	in
una	a
mano	hand
que también cae	that will also
convertida en polvo.	crumble into dust.

5 / ODE TO AIR

Oda al aire

TRANSLATED BY ILAN STAVANS

Andando en un camino
encontré al aire,
lo saludé y le dije
con respeto:
«Me alegro
de que por una vez
dejes tu transparencia,
así hablaremos».
El incansable
bailó, movió las hojas,
sacudió con su risa
el polvo de mis suelas,
y levantando toda
su azul arboladura,
su esqueleto de vidrio,
sus párpados de brisa,
inmóvil como un mástil
se mantuvo escuchándome.
Yo le besé su capa
de rey del cielo,
me envolví en su bandera
de seda celestial
y le dije:
monarca o camarada,
hilo, corola o ave,
no sé quién eres, pero
una cosa te pido,

Wandering on a road
I found air,
I greeted it and said
with respect:
"I'm glad
for once you've left
your transparency,
so we can talk."
The inexhaustible air
danced, caressed the leaves
shaking with laughter,
the dust on the soles of my shoes,
and, raising its entire
blue tree dome,
its crystal skeleton,
its eyelids of breeze,
immobile like a mast,
it kept listening to me.
I kissed its cape
of a heavenly king,
I wrapped myself in its celestial
silk flag,
and said:
monarch or comrade,
thread, corolla, or bird,
I don't know who you are, but
I ask one thing:

no te vendas.
El agua se vendió
y de las cañerías
en el desierto
he visto
terminarse las gotas
y el mundo pobre, el pueblo
caminar con su sed
tambaleando en la arena.
Vi la luz de la noche
racionada,
la gran luz en la casa
de los ricos.
Todo es aurora en los
nuevos jardines suspendidos.
Todo es oscuridad
en la terrible
sombra del callejón.
De allí la noche,
madre madrastra,
sale
con un puñal en medio
de sus ojos de búho,
y un grito, un crimen,
se levantan y apagan
tragados por la sombra.
No, aire,
no te vendas,
que no te canalicen,
que no te entuben,
que no te encajen
ni te compriman,
que no te hagan tabletas,
que no te metan en una botella,
cuidado!
llámame

don't sell yourself.
Water sold itself
and I have seen,
in the desert,
sewer-systems'
drops drying up
and the world impoverished, people
walking in thirst,
faltering on the sand.
I saw the night light
rationed,
the great light in the house
of the rich.
Everything is aurora in the
newly suspended gardens.
Everything is darkness
in the terrible
shadow of the alley.
From there on, the night,
stepmotherly mother,
comes out
holding a dagger
in the middle of its owl eyes,
and a scream, a crime,
emerge and turn off
swallowed by the shadow.
No, air,
don't sell yourself,
don't let yourself be channeled,
don't let yourself be forced into tubes,
don't let yourself be pinned down
or compressed,
don't let yourself be turned into tablets,
don't let yourself be put in a bottle,
beware!
call me

cuando me necesites,
yo soy el poeta hijo
de pobres, padre, tío,
primo, hermano carnal
y concuñado
de los pobres, de todos,
de mi patria y las otras,
de los pobres que viven junto al río
y de los que en la altura
de la vertical cordillera
pican piedra,
clavan tablas,
cosen ropa,
cortan leña,
muelen tierra,
y por eso
yo quiero que respiren,
tú eres lo único que tienen,
por eso eres
transparente,
para que vean
lo que vendrá mañana,
por eso existes,
aire,
déjate respirar,
no te encadenes,
no te fíes de nadie
que venga en automóvil
a examinarte,
déjalos,
ríete de ellos,
vuélales el sombrero,
no aceptes
sus proposiciones,
vamos juntos
bailando por el mundo,

when you need me:
I'm the poet child
of the poor, father, uncle,
cousin, blood sibling
and brother-in-law
of the poor, of everyone,
of my country and of others,
of the poor living near the river
and of those on the heights
of vertical cordilleras
who carve stone,
hammer tables,
sew clothes,
cut wood,
grind earth,
that's why
I want them to breathe,
you are everything they have,
that's why you are
translucent,
so that they see
what tomorrow will bring,
that's why you exist,
air:
allow yourself to be breathed,
don't let yourself be chained,
don't trust anyone
coming in an automobile
to examine you,
get away,
laugh at them,
make their hats fly,
don't accept
their propositions,
let's go together
dancing around the world,

derribando las flores
del manzano,
entrando en las ventanas,
silbando juntos,
silbando
melodías
de ayer y de mañana,
ya vendrá un día
en que libertaremos
la luz y el agua,
la tierra, el hombre,
y todo para todos
será, como tú eres.
Por eso, ahora,
cuidado!
y ven conmigo,
nos queda mucho
que bailar y cantar,
vamos
a lo largo del mar,
a lo alto de los montes,
vamos
donde esté floreciendo
la nueva primavera
y en un golpe de viento
y canto
repartamos las flores,
el aroma, los frutos,
el aire
de mañana.

bringing down the flowers
of the apple tree,
entering through windows,
whistling together,
whistling
melodies
of yesterday and tomorrow,
the day will come
in which we'll set free
light and water,
earth, man,
and everything for everyone
will be, be yourself.
That's why, now,
you must beware!
come with me,
we still have much
to dance and sing,
let's go
across the sea,
to the top of the hills,
let's go
where a new spring
is flowering
and in a bump from the wind
and the song,
let us give flowers away,
aroma, fruit,
the air
of tomorrow.

6 / ODE TO THE AMERICAS

Oda a las Américas

TRANSLATED BY MARGARET SAYERS PEDEN

Américas purísimas,	Oh, pure Americas,
tierras que los océanos	ocean-guarded lands
guardaron	kept
intactas y purpúreas,	purple and intact,
siglos de colmenares silenciosos,	centuries of silent apiaries,
pirámides, vasijas,	pyramids and earthen vessels,
ríos de ensangrentadas mariposas,	rivers of bloodstained butterflies,
volcanes amarillos	yellow volcanoes
y razas de silencio,	and silent peoples,
formadoras de cántaros,	shapers of pitchers,
labradoras de piedra.	workers of stone.
Y hoy, Paraguay, turquesa	Today, Paraguay, water-formed
fluvial, rosa enterrada,	turquoise, buried rose,
te convertiste en cárcel.	you have become a prison.
Perú, pecho del mundo,	Peru, heart of the world,
corona	eagles'
de las águilas,	aerie,
existes?	are you alive?
Venezuela, Colombia,	Venezuela, Colombia,
no se oyen	no one hears
vuestras bocas felices.	your happy voices.
Dónde ha partido el coro	What has become of
de plata matutina?	your silvery morning chorus?
Sólo los pájaros	Only the birds
de antigua vestidura,	of ancient plumage,
sólo las cataratas	only the waterfalls,

mantienen su diadema.
La cárcel ha extendido
sus barrotes.
En el húmedo reino
del fuego y la esmeralda,
entre
los ríos paternales,
cada día
sube un mandón y con su sable corta,
hipoteca y remata tu tesoro.
Se abre la cacería
del hermano.
Suenan tiros perdidos en los puertos.
Llegan de Pennsylvania
los expertos,
los nuevos
conquistadores,
mientras tanto
nuestra sangre
alimenta
las pútridas
plantaciones o minas subterráneas,
los dólares resbalan
y
nuestras locas muchachas
se descaderan aprendiendo el baile
de los orangutanes.
Américas purísimas,
sagrados territorios,
qué tristeza!
Muere un Machado y un Batista nace.
Permanece un Trujillo.
Tanto espacio
de libertad silvestre,
Américas,

display their diadems.
Prison bars have
multiplied.
In the humid kingdom of
fire and emerald,
between
paternal rivers,
each day
a new despot arises and with his saber
lops off mortgages and auctions your
treasure.
Brother begins
to hunt brother.
Stray shots sound in the ports.
Experts arrive
from Pennsylvania,
the new
conquistadors,
meanwhile,
our blood
feeds
the putrid
plantations and the buried mines,
the dollars flow,
and
our silly young girls
slip a disk learning the dance
of the orangutan.
Oh, pure Americas,
sacred lands,
what sadness!
A Machado dies and a Batista is born.
A Trujillo remains in power.
So much room
for sylvan freedom,
Americas,

tanta
pureza, agua
de océano,
pampas de soledad, vertiginosa
geografía
para que se propaguen los minúsculos
negociantes de sangre.
Qué pasa?
Cómo puede
continuar el silencio
entrecortado
por sanguinarios loros
encaramados en las enramadas
de la codicia panamericana?
Américas heridas
por la más ancha espuma,
por los felices mares
olorosos
a la pimienta de los archipiélagos,
Américas
oscuras,
inclinada
hacia nosotros surge
la estrella de los pueblos,
nacen héroes, se cubren
de victoria
otros caminos,
existen otra vez
viejas naciones,
en la luz más radiante
se traspasa el otoño,
el viento se estremece
con las nuevas banderas.
Que tu voz y tus hechos,
América,
se desprendan

so much
purity, ocean
waters,
solitary pampas, dizzying
geography, why do
insignificant blood merchants
breed and multiply?
What is happening?
How can the
silence continue
interrupted
by bloodthirsty parrots
perched in the branches
of Pan-American greed?
Americas, assailed
by broadest expanse of foam,
by felicitous seas
redolent
of the pepper of the archipelagos,
dark
Americas,
in our orbit
the star of the people
is rising,
heroes are being born,
new paths being garlanded
with victory,
the ancient nations
live again,
autumn passes
in the most radiant light,
new flags
flutter on the wind.
May your voice and your deeds,
America,
rise free from your

de tu cintura verde,
termine
tu amor encarcelado,
restaures el decoro
que te dio nacimiento
y eleves tus espigas sosteniendo
con otros pueblos
la irresistible aurora.

green girdle,
may there be an end
to love imprisoned,
may your native dignity
be restored,
may your grain rise toward the sky
awaiting with other nations
the inevitable dawn.

7 / ODE TO THE ANCHOR

Oda al ancla

TRANSLATED BY ILAN STAVANS

Estuvo allí, un pesado
fragmento fugitivo,
cuando murió la nave
la dejaron
allí, sobre la arena,
ella no tiene muerte:
polvo de sal en su esqueleto,
tiempo en la cruz de su esperanza,
se fue oxidando como la herradura
lejos de su caballo,
cayó el olvido en su soberanía.

La bondad de un amigo
la levantó de la perdida arena
y creyó de repente
que el temblor de un navío
la esperaba,
que cadenas sonoras
la esperaban
y a la ola infinita,
al trueno de los mares volvería.

Atrás quedó la luz de Antofagasta,
ella iba por los mares pero herida,
no iba atada a la proa,
no resbalaba por el agua amarga.
Iba, herida y dormida

It was there, a heavy
fugitive fragment,
when the ship died
she was abandoned
there, on the sand,
she has no death:
her skeleton is salt powder,
time on the cross of its hope,
it rusted like the horseshoe
far from its horse,
oblivion descended on its sovereignty.

A friend's goodness
picked her up from the lost sand
and suddenly she believed
a ship's tremor
awaited her,
sonorous chains
awaited her
and to the infinite wave,
to the ocean thunder she would return.

The Antofagasta light was left behind,
she navigated the seas but was injured,
she wasn't tied to the prow,
she didn't slip through the bitter water.
She went injured and, a sleeping

pasajera,
iba hacia el Sur, errante
pero muerta,
no sentía su sangre,
su corriente,
no palpitaba al beso del abismo.

Y al fin en San Antonio
bajó, subió colinas,
corrió un camión con ella,
era en el mes de octubre, y orgullosa
cruzó sin penetrarse
el río,
el reino de la primavera,
el caudaloso aroma
que se ciñe a la costa
como la red sutil de la fragancia,
como el vestido claro de la vida.
En mi jardín reposa
de las navegaciones
frente al perdido océano
que cortó como espada,
y poco a poco las enredaderas
subirán su frescura
por los brazos de hierro,
y alguna vez florecerán claveles
en su sueño terrestre,
porque llegó para dormir
y ya no puedo restituirla al mar.

Ya no navegará nave ninguna.

Ya no anclará sino en mis duros sueños.

passenger,
she went to the South, wandering
but dead,
didn't feel her blood,
her current,
the kiss of the abyss didn't palpitate.

Finally, in San Antonio,
she descended, climbed hills,
was taken on a bus,
it was the month of October, and proudly
she crossed without penetrating
the river,
the spring kingdom,
the rich aroma
clinging to the coast
like the subtle red of a fragrance,
like the clear dress of life.
In my garden she rests
from her navigations
before the lost ocean
cut by the sword,
and little by little the bindweed
will climb her freshness
through her iron arms,
and someday carnations will flower
in her terrestrial dream,
because she came to sleep
and I can't return her to the sea.

She will not navigate with any ship.

She will no longer anchor but in my
stubborn dreams.

8 / ODE TO THE ANDEAN CORDILLERA

Oda a la cordillera andina

TRANSLATED BY ILAN STAVANS

De nuevo desde arriba,
desde el cielo
volando,
apareciste, cordillera
blanca y oscura de la patria mía.
Antes el grande avión
cruzó los grandes mares,
las selvas, los desiertos.
Todo fue simetría,
todo sobre la tierra
preparado,
todo desde la altura
era camino
hasta que en medio
de la tierra y del cielo
se interpuso
tu nieve planetaria
congelando las torres de la tierra.
Volcanes, cicatrices,
socavones,
nieves ferruginosas,
titánicas alturas
desolladas,
cabezas de los montes,
pies del cielo,
abismos del abismo,
cuchilladas

Once again, from up high,
flying over
the sky,
you appeared, white and obscure
cordillera of my homeland.
Before then, the great airplane
crossed great seas,
jungles, deserts.
Everything was symmetry,
everything was ready
on the earth's surface,
everything from above
was path,
until, in the middle
of heaven and earth,
your planetary snow
lodged itself,
freezing the towers of earth.
Volcanoes, scars,
caves,
ferruginous snows,
skinned
titanic heights,
heads of mountains,
feet of sky,
abyss of the abyss,
stabs

que cortaron
la cáscara terrestre
y el sol
a siete mil
metros de altura,
duros como un diamante
sobre
las venas, los ramales
de la sombra y la nieve
sobre la enfurecida
tormenta de los mundos
que se detuvo hirviendo
y en el silencio
colosal
impuso
sus mares de granito.

Patria, puso la tierra
en tus manos delgadas
su más duro estandarte,
la cordillera andina,
hierro nevado, soledades puras,
piedra y escalofrío,
y en tu costado
como flor infinita el mar te ofrece
su derramada espuma.
Oh mar, oh nieve,
oh cielo
de mi pequeña patria,
al hombre, al compatriota,
al camarada
darás,
darás un día
el pan de tu grandeza,
lo unirás al destino
de la nieve,

cutting
the terrestrial shell,
and the sun,
at seven thousand
meters
hard like a diamond
on
the veins, the branchcs
of shadow and the snow
on the enraged
storm of the worlds,
stopping while boiling,
and the colossal
silence
imposed
its granite seas.

Homeland, the earth placed
on your slim hands
its toughest banner,
the Andean cordillera,
snowed blade, pristine solitudes,
stone and shiver,
and on your side
like an infinite flower the sea offers you
its spilled foam.
Oh sea, oh snow,
oh sky
of my small country,
to man, to the compatriot,
the comrade
you shall give,
you shall give one day
the bread of your grandeur,
you shall unite it to the fate
of snow,

al esplendor sagrado
del mar y su energía.
Dura morada,
un día
te abrirás
entregando
la secreta
fecundidad,
el rayo de tus dones,
y entonces
mi pequeño
compatriota,
malherido en su reino,
desdichado
en su propia fortaleza,
harapiento en su ámbito de oro,
recibirá
el tesoro
conquistándolo,
defendiendo la nieve de su estrella,
multiplicando el mar y sus racimos,
extendiendo el silencio de los frutos.
Cordillera, colegio
de piedra,
en esta hora
tu magnitud
celebro,
tu dureza,
el candelabro frío
de tus altas
soledades de nieve,
la noche,
estuario inmóvil,
navegando
sobre
las piedras de tu sueño,

to the sacred splendor
of the sea and its energy.
Hard dwelling,
one day
you shall open up
delivering
the secret
fecundity,
the ray of your qualities,
and then
my small
compatriot,
injured severely in your kingdom,
wretched
in its own fortitude,
ragged in its confines of gold,
it shall receive
the treasure
while conquering it,
defending the snow of its star,
multiplying the sea and its branches,
extending the silence of fruit.
Cordillera, school
of stone,
I celebrate
your magnitude
in this hour,
your toughness,
the cold candelabra
of your elevated
solitudes of snow,
the night,
motionless estuary,
navigating
on
the stones of your sleep,

el día
transparente
en tu cabeza
y en ella, en la nevada
cabellera
del mundo,
el cóndor
levantando
sus alas
poderosas,
su vuelo
digno
de las acérrimas alturas.

the translucent
day
on your head
and on it, white hair
snow on top
of the world,
the condor
raising
his powerful
wings,
his dignified
flight
above vigorous heights.

9 / ODE TO ÁNGEL CRUCHAGA

Oda a Ángel Cruchaga

TRANSLATED BY ILAN STAVANS

Ángel, recuerdo	Ángel, I remember
en mi infancia	in my childhood,
austral y sacudida	southern and shaken
por la lluvia y el viento,	by rain and wind,
de pronto,	suddenly
tus alas,	your wings,
el vuelo	the flight
de tu centelleante poesía,	of your sparkling poetry,
la túnica	the starry
estrellada	tunic
que llenaba la noche, los caminos,	filling the night, the roads,
con un fulgor fosfórico,	with phosphoric resplendence,
eras	you were
un palpitante río	a pulsating river
lleno de peces,	full of fish,
eras	you were
la cola plateada	the silvery tail
de una sirena verde	of a green mermaid
que atravesaba el cielo	crossing the sky
de oeste	from west
a este,	to east,
la forma de la luz	the shape of light
se reunía	gathered
en tus alas, y el viento	in your wings, and the wind
dejaba caer lluvia y hojas negras	allowing rain and black leaves to fall
sobre tu vestidura.	on your clothes.
Así era	So it was

allá lejos,	far away,
en mi infancia,	in my childhood,
pero tu poesía,	but your poetry,
no sólo	not only
paso de muchas alas,	a step made of many wings,
no sólo	not only
piedra errante,	wandering stone,
meteoro	meteor
vestido de amaranto y azucena,	dressed in colors of amaranth and white lily,
ha sido y sigue siendo,	was and still is,
sino planta florida,	but a flowering plant,
monumento	monument
de la ternura humana,	to human tenderness,
azahar	orange blossom
con raíces	with roots
en el hombre.	in man.
Por eso,	That's why,
Ángel,	Ángel,
te canto,	I sing to you,
te he cantado	I have sung to you
como canté todas las cosas puras,	the way I sang to all pure things,
metales,	metals,
aguas,	waters,
viento!	wind!
Todo lo que es lección para las vidas,	Everything becomes a lesson in living,
crecimiento	growth
de dureza o dulzura,	through hardship and sweetness,
como es tu poesía, el infinito	as in your poetry, the infinite
pan impregnado en llanto	bread pregnant with the tears
de tu pasión, las nobles	of your passion, the noble
maderas olorosas	fragrant woods
que tus divinas manos elaboran.	your divine hands shape.
Ángel,	Ángel,
tú, propietario	you, owner
de los más extendidos jazmineros,	of the widest jasmine trees,
permite que tu hermano	allow your younger

menor deje en tu pecho
esta rama con lluvias
y raíces.
Yo la dejo en tu libro
para que así se impregne
de paz, de transparencia y de hermosura,
viviendo en la corola
de tu naturaleza diamantina.

brother to leave on your chest
these branches with rain
and roots.
I leave them in your book
so it becomes pregnant
with peace, transparency, and beauty,
living in the corolla
of your adamantine nature.

10 / ODE TO THE APPLE

Oda a la manzana

TRANSLATED BY ILAN STAVANS

A ti, manzana,
quiero
celebrarte
llenándome
con tu nombre
la boca,
comiéndote.
Siempre
eres nueva como nada
o nadie,
siempre
recién caída
del Paraíso:
plena
y pura
mejilla arrebolada
de la aurora!

Qué difíciles
son
comparados
contigo
los frutos de la tierra,
las celulares uvas,
los mangos
tenebrosos,
las huesudas

You, apple,
I want
to celebrate you
by filling
my mouth
with your name,
by eating you.
You're always
new like nothing else,
or no one,
always
as if just fallen
from Paradise:
plentiful
and pristine,
reddened cheek
of aurora!

How unappealing
are
the fruits of earth
compared
to you,
the grainy grapes,
the gloomy
mangos,
the seedy

ciruelas, los higos
submarinos:
tú eres pomada pura,
pan fragante,
queso
de la vegetación.

plums, the submarine
figs:
you are pure ointment,
fragrant bread,
cheese
of vegetation.

Cuando mordemos
tu redonda inocencia
volvemos
por un instante
a ser
también recién creadas criaturas:
aún tenemos algo de manzana.

When we bite
into your rounded innocence,
for an instant
we return
to being
newly created creatures again:
somehow we remain apple.

Yo quiero
una abundancia
total, la multiplicación
de tu familia,
quiero
una ciudad,
una república,
un río Missisipi
de manzanas,
y en sus orillas
quiero ver
a toda
la población
del mundo
unida, reunida,
en el acto más simple de la tierra:
mordiendo una manzana.

I want
a total
abundance, the multiplication
of your family,
I want
a city,
a republic,
a Mississippi River
of apples,
and on its shores
I want to see
the entire
population
of the world
united, reunited,
in the simplest act on earth:
biting an apple.

11 / ODE TO THE ARAUCANIAN ARAUCARIA

Oda a la araucaria araucana

TRANSLATED BY ILAN STAVANS

Alta sobre la tierra
te pusieron,
dura, hermosa araucaria
de los australes
montes,
torre de Chile, punta
del territorio verde,
pabellón del invierno,
nave
de la fragancia.

Ahora, sin embargo,
no por bella
te canto,
sino por el racimo de tu especie,
por tu fruta cerrada,
por tu piñón abierto.

Antaño,
antaño fue
cuando
sobre los indios
se abrió
como una rosa de madera
el colosal puñado
de tu puño,
y dejó

Tall on earth
you were placed,
tough, beautiful Araucaria
of the southern
mountains,
tower of Chile, promontory
of the green territory,
pavilion of winter,
ship
of fragrance.

Now, nevertheless,
I don't sing to you
for your beauty,
but as the cluster of your species,
for your closed fruit,
for your open pine nut.

In days gone by,
in days gone by it was
when
the colossal handful
of your fist
like a wooden rose
opened up
over the Indians,
and left

sobre
la mojada tierra
los piñones:
harina, pan silvestre
del indomable
Arauco.

Ved la guerra:
armados
los guerreros
de Castilla
y sus caballos
de galvánicas
crines
y frente
a ellos
el grito
de los
desnudos
héroes,
voz del fuego, cuchillo
de dura piedra parda,
lanzas enloquecidas
en el bosque,
tambor,
tambor
sagrado,
y adentro
de la selva
el silencio,
la muerte
replegándose,
la guerra.

Entonces, en el último
bastión verde,

pine nuts
on
the wet soil:
flour, peasant bread
of the indomitable
Arauco.

Look at war:
armed
the warriors
of Castile
and their horses
with galvanic
manes
and before
them
the scream
of the
naked
heroes,
voice of fire, knife
of hard brown stone,
crazed spear
in the forest,
drum,
sacred
drum,
and inside
the jungle
silence,
death
withdrawing,
war.

Then, in the last
green bastion,

dispersas	dispersed
por la fuga,	in the fugue,
las lanzas	the spears
de la selva	of the jungle
se reunieron	gathered
bajo las araucarias	under the thorny
espinosas.	Araucarias.
La cruz,	The cross,
la espada,	the spear,
el hambre	hunger
iban diezmando	were decimating
la familia salvaje.	the savage family.
Terror,	Terror,
terror de un golpe	terror from a
de herraduras,	horseshoe sound,
latido de una hoja,	the howling from a leaf,
viento,	wind,
dolor	pain
y lluvia.	and rain.
De pronto	Suddenly,
se estremeció allá arriba	high on top
la araucaria	the Araucanian
araucana,	Araucaria
sus ilustres	shook its illustrious
raíces,	roots,
las espinas	the wiry
hirsutas	thorns
del poderoso	of the powerful
pabellón	pavilion
tuvieron	had
un movimiento	a black
negro	battle
de batalla:	movement:

rugió como una ola
de leones
todo el follaje
de la selva
dura
y entonces
cayó
una marejada
de piñones:
los anchos
estuches
se rompieron
contra la tierra, contra
la piedra defendida
y desgranaron
su fruta, el pan postrero
de la patria.

Así la Araucanía
recompuso
sus lanzas de agua y oro,
zozobraron los bosques
bajo el silbido
del valor
resurrecto
y avanzaron
las cinturas
violentas como rachas,
las
plumas
incendiarias del Cacique:
piedra quemada
y flecha voladora
atajaron
al invasor de hierro
en el camino.

the entire foliage
of the harsh
jungle
roared like a wave
of lions
and then
a swelling
of pine nuts
fell:
their wide
shells
broke
against the earth, against
the defending stone
and scattered
its fruit, the final bread
of the homeland.

So the Araucanía
repaired
its spears of water and gold,
the forests capsized
under the whistle
of resurrected
valor
and the violent
waists
advanced like gusts,
the
incendiary
plumes of the Cacique:
burnt stone
and flying arrow
caught
the invader of iron
on the road.

Araucaria,
follaje
de bronce con espinas,
gracias
te dio
la ensangrentada estirpe,
gracias
te dio
la tierra defendida,
gracias,
pan de valientes,
alimento
escondido
en la mojada aurora
de la patria:
corona verde,
pura
madre de los espacios,
lámpara
del frío
territorio,
hoy
dame
tu
luz sombría,
la imponente
seguridad
enarbolada
sobre tus raíces
y abandona en mi canto
la herencia
y el silbido
del viento que te toca,
del antiguo
y huracanado viento
de mi patria.

Araucaria,
foliage
of bronze with thorns,
the bloodstained stock
thanked
you,
the defended land
thanked
you,
thank you,
bread of the brave,
hidden
breath
in the wet aurora
of the homeland:
green crown,
pure
mother of spaces,
lamp
of the cold
territory,
give me
your
shady light
today,
the imposing
security
brandished
over the roots
and leave in my song
the heritage
and whistle
of the wind touching you,
of the ancient
and hurricane-driven wind
of my homeland.

Deja caer
en mi alma
tus granadas
para que las legiones
se alimenten
de tu especie en mi canto.
Árbol nutricio, entrégame
la terrenal argolla que te amarra
a la entraña lluviosa
de la tierra,
entrégame
tu resistencia, el rostro
y las raíces
firmes
contra la envidia,
la invasión, la codicia,
el desacato.
Tus armas deja y vela
sobre mi corazón,
sobre los míos,
sobre los hombros
de los valerosos,
porque a la misma luz de hojas y aurora,
arenas y follajes,
yo voy con las banderas
al llamado
profundo de mi pueblo!
Araucaria araucana,
aquí me tienes!

Allow
your grenades to fall
on my soul
so her legions
may feed
from your species in my song.
Nourishing tree, deliver me
the terrestrial ring binding you
to the rainy entrails
of the land,
deliver me
your resistance, the face
and roots
firm
against envy,
invasion, greed,
incivility.
Leave your weapons aside and watch over
my heart,
my beloved,
the shoulders
of those with courage,
because from the same light of leaves and
aurora,
sand and foliage,
I walk with the flags
to the profound
call of my people!
Araucanian Araucaria,
I'm at your disposal!

12 / ODE TO THE ARTICHOKE

Oda a la alcachofa

TRANSLATED BY ILAN STAVANS

La alcachofa
de tierno corazón
se vistió de guerrero,
erecta, construyó
una pequeña cúpula,
se mantuvo
impermeable
bajo
sus escamas,
a su lado
los vegetales locos
se encresparon,
se hicieron
zarcillos, espadañas,
bulbos conmovedores,
en el subsuelo
durmió la zanahoria
de bigotes rojos,
la viña
resecó los sarmientos
por donde sube el vino,
la col
se dedicó
a probarse faldas,
el orégano
a perfumar el mundo,
y la dulce

The tenderhearted
artichoke,
dressed as a warrior,
erect, built
a small cupola,
stood
impermeable
under
its lamina of scales,
at her side,
the maddening vegetables
riffed their leaves,
turned themselves
into earrings, cattails,
moving bulbs,
underground
slept the carrot
with red whiskers,
the vineyard
dried up the shoots
whence came the wine,
the cabbage
preened itself
on trying skirts,
the oregano
on perfuming the world,
and the sweet

alcachofa
allí en el huerto,
vestida de guerrero,
bruñida
como una granada,
orgullosa,
y un día
una con otra
en grandes cestos
de mimbre, caminó
por el mercado
a realizar su sueño:
la milicia.
En hileras
nunca fue tan marcial
como en la feria,
los hombres
entre las legumbres
con sus camisas blancas
eran
mariscales
de las alcachofas,
las filas apretadas,
las voces de comando,
y la detonación
de una caja que cae,
pero
entonces
viene
María
con su cesto,
escoge
una alcachofa,
no le teme,
la examina, la observa
contra la luz como si fuera un huevo,

artichoke
there in the garden,
dressed as a warrior,
polished
like a grenade,
proud,
and one day
one with the other
in big willow
baskets, walked
through the market
to fulfill a dream:
the army.
In the ranks
it never was as soldierly
as at the fair,
white-shirted
men
with their greens
were
marshals
of the artichokes,
in tight rows,
shouting commands,
and the detonation
of a falling crate,
but
then
comes
María
with her shopping basket,
selects
an artichoke,
is not afraid,
examines it, observes it
against the light as if it were an egg,

la compra,
la confunde
en su bolsa
con un par de zapatos,
con un repollo y una
botella
de vinagre
hasta
que entrando a la cocina
la sumerge en la olla.
Así termina
en paz
esta carrera
del vegetal armado
que se llama alcachofa,
luego
escama por escama
desvestimos
la delicia
y comemos
la pacífica pasta
de su corazón verde

buys it,
confuses it
in her bag
with a pair of shoes,
with a cabbage head and a
bottle
of vinegar
until
entering the kitchen
she submerges it in the pot.
Thus ends
in peace
this race
of armored vegetable
known as artichoke,
then
scale by scale
we undress
its deliciousness
and eat
the peaceful paste
of its green heart.

13 / ODE TO THE ATOM

Oda al átomo

TRANSLATED BY MARGARET SAYERS PEDEN

Pequeñísima
estrella,
parecías
para siempre
enterrada
en el metal: oculto,
tu diabólico
fuego.
Un día
golpearon
en la puerta
minúscula:
era el hombre.
Con una
descarga
te desencadenaron,
viste el mundo,
saliste
por el día,
recorriste
ciudades,
tu gran fulgor llegaba
a iluminar las vidas,
eras
una fruta terrible,
de eléctrica hermosura,
venías

Infinitesimal
star,
you seemed
forever
buried
in metal, hidden,
your diabolic
fire.
One day
someone knocked
at your tiny
door:
it was man.
With one
explosion
he unchained you,
you saw the world,
you came out
into the daylight,
you traveled through
cities,
your great brilliance
illuminated lives,
you were a
terrible fruit
of electric beauty,
you came to

a apresurar las llamas
del estío,
y entonces
llegó
armado
con anteojos de tigre
y armadura,
con camisa cuadrada,
sulfúricos bigotes,
cola de puerco espín,
llegó el guerrero
y te sedujo:
duerme,
te dijo,
enróllate,
átomo, te pareces
a un dios griego,
a una primaveral
modista de París,
acuéstate
en mi uña,
entra en esta cajita,
y entonces
el guerrero
te guardó en su chaleco
como si fueras sólo
píldora
norteamericana,
y viajó por el mundo
dejándote caer
en Hiroshima.

Despertamos.

La aurora
se había consumido.

hasten the flames
of summer,
and then
wearing
a predator's eyeglasses,
armor,
and a checked shirt,
sporting sulfuric mustaches
and a prehensile tail,
came
the warrior
and seduced you:
sleep,
he told you,
curl up,
atom, you resemble
a Greek god,
a Parisian modiste
in springtime,
lie down here
on my fingernail,
climb into this little box,
and then
the warrior
put you in his jacket
as if you were nothing but
a North American
pill,
and he traveled through the world
and dropped you
on Hiroshima.

We awakened.

The dawn
had been consumed.

Todos los pájaros
cayeron calcinados.
Un olor
de ataúd,
gas de las tumbas,
tronó por los espacios.
Subió horrenda
la forma del castigo
sobrehumano,
hongo sangriento, cúpula,
humareda,
espada
del infierno.
Subió quemante el aire
y se esparció la muerte
en ondas paralelas,
alcanzando
a la madre dormida
con su niño,
al pescador del río
y a los peces,
a la panadería
y a los panes,
al ingeniero
y a sus edificios,
todo
fue polvo
que mordía,
aire
asesino.

La ciudad
desmoronó sus últimos alvéolos,
cayó, cayó de pronto,
derribada,
podrida,

All the birds
burned to ashes.
An odor
of coffins,
gas from tombs,
thundered through space.
The shape of punishment arose,
hideous,
superhuman,
bloody mushroom, dome,
cloud of smoke,
sword
of hell.
Burning air arose,
spreading death
on parallel waves,
reaching
the mother sleeping
with her child,
the river fisherman
and the fish,
the bakery
and the bread,
the engineer
and his buildings;
everything
was acid
dust,
assassin
air.

The city
crumbled its last honeycombs
and fell, fell suddenly,
demolished,
rotten:

los hombres
fueron súbitos leprosos,
tomaban
la mano de sus hijos
y la pequeña mano
se quedaba en sus manos.
Así, de tu refugio,
del secreto
manto de piedra
en que el fuego dormía
te sacaron,
chispa enceguecedora,
luz rabiosa,
a destruir las vidas,
a perseguir lejanas existencias,
bajo el mar,
en el aire,
en las arenas,
en el último
recodo de los puertos,
a borrar
las semillas,
a asesinar los gérmenes,
a impedir la corola,
te destinaron, átomo,
a dejar arrasadas
las naciones,
a convertir el amor en negra pústula,
a quemar amontonados corazones
y aniquilar la sangre.

Oh chispa loca,
vuelve
a tu mortaja,
entiérrate
en tus manos minerales,

men
were instant lepers,
they took
their children's hand
and the little hand
fell off in theirs.
So, from your refuge
in the secret
mantle of stone
in which fire slept
they took you,
blinding spark,
raging light,
to destroy lives,
to threaten distant existences,
beneath the sea,
in the air,
on the sands,
in every twist and turn
of the ports,
to destroy
seeds,
to kill cells,
to stunt the corolla,
they destined you, atom,
to level
nations,
to turn love into a black pustule,
to burn heaped-up hearts
and annihilate blood.

Mad spark,
go back
to your shroud,
bury yourself
in your mineral mantle,

vuelve a ser piedra ciega,
desoye a los bandidos,
colabora
tú, con la vida, con la agricultura,
suplanta los motores,
eleva la energía,
fecunda los planetas.
Ya no tienes
secreto,
camina
entre los hombres
sin máscara
terrible,
apresurando el paso
y extendiendo
los pasos de los frutos,
separando
montañas,
enderezando ríos,
fecundando,
átomo,
desbordada
copa
cósmica,
vuelve
a la paz del racimo,
a la velocidad de la alegría,
vuelve al recinto
de la naturaleza,
ponte a nuestro servicio
y en vez de las cenizas
mortales
de tu máscara,
en vez de los infiernos desatados
de tu cólera,
en vez de la amenaza

be blind stone once again,
ignore the outlaws,
and collaborate
with life, with growing things,
replace motors,
elevate energy,
fertilize planets.
You have no secret
now,
walk
among men
without your terrible
mask,
pick up your pace
and pace
the picking of the fruit,
parting
mountains,
straightening rivers,
making fertile,
atom,
overflowing
cosmic
cup,
return
to the peace of the vine,
to the velocity of joy,
return to the province
of nature,
place yourself at our service,
and instead of the fatal
ashes
of your mask,
instead of the unleashed infernos
of your wrath,
instead of the menace

de tu terrible claridad, entréganos
tu sobrecogedora
rebeldía
para los cereales,
tu magnetismo desencadenado
para fundar la paz entre los hombres,
y así no será infierno
tu luz deslumbradora,
sino felicidad,
matutina esperanza,
contribución terrestre.

of your terrible light, deliver to us
your amazing
rebelliousness
for our grain,
your unchained magnetism
to found peace among men,
and then your dazzling light
will be happiness,
not hell,
hope of morning,
gift to earth.

14 / ODE TO AUTUMN

Oda al otoño

TRANSLATED BY ILAN STAVANS

Ay cuánto tiempo	Oh how could earth
tierra	endure
sin otoño,	without autumn
cómo	for such
pudo vivirse!	a long time!
Ah qué opresiva	Ah how oppressive
náyade	was the naïad
la primavera	of spring,
con sus escandalosos	with its scandalous
pezones	nipples,
mostrándolos en todos	showing us all
los árboles del mundo,	the trees of the world,
y luego	and then
el verano,	the summer,
trigo,	wheat,
trigo,	wheat,
intermitentes	intermittent
grillos,	crickets,
cigarras,	cicadas,
sudor desenfrenado.	frantic sweat.
Entonces	Then
el aire	the air
trae por la mañana	bringing in the morning
un vapor de planeta.	a planet's vapor.
Desde otra estrella	From another star,
caen gotas de plata.	silver drops fall.
Se respira	One breathes

el cambio
de fronteras,
de la humedad al viento,
del viento a las raíces.
Algo sordo, profundo,
trabaja bajo la tierra
almacenando sueños.
La energía se ovilla,
la cinta
de las fecundaciones
enrolla
sus anillos.

Modesto es el otoño
como los leñadores.
Cuesta mucho
sacar todas las hojas
de todos los árboles
de todos los países.
La primavera
las cosió volando
y ahora
hay que dejarlas
caer como si fueran
pájaros amarillos.
No es fácil.
Hace falta tiempo.
Hay que correr por todos
los caminos,
hablar idiomas,
sueco,
portugués,
hablar en lengua roja,
en lengua verde.
Hay que saber
callar en todos

the change
of borders,
from humidity to wind,
from wind to roots.
Something deaf, profound,
labors under the earth,
collecting dreams.
The energy curls,
the strip
of fecundity
rolls
its rings.

Autumn is modest
like the woodcutters.
It's hard
to remove all the leaves
of all the trees
of all the countries.
Spring
sewed them together on the fly
and now
one must allow them
to fall as if they were
yellow birds.
It isn't easy.
There's not enough time.
One must run down all
the roads,
speak languages,
Swedish,
Portuguese,
speak in the red tongue,
the green tongue.
One must know
how to be quiet in all

los idiomas
y en todas partes,
siempre
dejar caer,
caer,
dejar caer,
caer,
las hojas.

Difícil
es
ser otoño,
fácil ser primavera.
Encender todo
lo que nació
para ser encendido.
Pero apagar el mundo
deslizándolo
como si fuera un aro
de cosas amarillas,
hasta fundir olores,
luz, raíces,
subir vino a las uvas,
acuñar con paciencia
la irregular moneda
del árbol en la altura
derramándola luego
en desinteresadas
callas desiertas,
es profesión de manos
varoniles.

Por eso,
otoño,
camarada alfarero,
constructor de planetas,

the languages
and everywhere,
always
allowing
the leaves to fall,
fall,
allowing them to fall,
fall.

It's difficult
to
be autumn,
easy to be spring.
To ignite everything
that is born
to be ignited.
But to turn the world off,
sliding it
as if it were a hoop
of yellow things,
until colors are melted,
light, root,
bringing wine to grapes,
to meld with patience
the irregular coin
of the tree on the height,
then spilling it
over disinterested
deserted streets,
a profession for male
hands.

That's why,
autumn,
comrade potter,
planet builder,

electricista,
preservador de trigo,
te doy mi mano de hombre
a hombre
y te pido me invites
a salir a caballo,
a trabajar contigo.
Siempre quise
ser aprendiz de otoño,
ser pariente pequeño
del laborioso
mecánico de altura,
galopar por la tierra
repartiendo
oro,
inútil oro.
Pero, mañana,
otoño,
te ayudaré a que cobren
hojas de oro
los pobres del camino.

Otoño, buen jinete,
galopemos,
antes que nos ataje
el negro invierno.
Es duro
nuestro largo trabajo.
Vamos
a preparar la tierra
y a enseñarla
a ser madre,
a guardar las semillas
que en su vientre
van a dormir cuidadas
por dos jinetes rojos

electrician,
wheat preserver,
I give you my hand from man
to man
and ask that you invite me
to go out for a horse ride,
to work with you.
I always wanted
to be the autumn's apprentice,
to be a small relation
of the laborious
mechanic of the heights,
to gallop across the earth
sharing
gold,
useless gold.
But, tomorrow,
autumn,
I will help you to pay
the poor on the road
with golden leaves.

Autumn, fine horseman,
let us gallop
before the black winter
captures us.
Our strenuous work
is hard.
Let us
prepare the earth
and teach it
how to be a mother,
to save the seeds
in her womb
that sleep protected
by two red horsemen

que corren por el mundo:
el aprendiz de otoño
y el otoño.

Así de las raíces
oscuras y escondidas
podrán salir bailando
la fragancia
y el velo verde de la primavera.

traveling the world:
the autumn's apprentice
and autumn.

Thus, out of the dark
and hidden leaves
the fragrance
and the green veil of spring
will emerge dancing.

15 / ODE TO THE AZURE FLOWER

Oda a la flor azul

TRANSLATED BY ILAN STAVANS

Caminando hacia el mar
en la pradera
—es hoy noviembre—,
todo ha nacido ya,
todo tiene estatura,
ondulación, fragancia.
Hierba a hierba
entenderé la tierra,
paso a paso
hasta la línea loca
del océano.
De pronto una ola
de aire agita y ondula
la cebada salvaje:
salta
el vuelo de un pájaro
desde mis pies, el suelo
lleno de hilos de oro,
de pétalos sin nombre,
brilla de pronto como rosa verde,
se enreda con ortigas que revelan
su coral enemigo,
esbeltos tallos, zarzas
estrelladas,
diferencia infinita
de cada vegetal que me saluda
a veces con un rápido
centelleo de espinas

Walking to the sea,
across the prairie
—it's now November—
everything's born already,
everything has height,
undulation, fragrance.
Blade by blade,
step by step,
I shall understand the earth,
all the way to the crazy line
of the ocean.
Suddenly, a wave
of air shakes and ripples
the wild barley:
a bird
leaps into flight
at my feet; the earth
is teeming with golden threads,
nameless petals,
it shines suddenly like a green rose,
wreathed with spines, revealing
its enemy coral,
slim stems, starry
canes,
infinite difference
of each vegetable greeting me
sometimes with a quick
flashing of thorns,

o con la pulsación de su perfume
fresco, fino y amargo.
Andando a las espumas
del Pacífico
con torpe paso por la baja hierba
de la primavera escondida,
parece
que antes de que la tierra se termine
cien metros antes del más grande océano
todo se hizo delirio,
germinación y canto.
Las minúsculas hierbas
se coronaron de oro,
las plantas de la arena
dieron rayos morados
y a cada pequeña hoja de olvido
llegó una dirección de luna o fuego.
Cerca del mar, andando,
en el mes de noviembre,
entre los matorrales que reciben
luz, fuego y sal marinas
hallé una flor azul
nacida en la durísima pradera.
De dónde, de qué fondo
tu rayo azul extraes?
Tu seda temblorosa
debajo de la tierra
se comunica con el mar profundo?
La levanté en mis manos
y la miré como si el mar viviera
en una sola gota,
como si en el combate
de la tierra y las aguas
una flor levantara
un pequeño estandarte
de fuego azul, de paz irresistible,
de indómita pureza.

or with the pulsation of fresh
perfume, fine and sour.
Walking to the foam
of the Pacific
through the low green
of the hidden spring
with a clumsy step,
just before the land ends,
a hundred meters from the largest ocean
apparently all becomes delirium,
germination and song.
The tiny green
has been crowned with gold,
the sand plants
projected purple rays,
and each small leaf of forgetting
was greeted by an arrow of moon or fire.
Near the sea, walking
in the month of November,
among the bushes receiving
light, fire, and marine salts,
I find an azure flower,
born in the arid prairie.
From where, from what source
do you extract your blue ray?
Does your trembling silk
communicate with the deep sea
under the soil?
Picking it up in my hands,
I look at it as if the sea
could live in a single drop,
as if in the fight
between land and water
a flower could raise
a small flag
of azure fire, of irresistible peace,
of indomitable purity.

16 / ODE TO THE BAD BLIND MAN

Oda al mal ciego

TRANSLATED BY ILAN STAVANS

Oh ciego sin guitarra
y con envidia,
cocido
en
tu
veneno,
desdeñado
como
esos
zapatos
entreabiertos y raídos
que a veces
abren la boca como si quisieran
ladrar, ladrar desde la acequia sucia.
Oh atado
de lo que nunca fue, no pudo serlo,
de lo que no será, no tendrá boca,
ni voz, ni voto,
ni recuerdo,
porque así suma y resta
la vida en su pizarra:
al inocente el don,
al nudo ciego
su cuerda y su castigo.

Yo pasé y no sabía
que allí estaba esperando
con su brasa,

Oh, blind man without a guitar
and with envy,
cooked
in
your
poison,
scorned
like
those
half-open and threadbare
shoes
sometimes
opening their mouths as if they were ready
to bark, bark from the dirty trench.
Oh tied
to what never was, could not be,
to what will not be, will not have a mouth,
nor voice, nor vote,
nor memory,
because thus he adds and subtracts
life on the blackboard:
talent to the innocent,
to the blind knot
a string and a punishment.

I passed
and didn't know he was waiting there
with his ember,

y como no podía	and since he couldn't
quemarme	burn me
y me buscaba	and sought me
adentro de su sombra,	inside his shadow,
me fui	I left
con mis canciones	with my songs
a la luz	under the light
de la vida.	of life.
Pobre!	Poor man!
Allí transcurre,	He happens there,
allí está transcurrido,	he is happening there,
preparando	preparing
su sopa de vinagre,	his vinegar soup,
su queso de escorbuto,	his scurvy cheese,
cociéndose	cooking himself
en su nata corrosiva,	in corrosive cream,
en esa oscura olla	in his dark pot
en que cayó	into which he fell
y fue condenado	and was condemned
a consumir su propio	to consume his own
vitalicio brebaje.	foul drink.

17 / ODE TO BARBED WIRE

Oda al alambre de púa

TRANSLATED BY ILAN STAVANS

En mi país
alambre, alambre . . .

Tú recorres
el largo
hilo de Chile,
pájaros,
soledades,
y a lo largo,
a lo ancho,
extensiones baldías,
alambre,
alambre . . .

En otros sitios
del planeta
los cereales
desbordan,
trémulas olas
hace el viento
sobre el trigo.
En otras
tierras
muge
nutricia y poderosa
en las praderas
la ganadería:
aquí,
montes desiertos,

In my country
wire, wire . . .

You move across
Chile's
long thread,
birds,
solitudes,
and far,
and wide,
untilled extensions,
wire,
wire . . .

In other places
on the planet
grain
overflows,
the wind makes
quivering waves
on the wheat.
In other
lands
the livestock
moos
nourished and portentous
on the meadows:
here,
empty hills,

latitudes,
no hay hombres,
no hay caballos,
sólo cercados,
púas,
y la tierra
vacía.

En otras partes
cunden
los repollos,
los quesos,
se multiplica
el pan,
el humo
asoma
su penacho
en los techos
como el tocado
de la codorniz,
aldeas
que ocultan,
como la gallina
sus huevos,
un nido de tractores:
la esperanza.
Aquí
tierras
y tierras,
tierras enmudecidas,
tierras ciegas,
tierras sin corazón,
tierras sin surco.

En otras partes pan,
arroz, manzanas . . .

En Chile alambre, alambre . . .

latitudes,
there are no men,
there are no horses,
only enclosures,
barbs,
and the empty
land.

In other places
cabbages
spread,
cheeses,
bread
multiplies,
smoke
peeps
its crest
on the roofs
like the quail's
headgear,
villages
hiding,
like the hen
its eggs,
a tractor's nest:
hope.
Here
land
and land,
silenced earth,
blinded earth,
earth without heart,
earth without furrow.

In other places bread,
rice, apples . . .

In Chile, wire, wire . . .

18 / ODE TO A BEAUTIFUL NUDE

Oda a la bella desnuda

TRANSLATED BY NATHANIEL TARN

Con casto corazón, con ojos
puros,
te celebro, belleza,
reteniendo la sangre
para que surja y siga
la línea, tu contorno,
para
que te acuestes en mi oda
como en tierra de bosques o en espuma:
en aroma terrestre
o en música marina.

Bella desnuda,
igual
tus pies arqueados
por un antiguo golpe
del viento o del sonido
que tus orejas,
caracolas mínimas
del espléndido mar americano.
Iguales son tus pechos
de paralela plenitud, colmados
por la luz de la vida,
iguales son
volando
tus párpados de trigo
que descubren

With a chaste heart,
with pure eyes,
I celebrate your beauty
holding the leash of blood
so that it might leap out
and trace your outline
where
you lie down in my ode
as in a land of forests, or in surf:
in aromatic loam
or in sea-music.

Beautiful nude:
equally beautiful
your feet
arched by primeval tap
of wind or sound;
your ears
small shells
of the splendid American sea;
your breasts
of level plenitude full-
filled by living light;
your flying
eyelids of wheat
revealing

o cierran	or enclosing
dos países profundos en tus ojos.	the two deep countries of your eyes.
La línea que tu espalda	The line your shoulders
ha dividido	have divided
en pálidas regiones	into pale regions
se pierde y surge	loses itself and blends
en dos tersas mitades	into the compact halves
de manzana	of an apple,
y sigue separando	continues separating
tu hermosura	your beauty down
en dos columnas	into two columns
de oro quemado, de alabastro fino,	of burnished gold, fine alabaster,
a perderse en tus pies como en dos uvas,	to sink into the two grapes of your feet,
desde donde otra vez arde y se eleva	where your twin symmetrical tree
el árbol doble de tu simetría,	burns again and rises:
fuego florido, candelabro abierto,	flowering fire, open chandelier,
turgente fruta erguida	a swelling fruit
sobre el pacto del mar y de la tierra.	over the pact of sea and earth.
Tu cuerpo, en qué materia,	From what materials—
ágata, cuarzo, trigo,	agate, quartz, wheat—
se plasmó, fue subiendo	did your body come together,
como el pan se levanta	swelling like baking bread
de la temperatura,	to signal silvered
y señaló colinas	hills,
plateadas,	the cleavage of one petal,
valles de un sólo pétalo, dulzuras	sweet fruits of a deep velvet,
de profundo terciopelo,	until alone remained,
hasta quedar cuajada	astonished,
la fina y firme forma femenina?	the fine and firm feminine form?
No sólo es luz que cae	It is not only light that falls
sobre el mundo	over the world,
la que alarga en tu cuerpo	spreading inside your body
su nieve sofocada,	its suffocated snow,

sino que se desprende
de ti la claridad como si fueras
encendida por dentro.

Debajo de tu piel vive la luna.

so much as clarity
taking its leave of you
as if you were
on fire within.

The moon lives in the lining of your skin.

19 / ODE TO THE BED

Oda a la cama

TRANSLATED BY ILAN STAVANS

De cama en cama en cama	From bed to bed to bed
es este viaje	in this journey
el viaje de la vida.	the journey of life.
El que nace, el herido	He who is born, he who is injured,
y el que muere,	and he who dies,
el que ama y el que sueña	he who loves and he who dreams
vinieron y se van de cama en cama,	came and went from bed to bed,
vinimos y nos vamos	we came and left
en este tren, en esta nave, en este	in this train, in this ship, in
río común	this common river
a toda	steaming
vida,	with life,
común	common
a toda muerte.	to every death.
La tierra es una cama	The earth is a bed
florida por amor, sucia de sangre,	flowered with love, dirty with blood,
las sábanas del cielo	the sky sheets
se secan	dry out
desplegando	unfolding
el cuerpo de septiembre y su blancura,	the September body and its whiteness,
el mar	the sea
cruje	crunches
golpeado	hitting
por la	through the
cúpula	green
verde	cupola

del
abismo
y mueve ropa blanca y ropa negra.

Oh mar, cama terrible,
agitación perpetua
de la muerte y la vida,
del aire encarnizado y de la espuma,
duermen en ti los peces,
la noche,
las ballenas,
yace en ti la ceniza
centrífuga y celeste
de los agonizantes meteoros:
palpitas, mar, con todos
tus dormidos,
construyes y destruyes
el tálamo incesante de los sueños.

De pronto sale un rayo
con dos ojos de puro nomeolvides,
con nariz de marfil o de manzana,
y te muestra el sendero
a suaves sábanas
como estandartes claros de azucena
por donde resbalamos
al enlace.
Luego
viene a la cama
la muerte con sus manos oxidadas
y su lengua de yodo
y levanta su dedo
largo como un camino
mostrándonos la arena,
la puerta de los últimos dolores.

of the
abyss
and moves white clothes and black clothes.

Oh sea, terrible bed,
perpetual agitation
of death and life,
of bitter air and of foam,
the fish sleep in you,
the night,
the whales,
in you lie the ashes
centrifugal and celestial
of the agonizing meteors:
you palpitate, sea, with all
your sleepy beings,
you build and destroy
the incessant thalamus of dreams.

Suddenly a ray emerges
with two eyes of pure forget-me-not,
with nose of ivory or apple,
and they show you the path
to the soft sheets
like clear white-lily banners
through which we slip
toward a bond.
Then
comes to the bed
death with its rusty hands
and its iodine tongue
and raises its finger
long like a road
showing us the sand,
the door of the latest pain.

20 / ODE TO BEES

Oda a la abeja

TRANSLATED BY MARGARET SAYERS PEDEN

Multitud de la abeja!
Entra y sale
del carmín, del azul,
del amarillo,
de la más suave
suavidad del mundo:
entra en
una corola
precipitadamente,
por negocios,
sale
con traje de oro
y cantidad de botas
amarillas.

Perfecta
desde la cintura,
el abdomen rayado
por barrotes oscuros,
la cabecita
siempre
preocupada
y las
alas
recién hechas de agua:
entra
por todas las ventanas olorosas,

Multitude of bees!
In and out of the
crimson, the blue,
the yellow,
of the softest
softness in the world;
you tumble
headlong
into a corolla
to conduct your business,
and emerge
wearing a golden suit
and quantities of
yellow boots.

The waist,
perfect,
the abdomen striped
with dark bars,
the tiny,
ever-busy
head,
the
wings,
newly made of water;
you enter
every sweet-scented window,

abre
las puertas de la seda,
penetra por los tálamos
del amor más fragante,
tropieza
con
una
gota
de rocío
como con un diamante
y de todas las casas
que visita
saca
miel
misteriosa,
rica y pesada
miel, espeso aroma,
líquida luz que cae en goterones,
hasta que a su
palacio
colectivo
regresa
y en las góticas almenas
deposita
el producto
de la flor y del vuelo,
el sol nupcial seráfico y secreto!
Multitud de la abeja!
Elevación
sagrada
de la unidad,
colegio
palpitante!

Zumban
sonoros

open
silken doors,
penetrate the bridal chamber
of the most fragrant
love,
discover
a
drop
of diamond
dew,
and from every house
you visit
you remove
honey,
mysterious,
rich and heavy
honey, thick aroma,
liquid, guttering light,
until you return
to your
communal
palace
and on its gothic parapets
deposit
the product
of flower and flight,
the seraphic and secret nuptial sun!
Multitude of bees!
Sacred
elevation
of unity,
seething
schoolhouse.

Buzzing,
noisy

números
que trabajan
el néctar,
pasan
veloces
gotas
de ambrosía:
es la siesta
del verano en las verdes
soledades
de Osorno. Arriba
el sol clava sus lanzas
en la nieve,
relumbran los volcanes,
ancha
como
los mares
es la tierra,
azul es el espacio,
pero
hay algo
que tiembla, es
el quemante
corazón
del verano,
el corazón de miel
multiplicado,
la rumorosa
abeja,
el crepitante
panal
de vuelo y oro!

Abejas,
trabajadoras puras,
ojivales

workers
process
the nectar,
swiftly
exchanging
drops
of ambrosia;
it is summer
siesta in the green
solitudes
of Osorno. High above,
the sun casts its spears
into the snow,
volcanoes glisten,
land
stretches
endless
as the sea,
space is blue,
but
something
trembles, it is
the fiery
heart
of summer,
the honeyed heart
multiplied,
the buzzing
bee,
the crackling
honeycomb
of flight and gold!

Bees,
purest laborers,
ogival

obreras,
finas, relampagueantes
proletarias,
perfectas,
temerarias milicias
que en el combate atacan
con aguijón suicida,
zumbad,
zumbad sobre
los dones de la tierra,
familia de oro,
multitud del viento,
sacudid el incendio
de las flores,
la sed de los estambres,
el agudo
hilo
de olor
que reúne los días,
y propagad
la miel
sobrepasando
los continentes húmedos, las islas
más lejanas del cielo
del oeste.

Sí:
que la cera levante
estatuas verdes,
la miel
derrame
lenguas
infinitas,
y el océano sea
una
colmena,

workers,
fine, flashing
proletariat,
perfect,
daring militia
that in combat attack
with suicidal sting;
buzz,
buzz above
the earth's endowments,
family of gold,
multitude of the wind,
shake the fire
from the flowers,
thirst from the stamens,
the sharp,
aromatic
thread
that stitches together the days,
and propagate
honey,
passing over
humid continents, the most
distant islands of the
western sky.

Yes:
let the wax erect
green statues,
let honey
spill in
infinite
tongues,
let the ocean be
a
beehive,

la tierra
torre y túnica
de flores,
y el mundo
una cascada,
cabellera,
crecimiento
incesante
de panales!

the earth
tower and tunic
of flowers,
and the world
a waterfall,
a comet's tail, a
never-ending
wealth
of honeycombs!

21 / ODE TO BICYCLES

Oda a la bicicleta

TRANSLATED BY MARGARET SAYERS PEDEN

Iba	I was walking
por el camino	down
crepitante:	a sizzling road:
el sol se desgranaba	the sun popped like
como maíz ardiendo	a field of blazing maize,
y era	the
la tierra	earth
calurosa	was hot,
un infinito círculo	an infinite circle
con cielo arriba	with an empty
azul, deshabitado.	blue sky overhead.
Pasaron	A few bicycles
junto a mí	passed
las bicicletas,	me by,
los únicos	the only
insectos	insects
de aquel	in
minuto	that dry
seco del verano,	moment of summer,
sigilosas,	silent,
veloces,	swift,
transparentes:	translucent;
me parecieron	they
sólo	barely stirred
movimientos del aire.	the air.

Obreros y muchachas
a las fábricas
iban
entregando
los ojos
al verano,
las cabezas al cielo,
sentados
en los
élitros
de las vertiginosas
bicicletas
que silbaban
cruzando
puentes, rosales, zarza
y mediodía.

Pensé en la tarde cuando
los muchachos
se laven,
canten, coman, levanten
una copa
de vino
en honor
del amor
y de la vida,
y a la puerta
esperando
la bicicleta
inmóvil
porque
sólo
de movimiento fue su alma
y allí caída
no es
insecto transparente

Workers and girls
were riding to their
factories,
giving
their eyes
to summer,
their heads to the sky,
sitting on the
hard
beetle backs
of the whirling
bicycles
that whirred
as they rode by
bridges, rosebushes, brambles
and midday.

I thought about evening when
the boys
wash up,
sing, eat, raise
a cup
of wine
in honor
of love
and life,
and waiting
at the door,
the bicycle,
stilled,
because
only moving
does it have a soul,
and fallen there
it isn't
a translucent insect

que recorre
el verano,
sino
esqueleto
frío
que sólo
recupera
un cuerpo errante
con la urgencia
y la luz,
es decir,
con
la
resurrección
de cada día.

humming
through summer
but
a cold
skeleton
that will return to
life
only
when it's needed,
when it's light,
that is,
with
the
resurrection
of each day.

22 / ODE TO BIRD MIGRATION

Oda a la migración de los pájaros

TRANSLATED BY ILAN STAVANS

Por la línea
del mar
hacia el Gran Norte
un
río
derramado
sobre el cielo:
son los pájaros
del Sur, del ventisquero,
que vienen de las islas,
de la nieve:
los halcones antárticos,
los cormoranes vestidos
de luto,
los australes petreles del exilio.
Y hacia
las rocas amarillas
del Perú, hacia las
aguas encendidas
de Baja California
el incesante río
de los pájaros
vuela.

Aparece
uno,
es

Along the sea
line
toward the Grand North
a
spilled
river
on the sky:
it's the birds
from the South, from the snowdrift,
coming from the islands,
from the snow:
Antarctic hawks,
cormorants dressed
in mourning,
austral petrels out of exile.
And toward
the yellow rocks
from Peru, toward
the hidden waters
of Baja California,
flies
the incessant river
of birds.

One
appears,
it is

un
punto
perdido
en el espacio abierto de la niebla:
detrás son las cohortes
silenciosas, la masa
del plumaje,
el tembloroso triángulo
que corre sobre
el océano frío,
el cauce
sagrado
que palpita,
la flecha
de la nave
migratoria.

an
intangible
point
in an open space of fog:
behind are the silent
cohorts, the mass
of plumage,
the trembling triangle
running over
the cold ocean,
the palpitating
sacred
channel,
the arrow
of the migrating
craft.

Cadáveres de pájaros marinos
cayeron
en la arena,
pequeños
bultos
negros
encerrados
por las alas bruñidas
como ataúdes
hechos
en el cielo.
Y junto
a las falanges
crispadas sobre
la inútil
arena,
el mar,
el mar que continúa
el trueno blanco y verde de la olas,
la eternidad borrascosa del cielo.

Cadavers of marine birds
fell
on the sand,
black
small
bumps
locked
by burnished wings
like coffins
made
in heaven.
And near
the pressured
phalanges over
the useless
sand,
the sea,
the sea continues
the white and green thunder of the waves,
the tempestuous eternity of the sky.

Pasan
las aves, como
el amor,
buscando fuego,
volando desde
el desamparo
hacia la luz y las germinaciones,
unidas en el vuelo
de la vida,
y sobre
la línea y las espumas de la costa
los pájaros que cambian de planeta
llenan
el mar
con su silencio de alas.

The birds
pass by, like
love,
searching for fire,
flying from
abandonment
toward light and burgeoning,
tied to the flight
of life,
and on
the line and foam of the coast
the birds changing the planet
fill
the sea
with their silence of wings.

23 / ODE TO THE BIRDS OF CHILE

Oda a las aves de Chile

TRANSLATED BY MARGARET SAYERS PEDEN

Aves de Chile, de plumaje negro,	Black-feathered birds of Chile,
nacidas	born
entre la cordillera y las espumas,	between foam and cordillera,
aves hambrientas,	hungry birds,
pájaros sombríos,	somber birds,
cernícalos, halcones,	hawks and falcons,
águilas de las islas,	island eagles,
cóndores coronados por la nieve,	snow-crowned condors,
pomposos buitres enlutados,	pompous, funereal vultures,
devoradores de carroña,	carrion gorgers,
dictadores del cielo,	dictators of the sky,
aves amargas,	bitter birds,
buscadoras de sangre,	blood hunters,
nutridas con serpientes,	snake eaters,
ladronas,	thieves,
brujas del monte,	mountain witches,
sangrientas	bloodthirsty
majestades,	majesties,
admiro	I marvel
vuestro vuelo.	at your flight.
Largo rato interrogo	Long hours I scan
el espacio extendido	the vast sky
buscando el movimiento	searching for the motion
de las alas:	of your wings:
allí estáis,	I see you,
naves negras	black birds
de aterradora altura,	of alarming altitudes,

silenciosas estirpes
asesinas,
estrellas sanguinarias.
En la costa
la espuma sube al ala.
Ácida luz
salpica
el vuelo
de las aves marinas,
rozando el agua cruzan
migratorias,
cierran de pronto
el vuelo
y caen como flechas
sobre el volumen verde.

Yo navegué sin tregua
las orillas,
el desdentado litoral, la calle
entre las islas
del océano,
el grande mar Pacífico,
rosa azul de pétalos rabiosos,
y en el Golfo de Penas
el cielo
y el albatros,
la soledad del aire y su medida,
la ola negra del cielo.
Más allá,
sacudido
por olas y por alas,
cormoranes,
gaviotas y piqueros,
el océano vuela,
las abruptas
rocas golpeadas por el mar se mueven

silent breed,
murderers,
sanguinary stars.
Along the coast
foam takes wing.
Acid light
spatters
the flight
of migrating seabirds
skimming
the surface of the water;
suddenly they close
formation
and fall like arrows
upon voluminous green.

Tirelessly I navigated
the shorelines,
the toothless littoral, the street
between the islands
of the ocean,
the great Pacific sea,
blue rosebush of raging petals,
and in the Golfo de Penas
the sky
and the albatross,
the solitude of air and its vastness,
the black wave of the sky.
Ahead,
shaken
by waves and wings,
cormorants,
gulls and pikemen,
the ocean takes wing,
steep rocks,
pounded by the sea, stir,

palpitantes de pájaros,
se desborda la luz, el crecimiento,
atraviesa los mares hacia el norte
el vuelo de la vida.

Pero no sólo mares
o tempestuosas
cordilleras andinas
procreadoras
de pájaros terribles,
eres,
oh delicada patria mía:
entre tus brazos verdes se deslizan
las diucas matutinas,
van a misa
vestidas con sus mantos diminutos,
tordos ceremoniales
y metálicos loros,
el minúsculo
siete colores de los pajonales,
el queltehue
que al elevar el vuelo
despliega su abanico
de nieve blanca y negra,
el canastero y el matacaballo,
el fringilo dorado,
el jacamar y el huilque,
la torcaza,
el chincol y el chirigüe,
la tenca cristalina,
el zorzal suave,
el jilguero que danza sobre el hilo
de la música pura,
el cisne austral, nave
de plata

beating with birds,
light overflows, swells,
the flight of life
crosses the seas to the north.

But, my delicate land,
you are
more than seas
and stormy
Andean cordilleras,
begetters
of terrible birds;
through your green branches
in early morning
slip finches
in diminutive robes
on their way to mass,
ceremonial starlings
and metallic parrots pass,
the tiny
tanager of the harvested fields,
the *queltehue*
that rising in flight
unfolds a fan
of snowy white and black,
the weaverbird and the *ani-cuckoo*,
the golden bunting,
the jacamar, the *huilque,*
the ringdove,
crown sparrow and *chirigue*,
the crystalline mockingbird,
the dulcet thrush,
the goldfinch dancing on a thread
of purest music,
the southern swan, ship
of silver

y enlutado terciopelo,
la perdiz olorosa y el relámpago
de los fosforescentes picaflores.
En la suave cintura de mi patria,
entre las monarquías iracundas
del volcán y el océano,
aves de la dulzura,
tocáis el sol, el aire,
sois el temblor de un vuelo en el verano
del agua a mediodía,
rayos de luz violeta en la arboleda,
campanitas redondas,
pequeños aviadores polvorientos
que regresan del polen,
buzos en la espesura de la alfalfa.

Oh vivo vuelo!

Oh viviente hermosura!

Oh multitud del trino!

Aves de Chile, huracanadas
naves carniceras
o dulces y pequeñas
criaturas
de la flor y las uvas,
vuestros nidos construyen
la fragante unidad del territorio:
vuestras vidas errantes
son el pueblo del cielo
que nos canta,
vuestro vuelo
reúne las estrellas de la patria.

and mourning velvet,
the fragrant partridge and a flash
of phosphorescent hummingbird.
In the soft girdle of my country,
between wrathful monarchies
of volcano and sea,
sweet, gentle birds,
you touch the sun, the sky,
you are the tremor of a summer flight
from water to midday,
rays of violet in the woodland,
tiny round bells,
small, homebound aviators
dusted with pollen,
deep-sea divers in densest alfalfa.

Vivid flight!

Living beauty!

Multitude of song!

Birds of Chile, hurricanes,
carnivorous birdships
or sweet, small
creatures
of flower and grape,
your nests structure
the fragrant unity of the land:
your winging lives
compose the nation of the sky
and sing to us,
your flight
unites my country's stars.

24 / ODE TO BIRD-WATCHING

Oda a mirar pájaros

TRANSLATED BY ILAN STAVANS

Ahora
a buscar pájaros!
Las altas ramas férreas
en el bosque,
la espesa
fecundidad del suelo,
está mojado
el mundo,
brilla
lluvia o rocío, un astro
diminuto
en las hojas:
fresca
es la matutina
tierra madre,
el aire
es como un río
que sacude
el silencio,
huele a romero,
a espacio
y a raíces.
Arriba
un canto loco,
una cascada,
es un pájaro.
Cómo

Now
let's look for birds!
The high, ferrous treetops
of the forest,
the dense
fecund underground,
the world
is drenched,
rain or dew
shine, a tiny
planet
among leaves:
fresh
is the dawn-light
mother earth,
the air
is like a river
winnowing
silence,
smelling of rosemary,
space
and roots.
Above
a crazy song,
a waterfall,
is a bird.
How

de su garganta
más pequeña que un dedo
pueden caer las aguas
de su canto?
Facultad luminosa!
Poderío
invisible,
torrente
de la música
en la hojas,
conversación sagrada!

Limpio, lavado, fresco
es este día,
sonoro
como cítara verde,
yo entierro
los zapatos
en el lodo,
salto los manantiales,
una espina
me muerde y una ráfaga
de aire como una ola
cristalina
se divide en mi pecho.
Dónde
están los pájaros?
Fue tal vez
ese
susurro en el follaje
o esa huidiza bola
de pardo terciopelo
o ese desplazamiento
de perfume? Esa hoja
que desprendió el canelo
fue un pájaro? Ese polvo

can this song
fall from a
throat
narrower than a finger width?
Luminous asset!
Invisible
wealth,
torrent
of music
in the leaves,
sacred conversation!

Clean, washed, fresh
is this day,
resonant
like a green zither,
I sink
my shoes
in the glebe,
jump over water holes,
a thorn
bites me and gusts
of air like crystal
waves
break in my chest.
Where
are the birds?
Perhaps it was
that
murmur in the foliage
or the fleeing ball
of reddish velvet
or the shift
of perfume? That leaf
lost by the cinnamon tree
was a bird? The dust

de magnolia irritada
o esa fruta
que cayó resonando,
eso fue un vuelo?
Oh pequeños cretinos
invisibles,
pájaros del demonio,
vàyanse
al diablo
con su sonajera,
con sus plumas inútiles!
Yo que sólo quería
acariciarlos,
verlos resplandeciendo,
no quiero
en la vitrina
ver los relámpagos embalsamados,
quiero verlos vivientes,
quiero tocar sus guantes
de legítimo cuero,
que nunca olvidan en las ramas,
y conversar con ellos
en los hombros
aunque me dejen como a ciertas estatuas
inmerecidamente blanqueado.

Imposible.
No se tocan,
se oyen
como un celeste
susurro o movimiento,
conversan
con precisión,
repiten
sus observaciones,
se jactan

of irritated magnolia
or that fruit
echoing in its fall,
was that a flight?
Oh tiny, invisible
cretins,
birds of the demon,
go
to hell
with your chimes,
with your useless feathers!
I who only wished
to express affection,
to admire their glow,
I don't want to see them
become embalmed flashes of light
locked in a cage,
I want to see them alive,
touch their gloves
of genuine leather,
which they never leave behind in branches,
and converse with them
on my shoulders
even though they leave like certain statues
unjustly whitewashed.

Impossible.
Not to be touched,
they can be heard
like a celestial
whisper or movement,
they talk
with precision,
repeating
their remarks,
brag

de cuanto hacen,
comentan
cuanto existe,
dominan
ciertas ciencias
como la hidrografía
y a ciencia cierta saben
dónde están cosechando
cereales.
Ahora bien,
pájaros
invisibles
de la selva, del bosque,
de la enramada pura,
pájaros de la acacia
y de la encina,
pájaros
locos, enamorados,
sorpresivos,
cantantes
vanidosos,
músicos migratorios,
una palabra
última
antes
de volver
con zapatos mojados, espinas
y hojas secas
a mi casa:
vagabundos,
os amo
libres,
lejos de la escopeta y de la jaula,
corolas
fugitivas,
así

of what they do,
comment
on whatever is in existence,
master
certain sciences
like hydrography
and know for sure
where cereals
are being harvested.
Well then,
invisible
birds
of the jungle, of the forest,
of a perfect canopy,
birds of acacia
and oak,
crazy
birds, lovesick,
surprised,
conceited
singers,
migrating musicians,
one last
word
before
I return
home
with my wet shoes, thorns
and dry leaves:
tramps,
I love you
free,
far from the gun and the cage,
fugitive
corollas,
I love you

os amo,
inasibles,
solidaria y sonora
sociedad de la altura,
hojas
en libertad,
campeones
del aire,
pétalos
del humo,
libres,
alegres
voladores y cantores,
aéreos y terrestres,
navegantes del viento,
felices
constructores
de suavísimos nidos,
incesantes
mensajeros del polen,
casamenteros
de la flor, tíos
de la semilla,
os amo,
ingratos:
vuelvo
feliz de haber vivido con vosotros
un minuto
en el viento.

thus,
unreachable,
solitary and musical
society of heights,
leaves
of freedom,
champions
of the air,
petals
of smoke,
free,
happy
fliers and singers,
air-free and earthbound,
navigators of the wind,
cheerful
builders
of delicate nests,
incessant
messengers of pollen,
matchmakers
of the flower, uncles
of seed,
I love you,
damn it:
I happily
return from having lived with you
a moment
in the wind.

25 / ODE TO A BLACK PANTHERESS

Oda a la pantera negra

TRANSLATED BY MARGARET SAYERS PEDEN

Hace treinta y un años,
no lo olvido,
en Singapur, la lluvia
caliente como sangre
caía
sobre
antiguos muros blancos
carcomidos
por la humedad que en ellos
dejó besos leprosos.
La multitud oscura
relucía
de pronto en un relámpago,
los dientes
o los ojos
y el sol de hierro arriba
como
lanza implacable.
Vagué por calles inundadas
de olor,
betel, *las nueces rojas*
elevándose
sobre
camas de hojas fragantes,
y el fruto Dorian
pudriéndose en la siesta bochornosa.
De pronto estuve

Thirty-one years ago
in Singapore
—I still remember—
blood-warm
rain
was falling
on ancient
white walls
pocked and pitted
by humid, leprous kisses.
Suddenly a flash
of teeth
or eyes
would light
the dark multitude,
while overhead
a leaden sun cast down
its inexorable spear.
I wandered teeming alleyways:
betel, the red nut,
couched on beds of
fragrant leaves,
through the sweltering siesta
the *dorian* fruit
decayed.
Two eyes stopped me,
a stare, a gaze,

frente a una mirada,
desde una jaula
en medio de la calle
dos círculos
de frío,
dos imanes,
dos electricidades enemigas,
dos ojos
que entraron en los míos
clavándome
a la tierra
y a la pared leprosa.
Vi entonces
el cuerpo que ondulaba
y era
sombra de terciopelo,
elástica pureza,
noche pura.
Bajo la negra piel
espolvoreados
apenas la irisaban
no supe bien
si rombos de topacio
o hexágonos de oro
que se translucían
cuando
la presencia
delgada
se movía.
La pantera
pensando
y palpitando
era
una
reina
salvaje

a cage
in the middle of the street;
two icy
circles,
two magnets,
twin points
of hostile electricity,
two piercing eyes
transfixed me,
nailed me to the ground
before the leprous wall.
Then
I saw
undulating muscle,
velvet shadow,
flexed perfection,
incarnate night.
Blinking in that black pelt,
dusting it with iridescence,
either—I never knew for sure—
two topaz lozenges
or hexagons of gold
that glittered
as
the
lissome
presence
stirred.
A
pensive,
pulsating
pantheress;
a
savage
queen

en un cajón	caged
en medio	in the middle
de la calle	of the miserable
miserable.	street.
De la selva perdida,	Of the lost jungle
del engaño,	where she knew deceit,
del espacio robado,	of her freedom, lost forever,
del agridulce olor	of the acrid, sweetish odor
a ser humano	of human creatures
y casas polvorientas	and their dusty dwellings,
ella	only
sólo expresaba	mineral
con ojos	eyes
minerales	revealed
su desprecio, su ira	her scorn,
quemadora,	her
y eran sus ojos	scathing rage,
dos	two
sellos	jewel-like seals
impenetrables	that closed
que cerraban	until eternity
hasta la eternidad	a savage
una puerta salvaje.	door.
Anduvo	She moved like fire,
como el fuego, y, como el humo,	and when she closed her eyes,
cuando cerró los ojos	like smoke she disappeared,
se hizo invisible, inabarcable noche.	invisible, elusive night.

26 / ODE TO THE BOOK I

Oda al libro I

TRANSLATED BY EDWARD HIRSCH

Libro, cuando te cierro
abro la vida.
Escucho
entrecortados gritos
en los puertos.
Los lingotes del cobre
cruzan los arenales,
bajan a Tocopilla.
Es de noche.
Entre las islas
nuestro océano
palpita con sus peces.
Toca los pies, los muslos,
las costillas calcáreas
de mi patria.
Toda la noche pega en sus orillas
y con la luz del día
amanece cantando
como si despertara una guitarra.

A mí me llama el golpe
del océano. A mí
me llama el viento,
y Rodríguez me llama,
José Antonio,
recibí un telegrama
del sindicato «Mina»

Book, when I close you
life itself opens.
I hear
broken screams
in the harbor.
The copper slugs
cross the sandy areas,
descending to Tocopilla.
It is night.
Between the islands
our ocean
palpitates with fish.
It touches the feet, the thighs,
the chalky ribs
of my homeland.
Night touches the shoreline
and rises while singing
at daybreak
like a guitar awakening.

I feel the irresistible force
of the ocean's call. I am
called by the wind,
and called by Rodríguez,
José Antonio,
I received a telegram
from the "Mina" worker's union

27 / ODE TO THE BOOK II

Oda al libro II

TRANSLATED BY EDWARD HIRSCH

Libro	Book,
hermoso,	beautiful
libro,	book,
mínimo bosque,	little forest,
hoja	leaf
tras hoja,	after leaf,
huele	your paper
tu papel	smells
a elemento,	of the elements,
eres	you are
matutino y nocturno,	daily and nocturnal,
cereal,	grain,
oceánico,	ocean;
en tus antiguas páginas	in your ancient pages
cazadores de osos,	bear hunters,
fogatas	bonfires
cerca del Missisipi,	along the Mississippi,
canoas	canoes
en las islas,	in the islands;
más tarde	later on
caminos	roads
y caminos,	and more roads,
revelaciones,	revelations,
pueblos	rebellious
insurgentes,	towns,
Rimbaud como un herido	Rimbaud, like an injured
pez sangriento	blood-soaked fish

palpitando en el lodo,
y la hermosura
de la fraternidad,
piedra por piedra
sube el castillo humano,
dolores que entretejen
la firmeza,
acciones solidarias,
libro
oculto
de bolsillo
en bolsillo,
lámpara
clandestina,
estrella roja.

Nosotros
los poetas
caminantes
exploramos
el mundo,
en cada puerta
nos recibió la vida,
participamos
en la lucha terrestre.
Cuál fue nuestra victoria?
Un libro,
un libro lleno
de contactos humanos,
de camisas,
un libro
sin soledad, con hombres
y herramientas,
un libro
es la victoria.

gasping in the mud,
and the beauty
of brotherhood,
stone by stone
building the human castle,
grief interwoven
with firmness,
solidarity;
occult
book
passed from pocket
to pocket,
a secret
lamp,
a red star.

We
the wandering
poets
explored
the world,
life welcomed us
at every door,
we joined
in the earthly struggle.
What was our victory?
A book,
a book filled
with human connections,
with shirts,
without isolation, with men
and tools,
a book
is our victory.

Vive y cae
como todos los frutos,
no sólo tiene luz,
no sólo tiene
sombra,
se apaga,
se deshoja,
se pierde
entre las calles,
se desploma en la tierra.
Libro de poesía
de mañana,
otra vez
vuelve
a tener nieve o musgo
en tus páginas
para que las pisadas
o los ojos
vayan grabando
huellas:
de nuevo
descríbenos el mundo,
los manantiales
entre la espesura,
las altas arboledas,
los planetas
polares,
y el hombre
en los caminos,
en los nuevos caminos,
avanzando
en la selva,
en el agua,
en el cielo,
en la desnuda soledad marina,
el hombre

A book ripens and falls
like all fruits,
it has light
and shadow,
but its pages
are torn away,
it gets lost
in the streets,
buried in the earth.
Book of poetry
dawning,
come back again
to hold snow or moss
in your pages
so that the footsteps
or the eyes
can leave
their traces;
once again
describe the world for us
of freshwater springs
in the thickets,
groves of tall trees,
the polar
planets,
and human beings
on the roads,
on the new roads,
advancing
in the jungle,
on the water,
in the sky,
in the naked solitude of the sea,
human beings

descubriendo	discovering
los últimos secretos,	the ultimate secrets,
el hombre	human beings
regresando	returning
con un libro,	with a book,
el cazador de vuelta	the hunter coming home
con un libro,	with a book,
el campesino	the farmer
arando	working the land
con un libro.	with a book.

28 / ODE TO A BOUQUET OF VIOLETS

Oda a un ramo de violetas

TRANSLATED BY ILAN STAVANS

Crespo ramo en la sombra
sumergido:
gotas de agua violeta
y luz salvaje
subieron con tu aroma:
una fresca hermosura
subterránea
trepó con tus capullos
y estremeció mis ojos y mi vida.

Una por una, flores
que alargaron
metálicos pedúnculos,
acercando en la sombra
rayo tras rayo de una luz oscura
hasta que coronaron
el misterio
con su masa profunda de perfume,
y unidas
fueron una sola estrella
de olor remoto y corazón morado.

Ramo profundo,
íntimo
olor
de la naturaleza,
pareces

Crisp bouquet drowned
in shadow:
drops of violent water
and wild light
ascended with your aroma:
a fresh subterranean
rapture
seeped into your buds
shaking my eyes and my life.

One by one,
flowers elongating
metallic peduncles,
approaching in the shadow
ray after ray with darkened light
until they crowned
the mystery
with a deep mass of perfume,
and united
were a single star
of distant smell and purple heart.

Passionate bouquet,
intimate
smell
of nature,
you resemble

la onda, la caballera,
la mirada
de una náyade rota
y submarina,
pero de cerca,
en plena
temeridad azul de tu fragancia,
tierra, flor de la tierra,
olor terrestre
desprendes, y tu rayo
ultravioleta
es combustión lejana de volcanes.

Sumerjo en tu hermosura
mi viejo rostro tantas
veces hostilizado por el polvo
y algo desde la tierra
me transmites,
y no es sólo el grito puro
de tu color total, es más bien
una palabra con rocío,
una humedad florida con raíces.

Frágil haz de violetas
estrelladas,
pequeño, misterioso
planetario
de fósforo marino,
nocturno ramo entre las hojas verdes,
la verdad es
que no hay palabra azul para expresarte:

más que toda palabra
te describe un latido de tu aroma.

the fluctuation, the hair,
the gaze
of a broken aquamarine
water nymph,
but up close,
in full
temerity of your blue fragrance,
earth, flower of the earth,
you distill
an earthly smell, and your ultraviolet
ray
is a distant convulsion of volcanoes.

I bury in your beauty
my old face so often
harassed by the dust
and you transmit to me
something from the earth,
and it isn't only the sheer scream
of your integral color, it is
more like a dew-drench word,
a florid humidity with roots.

Delicate bundle of exploding
violets,
small, planetary
mystery
of sea's phosphorescence,
nocturnal bouquet among green leaves,
truth is
there is no blue word to express you:

more than any word
the beat of your aroma describes you.

29 / ODE TO A BOX OF TEA

Oda a la caja de té

TRANSLATED BY KEN KRABBENHOFT

Caja de té	Box of tea
de aquel	from
país de los elefantes,	elephant country,
ahora costurero	now a worn
envejecido,	sewing box,
pequeño planetario de botones,	small planetarium of buttons:
como de otro planeta	you brought
a la casa	into the house
trajiste	a sacred,
un aroma sagrado,	unplaceable scent,
indefinible.	as if you had come from another planet.
Así llegó de lejos	With you my weary young heart
regresando	arrived from far-off places,
de las islas	returning
mi corazón de joven fatigado.	from the islands.
La fiebre me tenía	I had lain sweating
sudoroso	with fever
cerca del mar, y un	by the ocean shore, while a
ramo de palmeras	palm frond
sobre mí se movía	waved back and forth above me,
refrescando	soothing
con aire verde y canto	my emotions
mis pasiones.	with its green air and song.
Caja	Exquisite
de latón, primorosa,	tin box,
ay	oh

me recuerdas	how you remind me of
las olas de otros mares,	the swell of other seas,
el anuncio	the roar
del	of
monzón sobre el Asia,	monsoons over Asia
cuando se balancean	when
como	countries
navíos	rock
los países	like ships
en las manos del viento	at the hands of the wind
y Ceylán desparrama	and Ceylon scatters
sus olores	its scents
como una	like a head of
combatida	storm-tossed
cabellera.	hair.
Caja de té,	Box of tea,
como mi	like my
corazón	own heart
trajiste	you arrived bearing
letras,	stories,
escalofríos,	thrills,
ojos	eyes
que contemplaron	that had held
pétalos fabulosos	fabulous petals in their gaze
y también ay!	and also, yes,
aquel	that
olor perdido	lost scent
a té, a jazmín, a sueños,	of tea, of jasmine and of dreams,
a primavera errante.	that scent of wandering spring.

30 / ODE TO BREAD

Oda al pan

TRANSLATED BY KEN KRABBENHOFT

Pan,	Bread,
con harina,	you rise
agua	from flour,
y fuego	water
te levantas.	and fire.
Espeso y leve,	Dense or light,
recostado y redondo,	flattened or round,
repites	you duplicate
el vientre	the mother's
de la madre,	rounded womb,
equinoccial	and earth's
germinación	twice-yearly
terrestre.	swelling.
Pan,	How simple
qué fácil	you are, bread,
y qué profundo eres:	and how profound!
en la bandeja blanca	You line up
de la panadería	on the baker's
se alargan tus hileras	powdered trays
como utensilios, platos	like silverware or plates
o papeles,	or pieces of paper,
y de pronto,	and suddenly
la ola	life washes
de la vida,	over you,
la conjunción del germen	there's the joining of seed
y del fuego,	and fire,
creces, creces	and you're growing, growing

de pronto	all at once
como	like
cintura, boca, senos,	hips, mouths, breasts,
colinas de la tierra,	mounds of earth,
vidas,	or people's lives.
sube el calor, te inunda	The temperature rises, you're overwhelmed
la plenitud, el viento	by fullness, the roar
de la fecundidad,	of fertility,
y entonces	and suddenly
se inmoviliza tu color de oro,	your golden color is fixed.
y cuando se preñaron	And when your little wombs
tus pequeños vientres	were seeded,
la cicatriz morena	a brown scar
dejó su quemadura	laid its burn the length
en todo tu dorado	of your two halves'
sistema	toasted
de hemisferios.	juncture.
Ahora,	Now,
intacto,	whole,
eres	you are
acción de hombre,	mankind's energy,
milagro repetido,	a miracle often admired,
voluntad de la vida.	the will to live itself.
Oh pan de cada boca,	O bread familiar to every mouth,
no	we will not
te imploraremos,	kneel before you:
los hombres	men
no somos	do not
mendigos	implore
de vagos dioses	unclear gods
o de ángeles oscuros:	or obscure angels:
del mar y de la tierra	we will make our own bread
haremos pan,	out of sea and soil,
plantaremos de trigo	we will plant wheat
la tierra y los planetas,	on our earth and the planets,

el pan de cada boca,
de cada hombre,
en cada día,
llegará porque fuimos
a sembrarlo
y a hacerlo,
no para un hombre sino
para todos,
el pan, el pan
para todos los pueblos
y con él lo que tiene
forma y sabor de pan
repartiremos:
la tierra,
la belleza,
el amor,
todo eso
tiene sabor de pan,
forma de pan,
germinación de harina,
todo
nació para ser compartido,
para ser entregado,
para multiplicarse.

Por eso, pan,
si huyes
de la casa del hombre,
si te ocultan,
te niegan,
si el avaro
te prostituye,
si el rico
te acapara,
si el trigo
no busca surco y tierra,

bread for every mouth,
for every person,
our daily bread.
Because we plant its seed
and grow it
not for one man
but for all,
there will be enough:
there will be bread
for all the peoples of the earth.
And we will also share with one another
whatever has
the shape and the flavor of bread:
the earth itself,
beauty
and love—
all
taste like bread
and have its shape,
the germination of wheat.
Everything
exists to be shared,
to be freely given,
to multiply.

This is why, bread,
if you flee
from mankind's houses,
if they hide you away
or deny you,
if the greedy man
pimps for you or
the rich man
takes you over,
if the wheat
does not yearn for the furrow and the soil:

pan,
no rezaremos,
pan,
no mendigaremos,
lucharemos por ti con otros hombres,
con todos los hambrientos,
por todos los ríos y el aire
iremos a buscarte,
toda la tierra la repartiremos
para que tú germines,
y con nosotros
avanzará la tierra:
el agua, el fuego, el hombre
lucharán con nosotros.
Iremos coronados
con espigas,
conquistando
tierra y pan para todos,
y entonces
también la vida
tendrá forma de pan,
será simple y profunda,
innumerable y pura.
Todos los seres
tendrán derecho
a la tierra y la vida,
y así será el pan de mañana
el pan de cada boca,
sagrado,
consagrado,
porque será el producto
de la más larga y dura
lucha humana.

then, bread,
we will refuse to pray:
bread,
we will refuse to beg.
We will fight for you instead, side by side
with the others,
with everyone who knows hunger.
We will go after you
in every river and in the air.
We will divide the entire earth among
ourselves
so that you may germinate,
and the earth will go forward
with us:
water, fire, and mankind
fighting at our side.
Crowned
with sheafs of wheat,
we will win
earth and bread for everyone.
Then
life itself
will have the shape of bread,
deep and simple,
immeasurable and pure.
Every living thing
will have its share
of soil and life,
and the bread we eat each morning,
everyone's daily bread,
will be hallowed
and sacred,
because it will have been won
by the longest and costliest
of human struggles.

No tiene alas
la victoria terrestre:
tiene pan en sus hombros,
y vuela valerosa
liberando la tierra
como una panadera
conducida en el viento.

This earthly *Victory*
does not have wings:
she wears bread on her shoulders instead.
Courageously she soars,
setting the world free,
like a baker
born aloft on the wind.

31 / ODE TO BROKEN THINGS

Oda a las cosas rotas

TRANSLATED BY ILAN STAVANS

Se van rompiendo cosas
en la casa
como empujadas por un invisible
quebrador voluntario:
no son las manos mías,
ni las tuyas,
no fueron las muchachas
de uña dura
y pasos de planeta:
no fue nada ni nadie,
no fue el viento,
no fue el anaranjado mediodía
ni la noche terrestre,
no fue ni la nariz ni el codo,
la creciente cadera,
el tobillo
ni el aire:
se quebró el plato, se cayó la lámpara,
se derrumbaron todos los floreros
uno por uno, aquél
en pleno octubre
colmado de escarlata,
fatigado por todas las violetas,
y otro vacío
rodó, rodó, rodó
por el invierno
hasta ser sólo harina

Things get broken
at home
as if seized by the whim
of invisible havoc:
not by my hands,
or yours,
or the girls
with obstinate nails
or the course of planets:
not by someone or something,
not by the summer,
not the meridian ocher
or the earthly darkness,
not the nose or the elbow,
not the expanding hip,
the ankle
or the gust of wind:
the plate smashed, the lamp knocked over,
all flowerpots, one after another,
broken to pieces, one of them
coloring mid-October
in scarlet,
wan in the surplus of violets,
another waiting in emptiness
rolling and rolling
in winter
until the flowerpot became

de florero,
recuerdo roto, polvo luminoso.
Y aquel reloj
cuyo sonido
era
la voz de nuestras vidas,
el secreto
hilo
de las semanas,
que una a una
ataba tantas horas
a la miel, al silencio,
a tantos nacimientos y trabajos,
aquel reloj también
cayó y vibraron
entre los vidrios rotos
sus delicadas vísceras azules,
su largo corazón
desenrollado.

La vida va moliendo
vidrios, gastando ropas,
haciendo añicos,
triturando
formas,
y lo que dura con el tiempo es como
isla o nave en el mar,
perecedero,
rodeado por los frágiles peligros,
por implacables aguas y amenazas.

Pongamos todo de una vez, relojes,
platos, copas talladas por el frío,
en un saco y llevemos
al mar nuestros tesoros:

a pile of dirt,
a broken memory, a luminous dust.
And that clock
whose sound
gave
voice to our lives,
the secret
thread
uniting weeks,
tying together,
hour and hour,
honey, silence,
births and endless endeavors,
even the clock
plunged downward
and its delicate blue viscera
pulsed amid the broken glass,
its long heart
unfolding.

Life grinds
on the glass, wears out the clothing,
shattering,
pounding
the forms,
and what survives with time is like
an island or an ocean ship,
perishing,
surrounded by fragile hazards
ringed by implacable waters and threats.

Let us collect everything once and for all,
clocks,
plates, cups carved in cold,
into a poke and let's give
all our belongings to the sea:

que se derrumben nuestras posesiones
en un solo alarmante quebradero,
que suene como un río
lo que se quiebra
y que el mar reconstruya
con su largo trabajo de mareas
tantas cosas inútiles
que nadie rompe
pero se rompieron.

let our possessions be undone
in one single alarming destruction,
allowing things to sound
like a river
and let the sea
with its arduous labor of tides
reconstruct the many useless things
that no hand ever breaks
but just keep breaking.

32 / ODE TO THE BUILDING

Oda al edificio

TRANSLATED BY ILAN STAVANS

Socavando
en su sitio,
golpeando
en una punta,
extendiendo y puliendo
sube la llamarada construida,
la edificada altura
que creció para el hombre.

Oh alegría
del equilibrio y de las proporciones.
Oh peso utilizado
de huraños materiales,
desarrollo del lodo
a las columnas,
esplendor de abanico
en las escales.
De cuántos sitios
diseminados en la geografía
aquí bajo la luz vino a elevarse
la unidad vencedora.

La roca fragmentó su poderío,
se adelgazó el acero, el cobre vino
a mezclar su salud con la madera
y ésta, recién llegada de los bosques,
endureció su grávida fragancia.

Excavating
on site,
hitting
a headland,
extending and polishing
the built blaze reaches up,
the edified height
raised for man.

Oh happiness
of equilibrium and proportions.
Oh weight used
from disdained materials,
mud's development
turned columns,
a fan's splendor
on the scales.
From how many places
disseminated across the geography
light from here underachieved its elevation
in triumphant unity.

The rock fragmented its riches,
steel became slim, copper managed
to mix its health with wood
and this, just arrived from the forests,
hardened its pregnant fragrance.

Cemento, hermano oscuro,
tu pasta los reúne,
tu arena derramada
aprieta, enrolla, sube
venciendo piso a piso.
El hombre pequeñito
taladra,
sube y baja.
Dónde está el individuo?
Es un martillo, un golpe
de acero en el acero,
un punto del sistema
y su razón se suma
al ámbito que crece.
Debió dejar caídos
sus pequeños orgullos
y elevar con los hombres una cúpula,
erigir entre todos
el orden
y compartir la sencillez metálica
de las inexorables estructuras.
Pero
todo sale del hombre.
A su llamado
acuden piedras y se elevan muros,
entra la luz a las salas,
el espacio se corta y se reparte.

El hombre
separará la luz de las tinieblas
y así
como venció su orgullo vano
e implantó su sistema
para que se elevara el edificio,
seguirá construyendo

Cement, dark brother,
your paste unites them,
your spilled sand
tightens, curls up, ascends
winning level after level.
The very tiny man
drills,
up and down.
Where is the individual?
It is a hammer, a hit
of steel on steel,
a point in the system
and its reason is added
to the growing realm.
He should have dispensed
with its petty prides
and raise a cupola with men,
to erect
order among all
and share the metallic simplicity
of inexorable structures.
But
everything comes from man.
His call
is heard by stones and they raise
    themselves into walls,
in the midst of the living rooms,
space is fragmented and spread out.

Man
separates light from darkness
and hence
since he defeated his vain pride
and implanted a system
for the building to be erected,
will continue to build

la rosa colectiva,
reunirá en la tierra
el material huraño de la dicha
y con razón y acero
irá creciendo
el edificio de todos los hombres.

the collective rose,
will reunite on earth
joy's disdainful material
and with reason and steel
all the building of men
will continue to grow.

33 / ODE AND BURGEONINGS

Oda y germinaciones

TRANSLATED BY DONALD D. WALSH

1

El sabor de tu boca y el color de tu piel,
piel, boca, fruta mía de estos días veloces,
dímelo, fueron sin cesar a tu lado
por años y por viajes y por lunas y soles
y tierra y llanto y lluvia y alegría
o sólo ahora, sólo
salen de tus raíces
como a la tierra seca el agua trae
germinaciones que no conocía
o a los labios del cántaro olvidado
sube en el agua el gusto de la tierra?

No sé, no me lo digas, no lo sabes.
Nadie sabe estas cosas.
Pero acercando todos mis sentidos
a la luz de tu piel, desapareces,
tu fundes como el ácido
aroma de una fruta
y el calor de un camino,
el olor del maíz que se desgrana,
la madreselva de la tarde pura,
los nombres de la tierra polvorienta,

1

The taste of your mouth and the color of
your skin,
skin, mouth, fruit of these swift days,
tell me, were they always beside you
through years and journeys and moons
and suns
and earth and weeping and rain and joy
or is it only now that
they come from your roots,
only as water brings to the dry earth
burgeonings that it did not know,
or as to the lips of the forgotten jug
the taste of the earth rises in the water?

I don't know, don't tell me, you don't
know.
Nobody knows these things.
But bringing all my senses close
to the light of your skin, you disappear,
you melt like the acid
aroma of a fruit
and the heat of a road,
and the smell of corn being stripped,
the honeysuckle of the pure afternoon,
the names of the dusty earth,

el perfume infinito de la patria:
magnolia y matorral, sangre y harina,
galope de caballos,
la luna polvorienta de la aldea,
el pan recién nacido:
ay todo de tu piel vuelve a mi boca,
vuelve a mi corazón, vuelve a mi cuerpo,
y vuelvo a ser contigo
la tierra que tú eres:
eres en mí profunda primavera:
vuelvo a saber en ti cómo germino.

the infinite perfume of our country:
magnolia and thicket, blood and flour,
the gallop of horses,
the village's dusty moon,
newborn bread:
ah from your skin everything comes back to my mouth,
comes back to my heart, comes back to my body,
and with you I become again
the earth that you are:
you are deep spring in me:
in you I know again how I am born.

2

Años tuyos que yo debí sentir
crecer cerca de mí como racimos
hasta que hubieras visto cómo el sol y la tierra
a mis manos de piedra te hubieran destinado,
hasta que uva con uva hubieras hecho
cantar en mis venas el vino.
El viento o el caballo
desviándose pudieron
hacer que yo pasara por tu infancia,
el mismo cielo has visto cada día,
el mismo barro del invierno oscuro,
la enramada sin fin de los ciruelos
y su dulzura de color morado.
Sólo algunos kilómetros de noche,
las distancias mojadas
de la aurora campestre,

2

Years of yours that I should have felt
growing near me like clusters
until you had seen how the sun and the earth
had destined you for my hands of stone,
until grape by grape you had made
the wine sing in my veins.
The wind or the horse
swerving were able
to make me pass through your childhood,
you have seen the same sky each day,
the same dark winter mud,
the endless branching of the plum trees
and their dark-purple sweetness.
Only a few miles of night,
the drenched distances
of the country dawn,

un puñado de tierra nos separó, los muros
transparentes
que no cruzamos, para que la vida,
después, pusiera todos
los mares y la tierra
entre nosotros, y nos acercáramos
a pesar del espacio,
paso a paso buscándonos,
de un océano a otro,
hasta que vi que el cielo se incendiaba
y volaba en la luz tu cabellera
y llegaste a mis besos con el fuego
de un desencadenado meteoro
y al fundirte en mi sangre, la dulzura
del ciruelo salvaje
de nuestra infancia recibí en mi boca,
y te apreté a mi pecho como
si la tierra y la vida recobrara.

a handful of earth separated us, the transparent
walls
that we did not cross, so that life,
afterward, could put all
the seas and the earth
between us, and we could come together
in spite of space,
step by step seeking each other,
from one ocean to another,
until I saw that the sky was aflame
and your hair was flying in the light
and you came to my kisses with the fire
of an unchained meteor
and as you melted in my blood, the sweetness
of the wild plum
of our childhood I received in my mouth,
and I clutched you to my breast as
if I were regaining earth and life.

3

Mi muchacha salvaje, hemos tenido
que recobrar el tiempo
y marchar hacia atrás, en la distancia
de nuestras vidas, beso a beso,
recogiendo de un sitio lo que dimos
sin alegría, descubriendo en otro
el camino secreto
que iba acercando tus pies a los míos,
y así bajo mi boca
vuelves a ver la planta insatisfecha
de tu vida alargando sus raíces

3

My wild girl, we have had
to regain time
and march backward, in the distance
of our lives, kiss after kiss,
gathering from one place what we gave
without joy, discovering in another
the secret road
that gradually brought your feet close to mine,
and so beneath my mouth
you see again the unfulfilled plant
of your life putting out its roots

hacia mi corazón que te esperaba.
Y una a una las noches
entre nuestras ciudades separadas
se agregan a la noche que nos une.
La luz de cada día,
su llama o su reposo
nos entregan, sacándolos del tiempo,
y así se desentierra
en la sombra o la luz nuestro tesoro,
y así besan la vida nuestros besos:
todo el amor en nuestro amor se encierra:
toda la sed termina en nuestro abrazo.
Aquí estamos al fin frente a frente,
nos hemos encontrado,
no hemos perdido nada.
Nos hemos recorrido labio a labio,
hemos cambiado mil veces
entre nosotros la muerte y la vida,
todo lo que traíamos
como muertas medallas
lo echamos al fondo del mar,
todo lo que aprendimos
no nos sirvió de nada:
comenzamos de nuevo,
terminamos de nuevo
muerte y vida.
Y aquí sobrevivimos,
puros, con la pureza que nosotros creamos,
más anchos que la tierra que no pudo
    extraviarnos,
eternos como el fuego que arderá
cuanto dure la vida.

toward my heart that was waiting for you.
And one by one the nights
between our separated cities
are joined to the night that unites us.
The light of each day,
its flame or its repose,
they deliver to us, taking them from time,
and so our treasure
is disinterred in shadow or light,
and so our kisses kiss life:
all love is enclosed in our love:
all thirst ends in our embrace.
Here we are at last face to face,
we have met,
we have lost nothing.
We have felt each other lip to lip,
we have changed a thousand times
between us death and life,
all that we were bringing
like dead medals
we threw to the bottom of the sea,
all that we learned
was of no use to us:
we begin again,
we end again
death and life.
And here we survive,
pure, with the purity that we created,
broader than the earth that could not lead
    us astray,
eternal as the fire that will burn
as long as life endures.

4

Cuando ha llegado aquí se detiene mi mano.
Alguien pregunta: —Dime por qué, como las olas
en una misma costa, tus palabras
sin cesar van y vuelven a su cuerpo?
Ella es sólo la forma que tú amas?
Y respondo: mis manos no se sacian
en ella, mis besos no descansan,
por qué retiraría las palabras
que repiten la huella de su contacto amado,
que se cierran guardando
inútilmente como en la red el agua,
la superficie y la temperatura
de la ola más pura de la vida?
Y, amor, tu cuerpo no sólo es la rosa
que en la sombra o la luna se levanta,
o sorprendo o persigo.
No sólo es movimiento o quemadura,
acto de sangre o pétalo del fuego,
sino que para mí tú me has traído
mi territorio, el barro de mi infancia,
las olas de la avena,
la piel redonda de la fruta oscura
que arranqué de la selva,
aroma de maderas y manzanas,
color de agua escondida donde caen
frutos secretos y profundas hojas.
Oh amor, tu cuerpo sube
como una línea pura de vasija
desde la tierra que me reconoce
y cuando te encontraron mis sentidos
tú palpitaste como si cayeran
dentro de ti la lluvia y las semillas!
Ay que me digan cómo

4

When I have reached here my hand
stops.
Someone asks: "Tell me, why, like
waves
on a single coast, do your words
endlessly go and return to her body?
Is she the only form that you love?"
And I answer: "My hands never tire
of her, my kisses do not rest,
why should I withdraw the words
that repeat the trace of her beloved
contact,
words that close, uselessly
holding like water in a net
the surface and the temperature
of the purest wave of life?"
And, love, your body is not only the
rose
that in shadow or moonlight rises,
it is not only movement or burning,
act of blood or petal of fire,
but to me you have brought
my territory, the clay of my childhood,
the waves of oats,
the round skin of the dark fruit
that I tore from the forest,
aroma of wood and apples,
color of hidden water where secret
fruits and deep leaves fall.
Oh love, your body rises
like the pure line of a goblet
from the earth that knows me
and when my senses found you
you throbbed as though within you
rain and seeds were falling.
Ah let them tell me how

pudiera yo abolirte
y dejar que mis manos sin tu forma
arrancaran el fuego a mis palabras!
Suave mía, reposa
tu cuerpo en estas líneas que te deben
más de lo que me das en tu contacto,
vive en estas palabras y repite
en ellas la dulzura y el incendio,
estremécete en medio de sus sílabas,
duerme en mi nombre como te has dormido
sobre mi corazón, y así mañana
el hueco de tu forma
guardarán mis palabras
y el que las oiga un día recibirá una ráfaga
de trigo y amapolas:
estará todavía respirando
el cuerpo del amor sobre la tierra!

I could abolish you
and let my hands without your form
tear the fire from my words.
My gentle one, rest
your body in these lines that owe you
more than you give me through your touch,
live in these words and repeat
in them the sweetness and the fire,
tremble amid their syllables,
sleep in my name as you have slept
upon my heart, and so tomorrow
my words will keep
the hollow of your form
and he who hears them one day will
    receive a gust
of wheat and poppies;
the body of love will still
be breathing upon earth!

5

Hilo de trigo y agua,
de cristal o de fuego,
la palabra y la noche,
el trabajo y la ira,
la sombra y la ternura,
todo lo has ido poco a poco consiendo
a mis bolsillos rotos,
y no sólo en la zona trepidante
en que amor y martirio son gemelos
como dos campanas de incendio,
me esperaste, amor mío,
sino en las más pequeñas
obligaciones dulces.
El aceite dorado de Italia hizo tu nimbo,

5

Thread of wheat and water,
of crystal or of fire,
word and night,
work and anger,
shadow and tenderness,
little by little you have sewn it all
into my threadbare pockets,
and not only in the tremorous zone
in which love and martyrdom are twins
like two fire bells,
did you wait for me, my love,
but in the tiniest
sweet duties.
The golden oil of Italy made your nimbus,

santa de la cocina y la costura,
y tu coquetería pequeñuela,
que tanto se tardaba en el espejo,
con tus manos que tienen
pétalos que el jazmín envidiaría
lavó los utensilios y mi ropa,
desinfectó las llagas.
Amor mío, a mi vida
llegaste preparada
como amapola y como guerrillera:
de seda el esplendor que yo recorro
con el hambre y la sed
que sólo para ti traje a este mundo,
y detrás de la seda
la muchacha de hierro
que luchará a mi lado.
Amor, amor, aquí nos encontramos.
Seda y metal, acécate a mi boca.

saint of kitchen and sewing,
and your tiny coquetry,
that tarried so long at the mirror,
with your hands that have
petals that jasmine would envy,
washed the dishes and my clothes,
disinfected wounds.
My love, to my life
you came prepared
as a poppy and as a guerilla fighter:
silken is the splendor that I stroke
with the hunger and thirst
that I brought to this world only for you,
and behind the silk
the girl of iron
who will fight at my side.
Love, love, here we are.
Silk and metal, come close to my mouth.

6

Y porque Amor combate
no sólo en su quemante agricultura,
sino en la boca de hombres y mujeres,
terminaré saliéndole al camino
a los que entre mi pecho y tu fragancia
quieran interponer su planta oscura.
De mí nada más malo,
te dirán, amor mío,
de lo que yo te dije.
Yo viví en las praderas
antes de conocerte
y no esperé el amor sino que estuve
acechando y salté sobre la rosa.

6

And because Love fights
not only in its burning agriculture
but in the mouths of men and women,
I shall end up by attacking
those who between my breast and your
fragrance
try to interpose their dark foot.
They will tell you nothing
worse about me, my love,
than what I told you.
I lived in the meadows
before I knew you
and I did not wait for love but lay
in ambush and jumped upon the rose.

Qué más pueden decirte?
No soy bueno ni malo sino un hombre,
y agregarán entonces el peligro
de mi vida, que conoces
y que con tu pasión has compartido.
Y bien, este peligro
es peligro de amor, de amor completo
hacia toda la vida,
hacia todas las vidas,
y si este amor nos trae
la muerte o los prisiones,
yo estoy seguro que tus grandes ojos,
como cuando los beso
se cerrarán entonces con orgullo,
en doble orgullo, amor,
con tu orgullo y el mío.
Pero hacia mis orejas vendrán antes
a socavar la torre
del amor dulce y duro que nos liga,
y me dirán: —«Aquella
que tú amas,
no es mujer para ti,
por qué la quieres? Creo
que podrías hallar una más bella,
más seria, más profunda,
más otra, tú me entiendes, mírala qué ligera,
y qué cabeza tiene,
y mírala cómo se viste
y etcétera y etcétera».
Y yo en estas líneas digo:
así te quiero, amor,
amor, así te amo,
así como te vistes
y como se levanta
tu cabellera y como

What more can they tell you?
I am not good or bad, just a man,
and they will then add the danger
of my life, which you know
and which with your passion you have
shared.
Well, this danger
is danger of love, of complete love
toward all of life,
toward all lives,
and if this love brings
death or prison,
I am sure that your big eyes,
as when I kiss them,
will then close with pride,
with double pride, my love,
with your pride and mine.
But toward my ears they will first come
to undermine the tower
of the sweet and harsh love that binds us,
and they will say: "That one
that you love
is no woman for you,
why do you love her? I think
you could find one more beautiful,
more serious, more profound,
more other, you understand, look at
her how flighty,
and what a head she has,
and look at her how she dresses
and so on and on."
And I in these lines say:
thus I love you, love,
love, thus I love you,
thus as you dress
and as your hair

tu boca se sonríe,
ligera como el agua
del manantial sobre las piedras puras,
así te quiero, amada.
Al pan yo no le pido que me enseñe
sino que no me falte
durante cada día de la vida.
Yo no sé nada de la luz, de dónde
viene ni dónde va,
yo sólo quiero que la luz alumbre,
yo no pido a la noche
explicaciones,
yo la espero y me envuelve,
y así tú, pan y luz
y sombra eres.
Has venido a mi vida
con lo que tú traías,
hecha
de luz y pan y sombra te esperaba,
y así te necesito,
así te amo,
y a cuantos quieran escuchar mañana
lo que no les diré, que aquí lo lean,
y retrocedan hoy porque es temprano
para estos argumentos.
Mañana sólo les daremos
una hoja del árbol de nuestro amor, una hoja
que caerá sobre la tierra
como si la hubieran hecho nuestros labios,
como un beso que cae
desde nuestras alturas invencibles
para mostrar el fuego y la ternura
de un amor verdadero.

lifts up and as
your mouth smiles,
light as the water
from the spring upon the pure stones,
thus I love you, beloved.
Of bread I do not ask that it teach me
but that it not fail me
during each day of life.
I know nothing of light, where
it comes from or where it goes,
I only want light to light,
I do not ask explanations
of the night,
I wait for it and it envelops me,
and thus you are, bread
and light and shadow.
You came into my life
with what you brought,
I waited for you,
made of light and bread and shadow,
and thus I need you,
thus I love you,
and all those who want to hear tomorrow
what I shall not tell them, let them read it
here,
and let them retreat today because it's too
early
for these arguments.
Tomorrow we shall give them only
a leaf from the tree of our love, a leaf
that will fall upon the earth
as if our lips had made it,
like a kiss that falls
from our invincible heights
to show the fire and the tenderness
of a true love.

34 / ODE TO THE BUTTERFLY

Oda a la mariposa

TRANSLATED BY ILAN STAVANS

A la de Muzo, aquella	For the one from Muzo, that
mariposa	butterfly
colombiana,	of Colombia,
hoguera azul, que el aire	the blue bonfire, which air
agregó metal vivo	combined with the vital metal,
y a la otra	and the other one
de las lejanas islas,	from the distant islands,
Morpho, Monarca, Luna,	*Morpho, Monarch, Moon-Butterfly,*
plateadas como peces,	silvered like fish,
dobles como tijeras,	paired like scissors,
alas abrasadoras,	embracing wings,
presencias amarillas,	yellow presences,
azufradas en las minas del cielo,	sulfured in the mines of heaven,
eléctricas, efímeras	electric, ephemeral,
que el viento lleva en lo alto de la frente	raised up to the forehead by the wind
y deja como lluvias o pañuelos	and falling like rain or handkerchiefs
caer entre las flores!	among the flowers!
Oh celestes	Oh, celestial ones,
espolvoreadas con humo de oro,	dusty with golden smoke,
de pronto	suddenly
elevan	they
un ojo de diamante negro	raise
sobre la luz del ala	an eye of black diamond
a una	over the wing's light,
calavera anunciatoria	that announces
de la fugacidad, de las tinieblas.	flightiness and shadows.

Aquella
que recuerdo
llega de las más lejanas zonas,
formada por la espuma,
nacida
en la claridad de la esmeralda,
lanzada al corto cielo
de la rápida aurora
y en ella
tú, mariposa, fuiste
centro
vivo,
volante agua marina,
monja verde.

Pero un día
sobre el camino
volaba otro camino.
Eran
las mariposas de la pampa.
Galopábamos desde
Venado Tuerto
hacia las alturas
de la caliente Córdoba.
Y contra los caballos
galopaban
las mariposas,
millones de alas blancas y amarillas,
oscureciendo el aire, palpitando
como una red que nos amenazaba.
Era espesa
la pared
temblorosa
de polen y papel, de estambre y luna,
de alas y alas y alas,
y contra

The one
I remember
came from the most distant zones,
shaped by the foam,
born
in the clarity of emerald,
thrown to the short sky
of the sudden sunrise
and in it
you were butterfly,
living
center,
flying seawater,
green nun.

But one day,
on the road,
another road was flying.
These were
the butterflies from the pampa.
We galloped from
Venado Tuerto
to the heights
of heated Córdoba.
And against the horses,
the butterflies
galloped,
millions of white and yellow wings
darkening the sky, palpitating
like a net they menaced us.
The wall
was dense,
trembling
with pollen and paper, yarn and moon,
wings and wings and wings,
and, against

la voladora masa	the flying mass,
apenas avanzaban	our horses
nuestras cabalgaduras.	could barely advance.
Quemaba el día con un rayo rojo	A red ray burned the day,
apuntado al camino	dazzling the road;
y contra el río aéreo,	and against the river of air,
contra la inundación	against this inundation
de mariposas	of butterflies,
cruzábamos las pampas argentinas.	we crossed the Argentine pampas.
Ya habían devorado	Already they had devoured
la alfalfa de las vacas,	the cows' alfalfa,
y a lo largo del ancho territorio	the green plantations
eran sólo esquelto	were just skeletons
las verdes plantaciones:	the whole wide territory:
hambre para el vacuno	the cattle possessed by hunger
iba en el río de las mariposas.	met the torrent of butterflies.
Fumígalas, incéndialas!	Kill them, burn them,
dije al paisano Aráoz,	I told my *paisano* Aráoz,
barre el cielo	sweep the sky
con una escoba grande,	with an enormous broom,
reunamos	let us gather
siete millones de alas,	seven million wings,
incendiemos	let us burn
el cauce de malignas	the source of evil
mariposas,	butterflies;
carbonízalas, dije,	incinerate them, I said,
que la pompa del aire	let pomp of air
ceniza de oro sea,	be ash of gold;
que vuelvan, humo al cielo,	let smoke go back to the sky,
y gusano a la tierra.	and worm to the earth.
Mariposa serás,	Butterfly, you shall be
tembloroso	the trembling
milagro de las flores,	miracle of flowers;
pero	but
hasta aquí llegaste:	you have reached your end:

no atacarás al hombre y a su herencia,
al campesino y a sus animales,
no te conviene
ese papel de tigre
y asi como celebro
tu radiante
hermosura,
contra
la multiplicación devoradora
yo llevaré el incendio, sin tristeza,
yo llevaré la chispa del castigo
a la montaña de las mariposas.

you shall not attack man and his legacy,
the peasant and his animals,
the role of tiger
does not suit you,
and just as I celebrate
your radiant
beauty
against
the multitude that devours,
I shall bring fire, without sadness,
I shall carry the spark of punishment
to the butterfly mountain.

35 / ODE TO THE CARNATION

Oda al alhelí

TRANSLATED BY ILAN STAVANS

Cuando envuelto en papeles,	When wrapped in paper,
devorador siniestro	sinister devourer
de libros y libracos,	of books good and bad,
llegué a la Isla, al sol	I arrived at Isla, at the sun
y sal marina,	and sea salt,
arranqué del pequeño	I yanked
jardín	the carnations
los alhelíes.	out of the little garden.
Los tiré a la barranca,	I threw them down the ravine,
los increpé	reprimanded them
contándoles	telling them about
mis pasiones contrarias:	my contrarian passions:
plantas de mar, espinas	flowers of the sea, thorns
coronadas	crowned
de purpúreos relámpagos:	with purple lighting:
así dispuse	So I arranged
mi jardín de arena.	my garden of sand.
Declaré suburbana	I declared
la fragancia	the fragrance of carnation the wind
del alhelí que el viento	spread there with invisible fingers
allí esparció con invisibles dedos.	to be suburban.
Hoy he vuelto	Today I'm back
después de largos	after long
meses,	months,
parecidos a siglos, años	like centuries, years

de sombra, luz y sangre,
a plantar
alhelíes
en la Isla:
tímidas flores,
apenas
luz fragante,
protagonistas puras
del silencio:
ahora
os amo
porque
aprendí
la claridad
andando
y tropezando
por la tierra,
y
cuando caí con la cabeza
golpeada, un
resplandor
morado,
un rayo blanco,
un olor infinito de pañuelo
me recibió:
los pobres alhelíes
de fiel aroma, de perdida nieve
me esperaban: rodearon
mi cabeza
con estrellas o manos
conocidas,
reconocí
el aroma
provinciano,
volví a vivir aquella
intimidad fragante.

of darkness, light and blood,
to plant
carnations
on the Isla:
bashful flowers,
little more than
fragrant light,
perfect protagonists
of silence:
I love you
now
because
I've learned
what clarity is
while tripping
and falling
and
banging
my head
on the earth,
a purple
radiance,
a white ray,
the infinite smell of handkerchief
greeted me:
the humble carnations
of loyal aroma, of lost snow
awaited me: they surrounded
my head
with stars and familiar
hands,
I recognized
the aroma
of the countryside,
once again lived that
fragrant intimacy.

Amados alhelíes
olvidados,
perdonadme.
Ahora
vuestras
celestiales flores
crecen
en mi jardín de arena,
impregnando
mi corazón
de aromas amorosos:
en la tarde
derrama
el cristalina viento del océano
gotas de sal azul,
nieve marina.

Todo a la claridad ha regresado!
Me parece
de pronto
que el mundo
es más
sencillo,
como
si se hubiera llenado
de alhelíes.
Dispuesta
está
la tierra.
Empieza
simplemente
un nuevo día de alhelíes.

Beloved, neglected
carnations,
forgive me.
Your
heavenly blossoms
grow
now
in my garden of sand,
impregnating
my heart
with loving aromas:
in the afternoon
the crystal-clear ocean breeze
spills
drops of blue salt,
marine snow.

Everything is bright again!
It seems
to me
the world
suddenly
is
simpler,
as if
filled
with carnations.
The earth
is ready.
A new day of carnations
begins
in simple terms.

36 / ODE TO THE CAT

Oda al gato

TRANSLATED BY KEN KRABBENHOFT

Los animales fueron
imperfectos,
largos de cola, tristes
de cabeza.
Poco a poco se fueron
componiendo,
haciéndose paisaje,
adquiriendo lunares, gracia, vuelo.
El gato,
sólo el gato
apareció completo
y orgulloso:
nació completamente terminado,
camina solo y sabe lo que quiere.

El hombre quiere ser pescado y pájaro,
la serpiente quisiera tener alas,
el perro es un león desorientado,
el ingeniero quiere ser poeta,
la mosca estudia para golondrina,
el poeta trata de imitar la mosca,
pero el gato
quiere ser sólo gato
y todo gato es gato
desde bigote a cola,
desde presentimiento a rata viva,
desde la noche hasta sus ojos de oro.

There was something wrong
with the animals:
their tails were too long, and they had
unfortunate heads.
Then they started coming together,
little by little
fitting together to make a landscape,
developing birthmarks, grace, pep.
But the cat,
only the cat
turned out finished,
and proud:
born in a state of total completion,
it sticks to itself and knows what it wants.

Men would like to be fish or fowl,
snakes would rather have wings,
and dogs are would-be lions.
Engineers want to be poets,
flies emulate swallows,
and poets try hard to act like flies.
But the cat
wants nothing more than to be a cat,
and every cat is pure cat
from its whiskers to its tail,
from sixth sense to squirming rat,
from nighttime to its golden eyes.

No hay unidad
como él,
no tienen
la luna ni la flor
tal contextura:
es una sola cosa
como el sol o el topacio,
y la elástica línea en su contorno
firme y sutil es como
la línea de la proa de una nave.
Sus ojos amarillos
dejaron una sola
ranura
para echar las monedas de la noche.

Oh pequeño
emperador sin orbe,
conquistador sin patria,
mínimo tigre de salón, nupcial
sultán del cielo
de las tejas eróticas,
el viento del amor
en la intemperie
reclamas
cuando pasas
y posas
cuatro pies delicados
en el suelo,
oliendo,
desconfiando
de todo lo terrestre,
porque todo
es inmundo
para el inmaculado pie del gato.

Nothing hangs together
quite like a cat:
neither flowers nor the moon
have
such consistency.
It's a thing by itself,
like the sun or a topaz,
and the elastic curve of its back,
which is both subtle and confident,
is like the curve of a sailing ship's prow.
The cat's yellow eyes
are the only
slot
for depositing the coins of night.

O little
emperor without a realm,
conqueror without a homeland,
diminutive parlor tiger, nuptial
sultan of heavens
roofed in erotic tiles:
when you pass
in rough weather
and poise
four nimble paws
on the ground,
sniffing,
suspicious
of all earthly things
(because everything
feels filthy
to the cat's immaculate paw),
you claim
the touch of love in the air.

Oh fiera independiente
de la casa, arrogante
vestigio de la noche,
perezoso, gimnástico
y ajeno,
profundísimo gato,
policía secreta
de las habitaciones,
insignia
de un
desaparecido terciopelo,
seguramente no hay
enigma
en tu manera,
tal vez no eres misterio,
todo el mundo te sabe y perteneces
al habitante menos misterioso,
tal vez todos lo creen,
todos se creen dueños,
propietarios, tíos
de gatos, compañeros,
colegas,
discípulos o amigos
de su gato.

Yo no.
Yo no suscribo.
Yo no conozco al gato.
Todo lo sé, la vida y su archipiélago,
el mar y la ciudad incalculable,
la botánica,
el gineceo con sus extravíos,
el por y el menos de la matemática,
los embudos volcánicos del mundo,

O freelance household
beast, arrogant
vestige of night,
lazy, agile
and strange,
O fathomless cat,
secret police
of human chambers
and badge
of
vanished velvet!
Surely there is nothing
enigmatic
in your manner,
maybe you aren't a mystery after all.
You're known to everyone, you belong
to the least mysterious tenant.
Everyone may believe it,
believe they're master,
owner, uncle
or companion
to a cat,
some cat's colleague,
disciple or friend.

But not me.
I'm not a believer.
I don't know a thing about cats.
I know everything else, including life and
its archipelago,
seas and unpredictable cities,
plant life,
the pistil and its scandals,
the pluses and minuses of math.
I know the earth's volcanic protrusions

la cáscara irreal del cocodrilo,
la bondad ignorada del bombero,
el atavismo azul del sacerdote,
pero no puedo descifrar un gato.
Mi razón resbaló en su indiferencia,
sus ojos tienen números de oro.

and the crocodile's unreal hide,
the fireman's unseen kindness
and the priest's blue atavism.
But cats I can't figure out.
My mind slides on their indifference.
Their eyes hold ciphers of gold.

37 / ODE TO CÉSAR VALLEJO

Oda a César Vallejo

TRANSLATED BY ILAN STAVANS

A la piedra en tu rostro,	The stone in your face,
Vallejo,	Vallejo,
a las arrugas	the wrinkles
de las áridas sierras	of arid sierras
yo recuerdo en mi canto,	I remember in my song,
tu frente	the gigantic
gigantesca	forehead
sobre tu cuerpo frágil,	over your fragile body,
el crepúsculo negro	the black sunset
en tus ojos	just unearthed
recién desenterrados,	in your eyes;
días aquéllos,	those days,
bruscos,	rough,
desiguales,	uneven,
cada hora tenía	each hour with
ácidos diferentes	different acids
o ternuras	or remote
remotas,	tenderness.
las llaves	The keys
de la vida	of life
temblaban	tremble
en la luz polvorienta	in the dusty light
de la calle,	of the street.
tú volvías	You were coming back
de un viaje	from a trip,
lento, bajo la tierra,	slow, under the earth,
y en la altura	and, at the height

de las cicatrizadas cordilleras
yo golpeaba las puertas,
que se abrieran
los muros,
que se desenrollaran
los caminos,
recién llegado de Valparaíso
me embarcaba en Marsella,
la tierra
se cortaba
como un limón fragante
en frescos hermisferios amarillos,
te quedabas
tú
allí, sujeto
a nada,
con tu vida
y tu muerte,
con tu arena
cayendo,
midiéndote
y vaciándote,
en el aire,
en el humo,
en las callejas rotas
del invierno.

Era en París, vivías
en los descalabrados
hoteles de los pobres.
España
se desangraba.
Acudíamos.
Y luego
te quedaste
otra vez en el humo

of the scarred cordilleras,
I banged at the door,
asking for walls
to open up,
for roads
to unravel.
I was recently arrived from Valparaíso,
about to set sail for Marseille.
The planet
was cut
like a fragrant lemon
into cool yellow hemispheres.
You stayed
there,
attached
to nothing,
with your life
and your death,
with your falling sand,
falling,
measuring yourself
and emptying yourself
in the air,
in the smoke,
in the broken alleys
of winter.

It was in Paris. You
lived in the broken-down
hotels of poor people.
Spain
was bleeding.
We responded
and then
you stayed behind,
again, in the smoke.

y así cuando
ya no fuiste, de pronto,
no fue la tierra
de las cicatrices,
no fue
la piedra andina
la que tuvo tus huesos,
sino el humo,
la escarcha
de París en invierno.

Dos veces desterrado,
hermano mío,
de la tierra y el aire,
de la vida y la muerte,
desterrado
del Perú, de tus ríos,
ausente
de tu arcilla.
No me faltaste en vida,
sino en muerte.
Te busco
gota a gota,
polvo a polvo,
en tu tierra,
amarillo
es tu rostro,
escarpado
es tu rostro,
estás lleno
de viejas pedrerías,
de vasijas
quebradas,
subo
las antiguas
escalinatas,

And, suddenly,
when you were no more,
the scarring earth was no more,
and the Andean stone
that held your bones
was no more.
Only smoke
and frost
were left behind
in a Paris winter.

Twice exiled,
my brother,
from land and air,
from life and death,
exiled
from Peru, from your rivers,
absent
from your own clay.
You didn't miss me in life,
only in death.
I look for you,
drop by drop,
dust to dust,
in your land.
Your face
is yellow,
your face
is steep,
you are filled
with precious stones,
with broken
vessels.
I climb
ancient
stairways,

tal vez
estés perdido,
enredado
entre los hilos de oro,
cubierto
de turquesas,
silencioso,
o tal vez
en tu pueblo,
en tu raza,
grano
de maíz extendido,
semilla
de bandera.
Tal vez, tal vez ahora
transmigres
y regreses,
vienes
al fin
de viaje,
de manera
que un día
te verás en el centro
de tu patria,
insurrecto,
viviente,
cristal de tu cristal, fuego en tu fuego,
rayo de piedra púrpura.

maybe
I'm lost,
entangled
in threads of gold,
covered
with turquoise jewels,
silent.
Or maybe
I'm in your pueblo,
in your race,
in your scattered
corn,
a seed
of flag.
Maybe, maybe now
you'll
transmigrate
and return.
You're
at the end
of the journey,
so you'll find yourself
at the heart of your
homeland,
in rebellion,
alive,
crystal of your own crystal, fire in your
own fire,
ray of purple stone.

38 / ODE TO THE CHAIR

Oda a la silla

TRANSLATED BY KEN KRABBENHOFT

Una silla en la selva:
bajo las lianas duras
cruje un tronco sagrado,
sube una enredadera,
aúllan en la sombra
bestias ensangrentadas,
del cielo verde caen grandes hojas,
suenan los cascabeles
secos de la serpiente,
como un flechazo contra una bandera
atravesó un pájaro el follaje,
las ramas levantaron sus violines,
rezan inmóviles
los insectos
sentados en sus flores,
se hunden los pies
en
el sargazo negro
de la selva marina,
en las nubes caídas de la selva,
y sólo pido
para el extranjero,
para el explorador desesperado
una silla
en el árbol de las sillas,
un trono
de felpa desgreñada,
el terciopelo de un sillón profundo
carcomido por las enredaderas.

A chair in the jungle:
under the severe lianas
a sacred tree trunk creaks,
tangles of vines press high,
in the shadows
bloody beasts cry out,
majestic leaves descend from the green
sky,
the rattles of snakes
quiver like bells.
A bird spanned the sprawling greenness,
like an arrow shot through a flag,
and branches hoisted high their violins.
Insects
pray in stillness,
seated on their wild bouquets.
Feet sink into
the black Sargasso
of the watery jungle,
into the rain forest's tumbled clouds.
I only request one thing
for the stranger,
for the desperate
explorer,
a chair in the tree of chairs,
a throne,
disheveled and plush,
the velvet of a deep easy chair,
eaten away by creepers.

Sí,
una silla,
la silla
que ama el universo
para el hombre que anda,
la fundación
segura,
la dignidad
suprema
del reposo!

Yes,
a chair,
loving the universe,
for the walkabout man,
the sure
foundation,
the supreme
dignity
of rest!

Atrás tigres sedientos,
muchedumbre de moscas sanguinarias,
atrás negra espesura
de fantasmales hojas,
atrás aguas espesas,
hojas ferruginosas,
sempiternas serpientes,
en medio
de los truenos,
una silla,
una silla
para mí, para todos,
una silla no sólo
para alivio
del cuerpo fatigado,
sino
que para todo
y para todos,
para la fuerza perdida
y para el pensamiento.

Behind thirsty tigers,
bands of bloodthirsty flies,
behind the black expanse
of ghost-ridden leaves,
behind the low waters,
the thicket like iron,
perpetual snakes,
in the middle
of the thunder,
a chair,
a chair,
for me,
for everyone,
a chair not
only for the weary body's
rescue,
but also for everything,
and for everybody,
to renew lost strength,
and for meditation.

La guerra es ancha como selva oscura.
La paz
comienza
en
una sola
silla.

War is wide like the light-starved jungle.
Peace
begins
in
a
single
chair.

39 / ODE TO A CHESTNUT ON THE GROUND

Oda a una castaña en el suelo

TRANSLATED BY STEPHEN MITCHELL

Del follaje erizado
caíste
completa,
de madera pulida,
de lúcida caoba,
lista
como un violín que acaba
de nacer en la altura,
y cae
ofreciendo sus dones encerrados,
su escondida dulzura,
terminada en secreto
entre pájaros y hojas,
escuela de la forma,
linaje de la leña y de la harina,
instrumento ovalado
que guarda en su estructura
delicia intacta y rosa comestible.
En lo alto abandonaste
el erizado erizo
que entreabrió sus espinas
en la luz del castaño,
por esa partidura
viste el mundo,
pájaros
llenos de sílabas,
rocío

Out of the bristling foliage
you fell
complete:
polished wood,
glistening mahogany,
perfect
as a violin that has just
been born in the treetops
and falls
offering the gifts locked inside it,
its hidden sweetness,
finished in secret among
birds and leaves,
the school of form,
lineage of firewood and flour,
oval instrument
that holds in its structure
unblemished delight and edible rose.
Up there, you abandoned
the bristling husk
that half-opened its barbs
in the light of the chestnut tree,
through that opening
you saw the world,
birds
filled with syllables,
starry

con estrellas,	dew,
y abajo	and down below
cabezas de muchachos	the heads of boys
y muchachas,	and girls,
hierbas que tiemblan sin reposo,	grasses that fluttered restlessly,
humo que sube y sube.	smoke that rises and rises.
Te decidiste,	You made up your mind,
castaña,	chestnut,
y saltaste a la tierra,	and you leapt down to earth,
bruñida y preparada,	burnished and prepared,
endurecida y suave	firm and smooth
como un pequeño seno	as a small breast
de las islas de América.	in the islands of America.
Caíste	You fell
golpeando	hitting
el suelo	the ground
pero	but
nada pasó,	nothing happened,
la hierba	the grass
siguió temblando, el viejo	went on fluttering, the old
castaño susurró como las bocas	chestnut tree whispered like the mouths
de toda una arboleda,	of a hundred trees,
cayó una hoja del otoño rojo,	one leaf fell from red autumn,
firme siguieron trabajando	steadily the hours kept on working
las horas en la tierra.	upon the earth.
Porque eres	Because you are
sólo	just
una semilla,	a seed:
castaño, otoño, tierra,	chestnut tree, autumn, earth,
agua, altura, silencio	water, heights, silence
prepararon el germen,	prepared the embryo,
la harinosa espesura,	the floury thickness,
los párpados maternos	the maternal eyelids,
que abrirán, enterrados,	which, buried, will open again
de nuevo hacia la altura	toward the heights
la magnitud sencilla	the simple magnificence

de un follaje,
la oscura trama húmeda
de unas nuevas raíces,
las antiguas y nuevas dimensiones
de otro castaño en la tierra.

of foliage,
the dark, damp network
of new roots,
the ancient and new dimensions
of another chestnut tree in the earth.

40 / ODE TO CLARITY

Oda a la claridad

TRANSLATED BY ILAN STAVANS

La tempestad dejó	The tempest left
sobre la hierba	on the leaves
hilos de pino, agujas,	threads of pine, needles,
y el sol en la cola del viento.	and the sun in the wind's tail.
Un azul dirigido	A straight azure
llena el mundo.	permeates the world.
Oh día pleno,	Oh plentiful day,
oh fruto	of fruit
del espacio,	of space,
mi cuerpo es una copa	my body is a cup
en que la luz y el aire	in which light and air
caen como cascadas.	fall like cascades.
Toco	I touch
el agua marina.	the sea water.
Sabor	The new waves
de fuego verde,	have
de beso ancho y amargo	the flavor
tienen las nuevas olas	of green fire,
de este día.	of a wide and bitter kiss.
Tejen su trama de oro	The cicadas
las cigarras	knit in the sonorous height
en la altura sonora.	their plot of gold.
La boca de la vida	The mouth of life
besa mi boca.	kisses my mouth.
Vivo,	I live,
amo	I love

y soy amado.	and I'm loved.
Recibo	I receive in my being
en mi ser cuanto existe.	whatever is in existence.
Estoy sentado	I'm sitting
en una piedra:	on a rock:
en ella	it's
tocan	touched
las aguas y las sílabas	by the waters and syllables
de la selva,	of the jungle,
la claridad sombría	the somber clarity
del manantial que llega	of the spring arriving
a visitarme.	to visit me.
Toco	I touch
el tronco de cedro	the cedar's trunk,
cuyas arrugas me hablan	its creases speak to me
del tiempo y de la tierra.	of time and the earth.
Marcho	I march
y voy con los ríos	and go along with the rivers
cantando	singing
con los ríos,	with the rivers,
ancho, fresco y aéreo	wide, fresh and aerial
en este nuevo día,	in this new day,
y lo recibo,	and I receive it,
siento	feeling
cómo	as if
entra en mi pecho, mira con mis ojos.	it enters my chest, it sees through my eyes.
Yo soy,	I am,
yo soy el día,	I am the day,
soy	am
la luz.	the light.
Por eso	That's why
tengo	I have
deberes de mañana,	morning duties,
trabajos de mediodía.	noon labors.
Debo	I must

andar
con el viento y el agua,
abrir ventanas,
echar abajo puertas,
romper muros,
iluminar rincones.

No puedo
quedarme sentado.
Hasta luego.
Mañana
nos veremos.
Hoy tengo muchas
batallas que vencer.
Hoy tengo muchas sombras
que herir y terminar.
Hoy no puedo
estar contigo, debo
cumplir mi obligación
de luz:
ir y venir por las calles,
las casas y los hombres
destruyendo
la oscuridad. Yo debo
repartirme
hasta que todo sea día,
hasta que todo sea claridad
y alegría en la tierra.

walk
with the wind and the water,
open windows,
break down doors,
break walls,
illuminate corners.

I can't
sit still.
So long.
Tomorrow
we'll see each other.
Today I have many
battles to win.
Today I have many shadows
to injure and finish.
I can't be with you
today, I must
fulfill my obligation
of light:
come and go on the streets,
the houses and men
destroying
darkness. I must
share myself
until everything is day,
until everything is clarity
and happiness on earth.

41 / ODE TO THE CLOTHES

Oda al traje

TRANSLATED BY W. S. MERWIN

Cada mañana esperas,	Every morning you wait,
traje, sobre una silla	clothes, over a chair,
que te llene	for my vanity,
mi vanidad, mi amor,	my love,
mi esperanza, mi cuerpo.	my hope, my body
Apenas	to fill you.
salgo del sueño,	I have scarcely
me despido del agua,	left sleep,
entro en tus mangas,	I say goodbye to the water
mis piernas buscan	and enter your sleeves,
el hueco de tus piernas	my legs look for
y así abrazado	the hollow of your legs,
por tu fidelidad infatigable	and thus embraced
salgo a pisar el pasto,	by your unwearying fidelity
entro en la poesía,	I go out to tread the fodder,
miro por las ventanas,	I move into poetry,
las cosas,	I look through windows,
los hombres, las mujeres,	at things,
los hechos y las luchas	men, women,
me van formando,	actions and struggles
me van haciendo frente	keep making me what I am,
labrándome las manos,	opposing me,
abriéndome los ojos,	employing my hands,
gastándome la boca	opening my eyes,
y así,	putting taste in my mouth,
traje,	and thus,
	clothes,

yo también voy formándote,	I make you what you are,
sacándote los codos,	pushing out your elbows,
rompiéndote los hilos,	bursting the seams,
y así tu vida crece	and so your life swells
a imagen de mi vida.	the image of my life.
Al viento	You billow
ondulas y resuenas	and resound in the wind
como si fueras mi alma,	as though you were my soul,
en los malos minutos	at bad moments
te adhieres	you cling
a mis huesos	to my bones
vacíos, por la noche	empty, at night
la oscuridad, el sueño	the dark, sleep,
pueblan con sus fantasmas	people with their phantoms
tus alas y las mías.	your wings and mine.
Yo pregunto	I ask
si un día	whether one day
una bala	a bullet
del enemigo	from the enemy
te dejará una mancha de mi sangre	will stain you with my blood
y entonces	and then
te morirás conmigo	you will die with me
o tal vez	or perhaps
no sea todo	it may not be
tan dramático	so dramatic
sino simple,	but simple,
y te irás enfermando,	and you will sicken gradually,
traje,	clothes,
conmigo,	with me, with my body
envejeciendo	and together
conmigo, con mi cuerpo	we will enter
y juntos	the earth.
entraremos	At the thought of this
a la tierra.	every day
Por eso	
cada día	

te saludo
con reverencia y luego
me abrazas y te olvido,
porque uno solo somos
y seguiremos siendo
frente al viento, en la noche,
las calles o la lucha
un solo cuerpo
tal vez, tal vez, alguna vez inmóvil.

I greet you
with reverence, and then
you embrace me and I forget you
because we are one
and will go on facing
the wind together, at night,
the streets or the struggle,
one body,
maybe, maybe, one day motionless.

42 / ODE TO CLOUDS

Oda a las nubes

TRANSLATED BY KEN KRABBENHOFT

Nubes del cielo Sur,	Clouds of southern skies,
nubes aladas,	winged clouds,
nubes	clouds
de impecable vapor, trajes del cielo,	of whitest steam, heaven's clothing,
pétales, peces puros	petals, perfect fish
del estío,	of summertime:
boca arriba en el pasto, en las arenas	you are heavenly girls
de todo el cielo sois	lying on your backs in grass and on beaches
las muchachas celestes,	of spreading sky,
la seda al sol, la primavera blanca,	silk in sunlight, white springtime,
la juventud del cielo.	the sky's childhood.
Derramadas, corriendo	Splashed across the heavens, rushing by
apenas	lofted
sostenidas	lightly
por el aire,	on air,
plumones	giant feathers
de la luz, nidos	of light, nests
del agua!	of water,
Ahora un solo	and now a single
ribete	filament
de combustión, de ira	of flame or rage
enciende	ignites
las praderas	meadows
celestiales	of sky
y los almendros	and blooming
en flor,	almond trees.
la equinoccial	Every equinox

lavandería
es devorada
por leopardos
verdes,
cortadas por alfanjes,
atacadas por
bocas
incendiarias.
Nubes desesperadas
y puntuales
en el fallecimiento
del sol
de cada día,
baile
ritual
de todo
el horizonte,
apenas
si cruzan el espacio
lentas aves del mar, vuelos
sobre la perspectiva,
se desgarran las nubes,
se disuelve
la luz del abanico delirante,
vida y fuego no existen, eran sólo
ceremonias del cielo.
Pero a ti, nubarrona
de tempestad, reservo
aquel espacio
de monte o mar, de sombra,
de pánico y tinieblas sobre el mundo,
sea sobre las haces
de la espuma
en la noche iracunda
del océano

this laundry
is devoured
by green
leopards,
slashed by scimitars,
attacked by
fire
hydrants.
Clouds that arrive on time
but without hope
for the sun's
daily
demise,
the whole
horizon's
ritual
dance:
no sooner
have sluggish seabirds
crossed this space, flying
above the view,
than clouds are ripped apart,
light from this frenzied fan
falls apart,
there is no more life or fire: they were simply
the sky's celebration.
But for you, swollen
storm cloud, I am holding
that space
over mountain and sea, that space of shadows,
of panic and darkness above the world.
And whether you stand above sheaves
of sea spray
in the ocean's
outraged night,

o sobre la callada
cabellera
de los bosques nocturnos,
nube, tinta de acero
desparramas,
algodones de luto en que se ahogan
las pálidas estrellas.

De tu paraguas cae
con densidad de plomo
la oscuridad y pronto
agua eléctrica y humo
tiemblan como banderas
oscuras, sacudidas
por el miedo.

Riegas
y unes
tu oscuridad al sueño
de las negras raíces,
y así de la tormenta
sale a la luz
de nuevo
el esplendor terrestre.

Nube
de primavera, nave
olorosa, pura
azucena
del cielo,
manto de viuda desdichada,
negra madre del trueno,
quiero un traje de nube,
una camisa
de vuestros materiales,
y llevadme en el hilo

or above the muted
mane
of nocturnal forests,
you, cloud, shed
a steely ink
and cotton puffs of mourning in which
the pale stars drown.

Darkness falls
from your umbrella
with the heaviness of lead, then
electrified water and smoke
tremble like dark
flags, shaken
by fear.

You water
your darkness
and join it to the sleep
of black roots:
this is how earth's splendor
emerges to sparkle
again
after storms.

Spring's
cloud, fragrant
vessel, perfect
lily
of heaven,
unfortunate widow's cloak,
black mother of thunder:
I want a suit of clouds,
a shirt
of your substance.
Sweep me along the edge

de la luz o en el
caballo de la sombra
a recorrer el cielo, todo el cielo.

Así tocaré bosques, arrecifes,
cruzaré cataratas y ciudades,
veré la intimidad del universo,
hasta que con la lluvia
regresaré a la tierra
a conversar en paz con las raíces.

of light, or mount me
on a steed of shadow
to race the length of the sky.

Thus will I touch reefs and forests,
scale waterfalls and cities,
peer into the world's secret heart,
and when I'm done I'll return
to earth with the rain,
and commune quietly with roots.

43 / ODE TO THE COASTAL FLOWERS

Oda a las flores de la costa

TRANSLATED BY ILAN STAVANS

Han abierto las flores
silvestres de Isla Negra,
no tienen nombre, algunas
parecen azahares de la arena,
otras
encienden
en el suelo un relámpago amarillo.

Soy pastoral poeta.
Me alimento
como los cazadores,
hago fuego
junto al mar, en la noche.

Sólo esta flor, sólo estas
soledades marinas
y tú, alegre,
y simple como rosa de la tierra.

La vida
me pidió que combatiera
y organicé mi corazón luchando
y levantando la esperanza:
hermano
del hombre soy, de todos.
Deber y amor se llaman
mis dos manos.

The Isla Negra wildflowers
are blooming,
they have no names, some
seem like sand crocuses,
others
illuminate
the ground with yellow lighting.

I'm a pastoral poet.
I feed myself
like a hunter;
near the sea, at night,
I build a fire.

Only this flower, only this
marine solitude;
and you, glad,
simple, like an earthly rose.

Life
begged me to be a fighter;
I organized my heart around struggle,
and keeping hope alive:
I'm a brother
to man, to everyone.
My two hands
are named duty and love.

Mirando	I stare
entre las piedras	at the coastal
de la costa	stones,
las flores que esperaron	while the flowers that lasted
a través del olvido	through oblivion
y del invierno	and winter
para elevar un rayo diminuto	to raise a tiny ray
de luz y de fragancia,	of light and fragrance
al despedirme	to tell me farewell
una vez más	yet again
del fuego,	farewell to the sand,
de la leña,	the wood,
del bosque,	the fire
de la arena,	of the forest,
me duele dar un paso,	the sand
aquí	it hurts to walk along.
me quedaría,	I would rather stay here,
no en las calles.	not on the streets.
Soy pastoral poeta.	I'm a pastoral poet.
Pero deber y amor son mis dos manos.	But duty and love are my two hands.

44 / ODE TO THE COLOR GREEN

Oda al color verde

TRANSLATED BY ILAN STAVANS

Cuando la tierra
fue
calva y callada,
silencio y cicatrices,
extensiones
de lava seca
y piedra congelada,
apareció
el verde,
el color verde,
trébol,
acacia,
río
de agua verde.

Se derramó el cristal
inesperado
y crecieron
y se multiplicaron
los numerosos
verdes,
verdes de pasto y ojos,
verdes de amor marino,
verdes
de campanario,
verdes
delgados, para
la red, para las algas, para el cielo,

While the earth
was
barren and calm,
stillness and scars,
extensions
of parched lava
and frozen stone,
green
appeared,
the color green,
clover,
acacia,
river
of green water.

The unexpected crystal
melted away
and numerous
greens
swelled
and multiplied:
greens of grass and eyes,
greens of sea love,
belfry
greens,
thin
greens, for
the net, for algae, the sky,

para la selva
el verde tembloroso,
para las uvas
un ácido verde.

Vestido
de la tierra,
población del follaje,
no sólo
uno
sino
la multiplicación
del ancho verde,
ennegrecido como
noche verde,
claro y agudo
como
violín verde,
espeso en la espesura,
metállco, sulfúrico
en la mina
de cobre, venenoso
en las lanzas
oxidadas,
húmedo en el abrazo
de la ciénaga,
virtud de la hermosura.

Ventana de la luna en movimiento,
cárdenos, muertos verdes
que enrojecen
a la luz del otoño
en el puñal del eucaliptus, frío
como piel de pescado,
enfermedades verdes,
neones saturnianos
que te afligen

trembling greens
for the jungle,
an acid green
for grapes.

Earth's
raiment,
population of leaves,
not
one alone
but
a broad amplification
of greens
blackened
like green night,
clear and sharp
like
a green violin,
thick in thickness,
metallic, sulfuric
in copper
mines, poisonous
in rusty
spears,
damped with the bog's
embrace,
virtue of beauty.

Window of the moon in motion,
opalescent, dead green
blushing
in autumn light
in the knife of eucalyptus, frigid
as fish skin,
green illnesses,
saturnine neons
they assail

con agobiante luz,
verde volante
de la nupcial luciérnaga,
y tierno
verde
suave
de la lechuga cuando
recibe sol en gotas
de los castos limones
exprimidos
por una mano verde.

El verde
que no tuve,
no tengo
ni tendría,
el fulgor submarino y subterráneo,
la luz
de la esmeralda,
águila verde entre las piedras, ojo
del abismo, mariposa helada,
estrella que no pudo
encontrar cielo
y enterró
su ola verde
en
la más honda
cámara terrestre,
y allí
como rosario
del infierno,
fuego del mar o corazón de tigre,
espléndida dormiste, piedra verde,
uña de las montañas,
río fatuo,
estatua hostil, endurecido verde.

with overpowering light,
the flying green
of the nuptial lightning bug,
and tender
green
of lettuce,
soft when
it receives the sun,
in slice drops of chaste lemon
squeezed
by a green hand.

The green
I didn't grasp,
I don't hold,
and I won't,
underwater and underground gleaming,
light of
emerald,
green eagle among stones, eye
of the abyss, gelid butterfly,
star incapable
of finding sky,
they buried
its green wave
in
the deepest
chambers of earth;
and there,
like a rosary
from hell,
sea fire and tiger's heart,
you slept splendidly, green stone,
mountain fingernail,
fatuous river,
hostile statue—green that turned to stone.

45 / ODE TO CONGER CHOWDER

Oda al caldillo de congrio

TRANSLATED BY MARGARET SAYERS PEDEN

En el mar
tormentoso
de Chile
vive el rosado congrio,
gigante anguila
de nevada carne.
Y en las ollas
chilenas,
en la costa,
nació el caldillo
grávido y suculento,
provechoso.
Lleven a la cocina
el congrio desollado,
su piel manchada cede
como un guante
y al descubierto queda
entonces
el racimo del mar,
el congrio tierno
reluce
ya desnudo,
preparado
para nuestro apetito.
Ahora
recoges
ajos,

In the storm-tossed
Chilean
sea
lives the rosy conger,
giant eel
of snowy flesh.
And in Chilean
stewpots,
along the coast,
was born the chowder,
thick and succulent,
a boon to man.
You bring the conger, skinned,
to the kitchen
(its mottled skin slips off
like a glove,
leaving the
grape of the sea
exposed to the world),
naked,
the tender eel
glistens,
prepared
to serve our appetites.
Now
you take
garlic,

acaricia primero
ese marfil
precioso,
huele
su fragancia iracunda,
entonces
deja el ajo picado
caer con la cebolla
y el tomate
hasta que la cebolla
tenga color de oro.
Mientras tanto
se cuecen
con el vapor
los regios
camarones marinos
y cuando ya llegaron
a su punto,
cuando cuajó el sabor
en una salsa
formada por el jugo
del océano
y por el agua clara
que desprendió la luz de la cebolla,
entonces
que entre el congrio
y se sumerja en gloria,
que en la olla
se aceite,
se contraiga y se impregne.
Ya sólo es necesario
dejar en el manjar
caer la crema
como una rosa espesa,
y al fuego
lentamente

first, caress
that precious
ivory,
smell
its irate fragrance,
then
blend the minced garlic
with onion
and tomato
until the onion
is the color of gold.
Meanwhile
steam
our regal
ocean prawns,
and when
they are
tender,
when the savor is
set in a sauce
combining the liquors
of the ocean
and the clear water
released from the light of the onion,
then
you add the eel
that it may be immersed in glory,
that it may steep in the oils
of the pot,
shrink and be saturated.
Now all that remains is to
drop a dollop of cream
into the concoction,
a heavy rose,
then slowly
deliver

entregar el tesoro
hasta que en el caldillo
se calienten
las esencias de Chile,
y a la mesa
lleguen recién casados
los sabores
del mar y de la tierra
para que en ese plato
tú conozcas el cielo.

the treasure to the flame,
until in the chowder
are warmed
the essences of Chile,
and to the table
come, newly wed,
the savors
of land and sea,
that in this dish
you may know heaven.

46 / ODE TO COPPER

Oda al cobre

TRANSLATED BY ILAN STAVANS

El cobre ahí	Copper lies
dormido.	asleep there.
Son los cerros del Norte	Those are the hills
desolado.	of the desolate North.
Desde arriba	From above
las cumbres	the summits
del cobre,	of copper,
cicatrices hurañas,	disdainful scars,
mantos verdes,	green mantles,
cúpulas carcomidas	cupolas in decay
por el ímpetu	a result of the burning
abrasador del tiempo,	impetus of time,
cerca	near
de nosotros	us
la mina:	the mine:
la mina es sólo el hombre,	the mine is only man,
no sale	the mineral
de la tierra	doesn't emerge
el mineral,	from the earth,
sale	it leaves
del pecho humano,	the human chest,
allí	there
se toca	one touches
el bosque muerto,	the dead forest,
las arterias	the arteries
del volcán	of the suspended
detenido,	volcano,

se averigua
la veta,
se perfora
y
estalla
la dinamita,
la roca se derrama,
se purifica:
va naciendo
el cobre.
Antes nadie sabrá
diferenciarlo
de la piedra materna.
Ahora
es hombre,
parte del hombre,
pétalo pesado
de su gloria.
Ahora
ya no es verde,
es rojo,
se ha convertido en sangre,
en sangre dura,
en corazón terrible.

Veo
caer los montes,
abrirse
el territorio
en iracundas
cavidades pardas,
el desierto, las casas
transitorias.
El mineral
a fuego
y golpe

the vein
is identified,
perforation takes place
and
dynamite
explodes,
the rock is spilled,
purified:
copper
is being born.
No one will know how to
differentiate it
from the mother rock.
Now
it is man,
part of man,
heavy petal
of its glory.
Now
it is no longer green,
it is red,
it has become blood,
hard blood,
terrible heart.

I see
the mountains fall,
open up
the territory
in angry
grayish cavities,
the desert, the transitory
houses.
The mineral
on fire
and shaped

y mano	and handled
se convirtió en lingotes militares,	became military ingots,
en batallones de mercaderías.	in battalions of merchandise.
Se fueron los navíos.	The ships departed.
A donde llegue	Wherever copper
el cobre,	arrives,
utensilio o alambre,	utensil or wire,
nadie	no one
que lo toque	touching it
verá las escarpadas	will see the rugged
soledades de Chile,	solitudes of Chile,
o las pequeñas casas a la orilla	or the small houses on the edge
del desierto,	of the desert,
o los picapedreros orgullosos,	or the proud stonecutters,
mi pueblo, los mineros	my people, the miners
que bajan a la mina.	who descend to the mine.
Yo sufro.	I suffer.
Yo conozco.	I know.
Sucede	It happens
que de tanta dureza,	that from so much hardship,
de las excavaciones,	from the excavations,
herida y explosión, sudor y sangre,	injury and explosion, sweat and blood,
cuando el hombre,	when man,
mi pueblo,	my people,
Chile,	Chile,
dominó la materia,	domesticated the matter,
apartó de la piedra	it cut from the stone
el mineral yacente,	the recumbent mineral,
éste se fue a Chicago	this one went to Chicago
de paseo,	on vacation,
el cobre	copper
se convirtió en cadenas,	was transformed into chains,
en maquinaria tétrica	in the gloomy machinery
del crimen,	of crime,
después de tantas luchas	after so many struggles
para que mi patria lo pariera,	so that my homeland would give birth to it,

después de su glorioso,
virginal nacimiento,
lo hicieron ayudante de la muerte,
lo endurecieron y lo designaron
asesino.

Pregunto
a la empinada cordillera,
al desértico
litoral sacudido
por la espuma
del desencadenado mar de Chile:
para eso
el cobre nuestro
dormía
en el útero verde
de la piedra?
Nació para la muerte?
Al hombre
mío,
a mi hermano
de la cumbre erizada,
le pregunto:
para eso
le diste nacimiento entre dolores?
Para que fuera
ciclón amenazante,
tempestuosa desgracia?
Para que demoliera
las vidas
de los pobres,
de otros pobres,
de tu propia familia
que tal vez no conoces
y que está derramada
en todo el mundo?

after its glorious,
virginal birth,
it became a companion of death,
they hardened it and designated it
an assassin.

I ask
the tipped-up cordillera,
the desertlike
coast shaken
by the foam
of the unchained sea of Chile:
is that why
our copper
lay
in the green womb
of the stone?
Was it born for death's sake?
My
man,
my brother
of the rooted summit,
I ask:
for this
did you give it
birth amid the pains?
So it became
a menacing cyclone,
tempestuous misfortune?
So it demolished
the lives
of the poor,
the other poor,
your own family
that perhaps you're unacquainted with,
and spreads out across the world?

Es hora	It's time
de dar el mineral	to give the mineral
a los tractores,	back to the tractors,
a la fecundidad	to the fecundity
de la tierra futura,	of the future earth,
a la paz del sonido,	to the peace of sound,
a la herramienta,	to the tool,
a la máquina clara	to the clear machine
y a la vida.	and to life.
Es hora	It's time
de dar	to give
la huraña	copper's
mano abierta del cobre	intractable hand
a todo ser humano.	to every human being.
Por eso,	That's why,
cobre,	copper,
serás nuestro,	you shall be ours,
no seguirán jugando	the cardsharp
contigo	of butchery
a los dados	will no longer play
los tahúres	dice
de la carnicería!	with you!
De los cerros	From the abrupt
abruptos,	hills,
de la altura	the green
verde,	heights,
saldrá el cobre de Chile,	the copper of Chile shall emerge,
la cosecha	the hardest
más dura	harvest
de mi pueblo,	of my people,
la corola	the blazing
incendiada,	corolla,
irradiando	irradiating
la vida	life
y no la muerte,	not death,
propagando la espiga	propagating the head of corn

y no la sangre,
dando a todos los pueblos
nuestro amor
desenterrado,
nuestra montaña verde
que al contacto
de la vida y el viento
se transforma
en corazón sangrante,
en piedra roja.

and not blood,
giving all the people
our unearthed
love,
our green mountain
in touch
with life and wind
that is transformed
into a bleeding heart,
into red stone.

47 / ODE TO A COUPLE

Oda a la pareja

TRANSLATED BY MARGARET SAYERS PEDEN

I

Reina, es hermoso ver
marcando mi camino
tu pisada pequeña
o ver tus ojos
enredándose
en todo lo que miro,
ver despertar tu rostro
cada día,
sumergirse
en el mismo
fragmento
de sombra
cada noche.
Hermoso
es ver
el tiempo
que corre
como el mar
contra una sola proa
formada por tus senos y mi pecho,
por tus pies y mis manos.
Pasan por tu perfil
olas del tiempo,
las mismas que me azotan
y me encienden,
olas como furiosas

I

My queen, how beautiful
to follow the path of
your small footprints,
how beautiful to see
your eyes
everywhere I look,
how beautiful your face
greeting each new day,
and sinking
every night
into the same
fragment
of shadow.
How beautiful
to see
time
running
like the sea
breaking over the prow
formed by your breasts and my chest,
by your feet and my hands.
The waves of time
wash over your profile,
the same waves that lash
and inflame me,
cold waves

dentelladas de frío
y olas como los granos
de la espiga.
Pero
estamos juntos,
resistimos,
guardando
tal vez
espuma negra o roja
en la memoria,
heridas
que palpitaron como labios o alas.
Vamos andando juntos
por calles y por islas,
bajo el violín quebrado
de las ráfagas,
frente a un dios enemigo,
sencillamente juntos
una mujer y un hombre.

with gnashing teeth,
and waves like the grains
of a head of wheat.
But
we are together,
we endure,
guarding
perhaps
black or red sea foam
in our memories,
wounds
throbbing like lips or wings.
We walk together
through streets and islands,
beneath the splintered violin
of the raging wind,
facing an enemy deity,
quietly together,
a man and a woman.

II

Aquellos
que no han sentido cada
día del mundo
caer
sobre la doble
máscara del navío,
no la sal sino el tiempo,
no la sombra
sino el paso desnudo
de la dicha,
cómo podrán cerrar
los ojos,
los ojos solitarios y dormir?

II

Those
who have never felt
the weight of day
fall
upon the ship's
twin figureheads,
not salt but time,
not shadow
but the naked footsteps
of happiness,
how can they
ever close
their lonely eyes in sleep?

No me gusta
la casa sin tejado,
la ventana sin vidrios.
No me gusta
el día sin trabajo,
ni la noche sin sueño.
No me gusta
el hombre
sin mujer,
ni la mujer
sin hombre.

Complétate,
hombre o mujer, que nada
te intimide.
En algún sitio
ahora
están esperándote.
Levántate:
tiembla
la luz en las campanas,
nacen
las amapolas,
tienes
que vivir
y amasar
con barro y luz tu vida.

Si sobre dos cabezas
cae la nieve
es dulce el corazón
caliente de la casa.
De otra manera,
en la intemperie, el viento
te pregunta:
dónde está la que amaste?

I don't like a house
without a roof,
or a window without panes.
I don't like
a day without work
or a night without sleep.
I don't like
a man
without a woman,
or a woman
without a man.

Complete yourself,
man or woman, let nothing
intimidate you.
Somewhere,
even now,
someone waits for you.
Get up,
light
is trembling on the bells,
poppies
are opening,
you must
live
and mold your life
with clay and light.

If snow falls
upon two heads,
the heart is sweet,
the house is warm.
If not,
in the storm, the wind
asks:
where is the woman you loved?

Y te empuja, mordiéndote, a buscarla.
Media mujer es una
y un hombre es medio hombre.
En media casa viven,
duermen en medio lecho.

Yo quiero
que las vidas se integren
encendiendo los besos
hasta ahora apagados.
Yo soy el buen poeta
casamentero. Tengo
novias
para todos los hombres.
Todos los días veo
mujeres solitarias
que por ti me preguntan.
Te casaré, si quieres,
con la hermana
de la sirena reina de las islas.
Por desgracia, no puedes
casarte con la reina,
porque me está esperando.
Se casará conmigo.

and nipping at your heels
will press you to seek her.
Half a woman is one woman
and one man is half a man.
Each lives in half a house,
each sleeps in half a bed.

I want
lives to blend together,
kindling kisses
unknown until now.
I am the good matchmaker
poet. I have
a sweetheart
for every man.
Every day I see
lonely women
who ask me about you.
If you want, I will wed you
to the sister
of the siren queen of the islands.
Unfortunately, you can't
marry the queen;
she is waiting for me.
She will marry me.

48 / ODE TO THE CRANIUM

Oda al cráneo

TRANSLATED BY MARGARET SAYERS PEDEN

No lo sentí	I never noticed it
sino	until
cuando caía,	I fell,
cuando perdí	until I lost
existencia	consciousness
y rodé	and rolled
fuera	outside
de mi ser como el hueso	my being like the pit
de una fruta	of some squashed
aplastada:	fruit;
no supe	all was
sino sueño	sleep
y oscuridad,	and darkness,
luego	then
sangre y camino,	blood and motion,
súbita	sudden
luz	intense
aguda:	light:
los viajeros	the messengers
que levantan tu sombra.	that dispel your shadow.
Más tarde el lienzo de la cama	Later, the linen of my bed
blanca como la luna	white as the moon
y el sueño al fin pegándose	and, finally, sleep clinging
a tu herida	to your wound
como un algodón negro.	like black cotton.
Esta mañana	This morning
extendí un dedo sigiloso,	a cautious finger emerged,

bajé por las costillas
al cuerpo
maltratado
y únicamente
encontré
firme
como un casco
mi pobre
cráneo.
Cuánto
en mi edad, en viajes, en amores,
me miré cada pelo,
cada arruga
de mi frente,
sin ver la magnitud
de la cabeza,
la huesuda
torre del pensamiento,
el coco duro,
la bóveda de calcio
protectora
como una caja de reloj
cubriendo
con su espesor de muro
minúsculos tesoros,
vasos, circulaciones
increíbles,
pulsos de la razón, venas del sueño,
gelatinas del alma,
todo
el pequeño océano
que eres,
el penacho profundo
del cerebro,
las circunvoluciones arrugadas
como una cordillera sumergida
y en ellas

crept along my ribs,
over my abused
body,
and found
the one thing
sound as a walnut
was
my poor
cranium.
How often in my mature years,
in travels, in love affairs,
I examined every hair,
every wrinkle
on my brow,
without noticing the grandness
of my head,
boned
tower of thought,
tough coconut,
calcium dome
protecting
the clockworks,
thick wall
guarding
treasures infinitesimal,
arteries, incredible
circulations,
pulses of reason, veins of sleep,
gelatin of the soul,
all
the miniature ocean
you are,
proud crest
of the mind,
the wrinkled convolutions
of an undersea cordillera
and in them

la voluntad, el pez del movimiento,
el eléctrica corola
del estímulo,
las algas del recuerdo.

Me toqué la cabeza,
descubriéndola,
como en la geología
de un monte
ya sin hojas,
sin temblorosa melodía de aves,
se descubre
el duro
mineral,
la osamenta
de la tierra,
y
herido aún,
en este
canto alabo
el cráneo, el tuyo,
el mío,
el cráneo,
la espesura
protectora,
la caja fuerte, el casco
de la vida,
la nuez de la existencia.

will, the fish of movement,
the electric corolla
of stimulus,
the seaweed of memory.

I touched my head,
discovering it,
as in the geology
of a mountain
now stripped bare of leaves
and the tremulous song of birds
one discovers
the hard
metal,
the skeleton
of the earth;
and so,
wounded still,
in this song
I praise
the cranium, yours,
mine,
the cranium,
guardian
thickness,
strongbox, the casque
of life,
the kernel of existence.

49 / ODE TO CRITICISM

Oda a la crítica

TRANSLATED BY MARGARET SAYERS PEDEN

Yo escribí cinco versos:	I wrote five poems:
uno verde,	one was green,
otro era un pan redondo,	another a round wheaten loaf,
el tercero una casa levantándose,	the third was a house, abuilding,
el cuarto era un anillo,	the fourth was a ring,
el quinto verso era	and the fifth was
corto como un relámpago	brief as a lightning flash,
y al escribirlo	and as I wrote it,
me dejó en la razón su quemadura.	it branded my reason.
Y bien, los hombres,	Well, then, men
las mujeres,	and women
vinieron y tomaron	came and took
la sencilla materia,	my simple materials,
brizna, viento, fulgor, barro, madera	breeze, wind, radiance, clay, wood,
y con tan poca cosa	and with such ordinary things
construyeron	constructed
paredes, pisos, sueños.	walls, floors, and dreams.
En una línea de mi poesía	On one line of my poetry
secaron ropa al viento.	they hung out the wash to dry.
Comieron	They ate my words
mis palabras,	for dinner,
las guardaron	they kept them
junto a la cabecera,	by the head of their beds,
vivieron con un verso,	they lived with poetry,
con la luz que salió de mi costado.	with the light that escaped from my side.
Entonces,	Then

llegó un crítico mudo
y otro lleno de lenguas,
y otros, otros llegaron
ciegos o llenos de ojos,
elegantes algunos
como claveles con zapatos rojos,
otros estrictamente
vestidos de cadáveres,
algunos partidarios
del rey y su elevada monarquía,
otros se habían
enredado en la frente
de Marx y pataleaban en su barba,
otros eran ingleses,
sencillamente ingleses,
y entre todos
se lanzaron
con dientes y cuchillos,
con diccionarios y otras armas negras,
con citas respetables,
se lanzaron
a disputar mi pobre poesía
a las sencillas gentes
que la amaban:
y la hicieron embudos,
la enrollaron,
la sujetaron con cien alfileres,
la cubrieron con polvo de esqueleto,
la llenaron de tinta,
la escupieron con suave
benignidad de gatos,
la destinaron a envolver relojes,
la protegieron y la condenaron,
le arrimaron petróleo,
le dedicaron húmedos tratados,
la cocieron con leche,

came a mute critic,
then another babbling tongues,
and others, many others, came,
some blind, some all-seeing,
some of them as elegant
as carnations with bright red shoes,
others as severely
clothed as corpses,
some were partisans
of the king and his exalted monarchy,
others had been snared
in Marx's brow
and were kicking their feet in his beard,
some were English,
plain and simply English,
and among them
they set out
with tooth and knife,
with dictionaries and other dark weapons,
with venerable quotes,
they set out
to take my poor poetry
from the simple folk
who loved it.
They trapped and tricked it,
they rolled it in a scroll,
they secured it with a hundred pins,
they covered it with skeleton dust,
they drowned it in ink,
they spit on it with the suave
benignity of a cat,
they used it to wrap clocks,
they protected it and condemned it,
they stored it with crude oil,
they dedicated damp treatises to it,
they boiled it with milk,

le agregaron pequeñas piedrecitas,
fueron borrándole vocales,
fueron matándole
sílabas y suspiros,
la arrugaron e hicieron
un pequeño paquete
que destinaron cuidadosamente
a sus desvanes, a sus cementerios,
luego
se retiraron uno a uno
enfurecidos hasta la locura
porque no fui bastante
popular para ellos
o impregnados de dulce menosprecio
por mi ordinaria falta de tinieblas,
se retiraron
todos
y entonces,
otra vez,
junto a mi poesía
volvieron a vivir
mujeres y hombres,
de nuevo
hicieron fuego,
construyeron casas,
comieron pan,
se repartieron la luz
y en el amor unieron
relámpago y anillo.
Y ahora,
perdonadme, señores,
que interrumpa este cuento
que les estoy contando
y me vaya a vivir
para siempre
con la gente sencilla.

they showered it with pebbles,
and in the process erased vowels from it,
their syllables and sighs
nearly killed it,
they crumbled it and tied it up in a
little package
they scrupulously addressed
to their attics and cemeteries,
then,
one by one, they retired,
enraged to the point of madness
because I wasn't
popular enough for them,
or saturated with mild contempt
for my customary lack of shadows,
they left,
all of them,
and then,
once again,
men and women
came to live
with my poetry,
once again
they lighted fires,
built houses,
broke bread,
they shared the light
and in love joined
the lightning flash and the ring.
And now,
gentlemen, if you will excuse me
for interrupting this story
I'm telling,
I am leaving to live
forever
with simple people.

50 / ODE TO CRITICISM II

Oda a la crítica II

TRANSLATED BY ILAN STAVANS

Toqué mi libro:
era
compacto,
firme,
arqueado
como una nave blanca,
entreabierto
como una nueva rosa,
era
para mis ojos
un molino,
de cada hoja
la flor del pan crecía
sobre mi libro:
me cegué con mis rayos,
me sentí demasiado
satisfecho,
perdí tierra,
comencé a caminar
envuelto en nubes
y entonces,
camarada,
me bajaste
a la vida,
una sola palabra
me mostró de repente
cuanto dejé de hacer

I touched my book:
it was
compact,
firm,
arched
like a white craft,
half-opened
like a new rose,
it was
a mill
for my eyes,
from each sheet
the flower of bread grew
over my book:
I was blinded by my rays,
I felt overly
satisfied,
I lost ground,
I started to walk
wrapped up in clouds
and then,
comrade,
you brought me down
to life,
a single word
suddenly showed me
how much I had ceased doing

y cuanto pude
avanzar con mi fuerza y mi ternura,
navegar con la nave de mi canto.

and how much I could
advance with my strength and my tenderness,
navigate with the craft of my song.

Volví más verdadero,
enriquecido,
tomé cuanto tenía
y cuanto tienes,
cuanto anduviste tú
sobre la tierra,
cuanto vieron
tus ojos,
cuanto
luchó tu corazón día tras día
se dispuso a mi lado,
numeroso,
y levanté la harina
de mi canto,
la flor del pan acrecentó su aroma.

I returned more truthful,
enriched,
I took what I had
and what you have,
what you traveled
through the earth,
what your eyes
saw,
what
your heart accomplished day by day
was at my side,
plentiful,
and I raised the flour
of my song,
the flower of bread increased its aroma.

Gracias te digo,
crítica,
motor claro del mundo,
ciencia pura,
signo
de la velocidad, aceite
de la eterna rueda humana,
espada de oro,
piedra
de la estructura.
Crítica, tú no traes
la espesa gota
sucia
de la envidia,
la personal guadaña
o el ambiguo, encrespado

I give you thanks,
criticism,
clear engine of the world,
pure science,
sign
of speed, oil
of the eternal human wheel,
sword of gold,
cornerstone
of structure.
Criticism, don't deal with
the thick drop
dirty
from envy,
the scythe person,
or the one torn by ambivalence, curly

gusanillo	worm
del café rencoroso:	of rancorous coffee:
no eres tampoco el juego	neither are you the game
del viejo tragasables y su tribu,	of the old magician and his tribe,
ni la pérfida	nor the perfidious
cola	tail
de la feudal serpiente	of the feudal serpent
siempre enroscada en su exquisita rama.	always curled up in its exquisite branch.
Crítica, eres	Criticism, you are
mano	a constructive
constructora,	hand,
burbuja del nivel, línea de acero,	leveling bubble, iron line,
palpitación de clase.	palpitation of class.
Con una sola vida	In a single life
no aprenderé bastante.	I won't learn enough.
Con la luz de otras vidas	In the light of other lives
vivirán otras vidas en mi canto.	other lives shall live in my song.

51 / ODE TO A DAY OF VICTORIES: SEVENTH OF NOVEMBER

Oda a un día de victorias: Siete de noviembre

TRANSLATED BY DONALD D. WALSH

Este doble aniversario, este día, esta noche,
hallarán un mundo vacío, encontrarán un torpe
hueco de corazones desolados?
No, más que un
día con horas,
es un paso de espejos y de espadas,
es una doble flor que golpea la noche
hasta arrancar el alba de su cepa nocturna!

Día de España que del sur
vienes, valiente día
de plumaje férreo,
llegas de allí, del último que cae con la frente
quebrada
con tu cifra de fuego todavía en la boca!

Y vas allí con nuestro
recuerdo insumergido:
tú fuiste el día, tú eres
la lucha, tú sostienes
la columna invisible, el ala

This double anniversary, this day, this
night,
will they find an empty world, will
they meet a crude
hollow of desolate hearts?
No, more
than a day with hours,
it is a procession of mirrors and swords,
it is a double flower that beats upon the
night
until it tears daybreak from its night
roots!

Day of Spain coming from the
south, valiant day
of iron plumage,
you arrive from there, from the last
man that falls with shattered brow
and with your fiery number still in his
mouth!

And you go there with our
memory unsubmerged:
you were the day, you are
the struggle, you support
the invisible column, the wing

de donde va a nacer, con tu número, el
vuelo!

Siete, noviembre, en dónde vives?
En dónde arden los pétalos, en dónde tu
silbido
dice al hermano: sube!, y al caído:
levántate!
En dónde tu laurel crece desde la
sangre
y atraviesa la pobre carne del hombre y
sube
a construir el héroe?
En ti, otra vez, Unión,
en ti, otra vez, hermana de los pueblos del
mundo,
Patria pura y soviética, vuelve a ti tu semilla
grande como un follaje derramado en la
tierra!

No hay llanto para ti, Pueblo, en tu lucha!
Todo ha de ser de hierro, todo ha de andar y
herir,
todo, hasta el impalpable silencio, hasta la
duda,
hasta la misma duda que con mano de invierno
nos busque el corazón para helarlo y
hundirlo,
todo, hasta la alegría, todo sea de hierro
para ayudarte, hermana y madre, en la victoria!

Que el que reniega hoy sea escupido!
Que el miserable hoy tenga su castigo en la
hora
de las horas, en la sangre total,
que el
cobarde retorne

from which flight, with your number,
will be born!

Seven, November, where do you dwell?
Where do the petals burn, where does
your whisper
say to the brother: go up! and to the
fallen: arise!
Where does your laurel grow from the
blood
and cross the frail flesh of man and go up
to fashion the hero?
In you, once more, Union,
in you, once more, sister of the peoples of
the world,
pure and Soviet fatherland. To you
returns your seed
in a leafy flood scattered upon the earth!

There are no tears for you, People, in your
struggle!
All must be of iron, all must march and
wound,
all, even impalpable silence, even doubt,
even the very doubt that with wintry hand
seeks our hearts to freeze them and sink
them,
all, even joy, all must be of iron
to help you, sister and mother, in victory!

May today's renegade be spat upon!
May the wretch today meet his
punishment in the hour
of hours, in the total blood,
may the
coward return

a las tinieblas, que los laureles pasen al valiente,
al valiente camino, a la valiente nave
de nieve y sangre que defiende el mundo!

Yo te saludo, Unión Soviética, en este día,
con humildad: soy escritor y poeta.
Mi padre era ferroviario: siempre fuimos pobres.
Estuve ayer contigo, lejos, en mi pequeño
país de grandes lluvias. Allí creció tu nombre
caliente, ardiendo en el pecho del pueblo,
hasta tocar el alto cielo de mi república!

Hoy pienso en ellos, todos están contigo!
De taller a taller, de casa a casa,
vuela tu nombre como un ave roja!

Alabados sean tus héroes, y cada gota
de tu sangre, alabada
sea la desbordante marejada de pechos
que defienden tu pura y orgullosa morada!

Alabado sea el heroico y amargo
pan que te nutre, mientras la puertas del tiempo se abren
para que tu ejército de pueblo y de hierro marche cantando
entre ceniza y páramo, sobre los asesinos
a plantar una rosa grande como la luna
en la fina y divina tierra de la victoria!

to darkness, may the laurels go to the valiant,
the valiant highway, the valiant ship
of snow and blood that defends the world!

I greet you, Soviet Union, on this day,
with humility: I am a writer and a poet.
My father was a railroad worker: we were always poor.
Yesterday I was with you, far off, in my little
country of great rains. There your name grew
hot, burning in the people's breasts
until it touched my country's lofty sky!

Today I think of them, they are all with you!
From factory to factory, from house to house,
your name flies like a red bird!

Praised be your heroes, and each drop
of your blood, praised
be the overflowing tide of hearts
that defend your pure and proud dwelling!
Praised be the heroic and bitter
bread that nourishes you, while the doors of time open
so that your army of people and iron may march, singing
among ashes and barren plain, against the assassins,
to plant a rose enormous as the moon
upon the fine and divine land of victory!

52 / ODE TO A DEAD CAROB TREE

Oda al algarrobo muerto

TRANSLATED BY MARGARET SAYERS PEDEN

Caminábamos desde
Totoral, polvoriento
era nuestro planeta:
la pampa circundada
por el celeste cielo:
calor y clara luz en el vacío.
Atravesábamos
Barranca Yaco
hacia las soledades Ongamira
cuando
tendido sobre la pradera
hallamos
un árbol derribado,
un algarrobo muerto.

La tempestad
de anoche
levantó sus raíces
argentinas
y las dejó crispadas
como una cabellera de frenéticas crines
clavadas en el viento.
Me acerqué y era tal
su fuerza herida,
tan heroicas sus ramas en el suelo,
irradiaba su copa
tal majestad terrestre,

We were traveling from
Totoral, dusty
was our planet,
pampa encircled
by azure sky:
heat and light in emptiness.
It was
passing through
Yaco Barranca
toward forsaken Ongamira
that we saw
horizontal on the prairie
a toppled giant,
a dead carob tree.

Last night's
storm
ripped out its silvery
roots,
left them twisted
like tangled hair, a tortured mane
unmoving in the wind.
I walked closer, and such
was its ruined strength,
so heroic the branches on the ground,
the crown radiating such
earthy majesty,

que cuando
toqué su tronco
yo sentí que latía
y una ráfaga
del corazón del árbol
me hizo cerrar los ojos
y bajar
la cabeza.

Era duro y arado
por el tiempo, una firme
columna trabajada
por la lluvia y la tierra,
y como un candelabro repartía
sus redondeados
brazos de madera
desde donde
luz verde y sombra verde
prodigó a la llanura.

Al algarrobo
duro, firme
como
una copa de hierro,
llegó
la tempestad americana,
el aquilón
azul
de la pradera
y de un golpe de cielo
derribó su hermosura.

Allí quedé mirando
lo que hasta ayer
enarboló
rumor silvestre y nidos

that when
I touched its trunk
I felt it throbbing,
and a surge
from the heart of the tree
made me close my eyes
and bow
my head.

It was sturdy and furrowed
by time, a strong
column carved
by earth and rain,
and like a candelabrum
it had spread its rounded
arms of wood
to lavish
green light and shadow
on the plain.

The American
storm, the
blue
north wind
of the prairie,
had overtaken
this sturdy carob,
goblet
strong as iron,
and with a blast from the sky
had felled its beauty.

I stood there staring
at what only yesterday
had harbored
forest sounds and nests,

y no lloré
porque mi hermano muerto
era tan bello en muerte como en vida.
Me despedí. Y allí quedó
acostado
sobre la tierra madre.

Dejé al viento
velándolo y llorándolo
y desde lejos vi
que
aún
acariciaba su cabeza.

but I did not weep
because my dead brother
was as beautiful in death as in life.
I said good-bye. And left it
lying there
on the mother earth.

I left the wind
keeping watch and weeping,
and from afar I saw
the
wind
caressing its head.

53 / ODE TO THE DEAD MILLIONAIRE

Oda a un millonario muerto

TRANSLATED BY ILAN STAVANS

Conocí a un millonario.
Era estanciero, rey
de llanuras grises
en donde se perdían
los caballos.
Paseábamos su casa,
sus jardines,
la piscina con una torre blanca
y aguas
como para bañar a una ciudad.
Se sacó los zapatos,
metió los pies
con cierta
severidad sombría
en la piscina verde.

No sé por qué
una a una
fue descartando
todas sus mujeres.
Ellas
bailaban en Europa
o atravesaban rápidas la nieve
en trineo, en Alaska.

S. me contó cómo
cuando niño

I knew a millionaire.
He was a rancher, king
of gray plains
where horses
got lost.
We went for walks in his house,
his gardens,
his swimming pool like a white tower
and water
enough to bathe a city.
He took his shoes off,
introduced his feet
to the green pool
with a certain
somber severity.

I don't know why
he got rid
of all his women
one by one.
They
danced in Europe
or quickly crossed the Alaskan
snow on sleds.

S. told me how
as a child

vendía diarios
y robaba panes.
Ahora sus periódicos
asaltaban las calles temblorosas,
golpeaban a la gente con noticias
y decían con énfasis
sólo sus opiniones.

Tenía bancos, naves,
pecados y tristezas.

A veces con papel,
pluma, memoria,
se hundía en su dinero,
contaba,
sumando, dividiendo,
multiplicando cosas,
hasta que se dormía.

Me parece
que el hombre nunca pudo
salir de su riqueza
—lo impregnaba,
le daba
aire, color abstracto—,
y él se veía
adentro
como un molusco ciego
rodeado
de un muro impenetrable.

A veces, en sus ojos,
vi un fuego
frío, lejos,
algo desesperado que moría.

he sold newspapers
and stole bread.
Now his newspapers
assaulted the tremulous streets,
beating people with the news
and emphatically reported
only his own opinions.

He owned banks, ships,
sins and sadness.

Sometimes with paper,
pen, memory,
he drowned in his money,
counting,
adding, dividing,
multiplying things,
until he fell asleep.

I think
the man was never able
to emerge from his wealth
—it impregnated him,
it gave him
air, abstract color—,
and he saw himself
inside
like a blind mollusk
surrounded
by an impenetrable wall.

Sometimes, in his eyes,
I saw a fire,
cold, far away,
something desperate dying.

Nunca supe si fuimos enemigos.

Murió una noche
cerca de Tucumán.
En la catástrofe
ardió su poderoso Rolls
como cerca del río
el catafalco
de una
religión oscura.

Yo sé
que todos
los muertos son iguales,
pero no sé, no sé,
pienso
que aquel
hombre, a su modo, con la muerte
dejó de ser un pobre prisionero.

I never knew if we were enemies.

He died one night
near Tucumán.
In the catastrophe
his powerful Rolls burned down
near a river
like the catafalque
of an
obscure religion.

I know
all the dead
are alike,
but I don't know, don't know,
I think
this
man, in his way, in death
stopped being a poor prisoner.

54 / ODE TO THE DICTIONARY

Oda al diccionario

TRANSLATED BY ILAN STAVANS

Lomo de buey, pesado
cargador, sistemático
libro espeso:
de joven
te ignoré, me vistió
la suficiencia
y me creí repleto,
y orondo como un
melancólico sapo
dictaminé: «Recibo
las palabras
directamente
del Sinaí bramante.
Reduciré
las formas a la alquimia.
Soy mago».

Back like an ox, beast
of burden, systematic
dense book:
young
I ignored you, I was visited
by smugness
and I thought myself complete,
and plump like a
melancholy toad
I proclaimed: "I receive
words
directly
from the roaring Mount Sinai.
I shall reduce
forms into alchemy.
I am a magus."

El gran mago callaba.

The great magus said nothing.

El Diccionario,
viejo y pesado, con su chaquetón
de pellejo gastado,
se quedó silencioso
sin mostrar sus probetas.
Pero un día,
después de haberlo usado
y desusado,

The Dictionary,
old and heavy, with its scruffy
leather jacket,
was silent,
its test tubes undisplayed.
But one day,
after having used it
and perused it,

después
de declararlo
inútil y anacrónico camello,
cuando por largos meses, sin protesta,
me sirvió de sillón
y de almohada,
se rebeló y plantándose
en mi puerta
creció, movió sus hojas
y sus nidos,
movió la elevación de su follaje:
árbol
era,
natural,
generoso
manzano, manzanar *o* manzanero,
y las palabras,
brillaban en su copa inagotable,
opacas o sonoras,
fecundas en la fronda del lenguaje,
cargadas de verdad y de sonido.

Aparto una
sola de
sus
páginas:
Caporal
Capuchón
qué maravilla
pronunciar estas sílabas
con aire,
y más abajo
Cápsula
hueca, esperando aceite o ambrosía,
y junto a ellas
Captura Capucete Capuchina

after
declaring it
a useless and anachronistic camel,
when for long months, without protest,
it served as an armchair
and a pillow,
it rebelled, and planted itself
in my doorstep,
it expanded, shook its leaves
and nests,
it moved the elevation of its foliage:
it was
tree,
neutral,
generous,
apple tree, *apple orchard*, or *apple blossom*,
and the words
shining in their inexhaustible cup,
opaque or sonorous,
fertile in the lodging of language,
charged with truth and sound.

I turn
to a single one
of its
pages:
Cape
Cartridge
how wonderful
to pronounce these syllables
with air,
and further on,
Capsule
hollow, awaiting oil or ambrosia,
and near them
Captivate Capture Capuchin

Caprario Captatorio
palabras
que se deslizan como suaves uvas
o que a la luz estallan
como gérmenes ciegos que esperaron
en las bodegas del vocabulario
y viven otra vez y dan la vida:
una vez más el corazón las quema.

Diccionario, no eres
tumba, sepulcro, féretro,
túmulo, mausoleo,
sino preservación,
fuego escondido,
plantación de rubíes,
perpetuidad viviente
de la esencia,
granero del idioma.
Y es hermoso
recoger en tus filas
la palabra
de estirpe,
la severa
y olvidada
sentencia,
hija de España,
endurecida
como reja de arado,
fija en su límite
de anticuada herramienta,
preservada
con su hermosura exacta
y su dureza de medalla.
O la otra
palabra
que allí vimos perdida

Carousel Carpathian
words
as slippery as smooth grapes
or exploding in the light
like blind seeds awaiting
in the storehouse of vocabulary
alive again and given life:
once again the heart is burning them.

Dictionary, you are not
tomb, sepulcher, coffin,
tumulus, mausoleum,
but preservation,
hidden fire,
plantation of rubies,
living eternity
of essence,
granary of language.
And it is wonderful
to harvest in your fields
a lineage
of words,
the severe
and forgotten
sentence,
daughter of Spain,
hardened
like a plow blade,
fixed in its limit
of antiquated tool,
preserved
in its exact beauty
and the immutability of a medallion.
Or another
word
we find hiding

entre renglones
y que de pronto
se hizo sabrosa y lisa en nuestra boca
como una almendra
o tierna como un higo.

Diccionario, una mano
de tus mil manos, una
de tus mil esmeraldas,
una
sola
gota
de tus vertientes virginales,
un grano
de
tus
magnánimos graneros
en el momento
justo
a mis labios conduce,
al hilo de mi pluma,
a mi tintero.
De tu espesa y sonora
profundidad de selva,
dame,
cuando lo necesite,
un solo trino, el lujo
de una abeja,
un fragmento caído
de tu antigua madera perfumada
por una eternidad de jazmineros,
una
sílaba,
un temblor, un sonido,
una semilla:
de tierra soy y con palabras canto.

between lines
that suddenly seems
as delicious and smooth in our mouths
as an almond
or as tender as a fig.

Dictionary, let one
of your thousand hands, one
of your thousand emeralds,
a
single
drop
of your virginal springs,
one grain
of
your
magnanimous granaries
fall
at the right moment
on my lips,
the thread of my pen,
into my inkwell.
From the dense and sonorous
depths of your jungle,
give me,
when I need it,
a single birdsong, the luxury
of a bee,
the fallen fragment
of your ancient wood perfumed
by an eternity of jasmine,
one
syllable,
one tremor, one sound,
one seed:
I am made of earth and with words I sing.

55 / ODE TO THE DISPLACED CACTUS

Oda al cactus desplazado

TRANSLATED BY ILAN STAVANS

Trajimos un gran cactus	We brought a great cactus
de tierra adentro	from inland
hasta la playa verde.	to the green beach.
Tenía las raíces	The giant
el gigante	had its roots
metidas	inserted
en la piedra	in the stone
y se agarraba	and held itself
a aquella dura	to that harsh
maternidad	maternity
con subterráneos,	with subterranean,
implacables	implacable
vínculos.	ties.
La picota	The pillory
caía	fell
alzando	raising
polvo	dust
y fuego,	and fire,
la roca	the rock
se estremecía como	shook as if
si pariera,	giving birth,
y apenas	and the green obelisk
se movía	barely
el obelisco verde,	moved,
acorazado	like steel

con todas las espiras	with all the thorns
de la tierra,	on earth,
hasta	until
que con un lazo	we tied it
lo amarramos	with a lasso
arriba	from above
y tirando	and pulling
entre todos	all together
derribamos	we brought down
la sagrada columna	the sacred column
de los montes.	of the mountains.
Entonces	So
custodiado	guarded
y detenido,	and sustained,
envuelto en	wrapped in
saco y cuerdas	a sack and strings
arrastramos	we dragged
su erizada	its urchin-like
estatura,	height,
pero	but no sooner
apenas	did
alguien	someone
acercó la mano	move
al vegetal ardiente,	his hand
éste	to the blazing vegetable
la clavó sus espinas	than its thorns got into him
y con sangre marcó la mordedura.	and blood colored the sting.
Lo plantamos	We planted it
mirando al mar sombrío,	facing the gloomy sea,
alto	high
contra	against
las olas,	the waves,
enemigo,	an enemy,
erizado por todas	spiked by all
las púas	the thorns

del orgullo,
majestuoso
en su nueva
solemnidad de estatua.
Y allí
quedamos
repentinamente
tristes,
los hombres
de la hazaña,
mirando
el alto
cactus
de la montaña andina
trasladado
a la arena.

of pride,
majestic
in its new
statuesque solemnity.
And there
we stood
unexpectedly
sad,
the participants
in the feat,
looking
at the high
cactus
of the Andean mountain
transposed
to the sand.

Él continuó
su
áspera
existencia:
nosotros
nos miramos
como humillados,
viejos
carceleros.

It continued
its
rugged
existence:
we looked
at each other
as if humiliated,
old
jailers.

Viento amargo
del mar
balanceó
la delgada
silueta
del alto solitario con espinas:
Él saludó
al océano
con

The sour wind
of the sea
swung
the delicate
silhouette
of the tall solitary form with thorns:
he greeted
the ocean
with

un
im-
per-
cep-
ti-
ble
mo-
vi-
mien-
to
y
si-
guió
allí
ele-
va-
do
en
su
mis-
te-
rio.

an
im-
per-
cep-
ti-
ble
move-
ment
and
con-
tin-
ued
there
el-
e-
vat-
ed
in
its
mys-
ter-
y.

56 / ODE TO THE DIVER

Oda al buzo

TRANSLATED BY ILAN STAVANS

Salió el hombre de goma	The rubber man emerged
de los mares.	from the seas.
Sentado	Seated,
parecía	he looked
rey	like the king
redondo	of the waters,
del agua,	secret
pulpo	and bulbous
secreto	octopus,
y gordo,	the truncated
talle	waist
tronchado	of
de invisible alga.	invisible algae.
Del oceánico bote	From the oceanic boat
bajaron	ragged
pescadores	fishermen
harapientos,	descended,
morados	blue
por la noche	with the night
en el océano,	of the ocean,
bajaron	large phosphorescent fish
levantando	raised
largos peces fosfóricos	near them
como	like
fuego voltaico,	volcanic fire,
los erizos cayendo	the falling sea urchins
amontonaron	piled

sobre las arenas
el rencor quebradizo
de sus púas.

El hombre
submarino
sacó sus grandes piernas,
torpemente
tambaleó entre intestinos
horribles de pescado.
Las gaviotas cortaban
el aire libre con
sus veloces tijeras,
y el buzo
como un ebrio
caminaba
en la playa,
torpe
y hosco,
enfundado
no sólo
en su vestido de cetáceo,
sino aún
medio mar
y medio tierra,
sin saber cómo
dirigir los inmensos
pies de goma.

Allí estaba naciendo.
Se desprendió
del mar
como del útero,
inocente,
y era sombrío, débil
y salvaje,
como

the silt
with the splintering rancor
of their quills.

The submarine
man
showed his long legs,
clumsily
waving them amid the horrible
guts of fish.
Seagulls splashed
through the limitless air
like speedy scissors,
and the diver
swarthy
and sullen
like a drunkard
toiled
through the beach,
locked
not only
in his cetacean clothes,
but even
half sea
and half earth,
not knowing where to move
the rubbery bulk
of his feet.

He was being born there.
He removed himself
from the sea
as if from the uterus,
innocent,
and he was gloomy, weak
and brute,
like

un	the
recién	newly
nacido.	born.
Cada vez	Time after time
le tocaba	he was due
nacer	to be reborn
para las aguas	amid the water
o la arena.	or sand.
Cada día	Each day,
bajando	descending
de la proa	from the prow
a las crueles	to the pitiless
corrientes,	currents,
al frío	the Pacific and
del Pacífico	Chilean
chileno,	cold,
el buzo	the diver
tenía	needed
que nacer,	to practice
hacerse	his birth again,
monstruo,	make himself
sombra,	into a monster,
avanzar	a silhouette,
con cautela,	advance
aprender	with caution,
a moverse	learn
con lentitud	to move
de luna	at the slothful speed
submarina,	of a submarine
tener	moon,
apenas	even
pensamientos	his thoughts must be
de agua,	made of water,
recoger	he must harvest
los hostiles	the hostile
frutos, estalactitas	fruit, stalactites,

o tesoros	treasures
de la profunda soledad	of profound solitude,
de aquellos	drenched
mojados	with
cementerios,	the wash
como si recogiera	of cemeteries,
coliflores,	as if he were gathering
y cuando como un globo	cauliflowers,
de aire negro	and when, like a balloon
subía	of black air,
hacia	he came up
la luz, hacia	to the light,
su Mercedes,	toward his Mercedes,
su Clara, su Rosaura,	his Clara, his Rosaura,
era difícil	it was painful
andar,	to walk,
pensar, comer	think, eat
de nuevo.	again.
Todo	Everything
era comienzo	was a beginning again
para	for
aquel hombre tan grande	a man so big
todavía inconcluso,	still unfinished,
tambaleante	unsteady
entre la oscuridad	between the darkness
de dos abismos.	of two abysses.
Como todas las cosas	This
que aprendí	I've learned
en mi existencia,	as all things in my life,
viéndolas, conociendo,	looking at them, studying them,
aprendí que ser buzo	thus I've wondered
es un oficio	if the diver's is
difícil? No!	a hazardous trade. No!
Infinito.	Infinite!

57 / ODE TO THE DOG

Oda al perro

TRANSLATED BY GEORGE D. SCHADE

El perro me pregunta	The dog asks me
y no respondo.	and I have no answer.
Salta, corre en el campo y me pregunta	He jumps, scampers through the fields
sin hablar	and wordlessly asks me,
y sus ojos	and his eyes
son dos preguntas húmedas, dos llamas	are two wet question marks, two liquid
líquidas que interrogan	interrogating flames,
y no respondo,	and I've no answer,
no respondo porque	no answer because
no sé, no puedo nada.	I don't know, I just can't.
A campo pleno vamos	Cross country we go
hombre y perro.	man and dog.
Brillan las hojas como	The leaves glisten as
si alguien	if someone
las hubiera besado	had kissed them
una por una,	one by one,
suben del suelo	all the oranges
todas las naranjas	climb from the ground
a establecer	to establish
pequeños planetarios	little planetariums
en árboles redondos	in trees round
como la noche, y verdes,	as the night, and green,
y perro y hombre vamos	and man and dog we go
oliendo el mundo, sacudiendo el trébol,	sniffing the world, parting the clover,
por el campo de Chile,	through the fields of Chile,

entre los dedos claros de septiembre.
El perro se detiene,
persigue las abejas,
salta el agua intranquila,
escucha lejanísimos
ladridos,
orina en una piedra
y me trae la punta de su hocico,
a mí, como un regalo.
Es su frescura tierna,
la comunicación de su ternura,
y allí me preguntó
con sus dos ojos,
por qué es de día, por qué vendrá la noche,
por qué la primavera
no trajo en su canasta
nada
para perros errantes,
sino flores inútiles,
flores, flores y flores.
Y así pregunta
el perro
y no respondo.

Vamos
hombre y perro reunidos
por la mañana verde,
por la incitante soledad vacía
en que sólo nosotros
existimos,
esta unidad de perro con rocío
y el poeta del bosque,
porque no existe el pájaro escondido,
ni la secreta flor,
sino trino y aroma
para dos compañeros,

between September's clear fingers.
The dog comes to a halt,
chases after bees,
leaps over gushing brooks,
perks up his ears at far-off
barking,
urinates on a rock,
and brings me the point of his nose,
like a gift.
It's his tender coolness,
conveying his tenderness,
and there he asked me
with his two eyes,
why it's daytime, why night comes,
why spring brought
nothing
in its basket
for roaming dogs,
but useless flowers,
flowers, flowers, flowers.
And so the dog
asks
and I have no answer.

We go
man and dog together
through the green morning,
the rousing empty solitude
where only we
exist,
this unity of dew and dog
and poet of the forest,
for the hidden bird does not exist,
nor the secret flower,
just trill and fragrance
for the two companions,

para dos cazadores compañeros:
un mundo humedecido
por las destilaciones de la noche,
un túnel verde y luego
una pradera,
una ráfaga de aire anaranjado,
el susurro de las raíces,
la vida caminando,
respirando, creciendo,
y la antigua amistad,
la dicha
de ser perro y ser hombre
convertida
en un solo animal
que camina moviendo
seis patas
y una cola
con rocío.

the two hunting companions:
a world humid
with the essences of night,
a green tunnel and then
a meadow,
a whiff of orange-scented air,
the rustle of roots,
life walking,
breathing, growing,
and the age-old friendship,
the joy
of being man and dog
converted
into a single animal
walking along moving
six legs
and a tail
splashed with dew.

58 / ODE TO DON JORGE MANRIQUE

Oda a don Jorge Manrique

TRANSLATED BY ILAN STAVANS

Adelante, le dije,
y entró el buen caballero
de la muerte.

Era de plata verde
su armadura
y sus ojos
eran
como el agua marina.
Sus manos y su rostro
eran de trigo.

Habla, le dije, caballero
Jorge,
no puedo
oponer sino el aire
a tus estrofas.
De hierro y sombra fueron,
de diamantes
oscuros
y cortadas
quedaron
en el frío
de las torres
de España,
en la piedra, en el agua,
en el idioma.

Come in, I said to him,
and the good *caballero*
of death came in.

His shining armor
was made of green silver
and his eyes
were
like seawater.
His hands and face
were made of wheat.

Speak, I said to him, *caballero*
Jorge,
I can only
counter your stanzas
with air.
They were of iron and shadow,
obscure
diamonds
tailored
that remained
in the cold
towers
of Spain,
in the stone, in water,
in language.

Entonces, él me dijo:
«Es la hora
de la vida.
Ay
si pudiera
morder una manzana,
tocar la polvorosa
suavidad de la harina.
Ay si de nuevo
el canto . . .
No a la muerte
daría
mi palabra . . .
Creo
que el tiempo oscuro
nos cegó
el corazón
y sus raíces
bajaron y bajaron
a las tumbas,
comieron
con la muerte.
Sentencia y oración fueron las rosas
de aquellas enterradas
primaveras
y, solitario trovador,
anduve
callado en las moradas
transitorias:
todos los pasos iban
a una solemne
eternidad
vacía.
Ahora
me parece
que no está solo el hombre.

Then he said to me:
"It is time
to live.
Ay
if I could only
bite an apple,
touch the dusty
tenderness of flour.
Ay if my song
could live again . . .
I would not give
my word
to death . . .
I trust
that dark times
blinded
our heart
and its roots
descended and descended
to the tombs,
they ate with death.
Sentence and oration were the flowers
of buried
springs
and, lonesome troubadour,
I wandered
quietly
in transient
dwellings:
all steps moved toward
an empty
solemn
eternity.
Now
it seems to me
that man is not alone.

En sus manos
ha elaborado
como si fuera un duro
pan, la esperanza,
la terrestre
esperanza».

Miré y el caballero
de piedra
era de aire.

Ya no estaba en la silla.

Por la abierta ventana
se extendían las tierras,
los países,
la lucha, el trigo,
el viento.

Gracias, dije, don Jorge, caballero.

Y volví a mi deber de pueblo y canto.

In his hands
he has elaborated,
as if it were hardened
bread, hope,
terrestrial
hope."

I looked and the knight
of stone
was made of air.

He was no longer on the chair.

In the open window,
I saw the extended lands,
countries,
struggle, wheat,
wind.

Thank you, I said, Don Jorge, *caballero.*

And I returned to my duties of people and song.

59 / ODE TO THE EARTH

Oda a la tierra

TRANSLATED BY MARGARET SAYERS PEDEN

Yo no la tierra pródiga	I do not sing to the prodigal
canto,	earth,
la desbordada	the profligate
madre de las raíces,	mother of roots,
la despilfarradora,	the squanderer
espesa de racimos y de pájaros,	choked with fruits and birds,
lodos y manantiales,	with mud and flowing springs,
patria de los caimanes,	homeland of the caiman,
sultana de anchos senos	full-breasted sultana
y diadema erizada,	with spiky diadem,
no al origen	not to the birthplace
del tigre en el follaje	of the jungle cat,
ni a la grávida tierra de labranza	to the tilled and gravid earth,
con su semilla como	its every seed a
un minúsculo nido	tiny nest ready
que cantará mañana,	to greet the dawn with song,
no, yo alabo	no, I praise
la tierra mineral, la piedra andina,	mineral earth, Andean rock,
la cicatriz severa	the severe scar
del desierto lunar, las espaciosas	of the lunar desert, the spacious
arenas de salitre,	nitrate sands,
yo canto	I sing
el hierro,	to iron,
la encrespada cabeza	to the rippling of veins
del cobre y sus racimos	of copper and its clusters
cuando emerge	as it emerges,
envuelto en polvo y pólvora	blasted and dusty,

recién desenterrado
de la geografía.
Oh tierra, madre dura,
allí escondiste
los metales profundos,
de allí los arañamos
y con fuego
el hombre,
Pedro,
Rodríguez o Ramírez
los convirtió de nuevo
en luz original, en lava líquida,
y entonces
duro contigo, tierra,
colérico metal,
te hiciste por la fuerza
de las pequeñas manos de mi tío,
alambre o herradura,
nave o locomotora,
esqueleto de escuela,
velocidad de bala.
Árida tierra, mano
sin signos en la palma,
a ti te canto,
aquí no diste trinos
ni te nutrió la rosa
de la corriente que canta
seca, dura y cerrada,
puño enemigo, estrella
negra,
a ti te canto
porque el hombre
te hará parir, te llenará de frutos,
buscará tus ovarios,
derramará en tu copa secreta
los rayos especiales,

newly unearthed
from its geography.
Oh, earth, harsh mother,
here is where you hid
your buried metals, and
here we scratched them out,
and then with fire,
men,
a Pedro,
a Rodríguez or Ramírez,
restored them
to primeval light, to liquid lava,
and then
hard like you, earth,
choleric metal,
you willed yourself
in the small strong hands of my uncle
into wire or horseshoe,
ship or locomotive,
the skeleton of a school,
the speed of a bullet.
Arid earth, palm
without a lifeline,
I sing to you,
here barren of birdsong,
bereft of the rose
of the current that runs
dry and hard and silent,
enemy fist, black
star,
I sing to you
because man
will make you yield, will make you bear,
he will expose your ovaries,
he will spill his special rays
into your secret cup,

tierra de los desiertos,
línea pura,
a ti las escrituras de mi canto
porque pareces muerta
y te despierta
el ramalazo de la dinamita,
y un penacho de humo sangriento
anuncia el parto
y saltan los metales hacia el cielo.
Tierra, me gustas
en la arcilla y la arena,
te levanto y te formo,
como tú me formaste,
y ruedas de mis dedos
como yo desprendido
voy a volver a tu matriz extensa.
Tierra, de pronto
me parece tocarte
en todos tus contornos
de medalla porosa,
de jarra diminuta,
y en tu forma paseo
mis manos
hallando la cadera de la que amo,
los pequeñitos senos,
el viento como un grano
de suave y tibia avena
y a ti me abrazo, tierra,
junto a ti, duermo,
en tu cintura se atan mis brazos y mis labios,
duermo contigo y siembro mis más profundos besos.

desert land,
lineal purity,
to you the lines of my song,
and though you lie dormant now,
the dynamite's scourge
will shake you,
and as metals leap toward the sky,
a plume of bloody smoke
will signal birth.
Earth, I like you
as clay and sand,
I hold you and shape you
as you shaped me,
you slip from my fingers
as I, freed, will return
to your encompassing womb.
Earth, suddenly
I seem to embrace you
in all your contours,
porous medallion,
common clay jug,
I run my hand
over your body
tracing the hips of the woman I love,
the small breasts,
wind like a grain
of smooth, sun-warmed oats,
and I cling to you, earth,
I sleep beside you,
my arms and lips caress your waist,
I lie beside you, sowing my warmest kisses.

60 / ODE TO THE EARTH II

Oda a la tierra II

TRANSLATED BY ILAN STAVANS

Tierra, quién	Earth, who was it
te midió y te puso	who measured and divided you
muros,	with walls,
alambre,	wire,
cierros?	enclosures?
Naciste dividida?	Were you born divided?
Cuando los meteoros te cruzaron	When meteors cruised through you
y tu rostro crecía	and your semblance grew
desmoronando mares y peñascos,	above dismantled seas and large crags,
quién repartió tus dones	who divided your assets
entre unos cuantos seres?	among a handful of creatures?
Yo te acuso,	I blame you,
tuviste	you
sacudidas de muerte,	underwent tremors of death,
temblores de catástrofe,	earthquakes of catastrophe,
hiciste polvo	turned cities
las ciudades, los pueblos,	into dust, towns,
las pobres casas ciegas	the blind and humble houses
de Chillán, destruiste	in Chillán, destroyed
los arrabales de Valparaíso,	the slums of Valparaíso,
fuiste cólera	you were rapture
de iracunda potra	of enraged fury
contra los apacibles habitantes	against the gentle inhabitants
de mi patria,	of my country,
y en cambio	and meanwhile
soportaste	you endured

la división injusta
de tus predios,
no crepitó la lanza
del volcán encendido
contra el usurpado de territorio,
y en ti cayó no sólo el muerto justo,
el que cumplió sus días,
sino el acribillado
perseguido
a quien robaron campos y caballos,
y que por fin se desangró cayendo
sobre tu piel impasible.

Tu duro invierno al pobre diste,
la mina negra al buscador herido,
la cueva fue para el abandonado,
el quemante calor al hijo del desierto,
y así tu sombra injusta no dio consuelo a todos,
y tu fuego no fue bien repartido.

Tierra, escucha y medita
estas palabras,
las doy al viento para que vuelen,
caerán en tu vientre a germinar,
no más batallas, basta,
no queremos pagar tierra con sangre:
te queremos amar,
madre fecunda,
madre del pan y del hombre,
pero
madre de todo el pan y de todos los hombres.

the unfair fragmentations
of your estate,
the volcano's burning spear
didn't crack
against the land's usurper,
and not only did the righteous dead
fall on you,
those whose days were already over,
but also the tormented,
the persecuted
whose fields and horses were stolen
and who finally bled away while
crumbling
on their impassible skin.

You gave the poor your tough winter,
the wounded searcher the dark mine,
the cave to the abandoned,
the blazing sun to the desert's child,
and so your unjust shadow offered no
consolation to any,
your fire wasn't fairly divided.

Earth, listen and reflect on
these words,
I let them free so they can fly,
let them fall on your wound and
germinate,
no more battles, enough,
we don't want to pay blood for land:
we want to love you,
fertile mother,
mother of bread and man,
but
mother of all the bread and every man.

61 / ODE TO THE ELEPHANT

Oda al elefante

TRANSLATED BY ILAN STAVANS

Espesa bestia pura,	Thick, pristine beast,
San Elefante,	Saint Elephant,
animal santo	sacred animal
del bosque sempiterno,	of perennial forests,
todo materia fuerte,	sheer strength,
fina	fine
y equilibrada,	and balanced
cuero	leather
de talabartería planetaria,	of
marfil	global saddle-makers,
compacto, satinado,	compact,
sereno	satin-finished ivory,
como	serene
la carne de la luna,	like
ojos mínimos	the moon's flesh,
para mirar, no para ser mirados,	with minuscule eyes
y trompa	to see—and not be seen—
tocadora,	and a singing trunk,
corneta	a blowing horn,
del contacto,	hose
manguera	of
del	the
animal	creature
gozoso	rejoicing
en	in
su	its own
frescura,	freshness,

máquina movediza,	shaking machine
teléfono del bosque,	and forest telephone,
y así	this is how
pasa tranquilo	the elephant passes by,
y bamboleante	tranquil,
con su vieja envoltura,	parading his ancient façade,
con su ropaje	his costume
de árbol arrugado,	made of wrinkled trees,
su pantalón	his pants
caído	falling down,
y su colita.	and his teeny tail.
No nos equivoquemos.	Make no mistake:
La dulce y grande bestia de la selva	this gentle, huge jungle beast
no es el clown,	is not a clown
sino el padre,	but a father,
el padre en la luz verde,	a priest of green light,
es el antiguo	an earthly progenitor,
y puro	ancient
progenitor terrestre.	and whole.
Total fecundación,	Bountiful
tantálica	in its tantalizing
codicia,	avarice,
fornicación	made
y piel	of abundant skins
mayoritaria,	and fornication,
costumbres	the elephant kingdom
en la lluvia	grew
rodearon	accustomed
el reino	to the rain.
de los elefantes,	But then came
y fue	a universal war,
con sal	bringing
y sangre	silence
la genérica guerra	with salt
en el silencio.	and blood.

Las escamosas formas,
el lagarto león,
el pez montaña,
el milodonto cíclope,
cayeron,
decayeron,
fueron fermento verde en el pantano,
tesoro
de las tórridas moscas,
de escarabajos crueles.
Emergió el elefante
del miedo destronado.
Fue casi vegetal, oscura torre
del firmamento verde,
y de hojas dulces, miel
y agua de roca
se alimentó su estirpe.

Iba pues por la selva
el elefante con su paz profunda.
Iba condecorado
por
las órdenes más claras
del rocío,
sensible
a la
humedad
de su universo,
enorme, triste y tierno
hasta que lo encontraron
y lo hicieron
bestia de circo envuelta
por el olor humano,
sin aire para su intranquila trompa,
sin tierra para sus terrestres patas.
Lo vi entrar aquel día,
y lo recuerdo como a un moribundo,

The scaly forms
of lizard lion,
mountain fish,
magisterial Cyclops,
fell away,
decayed,
fresh ferment on the marsh,
a treasure
for torrid flies
and cruel beetles.
The elephant awakened
from its dethroned fear.
But almost vegetative,
a dark tower
in the olive firmament, his lineage
nurtured by sweet leaves,
honey and rock water.

Thus he wandered through the forest
in weighty peace,
sensitive to the humidity of the universe,
decorated
with
the clearest commands
of the dew,
enormous,
sad and tender
until they found him
and turned him
into a circus beast
wrapped in human smells,
unable to breathe
through his restless trunk,
without earth
for his earthly feet.
I saw him coming in that day.
I remember his agony.

lo vi entrar al Kraal, al perseguido.
Fue en Ceylán, en la selva.
Los tambores,
el fuego,
habían desviado
su ruta de rocío,
y allí fue rodeado.
Entre el aullido y el silencio entró
como un inmenso rey. No comprendía.
Su reino era una cárcel, sin embargo
era el sol como siempre, palpitaba
la luz libre, seguía verde el mundo,
con lentitud tocó la empalizada,
no las lanzas, y a mí,
a mí entre todos,
no sé, tal vez no pudo ser, no ha sido,
pero a mí me miró
con sus ojos secretos
y aún me duelen
los ojos
de aquel encarcelado,
de aquel inmenso rey preso en su selva.

Por eso hoy rememoro tu mirada,
elefante perdido
entre las duras lanzas
y las hojas
y en tu honor, bestia pura,
levanto los collares
de mi oda
para que te pasees
por el mundo
con mi infiel poesía
que entonces no podía defenderte,

I saw the damned creature entering the
Kraal.
In the jungle of Ceylon.
Drums and fire
had changed his path of dew,
and he was surrounded.
Like an immense king
he arrived,
caught between howl and silence.
He understood nothing.
His kingdom was a prison,
yet the sun was still the sun,
palpitating free light,
and the world was still verdant.
Slowly, the elephant touched the stockade
and chose me from everyone else.
I don't know why. Maybe it wasn't so,
could not have been,
but he looked at me
between the stakes
with his secret eyes.
His eyes
still pain me,
a prisoner's eyes,
the immense king captive in his own jungle.

That's why I invoke your gaze today,
elephant,
lost between the hard stakes
and the leaves.
In your honor, pristine beast,
I lift the collar
of my ode
so you may walk
through the world again.
My unfaithful poetry
was unable to defend you then.

pero que ahora
junta
en el recuerdo
la empalizada en donde aprisionaron
el honor animal de tu estatura
y aquellos dulces ojos de elefante
que allí perdieron todo lo que habían amado.

Now I bring you back
through memory,
along with the stockade caging
your animal honor,
measured only by your height,
and those gentle eyes,
deprived forever of all they had once
loved.

62 / ODE TO ENCHANTED LIGHT

Oda a la luz encantada

TRANSLATED BY MARK STRAND

La luz bajo los árboles,
la luz del alto cielo.
La luz
verde
enramada
que fulgura
en la hoja
y cae como fresca
arena blanca.

Una cigarra eleva
su son de aserradero
sobre la transparencia.

Es una copa llena
de agua
el mundo.

The light under the trees,
the light from high heaven.
The green
arbor
light
that flashes
in the leaf
and falls like fresh
white sand.

A grasshopper lifts
its sawing sound
over the clearness.

The world
is a full glass
of water.

63 / ODE TO ENERGY

Oda a la energía

TRANSLATED BY KEN KRABBENHOFT

En el carbón tu planta
de hojas negras
parecía dormida,
luego
excavada
anduvo,
surgió,
fue
lengua loca
de fuego
y vivió adentro
de la locomotora
o de la nave,
rosa roja escondida,
víscera del acero,
tú que de los secretos
corredores
oscuros
recién llegada, ciega,
te entregabas
y motores
y ruedas,
maquinarias,
movimiento,
luz y palpitaciones,
sonidos,
de ti, energía,

Your black-leafed plant
seemed to slumber
within the heart of coal.
Later,
released,
it stirred,
surged forward,
became
a mad tongue
of fire.
It dwelt inside
locomotives
and steamships,
red rose hidden away,
entrails of steel.
And you, coming straight
from the secret
black
shafts, blind—
you gave yourself up.
Engines,
wheels
and machinery,
movement,
light, shudderings
and sounds
began pouring

de ti, madre energía,
fueron naciendo,
a golpes
los pariste,
quemaste los fogones
y las manos
del azul fogonero,
derribaste distancias
aullando adentro
de tu jaula
y hasta donde tú fuiste
devorándote,
donde alcanzó tu fuego,
llegaron los racimos,
crecieron
las ventanas,
las páginas se unieron como plumas
y volaron las alas de los libros:
nacieron hombres y cayeron árboles,
fecunda fue la tierra.
Energía, en la uva
eres redonda gota
de azúcar enlutado,
transparente
planeta,
llama líquida, esfera
de frenética púrpura
y aún multiplicado
grano de especie,
germen del trigo,
estrella cereal, piedra viviente
de imán o acero, torre
de los hilos eléctricos,
aguas en movimiento,
concentrada
paloma

out of you, energy,
mother energy.
You gave birth to them
in spasms,
you singed the firebox
and the blue stoker's
hands,
you annihilated distance
howling howling
in your cage,
and there, where you
burned yourself up,
in that place touched by your fire,
clusters of fruit also arrived,
windows
multiplied,
pages came together like feathers,
and the wings of books took flight.
Men were born and trees fell to the ground,
and the soil was fertile.
Energy, in a grape's shape
you are fat drops
of sugar dressed in mourning,
a transparent
planet,
liquid flame, sphere
of frenzied purple.
You are also repeated
seeds of spice,
wheat germ,
cereal star, living
lodestone and living steel, towers
hung with humming wires,
waters in motion,
taut
silent

sigilosa
de la energía, fondo
de los seres, te elevas
en la sangre del niño,
creces como una planta
que florece en sus ojos,
endureces sus manos
golpeándolo, extendiéndolo
hasta que se hace hombre.

Fuego que corre y canta,
agua que crea,
crecimiento,
transforma nuestra vida,
saca
pan de las piedras,
oro del cielo,
ciudades del desierto,
danos,
energía,
lo que guardas,
extiende tus dones de fuego
allá
sobre la estepa,
fragua la fruta, enciende
el tesoro del trigo,
rompe la tierra, aplana
montes, extiende
las nuevas
fecundaciones
por la tierra
para que desde entonces,
desde allí,
desde donde
cambió la vida,
ahora

dove
of energy, source
of beings. You exalt
the little boy's blood,
you grow like a plant that blossoms
    in his eyes,
you harden his hands
beating and stretching him
until he grows into a man.

Fire that rushes and sings,
water of creation,
growth itself:
change our lives,
draw
bread from stones,
gold from the sky,
cities from the desert.
Give us,
energy,
the essence you are hoarding,
project your gifts of fire
far away,
to the steppes,
forge fruits, set ablaze
treasuries of wheat,
break the soil, level
mountains, deliver
fresh
fertility
to all the earth
so that from now on,
beginning over there,
from the place where
life was transformed,
the earth will

cambie la tierra,
toda
la tierra,
las islas,
el desierto
y cambie el hombre.

Entonces, oh energía,
espada ígnea,
no serás
enemiga,
flor y fruto completo
será tu dominada
cabellera,
tu fuego
será paz, estructura,
fecundidad, paloma,
extensión de racimos,
praderas de pan fresco.

be changed,
the whole
earth,
islands
and deserts,
and mankind, too.

Then, O energy,
sword of fire,
you will cease being
our enemy:
your tamed
mane will be
all fruit and flower,
your flames
will bring peace and order,
fertility and doves,
an abundance of fruit
and fresh bread from the plains.

64 / ODE TO ENVY

Oda a la envidia

TRANSLATED BY KEN KRABBENHOFT

Yo vine
del Sur, de la Frontera.
La vida era lluviosa.
Cuando llegué a Santiago
me costó mucho
cambiar de traje.
Yo venía vestido
de riguroso invierno.
Flores de la intemperie
me cubrían.
Me desangré mudándome
de casa.
Todo estaba repleto,
hasta el aire tenía
olor a gente triste.
En las pensiones
se caía el papel
de las paredes.
Escribí, escribí sólo
para no morirme.
Y entonces
apenas
mis versos de muchacho
desterrado
ardieron
en la calle
me ladró Teodorico

I had come
from the South, from the Frontier,
where life was drizzly.
When I arrived in Santiago,
I worked hard
at dressing differently.
My clothes were made
for harsh winters.
Flowers of bad weather
covered me.
I bled myself dry changing
addresses.
Everything was used up:
even the air
smelled like sadness.
Wallpaper peeled
from the walls
of cheap hotels,
but I wrote and kept on writing
in order to keep from dying.
And no sooner
had
my boyish poems
of exile
burned a path
through the streets
than little Teddy barked in my ear,

y me mordió Ruibarbo.
Yo me hundí
en el abismo
de las casas más pobres,
debajo de la cama,
en la cocina,
adentro del armario,
donde nadie pudiera examinarme,
escribí, escribí sólo
para no morirme.

Todo fue igual. Se irguieron
amenazantes
contra mi poesía,
con ganchos, con cuchillos,
con alicates negros.

Crucé entonces
los mares
en el horror del clima
que susurraba fiebre con los ríos,
rodeado de violentos
azafranes y dioses,
me perdí en el tumulto
de los tambores negros,
en las emanaciones
del crepúsculo,
me sepulté y entonces
escribí, escribí sólo
para no morirme.

Yo vivía tan lejos, era grave
mi total abandono,
pero aquí los caimanes
afilaban
sus dentelladas verdes.

and Ginger bit my leg.
I dove
into the abyss
of the poorest houses—
underneath the bed,
in the kitchen
or deep inside a closet
where nobody could probe me,
and I wrote on, simply
to keep from dying.

It made no difference. They rose up
threatening
my poetry
with hooks and knives
and black pliers.

So I crossed
oceans,
hating those climates
where fever whispers along the waters:
engulfed by shrill
saffron and vengeful gods,
I wandered lost in the din
of dark drums
and panting
twilights.
I buried myself alive,
then I kept on writing, simply
to keep from dying.

My home was so far away, that's
how completely I'd let go.
But here the alligators
were sharpening
their long green rows of teeth.

Regresé de mis viajes.
Besé a todos,
las mujeres, los hombres
y los niños.
Tuve partido, patria.
Tuve estrella.
Se colgó de mi brazo
la alegría.
Entonces en la noche,
en el invierno,
en los trenes, en medio
del combate,
junto al mar o las minas,
en el desierto o junto
a la que amaba
o acosado, buscándome
la policía,
hice sencillos versos
para todos los hombres
y para no morirme.

Y ahora
otra vez ahí están.
Son insistentes
como los gusanos,
son invisibles
como los ratones
de un navío,
van navegando
donde yo navego,
me descuido y me muerden
los zapatos,
existen porque existo.
Qué puedo hacer?
Yo creo
que seguiré cantando

I returned from my journeys,
kissed everybody hello—
kissed women, men,
and children.
I belonged, I had a homeland.
Luck was with me.
I walked arm in arm
with Joy.
From then on, at night
and in winter,
in trains and in the thick
of battle,
by seashores, in mine shafts
and in deserts, next to
the woman I loved
and on the run from
police,
I wrote simple poems
for all mankind,
to keep from dying.

And now
they're back:
they're as dogged
as earthworms,
as invisible
as rats
on a ship.
They sail
where I sail,
and if I'm careless they nip at
my heels.
They exist because I exist.
What can I do?
What else
but keep on singing

hasta morirme.	until I die.
No puedo en este punto	At this point I simply
hacerles concesiones.	can't give in.
Puedo, si lo desean,	Maybe they'd like
regalarles	a present
una paquetería,	wrapped in pretty paper,
comprarles un paraguas	or an umbrella
para que se protejan	to keep themselves dry
de la lluvia inclemente	in the nasty rain
que conmigo llegó de la Frontera,	that arrived with me from the Frontier.
puedo enseñarles a andar a caballo,	I could teach them how to ride horseback
o darles por lo menos	or encourage
la cola de mi perro,	them to pet my dog.
pero quiero que entiendan	But I want them to know
que no puedo	I cannot
amarrarme la boca	wire my mouth shut
para que ellos	so they can write poetry
sustituyan mi canto.	in my place.
No es posible.	That's not possible.
No puedo.	I really can't.
Con amor o tristeza,	Sadly or lovingly,
de madrugada fría,	in the chill of early morning,
a las tres de la tarde,	at three in the afternoon
o en la noche,	or in the middle of the night—
a toda hora,	at any hour of the day—
furioso, enamorado,	whether I'm enraged or basking in love,
en tren, en primavera,	on trains and in springtime,
a oscuras o saliendo	in the dark or as I leave
de una boda,	a wedding,
atravesando el bosque	walking through woods
o la oficina,	or through my study,
a las tres de la tarde	at three in the afternoon
o en la noche,	or in the middle of the night,
a toda hora,	at any hour of the day:
escribiré no sólo	I will go on writing not simply
para no morirme,	to keep from dying

sino para ayudar
a que otros vivan,
porque parece que alguien
necesita mi canto.
Seré,
seré implacable.
Yo les pido
que sostengan sin tregua el estandarte
de la envidia.
Me acostumbré a sus dientes.
Me hacen falta.
Pero quiero decirles
que es verdad:
me moriré algún día
(no dejaré de darles
esa satisfacción postrera),
no hay duda,
pero
me moriré cantando.
Y estoy casi seguro,
aunque no les agrade esta noticia,
que seguirá
mi canto
más acá de la muerte,
en medio
de mi patria,
será mi voz, la voz
del fuego o de la lluvia
o la voz de otros hombres,
porque con lluvia o fuego quedó escrito
que la simple
poesía
vive
a pesar de todo,
tiene una eternidad que no se asusta,
tiene tanta salud

but to help
others live,
because it seems someone
needs my song.
Relentless is what I'll be,
utterly relentless.
So I'll beg them
to make no truce
when defending the flag of envy,
for I've gotten used to its teeth.
In fact I need them.
But I want them also to know
(it's true)
that one day I will die
(I'll have to give them
this last satisfaction).
Of this there is no doubt.
But
I will go down singing.
And I am relatively certain
(though they won't like to hear it)
that my song
will be heard
on this side of death,
in the heart
of my country:
it will be my voice, a voice
of fire and rain,
and the voice of other people.
For it is written in fire and rain
that the truest
poetry
survives
against all odds.
It outlives fear,
it has the robust health

como una ordeñadora
y en su sonrisa tanta dentadura
como para arruinar las esperanzas
de todos los reunidos
roedores.

of a milkmaid
and enough teeth in its smile
to ruin the hopes
of all the rodents in the world,
all of them put together.

65 / ODE TO THE EROSION IN MALLECO PROVINCE

Oda a la erosión en la provincia de Malleco

TRANSLATED BY ILAN STAVANS

Volví a mi tierra verde	I came back to my green land
y ya no estaba,	and it was no more,
ya no	the earth
estaba	was not
la tierra,	there,
se había ido.	it was gone.
Con el agua	It had gone
hacia el mar	with the water
se había marchado.	to the sea.
Espesa	Dense
madre	mother
mía,	of mine,
trémulos, vastos bosques,	trembling, vast forests,
provincias montañosas,	mountainous provinces,
tierra y fragancia y humus:	earth and fragrance and humus:
un pájaro que silba,	a whistling bird,
una gruesa	a thick
gota	drop
cae,	falling,
el viento	the wind
en su caballo	on its translucent
transparente,	horse,
maitenes, avellanos,	*maiten* trees, hazelnuts,
tempestuosos raulíes,	tempestuous *raulí* trees,
cipreses	silvery

plateados,
laureles que en el cielo
desataron su aroma,
pájaros de plumaje
mojado por la lluvia
que un grito negro
daban
en la
fecundidad
de la espesura,
hojas
puras, compactas,
lisas como lingotes,
duras como cuchillos,
delgadas
como lanzas,
arañas
de la selva,
arañas mías,
escarabajos
cuyo
pequeño
fuego errante
duplicaba una gota
de rocío,
patria
mojada, cielo
grande, raíces,
hojas, silencio verde,
universo
fragante,
pabellón
del planeta:
ahora,
ahora
siente

cypresses,
laurels whose aroma
opened up in heaven,
birds of plumage
moistened by the rain
offering
a black shriek
in
thick
fecundity,
pure, compact
leaves,
flat like ingots,
tough like knives,
slim
like spears,
spiders
of the jungle,
my spiders,
beetles
whose
minor
wandering fire
duplicated a drop
of dew,
moistened
homeland, big
sky, green silence,
fragrant
universe,
pavilion
of the planet:
now,
now
my heart
feels

y toca
mi corazón
tus cicatrices,
robada
la capa germinal
del territorio,
como si lava o muerte
hubieran roto
tu sagrada substancia
o una guadaña
en tu materno rostro
hubiera escrito
las iniciales del infierno.

and touches
your scars,
the germinal cape
of the territory
having been stolen,
as if lava or death
had broken
your
sacred substance
or a scythe
had written
the initials of hell
on your maternal face.

Tierra,
qué darás a tus hijos,
madre mía,
mañana,
así
destruida,
así arrasada
tu naturaleza,
así deshecha
tu matriz materna,
qué
pan
repartirás
entre los hombres?

Earth,
what will you offer your children,
mother of mine,
tomorrow,
destroyed,
your nature
devastated,
your maternal womb
undone,
what
bread
will you
share
with man?

Los pájaros cantores,
en tu selva
no sólo
deletreaban
el hilo
sempiterno
de la gracia,

In your jungle,
the singing birds
not only
spelled
the everlasting
thread
of grace,

eran preservadores
del tesoro,
hijos de la madera,
rapsodas emplumados
del perfume.
Ellos
te previnieron.
Ellos
en su
canto
vaticinaron
la agonía.
Sordo
y cerrado
como
pared
de muertos
es el cerril oído
del
hacendado
inerte.
Vino
a quemar
el bosque,
a incendiar las entrañas
de la tierra,
vino
a sembrar
un
saco
de frejoles
y a dejarnos
una herencia
helada:
la eternidad del hambre.
Rozó con fuego

they were keepers
of the treasure,
offspring of wood,
feathered rhapsodies
of perfume.
They
warned you.
In
their
song
they foresaw
the agony.
Deaf
and closed
like
the wall
of the dead
is the stubborn ear
of
the lifeless
landowner.
It came
to burn
the forest,
to turn the guts
of the earth into ashes,
it came
to plant
a
sack
of beans
and leave behind
a frozen
legacy:
the eternity of man.
It rubbed with fire

el alto
nivel
de los maños,
el baluarte
del roble,
la ciudad del raulí, la rumorosa
colmena de los ulmos,
y ahora
desde las raíces quemadas,
se va la tierra,
nada la defiende,
bruscos
socavones,
heridas
que ya nada ni nadie
puede borrar del suelo:
asesinada
fue la tierra
mía,
quemada fue la copa originaria.

Vamos
a contener la muerte!

Chilenos de hoy,
araucas
de la lejanía,
ahora,
ahora mismo, ahora,
a detener el hambre
de mañana,
a renovar la selva
prometida,
el pan
futuro
de la patria

the top
level
of the *maño* trees,
the oak tree's
stronghold,
the *raulí* tree's city, the rumoring
beehive of the elm tree,
and now
from the burnt roots,
the earth can be seen,
nothing protects it,
brusque
hollows,
injuries
nothing or no one
can erase from the ground:
my land
was
assassinated,
the original cup was burned.

Let us
contain death!

Chileans of today,
Araucas
of distant regions,
now,
right now, now,
let us stop tomorrow's
hunger,
renew the promised
jungle,
the future
bread
of the narrow

angosta!
Ahora
a establecer raíces,
a plantar la esperanza,
a sujetar la rama
al territorio!

Es ésa
tu
conducta de soldado,
son ésos
tus deberes rumorosos
de poeta,
tu plenitud profunda
de ingeniero,
raíces,
copas verdes,
otra vez
las iglesias del follaje,
y con
el canto
de la pajarería,
que volverá del cielo,
regresará a la boca de tus hijos
el pan que ahora huye con la tierra.

homeland!
Establish roots
now,
plant hope,
connect the branch
to the soil.

That is
your
duty as a soldier,
those are
your rumored duties
as a poet,
your deep plenitude
as engineer,
roots,
green cups,
again
the churches of the foliage,
and with
the song
of abundant birds,
which shall return from the sky,
the bread escaping with the land
will return to your children's mouths.

66 / ODES FOR EVERYONE

Odas de todo el mundo

TRANSLATED BY MARGARET SAYERS PEDEN

Odas para el que pase	Odes for the person
galopando	galloping
bajo ramas mojadas	beneath wet branches
en invierno.	in wintertime.
Odas	Odes
de todos	of all
los colores y tamaños,	colors and sizes,
seráficas, azules	seraphic, azure
o violentas,	or violent,
para comer,	odes for eating,
para bailar,	odes for dancing,
para seguir las huellas en la arena,	odes to track in the sand,
para ser y no ser.	to be and not to be.
Yo vendo odas	I sell fine-stranded
delgadas	odes
en ovillo,	wound in a ball,
como alambre,	odes like wire,
otras como cucharas,	some like spoons,
vendo	I sell
algunas selváticas,	jungle odes
corren con pies de puma:	that run on puma feet:
se deben manejar	they must be handled
con precaución, con rejas:	with care, behind bars,
salieron	they come

de los antiguos bosques,
tienen hambre.

También escribo
para costureras
odas
de inclinación doliente,
cubiertas por
el
aroma
enterrado
de las lilas.

Otras
tienen
silvestres minerales,
dureza de los montes
de mi patria,
o simplemente
amor ultramarino.

En fin,
decidirán ustedes
lo que llevan:
tomates
o venados
o cemento,
oscuras alegrías infundadas,
trenes
que
silban
solos
transmigrando
por regiones
con frío y aguacero.

from age-old forests,
they are hungry.

I also write
for seamstresses
odes
of sorrowful disposition,
drenched in
the
buried
scent
of lilacs.

Others
contain
raw minerals,
harsh as the mountains
of my homeland,
or simply
love from across the seas.

Finally,
it will be you who decide
what is in them:
tomatoes
or deer
or cement,
obscure unfounded joy,
trains
that
whistle,
lonely,
transmigrating
through regions
of cold and showers.

De todo
un poco
tengo para todos.

Yo sé
que hay otras
y otras
cosas
rondando alrededor
de la noche o debajo
de los muebles o adentro
del corazón
perdido.
Sí,
pero
tengo tiempo,
tengo aún mucho tiempo
—tengo una caracola
que recoge
la tenaz melodía
del secreto
y la guarda
en su caja
convertida en martillo o mariposa—,

tiempo

para
mirar
piedras sombrías

o recoger
aún
agua olvidada

I have a little
of everything
for everyone.

I know
there are others,
other
things
prowling about
at night or beneath
the furniture or deep within
the forgotten
heart.
Yes,
but
I have time,
plenty of time still
—I have a conch shell
that collects
the lasting melody
of secrets
and hoards them
in its chamber,
now hammers or butterflies—

time

to
look at
somber stones

time still
to store
forgotten waters

y para darte
a ti
o a quien lo quiera
la primavera larga de mi lira.

Así, pues,
en tus manos
deposito
este atado
de flores herraduras

y adiós,

hasta más tarde:

hasta más pronto:
hasta que todo
sea
y sea canto.

and to give
to you
or whoever may want it
the long springtime of my lyre.

And, so,
in your hands
I place
this medley
of flowers and horseshoes

and so long,

see you later,

see you soon,
when all things
become,
become song.

67 / ODE TO THE EYE

Oda al ojo

TRANSLATED BY ILAN STAVANS

Poderoso eres, pero	Powerful—
una arenilla,	but a grain of sand,
una pata de mosca,	a fly's foot,
la mitad de un miligramo	half a milligram
de polvo	of dust
entró en tu ojo derecho	entered your right eye
y el mundo	and the world
se hizo negro y borroso,	became dark and foggy.
las calles	Streets
se volvieron escaleras,	became staircases,
los edificios se cubrieron de humo,	buildings were covered with smoke,
tu amor, tu hijo, tu plato	your love, your son, your dinner plate
cambiaron de color, se transformaron	changed color, turning
en palmeras o arañas.	into palm trees or spiders.
Cuida el ojo!	Protect the eye!
El ojo,	The eye,
globo de maravilla,	bubble of wonder,
pequeño	small
pulpo de nuestro abismo	octopus of our emptiness
que extrae	extracting
la luz de las tinieblas,	brightness from shade,
perla	polished
elaboradora,	pearl,
magnético	alluring

azabache,
maquinita
rápida
como nada o como nadie,
fotógrafo
vertiginoso,
pintor francés,
revelador de asombro.
Ojo,
diste nombre
a la luz de la esmeralda,
sigues
el crecimiento
del naranjo
y controlas
las leyes de la aurora,
mides,
adviertes el peligro,
te encuentras con el rayo
de otros ojos
y arde en el corazón la llamarada,
como un
milenario molusco,
te sobrecoges
al ataque del ácido,
lees,
lees
números de banqueros,
alfabetos
de tiernos colegiales de Turquía,
de Paraguay, de Malta,
lees
nóminas
y novelas,
abarcas olas, ríos,
geografías,

blackness of the sea,
swift
engine
like nothing and no one,
dizzying
photographer,
French painter,
revelator of oracle.
Eye,
you name
the emerald glow,
trace
the growth
of an orange tree,
control
the laws of sunrise.
You measure,
announce danger,
encounter the glimmer
of others.
And fire burns in the heart,
like
an ancient mollusk.
You sneer
at the attacking acid.
You read,
read
the banker's numbers,
ABCs
by tender students from Turkey,
Paraguay, Malta,
read
reports
and novels,
seize waves, rivers,
geographies.

exploras,
reconoces
tu bandera
en el remoto mar, entre los barcos,
guardas al náufrago
el retrato
más azul del cielo
y de noche
tu pequeña
ventana
que se cierra
se abre por otro lado como un túnel
a la indecisa patria de los sueños.

Yo vi un muerto
en la pampa
salitrera,
era
un hombre del salitre,
hermano de la arena.
En una huelga
mientras
comía
con sus compañeros
lo derribaron, luego
en su sangre
que otra vez
volvía a las arenas,
los hombres
empaparon
sus banderas
y por la dura pampa
caminaron
cantando
y desafiando a sus verdugos.
Yo me incliné

Explorer,
you sight
your flag
in the remote sea, among the ships,
giving the shipwrecked sailor
the bluest portrait
of the sky.
Then, at night,
your small
closing
window
opens up from the other end, like a tunnel,
to the unsettled homeland of dreams.

I saw a dead man
in the salt
pampa,
he was
a man
made of salt,
a brother of sand.
During a strike,
while
he ate
with his *compañeros*,
he was struck down.
So they
soaked
their flags
in his blood,
coming back to the sand.
Across the arid pampa
they walked,
singing,
defying their oppressors.
I bent down

para tocar su rostro	to touch his face.
y en las pupilas	In his dead
muertas,	pupils,
retratada,	I saw,
profunda,	photographed
vi	in their depth,
que se había quedado	that his flag
viviente	was still moving,
su bandera,	the same one taken
la misma que llevaban	by his brothers
al combate	into battle
sus hermanos	while they sang.
cantando,	There,
allí	in the
como en el pozo	well that holds
de toda	humankind
la eternidad humana	forever,
vi	I saw
su bandera	his flag,
como fuego escarlata,	like scarlet fire,
como una amapola	an indestructible
indestructible.	poppy.
Ojo,	Eye,
tú faltabas	you were missing
en mi canto	from his song.
y cuando una vez más hacia el océano	When I returned to the ocean
fui a dirigir las cuerdas de mi lira	I played my lyre's chords once again
y de mi oda,	and sang my ode.
tú delicadamente	You showed me,
me mostraste	delicately,
qué tonto soy: vi la vida, la tierra,	how foolish I am: I saw life, I saw the earth.
todo	I saw
lo vi,	everything—
menos mis ojos.	except my own eyes.
Entonces	Then

dejaste penetrar
bajo mis párpados
un átomo de polvo.
Se me nubló la vista.
Vi el mundo
ennegrecido.
El oculista
detrás de una escafandra
me dirigió su rayo
y me dejó caer
como a una ostra
una gota de infierno.
Más tarde,
reflexivo,
recobrando la vista y admirando
los pardos, espaciosos
ojos de la que adoro,
borré mi ingratitud con esta oda
que tus
desconocidos ojos
leen.

you let a particle of dust
hide behind my eyelids.
I lost my sight.
I saw the world grow
darker.
The eye doctor,
in his white uniform,
pointed his ray at me.
He allowed an infernal drop
to fall
down
like an oyster.
Later,
reflective,
having recovered my sight—and admiring
the brownish, spacious eyes
of my beloved—
I erased my ingratitude with this ode,
now being read,
mysteriously,
by you.

68 / ODE TO A FALLEN BELL

Oda a la campana caída

TRANSLATED BY GEORGE D. SCHADE

Se cayó el campanario.
Se cayó la campana
un día sin orgullo,
un día
que llegó como otros jueves
y se fue,
se fue, se fue con ella,
con la campana que cayó de bruces,
con el sonido sepultado.

Por qué cayó aquel día?

Por qué no fue anteayer ni ayer ni nunca,
por qué no fue mañana,
sino entonces?
Por qué tenía que caer de pronto
una campana entera,
firme, fiel y madura?
Qué pasó en el metal, en la madera,
en el suelo, en el cielo?
Qué pasó por la sombra,
por el día
por el agua?
Quién llegó a respirar y no lo vimos?
Qué iras del mar alzaron su atributo

The bell tower fell.
The bell fell
on a day just like other days,
a day
which came like other Thursdays,
and went away,
went away, away with the bell,
with the bell which fell face down,
with its sound buried.

Why did it fall on that day?

Why wasn't it the day before yesterday,
  or yesterday or never?
Why wasn't it tomorrow
instead of then?
Why did a strong bell,
firm, faithful and mature,
suddenly have to fall?
What happened in the metal, in the
  wood,
in the ground, in the sky?
What passed through the shadow,
the day,
and the water?
Who came to breathe unseen by us?
What rages of the sea raised up their
  force

hasta que derribaron	demolishing
el profundo	the profound
eco	echo
que contuvo en su cuerpo la campana?	that the bell held in its body?
Por qué se doblegó la estrella?	Why did the star yield?
Quiénes quebraron su soberanía?	Who broke its sovereignty?
El daño yace ahora.	The damage now lies there.
Mordió el espacio	The bell
la campana	bit space
con su labio redondo,	with its round lips,
ya nadie puede tocar su abismo,	and no-one can touch its abyss,
todas las manos son impuras:	all hands are impure:
ella era del aire,	the bell belonged to the air,
y cada mano nuestra	and each of our hands
tiene uñas,	have nails,
y las uñas del hombre	and man's nails
tienen polvo,	have dust,
polvo de ayer, ceniza,	yesterday's dust, ashes,
y duerme	and the bell sleeps
porque	because
nadie puede alcanzar su voz perdida,	no-one can reach its lost voice,
su alma	its soul
que ella manifestó en la transparencia,	manifested in transparency,
el sonido	the sound
enterrado	buried
en cada campanada y en el aire.	in each single peal and in the air.
Y así fue la campana:	And that's the way the bell was:
cantó cuando vivía	it sang while living
y ahora está en el polvo	and now its sound lies
su sonido.	in the dust.
El hombre y la campana	Man and bell
cantaron victoriosos en el aire,	sang victoriously up in the air,
después enmudecieron en la tierra.	then they became silent down on earth.

69 / ODE TO FEDERICO GARCÍA LORCA

Oda a Federico García Lorca

TRANSLATED BY ANGEL FLORES

Si pudiera llorar de miedo en una casa sola,
si pudiera sacarme los ojos y comérmelos,
lo haría por tu voz de naranjo enlutado
y por tu poesía que sale dando gritos.

Porque por ti pintan de azul los hospitales
y crecen las escuelas y los barrios marítimos,
y se pueblan de plumas los ángeles heridos,
y se cubren de escamas los pescados nupciales,
y van volando al cielo los erizos:
por ti las sastrerías con sus negras membranas
se llenan de cucharas y de sangre,
y tragan cintas rotas, y se matan a besos,
y se visten de blanco.

Cuando vuelas vestido de durazno,
cuando ríes con risa de arroz huracanado,
cuando para cantar sacudes las arterias y los
dientes,

If I could weep for fear in a lonely house,
if I could tear my eyes out and devour
them,
I would do it, for your voice of
mourning orange trees
and for your poetry that emerges
uttering cries.

Because for your sake they are painting
the hospitals blue
and schools and maritime suburbs grow,
and wounded angels preen themselves
with feathers,
and nuptial fishes coat themselves with
scales,
and sea-urchins fly skyward:
for your sake the tailor-shops with their
black membranes
fill themselves with spoons and blood,
and swallow broken ribbons, and kill
themselves with kisses,
and dress in white.

When you fly dressed in peach,
when you laugh with a laughter of
hurricaned rice,
when in order to sing you shake arteries
and teeth,

la garganta y los dedos,
me moriría por lo dulce que eres,
me moriría por los lagos rojos
en donde en medio del otoño vives
con un corcel caído y un dios ensangrentado,
me moriría por los cementerios
que como cenicientos ríos pasan
con agua y tumbas,
de noche, entre campanas ahogadas:
ríos espesos como dormitorios
de soldados enfermos, que de súbito crecen
hacia la muerte en ríos con números de mármol
y coronas podridas, y aceites funerales:
me moriría por verte de noche
mirar pasar las cruces anegadas,
de pie y llorando,
porque ante el río de la muerte lloras
abandonadamente, heridamente,
lloras llorando, con los ojos llenos
de lágrimas, de lágrimas, de lágrimas.

Si pudiera de noche, perdidamente solo,
acumular olvido y sombra y humo
sobre ferrocarriles y vapores,
con un embudo negro,
mordiendo las cenizas,
lo haría por el árbol en que creces,
por los nidos de aguas doradas que reúnes,
y por la enredadera que te cubre los huesos
comunicándote el secreto de la noche.

throat and fingers,
I could die for the sweetness that is you,
I could die by the red lakes
where, at mid-autumn, you live
with a fallen steed and a bloodstained god,
I could die by the cemeteries
which like ashy rivers flow
with water and tombs,
at night, amid drowned bells:
rivers full as barracks
of sick soldiers, which suddenly overflow
deathward, with marble numbers
and rotten crowns, and funeral oils:
I could die to see you at night
watching the flooded crosses go by,
standing and weeping,
for by the river of death you weep,
abandonedly, woundedly,
you weep weeping, with your eyes full
of tears, tears, tears.

If I could, at night, forlornly alone,
with a black funnel
heap shadow and smoke and forgetfulness
over trains and ships,
biting ashes,
I would do it, for the tree on which you grow,
for the nests of golden waters which you gather.
And for the vines that cling to your bones
telling you the secret of the night.

Ciudades con olor a cebolla mojada
esperan que tú pases cantando roncamente,
y silenciosos barcos de esperma te persiguen,
y golondrinas verdes hacen nido en tu pelo,
y además caracoles y semanas,
mástiles enrollados y cerezas
definitivamente circulan cuando asoman
tu pálida cabeza de quince ojos
y tu boca de sangre sumergida.

Si pudiera llenar de hollín las alcaldías
y, sollozando, derribar relojes,
sería para ver cuándo a tu casa
llega el verano con los labios rotos,
llegan muchas personas de traje agonizante,
llegan regiones de triste esplendor,
llegan arados muertos y amapolas,
llegan enterradores y jinetes,
llegan planetas y mapas con sangre,
llegan buzos cubiertos de ceniza,
llegan enmascarados arrastrando doncellas
atravesadas por grandes cuchillos,
llegan raíces, venas, hospitales,
manantiales, hormigas,
llega la noche con la cama en donde
muere entre las arañas un húsar solitario,
llega una rosa de odio y alfileres,
llega una embarcación amarillenta,
llega un día de viento con un niño,
llego yo con Oliverio, Norah,
Vincente Aleixandre, Delia,
Maruca, Malva Marina, María Luisa y Larco,
la Rubia, Rafael Ugarte,
Cotapos, Rafael Alberti,
Carlos, Bebé, Manolo Altolaguirre,

Cities with the smell of wet onions
wait for you to pass singing huskily,
and green swallows nest in your hair,
and silent ships of sperm pursue you,
and besides, snails and weeks,
coiled masts and cherries
definitively circulate when your pale head
looms with its fifteen eyes
and mouth submerged in blood.

If I could fill the town halls with soot
and, sobbing, tear down the clocks,
I would do it, that I might see how to
your house
comes summer with its broken lips,
come many persons in moribund dress,
come regions of sad splendor,
come dead ploughs and poppies,
come gravediggers and horsemen,
come planets and maps with blood,
come divers covered with ashes,
come masqueraders dragging maidens
pierced through by long knives,
come roots, veins, hospitals,
wells, ants,
comes night with the bed on which
a lonely hussar dies among the spiders,
comes a rose of hate and pins,
comes a yellowish ship,
comes a windy day with a child,
come I with Oliverio, Norah,
Vincente Aleixandre, Delia,
Maruca, Malva Marina, María Luisa
and Larco,
La Rubia, Rafael Ugarte,
Cotapos, Rafael Alberti,
Carlos, Bebé, Manolo Altolaguirre,

Molinari,
Rosales, Concha Méndez,
y otros que se me olvidan.

Ven a que te corone, joven de la salud
y de la mariposa, joven puro
como un negro relámpago perpetuamente
libre,
y conversando entre nosotros,
ahora, cuando no queda nadie entre las rocas,
hablemos sencillamente como eres tú y soy yo:
para qué sirven los versos si no es para el
rocío?

Para qué sirven los versos si no es para esa
noche
en que un puñal amargo nos averigua, para
ese día,
para ese crepúsculo, para ese rincón roto
donde el golpeado corazón del hombre se
dispone a morir?

Sobre todo de noche,
de noche hay muchas estrellas,
todas dentro de un río,
como una cinta junto a las ventanas
de las casas llenas de pobres gentes.

Alguien se las ha muerto, tal vez
han perdido sus colocaciones en las oficinas,
en los hospitales, en los ascensores,
en las minas,
sufren los seres tercamente heridos
y hay propósito y llanto en todas partes:

Molinari,
Rosales, Concha Méndez,
and others I forget.

Let me crown you, youth
of health and butterflies, youth pure
as a black streak of lightning perpetually
free,
and talking between ourselves,
now, when no one remains among the
rocks,
let our words be simple, as you are and
I am:
what are poems good for if not for the
dew?

What are poems good for if not for that
night
when a bitter poignard prods us, for that
day,
that twilight, that broken corner
where man's stricken heart prepares itself
for death?

Above all at night,
at night there are many stars,
all inside a river,
like a ribbon by the windows
of the houses full of poor people.

Someone has died, perhaps
they have lost their jobs in the offices,
in the hospitals, in the elevators,
in the mines,
human beings suffer brutally wounded
and there is purpose and weeping
everywhere,

mientras las estrellas corren dentro de un río
interminable
hay mucho llanto en las ventanas,
los umbrales están gastados por el llanto,
las alcobas están mojadas por el llanto
que llega en forma de ola a morder las alfombras.

Federico,
tú ves el mundo, las calles,
el vinagre,
las despedidas en las estaciones
cuando el humo levanta sus ruedas decisivas
hacia donde no hay nada sino algunas
separaciones, piedras, vías férreas.

Hay tantas gentes haciendo preguntas
por todas partes.
Hay el ciego sangriento, y el iracundo, y el
desanimado,
y el miserable, el árbol de las uñas,
el bandolero con la envidia a cuestas.

Así es la vida, Federico, aquí tienes
las cosas que te puede ofrecer mi amistad
de melancólico varón varonil.
Ya sabes por ti mismo muchas cosas,
y otras irás sabiendo lentamente.

while the stars run in an interminable
river
there is much weeping in the windows,
the thresholds are worn out with
weeping,
the rooms are wet with weeping
which comes like waves to lap the rugs.

Federico,
you see the world, the streets,
the vinegar,
the farewells in stations
when the smoke raises its decisive
wheels
toward where there are only
stones, rails, separations.

There are so many people asking
questions
everywhere.
There is the bloodstained blind man,
and the wrathful one, and the
dispirited one,
and the wretched one, the tree with
nails,
the bandit with envy on his back.

Thus is life, Federico—
this is all
the friendship of a melancholy manly
man can offer.
Already you have learned many things
by yourself
and others you will be learning
gradually, with time.

70 / ODE TO THE FERTILITY OF THE SOIL

Oda a la fertilidad de la tierra

TRANSLATED BY ILAN STAVANS

A ti, fertilidad, entraña
verde,
madre materia, vegetal tesoro,
fecundación, aumento,
yo canto,
yo, poeta,
yo, hierba,
raíz, grano, corola,
sílaba de la tierra,
yo agrego mis palabras a las hojas,
yo subo a las ramas y al cielo.
Inquietas
son
las semillas,
sólo parecen
dormidas.
Las besa el fuego, el agua
las toca con su cinta
y se agitan,
largamente se mueven,
se interrogan,
abajo lanzan ojos,
encrespadas volutas,
tiernas derivaciones,
movimiento, existencia.
Hay que ver un granero
colmado,

To you, fertility, tender
entrails,
mother matter, green treasure,
fecundity, increase,
I sing,
I, the poet,
I, the grass,
root, grain, corolla,
syllable of earth,
I add my words to the leaves,
I ascend to reach the branches and sky.
Restless
are
the seeds,
they only appear
asleep.
Fire kisses them, water
touches them with its strip
and they flutter,
they move copiously,
question each other,
look underneath,
curl their spirals,
tender derivations,
movement, existence.
One needs to see a granary
filled to the brim,

allí todo reposa	everything is in repose,
pero	but
los fuegos de la vida,	the fires of life,
los fermentos	fermentation
llaman,	calls,
fermentan,	ferment,
arden	the invisible threads
con hilos invisibles.	are burning.
Uno siente en los ojos	One feels in the eyes
y en los dedos	and fingers
la presión, la paciencia,	the pressure, the patience,
el trabajo	the labor
de gérmenes y bocas,	of sprouts and mouths,
de labios y matrices.	of lips and wombs.
El viento lleva ovarios.	The wind has ovaries.
La tierra entierra rosas.	The earth buries roses.
El agua brota y busca.	Water flows and searches.
El fuego hierve y canta.	Fire boils and sings.
Todo	Everything
nace.	is born.
Y eres,	And you are
fertilidad, una campana,	fertility, a bell,
bajo tu círculo	under your circle
la humedad y el silencio desarrollan	humidity and silence develop
sus lenguas de verdura,	languages of greenness,
sube la savia,	sap emerges,
estalla	the plant's form
la forma de la planta,	explodes,
crece	the path of life
la línea de la vida	grows,
y en su extremo se agrupan	and at its edges the flower
la flor y los racimos.	and bunches of grapes gather.
Tierra, la primavera	Earth, spring
se elabora en mi sangre,	develops in my blood,
siento	I feel
como si fuera	as if I were

árbol, territorio,	a tree, a territory,
cumplirse en mí los ciclos	the cycles of earth
de la tierra,	take shape in me,
agua, viento y aroma	water, wind and aroma
fabrican mi camisa,	make my shirt,
en mi pecho terrones	in my chest clods of earth
que allí olvidó el otoño	forgotten by autumn
comienzan a moverse,	start moving,
salgo y silbo en la lluvia,	I emerge and whistle in the rain,
germina el fuego en mis manos,	fire germinates in my hands,
y entonces	and then
enarbolo	I hoist
una bandera verde	the green flag
que me sale del alma,	raised from my soul,
soy semilla, follaje,	I am seed, foliage,
encino que madura,	ripening oak,
y entonces todo el día,	and then all day,
toda la noche canto,	all night I sing,
sube de la raíces el susurro,	the whisper lifts itself from the roots,
canta en el viento la hoja.	the leaf sings in the wind.
Fertilidad, te olvido.	Fertility, I forget you.
Dejé tu nombre escrito	I left your name written down
con la primera sílaba	with the first syllable
de este canto,	of this song,
eres tú más extensa,	you are more extensive,
más húmeda y sonora,	more humid and sonorous,
no puedo describirte,	I cannot describe you,
ven a mí,	come to me,
fertilízame,	fertilize me,
dame sabor de fruto cada día,	each day give me the flavor of fruit,
dame	give me
la secreta	the secret
tenacidad de las raíces,	tenacity of roots,
y deja que mi canto	and allow my song
caiga en la tierra y suban	to drop on the earth and its words
en cada primavera sus palabras.	to climb each spring.

71 / ODE TO A FEW YELLOW FLOWERS

Oda a unas flores amarillas

TRANSLATED BY ILAN STAVANS

Contra el azul moviendo sus azules,	Against the blue shaking its blue,
el mar, y contra el cielo,	the sea, and against the sea,
unas flores amarillas.	a few yellow flowers.
Octubre llega.	October arrives.
Y aunque sea	And although
tan importante el mar desarrollando	the developed sea is so important,
su mito, su misión, su levadura,	its myth, mission, yeast,
estalla	the gold
sobre la arena el oro	of a single yellow plant
de una sola	explodes on the sand
planta amarilla	and your eyes
y se amarran	are tied
tus ojos	to the ground,
a la tierra,	escaping from the magnanimous sea
huyen del magno mar y sus latidos.	and its whip.
Polvo somos, seremos.	We are dust, we shall become.
Ni aire, ni fuego, ni agua	Not air, or fire, or water
sino	but
tierra,	earth,
sólo tierra	we shall be
seremos	mere earth
y tal vez	and maybe
unas flores amarillas.	a few yellow flowers.

72 / ODE TO FIRE

Oda al fuego

TRANSLATED BY KEN KRABBENHOFT

Descabellado fuego,	Wild-haired fire,
enérgico,	jumpy
ciego y lleno de ojos,	and blind but studded with eyes,
deslenguado,	sassy,
tardío, repentino,	tardy, and unpredictable,
estrella de oro,	golden star,
ladrón de leña,	thief of wood,
callado bandolero,	silent outlaw,
cocedor de cebollas,	cooker of onions,
célebre pícaro de las chispitas,	renowned swindler cloaked in sparks,
perro rabioso de un millón de dientes,	rabid dog with a million teeth:
óyeme,	hear me,
centro de los hogares,	heart of hearths,
rosal incorruptible,	bush of undying roses,
destructor de las vidas,	destroyer of lives,
celeste padre del pan y del horno,	heavenly father of bread and ovens,
progenitor ilustre	famous forefather
de ruedas y herraduras,	of wheels and instruments,
polen de los metales,	breeder of metals,
fundador del acero,	refiner of steel,
óyeme,	fire,
fuego.	hear me.
Arde tu nombre,	Your name crackles with flame:
da gusto	it's a pleasure
decir fuego,	to say "fire,"
es mejor	much better
que decir piedra	than "stone"

o harina.
Las palabras son muertas
junto a tu rayo amarillo,
junto a tu cola roja,
junto a tus crines de luz amaranto,
son frías las palabras.
Se dice fuego,
fuego, fuego, fuego,
y se enciende
algo en la boca:
es tu fruta que quema,
es tu laurel que arde.

Pero sólo palabra
no eres,
aunque toda palabra
si no tiene
brasa
se desprende y se cae
del árbol del tiempo.
Tú eres
flor,
vuelo,
consumación, abrazo,
inasible substancia,
destrucción y violencia,
sigilo, tempestuosa
ala de muerte y vida,
creación y ceniza,
centella deslumbrante,
espada llena de ojos,
poderío,
otoño, estío súbito,
trueno seco de pólvora,
derrumbe de los montes,
río de humo,
oscuridad, silencio.

or "grain."
Words seem lifeless
next to your yellow blaze,
next to your red tail,
next to your bright amaranth mane.
Words are simply cold.
We say "fire"—
fire! fire! fire!—
and there's something
burning in our mouth:
it's your fruit that burns,
it's your laurel that crackles.

But you're not
just a word,
though words
entirely lacking
in flame
shake loose and fall
from the tree of time.
You are
flower,
fancy,
consummation, embrace,
and elusive substance.
You are violence and destruction,
secrecy, stormy
wing of death and life,
creation and ashes alike.
You are a dazzling spark,
a sword covered with eyes,
you are eminence,
autumn or sudden summer,
gunpowder's dry thunder,
collapse of mountain ranges,
river of smoke,
obscurity and silence.

Dónde estás, qué te hiciste?
Sólo el polvo impalpable
recuerda tus hogueras,
y en las manos la huella
de flor o quemadura.
Al fin te encuentro
en mi papel vacío,
y me obligo a cantarte,
fuego,
ahora
frente a mí,
tranquilo
quédate mientras busco
la lira en los rincones,
o la cámara
con relámpagos negros
para fotografiarte.

Al fin estás
conmigo
no para destruirme,
ni para usarte
en encender la pipa,
sino para tocarte,
alisarte
la cabellera, todos
tus hilos peligrosos,
pulirte un poco, herirte,
para que conmigo
te atrevas,
toro escarlata.
Atrévete,
quémame
ahora,
entra
en mi canto,
sube

Where are you, where have you gone?
There's nothing left of your bonfires
but drifting dust
and, on our hands, burn marks
or the imprint of flowers.
In the end I've found you
on the blank page in front of me.
I'll make myself sing your praise,
fire,
right now,
before my very eyes.
Keep
quiet while I search
the closets for my lyre,
also the camera
with the black lightning bolts,
so I can take your picture.

In the end you
stay with me
not to do me in,
not so I can make you
light my pipe,
but so I can touch you,
smooth
your hair—every
dangerous strand—
so I can spruce you up or wound you,
so you'll have the courage
to charge me,
scarlet bull.
Go ahead,
burn me
now,
flare
into my song,
course

por mis venas,	through my veins,
sal	exit
por mi boca.	through my mouth.
Ahora	Now
sabes	you know:
que no puedes	you're no match
conmigo:	for me.
yo te convierto en canto,	I'm turning you into song,
yo te subo y te bajo,	I can feel you up and down,
te aprisiono en mis sílabas,	trap you in syllables of my making.
te encadeno, te pongo	I'll put you in shackles, order you
a silbar,	to whistle
a derramarte en trinos,	or melt away in trills
como si fueras	as if you were
un canario enjaulado.	a caged canary.
No me vengas	I'm not impressed
con tu famosa túnica	by your famous firebird
de ave de los infiernos.	tunic from hell.
Aquí	Here
estás condenado	you're condemned
a vida y muerte.	to life and death.
Si me callo	If I fall silent
te apagas.	you vanish.
Si canto	If I sing
te derramas	you melt away,
y me darás la luz que necesito.	giving me all the light I need.
De todos	Of all
mis amigos,	my friends
de todos	and
mis enemigos,	enemies,
eres	you're
el difícil.	the hardest to handle.
Todos	Everybody else

te llevan amarrado,
demonio de bolsillo,
huracán escondido
en cajas y decretos.
Yo no.
Yo te llevo a mi lado
y te digo:
es hora
de que me muestres
lo que sabes hacer.
Ábrete, suéltate
el pelo
enmarañado,
sube y quema
las alturas del cielo.

Muéstrame
tu cuerpo
verde y anaranjado,
levanta
tus banderas,
arde
encima del mundo
o junto a mí, sereno
como un pobre topacio,
mírame y duerme.
Sube las escaleras
con tu pie numeroso.
Acéchame,
vive,
para dejarte escritos,
para que cantes
con mis palabras
a tu manera,
ardiendo.

carries you tied up,
a demon in their pockets,
a hurricane locked away
in boxes and decrees.
But not me.
I carry you right alongside me,
and I'm telling you this:
it's high time
you showed me
what you can do.
Open up, let down
your tangled
hair,
leap up and singe
the heights of heaven.

Show me
your green and orange
body,
raise
your flags,
crackle
on the surface of the earth
or right here by my side, as calm
as a pale topaz.
Look at me, then go to sleep.
Climb the stairs
on your multitude of feet.
Chase me,
come alive
so I can write you down,
so you can sing
with my words
in your own way,
burning.

73 / ODE TO FIREFOOT

Oda a Pies de Fuego

TRANSLATED BY MARGARET SAYERS PEDEN

Con esos
pies
pequeños
parecidos
a abejas,
cómo
gastas
zapatos!
Yo sé
que vas y vienes,
que corres las escalas,
que adelantas al viento.
Antes
de que
te llame
ya has llegado,
y junto a la agresiva
cintura de la costa,
arena, piedra, espinas,
vas
a mi lado,
en los bosques
pisando troncos, mudas
aguas verdes,
o en las calles
andando

You have
two little
feet
no bigger than
bees,
but oh, what
you do
to shoes!
I know,
all that coming and going,
up and down ladders,
you outstrip the wind.
Before
I can
call you,
you're there;
you walk the
forbidding coastline,
sand, stone, thorns,
by my side,
in the woods
you tramp through trees and
still green water,
in the suburbs
you stride along
unnavigable

intransitables
suburbios, pavimentos
de alquitrán fatigado,
a esa hora
en que la luz
del mundo
se deshilacha como
una bandera,
tú, por calles y bosques,
a mi lado
caminas,
bravía, inagotable
compañera,
pero,
Dios mío!
cómo gastas
zapatos!

Apenas
me parece
que llegaron
en su caja
y al abrirla
salieron
bruñidos
como dos
pequeñas herramientas
de combate,
intactos
como
dos monedas
de
oro,
como dos campanitas,
y hoy,

streets,
across pavements
of dejected tar,
and at that hour
when the light
of the world
unravels
like a flag,
in streets or woods,
you walk
beside me,
a dauntless, tireless
companion,
but
oh, my God!
What you do
to shoes!

It seems
only yesterday
you brought them home
in a box,
you opened it
and they emerged
gleaming
like
two army
pistols,
two
gold
coins
in mint
condition,
two little bells,
but today

qué veo?
En tus pies
dos erizos
arrugados,
dos puños entreabiertos,
dos informes
pepinos,
dos batracios
de cuero
desteñido,
eso,
eso
han llegado
a ser
los dos luceros
hace un mes, sólo un mes
salidos
de la zapatería.

Como
flor amarilla de hermosura,
abierta en la barranca,
o enredadera viva en el ramaje,
como
la calceolaria
o el copihue
o como el amaranto electrizado,
así,
mi cristalina, mi fragante,
así tú, floreciendo, me acompañas,
y una pajarería, una cascada
de los australes
montes
es
tu corazón
cantando

what do I see?
On your feet
two trodden
chestnut burrs,
two relaxed fists,
two shapeless
cucumbers,
two toads
of faded
leather,
that,
that's
what's
become of
two bright stars that
a month ago, only a month ago,
left
the store.

You are
a beautiful yellow flower
perfuming the ravine,
a vine flowering in the treetops,
calceolaria,
copihue,
vibrant amaranth,
crystalline,
fragrant,
blooming,
with me always,
the chorus of an aviary,
a waterfall
in southern
mountains,
your heart
sings

junto al mío,
pero,
cómo
te comes
los zapatos,
Pies de Fuego!

with mine,
but oh,
Firefoot,
how you
burn up
shoes!

74 / ODE TO THE FIREWOOD CAR

Oda al carro de la leña

TRANSLATED BY ILAN STAVANS

El carro de la leña	The firewood car
de los bosques!	in the forest!
Fragante atado	Fragrant bundle
de madera pura!	of pure wood!
Ninguna	Not a single
mano	hand
en este	in this
corazón	heart
se detuvo,	stopped,
sólo	only
el acero	the steel
de las hachas, el	of axes, the
vuelo repentino	sudden flight
de las aves y, con	of birds and, with
la muerte,	death,
el beso	the dark
oscuro de la tierra!	kiss of the earth!
Carros del monte,	Mountain carts,
leña	firewood
recién herida,	recently wounded,
huraños	wild
palos	sticks
cortados	chopped
y sangrantes,	and bleeding,

mudos,
en orden, bellos
como héroes muertos,
recostados
en el último
viaje
hacia
la hoguera.

Quebrachos, algarrobos,
robles, pinos, espinos,
troncos bruñidos
por
el crecimiento
de la vida en la tierra,
endurecidos como minerales
y sin embargo
tiernos
padres de los follajes,
del susurro, del nido,
caísteis
derrotados
por minúsculos
hombres
que parecían
larvas y que
de pronto
levantaron sus hachas
como aguijones:
luego
cayó el árbol, la tierra
sonó
como si la golpearan en los huesos
y levantó una ola
de polvo y de perfume,
de polvoriento aroma.

mute,
ordered, beautiful
like dead heroes,
lying
in the last
journey
toward
the bonfire.

Quebracho, carob,
oak, pine, hawthorn,
trunks burnished
by
the growth
of life on earth,
hardened by minerals
and nonetheless
tender
parents of foliage,
of murmurings of nests,
you fell down
defeated
by minuscule
men
who resembled
larvae and who
suddenly
raised their axes
like stings:
the tree
feel then, the earth
resounded
as if beaten to the bone,
and awakened a wave
of dust and perfume,
of dusty perfume.

A mí también
golpeaste en tu caída:
sobre
mi corazón
educado en la fría
sombra
de las montañas
el filo
de las hachas
cayó cortando ramas
y levantando vuelos y sonidos!

Ay quién
pudiera
detener
el curso
del río de la leña,
desandar el camino,
devolverlo a la selva:
enderezar
de nuevo
la majestad
antigua
sobre
la tierra asesinada
y esperar
que regresen
las aves encendidas,
el canto pleno y puro
de las hojas,
la fragante
salud
de la madera!

You also
beat me with your demise:
the axes' edge
fell
over
my heart
educated by the cold
shadow
of the mountains
cutting down branches
and igniting flights and sounds!

Ay who
could
stop
the course
of the river of firewood,
turn it back,
return it to the jungle:
straighten back
again
an ancient
majesty
over
the assassinated land
and wait
for the aroused birds
to return,
the pure and plentiful song
of the leaves,
the fragrant
health
of wood!

75 / ODE TO THE FIRST DAY OF THE YEAR

Oda al primer día del año

TRANSLATED BY ILAN STAVANS

Lo distinguimos	We identify it
como	as if
si fuera	it were
un caballito	a wooden horse
diferente de todos	different from
los caballos.	all horses.
Adornamos	We adorn
su frente	its forehead
con una cinta,	with a ribbon,
le ponemos	we hang
al cuello cascabeles colorados,	on its neck colorful rattles,
y a medianoche	and at midnight
vamos a recibirlo	we get ready to receive it
como si fuera	as if it were
explorador que baja de una estrella.	an explorer descending from a star.
Como el pan se parece	The way bread resembles
al pan de ayer,	yesterday's bread,
como un anillo a todos los anillos:	a ring all rings:
los días	the days
parpadean	blink
claros, tintineantes, fugitivos,	clearly, jingling, fleetingly,
y se recuestan en la noche oscura.	and lie down in the dark night.
Veo el último	I see the last
día	day
de este	of this

año
en un ferrocarril, hacia las lluvias
del distante archipiélago morado,
y el hombre
de la máquina,
complicada como un reloj del cielo,
agachando los ojos
a la infinita
pauta de los rieles,
a las brillantes manivelas,
a los veloces vínculos del fuego.

Oh conductor de trenes
desbocados
hacia estaciones
negras de la noche,
este final
del año
sin mujer y sin hijos,
no es igual al de ayer, al de mañana?
Desde las vías
y las maestranzas
el primer día, la primera aurora
de un año que comienza,
tiene el mismo oxidado
color de tren de hierro:
y saludan
los seres del camino,
las vacas, las aldeas,
en el vapor del alba,
sin saber
que se trata
de la puerta del año,
de un día
sacudido

year
on a train, toward the rains
of a distant purple archipelago,
and the man
on the machine,
complicated like a clock from heaven,
lowering his eyes
to the infinite
ruler of the rails,
to the shining handles,
to the nimble bonds of fire.

Oh conductor of trains
accelerating
toward the black
stations of the night,
this end
of the year,
without wife or children,
is it not the same for the one gone, the one
coming?
From the roads
and workshops,
the first day, the first dawn
of the starting year,
has the same rusty
color as the iron train:
and people along the way
greet it,
cows, villages,
the vapor of the first light of day,
without knowing
it is
the year's door,
a day
heralded

por campanas,
adornado con plumas y claveles.

La tierra
no lo
sabe:
recibirá
este día
dorado, gris, celeste,
lo extenderá en colinas,
lo mojará con
flechas
de transparente
lluvia,
y luego
lo enrollará
en su tubo,
lo guardará en la sombra.
Así es, pero
pequeña
puerta de la esperanza,
nuevo día del año,
aunque seas igual
como los panes
a todo pan,
te vamos a vivir de otra manera,
te vamos a comer, a florecer,
a esperar.
Te pondremos
como una torta
en nuestra vida,
te encenderemos
como candelabro,
te beberemos
como
si fueras un topacio.

by bells,
adorned with plumes and carnations.

The earth
does not
know it:
it will receive
that golden
day, gray, heavenly,
it will extend it over hills,
it will wet it with
arrows
of translucent
rain,
and then
it will curl it
in a tube,
will store it in the shadows.
It is thus, but
a small
door of hope,
new year's day,
although you are
like the bread
of all breads,
we will live you in a different way,
we will eat you, flower you,
wait for you.
We will place you
like a cake
in our lives,
we will light you
like candelabra,
we will drink you
as if
you were a topaz.

Día
del año
nuevo,
día eléctrico, fresco,
todas
las hojas salen verdes
del
tronco de tu tiempo.

Corónanos
con
agua,
con jazmines
abiertos,
con todos los aromas
desplegados,
sí,
aunque
sólo
seas
un día,
un pobre
día humano,
tu aureola
palpita
sobre tantos
cansados
corazones,
y eres,
oh día
nuevo,
oh nube venidera,
pan nunca visto,
torre
permanente!

New
Year's
Day,
electric day, fresh,
all the leaves
emerge green
from
the trunk of time.

Crown us
with
water,
with open
jasmine,
with all the aromas
deployed,
yes,
even though
you're
only
a day,
a poor
human day,
your halo
beats
over so many
tired
hearts,
and you are,
oh new
day,
oh forthcoming cloud,
bread unseen before,
permanent
tower!

76 / ODE TO THE FISHING BOAT

Oda al barco pesquero

TRANSLATED BY ILAN STAVANS

De pronto en noche pura
y estrellada
el corazón del barco, sus arterias,
saltaron,
y ocultas
serpentinas construyeron
en el agua
un castillo
de serpientes:
el fuego aniquiló cuanto tenía
entre sus manos
y cuando con su lengua
tocó
la cabellera
de la pólvora
estalló
como un trueno,
como aplastada cápsula,
la embarcación pesquera.
Quince
fueron los
muertos
pescadores,
diseminados
en
la noche fría.

Suddenly in the clear
and starry night
the boat's heart, its arteries,
jumped,
and hidden
serpentines built
on the water
a castle
of serpents:
fire destroyed everything
in its path
and when it touched it
with its tongue
the hair of powder
exploded
like
thunder,
like a crushed capsule,
the fishing vessel.
There
were fifteen
dead
fishermen,
disseminated
in
the cold night.

Nunca
volvieron de este viaje.
Ni un sólo dedo de hombre,
ni un sólo pie desnudo.

Es poca muerte quince
pescadores
para el terrible
océano
de Chile,
pero
aquellos
muertos errantes,
expulsados
del cielo y de la tierra
por tanta soledad en movimiento,
fueron
como ceniza
inagotable,
como aguas enlutadas
que caían
sobre
las uvas de mi patria,
lluvia,
lluvia
salada,
lluvia devoradora que golpea
el corazón de Chile y sus claveles.

Muchos
son,
sí,
los muertos
de tierra y mar,
los pobres
de la mina

They never
returned from that voyage.
Not a single human finger,
not a single naked leg.

Small deaths, fifteen
fishermen
in Chile's
terrible
ocean,
but
those
wandering dead,
thrown out of heaven and earth
because of so much solitude in movement,
were
as
if
inexhaustible,
like mourning waters
falling
over
the grapes of my country,
rain,
salty
rain,
devouring rain beating
Chile's heart and its carnations.

Many
are,
yes,
the dead
of land and sea,
the poor
from the mine

tragados	swallowed
por la negra	by the black
marea de la tierra,	wave of the earth,
comidos	eaten
por	by
los sulfúricos	the sulfuric
dientes	teeth
del mineral andino,	of the Andean mineral,
o en la	or on
calle,	the street,
en la usina,	in the plant,
en el	in the
tristísimo hospital	saddest hospital
del desamparo.	of abandonment.
Sí,	Yes,
son	it is
siempre	always
pobres	the poor
los elegidos	who are chosen
por la muerte,	by death,
los cosechados en racimo	those harvested in bunches
por las manos heladas	by the cold hands
de la cosechadora.	of the harvest machine.
Pero éstos	But these
aventados	adventurers
en plena, en plena sombra,	in plain, in full shadow,
con estrellas	with stars
hacia todas las aguas	having all the waters
del océano,	of the ocean,
quince	fifteen
muertos	wandering
errantes,	dead,
poco	little
a	by
poco	little

integrados
a la sal, a la ola,
a las espumas,
éstos
sin duda
fueron
quince
puñales
clavados
al corazón marino
de mi pobre
familia.

Sólo
tendrán el ancho
ataúd de agua negra,
la única luz
que velará
sus cuerpos
será
la eternidad
de las estrellas,
y mis años
viuda
vagará por el cielo
la noche del naufragio,
aquella noche.

Pero
del mar
y de la tierra
volverán
algún día
nuestros muertos.
Volverán
cuando

integrated
with the salt, the wave,
the foam,
they
were
no doubt
fifteen
daggers
stabbing
the ocean heart
of my poor
family.

They will
have only black water
as a wide coffin,
the only light
keeping vigil
over their bodies
will be
the eternity
of stars,
and for a thousand years
the shipwreck's night,
that night,
like a widow
will roam the sky.

But
at sea
and on land
one day
our dead
will return.
They will return
when

nosotros estemos
verdaderamente
vivos,
cuando
el hombre
despierte
y los pueblos
caminen,
ellos
dispersos, solos, confundidos
con el fuego y el agua,
ellos,
triturados, quemados,
en tierra o mar, tal vez
estarán reunidos
por fin
en nuestra sangre.
Mezquina
sería la victoria sólo muestra.
Ella es la flor final de los caídos.

we are
truly
alive,
when
man
awakes
and people
walk,
they,
dispersed, alone, confused
by fire and water,
they,
crushed, burned,
on land or at sea, perhaps
will be reunited
finally
in our blood.
A victory for us alone
would be petty.
She is the final flower of those who have fallen.

77 / ODE TO THE FLOWER

Oda a la flor

TRANSLATED BY ILAN STAVANS

Flores	A poor man's
de pobre	flowers
en las	in
ventanas	a poor man's
pobres,	window,
pétalos	petals
de sol pobre	of a poor man's sun
en las desmoronadas	in poverty's
casas de la pobreza.	tumbledown houses.
Yo veo cómo	I see how
la flor, su cabellera,	a flower, its head of hair,
su satinado pecho,	its satiny breast,
su apostura	its appearance
relucen en la tienda.	shine in the store.
Veo	I see
cómo de allí el color, la luz de seda,	how the color, silk light,
la torre de turgencia,	swelling tower,
el ramo de oro,	gold bouquet,
el pétalo violeta de la aurora,	the aurora's violet petal,
el pezón encendido de la rosa,	the rose's burning nipple,
vestidos y desnudos	dressed and naked
se preparan	prepare
para entrar a la casa de los ricos.	to enter the house of the rich.
La geografía desbordó sus dones,	Geography overflew its qualities,
el océano	the ocean

se transformó en camino,
la tierra entremezcló sus latitudes
y así la flor remota
navegó con su fuego,
y así llegó a tu puerta,
desde donde una mano presurosa
la retiró: «Tú no eres
flor de pobre, le dijo,
a ti te toca, flor,
brillar en medio
de la sala encerada,
no te metas en esa calle oscura,
incorpórate
a nuestro monopolio de alegría».

Y así voy por las calles
mirando las ventanas
donde el carmín caído
de un geranio
canta allí, en medio de las pobres vidas,
donde un clavel eleva
su flecha de papel y de perfume
junto a los vidrios rotos,
o donde una azucena
dejó su monasterio
y se vino a vivir con la pobreza.

Oh flor, no te condeno,
flor alta de encrespada investidura,
no te niego el derecho
de llevar el relámpago
que la tierra elevó con tu hermosura,
hasta la casa de los ricos.
Yo estoy seguro
que mañana
florecerás en todas

became the road,
the earth interwove its latitudes
and so the remote flower
steered with its fire,
and so it reaches your door,
from where a hurried hand
removed it: "You aren't
a poor man's flower," she told it,
"you're meant to shine, flower,
in the middle of the polished living
room,
don't enter that dark street,
embody yourself
in our monopoly of happiness."

And so I go through the streets
looking at the windows
where a geranium's
fallen carmine
sings, amid poor lives,
where a carnation raises
its arrow of paper and perfume
near the broken glasses,
or where a white lily
leaves its monastery
and comes to live with poverty.

Oh flower, I don't condemn you,
tall flower of curled investiture,
I don't deny you the right
to carry the flashing light
earth elevated with your beauty,
to the house of the rich.
I'm sure
tomorrow
you'll flourish in

las moradas del hombre.	the residences of man.
No tendrás miedo de la calle oscura,	You won't be frightened by the dark street,
ni habrá sobre la tierra	nor will there be on earth
guarida tenebrosa	a sinister recess
donde no pueda entrar la primavera.	where spring won't be allowed to enter.
Flor, no te culpo, estoy seguro de esto	Flower, I don't blame you, I'm sure of what
que te digo	I tell you
y para que florezcas donde debes	and so you flourish where you should
florecer, en todas las ventanas,	flourish, on every window,
flor,	flower,
yo lucho	I fight
y canto desde ahora, como canto,	and sing from now on, the way I sing,
en forma tan sencilla,	in such a simple way,
para todos,	for everyone,
porque yo distribuyo	because I distribute
las flores de mañana.	the flowers of tomorrow.

78 / ODE TO THE FLOWERS OF DATITLA

Oda a las flores de Datitla

TRANSLATED BY ILAN STAVANS

Bajo los pinos la tierra prepara	Under the pines, the earth concocts
pequeñas cosas puras:	small unsullied things:
hierbas delgadas	slim grasses
desde cuyos hilos	from whose threads
se suspenden minúsculos faroles,	minuscule lanterns hang,
cápsulas misteriosas	mysterious capsules
llenas de aire perdido,	plump with lost air,
y es otra allí	and shadows
la sombra,	are different there,
filtrada	filtered
y floreada,	and flowery,
largas agujas verdes esparcidas	long green needles scattered
por el viento que ataca y desordena	by the wind attacking and disheveling
el pelo de los pinos.	the hair of pine trees.
En la arena	On the sand
suceden	stand
pétalos fragmentarios,	fragmentary petals,
calcinadas cortezas,	calcified bark,
trozos azules	blue pieces
de madera muerta,	of dead wood,
hojas que la paciencia	leaves that the patience
de los escarabajos	of beetlelike
leñadores	woodcutters
cambia de sitio, miles	moves around, thousands
de copas mínimas	of minimal cups
el eucaliptus deja	left
caer	behind by the eucalyptus

sobre	over
su	your
fría y fragante	cold and fragrant
sombra	silhouette
y hay	and herbs
hierbas	are
afraneladas	like flannels
y plateadas	planted
con suavidad	with the softness
de guantes,	of gloves,
varas	sticks
de orgullosas espinas,	of proud spines,
hirsutos pabellones	wiry pavilions
de acacia oscura	of dark acacia
y flor color de vino,	and flowers the color of wine,
espadañas, espigas,	bulrush, heads of corn,
matorrales,	thickets,
ásperos tallos reunidos como	harsh stems united like
mechones de la arena,	locks on the sand,
hojas	round
redondas	stems
de sombrío verde	of somber green
cortado con tijeras,	cut with scissors,
y entre el alto amarillo	and amid the tall yellowness
que de pronto	suddenly
eleva	while shooting skyward
una silvestre	a rustic circumference of gold,
circunferencia de otro	the tiger flower flourishes
florece la tigridia	with three
con tres	tongues
lenguas de amor	of ultraviolet
ultravioleta.	love.
Arenas de Datitla	Datitla sand
junto	united
al abierto estuario	to the open statuary

de La Plata, en las primeras	of La Plata, in the first
olas del gris Atlántico,	waves of the gray Atlantic,
soledades amadas,	deliver
no sólo	beloved solitude,
al penetrante	you not only return me
olor y movimiento	to the penetrating
de pinares marinos	smell and movement
me devolvéis,	of sea pine,
no sólo	not only
a la miel del amor y su delicia,	to the honey of love and its deliciousness,
sino a las circunstancias	but to the purest circumstances
más puras de la tierra:	on earth:
a la seca y huraña	to the dry and wild
Flora del Mar, del Aire,	Flora of Sea, Air,
del Silencio.	and Silence.

79 / ODE TO THE FORTUNATE VOYAGE

Oda al viaje venturoso

TRANSLATED BY ILAN STAVANS

<table>
<tr><td>

Oh, viaje venturoso!
Dejé la primavera
trabajando en mi patria.
Los motores
del ave de aluminio
trepidaron
y fueron fuerza pura
resbalando en el cielo.
Así las cordilleras y los ríos
crucé, las extensiones argentinas,
los volcanes, las ciénagas, las selvas:
nuestro planeta verde.
Luego lanzó el avión sobre las nubes
su rectitud de plata
cruzando agua infinita, noches
cortadas
como copas o cápsulas azules,
días desconocidos cuya llama
se deslizó en el viento,
hasta que descendimos
en nuestra estrella errante
sobre la antigua nieve de Finlandia.
Sólo unos días
en
la rosa blanca, reclinada
en su nave de madera,
y Moscú

</td><td>

Oh, fortunate voyage!
I left spring
working in my homeland.
The motors
of the aluminum bird
shook
and were pure force
slipping from the sky.
Thus I crossed mountain ranges
and rivers, the Argentine extensions,
volcanoes, marshes, jungles:
our green planet.
Then, over the clouds, the plane
hurled its silvery rectitude,
crossing infinite water,
chopped
like cups or blue capsules,
unknown days like wool
slid on the wind,
until we descended
on our wandering star
over the old snow of Finland.
Only a few days
in
the white rose, reclined
on its wooden ship,
and Moscow

</td></tr>
</table>

abrió sus calles:
me esperaba
su claridad nocturna,
su vino transparente.
Viva es la luz del aire
y encendida es la tierra
a toda hora,
aunque el invierno
cierre con espadas
los mares y los ríos,
alguien espera, nos reconocemos:
arde la vida en medio de la nieve.

Y cuando
de regreso
brilló tu boca bajo los pinares
de Datitla y arriba
silbaron, crepitaron
y cantaron
extravagantes
pájaros,
bajo la luna de Montevideo,
entonces
a tu amor he regresado,
a la alegría
de tus anchos ojos:
bajé, toqué la tierra
amándote y amando
mi viaje venturoso!

opened its streets:
I was awaited by
its nocturnal clarity,
its transparent wine.
The air light is alive
and the earth is on fire
at all times,
though the winter
closes with its spears
the seas and the rivers,
someone waits, we recognize each other:
life burns amid the snow.

And when
on the way back
your mouth shone under the pine groves
in Datitla and up high
extravagant
birds
crackled
and sang,
under the Montevideo moon,
then
I returned to your love,
to the happiness
of your wide eyes:
I descended, I touched earth
loving you and loving
my fortunate voyage!

80 / ODE TO FRENCH FRIES

Oda a las papas fritas

TRANSLATED BY ILAN STAVANS

Chisporrotea
en el aceite
hirviendo
la alegría
del mundo:
las papas
fritas
entran
en la sartén
como nevadas
plumas
de cisne matutino
y salen
semidoradas por el crepitante
ámbar de las olivas.
El ajo
les añade
su terrenal fragancia,
la pimienta,
polen que atravesó los arrecifes,
y
vestidas
de nuevo
con traje de marfil, llenan el plato
con la repetición de su abundancia
y su sabrosa sencillez de tierra.

The world's
joy,
sputtering
in boiling
oil:
potatoes
about to be fried
enter
the skillet
like the snowy
wings
of a morning swan,
and they leave
half-braised from the olive's
crackling amber.
Garlic
adds to them
its homely fragrance,
pepper,
pollen traversing reefs,
and so,
dressed
again
in an ivory suit, they fill the plate
with the repetition of abundance
and the delicious simplicity of earth.

81 / ODE TO THE GENTLE BRICKLAYER

Oda al albañil tranquilo

TRANSLATED BY MARGARET SAYERS PEDEN

El albañil
dispuso
los ladrillos.
Mezcló la cal, trabajó
con arena.

Sin prisa, sin palabras,
hizo sus movimientos
alzando la escalera,
nivelando
el cemento.

Hombros redondos, cejas
sobre unos ojos
serios.

Pausado iba y venía
en su trabajo
y de su mano
la materia
crecía.
La cal cubrió los muros,
una columna
elevó su linaje,
los techos
impidieron la furia
del sol exasperado.

The bricklayer
laid out
his bricks.
He mixed the lime, working
it with sand.

Unhurried, silent,
he performed his task,
setting up the ladder,
leveling
the cement.

Rounded shoulders, eyebrows
above serious
eyes.

Deliberate, he came
and went in his work,
and beneath his hand
his creation
grew.
Plaster covered walls,
a column
thrust skyward,
a roof
forestalled the fury
of an angry sun.

De un lado a otro iba
con
tranquilas manos
el albañil
moviendo
materiales.
Y al fin
de
la semana,
las columnas, el
arco,
hijos de
cal, arena,
sabiduría y manos,
inauguraron
la sencilla firmeza
y la frescura.

Ay, qué lección
me dio con su trabajo
el albañil tranquilo!

Back and forth went
the bricklayer,
his gentle
hands
working
his materials.
And by the end
of
the week,
the columns and the
arch,
children of
lime, sand,
wisdom and hands,
celebrated
simplicity, solid
and cool.

Ah, what a lesson
I learned
from the gentle bricklayer!

82 / ODE TO THE GLOBE

Oda al globo terráqueo

TRANSLATED BY ILAN STAVANS

Redondo y liso,	Round and flat,
como	like
una manzana,	an apple,
globo	purified
purificado . . .	globe . . .
En tu tersura	In your smoothness,
las cordilleras	the rugged
ásperas, las puntas	cordilleras, the planet's tipping
del planeta, se hicieron	points, became
suavidad, las cavidades	gentleness, the cavities
que golpea el océano	that the ocean beats
o perpetra en la piedra	or the waterfall
la cascada,	perpetrates on the stone,
en ti contorno verde,	are in your green contour,
piel satinada son,	glossy skin
redonda cápsula	rounded cupola
de suaves continentes y contactos.	of gentle continents and contacts.
Nadie divisa	No one distinguishes
en tus bruñidos hemisferios,	in your hemispheric burnishes,
en el latón pulido	in the polished brass
del globo de la tierra,	of the earth's globe,
los terribles trabajos de los hombres.	the forbearing labors of man.
Nadie respira	No one breathes
polvo mortal, azufre	deadly dust, sulfur
en el desierto,	in the desert,

alquitrán en las charcas, cieno
de la naturaleza pestilente.
No vemos quién camina
en el ovario turbio
de los ríos
con lentitud pesada,
paso a paso, rodeado
por hojas y vapores
y raíces.

Cuando en la nieve
el frío
te acuchilla,
o en el mar
una ola
se descarga
como
repentina, violenta
dinamita,
no eres,
tierra,
redonda y tersa
uva,
sino
ferruginosa
cabellera,
látigo del abismo!

Y cuando los volcanes
abren
su caja
de secreto
fuego,
y la montaña
es
sangre,

tar on the ponds, sludge
of pestilent nature.
We don't see who walks
in the muddy ovary
of the rivers
with heavy sluggishness,
step by step, surrounded
by leaves and vapors
and roots.

When in the snow
the cold
stabs you,
or at sea
a wave
unloads
like
sudden, violent
dynamite,
you are not,
earth,
round and smooth
grape,
but
ferruginous
hair,
whip of the abyss!

And when the volcanoes
open
their treasure box
of secret
fire,
and the mountain
is
blood,

ceniza,
cicatrices,
trueno,
oh mapa mundi,
no eres
un globo
de
piel pura,
sino
un hirviente y hórrido
manantial
del infierno.

En tu papel,
verdes, rosados,
los países
se acuestan
transparentes
como algas,
pero
allí mismo,
graves
multitudes,
movimientos
del hombre, mitos,
sangre,
razón,
oscuridad,
historia,
tiemblan, se desarrollan
con movimiento eterno.

En cada una
de las verdes praderas
del mapa y sus regiones
se encienden

ash,
scars,
thunder,
oh *mapa mundi*,
you are not
a globe
of
unprocessed leather,
but
the boiling and horrid
spring
of hell.

On paper,
the countries,
green, pinkish,
lie down
translucent
like algae,
but
right there,
dangerous
multitudes,
movements
of man, myth,
blood,
reason,
darkness,
history,
tremble, develop
with eternal movement.

In each of the
map's green meadows
and its regions
lives

y se apagan
las vidas,
se reúnen,
se agotan,
y retornan después
a las
ásperas
manos
de la tierra.

Las ciudades
elevan
sus ladrillos,
sus lanzas,
sus signos
orgullosos,
sus
erizados
odios,
sus capas de miseria,
de abandono,
de lágrimas
y luchas,
y en tu redondo
vientre
planetario
no pasa
nada,
no germina
trigo,
ni se despeña
el agua
desmedida
de las inundaciones.

Tú, mapa mundi,
objeto,

are turned on
and off,
they gather,
exhaust themselves,
and return later
to the
rough
hands
of the earth.

The cities
elevate
their bricks,
spears,
proud
signs,
their
awakened
hatred,
their layers of misery,
abandonment,
tears
and struggle,
and in your round
planetary
womb
nothing
happens,
wheat
doesn't grow,
nor does
the overwhelming
floodwater
find recourse.

You, *mapa mundi*,
object,

eres
bello como
una paloma verde opulenta,
o como una
trascendente cebolla,
pero
no
eres
la tierra, no
tienes
frío, sangre,
fuego, fertilidades.
Una mujer, un hombre,
o la pequeña mano
de un niño
pobre o una
sencillísima
castaña,
representan
más que tu redondez
nuestro planeta.
No tienen paralelos,
nombres ni meridianos:
todo es estrella,
menos tu fría forma:
globo
bello,
todo tiene la tierra
que no tienes.

No sigas
engañando
con tu convexa piel, con tu tersura.
Yo quiero ver
el mundo
áspero
y verdadero

are
beautiful like
an opulent green dove,
or like a
transcendent onion,
but
you
are not
earth,
have no
warmth, blood,
fire, fertility.
A woman, a man,
or a poor
child's
small hand, or a
very simple
chestnut,
represent,
more than your roundness,
our planet.
There are no parallels,
names or meridians:
everything is star,
except your cold form:
beautiful
globe,
the earth has everything
you don't.

Don't go on
deceiving
with your convex skin, with your smoothness.
I want to see
the harsh
and true
world

porque no somos	because
puntos,	we are not points,
líneas,	lines,
signos,	signs,
de papel planetario.	on planetary paper.
Somos los hombres	We humans are
gérmenes	obscure
oscuros	germs
de claridad que desde nuestras manos	of clarity which through our hands
inundará la tierra.	will inundate the earth.

83 / ODE TO THE GOOD BLIND MAN

Oda al buen ciego

TRANSLATED BY ILAN STAVANS

La luz del ciego era su compañera.
Tal vez sus manos de artesano ciego
elaboraron con piedra perdida
aquel rostro de torre,
aquellos ojos que por él miraban.

Me vino a ver y en él
la luz del mar caía
cubriéndolo del miel, dando a su cuerpo
la pureza como una vestidura,
y su mirada no tenía fondo,
ni peces crueles en su abismo.

Tal vez aquella vez perdió la luz
como un hijo a su madre, pero siguió viviendo.
El hijo ciego de la luz mantuvo
la integridad del hombre con la sombra
y no fue soledad la oscuridad,
sino raíz del ser y fruta clara.

Ella con él venía,
bienamada,

The blind man's light was his
companion.
Perhaps his blind craftsman's hands
crafted, with a lost stone,
that towering face,
those eyes that saw on his behalf.

He came to see me and in him
the sea light descended,
covering him with honey, giving his
body
purity like vesture,
and his sigh had no bottom,
nor were there cruel fish in his abyss.

Perhaps he lost the light on that
occasion,
the way a son loses his mother, but he
went on living.
The light's blind son retained
the integrity of man accompanied by
shadow,
and darkness wasn't solitude
but root of being and clear fruit.

She came with him,
beloved,

esposa, amante	wife, lover
del muchacho ciego,	of the blind young man,
y cuando vacilaba su ternura,	and when her tenderness faltered,
ella tomó sus manos	she took his hands
y las puso en su rostro	and placed them on his face,
y fue como violetas el minuto,	and the minute was like violets.
toda la tierra allí se hizo fragante.	Oh beauty
Oh hermosura	of seeing the calamity floridly on high,
de ver alto y florido el infortunio,	of seeing the man whole
de ver completo el hombre	with flower and pain, and, suddenly,
con flor y con dolor, y ver de pronto	seeing
al héroe ciego	the blind hero
levantando el mundo,	raising the world,
haciéndolo de nuevo,	creating it anew,
anunciándolo,	announcing it,
nacido otra vez él en sus dolores	born again in his pain,
entero y estrellado	complete and starry,
con infinita luz de cielo oscuro.	with the infinite light of a dark sky.
Cuando se fue, a su lado	When he left, she was
ella era sombra pura	at his side like a sheer shadow,
que acompaña a los árboles de enero,	accompanying the trees in full,
la rumorosa sombra,	the rumored shadow,
la frescura,	the freshness,
el vuelo de la miel y sus abejas,	the flight of honey and its bees,
y se fueron	and they left
a todos sus trabajos,	everyone to his labor,
capaces de la vida,	capable of life,
profesores	professors
de sol, de luna, de madera, de agua,	of sun, of moon, of wood, of water,
de cuanto él abarcaba sin sus ojos,	of what he could embrace without his eyes,
dándote, ciego, inquebrantable luz	giving you, blind man, unshakable light
para que tú camines.	so you might walk.

84 / ODE TO GRATITUDE

Oda a las gracias

TRANSLATED BY ILAN STAVANS

Gracias a la palabra
que agradece.
Gracias a gracias
por
cuanto esta palabra
derrite nieve o hierro.

El mundo parecía amenazante
hasta que suave
como pluma
clara,
o dulce como pétalo de azúcar,
de labio en labio
pasa,
gracias,
grandes a plena boca
o susurrantes,
apenas murmulladas,
y el ser volvió a ser hombre
y no ventana,
alguna claridad
entró en el bosque:
fue posible cantar bajo las hojas.
Gracias, *eres la píladora*
contra
los óxidos cortantes del desprecio,
la luz contra el altar de la dureza.

Gracias to the word
that is thankful.
Thanks to *gracias*
for the extent
to which this word
melts snow or iron.

The world appeared threatening
until
soft
went
gracias
from lip to lip
as a clear-headed
pen,
or sweet like a sugar petal,
or whispering,
barely being voiced,
and a being became man again
and not a window,
some clarity
entered the forest,
able to sing amid the leaves.
Gracias, you're a pill
against
scorn's biting oxides,
light against the altar of harshness.

Tal vez
también tapiz
entre los más distantes hombres
fuiste.
Los pasajeros
se diseminaron
en la naturaleza
y entonces
en la selva
de los desconocidos,
merci,
mientras el tren frenético
cambia de patria,
borra las fronteras,
spasivo,
junto a los puntiagudos
volcanes, frío y fuego,
thanks, *sí,* gracias, *y entonces*
se transforma la tierra en una mesa:
una palabra la limpió,
brillan platos y copas,
suenan los tenedores
y parecen manteles las llanuras.

Gracias, gracias,
que viajes y que vuelvas,
que subas
y que bajes.
Está entendido, no
lo llenas todo,
palabra gracias,
pero
donde aparece
tu pétalo pequeño
se esconden los puñales del orgullo,
y aparece un centavo de sonrisa.

Perhaps
you were
also carpet
between the most distant men.
Passengers
are disseminated
in nature
and then
in the jungle
of unknown men,
merci,
while the frantic train
switches countries,
erases borders,
spasivo,
near the sharp-cusped
volcanoes, cold and fire,
thanks, yes, *gracias,* and then
the earth becomes a table,
a word swept it clean,
plates and cups shine,
forks jingle
and plains resemble tablecloths.

Thanks, *gracias,*
may you travel and return,
rise up
and come down.
It's understood that you,
word of *gracias,*
don't permeate all things,
but where
your small petal
appears,
proud daggers hide away
and a penny's worth of smiles emerges.

85 / ODE TO THE GREAT WALL IN THE FOG

Oda a la gran muralla de la niebla

TRANSLATED BY ILAN STAVANS

Lo cierto es que estas piedras	Truth is, these stones
duraron y duraron,	have lasted and lasted,
los minutos murieron como insectos,	the minutes died like insects,
el sol creció, fue rojo,	the sun grew, was red,
verde,	green,
azul,	blue,
negro,	black,
amaranto,	amaranth,
la nieve unió los ojos de los hombres	the snow united the eyes of men
y esta serpiente inútil	and this useless serpent
no comió sino tiempo.	only ate time.
Hoy la niebla	Today, fog
la cubre:	is covering it:
esta mañana el mundo,	this morning the world,
las montañas, los asnos	the mountains, the asses
que transportan las mismas piedras duras,	transporting the same stones,
todo	everything
es vapor,	is vapor,
temblor,	tremor,
neblina,	fog,
y sólo el prodigioso	and only the prodigious
son de flauta	sound of a hidden
de un pastor escondido	shepherd's flute
sube como una espada	rises like a spear
por los desfiladeros:	through the narrow mountain passes:

es el hombre que vive y come y canta
junto a la muerta serpiente.

Pero ella
cumplió con su destino.
Inmóvil, con la edad,
se olvidó de los hombres que la hicieron:
nació del artificio,
luego fue natural como la luna,
quedó desenterrada
como un cadáver demasiado grande.
Asciendo la osamenta, la costilla
del reino antiguo, de la luz secreta,
la cola del león de garras muertas.

Silencio, tiempo y niebla,
montes verdes, mojados,
y hacia la altura huraña
la Muralla,
la Muralla vacía.

Qué eres, muro?
Qué fuiste?
Oh gran separadora
de países,
fuiste siempre
inmutable
signo
que divisaron los planetas?
Quisiste ser camino?
La sangre derramada,
el silencio, la lluvia,
te convirtieron en reptil de piedra?

Oscuras mariposas entrevuelan,
se persiguen en la húmeda mañana,

it's the man living and eating and
singing near the dead serpent.

But the Wall carried out
its fate.
Motionless, with age,
it forgot the men who built it:
it was born from artifice,
was then natural like the moon,
ended up unearthed
like a bigger-than-required corpse.
I ascend the skeleton, the rib
of the ancient kingdom, the secret light,
the tail of the lion with dead claws.

Silence, time and fog,
green mountains, wet,
and toward the disdainful height
the Wall,
the empty Wall.

What are you, Wall?
What were you?
Oh great separator
of countries,
were you always
immutable
sign
observed by planets?
Did you want to be a road?
Spilled blood,
silence, rain,
turning you into a stone reptile?

Dark wrapped butterflies
pursue each other in the humid morning,

la soledad es grande y sigue sobre
tu cinta interminable,
Gran Muralla.
Me parece que allí donde creciste
como un río inhumano
se espantaron los nómades,
se estableció el silencio,
y un largo escalofrío
quedó sobre los montes
durando, duradero.

solitude is plentiful and continues
over your unending waist,
Great Wall.
I believe there where you grew
like an inhuman river
nomads were frightened,
silence was established,
and a lengthy shiver
lasted over the mountain,
enduring, enduring.

86 / ODE TO GUATEMALA

Oda a Guatemala

TRANSLATED BY ILAN STAVANS

Guatemala,
hoy
te
canto.

Sin razón,
sin objeto,
esta mañana
amaneció
tu nombre
enredado
a mi boca,
verde rocío,
frescura matutina,
recordé
las lianas
que atan
con su cordel silvestre
el tesoro sagrado
de tu selva.

Recordé en las alturas
los cauces invisibles
de tus aguas,
sonora
turbulencia secreta,
corolas amarradas

Guatemala,
today
I sing
to you.

Without reason,
without purpose,
this morning
your name
appeared
entangled
in my mouth,
green dew,
morning freshness,
I remembered
the lianas
tying
with their rustic cord
the sacred treasure
of your jungle.

I remembered in your heights
the invisible riverbeds
of your waters,
sonorous
secret turbulence,
corollas fastened

al follaje,	to the foliage,
un ave	a bird
como súbito zafiro,	like a sudden sapphire,
el cielo desbordado,	the overflowing sky,
lleno como una copa	full like a cup
de paz y transparencia.	of peace and transparency.
Arriba	Above
un lago	a lake
con un nombre de piedra.	with a name of stone.
Amatitlán se llama.	Amatitlán it's called.
Aguas, aguas del cielo	Waters, waters from heaven
lo llenaron,	filled it,
aguas, aguas de estrellas	waters, waters of stars
se juntaron	gathered together
en la profundidad aterradora	in the frightening depths
de su esmeralda oscura.	of a dark emerald.
En sus márgenes	In its margins
las tribus	the tribes
del Mayab	of Mayab
sobreviven.	survive.
Tiernos, tiernos	Tender, tender
idólatras	idolaters
de la miel, secretarios	of honey, secretaries
de los astros,	of heavenly bodies,
vencidos	beaten
vencedores	winners
del más antiguo enigma.	of the most archaic enigma.
Hermoso es ver	It is lovely to see
el vestido esplendor	the dressed-up splendor
de sus aldeas,	of its small villages,
ellos se atrevieron	they dared
a continuar llevando	to continue carrying
resplandecientes túnicas,	resplendent tunics,
bordados amarillos,	yellow embroideries,

calzones escarlatas,	scarlet panties,
colores	the colors
de la aurora.	of the aurora.
Antaño	In days gone by
los soldados	the soldiers
de Castilla enlutada	of a mourning Castile
sepultaron América,	buried America,
y el hombre	and to this day
americano	the American
hasta ahora	man
se pone la levita	wears the frock coat
del notario extremeño,	of a notary from Estremadura,
la sotana	Loyola's
de Loyola.	cassock.
España	Inquisitive
inquisitiva,	Spain,
purgatoria,	a purgatory,
enfundó los sonidos	sheathed the sounds
y colores,	and colors,
las estirpes de América,	the lineage of America,
el polen, la alegría,	the pollen, the happiness,
y nos dejó su traje	and left us behind
de salmantino luto,	its suit of Salamancan sorrow,
su armadura	its suit of armor
de trapo inexorable.	of inexorable rags.
El color sumergido	Only in you does
sólo en ti sobrevive,	the submerged color survive,
sobreviven, radiosos,	the plumage, radiant,
los plumajes,	survive,
sobrevive	your large-mouthed pitcher
tu frescura de cántaro,	survives in torrents,
profunda	profound
Guatemala,	Guatemala,
no te enterró la ola	you were not buried
sucesiva	by the successive wave

de la muerte,	of death,
las invasoras alas	the invading foreign
extrajeras,	wings,
los paños funerarios	funeral garments
no lograron	did not succeed
ahogar tu corola	in drowning your corolla
de flor resplandeciente.	of glittering flowers.

Yo vi en Quetzaltenango	I saw in Quetzaltenango
la muchedumbre	the fertile
fértil	crowd
del mercado,	in the market,
los cestos	the baskets
con el amor trenzados,	of plaited love,
con antiguos	the ancient
dolores,	sorrows,
las telas	the fabrics
de color turbulento,	of turbulent color,
raza roja,	red race,
cabezas de vasija,	vessel heads,
perfiles	profiles of
de metálica azucena,	metallic white lily,
graves miradas, blancas	grave glances, white
sonrisas como vuelos	smiles like a heron's
de garzas en el río,	flight on the river,
pies de color de cobre,	feet the color of copper,
gentes	peoples
de la tierra,	of the earth,
indios	dignified
dignos como	Indians like
monarcas de baraja.	a pack of monarchs.

Tanto	So much
humo cayó	smoke fell
sobre sus rostros, tanto	on their countenance, so much
silencio	silence

que no hablaron
sino con el maíz, con el tabaco,
con el agua,
estuvieron
amenazados por la tiranía
hasta en sus erizados territorios,
o en la costa
por invasores norteamericanos
que arrasaron la tierra,
llevándose los frutos.

Y ahora
Arévalo elevaba
un puñado de tierra
para ellos,
sólo un puñado
de polvo germinal, y es eso,
sólo eso, Guatemala,
un minúsculo
y fragante
fragmento de la tierra,
unas cuantas semillas
para sus pobres gentes,
un arado
para los campesinos.
Y por eso
cuando Arbenz
decidió la justicia,
y con la tierra repartió fusiles,
cuando los
cafeteros
feudales
y los aventureros de Chicago
encontraron
en la casa de gobierno
no un títere despótico,

they did not speak
but with corn, with tobacco,
with water,
they were
threatened by tyranny
even in their enrooted territories,
or on the coast
by invading North Americans
who devastated the land,
taking the fruit with them.

And now
Arévalo elevated
a handful of soil
for them,
just a handful
of germinating dust, that's all,
that's all, Guatemala,
a minuscule
and fragrant
fragment of land,
a few seeds
for the poor people,
a plow
for the peasants.
And that's why
when Arbenz
brought in justice,
and with the land gave out rifles,
when the
feudal
coffee growers
and the adventurers of Chicago
found
in the house of government
not a despotic puppet

sino un hombre,
entonces
fue la furia,
se llenaron
los periódicos
de comunicados:
ardía Guatemala.

Guatemala no ardía.
Arriba el lago
Amatitlán, quieto como mirada
de los siglos,
hacia el sol y la luna relucía,
el río Dulce
acarreaba
sus aguas primordiales,
sus peces y sus pájaros,
su selva,
su latido
desde el aroma original de América,
los pinos en la altura
murmuraban,
y el pueblo simple
como arena o harina
pudo, por vez primera,
cara a cara
conocer la esperanza.

Guatemala,
hoy te canto,
hoy a las desventuras del pasado
y a tu esperanza canto.
A tu belleza canto.
Pero quiero
que mi amor te defienda.
Yo conozco

but a man,
then
fury settled in,
they filled
newspapers
with communiqués:
Guatemala was burning.

Guatemala wasn't burning.
On top was Lake
Amatitlán, quiet with centuries-old
sight,
toward the sun and the moon it shone,
the Dulce River
carried
primordial waters,
fish and birds,
its jungle,
its beat
from the primordial aroma of America,
the pines in their heights
murmured,
and the simple people
like sand and flour
succeeded, for the first time,
at looking hope
in the face.

Guatemala,
I sing to you today,
I sing your past misfortunes
and your hope.
I sing your beauty.
But I want my love
to protect you.
I know

a los que te preparan una tumba
como la que cavaron a Sandino.
Los conozco. No esperes
piedad de los verdugos.
Hoy se preparan
matando pescadores,
asesinando peces de las islas.
Son implacables. Pero
tú, Guatemala, eres
un puño y un puñado
de polvo americano con semillas,
un pequeño puñado
de esperanza.
Defiéndelo, defiéndenos,
nosotros
hoy sólo con mi canto,
mañana con mi pueblo y con mi canto
acudiremos
a decirte «aquí estamos»,
pequeña hermana,
corazón caluroso,
aquí estamos dispuestos
a desangrarnos para
defenderte,
porque en la hora oscura
tú fuiste
el honor, el orgullo,
la dignidad de América.

those who prepare a tomb for you
like the one they dug for Sandino.
I know them. Don't expect
piety from your executioners.
Today they get ready
by killing fishermen,
assassinating fish in the islands.
They are implacable. But
you, Guatemala, are
a fist and a handful
of American dust with seeds,
a small handful
of hope.
Defend them, defend us,
we
today only with my song,
tomorrow with my people and my song
we shall arrive
to say to you, "Here we are,"
little sister,
warm heart,
we are ready now
to bleed to
defend you,
because in the dark hour
you were
the honor, the pride,
the dignity of America.

87 / ODE TO THE GUITAR

Oda a la guitarra

TRANSLATED BY ILAN STAVANS

Delgada
línea pura
de corazón sonoro,
eres la claridad cortada al vuelo:
cantando sobrevives:
todo se irá menos tu forma.

No sé si el llanto ronco
que de ti se desploma,
tus toques de tambor, tu
lenjambre de alas,
será de ti lo mío,
o si eres
en silencio
más decididamente arrobadora,
sistema de paloma
o de cadera,
molde que de su espuma
resucita
y aparece, turgente, reclinada
y resurrecta rosa.

Debajo de una higuera,
cerca del ronco y raúdo Bío Bío,
guitarra,
saliste de tu nido como un ave
y a unas manos

Slim
sheer line
of resonant heart,
you are clarity cut in flight:
you survive singing:
everything will vanish but your form.

I don't know if the hoarse lament
bulging out from you,
your drumbeats, your
swarm of wings,
will be mine in yours,
or if you are
in silence
more subtly captivating,
system of doves
or of waists,
mold reviving
from your foam
and appearing, turgescent, like a reclined
and resurrected rose.

Under a fig tree,
close to the hoarse, swift Biobío River,
guitar,
you emerged from your nest like a bird
and you delivered

morenas
entregaste
las citas enterradas,
los sollozos oscuros,
la cadena sin fin de los adioses.
De ti salía el canto,
el matrimonio
que el hombre
consumó con su guitarra,
los olvidados besos,
la inolvidable ingrata,
y así se transformó
la noche entera
en estrellada caja
de guitarra,
temblando el firmamento
con su copa sonora
y el río
sus infinitas cuerdas
afinaba
arrastrando hacia el mar
una marea pura
de aromas y lamentos.

Oh soledad sabrosa
con noche venidera,
soledad como el pan terrestre,
soledad con un río de guitarras!
El mundo se recoge
en una sola gota
de miel, en una estrella,
todo es azul entre las hojas,
toda la altura temblorosa canta.

Y la mujer que toca
la tierra y la guitarra

the buried appointments,
the dark sobs,
the unending chain of goodbyes
to a pair of swarthy
hands.
The song came out of you,
the wedding
that man
consummated with his guitar,
the forgotten kisses,
the unforgettable ingratitude of someone,
and so the entire night
was transformed
in the starry box
of the guitar,
the firmament trembling
with its resonant heart
and the river
its infinite strings
tuned to river
dragging toward the sea
a crystal tide
of aromas and laments.

Oh savory solitude
with authentic night,
solitude like terrestrial bread,
solitude with a river of guitars!
The world collects itself
in a single drop
of honey, in a star,
everything is blue amid the leaves,
the whole trembling height sings.

And the woman playing
the earth and the guitar

lleva en su voz
el duelo
y la alegría
de la profunda hora.
El tiempo y la distancia
caen a la guitarra:
somos un sueño,
un canto
entrecortado:
el corazón campestre
se va por los caminos a caballo:
sueña y sueña la noche y su silencio,
canta y canta la tierra y su guitarra.

carries in her voice
the grief
and happiness
of the painful hour.
Time and distance
fall onto the guitar:
we are a dream,
an interrupted
song:
the country son
wanders the roads on a horse:
dreams and dreams of the night and its silence,
sings and sings of the earth and its guitar.

88 / ODE TO HAPPINESS

Oda a la alegría

TRANSLATED BY ILAN STAVANS

Alegría,	Happiness,
hoja verde	green leaf
caída en la ventana,	fallen on the window,
minúscula	tiny
claridad	newborn
recién nacida,	clarity,
elefante sonoro,	melodious elephant,
deslumbrante	dazzling
moneda,	coin,
a veces	sometimes
ráfaga quebradiza,	breakable outburst of light,
pero	but
más bien	even better
pan permanente,	permanent bread,
esperanza cumplida,	fulfilled hope,
deber desarrollado.	developed duty.
Te desdeñe, alegría.	I scorned you, happiness.
Fui mal aconsejado.	I was badly advised.
La luna	The moon
me llevó por sus caminos.	took me on her roads.
Los antiguos poetas	The ancient poets
me prestaron anteojos	lent me glasses
y junto a cada cosa	and next to each thing
un nimbo oscuro	I placed
puse,	an obscure halo,
sobre la flor una corona negra,	on the flower a black crown,
sobre la boca amada	on the beloved mouth

un triste beso.
Aún es temprano.
Déjame arrepentirme.
Pensé que solamente
si quemaba
mi corazón
la zarza del tormento,
si mojaba la lluvia
mi vestido
en la comarca cárdena del luto,
si cerraba
los ojos a la rosa
y tocaba la herida,
si compartía todos los dolores,
yo ayudaba a los hombres.
No fui justo.
Equivoqué mis pasos
y hoy te llamo, alegría.

Como la tierra
eres
necesaria.

Como el fuego
sustentas
los hogares.

Como el pan
eres pura.

Como el agua de un río
eres sonora.

Como una abeja
repartes miel volando.

a sad kiss.
It is still early.
Let me regret.
I thought
if the bramble of torment
burned
my heart,
if the rain
wet my clothes
in the livid district of grief,
if I closed
my eyes to the rose
and touched the wound,
if I shared all my pains,
I would help men.
I wasn't fair.
I erred on my way
and today I call on you, happiness.

You are
necessary
like the earth.

Like fire
you support
the home.

Like bread
you are pure.

Like the water in the river
you are melodious.

Like the bee
you share honey.

Alegría,
fui un joven taciturno,
hallé tu cabellera
escandalosa.

No era verdad, lo supe
cuando en mi pecho
desató su cascada.

Hoy, alegría,
encontrada en la calle,
lejos de todo libro,
acompáñame:

contigo
quiero ir de casa en casa,
quiero ir de pueblo en pueblo,
de bandera en bandera.
No eres para mí solo.
A las islas iremos,
a los mares.
A las minas iremos,
a los bosques.
No sólo leñadores solitarios,
pobres lavanderas
o erizados, augustos
picapedreros,
me van a recibir con tus racimos,
sino los congregados,
los reunidos,
los sindicatos de mar o madera,
los valientes muchachos
en su lucha.

Contigo por el mundo!
Con mi canto!

Happiness,
I was a melancholy young man,
I found your hair
scandalous.

It wasn't true, I knew it
when it opened up a cascade
in my chest.

Today, happiness,
found on the street,
far from all books,
accompany me:

with you
I want to go from home to home,
I want to go from town to town,
from flag to flag.
You are not for me alone.
We are en route to the islands,
to the seas.
To the mines we will go,
to the forests.
Not only lonely woodcutters,
poor laundresses
or spiky, august
stonecutters
will receive me with their grapes,
but all those congregants,
the reunited,
the unions of sea and wood,
the brave young men
in their struggle.

With me through the world!
With my song!

Con el vuelo entreabierto
de la estrella,
y con el regocijo
de la espuma!

Voy a cumplir con todos
porque debo
a todos mi alegría.

No se sorprenda nadie porque quiero
entregar a los hombres
los dones de la tierra,
porque aprendí luchando
que es mi deber terrestre
propagar la alegría.
Y cumplo mi destino con mi canto.

With the star's
half-open flight,
and the joy
of the foam!

I will help everyone
because I owe
my happiness to all.

No one should be surprised
I want to give men
the fruits of the earth,
because I learned while fighting
that my earthly duty
is to disseminate happiness.
And I fulfill my destiny with my song.

89 / ODE TO THE HAPPY DAY

Oda al día feliz

TRANSLATED BY ILAN STAVANS

Esta vez dejadme	This time allow me
ser feliz,	to be happy,
nada ha pasado a nadie,	nothing has happened to anyone,
no estoy en parte alguna,	I am nowhere,
sucede solamente	it just happens
que soy feliz	I am happy
por los cuatro costados	in the four chambers
del corazón, andando,	of the heart, wandering around,
durmiendo o escribiendo.	sleeping or writing.
Qué voy a hacerle, soy	What can I do, I'm
feliz.	happy.
Soy más innumerable	I'm more innumerable
que el pasto	than the grass
en las praderas,	in the prairies,
siento la piel como un árbol rugoso	I feel my skin like a wrinkled tree
y el agua abajo,	and water underneath,
los pájaros arriba,	birds above,
el mar como un anillo	the sea like a notch
en mi cintura,	on my belt,
hecha de pan y piedra la tierra	made of bread and stone of earth
el aire canta como una guitarra.	the air sings like a guitar.
Tú a mi lado en la arena	At my side on the sand
eres arena,	you're sand,
tú cantas y eres canto,	you sing and are song,
el mundo	the world
es hoy mi alma,	is my soul today,

canto y arena,	song and sand,
el mundo	the world
es hoy tu boca,	is your mouth,
dejadme	let me
en tu boca y en la arena	be happy
ser feliz,	with your mouth and with the sand,
ser feliz porque sí, porque respiro	be happy just because, because I breathe
y porque tú respiras,	and because you breathe,
ser feliz porque toco	be happy because I touch
tu rodilla	your knee
y es como si tocara	and it's like touching
la piel azul del cielo	the blue skin of the sky
y su frescura.	and its freshness.
Hoy dejadme	Today let me
a mí solo	alone
ser feliz,	be happy,
con todos o sin todos,	with or without everyone,
ser feliz	be happy
con el pasto	with the grass
y la arena,	and the sand,
ser feliz	be happy
con el aire y la tierra,	with the air and the earth,
ser feliz,	be happy,
contigo, con tu boca,	with you, with your mouth,
ser feliz.	be happy.

90 / ODE TO A HARE-BOY

Oda al niño de la liebre

TRANSLATED BY PAUL MULDOON

A la luz del otoño
en el camino
el niño
levantaba en sus manos
no una flor
ni una lámpara,
sino una liebre muerta.

Los motores rayaban
la carretera fría,
los rostros no miraban
detrás
de los cristales,
eran ojos
de hierro,
orejas
enemigas,
rápidos dientes
que relampagueaban
resbalando
hacia el mar y las ciudades,
y el niño
del otoño
con su liebre,
huraño
como un cardo,
duro

In the light of autumn
and the open road,
the boy
holds up in his hands
not a blossom
nor a lantern
but a dead hare.

The automobiles scan
the freezing camber,
no faces showing
from behind
windshields,
their eyes
of iron,
their ears
set against everything,
their gear-teeth quick
as flashes of lightning,
skidding
towards the sea and the cities
while an autumn-
boy
with a hare,
standoffish
as a thistle,
hard

como una piedrecita,
allí
levantando
una mano
hacia la exhalación
de los viajeros.
Nadie
se detenía.

Eran pardas
las altas cordilleras,
cerros
color de puma
perseguido,
morado
era
el silencio
y como
dos ascuas
de diamante
negro
eran
los ojos
del niño con su liebre,
dos puntas
erizadas
de cuchillo,
dos cuchillitos negros,
eran los ojos
del niño,
allí perdido
ofreciendo su liebre
en el inmenso
otoño
del camino.

as a flint,
raises
there
a hand
to the shudder-sighs
of the cars.
Nobody
slows down.

They're dun-dullish,
the high ridges,
the hills
the color of a puma
on the run,
violet
now
the silence,
and like
two embers,
two
black
diamonds,
the eyes
of the hare-boy,
now
two points
set
on a knife,
two little black blade-tips,
the eyes
of the boy
who's all at a loss,
offering up his hare
to the huge
autumn
of the open road.

91 / ODE TO HER SCENT

Oda a su aroma

TRANSLATED BY ILAN STAVANS

Suave mía, a qué hueles,
a qué fruto,
a qué estrella, a qué hoja?

Cerca
de tu pequeña oreja
o en tu frente
me inclino,
clavo
la nariz entre el pelo
y la sonrisa
buscando, conociendo
la raza de tu aroma:
es suave, pero
no es flor, no es cuchillada
de clavel penetrante
o arrebatado aroma
de violentos
jazmines,
es algo, es tierra,
es
aire,
maderas o manzanas,
olor
de la luz en la piel,
aroma
de la hoja

Tender love of mine, what does your
smell invoke,
what fruit,
what star, what leaf?

Close
to your small ear
or on your forehead
I bend,
I stick
my nose in your hair
and the smile
searches, knowing
the
race of your aroma:
it's soft, but
it isn't a flower, it isn't a stab
of penetrating carnation
or snatched aroma
of violent jasmines,
it's something, it's earth,
it isn't only
air,
wood or apples,
smell
of light on the skin,
aroma
of leaf

del árbol
de la vida
con polvo
de camino
y frescura
de matutina sombra
en las raíces,
olor de piedra y río,
pero
más cerca
de un durazno,
de la tibia
palpitación secreta
de la sangre,
olor
a casa pura
y a cascada,
fragancia
de paloma
y cabellera,
aroma
de mi mano
que recorrió la luna
de tu cuerpo,
las estrellas
de tu piel estrellada,
el oro,
el trigo,
el pan de tu contacto,
y allí
en la longitud
de tu luz loca,
en tu circunferencia de vasija,
en la copa,
en los ojos de tus senos,
entre tus anchos párpados

of tree
of life
with dust
from the road
and freshness
of morning shadow
on the roots,
smell of stone and river,
but also,
even closer,
the secret
of a peach,
lukewarm palpitation
of blood,
smell
of pure house
and waterfall,
fragrance
of dove
and cavalry,
aroma
of my hand
traveling the moon
of your body,
stars
of your starry skin,
gold,
wheat,
the bread of your touch,
and from there on,
the longitude
of your crazy light,
your vessel's circumference,
in the goblet,
in the eyes of your breasts,
between your wide eyelids

y tu boca de espuma,
en todo
dejó,
dejó mi mano
olor de tinta y selva,
sangre y frutos perdidos,
fragancia
de olvidados planetas,
de puros
papeles vegetales,
allí
mi propio cuerpo
sumergido
en la frescura de tu amor, amada,
como en un manantial
o en el sonido
de un campanario
arriba
entre el olor del cielo
y el vuelo
de las últimas aves,
amor,
olor,
palabra
de tu piel, del idioma
de la noche en tu noche,
del día en tu mirada.

Desde tu corazón
sube
tu aroma
como desde la tierra
la luz hasta la cima del cerezo
en tu piel yo detengo
tu latido
y huelo

and your mouth of foam,
everything
leaves,
it leaves in my hand
the smell of ink and jungle,
blood and lost fruits,
scent
of forgotten planets,
pure
vegetable papers,
my own body
is
submerged there
in the freshness of your love, beloved one,
as in a spring
or the sound
of a rising bell tower
above
between the color of the sky
and the flight
of the last birds,
love,
smell,
word
of your skin, of the language
of night in your night,
of day in your gaze.

From your heart
your aroma
rises
as if from the earth,
light to the tip of the cherry tree:
in your skin, I stop
your beat
and smell

la ola de luz que sube,
la fruta sumergida
en su fragancia,
la noche que respiras,
la sangre que recorre
tu hermosura
hasta llegar al beso
que me espera
en tu boca.

the light-wave climbing,
the submerged fruit
of your fragrance,
the night you breathe,
the blood covering
your beauty
until it reaches the kiss
awaiting me
in your mouth.

92 / ODE TO HOPE

Oda a la esperanza

TRANSLATED BY ILAN STAVANS

Crepúsculo marino,
en medio
de mi vida,
las olas como uvas,
la soledad del cielo,
me llenas
y desbordas,
todo el mar,
todo el cielo,
movimiento
y espacio,
los batallones blancos
de la espuma,
la tierra anaranjada,
la cintura
incendiada
del sol en agonía,
tantos
dones y dones,
aves
que acuden a sus sueños,
y el mar, el mar,
aroma
suspendido,
coro del sal sonora,
mientras tanto,
nosotros,

Marine twilight,
in the midst
of my life,
waves like grapes,
the solitude of heaven,
you fill
and overwhelm me,
the whole sea,
the whole sky,
movement
and space,
white battalions
of foam,
orange soil,
the burned
waist
of the sun in agony,
many
qualities and qualities,
birds
gathering in your dreams,
and the sea, the sea,
suspended
aroma,
choir of resonant salt,
meanwhile,
we,

los hombres,
junto al agua,
luchando
y esperando
junto al mar,
esperando.

men,
near water,
struggling
and waiting
near the sea,
waiting.

Las olas dicen a la costa firme:
«Todo será cumplido».

The waves tell the solid coast:
"Everything will happen."

93 / ODE TO THE HORSE

Oda al caballo

TRANSLATED BY ILAN STAVANS

Aquel caballo solo y amarrado	That horse, lonesome and tied
en un pobre potrero	to a humble farm
de mi patria,	in my homeland,
aquel pobre caballo	that poor horse
es un recuerdo,	is a memory,
y ahora	and now
cuando todos los caballos	when all the horses convene
acuden al relámpago,	in the lightning flash,
a la luz repentina de mi oda,	the sudden light of my ode,
el olvidado viene,	the forgotten one comes,
el apaleado,	the beaten one,
el que acarreó la leña de los montes,	the one carrying the mountain firewood,
las piedras	the cruel
crueles	stones
de cantera y costa,	of quarry and coast,
él,	he,
no viene galopando	isn't galloping
con incendiarias crines	with fire-raising mane
ondulando en el viento,	waving in the wind,
no llega	doesn't come
intacta grupa como	the croup untouched like
manzana de la nieve,	a snow apple,
no,	no,
así no llega.	he doesn't come like this.
Llega rengueando, apenas	He comes grumbling, his four
sus cuatro patas andan	hooves barely moving
y su cabeza inmóvil	and his immobile head
es torre	is a tower

de tristeza,
y así
llega a mi oda,
así el caballo llega a que lo cante.

Trotó por todos los caminos duros,
comió mal con sus muelas amarillas,
bebió poco—su dueño
usaba más palo que pozo—,
está seco mi amigo
de lomo
puntiagudo,
y tiene un alma flaca de violín,
un corazón cansado,
el pelo de una alfombra suburbana.

Ay viéndolo, tocándolo,
se ven sus muchos huesos,
el arca que protegen las costillas,
los agobiados fémures caídos
en los trabajadores metatarsos
y el cráneo, catedral de hueso puro,
en cuyos dos altares
viven dos santos ojos de caballo.

Entonces me miraron con la prueba
de un extenso, de un ancho sufrimiento,
de un sufrimiento grave como el Asia,
caminando con sed y con arena,
y era aquel pobre y nómade caballo
con su bondad algo que yo buscaba,
tal vez
su religión sin ilusiones.

Desde entonces me buscó su mirada
dentro de mí, contra tantos dolores
padecidos por hombres y caballos,

of sadness,
and so
he comes to my ode,
the horse comes so I can turn him into song.

He trotted down all the hard roads,
ate badly with his yellow teeth,
drank little—his owner
used more stick than well—
my friend with the sharp-pointed
back
is dry,
and has the thin soul of a violin,
a tired heart,
the hair of a suburban carpet.

Ay, looking at him, touching him,
one sees his many bones,
the ark his ribs protect,
the fallen, weighed-down thighbones
in the working metatarsals
and the cranium, pure-bone cathedral,
on which two saintly horse eyes
live in its two altars.

Then they looked at me with the proof
of an extended, a wide suffering,
a grave suffering like Asia's,
walking with thirst and with sand,
and it was that poor nomadic horse
with its goodness I was looking for,
perhaps
his religion without illusions.

Since then his gaze peered
inside me, against so many sorrows
endured by men and horses,

y no me gusta, no, la suave liebre,
ni el león, ni el halcón,
ni los puñales de los tiburones,
sino aquella mirada,
aquellos ojos fijos
en la tranquilidad de la tristeza.

and I don't like it, no, the tender hare,
or the lion, or the hawk,
or the shark's daggers,
only that gaze,
those eyes fixated
in the tranquillity of sadness.

Tal vez alguien pregunte
por la forma
del alado y elástico
caballo, del puro
corcel de cabalgata,
orgullo del desfile,
bala de la carrera:
y bien, celebro
su donaire de avispa,
la flecha que con líneas lo dibuja
desde el belfo a la cola
y baja por metálicos tobillos
hasta nerviosos cascos presurosos.

Perhaps someone will ask
about the form
of the winged and elastic
horse, the pure
processional steed,
pride of the parade,
bullet of the race:
well then, I celebrate
his wasp's wit,
the arrow drawing him with lines
from the thick underlip to the tail
that descends through metallic ankles
to the nervous and hurried hooves.

Sí, tal vez es la vela del velero,
la claridad de una cadera amada,
la curva de la gruta de una ola,
lo que puede acercarse a la belleza,
al veloz arabesco de un caballo,
a su estampa acuñada sobre un vuelo,
dibujada en el sello del rocío.

Yes, perhaps it's the boat's sail,
the clarity of an armed hip,
the curve of a wave's grotto,
that which can approach beauty,
to the swift arabesque of a horse,
to his image stamped on a fly,
drawn on the seal of dew.

Pero no va mi oda
a volar con el viento,
a correr con la guerra
ni con los regocijos:
mi poesía se hizo paso a paso,
trotando por el mundo,
devorando caminos pedregosos,

But my ode
won't fly with the wind,
run with the war
or delights:
my poetry was made step by step,
trotting through the world,
devouring stony roads,

comiendo con
los miserables
en el mesón glacial de la pobreza,
y me debo
a esas piedras
del camino,
a la sed, al castigo del errante,
y si un nimbo saqué de aquella aurora,
si rescaté el dolor para cantar victoria,
ahora la corona
de laurel fresco para el sufrimiento,
la luz que conquisté
para las vidas
la doy para esa gloria de un caballo,
de uno que aguantó peso, lluvia y golpe,
hambre y remota soledad y frío
y que no sabe, no, para qué vive,
pero anda y anda y trae carga y lleva,
como nosotros, apaleados hombres,
que no tenemos dioses sino tierra,
tierra que arar, que caminar, y cuando
ya está bastante arada y caminada
se abre para los huesos del caballo
y para nuestros huesos.
Ay caballo
de pobre, caminante,
caminemos
juntos en este espacio duro
y aunque no sepas ni sabrás que sirva
mi razón para amarte, pobre hermano,
mi corazón para esta oda,
mis manos para pasarlas sobre tu suave hocico!

eating with
the indigent
in the glacial inn of poverty,
and I owe myself
to those stones
from the road,
to thirst, to the wanderer's punishment,
and if I earned a nimbus from that dawn,
if I rescued pain to sing victory,
I now grant the horse's glory
the fresh laurel crown of suffering,
the light I conquered
for the lives,
for he bore the weight, rain and blows,
hunger and remote loneliness and cold
and doesn't know, no, why he lives,
but walks and walks and carries the burden,
like us, men beaten,
who don't have gods but land,
land to plow, to walk, and when
it's been plowed and walked enough
it opens up for the horse's bones
and our bones.
Ay, poor man's
walking horse,
let us walk
together in this hard space
and though you don't know nor will know if my reason
is useful for love, poor brother,
my heart for this ode,
my hands to touch your tender muzzle!

94 / ODE TO THE HUMMINGBIRD

Oda al picaflor

TRANSLATED BY MARGARET SAYERS PEDEN

Al colibrí,	To the colibri,
volante	winged
chispa de agua,	liquid spark,
incandescente gota	a shimmering drop
de fuego	of America's
americano,	fire,
resumen	symbol
encendido	of a vivid
de la selva,	jungle,
arco iris	rainbow
de precisión	of celestial
celeste:	precision:
al	to the
picaflor	hummingbird,
un arco,	an arc,
un	a
hilo	thread
de oro,	of gold,
una fogata	green
verde!	conflagration!
Oh	Oh
mínimo	diminutive
relámpago	flash of
viviente,	lightning energy,
cuando	as
se sostiene	you

en el aire
tu
estructura
de polen,
pluma
o brasa,
te pregunto,
qué cosa eres,
en dónde
te originas?
Tal vez en la edad ciega
del diluvio,
en el lodo
de la fertilidad,
cuando
la rosa
se congeló en un puño de antracita
y se matricularon los metales,
cada uno en
su secreta
galería,
tal vez entonces
del reptil
herido
rodó un fragmento,
un átomo
de oro,
la última
escama cósmica, una
gota
del incendio terrestre
y voló
suspendiendo tu hermosura,
tu iridiscente
y rápido zafiro.

hover
in the
air,
pollen,
feather,
glowing coal,
I ask you,
how
and where
did you begin?
Perhaps in the dark days
before the Flood,
from the mud
of fertility,
when
the rose
hardened into a fist of coal,
and metals formed,
each
in its secret
chamber,
maybe there
from the dying
reptile
one fragment lived,
one atom
of gold,
the last cosmic
reptilian scale,
a drop
of terrestrial fire,
and it flew,
creating your beauty,
your vibrating
iridescent sapphire.

Duermes
en una nuez,
cabes en una
minúscula corola,
flecha,
designio,
escudo,
vibración
de la miel, rayo del polen,
eres
tan valeroso
que el halcón
con su negra emplumadura
no te amedrenta:
giras
como luz en la luz,
aire en el aire,
y entras
volando
en el estuche húmedo
de una flor temblorosa
sin miedo
de que su miel nupcial te decapite.
Del escarlata al oro espolvoreado,
al amarillo que arde,
a la rara
esmeralda cenicienta,
al terciopelo anaranjado y negro
de tu tornasolado corselete,
hasta el dibujo
que como
espina de ámbar
te comienza,
pequeño ser supremo,
eres milagro,
y ardes

You can sleep
in a nut,
disappear in
the smallest corolla,
arrow,
invention,
escutcheon,
quivering
honey, pollen's ray,
you are
so brave
the black-plumed
falcon
does not awe you:
you dart
like light in light,
air in air,
and plunge
into the moist jewel coffer
of a trembling flower
never fearing to lose your head
in its nuptial honey.
From gold-dusted scarlet
to flaming yellow,
from rare
ashen emerald
to the orange-tinted black velvet
of your sunflower corselet,
from the nib that like an
amber thorn
initiates
your outline,
greatest of small creatures,
you are a miracle,
and you blaze

desde	from
California caliente	sunny California
hasta el silbido	to the whistling
del viento amargo de la Patagonia.	icy winds of Patagonia.
Semilla del sol	Seed
eres,	of sunlight,
fuego	feathered
emplumado,	fire,
minúscula	smallest
bandera	flying
voladora,	flag,
pétalo de los pueblos que callaron,	petal of silenced peoples,
sílaba	syllable
de la sangre enterrada,	of buried blood,
penacho	feathered crest
del antiguo	of our ancient
corazón	subterranean
sumergido.	heart.

95 / ODE TO THE INCONSEQUENTIAL DAY

Oda al día inconsecuente

TRANSLATED BY ILAN STAVANS

Plateado pez	Silver fish
de cola	with orange
anaranjada,	tail,
día del mar,	day of the sea,
cambiaste	each hour
en cada hora	you changed
de vestido,	your clothes,
la arena	the sand
fue celeste,	was blue,
azul	your tie
fue tu corbata,	was azure,
en una nube	on a cloud
tus pies	your feet
eran espuma	were foam
y luego	and then
total	the green flight
fue el vuelo verde	of the rain
de la lluvia	over the pine trees
en los pinos:	was total:
una racha de acero	an iron spell
barrió	swept
las esperanzas	the western
del oeste,	slopes,
la última o la primera	the last or first
golondrina	swallow
brilló blanca y azul	shone white and blue
como un revólver,	like a revolver,
como un reloj nocturno	like a nocturnal watch

el cielo sólo
conservó un minutero
de platino,
turgente y negro el mar
cubrió su corazón
con terciopelo
mostrando de repente
la nevada sortija
o la encrespada
rosa de su radiante desvarío.

the sky only
preserved a platinum
minute hand,
well-rounded and black the sea
covered its heart
with velvet
suddenly showing
the snowy ring
or the curled
rose in its radiant delirium.

Todo esto
lo miré
inquietamente fijo
en mi ventana
cambiando de zapatos
para ir por la arena
llena de oro
o hundirme en la humedad, entre las hojas
del eucaliptus rojo,
corvas como puñales de Corinto,
y no pude
saber
si el Arco Iris,
que como una bandera mexicana
creció hacia Cartagena,
era anuncio
de dulce luz
o torre de tinieblas.
Un fragmento
de nube
como resto volante
de camisa
giraba
en el último umbral
del pánico celeste.

Restlessly fixed
I saw
all this
from my window
changing my shoes
to go through the sand
full of gold
or sink in the humidity, amid the leaves
of red eucalyptus,
curved like Corinthian daggers,
and I could not
know
if the Rainbow,
like a Mexican flag
bent toward Cartagena,
was an announcement
of sweet light
or a tower of darkness.
A fragment
of cloud
like the remnant
of a flying shirt
rotated
on the last threshold
of celestial panic.

El día
tembló de lado a lado,
un relámpago
corrió como un lagarto
entre las vestiduras
de la selva
y de golpe cayó todo el rocío
perdiéndose en el polvo
la diadema salvaje.
Entre las nubes y la tierra
de pronto
el sol
depositó su huevo duro,
blanco, liso, obstinado,
y un gallo verde
y alto
como un pino
cantó, cantó
como si desgranara
todo el maíz del mundo:
un río,
un río rubio
entró por las ventanas
más oscuras
y no la noche, no la tempestuosa
claridad indecisa
se estableció en la tierra,
sino sencillamente
un día más,
un día.

The day
trembled from side to side,
lightning
ran like an alligator
amid the clothing
of the jungle
and at once the entire dew fell down
disappearing in the dust
of the savage diadem.
Between the clouds and the earth
the sun
swiftly
laid its hard egg,
white, smooth, stubborn,
and a green and tall
rooster
like a pine
sang, sang
as if he were threshing
all the corn in the world:
a river,
a blond river
entered through the darkest
windows
and not the night, not the tempestuous
indecisive clarity
established over the earth,
but simply
another day,
a day.

96 / ODE TO IRONING

Oda para planchar

TRANSLATED BY ILAN STAVANS

La poesía es blanca:
sale del agua envuelta en gotas,
se arruga y se amontona,
hay que extender la piel de este planeta,
hay que planchar el mar de su blancura
y van y van las manos,
se alisan las sagradas superficies
y así se hacen las cosas:
las manos hacen cada dia el mundo,
se une el fuego al acero,
llegan el lino, el lienzo y el tocuyo
del combate de las lavanderías
y nace de la luz una paloma:
la castidad regresa de la espuma.

Poetry is white:
it comes from water swathed in drops,
it wrinkles and gathers,
this planet's skin has to spread out,
the sea's whiteness has to be ironed out,
and the hands keep moving,
the sacred surfaces get smoothed,
and things are done this way:
the hands make the world every day,
fire conjoins with steel,
linen, canvas and cotton arrive
from the scuffles in the laundries,
and from light a dove is born:
chastity returns out of the foam.

97 / ODE BEFORE THE ISLAND OF CEYLON

Oda frente a la isla de Ceylán

TRANSLATED BY ILAN STAVANS

Otra vez en los mares,	Once again at sea,
envuelto	wrapped
en lluvia,	in rain,
en oro,	in gold,
en vago amanecer,	in vague daybreak,
en ceniciento	in ashen
vapor de soledades calurosas.	vapor of warm solitudes.
Y allí	And there
surgiendo	emerging
como	like
una nueva ola verde,	a new green wave,
oh Ceylán,	oh Ceylon,
oh isla	oh sacred
sagrada,	island,
cofre	coffer
en donde palpitó	where my youthful,
mi joven, mi perdido	my lost, exiled
corazón	heart
desterrado!	palpitated!
Yo el solitario	I was the solitary figure
fui	in
de la floresta,	the rural landscape,
el testigo	a witness
de cuanto no pasaba,	to what was happening,
el director	a director

de sombras	of shadows
que sólo	living
en mí	only
existían.	in me.
Oh tiempos,	Oh times long gone,
oh tristezas,	oh sadness,
oh loca noche de agua	oh foolish night of water
y luna	and red
roja	moon
con un	with
olor	the smell
de sangre y de jazmines,	of blood and jasmine,
mientras allá,	while there,
más lejos,	far away,
la sombra redoblaba	the shadow rolled
sus tambores,	its drums,
trepidaba la tierra,	made the earth quiver,
entre las hojas	amid the leaves
bailaban los guerreros.	the warriors sang.
Y, ahora,	And, now,
acompañado	accompanied
por tus pequeñas manos	by your small hands
que van y van secando	continuing to shake
el sudor	the sweat
y las penas	and the afflictions
de mi frente,	on my forehead,
ahora	now
con otra voz	once again
segura,	assured,
con otro canto	with another song
hecho	delivered
por la luz de la vida,	by the light of life,
aquí	here
vengo a parar	I come to stand
de nuevo junto	again near

al mar que sólo fuera
soledad rumorosa,
al viento
de la noche
sobre los cocoteros
estrellados:
y nadie sabe ahora
lo que fui, lo que supe,
lo que sufrí,
sin nadie,
desangrándome.

Piso la calle
mía:
manchas de ausencia
o de humedad,
las plantas
se transformaron
en sombría espesura
y hay una sola
casa
que agoniza,
vacía.
Era mi casa, y hace
treinta años,
treinta
años. Toco
la puerta
de mis sueños,
los muros
carcomidos,
el tiempo
me esperaba,
el tiempo aquel
girando
con su rueda.

the sea that was only
a rumor of solitude,
the wind
of night
over the starry
coconut trees:
and no one knows now
who I was, what I knew,
what I suffered,
with no one,
bleeding.

I step over my
street:
stains of absence
and humidity,
the plants
are transformed
into a shady thickness
and there is only one
house
in agony,
empty.
It was my house, and
thirty years ago,
thirty
years. I knock
at the door
of my dreams,
the decayed
walls,
time
was waiting for me,
time
turning
on its wheel.

Aquí,
en la pobre calle
de la isla
me
esperó, todo:
palmeras, arrecifes,
siempre supieron
que yo volvería,
sólo yo no lo supe
y, de pronto,
todo volvió, las mismas
olas en las arenas,
la humedad, el rumor
del baile entre las hojas,
y supe, entonces,
supe
que sí, existí, que no era
mentira mi existencia,
que aquí estaba la casa,
el mar, la ausencia
y tú, amor, a mi lado.

Perdóname la vida,
perdóname las vidas.

Por esta calle
se fue al mar la tristeza.
Y tú y yo llevaremos
en nuestros labios
como un largo beso,
el retrato,
el sonido,
el color palpitante
de la isla,
y ahora, sí,
pasó, pasó

Here,
in the poor street
of the island
it waited for me,
everything:
palm trees, coral reefs,
always knew
I would come back,
only I didn't know
and, suddenly,
everything came back, the same
waves on the sand,
the humidity, the rumor
of dance amid the leaves,
and I knew, then,
I knew
that yes, I existed, my
existence wasn't a lie,
here was the house,
the sea, the absence
and you, my love, at my side.

Forgive my life,
forgive my lives.

Through this street
sadness disappeared into the sea.
And you and I will carry
on our lips
like a long kiss,
the portrait,
the sound,
the palpitating color
of the island,
and now, yes,
the past

el pasado,	is gone, gone,
cerraremos el cofre	we will close the empty
vacío	chest
en donde	where
sólo	only
vivirá todavía	the old
un viejo	smell
olor	or sea and jasmine
de mar y de jazmines.	will still live.

98 / ODE TO JEAN ARTHUR RIMBAUD

Oda a Jean Arthur Rimbaud

TRANSLATED BY ILAN STAVANS

Ahora,
en este octubre
cumplirás
cien años,
desgarrador amigo.
Me permites
hablarte?
Estoy solo,
en mi ventana
el Pacífico rompe
su eterno trueno oscuro.

Es de noche.

La leña que arde arroja
sobre el óvalo
de tu antiguo retrato
un rayo fugitivo.
Eres un niño
de mechones torcidos,
ojos semicerrados,
boca amarga.
Perdóname
que te hable
como soy, como creo
que serías ahora,
te hable de agua marina

Now,
this October
you will turn
a hundred,
harrowing friend.
May I speak
to you?
I'm alone,
through my window
the Pacific breaks
its eternal threatening thunder.

It is night.

The burning firewood casts
a fugitive ray
on the oval
of your old portrait.
You are a child
of twisted locks,
half-shut eyes,
sour mouth.
I apologize
if I talk to you
the way I am, the way
I trust you'd be today,
if I talk of marine water

y de leña que arde,	and burning firewood,
de simples cosas y sencillos seres.	of simple things and simple beings.
Te torturaron	They tortured you
y quemaron tu alma,	and burned your soul,
te encerraron	they imprisoned you
en los muros de Europa	in the walls of Europe
y golpeabas	and furiously
frenético	you banged
las puertas.	the doors.
Y cuando	And when you were
ya pudiste	finally
partir	able to depart
ibas herido,	you were injured,
herido y mudo,	injured and mute,
muerto.	dead.
Muy bien, otros poetas	Quite soon, other poets
dejaron	abandoned
un cuervo, un cisne,	a raven, a swan,
un sauce,	a willow,
un pétalo en la lira,	a lyre's petal,
tú dejaste un fantasma	you left behind a ripped
desgarrado	ghost
que maldice	who curses
y escupe	and spits
y andas	and walks
aún	still
sin rumbo,	directionless,
sin domicilio fijo,	with no fixed address,
sin número,	no number,
por las calles de Europa,	through the streets of Europe,
regresando a Marsella,	returning to Marseille,
con arena africana	with African sand
en los zapatos,	in his shoes,
urgente	urgent
como un escalofrío,	as a shiver,

sediento,
ensangrentado,
con los bolsillos rotos,
desafiante,
perdido,
desdichado.

No es verdad
que te robaste el fuego,
que corrías
con la furia celeste
y con la pedrería
ultravioleta
del infierno,
no es así,
no lo creo,
te negaban
la sencillez, la casa,
la madera,
te rechazaban,
te cerraban puertas,
y volabas entonces,
arcángel iracundo,
a las moradas
de la lejanía,
y moneda a moneda,
sudando y desangrando
tu estatura
querías
acumular el oro
necesario
para la sencillez, para la llave,
para la quieta esposa,
para el hijo,
para la silla tuya,
el pan y la cerveza.

thirsty,
bloody,
with his pockets broken,
defiant,
lost,
wretched.

It is not true
you stole the fire,
you ran
with celestial fury
and with an ultraviolet
chest of stones
from hell,
it is not so,
I don't believe it,
you we denied
simplicity, the house,
wood,
you were rejected,
doors closed on you,
and therefore you flew,
irate archangel,
to remote
lodgings,
and coin by coin,
sweating and bleeding
your height
you wanted
to accumulate the necessary
gold
for simplicity, for the key,
for the virtuous wife,
for the son,
for your chair,
for bread and beer.

En tu tiempo
sobre las telarañas
ancho
como un paraguas
se cerraba el crepúsculo
y el gas parpadeaba
soñoliento.
Por la Commune pasaste,
niño rojo,
y dio tu poesía
llamaradas
que aún suben castigando
las paredes
de los fusilamientos.
Con ojos
de puñal
taladraste
la sombra
carcomida,
la guerra, la errabunda
cruz de Europa.
Por eso hoy, a cien años
de distancia,
te invito
a la sencilla
verdad que no alcanzó
tu frente huracanada,
a América te invito,
a nuestros ríos,
al vapor de la luna
sobre las cordilleras,
a la emancipación
de los obreros,
a la extendida patria
de los pueblos,
al Volga

In your time
over the spiderwebs
wide
as an umbrella
the twilight was shutting down
and oil blinked
drowsily.
You passed by the Commune,
red child,
and your poetry gave
blazes of fire
still ascending while it punishes
the walls
used in executions.
With eyes
like a dagger
you drilled
the decayed
shadow,
war, the wandering
cross of Europe.
That is why today, with a distance
of one hundred years,
I invite you
to the simple
truth unattained
by your hurricane-shaped forehead,
I invite you to America,
to our rivers,
to the breath of the moon
over the cordillera,
to the emancipation
of the workers,
to the extended homeland
of the people,
to the electrified

electrizado
de los racimos y de las espigas,
a cuanto el hombre
conquistó sin misterio,
con la fuerza
y la sangre,
con una mano y otra,
con millones
de manos.

A ti te enloquecieron,
Rimbaud, te condenaron
y te precipitaron
al infierno.
Desertaste la causa
del germen, descubridor
del fuego, sepultaste
la llama
y en la desierta soledad
cumpliste
tu condena.
Hoy es más simple, somos
países, somos
pueblos,
los que garantizamos
el crecimiento de la poesía,
el reparto del pan, el patrimonio
del olvidado. Ahora
no estarías
solitario.

Volga River
with grape bunches and wheat shoots,
to what man
conquered without mystery,
with force
and blood,
with one hand and with the other,
with millions
of hands.

You were driven crazy,
Rimbaud, you were condemned
and hurried
to hell.
You deserted the germ's
cause, discoverer
of fire, you buried
the flame
and in desertlike solitude
you lived out
your sentence.
Today it's simpler, we are
countries, we're
peoples,
guaranteeing
the growth of poetry,
the distribution of bread, the patrimony
of oblivion. Now
you would not be
alone.

99 / ODE TO JUAN TARREA

Oda a Juan Tarrea

TRANSLATED BY ILAN STAVANS

Sí, conoce la América,
Tarrea.
La conoce.
En el desamparado
Perú, saqueó las tumbas.
Al pequeño serrano,
al indio andino,
el protector Tarrea
dio la mano,
pero la retiró con sus anillos.
Arrasó las turquesas.
A Bilbao se fue con las vasijas.
Después
se colgó de Vallejo,
le ayudó a bien morir
y luego puso
un pequeño almacén
de prólogos y epílogos.

Ahora
ha hablado con Pineda.
Es importante.
Algo andará vendiendo.
Ha «descubierto»
el Nuevo Mundo.
Descubramos nosotros
a estos descubridores!

Yes, you know America,
Tarrea.
You know it.
In helpless
Peru, you looted tombs.
Tarrea, protector,
lent his hand
to the small villager,
to the Andean Indian,
but then drew it back with its rings.
He destroyed wealth.
He left for Bilbao with the ships.
Later
he hung from Vallejo,
he was lucky to die
and then he opened
a small store
of prologues and epilogues.

Now
he has spoken with Pineda.
He is important.
He might be selling something.
He has "discovered"
the New World.
Let us discover
those discoverers!

A Pineda, muchacho
de quien leí
en su libro
verdades
y velorios,
ríos ferruginosos,
gente clara,
panes y panaderos,
caminos con caballos,
a nuestro americano
Pineda,
o a otro
desde España con boina
de sotacura y uñas
de prestamista,
Tarrea
llega
a enseñar
lo que es él, lo que soy
y lo que somos.

No sabe nada
pero
nos enseña.
«Así es América.
Éste es Rubén Darío»,
dice
poniendo sobre el mapa
la larga uña de Euzkadi.
Y escribe el pobrecillo
largamente.
Nadie puede leer
lo que repite,
pero incansable
sube
a las revistas,

Of Pineda, a young man
about whom I read
in his book
of truths
and wakes,
ferruginous rivers,
bright people,
breads and bakers,
roads with horses,
to our American
Pineda,
and to another
from Spain with a priest's
beret and moneylender's
nails,
Tarrea
arrives
to teach
what he is, what I am
what we are.

He knows nothing
but
he teaches us.
"America is like this.
This is Rubén Darío,"
he says,
placing on the map
the long nail of Euzkadi.
And the poor little one writes
endlessly.
He can't read
what he spews,
but unwearied
he climbs
toward the magazines,

se descuelga	he unhooks himself
entre los capitolios,	toward the capitols,
resbala	he slides down
desde las academias,	from the academies,
en todas partes	everywhere
sale con su discurso,	he emerges with a speech,
con su berenjenal	with a mess
de vaguedades,	of vagueness,
con su oscilante	with his oscillating
nube	cloud
de tontas teorías,	of foolish theories,
su baratillo viejo	his old junkyard
de saldos metafísicos,	of metaphysical balances,
de seudo magia	of black
negra	pseudo-magic
y de mesiánica	and messianic
quincallería.	trinkets.
Es lo que ahora llevan	This is what they carry around,
por nuestras inocentes	our innocent
poblaciones,	populations:
suplementos,	supplements,
revistas,	magazines,
los últimos	the last
o penúltimos	and next-to-last
filibusteros,	pirates,
y al pobre americano	and the poor American
le muestran	is shown
una inservible y necia	a useless and stubborn
baratija	knickknack
con	of worm
sueños	dreams
de gusano	and lies
o mentiras	of the false Apocalypse,
de falso Apocalipsis,	and they take
y se llevan	Pineda's

el oro	gold,
de Pineda,	the green
el vapor	vapor
verde	of our rivers,
de nuestros ríos,	the harsh
la piel	skin,
pura,	the pure
la sal	salt
de nuestras soledades espaciosas.	of our spacious solitudes.
Tarrea,	Tarrea,
ándate pronto.	go away soon.
No me toques. No toques	Don't touch me. Don't touch
a Darío, no vendas	Darío, don't sell
a Vallejo, no rasques	Vallejo, don't scratch
la rodilla	Neruda's
de Neruda.	knee.
Al español, a la española amamos,	We love Spanish, Spanishness,
a la sencilla gente	the simple people
que trabaja y discurre,	who work and wander,
al hijo luminoso	the luminous child
de la guerra	of the terrible
terrible,	war,
al capitán valiente	we desire
y al labrador	the brave captain
sincero	and the sincere
deseamos. Si quieren	farmer. If they want
roturar tierra o presidir los ríos,	to plow the land and preside over the rivers,
vengan,	come,
sí, vengan ellos,	yes, they should come,
pero	but
tú,	you,
Tarrea, vuelve	Tarrea, go back
a tu cambalache	to your barter
de Bilbao,	in Bilbao,
a la huesa	to the grave
del monasterio pútrido,	of the putrid monastery,

golpea
la puerta del Caudillo,
eres su emanación,
su nimbo negro,
su viudedad vacía.
Vuelve
a tus enterrados, al osario
con ociosos lagartos,
nosotros,
simples
picapedreros, pobres
comedores de manzanas,
constructores
de una casa sencilla,
no queremos
ser descubiertos,
no,
no deseamos
la cháchara perdida
del tonto de ultramar.
Vuélvete ahora
a tu epitafio
atlántico, a la ría
mercantil, marinera,
allí sal con tu cesta
de monólogos
y grita por las calles
a ver si alguien se apiada
y consume
tu melancólica mercadería.
Yo no puedo.

No acepto baratijas.

No puedo
preocuparme de ti, pobre Tarrea.

knock
at the Caudillo's door,
you are his emanation,
his black nimbus,
his vacuous widowhood.
Go back
to your buried, to the ossuary
of idle alligators,
we,
simple
stonecutters, poor
apple eaters,
builders
of a simple house,
don't want
to be discovered,
no,
we don't want
the lost chatter
of the dumb from overseas.
Go back now
to your Atlantic
epitaph, to the merchant's
inlet, sailor,
perform there with your basket
of monologues
and scream on the streets
to see if someone has mercy
and consumes
your melancholy goods.
I cannot.

I don't accept trifles.

I cannot
worry about you, poor Tarrea.

Tengo deberes de hombre.

Y tengo canto
para tanto tiempo
que te aconsejo
ahorres
uña y lengua.

Dura
fue mi madre,
la cordillera andina,
caudaloso
fue el trueno del océano
sobre mi nacimiento,
vivo en mi territorio,
me desangro
en la luz de mi batalla,
hago los muros
de mi propia casa,
contribuyo
a la piedra con mi canto,
y no te necesito,
vendedor
de muertos, capellán
de fantasmas,
pálido sacristán
espiritista,
chalán de mulas muertas,
yo no te doy
vasija
contra baratijo:
yo, para tu desgracia,
he andado, he visto,
canto.

I have a man's duties to fulfill.

I have sung
so long
I advise you
to save
nail and tongue.

My mother
was tough,
the Andean cordillera,
the ocean's thunder
flew
mightily
over my birth,
I live in my domain,
I bleed
in the light of battle,
I shape the walls
of my own home,
I build the stone with my song,
and I don't need you,
seller
of the dead, chaplain
of ghosts,
pale spiritualist
sexton,
dealer in dead mules,
I won't give you
a vessel
for your rubbish:
I, unfortunately for you,
have wandered, have seen,
sing.

100 / ODE TO A LABORATORY TECHNICIAN

Oda al laboratorista

TRANSLATED BY MARGARET SAYERS PEDEN

Hay un hombre
escondido,
mira
con un solo ojo
de cíclope eficiente,
son minúsculas cosas,
sangre,
gotas de agua,
mira
y escribe o cuenta,
allí en la gota
circula el universo,
la vía láctea tiembla
como un pequeño río,
mira
el hombre
y anota,
en la sangre
mínimos puntos rojos,
movedizos
planetas
o invasiones
de fabulosos regimientos blancos,
el hombre
con su ojo
anota,
escribe

An unseen man
sits
peering
with the single eye
of an efficient Cyclops
at minuscule objects,
blood,
drops of water;
he peers,
then writes or counts;
the universe circulates
in the drop,
the Milky Way quivers
like a miniature river,
the man
peers
and makes notes;
in the blood
minute red dots,
orbiting
planets
or invasions
of fabulous white regiments,
the man
with the eye
makes notes,
writes;

allí encerrado	captive there,
el volcán de la vida,	the volcano of life,
la esperma	sperm
con su titilación de firmamento,	with its twinkling firmament,
cómo aparece	a racing,
el rápido tesoro	vibrating
tembloroso,	treasure,
las semillitas de hombre,	the tiny seeds of man;
luego	then
en su círculo pálido	on his colorless disk
una gota	a drop
de orina	of urine
muestra países de ámbar	reveals amber lands,
o en tu carne	or in your flesh,
montañas de amatista,	amethyst mountains,
temblorosas praderas,	trembling meadows,
constelaciones verdes,	green constellations,
pero	but he only
él anota, escribe,	makes notes, writes,
descubre	discovers
una amenaza,	a threat,
un punto	a divided
dividido,	pinpoint,
un nimbo negro,	a black nimbus,
lo identifica, encuentra	he identifies it, checks
su prontuario,	his manual,
ya no puede escaparse,	it can't escape now,
pronto	soon
en tu cuerpo será la cacería,	the hunt will be in your body,
la batalla	the battle
que comenzó en el ojo	that began in the eye
del laboratorista:	of the technician:
será de noche, junto	it will be night, beside
a la madre la muerte,	the mother, death,
junto al niño las alas	beside the child, the wings

del invisible espanto,
la batalla en la herida,
todo
comenzó
con el hombre
y su ojo
que buscaba
en el cielo
de la sangre
una estrella maligna.
Allí con blusa blanca
sigue
buscando
el signo,
el número,
el color
de la muerte
o la vida,
descifrando
la textura
del dolor, descubriendo
la insignia de la fiebre
o el primer síntoma
del crecimiento humano.

Luego
el descubridor
desconocido,
el hombre
que viajó por tus venas
o denunció
un viajero enmascarado
en el sur o en el norte
de tus vísceras,
el temible
hombre con ojo

of invisible terror,
the battle in the wound,
everything
began
with the man
and the eye
that sought
in the sky
of blood
a malignant star.
There in his white coat
he continues
searching
for the sign,
the number,
the color,
of death
or life,
deciphering
the texture
of pain, discovering
the emblem of fever,
of the first symptom
of human growth.

Then
the undiscovered
discoverer,
the man
who voyaged through your veins,
or reported
a masked invader
in the South or North
of your viscera,
the fearsome
man with the eye

descuelga su sombrero,
se lo pone,
enciende un cigarrillo
y entra en la calle,
se mueve, se desprende,
se reparte en las calles,
se agrega a la espesura de los hombres,
por fin desaparece
como el dragón
el diminuto y circulante monstruo
que se quedó olvidado en una gota
en el laboratorio.

removes his hat from a peg,
dons it,
lights a cigarette,
and steps outside,
moves, breaks away,
is pumped through the streets,
assimilated into the crowds,
and finally disappears
like the dragon,
the diminutive and circulating monster,
left forgotten in a drop
in the laboratory.

101 / ODE WITH A LAMENT

Oda con un lamento

TRANSLATED BY DONALD D. WALSH

Oh niña entre las rosas, oh presión de palomas,
oh presidio de peces y rosales,
tu alma es una botella llena de sal sedienta
y una campana llena de uvas es tu piel.

Por desgracia no tengo para darte sino uñas
o pestañas, o pianos derretidos,
o sueños que salen de mi corazón a borbotones,
polvorientos sueños que corren como jinetes negros,
sueños llenos de velocidades y desgracias.

Sólo puedo quererte con besos y amapolas,
con guirnaldas mojadas por la lluvia,
mirando cenicientos caballos y perros amarillos.
Sólo puedo quererte con olas a la espalda,
entre vagos golpes de azufre y aguas ensimismadas,

Oh girl among the roses, oh crush of doves,
oh fortress of fishes and rosebushes,
your soul is a bottle filled with thirsty salt
and your skin a bell filled with grapes.

Unfortunately I have only fingernails to give you,
or eyelashes, or melted pianos,
or dreams that come spurting from my heart,
dusty dreams that run like black horsemen,
dreams filled with velocities and misfortunes.

I can love you only with kisses and poppies,
with garlands wet by the rain,
looking at ash-gray horses and yellow dogs.
I can love you only with waves at my back,
amid vague sulfur blows and brooding waters,

nadando en contra de los cementerios que corren en ciertos ríos
con pasto mojado creciendo sobre las tristes tumbas de yeso,
nadando a través de corazones sumergidos
y pálidas planillas de niños insepultos.

Hay mucha muerte, muchos acontecimientos funerarios
en mis desamparadas pasiones y desolados besos,
hay el agua que cae en mi cabeza,
mientras crece mi pelo,
un agua como el tiempo, un agua negra desencadenada,
con una voz nocturna, con un grito
de pájaro en la lluvia, con una interminable
sombra de ala mojada que protege mis huesos:
mientras me visto, mientras
interminablemente me miro en los espejos y en los vidrios,
oigo que alguien me sigue llamándome a sollozos
con una triste voz podrida por el tiempo.

Tú estás de pie sobre la tierra, llena
de dientes y relámpagos.
Tú propagas los besos y matas las hormigas.
Tú lloras de salud, de cebolla, de abeja,
de abecedario ardiendo.
Tú eres como una espada azul y verde
y ondulas al tocarte, como un río.

swimming against the cemeteries that run in certain rivers
with wet fodder growing over the sad plaster tombs,
swimming across submerged hearts
and pale lists of unburied children.

There is much death, many funereal events
in my forsaken passions and desolate kisses,
there is the water that falls upon my head,
while my hair grows,
a water like time, a black unchained water,
with a nocturnal voice, with a shout
of birds in the rain, with an interminable
wet-winged shadow that protects my bones:
while I dress, while
interminably I look at myself in mirrors and windowpanes,
I hear someone who follows me, sobbing to me
with a sad voice rotted by time.

You stand upon the earth, filled
with teeth and lightning.
You spread the kisses and kill the ants.
You weep with health, with onion, with bee,
with burning abacus.
You are like a blue and green sword
and you ripple, when I touch you, like a river.

Ven a mi alma vestida de blanco, con un ramo
de ensangrentadas rosas y copas de cenizas,
ven con una manzana y un caballo,
porque allí hay una sala oscura y un candelabro
roto,
unas sillas torcidas que esperan el invierno,
y una paloma muerta, con un número.

Come to my heart dressed in white,
with a bouquet
of bloody roses and goblets of ashes,
come with an apple and a horse,
because there is a dark room there and
a broken candleholder,
some twisted chairs waiting for winter,
and a dead dove, with a number.

102 / ODE TO A LARGE TUNA IN THE MARKET

Oda a un gran atún en el mercado

TRANSLATED BY MARGARET SAYERS PEDEN

En el mercado verde,	Among the market greens,
bala	a bullet
del profundo	from the ocean
océano,	depths,
proyectil	a swimming
natatorio,	projectile,
te vi,	I saw you,
muerto.	dead.
Todo a tu alrededor	All around you
eran lechugas,	were lettuces,
espuma	sea foam
de la tierra,	of the earth,
zanahorias,	carrots,
racimos,	grapes,
pero	but
de la verdad	of the ocean
marina,	truth,
de lo desconocido,	of the unknown,
de la	of the
insondable	unfathomable
sombra,	shadow, the
agua	depths
profunda,	of the sea,
abismo,	the abyss,

sólo tú sobrevivías
alquitranado, barnizado,
testigo
de la profunda noche.

Sólo tú, bala oscura
del abismo,
certera,
destruida
sólo en un punto,
siempre
renaciendo,
anclando en la corriente
sus aladas aletas,
circulando
en la velocidad,
en el transcurso
de
la
sombra
marina
como enlutada flecha,
dardo del mar,
intrépida aceituna.

Muerto te vi,
difunto rey
de mi propio océano,
ímpetu
verde, abeto
submarino,
nuez
de los maremotos,
allí,
despojo muerto,
en el mercado

only you had survived,
a pitch-black, varnished
witness
to deepest night.

Only you, well-aimed
dark bullet
from the abyss,
mangled
at one tip,
but constantly
reborn,
at anchor in the current,
winged fins
windmilling
in the swift
flight
of
the
marine
shadow,
a mourning arrow,
dart of the sea,
olive, oily fish.

I saw you dead,
a deceased king
of my own ocean,
green
assault, silver
submarine fir,
seed
of seaquakes,
now
only dead remains,
yet

era
sin embargo
tu forma
lo único dirigido
entre
la confusa derrota
de la naturaleza:
entre la verdura frágil
estabas
solo como una nave,
armado
entre legumbres,
con ala y proa negras y aceitadas,
como si aún tú fueras
la embarcación del viento,
la única
y pura
máquina
marina:
intacta navegando
las aguas de la muerte.

in all the market
yours
was the only
purposeful form
amid
the bewildering rout
of nature;
amid the fragile greens
you were
a solitary ship,
armed
among the vegetables,
fin and prow black and oiled,
as if you were still
the vessel of the wind,
the one and only
pure
ocean
machine:
unflawed, navigating
the waters of death.

103 / ODE TO THE LAST VOYAGE OF *LA BRETONA*

Oda al último viaje de "La Bretona"

TRANSLATED BY ILAN STAVANS

La barca se quebró contra la roca,
una pequeña barca
de formación errante,
la curva de una quilla que fue nube,
un pecho de paloma marinera.

El mar alzó su brío
y trituró la forma,
fue sólo un haz de espuma,
un rayo de magnolia que golpeaba
y allí quedó el despojo
de la despedazada vencedora:
cuatro tablas heridas
pequeñas como plumas
y junto a las inmóviles maderas
la eternidad del mar en movimiento.

Mi amigo las condujo
a su elevada casa sobre el monte
y un alto fuego coronó la muerte
de la pequeña embarcación amada.
Una por una las tablas reunidas,
aquellas que absorbieron
la libertad marina,
ardieron en la noche,

The boat smashed against the rock,
a small boat
of nomadic formation,
the curve of a keel that was cloud,
a marine dove's breast.

The sea raised its verve
and crushed the form,
it was barely a beam of foam,
a beating ray of magnolia
and the debris of the shattered conqueror
gathered there:
four injured tablets
small like feathers
and near the motionless wood
the eternity of sea in its movement.

My friend took them
to his elevated house on the hill
and a strong fire crowed the death
of the small beloved ship.
One by one the reunited tablets,
those absorbing
marine freedom,
burned at night,

y allí de pronto	and suddenly, right there
se hicieron milagro:	they became a miracle:
con un extraño azul se despidieron,	they said goodbye in a strange blue,
con un anaranjado indescriptible,	in an indescribable orange,
con lenguas de agua verde que salían	in tongues of green water emerging there,
a devolver la sal que consumieron.	seeking to return the salt they once consumed.
Y nos quedamos mudos:	And we were mute:
era la última fiesta,	it was the last fiesta,
la luz mortal de la pequeña nave	the small vessel's mortal light
que allí partía desplegando su alma.	departing then while unfolding its soul.
Y así fue su postrer navegación:	And thus it began its last voyage:
así se fue alejando y encendiendo	the ship began to move away,
con fosfóricos fuegos extraviados	the mortal light of the small craft
en el viaje final su arboladura.	in its final journey of masts and spars.

104 / ODE TO LAZINESS

Oda a la pereza

TRANSLATED BY WILLIAM CARLOS WILLIAMS

Ayer sentí que la oda
no subía del suelo.
Era hora, debía
por lo menos
mostrar una hoja verde.
Rosqué la tierra: «Sube,
hermana oda
—le dije—,
te tengo prometida,
no me tengas miedo,
no voy a triturarte,
oda de cuatro hojas,
oda de cuatro manos,
tomarás té conmigo.
Sube,
te voy a coronar entre las odas,
saldremos juntos, por la orilla
del mar, en bicicleta».
Fue inútil.

Entonces,
en lo alto de los pinos,
la pereza
apareció desnuda,
me llevó deslumbrado
y soñoliento,
me descubrió en la arena

Yesterday I felt this ode
would not get off the floor.
It was time, I ought
at least
show a green leaf.
I scratch the earth: "Arise,
sister ode
—said to her—
I have promised you,
do not be afraid of me,
I am not going to crush you,
four-leaf ode,
four-hand ode,
you shall have tea with me.
Arise,
I am going to crown you among the odes,
we shall go out together along the shores
of the sea, on a bicycle."
It was no use.

Then,
on the pine peaks,
laziness
appeared in the nude,
she led me dazzled
and sleepy,
she showed me upon the sand

pequeños trozos rotos
de substancias oceánicas,
maderas, algas, piedras,
plumas de aves marinas.
Busqué sin encontrar
ágatas amarillas.
El mar
llenaba los espacios
desmoronando torres,
invadiendo
las costas de mi patria,
avanzando
sucesivas catástrofes de espuma.
Sola en la arena
abría un rayo
una corola.
Vi cruzar los petreles plateados
y como cruces negras
los cormoranes
clavados en las rocas.
Liberté una abeja
que agonizaba en un velo de araña,
metí una piedrecita
en un bolsillo,
era suave, suavísima
como un pecho de pájaro,
mientras tanto en la costa,
toda la tarde,
lucharon sol y niebla.
A veces
la niebla se impregnaba
de luz
como un topacio,
otras veces caía
un rayo de sol húmedo
dejando caer gotas amarillas.

small broken bits
of ocean substance,
wood, algae, pebbles,
feathers of sea birds.
I looked for but did not find
yellow agates.
The sea
filled all spaces
crumbling towers,
invading
the shores of my country,
advancing
successive catastrophes of the foam.
Alone on the sand
a ray spread wide
its corolla.
I saw the silvery petrels crossing
and like black creases
the cormorants
nailed to the rocks.
I released a bee
that was agonizing in a spider's net.
I put a little pebble
in my pocket,
it was smooth, very smooth
as the breast of a bird,
meanwhile on the shore,
all afternoon
sun struggled with a mist.
At times
the mist was steeped
in thought,
topaz-like,
at others fell
a ray from the moist sun
distilling yellow drops.

En la noche,
pensando en los deberes de mi oda
fugitiva,
me saqué los zapatos
junto al fuego,
resbaló arena de ellos
y pronto fui quedándome
dormido.

At night,
thinking of the duties
of my fugitive ode,
I pull off my shoes
near the fire;
sand slid out of them
and soon I began to fall
asleep.

105 / ODE TO THE LEMON

Oda al limón

TRANSLATED BY STEPHEN MITCHELL

De aquellos azahares	From those flowers
desatados	loosened
por la luz de la luna,	by the moon's light,
de aquel	from that
olor de amor	smell of exasperated
exasperado,	love,
hundido en la fragancia,	sunk in fragrance,
salió	yellow
del limonero el amarillo,	emerged from the lemon tree,
desde su planetario	from its planetarium
bajaron a la tierra los limones.	lemons came down to the earth.
Tierna mercadería!	Tender merchandise!
Se llenaron las costas,	The coasts, the markets
los mercados,	filled up
de luz, de oro	with light, with barbaric
silvestre,	gold,
y abrimos	and we opened
dos mitades	two halves
de milagro,	of a miracle,
ácido congelado	congealed acid
que corría	that ran
desde los hemisferios	from the hemispheres
de una estrella,	of a star,
y el licor más profundo	and nature's most intense
de la naturaleza,	liqueur,
intransferible, vivo,	unchanging, alive,

irreductible,
nació de la frescura
del limón,
de su casa fragante,
de su ácida, secreta simetría.

En el limón cortaron
los cuchillos
una pequeña
catedral,
el ábside escondido
abrió a la luz los ácidos vitrales
y en gotas
resbalaron los topacios,
los altares,
la fresca arquitectura.

Así, cuando tu mano
empuña el hemisferio
del cortado
limón sobre tu plato,
un universo de oro
derramaste,
una
copa amarilla
con milagros,
uno de los pezones olorosos
del pecho de la tierra,
el rayo de la luz que se hizo fruta,
el fuego diminuto de un planeta.

irreducible,
was born from that coolness
of the lemon,
from its fragrant house,
from its acid and secret symmetry.

In the lemon
knives cut
a small
cathedral,
the hidden apse
opened acid windows
to the light
and drops poured out
the topazes,
the altars,
the cool architecture.

So, when your hand
grasps the hemisphere
of the cut
lemon above your plate
you spill
a universe of gold,
a
goblet yellow
with miracles,
one of the aromatic nipples
of the earth's breast,
the ray of light that became fruit,
a planet's minuscule fire.

106 / ODE TO LENIN

Oda a Lenin

TRANSLATED BY ILAN STAVANS

La revolución tiene 40 años. Tiene la edad de una joven madura. Tiene la edad de las madres hermosas.	*The revolution turns forty.* *It has the age of a ripe young woman.* *It has the age of the beautiful mothers.*
Cuando nació, en el mundo la noticia se supo en forma diferente.	*When it was born,* *the news spread* *in different ways* *around the world.*
—Qué es esto? —se preguntaban los obispos— se ha movido la tierra, no podremos seguir vendiendo cielo. Los gobiernos de Europa, de América ultrajada, los dictadores turbios, leían en silencio las alarmantes comunicaciones. Por suaves, por profundas escaleras subía un telegrama, como sube la fiebre en el termómetro: ya no cabía duda, el pueblo había vencido, se transformaba el mundo.	*"What is this?" asked the priests.* *"The earth has moved,* *we can no longer continue selling heaven."* *The governments of Europe,* *of an abused America,* *the shady dictators,* *read in silence* *the alarming communiqués.* *Through soft, through deep* *staircases* *a telegraph ascended,* *as the earthquake* *fever ascends:* *no more room for doubt,* *the people were victorious,* *the world was being transformed.*

I

Lenin, para cantarte
debo decir adiós a las palabras;
debo escribir con árboles, con ruedas,
con arados, con cereales.
Eres concreto como
los hechos y la tierra.
No existió nunca
un hombre más terrestre
que V. Uliánov.
Hay otros hombres altos
que como las iglesias acostumbran
conversar con las nubes,
son altos hombres solitarios.

Lenin sostuvo un pacto con la tierra.

Vio más lejos que nadie.
Los hombres,
los ríos, las colinas,
las estepas,
eran un libro abierto
y él leía,
leía más lejos que todos,
más claro que ninguno.
Él miraba profundo
en el pueblo, en el hombre,
miraba al hombre como a un pozo,
lo examinaba como
si fuera un mineral desconocido
que hubiera descubierto.
Había que sacar las aguas del pozo,
había que elevar la luz dinámica,
el tesoro secreto
de los pueblos,

I

Lenin, to sing to you
I must say farewell to words:
I must write with trees, with wheels,
with plows, with cereals.
You are concrete
as facts and earth.
There never was
a more earthly man
than V. Ulyanov.
There are other imposing men
who like churches are used to
conversing with the clouds,
they are tall, solitary men.

Lenin made a pact with the earth.

He came from farther away than anyone.
Men,
rivers, hills,
steppes,
were an open book
and he read,
read farther than anyone,
clearer than anyone.
He looked deeply
into the people, into man,
admired man like a well,
examined him as
if he were an unknown mineral
he had discovered.
Water needed to be taken from the well,
the dynamic light needed to be elevated,
the secret treasure
of the people,

para que todo germinara y naciera,
para ser dignos del tiempo y de la tierra.

so everything germinated and hatched,
to be worthy of time and earth.

II

Cuidad de confundirlo con un frío ingeniero,
cuidad de confundirlo con un místico ardiente.
Su inteligencia ardió sin ser jamás cenizas,
la muerte no ha helado aún su corazón de fuego.

II

Beware of confusing him with a frigid
engineer,
beware of confusing him with an
ardent mystic.
His intelligence blazed without
becoming ashes,
death has yet to freeze his heart of fire.

III

Me gusta ver a Lenin pescando en la
transparencia
del lago Razliv, y aquellas aguas son
como un pequeño espejo perdido entre
la hierba
del vasto norte frío y plateado:
soledades aquellas, hurañas soledades,
plantas martirizadas por la noche y la nieve,
el ártico silbido del viento en su cabaña.
Me gusta verlo allí solitario escuchando
el aguacero, el tembloroso vuelo
de las tórtolas,
la intensa pulsación del bosque puro.
Lenin atento al bosque y a la vida,
escuchando los pasos del viento y de la
historia
en la solemnidad de la naturaleza.

III

I like seeing Lenin fishing in the
clearness
of Lake Lakhta, and those waters are
like a small mirror lost amid the grass
of the vast, cold, organized north:
those solitudes, disdainful solitudes,
processing plants martyred by night
and snow,
the arctic whistle of the wind in its
cabin.
I like seeing him there alone listening
to the rain shower, the trembling flight
of turtledoves,
the intense pulsation of the pristine
forest.
Lenin attentive to the forest and life,
listening to the wind's steps and to
history
in the solemnity of nature.

IV

Fueron algunos hombres sólo estudio,
libro profundo, apasionada ciencia,
y otros hombres tuvieron
como virtud del alma el movimiento.
Lenin tuvo dos alas:
el movimiento y la sabiduría.
Creó en el pensamiento,
descifró los enigmas,
fue rompiendo las máscaras
de la verdad y el hombre
y estaba en todas partes,
estaba al mismo tiempo en todas partes.

IV

Some men were only good for studying,
deep book, passionate science,
and other men had
as their virtue the soul of the movement.
Lenin had two wings:
wisdom and the movement.
He created by means of thought,
deciphered enigmas,
went on breaking the masks
of truth and man
and was everywhere,
was simultaneously in all places.

V

Así, Lenin, tus manos trabajaron
y tu razón no conoció el descanso
hasta que desde todo el horizonte
se divisó una nueva forma:
era una estatua ensangrentada,
era una victoriosa con harapos,
era una niña bella como la luz,
llena de cicatrices, manchada por el humo.
Desde remotas tierras los pueblos la miraron:
era ella, no cabía duda,
era la Revolución.

El viejo corazón del mundo latió de otra manera.

V

So, Lenin, your labored hands
and mind didn't know rest
until from the horizon's other side
a new shape was discerned:
it was a bleeding statue,
victorious in its rags,
a girl beautiful as light,
full of scars, stained with smoke.
From faraway lands people looked at her:
it was her, no doubt,
it was the revolution.

The world's old heart beat in a different way.

VI

Lenin, hombre terrestre,
tu hija ha llegado al cielo.
Tu mano
mueve ahora
claras constelaciones.
La misma mano
que firmó decretos
sobre el pan y la tierra
para el pueblo,
la misma mano
se convirtió en planeta:
el hombre que tú hiciste me construyó
una estrella.

VI

Lenin, earthly man,
your daughter has reached the sky.
Your hand
moves now
tidy constellations.
The same hand
signing decrees
for the people
about bread and land,
the same hand
became a planet:
the man you forged built me a star.

VII

Todo ha cambiado, pero
fue duro el tiempo
y ásperos los días.
Durante cuarenta años aullaron
los lobos junto a las fronteras:
quisieron derribar la estatua viva,
quisieron calcinar sus ojos verdes,
por hambre y fuego
y gas y muerte
quisieron que muriera
tu hija, Lenin,
la victoria,
la extensa, firme, dulce, fuerte y alta
Unión Soviética.

No pudieron.
Faltó el pan, el carbón,

VII

Everything has changed, but
time was harsh
and the days rough.
For forty years wolves
howled near the borders:
they wanted to demolish the living statue,
they wanted to burn its green eyes,
because of hunger and fire
and gas and death
they wanted your daughter
to die, Lenin,
the extensive, firm, sweet, strong and
elevated
victory,
the Soviet Union.

They could not.
Bread was missing, coal,

faltó la vida,
del cielo cayó lluvia, nieve, sangre,
sobre las pobres casas incendiadas,
pero entre el humo
y a la luz del fuego
los pueblos más remotos vieron la estatua viva
defenderse y crecer crecer crecer
hasta que su valiente corazón
se transformó en metal invulnerable.

life was missing,
rain fell from the sky, snow, blood,
over the poor burned houses,
but amid the smoke
and in the light of fire
the most remote people saw the living
statue
defend itself and grow grow grow
until its courageous heart
became invulnerable metal.

VIII

Lenin, gracias te damos los lejanos.
Desde entonces, desde tus decisiones,
desde tus pasos rápidos y tus rápidos ojos
no están los pueblos solos
en la lucha por la alegría.
La inmensa patria dura,
la que aguantó el asedio,
la guerra, la amenaza,
es torre inquebrantable.
Ya no pueden matarla.
Y así viven los hombres
otra vida,
y comen otro pan
con esperanza,
porque en el centro de la tierra existe
la hija de Lenin, clara y decisiva.

VIII

Lenin, we who are far away thank you.
Since then, since your decision,
since your quick steps and quick eyes
the people aren't alone
in the struggle for happiness.
The immense harsh homeland,
the one bearing the siege,
war, the threat,
is an unbreakable tower.
They can't kill it anymore.
And thus men live
another life,
and eat another bread
with hope,
because at the center of the earth is
Lenin's daughter, clear and decisive.

IX

Gracias, Lenin,
por la energía y la enseñaza,

IX

Thank you, Lenin,
for the energy and the teachings,

gracias por la firmeza,
gracias por Leningrado y las estepas,
gracias por la batalla y por la paz,
gracias por el trigo infinito,
gracias por las escuelas,
gracias por tus pequeños
titánicos soldados,
gracias por este aire que respiro en tu tierra
que no se parece a otro aire:
es espacio fragante,
es electricidad de enérgicas montañas.

Gracias, Lenin,
por el aire y el pan y la esperanza.

thank you for the firmness,
thank you for Leningrad and the steppes,
thank you for the battle and for peace,
thank you for the infinite wheat,
thank you for the schools,
thank you for the little
titanic soldiers,
thank you for the air I breathe in your land
unlike all other air:
it is fragrant space,
it is electricity of energetic mountains.

Thank you, Lenin,
for the air and the bread and the hope.

107 / ODE TO LENINGRAD

Oda a Leningrado

TRANSLATED BY ILAN STAVANS

Suave tu piedra pura,	Soft is your pristine stone,
ancho tu cielo blanco,	wide your white sky,
hermosa	beautiful
rosa gris, espaciosa	gray rose, spacious
Leningrado,	Leningrad.
con qué tranquilidad	With what tranquillity
puse en tu antigua tierra	I set my shoes
mis zapatos,	on your ancient land,
de otra tierra	they came from
venían,	another land,
de la virgen América,	from virginal America,
mis pies habían pisado	my feet had stepped over
lodo de manantiales	elevated
en la altura,	wells of mud,
fragancias indecibles	unspeakable fragrances
en la gran cordillera	in the grand cordillera
de mi patria,	of my country,
habían	my shoes
tocado mis zapatos	had touched
otra nieve,	another snow,
las ráfagas	the gusts
de los Andes hirsutos	of the wiry Andes.
y ahora,	And now,
Leningrado,	Leningrad,
tu nieve,	your snow,
tu ilustre	your illustrious
sombra blanca,	white shadow,

el río con sus gradas sumergiéndose
en la corriente blanca,
la luz como una rama de durazno
dándote su blancura,
oh nave,
nave blanca,
navegando en invierno,
cuántas cosas
vivieron,
se movieron
conmigo
cuando entre tus cordajes
y tus velas de piedra
anduve,
cuando pisé las calles
que conocí en los libros,
me saturó la esencia
de la niebla y los mares,
el joven Pushkin
me tomó de la mano
con su mano enguantada
y en las solemnes edificaciones
del pasado,
en las colmenas
de la nueva vida,
entró mi corazón
americano
latiendo con respeto
y alegría,
escuchando los ecos
de mis pasos
como si despertaran
existencias
que dormían envueltas en la nieve
y de pronto vinieran
a caminar conmigo

the river with its steps submerged
in white current,
light like a peach branch
granting you whiteness,
oh ship,
white ship,
sailing in winter,
how many things
they did live through,
they moved
with me
when I wandered
amid your strings
and your stone sails,
when I stepped on the streets
I knew from books,
I became saturated with the essence
of fog and seas,
the young Pushkin
held me by the hand
with his gloved hand
and in solemn edifications
of the past,
in the hives
of our life,
my American heart
entered
beating with respect
and happiness,
hearing the echoes
of my steps
as if they awakened
lives
dormant while wrapped in snow
and suddenly came
to walk with me

pisando fuertemente en el silencio	stepping forcefully on silence
como sobre las tablas de un navío.	as if on a ship's planks.
Cuántas	How many
antiguas noches,	ancient nights,
allá lejos:	at a distance:
mi libro,	my book,
la lluvia	the rain
desde el cielo de la isla,	from the island sky
en Chiloé marino,	in marine Chiloé,
y ahora	and, now,
la misma	the same
sombra blanca	white shadow
acompañándome,	accompanying me,
Netochka Nezvanova,	Netochka Nezvanova,
la Perspectiva Nevsky,	Nevsky Avenue,
ancha, durmiendo,	wide, somnolent,
un coro ahogado	a drowned choir
y un violín perdido.	and a lost violin.
Antiguo tiempo, antiguo	Ancient time, ancient
dolor blanco,	white pain,
terribles seres de otra	terrible beings of another
ciudad, que aquí vivían,	city, who lived here,
tormentos desangrados,	sordid torments,
pálida	pale
rosa	rose
de neblina y nieve,	of fog and snow,
Netochka Nezvanova,	Netochka Nezvanova,
un insensato	a senseless
movimiento	movement
en la niebla,	in the fog,
en la nieve,	in the snow,
entrecortados	faltering
sufrimientos,	sufferings,
las vidas	lives
como pozos,	like wells,

el alma,	the soul,
el alma,	the soul,
ciénaga	marsh
de peces ciegos,	of blind fish,
el alma,	the soul,
lago	lake
de alcoholes dormidos,	of dormant alcohols,
de pronto	suddenly
enloquecidas	mad
ventanas	windows
delirando	delirious
en la noche,	at night,
sonatas	sonatas
de una sola cuerda	of a single string
enroscándose	curling up
a la cola	in the devil's
del diablo,	tail,
crímenes	crimes
largamente contados	long-told
y contados.	and retold.
Honor al alba fría!	Honor the cold daybreak!
Cambió el mundo!	The world changed!
Es de noche,	It is night,
clara	clear
soledad nocturna,	nocturnal solitude,
mañana	tomorrow
el día	the day
se poblará de cantos	will be populated with songs
y rostros encendidos,	and burning faces,
de seres	of beings
que navegan	who sail
en la nave	in the ship
de la nueva	of the new
alegría,	happiness,
de manos que golpean	of hands banging
los ardientes talleres,	the feverish workshops,

de blusas que acrecientan
la luz blanca,
de asuntos compartidos
como los panes de oro
por escuelas unánimes,
es eso,
ahora
los seres solitarios
de los libros
vienen a acompañarme
pero
la soledad no viene,
no existe,
arden
en la corola
de la vida,
viven
la organizada
dignidad
del trabajo,
la antigua angustia
separó sus hojas
como un árbol que el viento
inclinó, rechazando
la tormenta,
ahora
el caballo de bronce,
el caballero,
no están a punto de emprender el viaje,
regresaron,
el Neva no se va,
viene llegando
con noticias de oro,
con sílabas de plata.
Se fueron
los antiguos

of shirts amplifying
the white light,
of shared issues
like the breads of gold
through the unanimous followings,
that is it,
now,
the lonely beings
in the books
arrive to accompany me
but
solitude is not here,
it doesn't exist,
they burn
in the corolla
of life,
live
the organized
dignity
of labor,
the ancient angst
separated their pages
like a tree tilted
by the wind, rejecting
the storm,
now
the bronze horse,
the knight,
are not about to start the journey,
they return,
the Neva is not going,
it is arriving
with news of gold,
with syllables of silver.
The ancient
characters

personajes
enfundados
en niebla,
provistos de elevados
sombreros de humo,
las mujeres
talladas en la nieve
llorando en un pañuelo
sobre el río,
emigraron,
cayeron de los libros
y corrieron
los estudiantes locos
que esperaban
con un hacha en la mano
a la puerta
de una anciana,
aquel mundo
de frenéticos popes
y carcajadas muertas en la copa,
trineos
que raptaban la inocencia,
sangre y lobos oscuros en la nieve,
todo aquello
se cayó de los libros,
se fugó de la vida
como un maligno sueño,
ahora
las cúpulas deslizan
el anillo
de la luna creciente,
y otra vez una noche
clarísima
navega
junto con la ciudad,
subieron

sheathed
in fog
have left,
parading elevated
hats of smoke,
the women
carved in snow
crying on a handkerchief
on the river,
they emigrated,
fell from the books
and the crazed
students
waiting
ax in hand
at the old lady's door
ran,
that world
of frantic popes
and laughter dead in a cup,
sleds
kidnapping innocence,
blood and black wolves in the snow,
all that
fell from the books,
it ran away from life
like a bad dream,
now
the cupolas slide
the ring
of the crescent moon
and again the clearest
night
sails
near the city,
they brought up

las dos pesadas anclas
a los portones del Almirantazgo,
navega Leningrado,
aquellas sombras
se dispersaron, frías,
asustadas,
cuando en la escalinata
del Palacio de Invierno,
subió la Historia
con los pies del pueblo.
Más tarde a la ciudad
llegó la guerra,
la guerra con sus dientes
desmoronando
la belleza antigua,
glotona,
comiéndose una torta
de piedra gris y nieve
y sangre,
la guerra
silbando entre los muros,
llevándose a los hombres,
acechando a los hijos,
la guerra
con su saco vacío
y su tambor terrible,
la guerra
con los vidrios quebrados
y la muerte
en la cama,
rígida bajo el frío.
Y el valor alto,
más alto que un abeto,
redondo
como las graves cúpulas,
erguido

the two heavy anchors
to the great doors of the admiralty,
Leningrad sails,
the shadows
disperse, cold,
frightened,
when on the Winter Palace
staircase
History ascended
with the people's feet.
Later on, war came
to the city,
war with its teeth
demolishing
the ancient model of beauty,
gluttonous,
eating a cake
of gray stone and snow
and blood,
war
whistling amid the walls,
taking men away,
spying on children,
war
with its empty sack
and terrible drum,
war
with broken glasses
and death
in bed,
stiff under the cold.
And the high valor,
higher than a fir tree,
round,
like grave cupolas,
erected

como
las serenas columnas,
la resistencia
grave
como la simetría
de la piedra,
el coraje
como una llama viva
en medio
de la nieve
fue
una hoguera
indomable,
en Leningrado
el corazón
soviético.
Y hoy todo vive
y duerme,
la noche
de Leningrado cubre
no sólo
los palacios,
las verjas enrejadas,
las cornisas platónicas,
el esplendor antiguo,
no sólo
los motores
y las innumerables
casas frescas,
la vida
justa y ancha,
la construcción del mundo,
la noche, sombra clara
se unió a la antigua noche,
como el día,
como el olor del agua,

like
serene columns,
the grave
resistance
like symmetry
of stone,
courage
like a living flame
amid
the snow
was
an indomitable
bonfire,
in Leningrad,
the Soviet
heart.
And today everything lives
and sleeps,
the Leningrad
night covers
not only
the palaces,
the fenced iron gates,
the Platonic cornices,
the ancient splendor,
not only
the engines
and the countless
new homes,
life
far and wide,
the construction of the world,
night, clear shadow,
joined the ancient night,
like the day,
like the smell of water,

Pedro el Gigante y Lenin
el Gigante
se hicieron
unidad,
el tiempo
hizo una rosa,
una torre invencible.
Huele
a fuego
enterrado,
a flor inquebrantable,
circula por las calles
viva sangre sin tiempo,
lo que fue
y lo que viene
se unieron
en la rosa espaciosa,
y navega
la nave,
perfuma
la torre gris del Norte,
ancha y celeste, firme
en su reino de nieve,
poblada no por sombras
sino por la grandeza
de su sangre,
coronada
por el rumor marino
de su Historia,
brillando con orgullo, preparada
con toda su belleza
como un salón ilustre
para las reuniones de su pueblo.

Peter the Great and Lenin
the Great
became
a unit,
time
became a rose,
the invincible tower.
It smells
like buried
fire,
unbreakable flower,
circulates on the streets
the living, timeless blood,
what was
and what will be
became
one
in the spacious rose,
and the ship
sails,
it perfumes the gray tower of the north,
wide and celestial, firm
in its reign of snow,
populated not by shadows
but by the grandeur
of its blood,
crowned
by the marine rumor
of History,
shining with pride, prepared
with all its beauty
like an elegant salon
for its peoples' gatherings.

108 / ODE TO LIFE

Oda a la vida

TRANSLATED BY ILAN STAVANS

La noche entera
con una hacha
me ha golpeado el dolor,
pero el sueño
pasó lavando como un agua oscura
piedras ensangrentadas.
Hoy de nuevo estoy vivo.
De nuevo
te levanto,
vida,
sobre mis hombros.

Oh vida,
copa clara,
de pronto
te llenas
de agua sucia,
de vino muerto,
de agonía, de pérdidas,
de sobrecogedoras telarañas,
y muchos creen
que ese color de infierno
guardarás para siempre.

No es cierto.

Pasa una noche lenta,
pasa una solo minuto

The whole night,
armed with an ax,
has overwhelmed me with grief,
but the dream
passed by washing, like dark water,
bloodied stones.
Today I am alive again.
Again
I wake you,
life,
on my shoulders,

Oh life,
clear cup,
suddenly
you fill up
with dirty water,
with dead wine,
with agony, with losses,
with overhanging spiderwebs,
and many believe
you will keep
that hellish color forever.

It is not true.

A slow night passes,
a single minute passes

y todo cambia.
Se llena
de transparencia
la copa de la vida.
El trabajo espacioso
nos espera.
De un solo golpe nacen las palomas.
Se establece la luz sobre la tierra.

and everything changes.
The cup of life
brims
with translucence.
The spacious job
awaits us.
Doves are born in a lonesome burst.
Life on earth is established.

Vida, los pobres
poetas
te creyeron amarga,
no salieron contigo
de la cama
con el viento del mundo.

Life, the poor
poets
thought you were bitter,
they did not rise
from bed with you,
with the wind of the world.

Recibieron los golpes
sin buscarte,
se barrenaron
un agujero negro
y fueron sumergiéndose
en el luto
de un pozo solitario.

They received beatings
without looking for you,
scuttled
a black hole
and began to drown
in the mourning
of a solitary well.

No es verdad, vida,
eres
bella
como la que yo amo
y entre los senos tienes
olor a menta.

It is not true, life,
you are
beautiful
like my beloved
and between your breasts you distill
the smell of spearmint.

Vida,
eres
una máquina plena,
felicidad, sonido
de tormenta, ternura
de aceite delicado.

Life,
you are
a full machine,
happiness, sound
of a thunderstorm, tenderness
of delicate oil.

Vida,
eres como una viña:
atesoras la luz y la repartes
transformada en racimo.

El que de ti reniega
que espere
un minuto, una noche,
un año corto o largo,
que salga
de su soledad mentirosa,
que indague y luche, junte
sus manos a otras manos,
que no adopte ni halague
a la desdicha,
que la rechace dándole
forma de muro,
como a la piedra los picapedreros,
que corte la desdicha
y se haga con ella
pantalones.
La vida nos espera
a todos
los que amamos
el salvaje
olor a mar y menta
que tiene entre los senos.

Life,
you are like a vineyard:
treasuring light, distributing it
remixed in clusters of grapes.

He who evades you
let him wait
a minute, a night,
a short year, a long one,
exit
his lying solitude,
let him inquire and fight, bring
his hands to other hands,
he should not adopt or flatter
misery,
let him reject it giving it
the shape of a wall,
like the stone to the stonemason,
let him cut misery
and turn it into
a pair of pants.
Life awaits
us all
who love
the wild
perfume of the sea and the spearmint
it keeps between its breasts.

109 / ODE TO THE LIVER

Oda al hígado

TRANSLATED BY GEORGE D. SCHADE

Modesto,	Modest,
organizado	organized
amigo,	friend,
trabajador	hard
profundo,	worker,
déjame darte el ala	let me give you my winged
de mi canto,	song,
el golpe	the gust
de aire,	of air,
el santo	the lilt
de mi oda:	of my ode:
ella nace	it issued
de tu invisible	from your invisible
máquina,	machine,
ella vuela	takes flight
desde tu infatigable	from your tireless
y encerrado molino,	encircled mill,
entraña	delicate
delicada	and powerful
y poderosa,	organ,
siempre	always
viva y oscura.	alive and dark.
Mientras	While
el corazón suena y atrae	the heart beats attracting
la partitura de la mandolina,	the mandolin's partitura,
allí adentro	there deep inside
tú filtras	you filter

y repartes,	and dole,
separas	divide
y divides,	and separate,
multiplicas	multiply
y engrasas,	and grease,
subes	raise
y recoges	and gather
los hilos y los gramos	the threads and grams
de la vida, los últimos	of life, the final
licores,	liquors,
las íntimas esencias.	the intimate essences.
Víscera	Submarine
submarina,	viscera,
medidor	measurer
de la sangre,	of blood,
vives	you live
lleno de manos	full of hands
y de ojos,	and eyes,
midiendo y trasvasando	measuring and decanting
en tu escondida	in your hidden
cámara	alchemist's
de alquimista.	chamber.
Amarillo	Yellow
es tu sistema	is your system
de hidrografía roja,	of red hydrography,
buzo	diver
de la más peligrosa	into man's most
profundidad del hombre,	dangerous depths,
allí escondido	hidden there
siempre,	always,
sempiterno,	everlasting,
en la usina,	in the factory,
silencioso.	silent.
Y todo	And every
sentimiento	sentiment

o estímulo
creció en tu maquinaria,
recibió alguna gota
de tu elaboración
infatigable,
al amor agregaste
fuego o melancolía,
una pequeña
célula equivocada
o una fibra
gastada en tu trabajo
y el aviador se equivoca de cielo,
el tenor se derrumba en un silbido,
al astrónomo se le pierde un planeta.

Cómo brillan arriba
los hechiceros ojos
de la rosa,
los labios
del clavel
matutino!
Cómo ríe
en el río
la doncella!
Y abajo
el filtro y la balanza,
la delicada química
del hígado,
la bodega
de los cambios sutiles:
nadie
lo ve o lo canta,
pero,
cuando
envejece
o desgasta su mortero,

or stimulus
grew in your machinery,
received at least a drop
of your tireless
elaboration,
to love you added
fire or melancholy,
a tiny
mistaken cell
or a fiber
worn out in your work,
and the aviator errs in the sky,
the tenor caves in with a whistle,
the astronomer loses a planet.

How the spellbound eyes
of the rose
and the lips
of the morning
carnation
shine above!
How the maiden
laughs
in the river!
And down below
the filter and scale,
the delicate chemistry
of the liver,
the cellar
of subtle changes:
nobody
sees or sings its praise,
but,
when its mortar
grows old and worn,

los ojos de la rosa se acabaron,
el clavel marchitó su dentadura
y la doncella no cantó en el río.

Austera parte
o todo
de mí mismo,
abuelo
del corazón,
molino
de energía:
te canto
y temo
como si fueras juez,
metro,
fiel implacable,
y si no puedo
entregarme amarrado a la pureza,
si el excesivo
manjar
o el vino hereditario de mi patria
pretendieron
pertubar mi salud
o el equilibrio de mi poesía,
de ti,
monarca oscuro,
distribuidor de mieles y venenos,
regulador de sales,
de ti espero justicia:
Amo la vida: Cúmpleme! Trabaja!
No detengas mi canto.

the eyes of the rose become dim,
the carnation's teeth fade away,
the maid sings no more at the river.

Austere part
or all
of myself,
the heart's
grandfather,
energy
mill,
I sing your praise
and fear you
as if you were judge,
meter,
implacably faithful,
and if I cannot
surrender bound to purity,
if excessive
rich food
or my country's hereditary wine
try
to disturb my health
or the equilibrium of my poetry,
from you,
dark monarch,
distributor of honeys and venoms,
controller of salts,
from you I seek justice:
I love life: keep your promise! Work on!
Don't halt my song.

110 / ODE TO THE LIZARD

Oda a la lagartija

TRANSLATED BY MARGARET SAYERS PEDEN

Junto a la arena	On the sand
una	a
lagartija	lizard
de cola enarenada.	with a sandy tail.
Debajo	Beneath
de una hoja	a leaf,
su cabeza	a leaflike
de hoja.	head.
De qué planeta	From what planet,
o brasa	from what
fría y verde,	cold green ember
caíste?	did you fall?
De la luna?	From the moon?
Del más lejano frío?	From frozen space?
O desde	Or from
la esmeralda	the emerald
ascendieron tus colores	did your color
en una enredadera?	climb the vine?
Del tronco	On a rotting
carcomido	tree trunk
eres	you are
vivísimo	a living
retoño,	shoot,
flecha	arrow

de su follaje.
En la piedra
eres piedra
con dos pequeños ojos
antiguos:
los ojos de la piedra.
Cerca
del agua
eres
légamo taciturno
que resbala.
Cerca
de la mosca
eres el dardo
del dragón que aniquila.

Y para mí,
la infancia,
la primavera
cerca
del río
perezoso,
eres
tú!
lagartija
fría, pequeña
y verde:
eres una remota
siesta
cerca de la frescura,
con los libros cerrados.

El agua corre y canta.

El cielo, arriba, es una
corola calurosa.

of its foliage.
On a stone
you are a stone
with two small, ancient
eyes—
eyes of the stone.
By the
water
you are
silent, slippery
slime.
To
a fly
you are the dart
of an annihilating dragon.

And to me,
my childhood,
spring
beside
a lazy
river,
that's
you!
lizard,
cold, small
and green;
you are a long-ago
siesta
beside cool waters,
with books unopened.

The water flows and sings.

The sky, overhead, is a
warm corolla.

111 / ODE TO LOVE

Oda al amor

TRANSLATED BY ILAN STAVANS

Amor, hagamos cuentas.
A mi edad
no es posible
engañar o engañarnos.
Fui ladrón de caminos,
tal vez,
no me arrepiento.
Un minuto profundo,
una magnolia rota
por mis dientes
y la luz de la luna
celestina.
Muy bien, pero, el balance?
La soledad mantuvo
su red entretejida
de fríos jazmineros
y entonces
la que llegó a mis brazos
fue la reina rosada
de las islas.
Amor,
con una gota,
aunque caiga
durante toda y toda
la nocturna
primavera
o se forma el océano

Love, let's do the numbers.
At my age
it isn't possible to deceive or deceive
ourselves.
I was a highway thief,
perhaps,
I don't regret it.
A deep minute,
a magnolia broken
by my teeth
and the light of the moon's
go-between.
Very well, but, the balance?
Solitude kept
its net with interwoven
cold jasmine
and then
the one coming to my arms
was the pink-colored queen
of the islands.
Love,
with a drop,
even if it falls
during all and all
the nocturnal
spring
the ocean is not formed

y me quedé desnudo,
solitario, esperando.

Pero, he aquí que aquella
que pasó por mis brazos
como una ola,
aquella
que sólo fue un sabor
de fruta vespertina,
de pronto
parpadeó como estrella,
ardió como paloma
y la encontré en mi piel
desenlazándose
como la cabellera de una hoguera.
Amor, desde aquel día
todo fue más sencillo.
Obedecí las órdenes
que mi olvidado corazón me daba
y apreté su cintura
y reclamé su boca
con todo el poderío
de mis besos,
como un rey que arrebata
con un ejército desesperado
una pequeña torre donde crece
la azucena salvaje de su infancia.

Por eso, Amor, yo creo
que enmarañado y duro
puede ser tu camino,
pero que vuelves
de tu cacería
y cuando enciendes
otra vez el fuego,
como el pan en la mesa,

and I remain naked,
desolate, waiting.

But, I announce the one
passing through my arms
like a wave,
she
who was just a taste
of a twilight fruit,
suddenly
fluttered like a star,
sparkled fire like a dove
and I found her in my skin
unraveling like a blaze of hair.
Love, since that day
everything was simple.
I obeyed the orders
my forgotten heart was giving
and held her by the waist
and reclaimed her mouth
with all the power
of my kisses,
like a king ravishing
a small tower where
the savage white lily
of its childhood grows
with a desperate army.

That's why, Love, I trust
your path might
be hard and twisted,
because you return
from your hunt
and when you light
the fire again,
like bread on the table,

así, con sencillez,
debe estar lo que amamos.
Amor, eso me diste.
Cuando por vez primera
ella llegó a mis brazos
pasó como las aguas
en una despeñada primavera.
Hoy
la recojo.
Son angostas mis manos y pequeñas
las cuencas de mis ojos
para que ellas reciban
su tesoro,
la cascada
de interminable luz, el hilo de oro,
el pan de su fragancia
que son sencillamente, Amor, mi vida.

right there, simply,
must be what we love.
Love, you gave me that.
When she reached my arms
for the first time
she passed on like water
over the precipice of spring.
Today,
I take all this back.
My hands are narrow, and small
the cavities of my eyes,
so they receive
their treasure,
the cascade
of unending light, the thread of gold,
the bread of their fragrance
are simply, Love, my life.

112 / ODE TO THE MAGNOLIA

Oda a la magnolia

TRANSLATED BY ILAN STAVANS

Aquí en el fondo	Here in the depths
del Brasil profundo,	of deepest Brazil,
una magnolia.	a magnolia.
Se levantaban	The roots
como	rose up
boas negras	like
las raíces,	black boas,
los troncos de los árboles	trunks
eran	became
inexplicables	inexplicable
columnas con espinas.	columns with thorns.
Alrededor	Around
las copas	the tops of
de los mangos	mangoes
eran	were
ciudades	wide
anchas, con balcones,	cities, with balconies,
habitadas por	lived in by
pájaros	birds
y estrellas.	and stars.
Caían	Among the ashen
entre las hojas	leaves, old
cenicientas, antiguas	wigs
cabelleras,	descended,
flores terribles	terrible flowers
con bocas voraces.	with ravenous mouths.

Alrededor subía
el silencioso
terror
de animales, de dientes
que mordían:
patria desesperada
de sangre y sombra verde!

Una magnolia
pura,
redonda como un círculo
de nieve,
subió hasta mi ventana
y me reconcilió con la hermosura.
Entre sus lisas hojas
—ocre y verde—
cerrada,
era perfecta
como un huevo
celeste,
abierta
era la piedra
de la luna,
afrodita fragante,
planeta de platino.
Sus grandes pétalos me recordaron
las sábanas
de la primera luna
enamorada,
y su pistilo
erecto
era torre nupcial
de las abejas.

Oh blancura
entre

Everywhere
the silent
terror
of animals arose, with biting
teeth:
desperate homeland
of blood and green shadow!

A pure
magnolia,
round like a circle
of snow,
came up my window,
consoling me with its beauty.
Hidden
between its smooth leaves
—ochre and green—,
it was perfect:
a celestial
egg,
like the moon's
stone,
opened,
fragrant Aphrodite,
platinum planet.
Its great petals reminded me
of the sheets
of the early moon
in love,
its erect
pistil
a nuptial tower
for bees.

Oh, whiteness
amid

todas las blancuras,
magnolia inmaculada,
amor resplandeciente,
olor de nieve blanca
con limones,
secreta secretaria
de la aurora,
cúpula
de los cisnes,
aparición radiante!

Cómo
cantarte sin
tocar
tu
piel purísima,
amarte
sólo
al pie
de tu hermosura,
y llevarte
dormida
en el árbol de mi alma,
resplandeciente, abierta,
deslumbrante,
sobre la selva oscura
de los sueños!

all whiteness,
immaculate magnolia,
resplendent love,
odor of white snow
with lemons,
secret secretary
of dawn,
cupola
of swans,
radiant apparition!

How
to sing to you without
touching
your
purest skin,
mere
lover
at the feet
of your beauty,
now take you
asleep
into the tree of my soul,
resplendent, open,
above
the dark wood
of dreams!

113 / ODE TO MAIZE

Oda al maíz

TRANSLATED BY MARGARET SAYERS PEDEN

América, de un grano
de maíz te elevaste
hasta llenar
de tierras espaciosas
el espumoso
océano.
Fue un grano de maíz tu geografía.
El grano
adelantó una lanza verde,
la lanza verde se cubrió de oro
y engalanó la altura
del Perú con su pámpano amarillo.

Pero, poeta, deja
la historia en su mortaja
y alaba con tu lira
al grano en sus graneros:
canta al simple maíz de las cocinas.

Primero suave barba
agitada en el huerto
sobre los tiernos dientes
de la joven mazorca.
Luego se abrió el estuche
y la fecundidad rompió sus velos
de pálido papiro
para que se desgrane
la risa del maíz sobre la tierra.

America, from a grain
of maize you grew
to crown
with spacious lands
the ocean
foam.
A grain of maize was your geography.
From the grain
a green lance rose,
was covered with gold,
to grace the heights
of Peru with its yellow tassels.

But, poet, let
history rest in its shroud;
praise with your lyre
the grain in its granaries:
sing to the simple maize in the kitchen.

First, a fine beard
fluttered in the field
above the tender teeth
of the young ear.
Then the husks parted
and fruitfulness burst its veils
of pale papyrus
that grains of laughter
might fall upon the earth.

A la piedra
en tu viaje, regresabas.
No la piedra terrible,
al sanguinario
triángulo de la muerte mexicana,
sino a la piedra de moler,
sagrada
piedra de nuestras cocinas.
Allí leche y materia,
poderosa y nutricia
pulpa de los pasteles
llegaste a ser movida
por milagrosas manos
de mujeres morenas.

Donde caigas, maíz,
en la olla ilustre
de las perdices o entre los fréjoles
campestres, iluminas
la comida y le acercas
el virginal sabor de tu substancia.

Morderte,
panocha de maíz, junto al océano
de cantata remota y vals profundo.
Hervirte
y que tu aroma
por las sierras azules
se despliegue.

Pero, dónde
no llega
tu tesoro?

En las tierras marinas
y calcáreas,
peladas, en las rocas

To the stone,
in your journey, you returned.
Not to the terrible stone,
the bloody
triangle of Mexican death,
but to the grinding stone,
sacred
stone of our kitchens.
There, milk and matter,
strength-giving, nutritious
cornmeal pulp,
you were worked and patted
by the wondrous hands
of dark-skinned women.

Wherever you fall, maize,
whether into the
splendid pot of partridge, or among
country beans, you light up
the meal and lend it
your virginal flavor.

Oh, to bite into
the steaming ear beside the sea
of distant song and deepest waltz.
To boil you
as your aroma
spreads through
blue sierras.

But is there
no end
to your treasure?

In chalky, barren lands
bordered
by the sea, along

del litoral chileno,	the rocky Chilean coast,
a la mesa desnuda	at times
del minero	only your radiance
a veces sólo llega	reaches the empty
la claridad de tu mercadería.	table of the miner.
Puebla tu luz, tu harina, tu esperanza,	Your light, your cornmeal, your hope
la soledad de América,	pervades America's solitudes,
y el hambre	and to hunger
considera tus lanzas	your lances
legiones enemigas.	are enemy legions.
Entre tus hojas como	Within your husks,
suave guiso	like gentle kernels,
crecieron nuestros graves corazones	our sober provincial
de niños provincianos	children's hearts were nurtured,
y comenzó la vida	until life began
a desgranarnos.	to shuck us from the ear.

114 / ODE TO THE MALVENIDA

Oda a la malvenida

TRANSLATED BY ILAN STAVANS

Planta de mi país, rosa de tierra,	Plant of my country, rose of earth,
estrella trepadora,	climbing star,
zarza negra,	blackberry bush,
pétalo de la luna en el océano	moon petal in the ocean
que amé con sus desgracias y sus olas,	I loved with its misfortunes and its waves,
con sus puñales y sus callejones,	its daggers and narrow lanes,
amapola	bristled
erizada,	poppy,
clavel de nácar negro,	carnation of mother-of-pearl,
por qué	why
cuando mi copa	when my cup
desbordó y cuando	was overwhelmed and when
mi corazón cambió de luto a fuego,	my heart changed from mourning to fire,
cuando no tuve para ti, para ofrecerte,	when I had nothing to offer you
lo que toda la vida te esperaba,	of what life had in store for you,
entonces	then
tú llegaste,	you came,
cuando letras quemantes	when kindling letters
van ardiendo en mi frente,	keep burning on my forehead,
por qué la línea pura	why did the pure line
de tu nupcial contorno	of your nuptial contour
llegó como un anillo	arrive like a ring,
rodando por la tierra?	rolling over the earth?
No debías	All in all,
de todas y de todas	you shouldn't have come
llegar a mi ventana	at my window
como un jazmín tardío.	like late jasmine.

No eras, oh llama oscura,
la que debió tocarme
y subir con mi sangre
hasta mi boca.
Ahora
qué puedo contestarte?
Consúmete,
no esperes,
no hay espera
para tus labios de piedra nocturna.
Consúmete,
tú en tu llama,
yo en mi fuego,
y ámame
por el amor que no pudo esperarte,
ámame en lo que tú y yo
tenemos de piedra o de planta:
seguiremos viviendo
de lo que no nos dimos:
del hombro en que no pudo reclinarse una rosa,
de una flor que su propia quemadura ilumina.

You weren't, oh dark flame,
meant to touch me
and rise with my blood
in my mouth.
Now
what can I answer you?
Consume yourself!
Don't wait,
there's no wait
for your lips of nocturnal stone.
Consume yourself!
You in your flame,
I in my fire,
and love me
for the love that couldn't wait for you.
Love me in what you and I
have of stone and plant:
we'll continue living
from what we didn't give each other:
from the shoulder on which a rose
could not recline,
from a flower illuminated by its
own burn.

115 / ODE TO MARINE LIGHT

Oda a la luz marina

TRANSLATED BY ILAN STAVANS

Otra vez, espaciosa	Once again, spacious
luz marina	marine light,
cayendo de los cántaros	falling in heavenly
del cielo,	torrents,
subiendo de la espuma,	climbing through the foam,
de la arena,	sand,
luz agitada sobre	nervous light over
la extensión del océano,	the ocean's extent,
como un	like a
combate de cuchillos	fight of knives
y relámpagos,	and lightning,
luz de la sal caliente,	light of warm salt,
luz del cielo	light of the elevated
elevado	sky
como torre del mar sobre las aguas.	like a firehouse over water.
Dónde	Where
están las tristezas?	is sadness?
El pecho se abre	My chest opens
convertido	transformed
en rama,	into branch,
la luz sacude	light shakes
en nuestro	in our
corazón	heart
sus amapolas,	its poppy flowers,
brillan	during the day

en el día del mar
las cosas
puras,
las piedras
visitadas
por la ola,
los fragmentos
vencidos
de botellas,
vidrios
del agua,
suaves,
alisados
por sus dedos
de estrella.
Brillan
los
cuerpos
de los hombres salobres,
de las mujeres
verdes,
de los niños
como algas,
como
peces que saltan
en el cielo,
y cuando
una ventana
clausurada, un traje,
un monte oscuro,
se atreven
a competir
manchando la blancura,
llega la claridad a borbotones,
la luz
extiende sus mangueras

crystalline
ocean things
shine,
stones
visited
by waves,
defeated
fragments
of a bottle,
water
glass,
soft,
smoothed
by its starry
fingers.
The bodies
of
salty men
shine,
of green
women,
of children
like algae,
like
fish jumping
in the sky,
and when
a closed-up
window, a suit,
a dark mountain,
dares
to compete
staining the whiteness,
clarity arrives bubbling,
light
extends its hoses

y ataca la insolente
sombra
con brazos blancos,
con manteles,
con talco y olas de oro,
con estupenda espuma,
con carros de azucena.

Poderío
de la luz madurando en el espacio,
ola que nos traspasa
sin mojarnos, cadera
del universo,
                    rosa
renacedora, renacida:
abre
cada día tus pétalos,
tus párpados,
que la velocidad de tu pureza
extienda nuestros ojos
y nos enseñe a ver ola por ola
el mar
y flor a flor la tierra.

and attacks the insolent
shadow
with white arms,
with tablecloths,
with powder and waves of gold,
with superb foam,
with carts of white lilies.

Domain
of light maturing in space,
wave passing through
without wetting us, hip
of the universe,
                    rose,
renewing, reborn:
each day
open its petals,
your eyelids,
so the speed of your purity
extends our eyes
and teaches us to see wave by wave
the sea
and the earth one flower at a time.

116 / ODE TO MARINE SPACE

Oda al espacio marino

TRANSLATED BY ILAN STAVANS

Húmedo el corazón, la ola	Humid is the heart, the wave
golpea	beats
pura, certera, amarga.	pure, sharp, sour.
Dentro de ti la sal,	Inside you salt,
la transparencia,	transparency,
el agua se repiten:	water get repeated:
la multitud del mar	the sea's multitude
lava tu vida	washes your life
y no sólo la playa	and not only the beach
sino tu corazón es coronado	but your heart is crowned
por la insistente espuma.	by the insistent foam.
Diez años o quince años,	Ten years or fifteen years,
no recuerdo,	I don't remember,
llegué a estas soledades,	I came to these solitudes,
fundé	I founded
mi casa	my house
en la perdida arena,	in the lost sand,
y como arena fui desmenuzando	and like sand I sifted
las horas de mi vida	through the hours of my life
grano a grano:	grain by grain:
luz, sombra, sangre, trigo,	light, shadow, blood, wheat,
repulsión o dulzura.	repulsion and sweetness.
Los muros,	The walls,
las ventanas,	windows,
los ladrillos, las puertas de la casa,	bricks, house doors,
no sólo	not only

se gastaron
con la humedad y el paso
del viajero,
sino que con mi canto
y con la espuma
que insiste en las arenas.
Con mi canto y el viento
se gastaron
los muros
y del mar y las piedras
de la costa
recogí resistencia,
espacio y alas
para el sonido,
recogí la sustancia
de la noche marina.

Aquí primero
de la arena,
extasiado,
levanté el alga fría
ondulada en la ola
o el caracol de Chile,
rosa dura,
sumergida cadera
de paloma,
o el ágata
marina,
translúcida
como vino amarillo.
Luego
busqué
las plantas procelarias,
el firmamento fino
de las flores
perdidas en la duna,

grew old
with the humanity and the passing
of the traveler,
but with my song
and the foam
insistent on the sand.
With my song and the wind
the walls
grew old
and I gathered resistance
in the sea and stones
from the coast,
space and wings
for the sound,
I gathered the substance
of the marine night.

Here I first
raised the cold algae
undulating
in the wave
or the snail of Chile
on the ecstatic sand,
harsh rose,
submerged waist
of a dove,
or the marine
agate,
translucent
like yellow wine.
Then
I looked
for porcelain plants,
the fine firmament
of lovers
lost in the dune,

en la calcárea
virginidad rocosa:
amé la flora
de la ardiente arena,
gruesas hojas, espinas,
flores de la intemperie,
diminutas
estrellas
invariables
pegadas a la tierra.

Sí, las flores,
las algas,
las arenas,
pero detrás de todo
el mar como un caballo
desbocado
en el viento,
caballo azul, caballo
de cabellera blanca,
siempre
galopando,
el mar,
marmita
siempre
cocinando,
el mar
mucho más ancho
que las islas,
cinturón frenético
de tierra y cielo.
En las orillas
piedras
a puñados,
edificios
de roca

in the calcareous
craggy virginity:
I loved the flora
of the burning sand,
thick leaves, thorns,
open-air flowers,
minuscule
invariable
stars
patched to the earth.

Yes, the flowers,
algae,
sand,
but behind all this
the sea like a horse
running wild
in the wind,
blue horse, horse
with white hair,
the sea
always
galloping,
kettle pot
always
cooking,
the sea
much wider
than the islands,
frantic belt
of land and sky.
On the shores
stones
by the handful,
buildings
of rock

dispuestos contra el mar y su batalla
socavados por una misma gota
repetida en los siglos.

Contra el granito gris
el mar estalla:
invasiones de espuma,
ejércitos de sal,
soldados verdes
derribando racimos invisibles.
Espesos buzos
bajan,
militantes
de la profundidad:
la nave espera
en el vaivén del seno de la ola,
vuelven
con
un puñado
de palpitantes
frutos
submarinos,
góticas caracolas,
erizados erizos:
el buzo
emerge
de la mitología
en su escafandra, pudo
bailar con las medusas,
quedarse
en el profundo hotel
de las sirenas,
pero ha vuelto: un pequeño
pescador de la orilla
sale de sus zapatos
y es aéreo

ready against the sea and its bottle
undermined by the same drop
repeated over centuries.

The sea crashes
against gray granite:
invasions of foam,
armies of salt,
green soldiers
bringing down invisible bunches.
Thick divers
descend,
militants
of the depths:
the ship awaits
the coming and going of the wave's breast,
they return
with
a handful
of palpitating
submarine
fruit,
gothic shells,
stiffened sea urchin:
the diver
emerges
from mythology
in his diving suit, he
danced with the jellyfish,
stayed
in the mermaids'
deep hotel,
but has come back: a small
fisherman on the shore
comes out of his shoes
and is aerial

como un papel o un pájaro.
Rápida raza
de mis compañeros,
más que el mar es la tos
quien los golpea
y como en redes rotas
sus difíciles vidas
sin unidad, resbalan
a la muerte.

El hombre
de la costa
se ve minúsculo
como pulga marina.
No es verdad.
Ha colgado
como araña
en las piedras, en
el erial marino
su mansión miserable,
el hombre
de las tierras desdentadas
con trozos de latón, con tablas rotas
puso el techo sobre los hijos
y salió cada día
al martillo, al cemento,
a los navíos.
Aquí están
los puertos,
las casas, las aduanas:
el hombrecito
de la costa elevó las estructuras
y regresó a los cerros,
a su cueva.

Sí, océano, solemne
es tu insistente

like paper or a bird.
Quick race
of my fellow men,
more than the sea it is the cough
that beats them
and as in broken nets
their difficult lives
without unity, slide
toward death.

The man
from the coast
is as minuscule
as a sea flea.
It isn't true.
He has hung
like a spider
from the stones, in
the uncultivated marine land
his miserable mansion,
the man
from the toothless lands
with pieces of brass, with broken boards
put a roof over his children
and goes back every day
to the hammer, the cement,
the ships.
There are
the ports,
houses, customs offices:
the little man
from the coast lifted the structures
and returned to the hills,
to his cave.

Yes, ocean, solemn
is your insistent

vaticinio, la eternidad
del canto en movimiento,
tu coro
entra en mi corazón, barre las hojas
del fallecido otoño.
Océano,
tu desbordante copa
abre
como en la roca
su agujero
en mi pequeña frente de poeta,
y arena, flores duras, aves
de tempestad, silbante cielo,
rodean mi existencia.
Pero el minúsculo
hombre de las arenas
es para mí más grande.
Ahora, vedlo:
pasa con su mujer, con cinco perros
hambrientos, con su carga
de mar, algas, pescados.

Yo no soy mar, soy hombre.

Yo no conozco al viento.

Qué dicen estas olas?

Y cierro mi ventana.

Océano,
bella es tu voz, de sal y sol tu estatua,
pero
para el hombre es mi canto.

prophecy, the eternity
of song in movement,
your chorus
enters my heart, sweeps the leaves
of the dead autumn.
Ocean,
your boundless cup
opens
its hole
in my small poet's forehead
as in the rock,
and sand, hard fruit, birds
of tempest, whistling sky,
steal my existence.
But the minuscule
man of the sands
is to me bigger.
See it now:
he passes with his wife, with five hungry
dogs, with the sea
as his burden, algae, fish.

I am not the sea, I am man.

I do not know the wind.

What do the waves say?

And I close my window.

Ocean,
your voice is beautiful, your statue is made of
salt and sun,
but
my song is for man.

117 / ODE TO A *MIRABILIS JALAPA*: THE NIGHT-BLOOMING FOUR O'CLOCK

Oda a don Diego de la Noche

TRANSLATED BY MARGARET SAYERS PEDEN

Don Diego	Don *Mirabilis*
de la Noche,	*Jalapa*,
buenos días,	hello,
don Diego,	Don *Mirabilis*,
buenas noches:	good evening:
Yo soy	I am a poet
un poeta perdido.	who has lost his way.
Aquella puerta	That door back there
era	was
un agujero.	a hole.
La noche	Night
me golpeó la nariz	struck me on the nose
con esa rama	with that branch,
que yo tomé por una	which I had mistaken
criatura excelente.	for some well-bred creature.
La oscuridad es madre	Darkness is mother
de la muerte	to death,
y en ella	and in darkness
el poeta perdido	this lost poet
navegaba	steered a course
hasta	until a
que una estrella de fósforo	phosphorescent star
subió o bajó—no supe—	rose or set—I knew not which—
en las tinieblas.	in the darkness.
Estaba yo en el cielo,	Was I in heaven,

fallecido?
A quién
debía dirigirme,
entonces?
Mi único
amigo celestial
murió hace tanto tiempo
y anda con armadura:
Garcilaso.
En el infierno,
como dos lechuzas,
Baudelaire y Edgar Poe,
tal vez
ignorarán mi nombre!
Miré la estrella
y ella
me miraba:
la toqué
y era flor,
era don Diego,
y en la mano
su aroma
se me quedó prendido
traspasándome
el alma.

Terrestre
estrella,
gracias
por
tus cuatro
pétalos
de claridad fragante,
gracias
por

passed beyond?
To whom, then,
could I
turn?
My only
friend in heaven
died centuries ago
and still wears armor:
noble Garcilaso.
In hell,
like two owls,
Baudelaire and Edgar Poe
might not even know
my name!
I looked at the star
and it
gazed at me:
I touched it,
it was a flower,
Don *Mirabilis*,
and its fragrance
clung
to my fingers,
piercing
my soul.

Star
of earth,
thank you
for
your
four
petals
of fragrant radiance,
thank you
for

tu blancura
en las tinieblas,
gracias, estrella, por tus cuatro rayos,
gracias, flor,
por tus pétalos,
y gracias
por tus cuatro
espadas,
Caballero.

your whiteness
in the dark,
thank you, star, for your four rays,
thank you, flower,
for your petals,
and for your four
swords,
thank you,
Caballero.

118 / ODE TO THE MONTH OF AUGUST

Oda al mes de agosto

TRANSLATED BY ILAN STAVANS

Otra vez vuelvo	Once again I return
al claro	to the clarity
de la tierra,	of the land,
a mirar	to look
y tocar	and touch
piedras silvestres,	wild stones,
arena, ramas, luna.	sand, branches, moon.
Agosto	Southern
austral,	August,
agosto	August
limpio y frío,	clean and cold,
tu columna	your column
se eleva	raises
desde la tierra al cielo	from the earth to the sky
y te coronan	and you are crowned
las piedras estrelladas,	by the starry rocks,
la noche del zafiro.	the sapphire night.
Oh	Oh
invierno	clear
claro,	winter,
veo	I see
florecer tu rectángulo	your rectangle flourish
en una	in a
sola	single
rosa,	rose,
la nieve,	the snow,

y blanco, azul, me enseña	and white, azure, your pure
tu pura	geometry
geometría	teaches me
una lección	an open
abierta:	lesson:
el mundo está sin hojas,	the world is without leaves,
sin latidos,	without beat,
despojado de todo	deprived of everything
lo que muere:	that dies:
es sólo	it is only
piedra y frío,	stone and cold,
libro desnudo de cristal en donde	naked book of crystal where
las largas letras de la luz se elevan.	the long letters of light ascend.
Agosto sin	August without
calles, sin	streets, without
números,	numbers,
agosto sin zapatos	August without shoes
que caminan	walking
hacia los sufrimientos,	toward pain,
vuelvo	I return
a tu soledad	to your solitude
no	not
para	to
ahogarme	drown
en ella,	in it,
sino	but
para	to
lavarme con tus aguas,	wash myself in your waters,
para que en mí	so in me
resbale	the cold
luna	moon
fría,	may slide,
y pise por los bosques	and step on stones
piedras, hojas	in the forests, fallen
caídas	leaves

de agosto, y todo tenga
extensión limpia,
sabor de cielo, altura
de joven corazón bajo la lluvia.

Oh
plena potencia,
claridad
despojada
de la tierra,
amo
tu
abstracta
paz
en los caminos.
Quiero
estar
solo
en medio
de la luz de agosto
y ver
así
sin sangre
por una vez
la vida:
verla
como una
nave
deshabitada
y bella,
sin más aroma que el aire marino
o el invisible de un romero amargo.
Paso a paso,
sin nada:
no hay sino
luna y nieve.

of August, and everything has
a stainless expanse,
sky flavor, height
of a youthful heart under the rain.

Oh
full potency,
clarity
stripped
from the earth,
I love
your
abstract
peace
on the roads.
I want
to be
alone
in the middle
of you, August light,
and hence
see
life
for once
without blood:
see it
like
an uninhabited
and beautiful
ship,
with no more aroma than the marine air
or the invisible scent of sour rosemary.
Step by step,
without a thing:
there is nothing but
moon and snow.

Y ando
hasta sin mí,
por fin,
en la más clara
claridad de la tierra!

And I wander
without myself, even
finally,
in the clearest
clarity of the earth!

119 / ODE TO THE MOON

Oda a la luna

TRANSLATED BY ILAN STAVANS

Reloj del cielo,	Clock of the sky,
mides	you measure
la eternidad celeste,	celestial eternity,
una hora	one white
blanca,	hour,
un siglo	one century
que resbala	sliding
en tu nieve,	on your snow,
mientras tanto	meanwhile
la tierra	the earth,
enmarañada,	entangled,
húmeda,	is humid,
calurosa:	warm:
los martillos	the hammers
golpean,	hit,
arden	the tall ovens
los altos hornos,	burn,
se estremece en su lámina	the petroleum
el petróleo,	shakes in its plate,
el hombre busca, hambriento,	man searches, hungry,
la materia,	for matter,
se equivoca,	falters,
corrige	corrects
su estandarte,	his banner,
se agrupan los hermanos,	siblings gather,
caminan,	walk,
escuchan,	hear,

surgen
las ciudades,
en la altura
cantaron
las campanas,
las telas se tejieron,
saltó
la transparencia
a los cristales.
Mientras tanto
jazmín
o luz
nevada,
luna,
clarísima,
alta
acción de platino,
suave
muerta,
resbalas
por la noche
sin que sepamos
quiénes
son tus hombres,
si tienes
mariposas,
si en la mañana
vendes
pan de luna,
leche de estrella blanca,
si eres
de vidrio,
de corcho anaranjado,
si respiras,
si en tus praderas corren
serpientes biseladas,
quebradizas.

cities
emerge,
bells
sing
in the heights,
cloths are woven,
transparency
jumps
onto the crystals.
Meanwhile,
jasmine
or snowy
light,
moon,
bright clear,
tall,
action made from platinum,
gentle
dead,
you slide
through the night
without us knowing
who
your men are,
if you have
butterflies,
if in the morning
you sell
sweet bread,
white-star milk,
if you are
made of glass,
of orange cork,
if you breathe,
if in your meadows
beveled, fragile
serpents slither.

Queremos
acercarte,
miramos
hasta quedar ciegos
tu implacable
blancura,
ajustamos
al monte el telescopio
y pegamos el ojo
hasta dormirnos:
no hablas,
no te desvistes,
no enciendes
una sola fogata,
miras
hacia otro lado,
cuentas,
cuentas
el tiempo
de la noche,
tic
tac
suave,
suave
tac
tic
tac
como gota en la nieve,
redondo
reloj de agua,
corola
del tiempo
sumergida
en el cielo.

No será, no será
siempre,

We want
to bring you near,
we look
at your impeccable
whiteness
until we're blind,
we adjust
the telescope on the mountain
and set the eye
until we fall asleep:
you don't talk,
you don't undress,
you don't light
a single bonfire,
you look
at the other side,
you count,
you count
the time
of night,
gentle
tick
tock,
gentle
tock
tick
tock
like a drop on the snow,
round,
clock of water,
corolla
of time,
submerged
in the sky.

It won't be that way,
it won't always be,

prometo
en nombre
de todos
los poetas
que te amaron
inútilmente:
abriremos
tu paz de piedra pálida,
entraremos
en tu luz subterránea,
se encenderá
fuego
en tus ojos muertos,
fecundaremos
tu estatura helada,
cosecharemos
trigo
y aves
en tu frente,
navegaremos
en tu océano blanco,
y marcarás
entonces
las horas
de los hombres,
en la altura
del cielo:
serás
nuestra,
habrá en tu nieve
pétalos
de mujeres,
descubrimiento
de hombres,
y no serás inútil
reloj

I promise,
in the name
of all
the poets
who loved you
uselessly:
we shall open
your peace of pallid stone,
we shall enter
into your subterranean light,
fire
will light up
your dead eyes.
We'll inseminate
your frozen statue,
we shall harvest
wheat
and birds
in your forehead,
we shall navigate
on your white ocean.
And then
you will mark
the hours
of men,
in the heights
of the sky:
you will be
ours,
petals
of women
will be found
in your snow,
discovery of men,
and you will not be a useless
nocturnal

nocturno,	watch,
magnolia	magnolia
del árbol de la noche,	of the tree of night,
sino sólo	but only
legumbre,	legume,
queso puro,	only cheese,
vaca celeste,	celestial cow,
ubre	spilt
derramada,	udder,
manantial	spring
de la leche,	of milk,
útil	useful
como la espiga,	like the head of corn,
desbordante,	boundless,
reinante	reigning
y necesaria.	and necessary.

120 / ODE TO THE MOON OF THE SEA

Oda a la luna del mar

TRANSLATED BY MARGARET SAYERS PEDEN

Luna	City
de la ciudad,	moon,
me pareces	you look tired
cansada,	to me,
oscura	you look
me pareces	dark
o amarilla,	or yellowed,
con algo	a broken
de uña gastada	fingernail,
o gancho de candado,	a padlock's "u,"
cadavérica,	cadaverous,
vieja,	time worn,
borrascosa,	squally,
tambaleante	tumbling
como una	like a tarnished
religiosa oxidada	silver nun
en el transcurso	through
de las metálicas	metallic
revoluciones:	revolutions:
luna	transmigratory
transmigratoria,	moon,
respetable,	respectable,
impasible:	impassive,
tu	your
palidez	pallor
ha visto	has witnessed
barricadas	bloody

sangrientas,
motines
del pueblo que sacude
sus cadenas,
amapolas
abiertas
sobre
la guerra
y sus
exterminados
y allí, cansada, arriba,
con tus párpados viejos
cada vez
más cansada,
más
triste,
más rellena con humo,
con sangre, con tabaco,
con infinitas interrogaciones,
con el sudor nocturno
de las panaderías,
luna
gastada
como
la única muela
del cielo
de la noche
desdentada.

De pronto
llego
al mar
y otra luna
me pareces,
blanca,
mojada

barricades,
rebellions
of peoples shaking off
their chains,
seen full-blown
poppies
open
over
fields
of war dead,
there, aloft, exhausted,
your bleary eyelids
ever
lower,
sadder,
more
teary from smoke,
from blood, tobacco,
from endless interrogations,
the dripping sweat of
all-night bakeries,
ground-
down
moon,
the one remaining
tooth
in the gums
of night.

But when
I reach
the sea,
you seem
a different moon,
white,
moist

y fresca
como
yegua
reciente
que corre
en el rocío,
joven
como una perla,
diáfana
como frente
de sirena.
Luna
del mar,
te lavas
cada noche
y amaneces
mojada
por una aurora eterna,
desposándote
sin cesar con el cielo, con el aire,
con el viento marino,
desarrollado cada
nueva hora
por el interno impulso
vital de la marea,
limpia como las uñas
en la sal
del océano.

Oh, luna de los mares,
luna
mía,
cuando
de las calles
regreso,
de mi número

and cool
as
a
filly
frolicking
in the dew,
youthful
as a pearl,
diaphanous
as a siren's
brow.
Moon
of the sea,
each night
you wash yourself
and wake
misted
by eternal dawn,
wed ceaselessly
with sky, with air,
with sea wind,
gradually
expelled
by the rhythmic
contractions of the tide,
clean as fingernails
in ocean
brine.

Oh, moon of the seas,
my
moon,
when
I return
from the streets,
come back

vuelvo,
tú me lavas
el polvo,
el sudor
y las manchas
del camino,
lavandera
marina,
lavas
mi corazón cansado,
mi camisa.
En la noche
te miro,
pura,
encendida
lámpara
del cielo,
fresca, recién nacida
entre las olas,
y me duermo
bajo tu esfera limpia,
reluciente,
de universal reloj,
de rosa blanca.
Amanezco
nuevo, recién vestido,
lavado por tus manos,
lavandera,
buena para el trabajo
y la batalla.
Tal vez tu paz, tu nimbo
nacarado,
tu nave
entre las olas,
eterna, renaciendo
con la sombra,

from numbers,
you wash away
the dust,
the sweat,
the stains
of the highway,
marine
laundress,
you wash
my weary heart,
my shirt.
At night
I gaze at you,
pure
lighted
lamp
of the sky,
fresh, newborn
from the waves,
and I sleep
beneath your limpid,
shining sphere,
universal clock,
white rose.
I waken
new, newly clothed,
washed by your hands,
laundress,
ready for work
and battle.
Perhaps your peace, your
nacreous nimbus,
your ship
riding the waves,
eternal, reborn
with shadow,

tienen que ver conmigo
y a tu fresca
eternidad de plata
y de marea
debe mi corazón
su levadura.

affect me,
and to your fresh
eternity of silver
and tides
my heart owes
its leaven.

121 / ODE TO A MORNING IN BRAZIL

Oda a una mañana del Brasil

TRANSLATED BY KEN KRABBENHOFT

Ésta es una mañana	This is morning
del Brasil. Vivo adentro	in Brazil. I'm living
de un violento diamante,	inside a blazing diamond,
toda la transparencia	the world's
de la tierra	transparency
se materializó	has materialized
sobre	above
mi frente,	my head.
apenas si se mueve	The fringed greenness
la bordada verdura,	scarcely quivers,
el rumoroso cinto	this murmuring belt
de la selva:	of jungle:
ancha es la claridad, como una nave	there's a breadth of brightness, like a ship
del cielo, victoriosa.	of heaven, triumphant.
Todo crece,	Everything grows—
los árboles,	trees,
el agua,	water,
los insectos,	insects,
el día.	day itself.
Todo termina en hoja.	Everything ends in leaves.
Se unieron	All
todas	the cicadas
las cigarras	that have ever lived
que nacieron, vivieron	and died
y murieron	since the world's creation
desde que existe el mundo,	have banded together,
y aquí cantan	and they're singing

en un solo congreso
con voz de miel,
de sal,
de aserradero,
de violín delirante.

Las mariposas
bailan
rápidamente
un
baile
rojo
negro
naranja
verde
azul
blanco
granate
amarillo
violeta
en el aire,
en las flores,
en la nada,
volantes,
sucesivas
y remotas.

Deshabitadas
tierras,
cristal
verde
del mundo,
en alguna
región
un ancho río
se despeña
en plena soledad,

in one single voice
made of honey
and salt
and sawdust,
the voice of a screeching violin.

The butterflies
are doing
a fast dance,
a
dance
that is red
black
orange
green
blue
white
garnet
yellow
and violet,
dancing on the air
and on flowers
or in the emptiness,
flying by
one after another
in the distance.

Uninhabited
land,
the world's
green
glass:
some-
where
a wide river
plummets
in complete solitude,

los saurios cruzan
las aguas pestilentes,
miles de seres lentos
aplastados
por la
ciega espesura
cambian de planta, de agua,
de pantano, de cueva,
y atraviesan el aire
aves abrasadoras.

Un grito, un canto,
un vuelo,
una cascada
cruzan desde una copa
de palmera
hasta
la arboladura
del bambú innumerable.

El mediodía
llega
sosegado,
se extiende
la luz como si hubiera
nacido un nuevo río
que corriera y cantara
llenando el universo:
de pronto
todo
queda
inmóvil,
la tierra, el cielo, el agua
se hicieron transparencia,
el tiempo se detuvo
y todo entró en su caja de diamante.

lizards criss-cross
fever-bearing waters,
thousands of sluggish things
squashed
by the
forest's sightless mass
exchange plants, waterholes,
swamps and caves,
while blazing birds
wing through the air.

A cry, a song,
a flight,
a spray of water
leap from the crown
of a palm tree
into
the endless bamboo
forest.

Noon
arrives
relaxed,
light
stretches like
a river born
swiftly rushing and singing,
filling the universe.
All at once
everything
comes
to a halt:
earth, air and water
turn transparent,
time stops,
and the world retires to its diamond box.

122 / ODE TO A MORNING IN STOCKHOLM

Oda a una mañana en Stokholmo

TRANSLATED BY KEN KRABBENHOFT

Por los días del norte,	We're cruising, love,
amor, nos deslizamos.	through northern days.
Leningrado quedó	Leningrad was covered
nevado, azul, acero	in snow, blue and steely
debajo de sus nubes	beneath clouds
las columnas, las cúpulas,	pillars, domes,
el oro viejo, el rosa,	pink and weathered gold,
la luz ancha del río,	wide light on the river:
todo se fue en el viaje,	it all passed so fast,
se quedó atrás llorando.	was left behind in tears.
Se come al mar la tierra?	The earth: does it swallow the sea?
La tierra al firmamento?	The firmament: is it swallowed by the earth?
Diviso el cielo blanco	I spy the white sky
de Stokholmo, el tridente	of Stockholm, the trident
de una iglesia en las nubes,	of a church thrust into clouds.
ácidas copas verdes	Those bilious green crowns
con cúpulas, son senos	are domes, breasts
de ciudad oxidada,	of a rusting city.
y lo demás es vago,	All the rest is vague,
noche sin sombra o día	night without shadow, day
sin luz, cristal opaco.	without light, glass you can't see through.
Amor mío, a estas islas	My love, this heart brought you
dispersas en la bruma,	to these islands

a los acantilados
de nieve y alas negras,
mi corazón te trajo.

Y ahora como naves
silenciosas pasamos,
sin saber dónde fuimos
ni dónde iremos, solos
en un mundo de perlas
e implacables ladrillos.

Apágate hasta ser
sólo nieve o neblina,
clausuremos los ojos,
cerremos los sentidos
hasta salir al sol
a morder las naranjas.

scattered in fog,
to cliffs
of snow and coal-black wings.

And now we are moving on
like silent ships
not knowing where we've been
or where we're going, alone
in a world of pearls
and pitiless bricks.

It's best to shut down,
emulate snow and mist.
We'll retire our eyes
and stifle our senses
until we emerge in the sun
and bury our teeth in an orange.

123 / ODE TO THE MURMUR

Oda al murmullo

TRANSLATED BY ILAN STAVANS

Versos de amor, de luto,
de cólera o de luna,
me atribuyen:
de los que con trabajos,
manzanas y alegría,
voy haciendo,
dicen que no son míos,
que muestran la influencia
de Pitiney, de Papo,
de Sodostes.
Ay qué vamos a hacerle!
La vida
fue poniendo en mi mano
una paloma
y otra.
Aprendí el vuelo
y enseñé
volando.
Desde el cielo celeste
comprendí los deberes
de la tierra,
vi más grandes los hechos
de los hombres
que el vuelo
encarnizado
de los pájaros.
Amé la tierra, puse

Lines of love, of mourning,
of cholera or moon,
are attributed to me:
of the kind I go on making
with labor,
apples and happiness,
people say they aren't mine,
that the verses show the influence
of Pitiney, of Papo,
of Sodostes.
Ah, what are we to do!
Life
kept on placing one dove
in my hand,
and another.
I learned to fly
and taught
while flying.
From the celestial sky,
I understood the duties
of the earth.
I saw the happenings
of men
with more clarity than the bitter
flight
of birds.
I loved the soil, I set

en mi corazón la transparencia	the transparency of moving water
del agua que camina,	in my heart
formé	I formed,
de barro y viento la vasija	the vessel
de mi constante canto,	of my constant song out of mud and wind.
y entonces	And then
por los pueblos,	I began to conquer a human family
las casas,	from the towns,
los puertos	houses,
y las minas,	ports,
fui conquistando una familia humana,	and mines,
resistí con los pobres	I resisted poverty
la pobreza,	with the poor.
viví con mis hermanos.	I lived with my brothers.
Entonces	Then
cada ataque de ola negra,	each attack of black wave,
cada	each
pesado	heavy
manotón de la vida	slap of life
contra mis pobres huesos	against my poor bones
fue sonoro sonido de campana,	was the sonorous toll of the bell,
y me hice campanero,	and I became a bell ringer,
campanero	the bell ringer
de la tierra	of earth
y los hombres.	and men.
Ahora	Now
soy campanero,	I am a bell ringer.
me agarro	I hold the rope
con el alma	with my soul.
a los cordeles,	The earth
tiembla	makes my heart
la tierra	tremble
con mi corazón en el sonido,	with sound.
subo, recorro montes,	I climb, I cross mountains,
bajo,	I descend,

reparto
la alarma, la alegría,
la esperanza.
Por qué
cuando
tal vez estoy cansado,
cuando duermo,
cuando salgo a beber con mis amigos
el vino
de las tierras que amo y que defiendo,
por qué
me persigues, desquiciado
con una piedra,
con una
quijada de borrico
quieres amedrentarme,
si nadie
pudo
antes
hacer que me callara?
Tú crees
que poniendo en la calle
una resbaladiza
cáscara de manzana
o tu remota
producción de saliva
puedes
terminar con mi canto de campana
y con mi vocación de campanero?
Es hora
de que nos comprendamos:
acuéstate temprano,
preocúpate
de que paguen tu sastre
tu madre o tu cuñado,
déjame

I share
the alarm, the happiness,
the hope.
Why
when
I'm tired, perhaps,
when I sleep,
when I go out to drink with friends
the wine
of the lands I love and defend others,
why
do you persecute me, unhinged,
with a stone,
with the
jawbone of an ass
you want me frightened,
when no one
has been able
to silence me
until now?
Do you believe
that by laying
a slippery apple skin
in the street,
or your far-flung
production of saliva,
you might be able
to stop my bell song
and my bell ringer's calling?
It is time
for us to understand each other:
go to bed early,
making sure
your tailor is paid
by his mother and brother-in-law,
let me

subir por la escalera a mi campana:
arde el sol en el frío,
aún está caliente
el pan
en los mesones,
es fragante la tierra,
amanece,
y yo con mi campana,
con mi canto,
despierto y te despierto.
Ése es mi oficio
—aunque no quieras—,
despertarte
a ti y a los que duermen,
convencer
al nocturno
de que llegó la luz,
y esto
es tan sencillo
de hacer,
tan agradable como
repartir panes en la vía pública,
que hasta yo puedo hacerlo,
cantando como canto,
sonoro como el agua que camina,
y como un campanero,
inexorable.

climb the stairs to the bell:
while the sun burns in the cold,
and the bread
is still warm
in the inns,
the soil is fragrant.
It is daybreak,
and I, with my bell,
with my song,
wake and wake you.
That is my task
—even if I don't want to—
to wake
you and those who are sleeping;
to convince
the darkness
that light has arrived.
This
is easy
to do,
it's pleasant,
like giving out bread on the street,
so easy even I can do it,
singing the way I sing,
sonorous like moving water,
and, like a bell ringer,
inexorable.

124 / ODE TO THE MYRRH TREE

Oda al aromo

TRANSLATED BY ILAN STAVANS

Vapor o niebla o nube	Vapor or fog or cloud
me rodeaban.	surrounded me.
Iba por San Jerónimo	I was passing by San Jerónimo
hacia el puerto	on the way to the port,
casi dormido cuando	almost asleep, when
desde el invierno	from winter
una montaña	a mountain
de luz amarilla,	of yellow light,
una torre florida	a florid tower
salió al camino y todo	appeared on the road, all full
se llenó de perfume.	of perfume.
Era un aromo.	It was a myrrh tree.
Su altura	Its soaring
de pabellón florido	florid pavilion
se construyó	was built
con miel y sol y aroma	of honey and scent,
y en él	and in it
yo	I
vi	saw
la catedral del polen,	the cathedral of pollen,
la profunda	the deep
ciudad	city
de las abejas.	of the bees.
Allí me quedé mudo	I was rapt, speechless,
y eran los montes	the Chilean

de Chile, en el invierno,
submarinos,
remotos,
sepultados
en el agua invisible
del cielo plateado:
sólo
el árbol mimosa
daba en la sombra
gritos
amarillos
como si
de la primavera errante
se hubiera desprendido
una campana
y allí
estuviera
ardiendo
en
el
árbol sonoro,
amarillo,
amarillo
como ninguna cosa puede serlo,
ni el canario, ni el oro,
ni la piel del limón, ni la retama.

Aromo,
sol terrestre,
explosión
del perfume,
cascada,
catarata,
cabellera
de todo el amarillo
derramado
en una sola ola

mountains in winter before me
underwater,
remote,
buried
in the invisible water
of silver sky:
only
the mimosa tree
offered yellow
cries
in the shade,
as if,
in the wandering spring,
a bell
had come loose
and
fire
would shimmer
there,
in
the
resonant tree,
yellow,
as no other thing could be yellow,
not the canary's color, not gold,
not lemon peel, not broom.

Myrrh tree,
sun on earth,
explosion
of perfume,
cascade,
cataract,
hair
of all the yellow
spilled
into a single wave

de follaje,	of foliage,
aromo	myrrh tree,
adelantado	sentinel
en el	in the
austral	southern
invierno	winter,
como	like
un	a
valiente	valiant
militar	yellow
amarillo,	soldier
antes de la batalla,	before battle,
desnudo,	naked,
desarmado,	unarmed,
frente	facing
a los batallones de la lluvia,	battalions
aromo,	of rain,
torre	myrrh tree,
de	tower
la	of
luz	fragrant
fragante,	light,
previa	ancestral
fogata	bonfire
de la	of
primavera,	spring,
salud	hail!
salud	hail!
pesado es tu trabajo	your labor is hard
y un amarillo amor es tu espesura.	and yellow love is your hope.
Te proclamo	I proclaim you
panal	honeycomb

del mundo:
queremos
por un instante
ser
abejorros
silvestres,
elegantes, alcohólicas
avispas,
moscardones de miel
y terciopelo,
hundir
los ojos,
la camisa,
el corazón,
el pelo
en tu temblor fragante,
en tu copa
amarilla
hasta ser sólo aroma
en tu
planeta,
polen de honor, intimidad del oro,
pluma de tu fragancia.

of the world:
for an instant,
we want
to become
wild
beekeepers,
elegant, alcoholic
wasps,
hornets of honey
and velvet,
so that we may bury
our eyes,
shirt,
heart,
hair
in your aromatic trembling,
in your yellow
chalice,
till we become simple odor
on your
planet,
pollen of honor, intimacy of gold,
feather of your fragrance.

125 / ODE ABOUT MY SORROWS

Oda de mis pesares

TRANSLATED BY KEN KRABBENHOFT

Tal vez algún, algunos
quieren saber
de mí.

Yo me prohíbo
hablar de mis pesares.
Aún joven, casi viejo
y caminando
no puedo
sin
espinas
coronar
mi corazón
que tanto
ha trabajado,
mis ojos
que exploraron la tristeza
y volvieron sin llanto
de las embarcaciones
y las islas.

Voy a contarles cómo
cuando nací
los hombres, mis amigos,
amaban
la soledad, el aire
más lejano,
la ola de las sirenas.

It could be that somebody
would like to know
how I'm doing.

I won't let myself
list my sorrows.
Almost old, I'm still youthful
and spry:
without
thorns
I cannot
crown
my heart
(which has worked
so hard)
or my eyes
that have explored the land of sadness
and returned undimmed by grief
from those ships
and islands.

But I will tell you that,
at the time I was born,
mankind—I mean my friends—
loved
solitude, the most distant
air,
and the siren's watery wave.

Yo volví	I returned
de los	from
archipiélagos,	archipelagos,
volví de los jazmines,	I returned from jasmine
del desierto,	and deserts
a ser,	to simply being
a ser,	simply being
a ser	simply being
con otros seres,	with other beings,
y cuando fui no sombra,	and when I was no longer a shadow
ni evadido,	and no longer on the run,
humano, recibí los cargamentos	when I was fully human, I received the freight
del corazón humano,	of the human heart,
las alevosas piedras	treacherous stones
de la envidia,	of envy,
la ingratitud servil de cada día.	and common, fawning ingratitude.
Regresa, Don, susurran	"Sir, come back to us!" the sirens whisper
cada vez más lejanas las sirenas:	as they fade into the distance.
golpean las espumas	Their silvery
y cortan con sus colas	tails slap the spray
plateadas	and slice
el transparente	the transparent
mar	sea
de los recuerdos.	of memories.
Nácar y luz mojados	Mother-of-pearl and ocean light
como frutas gemelas	like twin fruits glistening
a la luz de la luna embriagadora.	in the light of an intoxicating moon.
Ay, y cierro los ojos!	Ah, I close my eyes!
El susurro del cielo se despide.	Heaven's whisper takes its leave.
Voy a mi puerta a recibir espinas.	I go to the door, to receive my thorns.

126 / ODE TO THE NAMES OF VENEZUELA

Oda a los nombres de Venezuela

TRANSLATED BY ILAN STAVANS

Los llanos requemados	The plains once again burned
de febrero,	in February,
ardiente en Venezuela	Venezuela is in flames
y el camino divide	and the path divides
su extensa llamarada,	the extensive blaze,
la luz fecundadora	the fertilizing light
despojó el poderío	dismantles the wealth
de la sombra.	of its shadow.
Cruzo por el camino,	I walk across the road,
mientras crece	while the planet
el planeta a cada lado,	grows on each side,
desde Barquisimeto	from Barquisimeto
hacia Acarigua.	to Acarigua.
Como un martillo	Like a hammer
el sol	the sun
pega	touches
en las ramas,	the branches,
clava	nails
clavos celestes	celestial nails
a la tierra,	onto the earth,
estudia los rincones	studies the corners
y como un gallo encrespa	and like a rooster curls up
su plumaje	its plumage
sobre las tejas verdes de Barinas,	over the green tiles of Barinas,
sobre los párpados de Suruguapo.	over the eyelids of Suruguapo.
Tus nombres, Venezuela,	Your names, Venezuela,
los ritos	the buried

enterrados,
el agua, las batallas,
el sombrío
enlace de jaguar y cordilleras,
los plumajes
de las desconocidas
aves condecoradas
por la selva,
las palabras
apenas
entreabiertas
como de pluma o polen,
o los duros
nombres de lanza o piedra:
Aparurén, Guasipati, Canaima,
Casiquiare, Mavaca,
o más lejos, Maroa,
donde los ríos bajo las tinieblas
combaten como espadas,
arrastran tu existencia,
madera, espacio, sangre,
hacia la espuma férrea del Atlántico.

Nombres de Venezuela
fragantes y seguros
corriendo como el agua
sobre la tierra seca,
iluminando
el rostro
de la tierra
como el araguaney cuando levanta
su pabellón de besos amarillos.

Ocumare,
eres ojo, espuma y perla,
Tocuyo, hijo de harina,
Siquisique, resbalas

rivers,
water, battles,
the somber
link between the jaguar and the cordillera,
the plumage
of unknown birds
in concordance
with the jungle,
words
barely
uttered
perhaps made of pen or pollen,
or the tough
names of lance or stone:
Aparurén, Guasipati, Canaima,
Casiquiare, Mavaca,
and further away, Maroa,
where the rivers under the darkness
fight with spears,
drag your existence,
wood, space, blood,
toward the iron foam of the Atlantic.

The names of Venezuela
fragrant and assured,
running like water
over dry land,
illuminating
the face
of the earth
like the Araguaney when raising
its pavilion of yellow kisses.

Ocumare,
you are eye, foam and pearl.
Tocuyo, child of flour.
Siquisique, you slide

como un jabón mojado y oloroso
y, si escogiera, el sol
nacería en el nombre de Carora,
el agua nacería en Cabudare,
la noche dormiría en Sabaneta.

En Chiriguare, en Guay, en Urucure,
en Coro, en Bucarai, en Moroturo,
en todas las regiones
de Venezuela desgranada
no recogí sino éste,
este tesoro:
las semillas ardientes de esos nombres
que sembraré en la tierra mía, lejos.

like wet and odorous soap
and, if I need to choose, the sun
would be born with the name of Carora,
water would be born in Cabudare,
the sleeping night in Sabaneta.

In Chiriguare, in Guay, in Urucure,
in Coro, in Bucarai, in Moroturo,
in all the regions
of a scattered Venezuela
I did not collect but this,
its treasure:
the ardent seeds of those names,
which I planted in my own land, far away.

127 / ODE TO NIGHT

Oda a la noche

TRANSLATED BY ILAN STAVANS

Detrás
del día,
de cada piedra y árbol,
detrás de cada libro,
noche,
galopas y trabajas,
o reposas,
esperando
hasta que tus raíces recogidas
desarrollan tu flor y tu follaje.
Como
una bandera
te agitas en el cielo
hasta llenar no sólo
los montes y los mares,
sino las más pequeñas cavidades,
los ojos
férreos del campesino fatigado,
el coral negro
de las bocas humanas
entregadas al sueño.
Libre corres
sobre el curso salvaje
de los ríos,
secretas sendas cubres, noche,
profundidad de amores constelados
por los cuerpos desnudos,

Behind
the day,
in each stone and tree,
behind each book,
night,
you gallop and labor,
or rest,
waiting
until your withdrawn roots
develop your flower and foliage.
Like
a flag
you flutter in the sky
until you fill not only
the hills and seas,
but the smallest cavities,
the tired peasant's
iron eyes,
the black coral
of human mouths
given to dreaming.
You run free
over the savage course
of rivers,
covering secret paths, night,
depths of loves star-stricken
by naked bodies,

crímenes que salpican
con un grito de sombra,
mientras tanto los trenes
corren, los fogoneros
tiran carbón nocturno al fuego rojo,
el atareado empleado de estadística
se ha metido en un bosque
de hojas petrificadas,
el panadero amasa
la blancura.
La noche también duerme
como un caballo ciego.
Llueve
de norte a sur,
sobre los grandes
árboles de mi patria,
sobre los techos
de metal corrugado,
suena
el canto de la noche,
lluvia y oscuridad son los metales
de la espada que canta,
y estrellas o jazmines
vigilan
desde la altura negra,
señales
que poco a poco
con lentitud de siglos
entenderemos.
Noche,
noche mía,
noche de todo el mundo,
tienes algo
dentro de ti, redondo
como un niño
que va a nacer, como una

crimes splashing
with the scream of a shadow,
meanwhile trains
run, the stokers
throw nocturnal coal on the red fire,
the busy statistician
has immersed himself in a forest
of petrified pages,
the baker kneads
whiteness.
Night also sleeps
like a black horse.
It rains
from north to south,
over the grand
trees of my country,
over the roofs
of corrugated metal,
the night's song
is heard,
the metal of the singing spear
is made of rain and darkness,
and stars and jasmine
guard
from the darkness above,
signs
we will understand
little by little
at the speed of centuries.
Night,
night of mine,
night of the entire world,
you have something
inside you, round
like a child
about to be born, like

semilla	a bursting
que revienta,	seed,
es el milagro,	it is the miracle,
es el día.	it is the day.
Eres más bella	You are more beautiful
porque alimentas con tu sangre oscura	because with your darker blood
la amapola que nace,	you feed the poppy being born,
porque trabajas con ojos cerrados	because you work with eyes closed
para que se abran ojos,	so eyes can open,
para que cante el agua,	so water can sing,
para que resuciten	so our lives
nuestras vidas.	might resuscitate.

128 / ODE TO A NOCTURNAL WASHERWOMAN

Oda a una lavandera nocturna

TRANSLATED BY ILAN STAVANS

Desde el jardín, en lo alto,
miré la lavandera.
Era de noche.
Lavaba, refregaba,
sacudía,
un segundo sus manos
brillaban en la espuma,
luego
caían en la sombra.
Desde arriba
a la luz de la vela
era en la noche la única
viviente,
lo único que vivía:
aquello
sacudiéndose
en la espuma,
los brazos en la ropa,
el movimiento,
la incansable energía:
va y viene
el movimiento,
cayendo y levantándose
con precisión celeste,
van y vienen
las manos sumergidas,
las manos, viejas manos

From the garden, high above,
I watched the washerwoman.
It was night.
She washed, scrubbed,
scrubbed,
her hands glittered
for a second in the suds,
then
descended into shadow.
Seen from above
under the candlelight
she was the only one
alive at night,
the only thing living:
something
shuddering
in the suds,
arms deep in washing,
the movement,
the tireless energy:
the movement
coming and going,
falling and rising
with celestial precision,
her submerged hands
coming and going,
hands, old hands

que lavan en la noche,	washing in the night
hasta tarde, en la noche,	till late at night,
que lavan	washing
ropa ajena,	other people's clothes,
que sacan en el agua	leaving in the water
la huella	the stain
del trabajo,	of labor,
la mancha	stains
de los cuerpos,	of bodies,
el recuerdo impregnado	the impregnated memory
de los pies que anduvieron,	of feet in motion,
las camisas,	of weary,
cansadas,	worn-out
los calzones	shirts,
marchitos,	faded underwear,
lava	she washes
y lava,	and washes,
de noche.	at night.
La nocturna	The night
lavandera	washerwoman
a veces	sometimes
levantaba	lifts
la cabeza	her head
y ardían en su pelo	and stars blaze
las estrellas	in her hair
porque	because
la sombra	the shadow
confundía	blurred
su cabeza	her head
y era la noche, el cielo	and the washerwoman
de la noche	is the night, the night
la cabellera	sky,
de la lavandera,	and her candle
y su vela	a tiny
un astro	planet

diminuto
que encendía
sus manos
que alzaban
y movían
la ropa,
subiendo
y
descendiendo,
enarbolando
el aire, el agua,
el jabón vivo,
la magnética espuma.

Yo no oía,
no oía
el susurro
de la ropa en sus manos.
Mis ojos
en la noche
la miraban
sola
como un planeta.
Ardía
la nocturna
lavandera,
lavando,
restregando
la ropa
trabajando
en el frío,
en la dureza,
lavando en el silencio nocturno del invierno,
lava y lava,
la pobre
lavandera.

lighting
her hands
that
raise
and scrub
the clothes,
rising
and
falling,
brandishing
air, water,
glowing soap,
magnetic suds.

I couldn't hear,
not hear
the whisper
of the clothes in her hands.
My eyes
in the night
saw her
alone
like a planet.
The night
washerwoman
blazed,
washing,
rubbing
the clothes,
working
in the cold,
in harshness,
washing in the nocturnal silence of
winter,
washing and washing,
poor
washerwoman.

129 / ODE WITH NOSTALGIA FOR CHILE

Oda con nostalgias de Chile

TRANSLATED BY ILAN STAVANS

En tierras argentinas *vivo y muero* *penando por mi patria,* *escogiendo* *de día lo que a Chile me recuerda,* *de noche las estrellas* *que arden al otro lado de la nieve.*	In Argentine lands I live and die, craving my country, choosing by day what Chile reminds me of, by night the stars blazing on the other side of the snow.
Andando las llanuras, *extraviado en la palma del espacio,* *descifrando las hierbas* *de la pampa, verbenas,* *matorrales, espinas,* *me parece que el cielo los aplasta:* *el cielo, única flor de la pradera.*	Walking through plains, astray in the palm of space, deciphering herbs in the pampa, verbena, thickets, thorns, it seems the sky is crushing them: the sky, sole flower of the prairie.
Grande es el aire vivo, la intemperie *total y parecemos* *desnudos, solos en el infinito* *y oloroso silencio.* *Plana es la tierra como* *tirante cuero de tambor: galopes,* *hombre, historia,* *desaparecen en la lejanía.*	Grand is the living air, the absolute openness, and we seem naked, alone in the infinite, aromatic silence. Flat is the land like a strained drumhead: galloping, man, history, disappear in the distance.
A mí dadme los verdes *laberintos,* *las esbeltas*	Give me the green labyrinths, the svelte

vertientes
de los Andes, y bajo los parrones,
amada, tu cintura
de guitarra!

slopes
of the Andes, and under the wild vine,
loved one, your guitar
waist!

A mí dadme las olas
que sacuden
el cuerpo cristalino
de mi patria,
dejadme al este ver cómo se eleva
la majestad del mundo
en un collar altivo de volcanes
y a mis pies sólo el sello
de la espuma,
nieve del mar, eterna platería!

Give me the waves
shaking
the crystalline body
of my country,
allow me to see in the east how
the majesty of the world is lifted
with a haughty necklace of volcanoes
and on my feet only the mark
of foam,
sea snow, the eternal shop of a silversmith.

Americano
soy
y se parece
a la pampa extendida
mi corazón, lo cruzan
los caminos
y me gusta
que en él enciendan fuego
y vuelen y galopen
pájaros y viajeros.

I am
American
and my heart
resembles
the spread-out pampa crossed
by roads
and I enjoy
birds and travelers
lighting a fire
and flying and galloping.

Pero mi cuerpo, Patria,
reclama tu substancia:
metálicas montañas desde donde
el habitante baja, enamorado,
entre vegetaciones minerales
hacia el susurro de los valles verdes.

But my body, Homeland,
requires your substance:
metallic mountains from where
the inhabitant descends, in love,
amid mineral vegetation
toward the whisper of green valleys.

Amor de mis amores,
tierra pura,

Love of my life,
land of purity,

cuando vuelva
me amarraré a tu proa
de embarcación terrestre,
y así navegaremos
confundidos
hasta que tú me cubras
y yo pueda, contigo, eternamente,
ser vino que regresa en cada otoño,
piedra de tus alturas,
ola de tu marino movimiento!

when I return
I shall bind myself to the prow
of your earthly embankment,
and that way we shall sail
confused
until you cover me
and I can become, with you, eternally,
wine returning every autumn,
stone of your heights,
wave of your marine movement!

130 / ODE TO NUMBERS

Oda a los números

TRANSLATED BY MARGARET SAYERS PEDEN

Qué sed
de saber cuánto!
Qué hambre
de saber
cuántas
estrellas tiene el cielo!

Nos pasamos
la infancia
contando piedras, plantas,
dedos arenas, dientes,
la juventud contando
pétalos, cabelleras.
Contamos
los colores, los años,
las vidas y los besos,
en el campo
los bueyes, en el mar
las olas. Los navíos
se hicieron cifras que se fecundaban.
Los números parían.
Las ciudades
eran miles, millones,
el trigo centenares
de unidades que adentro
tenían otros números pequeños,
más pequeños que un grano.

Oh, the thirst to know
how many!
The hunger
to know
how many
stars in the sky!

We spent
our childhood counting
stones and plants, fingers and
toes, grains of sand, and teeth,
our youth we passed counting
petals and comets' tails.
We counted
colors, years,
lives, and kisses;
in the country,
oxen; by the sea,
the waves. Ships
became proliferating ciphers.
Numbers multiplied.
The cities
were thousands, millions,
wheat hundreds
of units that held
within them smaller numbers,
smaller than a single grain.

El tiempo se hizo número.
La luz fue numerada
y por más que corrió con el sonido
fue su velocidad un 37.
Nos rodearon los números.
Cerrábamos la puerta,
de noche, fatigados,
llegaba un 800,
por debajo,
hasta entrar con nosotros en la cama,
y en el sueño
los 4000 y los 77
picándonos la frente
con sus martillos o sus alicates.
Los 5
agregándose
hasta entrar en el mar o en el delirio,
hasta que el sol saluda con su cero
y nos vamos corriendo
a la oficina,
al taller,
a la fábrica,
a comenzar de nuevo el infinito
número 1 de cada día.

Tuvimos, hombre, tiempo
para que nuestra sed
fuera saciándose,
el ancestral deseo
de enumerar las cosas
y sumarlas,
de reducirlas hasta
hacerlas polvo,
arenales de números.
Fuimos
empapelando el mundo

Time became a number.
Light was numbered
and no matter how it raced with sound
its velocity was 37.
Numbers surrounded us.
When we closed the door
at night, exhausted,
an 800 slipped
beneath the door
and crept with us into bed,
and in our dreams
4000s and 77s
pounded at our foreheads
with hammers and tongs.
5s
added to 5s
until they sank into the sea or madness,
until the sun greeted us with its zero
and we went running
to the office,
to the workshop,
to the factory,
to begin again the infinite
1 of each new day.

We had time, as men,
for our thirst slowly
to be sated,
the ancestral desire
to give things a number,
to add them up,
to reduce them
to powder,
wastelands of numbers.
We
papered the world

con números y nombres,
pero
las cosas existían,
se fugaban
del número,
enloquecían en sus cantidades,
se evaporaban
dejando
su olor o su recuerdo
y quedaban los números vacíos.

Por eso,
para ti
quiero las cosas.
Los números
que se vayan a la cárcel,
que se muevan
en columnas cerradas
procreando
hasta darnos la suma
de la totalidad del infinito.
Para ti sólo quiero
que aquellos
números del camino
te defiendan
y que tú los defiendas.
La cifra semanal de tu salario
se desarrolle hasta cubrir tu pecho.
Y del número 2 en que se enlazan
tu cuerpo y el de la mujer amada
salgan los ojos pares de tus hijos
a contar otra vez
las antiguas estrellas
y las innumerables
espigas
que llenarán la tierra transformada.

with numbers and names,
but
things survived,
they fled
from numbers,
went mad in their quantities,
evaporated,
leaving
an odor or a memory,
leaving the numbers empty.

That's why
for you
I want *things*.
Let numbers
go to jail,
let them march
in perfect columns
procreating
until they give the sum
total of infinity.
For you I want only
for the numbers
along the road
to protect you
and for you to protect them.
May the weekly figure of your salary
expand until it spans your chest.
And from the 2 of you, embraced,
your body and that of your beloved,
may pairs of children's eyes be born
that will count again
the ancient stars
and countless
heads of grain
that will cover a transformed earth.

131 / ODE TO AN OFFENDED PICARO

Oda al pícaro ofendido

TRANSLATED BY MARGARET SAYERS PEDEN

Yo sólo de la bruma,
de las
banderas
del invierno
marino, con su niebla,
traspasado
por la soberanía
de las olas,
hablé,
sólo de aquellas cosas
que acompañaron
mi destino.

El pícaro elevó
su nariz verde,
clavó su picotazo
y todo siguió como
había sido,
la bruma, el mar,
mi canto.
Al amor, a su caja
de palomas,
al alma y a la boca
de la que amo,
consagré
toda palabra, todo
susurro, toda tierra,
todo fuego en mi canto,

I wrote only of mist,
of the
banners
of the winter
sea, with its fog,
penetrated
by the sovereignty
of the waves,
only
of those things
that were a part of
my destiny.

The picaro raised
his envious nose and
struck a blow with his beak,
but everything continued as
before,
the fog, the sea,
my song.
To love, to its crate
of doves,
to the soul and the lips
of the woman I love,
I dedicated
every word, every
whisper, all the earth,
all the fire in my song,

porque el amor
sostengo
y me sostiene
y he de morir amándote,
amor mío.

El pícaro esperaba
en las esquinas turbias
y eruditas
para clavar su infame
dentadura
en
el
panal
abierto
y rumoroso.

Todo siguió como era, como deben
ser las cosas eternas,
la mujer
con su ramo
de rocío,
el hombre con su canto.
En el camino
el pueblo
iba desnudo
y me mostró
sus manos
desgarradas
por aguas y por minas.
Eran
aquellos
caminantes
miembros de mi familia:
no era mi sangre,
sol,
ni flor,

because I sustain
love
and its sustains me,
and I will die loving you,
my love.

The picaro waited
on his dark erudite
street corners
to sink his infamous
teeth
into
the
open
buzzing
honeycomb.

Everything remained the same, as
eternal things should,
the woman
with her dewy
bouquet,
the man with his song.
Along the road
ordinary folk
walked naked
and showed me
their hands
ravaged
by rain and mines.
They were,
those
travelers,
members of my family:
my blood was not
sun,
or flower,

ni cielo:	or sky;
eran aquellos hombres	they were, those men,
mis hermanos	my brothers
y para ellos	and for them
fue	was
la inquebrantable	the indestructible
materia de mi canto.	substance of my song.
El pícaro con otros	The picaro and assorted
adheridos	sycophants
cocinó en una marmita	simmered vile brews
sus resabios,	in his kettle,
los preparó con odio,	he stewed them with hatred,
con recortes	with clippings
de garras,	from claws,
estableció oficinas	he set up offices
con	with
amigos	frustrated
amargos	friends
y produjo	and produced
sangrienta y polvorienta	a bloody and dusty
picardía.	villainy.
Entre olas	Between waves
que llenaban	that flooded
de claridad y canto el universo,	the universe with light and song,
de pronto me detuve	I paused suddenly
y dediqué una línea	to dedicate a line
de mi oda,	of my ode,
una sola	a single
sentencia,	sentence,
apenas	barely
una	a
sílaba,	syllable,
al contumaz y pícaro	to my contumacious and villainous
enemigo	enemy
—en tantos años un solo saludo—,	—in so many years, a single remark—

el golpe de la espuma
de una ola.

Y enloqueció
de pronto
el pícaro
famoso,
el viejo ofendedor
se declaró
ofendido,
corrió por las esquinas
con su lupa
clavada
al
mínimo meñique de mi oda,
clamó ante los autores
y las autoridades
para que todo el mundo
me
desautorizara,
y cuando
nadie
se
hizo parte
de sus lamentaciones
enfermó de tristeza,
se hundió en la más letárgica
de las melancolías
y sólo de su cueva
sale a veces
a llenar oficinas con suspiros.

Moraleja:
no ofendas al poeta distraído
semana por semana, siglo a siglo,
porque de pronto puede
dedicarte un minuto peligroso.

the breath of the froth
of a wave.

Instantly
he went berserk,
this famous
picaro,
the former offender
declared himself
offended,
he ran through the streets
with his magnifying glass
glued
on the
little finger of my ode,
he railed before authors
and authorities
hoping everyone
would de-authorize
me,
but when
no
one
joined in
his lamentations,
he became ill with grief,
he sank into the most lethargic
of melancholies,
and only occasionally emerges
from his cave
to fill offices with sighs.

Moral:
do not insult the distracted poet
week after week, century after century,
because suddenly he may devote
one perilous minute to you.

132 / ODE TO OIL

Oda al aceite

TRANSLATED BY MARGARET SAYERS PEDEN

Cerca del rumoroso	Near the rustling
cereal, de las olas	grain, near the waves
del viento en las avenas,	of wind in the oatfields
el olivo	the olive tree
de volumen plateado,	of silvery volume,
severo en su linaje,	severe in its lineage,
en su torcido	in its twisted
corazón terrestre:	terrestrial heart:
las gráciles	graceful
olivas	olives
pulidas	polished
por los dedos	by the fingers
que hicieron	that made
la paloma	the dove
y el caracol	and the seashell:
marino:	green,
verdes,	innumerable,
innumerables,	pure, pure
purísimos	nipples
pezones	of nature,
de la naturaleza,	and there
y allí	in
en	the dry
los secos	olive groves,
olivares,	where
donde	

tan sólo
cielo azul con cigarras,
y tierra dura
existen,
allí
el prodigio,
la cápsula
perfecta
de la oliva
llenado
con sus constelaciones el follaje:
más tarde
las vasijas,
el milagro,
el aceite.

Yo amo
las patrias del aceite,
los olivares
de Chacabuco, en Chile,
en la mañana
las plumas de platino
forestales
contra las arrugadas
cordilleras,
en Anacapri, arriba,
sobre la luz tirrena,
la desesperación de los olivos,
y en el mapa de Europa,
España,
cesta negra de aceitunas
espolvoreada por los azahares
como por una ráfaga marina.

Aceite,
recóndita y suprema

only
blue sky with cicadas
and harsh land
exist,
there
the prodigy,
the perfect
capsule
of the olive
filling the foliage with its constellations:
later,
the casks,
the miracle,
oil.

I love
the homelands of oil,
the Chacabuco olive
groves, in Chile,
in the morning
the feathery forest
of platinum
against the wrinkled
mountain range,
in Anacapri, high above
over the Tyrrhenian lit sky,
the desperation of the olive trees,
and on the map of Europe,
Spain,
black basket of olives
dusted with orange blossoms
as if by a gust of wind from the sea.

Oil,
hidden and most important

condición de la olla,
pedestal de perdices,
llave celeste de la mayonesa,
suave y sabroso
sobre las lechugas
y sobrenatural en el infierno
de los arzobispales pejerreyes.
Aceite, en nuestra voz, en
nuestro coro,
con
íntima
suavidad poderosa
cantas:
eres idioma
castellano:
hay sílabas de aceite,
hay palabras
útiles y olorosas
como tu fragante materia.
No sólo canta el vino,
también canta el aceite,
vive en nosotros con su luz madura
y entre los bienes de la tierra
aparto,
aceite,
tu inagotable paz, tu esencia verde,
tu colmado tesoro que desciende
desde los manantiales del olivo.

ingredient of the stew,
base for partridges,
celestial key to mayonnaise,
smooth and savory
on lettuce leaves,
and supernatural in the hell
of archiepiscopal mackerel.
Oil, with our voice,
our chorus,
with
intimate
powerful smoothness
you sing:
you are the Castilian
tongue:
there are syllables of oil,
there are words,
useful and aromatic
like your fragrant substance.
Not only the wine sings,
but the oil sings too,
living in us with its mature light,
and among the riches of the earth,
I set you aside,
oil,
for your boundless peace, your green essence,
your abundant treasure flowing down
from the springs of the olive tree.

133 / ODE TO THE OLD MAPOCHO STATION, IN SANTIAGO, CHILE

Oda a la vieja Estación Mapocho, en Santiago de Chile

TRANSLATED BY ILAN STAVANS

Antiguo hangar echado
junto al río,
puerta del mar,
vieja Estación rosada,
bajo cuyas
ferruginosas cavidades
sueños y trenes
saliendo desbocados
trepidaron
hacia las olas y las ciudades.
El humo, el sueño, el hombre
fugitivo,
el movimiento,
el llanto,
el humo, la alegría
y el invierno
carcomieron tus muros,
corroyeron tus arcos,
y eres hoy una pobre
catedral que agoniza.

Se fugaron los dioses
y entran como ciclones

Ancient hangar laid over
near the river,
door to the sea,
old crimson station,
from whose
ferruginous cavities
dreams and trains
quiveringly departed
in hurried exit
toward the waves and cities.
Smoke, dream, furtive
man,
movement,
crying,
smoke, happiness
and winter
ruined your walls,
corroded your arcs,
and today you are a forgotten
cathedral dying out.

The gods escaped
and like cyclones the trains

los trenes ahuyentando las distancias.
De otro tiempo gentil
y miserable
eres
y tu nave de hierro
alimentó las crinolinas
y los sombreros altos,
mientras
sórdida era la vida de los pobres
que como un mar amargo
te rodeaba.
Era el pasado, el pueblo
sin banderas,
y tú resplanderecías
luminosa
como una jaula nueva:
con su cinta de barro
el río Mapocho
rascaba tus
paredes,
y los niños dormían
en las alas del hambre.

Vieja Estación, no sólo
transcurrían
las aguas del Mapocho
hacia el océano,
sino también
el tiempo.
Las elegantes
aves
que
partían
envejecieron o
murieron en París, de alcoholismo.
Otra gente

came driving away distances.
You are
from another gentle
and miserable time
and your iron vault
fed the crinolines
and top hats,
while
sordid was the life of the poor
who surrounded you
as in a sour sea.
You are the past, the people
without flags,
and you shone
luminous
like a new cage:
with a ribbon of clay
the Mapocho River
itched your
walls,
and children slept
in the wings of hunger.

Old station, not only
the Mapocho waters
passed
toward the ocean,
but time
as well.
The elegant
birds
who
took off
aged or
died in Paris, from alcohol.
Others

llegó,
llenó los trenes,
mal vestidos viajeros,
con canastos,
banderas
sobre amenazadoras multitudes,
y la vieja Estación
reaccionaria
se marchitó. La vida
creció y multiplicó su poderío
alrededor de todos los viajeros,
y ella, inmóvil, sagrada,
envejeció, dormida
junto al río.

Oh antigua
Estación,
fresca como un túnel,
fueron
contigo
hacia los siete océanos
mis sueños,
hacia Valparaíso,
hacia las islas
puras,
hacia el escalofrío de la espuma
bajo
la rectitud
de las palmeras!

En tus andenes
no sólo
los viajeros olvidaron
pañuelos,
ramos
de rosas apagadas,

came,
filled the trains,
poorly dressed travelers,
with baskets,
flags
over threatening crowds,
and the old reactionary
Station
withered. Life
grew and multiplied its power
around all the travelers,
and she, motionless, sacred,
aged, asleep
by the river.

Oh ancient
Station,
fresh like a tunnel,
my dreams
went
with you
toward the Seven Seas,
to Valparaíso,
toward the pristine
islands,
toward the shiver of the foam
under
the rectitude
of palm trees!

On your platforms
not only
travelers forgot
handkerchiefs,
bouquets
of toned-down roses,

llaves,
sino
secretos, vidas,
esperanzas.
Ay, Estación,
no sabe
tu silencio
que fuiste
las puntas de una estrella
derramada
hacia la magnitud
de las mareas,
hacia
la lejanía
en los caminos!

Te acostumbró
la noche
a su vestido
y el día
fue
terrible
para tu viejo rostro
allí
pintado falsamente
para una fiesta,
mientras tu subterráneo
corazón
se nutría
de distantes adioses
y raíces.

Te amo,
vieja Estación
que junto
al río oscuro,

keys,
but
secrets, lives,
hopes.
Ay, Station,
your silence
doesn't know
you were
the tips of a star
scattered
onto the magnitude
of tides,
toward
the distance
of roads!

Night
made its dress
common
and day
was
devastating
for your old face
falsely painted
for a party
there,
while your subterranean
heart
was nurtured
by distant goodbyes
and roots.

I love you
old Station,
for rising
near

a la corriente turbia
del Mapocho,
fundaste,
con sombras pasajeras,
tu propio río
de amor intermitente, interminable.

the dark,
troubled currents
of the Mapocho River,
the passing shadows
of your own river
of intermittent love, interminable.

134 / ODE TO THE ONION

Oda a la cebolla

TRANSLATED BY STEPHEN MITCHELL

Cebolla,	Onion,
luminosa redoma,	shining flask,
pétalo a pétalo	your beauty assembled
se formó tu hermosura,	petal by petal,
escamas de cristal te acrecentaron	they affixed crystal scales to you
y en el secreto de la tierra oscura	and your belly of dew grew round
se redondeó tu vientre de rocío.	in the secret depth of the dark earth.
Bajo la tierra	The miracle took place
fue el milagro	underground,
y cuando apareció	and when your lazy green stalk
tu torpe tallo verde,	appeared
y nacieron	and your leaves were born
tus hojas como espadas en el huerto,	like swords in the garden,
la tierra acumuló su poderío	the earth gathered its strength
mostrando tu desnuda transparencia,	exhibiting your naked transparency,
y como en Afrodita el mar remoto	and just as the distant sea
duplicó la magnolia	copied the magnolia in Aphrodite
levantando sus senos,	raising up her breasts,
la tierra	so the earth
así te hizo,	made you,
cebolla,	onion,
clara como un planeta,	as bright as a planet
y destinada	and fated
a relucir,	to shine,
constelación constante,	constant constellation,
redonda rosa de agua,	rounded rose of water,

sobre
la mesa
de las pobres gentes.

Generosa
deshaces
tu globo de frescura
en la consumación
ferviente de la olla,
y el jirón de cristal
al calor encendido del aceite
se transforma en rizada pluma de oro.

También recordaré cómo fecunda
tu influencia el amor de la ensalada
y parece que el cielo contribuye
dándote fina forma de granizo
a celebrar tu claridad picada
sobre los hemisferios de un tomate.
Pero al alcance
de las manos del pueblo,
regada con aceite,
espolvoreada
con un poco de sal,
matas el hambre
del jornalero en el duro camino.
Estrella de los pobres,
hada madrina
envuelta
en delicado
papel, sales del suelo,
eterna, intacta, pura
como semilla de astro,
y al cortarte
el cuchillo en la cocina

on
poor people's
dining tables.

Generously
you give up
your balloon of freshness
to the boiling consummation
of the pot,
and in the blazing heat of the oil
the shred of crystal
is transformed into a curled feather of gold.

I shall also proclaim how your influence
livens the salad's love,
and the sky seems to contribute
giving you the fine shape of hail
praising your chopped brightness
upon the halves of the tomato.
But within the people's
reach,
showered with oil,
dusted
with a pinch of salt,
you satisfy the worker's hunger
along the hard road home.
Poor people's star,
fairy godmother
wrapped
in fancy paper,
you rise from the soil,
eternal, intact, as pure
as a celestial seed,
and when the kitchen knife
cuts you

sube la única lágrima
sin pena.
Nos hiciste llorar sin afligirnos.
Yo cuanto existe celebré, cebolla,
pero para mí eres
más hermosa que un ave
de plumas cegadoras,
eres para mis ojos
globo celeste, copa de platino,
baile inmóvil
de anémona nevada

y vive la fragancia de la tierra
en tu naturaleza cristalina.

the only painless tear
is shed:
you made us weep without suffering.
I have praised every living thing, onion,
but for me you are
more beautiful than a bird
of blinding plumage;
to my eyes you are
a heavenly balloon, platinum cup,
the snowy anemone's
motionless dance.

The fragrance of earth is alive
in your crystalline nature.

135 / ODE TO THE ORANGE

Oda a la naranja

TRANSLATED BY KEN KRABBENHOFT

A semejanza tuya,
a tu imagen,
naranja,
se hizo el mundo:
redondo el sol, rodeado
por cáscaras de fuego:
la noche consteló con azahares
su rumbo y su navío.
Así fue y así fuimos,
oh tierra,
descubriéndote,
planeta anaranjado.
Somos los rayos de una sola rueda
divididos
como lingotes de oro
y alcanzando con trenes y con ríos
la insólita unidad de la naranja.

Orange,
the world was made
in your likeness
and image:
the sun was made round, surrounded
by peels of flame,
and night strewed its engine and its path
with your blossoms.
So it was, O earth,
orange planet,
and we went on
to discover you.
We are the spokes of a single wheel
fanning out
like tongues of molten gold.
Trains and rivers are the way we achieve
the orange's unmatched oneness.

Patria
mía,
amarilla
cabellera,
espada del otoño,
cuando
a tu luz
retorno,
a la desierta

Country
of my birth,
head of
yellow hair,
autumn sword:
when
I return
to your light,
to the vacant

zona | lunar landscape
del salitre lunario, | of saltpeter wastes,
a las aristas | to lacerating
desgarradoras | cliffs
del metal andino, | of Andean ore,
cuando | when
penetro | I penetrate
tu contorno, tus aguas, | your borders and your waters,
alabo | when I praise
tus mujeres, | your women
miro cómo los bosques | and admire how the woods
balancean | gently rock
aves y hojas sagradas, | the birds and sacred leaves,
el trigo se derrama en los graneros | how wheat pours into granaries
y las naves navegan | and ships find their way
por oscuros estuarios, | up dark estuaries:
comprendo que eres, | I understand that you,
planeta, | planet, are
una naranja, | an orange,
una fruta del fuego. | a fruit born of fire.

En tu piel se reúnen | Nations
los países | are united
unidos | within your rind
como sectores de una sola fruta, | like segments of a single fruit.
y Chile, a tu costado, | Chile, lying the length of your side,
eléctrico, | electric
encendido | and inflamed
sobre | above
los follajes azules | the Pacific's
del Pacífico | blue foliage,
es un largo recinto de naranjos. | is a long haven for orange trees.

Anaranjada sea | Give us
la luz | this day
de cada | orange daylight,

día,
y el corazón del hombre,
sus racimos,
ácido y dulce sea:
manantial de frescura
que tenga y que preserve
la misteriosa
sencillez
de la tierra
y la pura unidad
de una naranja.

and every day,
and may mankind's heart,
and its clusters of fruit,
be both bitter and sweet:
irrepressible source of freshness,
may it hold and protect
the earth's
mysterious
simplicity,
and the perfect oneness
of an orange.

136 / ODE TO A PAIR OF SCISSORS

Oda a las tijeras

TRANSLATED BY ILAN STAVANS

Prodigiosas
tijeras
(parecidas
a pájaros,
a peces),
bruñidas sois como las armaduras
de la caballería.

De dos cuchillos largos
y alevosos,
casados y cruzados
para siempre,
de dos
pequeños ríos
amarrados,
resultó una cortante criatura,
un pez que nada en tempestuosos lienzos,
un pájaro que vuela
en
las peluquerías.

Tijeras
olorosas
a
mano

Prodigious
scissors
(looking
like birds,
like fish),
you're polished like the knight's
shining armor.

From two knives long
and treacherous,
married and crossed
forever,
from two
small rivers
tied together,
a cutting creature resulted,
a fish swimming on tempestuous
canvases,
a bird flying
in
the barbershops.

Scissors
that smell
of
the hand

de la tía	of my seamstress
costurera,	aunt's
cuando con su metálico	when there a metallic
ojo blanco	white eye
miraron	spied
nuestra	our
arrinconada	cornered
infancia	childhood
contando	telling
a los vecinos	our neighbors
nuestros robos de besos y ciruelas.	about our thefts of kisses and plums.
Allí	There
en la casa	in the house
y dentro de su nido	and inside their own nest
las tijeras cruzaron	the scissors crossed
nuestras vidas	our lives
y luego	and so
cuánta	how much
tela	fabric
cortaron y cortaron	they cut and kept on cutting
para novias y muertos,	for brides and the dead,
para recién nacidos y hospitales	for newborns and hospitals
cortaron,	they cut
y cortaron,	and kept on cutting,
y el pelo	also the peasant's
campesino	hair
duro	like
como planta en la piedra,	a plant in stone,
y las banderas	and the flags
que luego	soon
fuego y sangre	stained and scorched
mancharon y horadaron,	by fire and blood,
y el tallo	and vine
de las viñas en invierno,	stacks in winter,

el hilo	the thread
de la	of
voz	voices
en el teléfono.	on the telephone.
Unas tijeras olvidadas	A forgotten pair of scissors
cortaron en tu ombligo	cut your mother's
el hilo	thread
de la madre	from the navel
y te entregaron para siempre	and handed you
tu separada parte de existencia:	your separate existence forever:
otras, no necesariamente	others, not necessarily
oscuras,	somber,
cortarán algún día	will someday cut
tu traje de difunto.	your shroud.
Las tijeras	Scissors
fueron	went
a todas partes:	everywhere:
exploraron	they explored
el mundo	the world
cortando	equally
por igual	cutting
alegría	happiness
y tristeza	and sorrow:
todo fue paño	everything has been cloth
para las tijeras:	for scissors to cut:
titánicas	titanic
tijeras	tailoring
de sastrería,	scissors,
bellas como cruceros,	beautiful like a schooner,
minúsculas	minuscule
que cortan uñas	that trim nails
dándoles forma de menguante luna,	giving them the shape of a waning moon,
delgadas,	slender,

submarinas tijeras	a surgeon's
del cirujano	submarine scissors
que cortan el enredo	cutting the tangle
o el nudo equivocado en tu intestino.	or the wrong knot in your intestine.
Y aquí con las tijeras	And now with the scissors
de la razón	of reason
corto mi oda,	I cut my ode,
para que no se alargue y no se encrespe,	so it doesn't lose shape and escape,
para que	so it
pueda	can
caber en tu bolsillo	fit in your pocket
plegada y preparada	folded and smoothed
como	like
un par	a pair
de tijeras.	of scissors.

137 / ODE TO A PAIR OF SOCKS

Oda a los calcetines

TRANSLATED BY MARK STRAND

Me trajo Maru Mori
un par
de calcetines
que tejió con sus manos
de pastora,
dos calcetines suaves
como liebres.
En ellos
metí los pies
como en
dos
estuches
tejidos
con hebras del
crepúsculo
y pellejo de ovejas.

Violentos calcetines,
mis pies fueron
dos pescados
de lana,
dos largos tiburones
de azul ultramarino
atravesados
por una trenza de oro,
dos gigantescos mirlos,
dos cañones:

Maru Mota brought me
a pair
of socks
that she knitted with her
shepherdess hands,
two socks soft
as rabbits.
I put my feet
into them
as into
two
cases
knitted
with threads of
twilight
and sheeps wool.

Wild socks,
my feet were
two wool
fish,
two big sharks
of ultramarine
crossed
by a golden braid,
two giant blackbirds,
two cannons:

mis pies
fueron honrados
de este modo
por
estos
celestiales
calcetines.
Eran
tan hermosos
que por primera vez
mis pies me parecieron
inaceptables
como dos decrépitos
bomberos, bomberos
indignos
de aquel fuego
bordado,
de aquellos luminosos
calcetines.

Sin embargo
resistí
la tentación aguda
de guardarlos
como los colegiales
preservan
las luciérnagas,
como los eruditos
coleccionan
documentos sagrados,
resistí
el impulso furioso
de ponerlos
en una jaula
de oro
y darles cada día

my feet
were honored
in this way
by these
heavenly
socks.
They were
so beautiful
that for the first time
my feet seemed to me
unacceptable
like two decrepit
firemen, firemen
unworthy
of that
embroidered
fire,
of those shining
socks.

Anyway
I resisted
the sharp temptation
to save them
the way schoolboys
keep
lightning bugs,
the way scholars
collect
rare books,
I resisted
the mad impulse
to put them
in a golden
cage
and each day

alpiste
y pulpa de melón rosado.
Como descubridores
que en la selva
entregan el rarísimo
venado verde
al asador
y se lo comen
con remordimiento,
estiré
los pies
y me enfundé
los
bellos
calcetines
y
luego los zapatos.

Y es ésta
la moral de mi oda:
dos veces es belleza
la belleza
y lo que es bueno es doblemente
bueno
cuando se trata de dos calcetines
de lana
en el invierno.

to feed them birdseed
and the meat of a rosy melon.
Like explorers
in the forest
who give up the finest
young deer
to the roasting spit
and eat it
with regret,
I stretched out
my feet
and put on
the
lovely
socks
and then
my shoes.

And this is
the moral of my ode:
beauty is twice
beautiful
and goodness is doubly
good
when
it concerns two wool
socks
in winter.

138 / ODE TO THE PAST

Oda al pasado

TRANSLATED BY MARGARET SAYERS PEDEN

Hoy, conversando,	Today, in conversation,
se salió de madre	the past
el pasado,	cropped up,
mi pasado.	my past.
Con indulgencia	Sleazy
las pequeñas	incidents
cosas sucias,	indulged,
episodios	vacuous
vacíos,	episodes,
harina negra,	spoiled flour,
polvo.	dust.
Te agachas	You crouch down,
suavemente	gently
inclinado	sink
en ti mismo,	into yourself,
sonríes,	you smile,
te celebras,	congratulate yourself,
pero	but
si se trata	when it's a matter
de otro, de tu amigo,	of someone else, some friend,
de tu enemigo,	some enemy,
entonces	then
te tornas despiadado,	you are merciless,
frunces el ceño:	you frown:
Qué cosas hizo ese hombre!	What a terrible life he had!
Esa mujer, qué cosas	That woman, what a life
hizo!	she led!

Te tapas	You hold
la nariz,	your nose,
visiblemente	visibly
te desagradan mucho	you disapprove of pasts
los pasados ajenos.	other than your own.
De lo nuestro miramos	Looking back, we view
con nostalgia	our worst days
los peores días,	with nostalgia,
abrimos	cautiously
con precaución el cofre	we open the coffer
y enarbolamos,	and run up the ensign
para que nos admiren,	of our feats
la proeza.	to be admired.
Olvidemos el resto.	Let's forget the rest.
Sólo es mala memoria.	Just a bad memory.
Escucha, aprende:	Listen and learn.
el tiempo	Time
se divide	is divided
en dos ríos:	into two rivers:
uno	one
corre hacia atrás, devora	flows backward, devouring
lo que vives,	life already lived;
el otro	the other
va contigo adelante	moves forward with you
descubriendo	exposing
tu vida.	your life.
En un solo minuto	For a single second
se juntaron.	they may be joined.
Es éste.	Now.
Ésta es la hora,	This is that moment,
la gota de un instante	the drop of an instant
que arrastrará el pasado.	that washes away the past.
Es el presente.	It is the present.
Está en tus manos.	It is in your hands.
Rápido, resbalando,	Racing, slipping,
cae como cascada.	tumbling like a waterfall.

Pero eres dueño de él.
Construyelo
con amor, con firmeza,
con piedra y ala,
con rectitud
sonora,
con cereales puros,
con el metal más claro
de tu pecho,
andando
a mediodía,
sin temer
a la verdad, al bien, a la justicia.
Compañeros de canto,
el tiempo que transcurre
tendrá forma
y sonido
de guitarra,
y cuando quieras
inclinarte al pasado,
el manantial del tiempo
transparente
revelará tu integridad cantando.
El tiempo es alegría.

But it is yours.
Help it grow
with love, with firmness,
with stone and flight,
with resounding
rectitude,
with purest grains,
the most brilliant metal
from your heart,
walking
in the full light of day
without fear
of truth, goodness, justice,
companions of song,
time that flows
will have the shape
and sound
of a guitar,
and when you want
to bow to the past,
the singing spring of
transparent time
will reveal your wholeness.
Time is joy.

139 / ODE TO PAUL ROBESON

Oda a Paul Robeson

TRANSLATED BY ILAN STAVANS

Antes	Before
él aún no existía.	he did not exist.
Pero su voz	Yet his voice
estaba	was there,
allí, esperando.	waiting.
La luz	Light
se apartó de la sombra,	parted from shadow,
el día	day
de la noche,	from night,
la tierra	land
de las primeras aguas.	from the primal waters.
Y la voz de Paul Robeson	And Paul Robeson's voice
se apartó del silencio.	separated from silence.
Las tinieblas querían	Darkness struggled
sustentarse. Y abajo	to endure. The roots
crecían las raíces.	grew underneath.
Peleaban	The blind plants
por conocer la luz	sought
las plantas ciegas,	to know the light,
el sol temblaba, el agua	the sun shivered, water
era una boca muda,	was a mute mouth,
los animales	animals
iban transformándose:	evolved:
lenta,	slow,

lentamente
se adaptaban al viento
y a la lluvia.

La voz del hombre fuiste
desde entonces
y el canto de la tierra
que germina,
el río, el movimiento
de la naturaleza.

Desató la cascada
su inagotable trueno
sobre tu corazón, como si un río
cayera en una piedra
y la piedra cantara
con la boca
de todos los callados,
hasta que todo y todos
en tu voz
levantaron
hacia la luz su sangre,
y tierra y cielo, fuego y sombra y agua,
subieron con tu canto.

Pero
más tarde
el mundo
se oscureció de nuevo.
Terror, guerra
y dolores
apagaron
la llama verde,
el fuego
de la rosa
y sobre

slowly
adapting to the wind
and rain.

From then on,
you were the voice of man
as well as the song of the earth
germinating,
the river, natural
movement.

The waterfall let loose
its inexhaustible thunder
on your heart, as if a river
fell on rock,
the stone singing
with the voice
of all those who are silenced,
until your voice
lifted
everything and everyone,
their blood to the daylight;
and earth and sky, fire and shadow and water,
arose with your song.

But
later
the world
was dark again.
Terror, war,
and pain
extinguished
the green flame,
the fire
inside the rose;
terrible

las ciudades
cayó
polvo
terrible,
ceniza
de los asesinados.
Iban
hacia los hornos
con un número
en la frente
y sin cabellos,
los hombres, las mujeres,
los ancianos, los niños
recogidos
en Polonia, en Ucrania,
en Amsterdam, en Praga.
Otra vez
fueron
tristes
las ciudades
y el silencio
fue grande,
duro,
como piedra de tumba
sobre un corazón vivo,
como una mano muerta
sobre la voz de un niño.

Entonces
tú, Paul Robeson,
cantaste.

Otra vez
so oyó sobre la tierra
la poderosa
voz

dust
descended
over
the cities,
the ash
of the assassinated.
They marched
into ovens
with a number
written in their forehead,
hairless,
men, women,
old, young,
all rounded up
in Poland, in Ukraine,
in Amsterdam, in Prague.
The cities
grieved
once
again;
silence
was great,
harsh,
like a tombstone
on a living heart,
like a dead hand
on a child's voice.

Then
you, Paul Robeson,
sang.

Once again,
the powerful
voice
of water

del agua	over fire
sobre el fuego,	was heard on earth:
la solemne, pausada, ronca, pura	the solemn, slow, harsh, pure
voz de la tierra	voice of the earth
recordándonos	reminding us
que aún	we were still
éramos hombres,	men,
que compartíamos	that we still share
el duelo y la esperanza.	sorrow and hope.
Tu voz	Your voice
nos separó del crimen,	distanced us from crime;
una vez más	once again
apartó	it separated
la luz de las tinieblas.	light from darkness.
Luego	Then
en Hiroshima	total silence dropped
cayó	over Hiroshima,
todo el silencio,	total silence,
todo.	total.
Nada	Nothing
quedó:	was left:
ni un pájaro	not a bird
equivocado en una	wandering in a
ventana fallecida,	dead window,
ni una madre	not a mother
con un	with a
niño que llora,	crying child,
ni el eco	or the echo
de una usina,	in a factory,
ni	or
la	the
voz	voice
de	of
un	an agonizing
violín	violin.

agonizante.
Nada.
Del cielo
cayó todo el silencio
de la muerte.

Y entonces
otra
vez,
padre,
hermano,
voz
del hombre
en su resurrección
sonora,
en su
profundidad,
en su esperanza,
Paul,
cantaste.
Otra vez
tu corazón de río
fue más alto,
más
ancho
que el silencio.

Yo sería
mezquino
si te coronara
rey de la voz
del negro,
sólo
grande en tu raza,
entre tu bella
grey

Nothing.
The utter silence
of death
fell
from the sky.

And then,
afresh,
father,
brother,
voice
of man
in its
sonorous
resurrection,
in its
depth,
in its hope,
Paul,
you sang.
Once again
your heart of river
was taller,
ampler
than
silence.

I would be
ungenerous
if I crowned you
king
of the black
voice,
giant only among your race,
among your beautiful
flock

de música y marfil,
que sólo para oscuros
niños
encadenados por los amos crueles,
cantas.

No,
Paul Robeson,
tú,
junto
a Lincoln
cantabas,
cubriendo
el cielo con tu voz sagrada,
no sólo
para negros,
para los pobres negros,
sino para los pobres
blancos,
para
los pobres
indios,
para todos
los pueblos.

Tú,
Paul
Robeson,
no
te quedaste mudo
cuando
a Pedro o a Juan
le pusieron los muebles
en la calle, en la lluvia,
o cuando
los milenarios sacrificadores

of music and ivory,
as though you sang only
for black
children
shackled by cruel masters.

No,
Paul Robeson,
you
sang
with
Lincoln,
covering
the sky with your sacred voice,
you do not sing
only for blacks,
for poor blacks,
but for poor
whites,
for
poor
Indians,
for all
people.

You,
Paul
Robeson,
did not
go silent
when
Pedro's and Juan's
furniture was put
over on the street, under the rain,
or when
the millenarian victimizers

quemaron	burned
el doble corazón	the double heart
de los que ardieron	of those on fire,
como cuando	as was the case
en mi patria	in my country,
el trigo crece en tierra de volcanes,	when wheat grew on volcanic land;
nunca	you never
dejaste	gave up
tu canción: caía	your song: man
el hombre y tú	stumbled and you
lo levantabas,	lifted him;
eras a veces	sometimes you were
un subterráneo	an underground
río,	river,
algo	a thing
que apenas	barely
sostenía la luz	sustaining the light
en las tinieblas,	amid the darkness,
la última	the last
espada	sword
del honor	of dying
que moría,	honor,
el postrer rayo	the last wounded
herido,	ray,
el trueno inextinguible.	the unquenchable thunder.
El pan del hombre,	Bread of man,
honor,	honor,
lucha,	struggle,
esperanza,	hope—
tú lo defiendes,	you defend us,
Paul	Paul
Robeson.	Robeson.
La luz del hombre,	Brightness of man,
hijo	child
del sol,	of the sun,
del nuestro,	of our

sol	sun
del suburbio	of the American
americano	suburb,
y de las nieves	and the red
rojas	snows
de los Andes:	of the Andes:
tú	you
proteges nuestra luz.	protect our light.
Canta,	Sing,
camarada,	comrade,
canta,	sing,
hermano	brother of
de la tierra,	earth,
canta,	sing,
buen	good
padre	father
del fuego,	of fire,
canta	sing
para todos nosotros,	for all of us,
los que viven	who live
pescando,	by fishing,
clavando clavos con	who hammer nails with
viejos martillos,	old hammers,
hilando	who spin
crueles	cruel
hilos de seda,	threads of silk,
machacando la pulpa	who pound the pulp
del papel, imprimiendo,	for paper, who print,
para	sing for all
todos	those
aquellos	barely
que	able
apenas	to close
pueden cerrar los ojos	their eyes
en la cárcel,	in jail,

despertados
a medianoche,
apenas
seres
humanos
entre dos torturas,
para los que combaten
con el cobre
en la desnuda
soledad andina,
a cuatro
mil
metros de altura.

Canta,
amigo
mío,
no dejes
de cantar:
tú
derrotaste
el silencio
de los ríos
que no tenían voz
porque llevaban
sangre,
tu voz habla por ellos,
canta,
tu voz
reúne
a muchos hombres
que no
se conocían.
Ahora
lejos,
en los magnéticos Urales

awakened
at midnight,
barely
human
between tortures,
sing for those who struggle
with copper
in
naked
Andean solitude,
four
thousand
meters high.

Sing,
my
friend,
never stop
singing:
you have
defeated
the silence
of the rivers
that had no voice
because they carried
blood—
your voice speaks for them;
sing,
for your voice
unites
many men
who don't know
each other.
Now,
at a distance,
in the magnetic Urals

y en la perdida
nieve
patagónica,
tú, cantando,
atraviesas
sombra,
distancia,
olores
de mar y matorrales,
y el oído
del
joven
fogonero,
del cazador errante,
del vaquero
que se quedó de pronto solo con su guitarra,
te escuchan.

Y en su prisión perdida, en Venezuela,
Jesús Faría,
el noble, el luminoso,
oyó el trueno sereno
de tu canto.

Porque tú cantas
saben que existe el mar
y que el mar canta.

Saben que es libre el mar, ancho y florido,
y así es tu voz, hermano.

Es nuestro el sol. La tierra será nuestra.
Torre del mar, tú seguirás cantando.

and the lost
Patagonian
snow,
singing,
cross through
shadow,
distance,
the aroma
of the sea and desert,
and the ear
of the
young
stoker,
the wandering hunter,
the cowboy
suddenly alone with his guitar,
all hear you.

And in his lost prison, in Venezuela,
Jesús Faría,
the noble, the luminous
heard the serene thunder
of your song.

Because you sing,
they know the sea exists,
the sea sings.

They know the sea is free, wide and fertile,
as your voice is, brother.

The sun is ours. The earth will be ours.
Tower of the sea, you will continue singing.

140 / ODE TO PEACE AND QUIET

Oda a la tranquilidad

TRANSLATED BY KEN KRABBENHOFT

Ancho	Deep
reposo,	restfulness,
agua	still
quieta,	water,
clara, serena sombra,	bright peaceful shade:
saliendo	emerging
de la acción como salen	from the fray, the way
lagos de las cascadas,	lakes emerge from waterfalls,
merecida merced,	merciful reward,
pétalo justo,	perfect petal.
ahora	I lie
boca arriba	face up
miro	and watch
correr el cielo,	the sky stream by.
se desliza	Its deep blue mass
su cuerpo azul profundo,	slides past.
adónde	Where
se dirige	is it headed,
con sus peces, sus islas,	with its fish, its islands
sus estuarios?	and estuaries?
El cielo	Above me
arriba,	the sky,
abajo	below me
un rumor	the rustling
de rosa seca	of a desiccated rose.
crujen	Small things
pequeñas cosas, pasan	fidget, insects

insectos como números:	flit by like numbers:
es la tierra,	this is the earth,
debajo	roots
trabajan	are at work
raíces,	down below,
metales,	minerals
aguas,	and water
penetran	seep into
nuestro cuerpo,	our bodies
germinan en nosotros.	and germinate inside us.
Inmóviles un día,	Lying there motionless,
bajo un árbol,	that day beneath the tree,
no lo sabíamos:	we knew nothing of this:
todas las hojas hablan,	the leaves were all talking,
se cuentan	trading
noticias de otros árboles,	news of other trees,
historias de la patria,	stories about their homeland,
de los árboles,	about trees.
algunos aún recuerdan	Some still remember
la forma sigilosa	the leopard's
del leopardo	stealthy shape
cruzando entre sus ramas,	moving like solid
como dura	mist
neblina,	through their branches;
otros	others recall
la nieve huracanada,	snow whipped by gales,
el cetro	the storm season's
del tiempo tempestuoso.	scepter.
Debemos	We should
dejar que hable	let all mouths
no sólo	speak,
la boca de los árboles,	not just
sino todas las bocas,	trees:
callar, callar en medio	we should sit still in the midst
del canto innumerable.	of this incalculable song.

Nada es mudo en la tierra:
cerramos
los ojos
y oímos
cosas que se deslizan,
criaturas que crecen,
crujidos
de madera invisible,
y luego
el mundo,
tierra, celestes aguas,
aire,
todo
suena
a veces como un trueno,
otras veces
como un río remoto.
Tranquilidad, reposo
de un minuto, de un día,
de tu profundidad recogeremos
metales,
de tu apariencia muda
saldrá la luz sonora.
Así será la acción purificada.
Así dirán los hombres, sin saberlo,
la opinión de la tierra.

Nothing on earth lacks a voice:
when we close
our eyes
we hear
things that slither,
creatures that are growing,
the creaking
of unseen wood,
and then
the world,
earth, heavenly waters,
air:
everything
sounds
like thunder at times,
other times
like a distant river.
Peace and quiet, a moment's
rest, or a day's:
from your depths we will gather
minerals,
from your unspeaking face
musical light will issue.
This is how we'll perfect our actions.
This is how men and women will speak
the earth's conviction, and never know it.

141 / ODE TO THE PEOPLE'S ARMY

Oda solar al ejército del pueblo

TRANSLATED BY RICHARD SCHAAF

Armas del pueblo! Aquí! La amenaza, el asedio
aún derraman la tierra mezclándola de muerte,
áspera de aguijones!
Salud, salud,
salud te dicen las madres del mundo,
las escuelas te dicen salud, los viejos
carpinteros,
Ejército del Pueblo, te dicen salud, con las
espigas,
la leche, las patatas, el limón, el laurel,
todo lo que es de la tierra y de la boca
del hombre.
Todo, como un collar
de manos, como una
cintura palpitante, como una obstinación de
relámpagos,
todo a ti se prepara, todo hacia ti converge!
Día de hierro,
azul fortificado!
Hermanos, adelante,
adelante por las tierras aradas,
adelante en la noche seca y sin sueño,
delirante y raída,
adelante entre vides, pisando el color frío
de las rocas,

Arms of the people! Here! The threat,
the siege
still overruns the land, mixing it with
death,
a harsh prodding of goads!
Salud, salud,
salud say the mothers of the world,
the schools say *salud* the old carpenter,
the People's Army say *salud* with spikes
of wheat,
with milk, potatoes, lemon, laurel,
all that is of the earth and of the mouth
of man.
Everything, like a collar
of hands, like a
throbbing waist, like an obstinacy of
lightning bolts,
everything is prepared for you,
everything converges on you!
Steeled day,
fortified blue!
Brothers, onward,
onward across the ploughed lands,
onward through the dry, sleepless,
delirious and frayed night,
onward amid the vines, treading upon
the cold color of rocks,

salud, salud, seguid. Más cortantes que la voz
del invierno,
más sensibles que el párpado, más seguros que
la punta del trueno,
puntuales como el rápido diamante, nuevamente
marciales,
guerreros según el agua acerada de las tierras
del centro,
según la flor y el vino, según el corazón espiral
de la tierra,
según las raíces de todas las hojas, de todas las
mercaderías fragantes de la tierra.

Salud, soldados, salud, barbechos rojos,
salud, tréboles duros, salud, pueblos parados
en la luz del relámpago, salud, salud, salud,
adelante, adelante, adelante, adelante,
sobre las minas, sobre los cementerios, frente
al abominable
apetito de muerte, frente al erizado
terror de los traidores,
pueblo, pueblo eficaz, corazón y fusiles,
corazón y fusiles, adelante.
Fotógrafos, mineros, ferroviarios, hermanos
del carbón y la piedra, parientes del martillo,
bosque fiesta de alegres disparos, adelante,
guerrilleros, mayores, sargentos, comisarios
políticos,
aviadores del pueblo, combatientes nocturnos,

salud, salud, press onward. More biting
than winter's voice,
more sensitive than the eyelid, more
sure than the thunderclap,
punctual as the swift diamond, newly
warlike,
fighters following the steeled waters
of the central lands,
following the flower, the wine, the
earth's spiraling heart,
following the roots of every leaf, every
fragrant product of the land.

Salud, soldiers, *salud*, red unploughed
lands,
salud, tough clover, *salud*, villages
nestled
in the lightning flash, *salud, salud, salud,*
onward, onward, onward, onward,
over the mines, the cemeteries, facing
death's
abominable appetite, facing the
unspeakable
terror of traitors,
people, effective people, hearts and
rifles,
hearts and rifles, onward.
Photographers, miners, railwaymen,
brothers
of coal and rock, relatives of the
hammer,
of the forest, wild happy partygoers,
onward,
guerrillas, majors, sergeants, political
commissars,
pilots of the people, combatants at
night,

combatientes marinos, adelante:
frente a vosotros
no hay más que una mortal cadena, un agujero
de podridos pescados: adelante!
no hay allí sino muertos moribundos,
pantanos de terrible pus sangrienta,
no hay enemigos: adelante, España,
adelante, campanas populares,
adelante, regiones de manzana,
adelante, estandartes cereales,
adelante, mayúsculos del fuego,
porque en la lucha, en la ola, en la pradera,
en la montaña, en el crepúsculo cargado de
acre aroma,
lleváis un nacimiento de permanencia, un hilo
de difícil dureza.
Mientras tanto,
raíz y guirnalda sube del silencio
para esperar la mineral victoria:
cada instrumento, cada rueda roja,
cada mango de sierra o penacho de arado,
cada extracción del suelo, cada temblor de
sangre
quiere seguir tus pasos, Ejército del Pueblo:
tu luz organizada llega a los pobres hombres
olvidados, tu definida estrella
clava sus roncos rayos en la muerte
y establece los nuevos ojos de la esperanza.

combatants at sea, onward:
facing you
there is but a mortal chain, a deep
hollow
filled with rotted fish: onward!
there are but dying deaths there,
marshes of foul bloody pus,
there are no enemies; onward, Spain,
onward, bells of the people,
onward, regions of apple orchards,
onward, banners of grains,
onward, capitals of fire,
because in the struggle, in the wave,
in the meadow,
in the mountain, in the twilight heavy
with an acrid aroma,
you carry a source of permanence,
a thread
of hard perseverance.
All the while,
root and garland rise from the silence
to wait for the mineral victory:
every instrument, every red wheel,
every saw handle or ploughshare,
every product of the soil, every
bloodthrob
wants to follow your footsteps,
the People's Army:
your organized light reaches the
humble, the forgotten
ones, your definitive star
thrusts its searing rays into death
and establishes the new eyes of hope.

142 / ODE TO THE PETRIFIED FOREST

Oda al bosque de las Petras

TRANSLATED BY ILAN STAVANS

Por la costa, entre los	Along the coast, amid the
eucaliptos azules	azure eucalyptus
y las mansiones nuevas	and the new carob
de Algarrobo,	mansions,
hay un bosque	a solemn forest
solemne:	stands:
un antiguo	a fossilized
puñado de árboles	gathering of trees
que olvidó la muerte.	that death forgot.
Los siglos	The centuries
retorcieron	have twisted
sus troncos, cicatrices	their trunks, scars
cubrieron cada rama,	covered all their branches,
ceniza y luto	ash and mourning
cayeron sobre sus antiguas copas,	fell on their old treetops,
se enmarañó el follaje	here
de uno y otro	and there foliage gets entangled
como telas titánicas	as in titanic spider
de araña	webs
y fueron los ramajes como dedos	and branches resembled knotted,
de agonizantes verdes	agonizing
anudados	green fingers,
unos en otros y petrificados.	intricate and petrified.
El viejo bosque vive	The old forest lives on,
aún, alguna nueva	an occasional new

hoja asoma en la altura,
un nido
palpitó
en la primavera,
una gota
de resina fragante
cae en el agua y muere.

Quieta, quieta es la sombra
y el silencio compacto
es
como
cristal negro
entre los viejos brazos
de los desfallecidos candelabros.
El suelo se levanta,
los pies nudosos se desenterraron
y son muertos de piedra,
estatuas rotas, huesos,
las raíces
que afloraron a la tierra.

De noche
allí el silencio
es un profundo lago
del que salen
sumergidas
presencias,
cabelleras
de musgos
y de lianas,
ojos
antiguos
con
luz
de turquesa,

leaf popping up in the heights,
a nest
palpitating
in spring,
a drop
of fragrant resin
falling on water, dying.

Still, still is the shadow,
compact is
the silence
like
black crystal
among the old arms
of defunct chandeliers.
The earth heaves,
the gnarled feet come to light
and stone dead
broken statues, bones,
the roots
that once bloomed in the earth.

At night,
the silence there
is a deep lake
from which
sunken
presences
arise,
hair
of moss
and lianas,
aged
eyes
with turquoise
light,

cenicientos lagartos olvidados,
anchas mujeres locamente muertas,
guerreros
deslumbradores,
ritos
araucanos.

Se puebla el viejo bosque
de las Petras
como un salón
salvaje
y luego
sombra,
lluvia,
tiempo,
olvido
caen
apagándolo.

Los invisibles seres
se recogen
y el viejo bosque
vuelve
a su inmovilidad, a su solemne
virtud de piedra y sueño.

forgotten lizards of ash,
ample women insanely dead,
shimmering
warriors,
Araucanian
rites.

The old stone
forest is inhabited
like a savage
salon,
shadow,
rain,
time,
forgetfulness
patiently
fall
and quench it.

The invisible beings
withdraw,
and the petrified forest
returns
to its immobility, its solemn
virtue of stone and dream.

143 / ODE TO THE PHARMACY

Oda a la farmacia

TRANSLATED BY ILAN STAVANS

Qué olor a bosque	What a smell of forest
tiene	the pharmacy
la farmacia!	has!
De cada	From each
raíz salió la esencia	root the essence emerged
a perfumar	to perfume
la paz	the apothecary's
del boticario,	peace,
se machacaron	crushing
sales	salts
que producen	producing
prodigiosos ungüentos,	prodigious ointments,
la seca solfatara	the dry solfège of
molió, molió, molió	grind, grind, grind
el azufre	the sulfur
en su molino	in its mill
y aquí está	and it is
junto	near
con la resina	the resin
del copal fabuloso:	of the fabulous copal:
todo	everything
se hizo cápsula,	became a capsule,
polvo,	dust,
partícula	impalpable
impalpable,	particle,
preservador	preserving
principio.	principle.

El mortero
machacó diminutos
asteriscos,
aromas,
pétalos de bismuto,
esponjas secas,
cales.

En el fondo
de su farmacia
vive
el alquimista
antiguo,
sus anteojos
encima
de una multiplicada
nariz,
su prestigio
en los frascos,
rodeado
por nombres
misteriosos:
la nuez vómica,
el álcali,
el sulfato,
la goma
de las islas,
el almizcle,
el ruibarbo,
la infernal belladona
y el arcangelical bicarbonato.
Luego las vitaminas
invadieron
con sus abecedarios
sabios anaqueles.
De la tierra,

The mortar
crushed minuscule
asterisks,
aromas,
petals of bismuth,
dry sponges,
lime powder.

At the back
of the pharmacy
lives
the ancient
alchemist,
his spectacles
atop
his multiplied
nose,
his prestige
in the bottles,
surrounded
by mysterious
names:
nux vomica,
alkali,
sulfate,
gum
from the islands,
musk,
rhubarb,
hellish belladonna
and angelic bicarbonate.
Then vitamins
invaded
the shelves
with their wise alphabets.
From the land

del humus,
de los hongos,
brotaron
los bastones
de la penicilina.
De cada
víscera
fallecida
volaron
como abejas
las hormonas
y ocuparon
su sitio en la farmacia.

A medida
que en el laboratorio
combatiendo
la muerte
avanza
la bandera
de la vida,
se registra
un movimiento
en el aroma
de la vieja farmacia:
los lentos
bálsamos
del pasado
dejan
sitio
a la instantánea caja
de inyecciones
y concentra una cápsula la nueva
velocidad
en la carrera
del hombre con la muerte.

of humus,
from mushrooms,
bud
penicillin sticks.
From each
deceased
entrail
the hormones
flew
like bees
and took up
their place
in the pharmacy.

While
in the laboratory
life's
flag
advances
its was against
death,
a movement
is noted
in the aroma
of the old pharmacy:
the slow
balsams
of the past
give
way
to an instantaneous box
of shots
and a capsule concentrating the new
speed
of the human race
against death.

Farmacia, qué sagrado
olor a bosque
y a conocimiento
sale de tus
estanterías,
qué diversa
profundidad de aromas
y regiones:
la miel
de una madera,
el purísimo polvo
de una rosa
o el luto
de un veneno.
Todo
en tu ámbito claro,
en tu universidad
de frascos y cajones,
espera
la hora de la batalla en nuestro cuerpo.

Farmacia, iglesia
de los desesperados,
con un pequeño
dios
en cada píldora:
a menudo eres
demasiado cara,
el precio
de un remedio
cierra tus claras puertas
y los pobres
con la boca apretada
vuelven al cuarto oscuro del enfermo,
que llegue un día
gratis
de farmacia,

Pharmacy, what a sacred
smell of forest
and knowledge
comes from your
shelves,
what diverse
depths of aromas
and regions:
a wood's
honey,
a rose's
purest powder,
or a poison's
mourning.
Everything
in your unmistakable confine,
in your university
of bottles and drawers,
awaits
the hour of battle inside our body.

Pharmacy, church
of the desperate,
with a small
god
in each pill:
often you're
too expensive,
a remedy's
price
closes your clear doors
and the poor
with tight mouth
return to the sick man's dark room,
there ought to be
a free day
at the pharmacy,

que no sigas
vendiendo
la esperanza,
y que sean
victorias
de la vida,
de toda
vida
humana
contra
la poderosa
muerte,
tus victorias.
Y así serán mejores
tus laureles,
serán más olorosos los sulfatos,
más azul el azul de metileno
y más dulce la paz de la quinina.

you shouldn't keep
selling
hope,
let
your
victories
be
life's victories,
all of
life's victories
against
mighty
death.
So will your laurels
be better,
your sulfates more fragrant,
the methylene's blue bluer
and the quinine's sweet sweeter.

144 / ODE TO THE PIANO

Oda al piano

TRANSLATED BY GEORGE D. SCHADE

Estaba triste el piano
en el concierto,
olvidado en su frac sepulturero,
y luego abrió la boca,
su boca de ballena:
entró el pianista al piano
volando como un cuervo,
algo pasó como si cayera
una piedra
de plata
o una mano
a un estanque
escondido:
resbaló la dulzura
como la lluvia
sobre una campana,
cayó la luz al fondo
de una casa cerrada,
una esmeralda recorrió el abismo
y sonó el mar,
la noche,
las praderas,
la gota del rocío,
el altísimo trueno,
cantó la arquitectura de la rosa,
rodó el silencio al lecho de la aurora.

The piano was sad
at the concert,
forgotten in its gravedigger's frock coat,
and then it opened its mouth,
whale mouth:
the pianist entered his piano
flying like a crow,
something happened, as if a silver
pebble
or a hand
had fallen
into a hidden
pond:
the sweetness skated
like rain
on a bell,
the light fell to the depths
of a locked-up house,
an emerald crossed the abyss,
and the sea gave forth its sound,
the night
and meadows too,
the drop of dew,
the highest notes of thunder,
the structure of the rose sang,
silence rolled to the bed of dawn.

Así nació la música
del piano que moría,
subió la vestidura
de la náyade
del catafalco
y de su dentadura
hasta que en el olvido
cayó el piano, el pianista
y el concierto,
y todo fue sonido,
torrencial elemento,
sistema puro, claro campanario.

Entonces volvió el hombre
del árbol de la música.
Bajó volando como
cuervo perdido
o caballero loco
cerró su boca de ballena el piano
y él anduvo hacia atrás,
hacia el silencio.

So was music born
in the dying piano,
the naiad's
tunic rose
from the coffin,
and from its row of teeth
piano, pianist and
concert sank into oblivion,
and all was sound,
torrential elements,
pure method, clear bell pealing.

Then the man returned
from the tree of music.
He came flying down
like a lost crow
or a crazy knight:
the piano closed its whale mouth
and he walked off, backing away
toward the silence.

145 / ODE TO THE PLATE

Oda al plato

TRANSLATED BY ILAN STAVANS

Plato,
disco central
del mundo,
planeta y planetario:
a mediodía, cuando
el sol, plato de fuego,
corona
el
alto
día,
plato, aparecen
sobre
las mesas en el mundo
tus estrellas,
las pletóricas
constelaciones,
y se llena de sopa
la tierra, de fragancia
el universo,
hasta que los trabajos
llaman de nuevo
a los trabajadores
y otra vez
el comedor es un vagón vacío,
mientras vuelvan los platos
a la profundidad de las cocinas.

Plate,
central disk
of the world,
planet and planetarium,
at noon, when
the sun, plate of fire,
crowns
the
tall
day,
plate, over
the world's tables
your star
will appear,
plethoric
of constellations,
and the earth is filled
with soup, the universe
with fragrance,
until workers
are called
back to work
and once again
the dining room is an empty wagon,
the plates returning
to the kitchen depths.

Suave, pura vasija,
te inventó el manantial en una piedra
luego la mano humana
repitió
el hueco puro
y copió el alfarero su frescura
para
que el tiempo con su hilo
lo pusiera
definitivamente
entre el hombre y la vida:
el plato, el plato, el plato,
cerámica esperanza,
cuenco santo,
exacta luz lunar en su aureola,
hermosura redonda de diadema.

Smooth, sheer vessel,
you were spawned by the spring in a stone
after which the human hand
repeated
the pure hole
and the potter copied its freshness
so that
time in its thread
could place it
definitively
between man and life:
the plate, the plate, the plate,
ceramic hope,
saintly earthen bowl,
precise lunar light in its halo,
rounded beauty of a diadem.

146 / ODE TO THE PLUM

Oda a la ciruela

TRANSLATED BY ILAN STAVANS

Hacia la cordillera	Nearing the cordillera
los caminos	the old
viejos	roads
iban cercados	were lined
por ciruelos,	with plum trees,
y a través	and
de la pompa	amid
del follaje,	the pageant of their leaves,
la verde, la morada	the green, the purple
población de las frutas	population of fruits
traslucía	projected
sus ágatas ovales,	its oval agates,
sus crecientes	its ripening
pezones.	nipples.
En el suelo	On the ground,
las charcas	puddles
reflejaban	reflected
la intensidad	the intensity
del duro	of the harsh
firmamento:	heaven:
el aire	the air
era una	was a
flor	flower,
total y abierta.	total and open.
Yo, pequeño	I, a young
poeta,	poet,
con los primeros	using the early

ojos
de la vida,
iba sobre
el caballo
balanceado
bajo la arboladura
de ciruelos.

Así en la infancia
pude
aspirar
en
un ramo,
en una rama,
el aroma del mundo,
su clavel
cristalino.

Desde entonces
la tierra, el sol, la nieve,
las rachas
de la lluvia, en octubre,
en los aminos,
todo,
la luz, el agua,
el sol desnudo,
dejaron
en mi memoria
olor
y transparencia
de ciruela:
la vida
ovaló en una copa
su claridad, su sombra,
su frescura.
Oh beso
de la boca

eyes
of life,
rode
a horse,
balancing
under a canopy
of plum trees.

Thus, in my infancy
I was able
to breathe
a bouquet,
on
a branch,
the aroma of the world,
its crystalline
carnation.

Since then,
the earth, the sun, the snow,
the rivulets
of rain, in October,
on the roads,
everything,
light, water,
the naked sun,
left
in my memory
the scent
and transparency
of a plum:
life
made its clarity, shadow,
freshness
into an oval cup.
Oh kiss
from the mouth

en la ciruela,
dientes
y labios
llenos
del ámbar oloroso,
de la líquida
luz de la ciruela!

Ramaje
de altos árboles
severos
y sombríos
cuya
negra
corteza
trepamos
hacia el nido
mordiendo
ciruelas verdes,
ácidas estrellas!

Tal vez cambie, no soy
aquel niño
a caballo
por
los
caminos de la cordillera.
Tal vez
más
de una
cicatriz
o quemadura
de la edad o la vida
me cambiaron
la frente,
el pecho,
el alma!

of the plum,
teeth
and lips
immersed
in scented amber,
in the plum's
liquid light!

Branches
of soaring trees,
severe
and somber,
their
dark
bark
we climb
up to the nest
eating
green plums,
sour stars!

Maybe I've changed, I'm no longer
the child of yesteryear,
riding my horse
on
the
roads of the cordillera.
Perhaps
more
than one
scar
or burn,
signs of age or life,
have altered
my forehead,
my breast,
my soul!

Pero, otra vez,
otra vez
vuelvo
a ser
aquel niño silvestre
cuando
en la mano levanto
una ciruela:
con su luz
me parece
que levanto
la luz del primer día
de la tierra,
el crecimiento
del fruto y del amor
en su delicia.

Sí,
en esta hora,
sea
cual sea, plena
como pan o paloma
o amarga
como
deslealtad de amigo,
yo para ti levanto una ciruela
y en ella, en su pequeña
copa
de ámbar morado y espesor fragante
bebo y brindo la vida
en honor tuyo,
seas quien seas, vayas donde vayas.

No sé quién eres, pero
dejo en tu corazón
una ciruela.

But again
and again
I
become
that wild child
each
time I take
a plum in my hand:
with its light
it seems
that I raise
the light of the first day
on earth,
the burgeoning
of fruit and love
in its lusciousness.

Yes,
in this moment,
be it
as it may, full
as bread or a dove
or sour
as
a friend's disloyalty,
I give a plum to you
and in it, in its tiny
cup
of purple amber and fragrant thickness,
I drink and toast to life
in your honor,
whoever you may be, wherever you may go.

I don't know who you are, but
I leave a plum
in your heart.

147 / ODE TO POETRY

Oda a la poesía

TRANSLATED BY GEORGE D. SCHADE

Cerca de cincuenta años	Almost fifty years
caminando	walking at
contigo, Poesía.	your side, Poetry.
Al principio	At first
me enredabas los pies	you entangled my feet
y caía de bruces	and I fell face down
sobre la tierra oscura	on the dark earth
o enterraba los ojos	or buried my eyes
en la charca	in the pool
para ver las estrellas.	to see the stars.
Más tarde te ceñiste	Later you encircled me
a mí con los dos brazos de la amante	with the arms of a lover
y subiste	and raced up
en mi sangre	through my blood
como una enredadera.	like a clambering vine.
Luego	Then
te convertiste en copa.	you became a cup.
Hermoso	Lovely
fue	it was
ir derramándote sin consumirte,	to spill and not consume you,
ir entregando tu agua inagotable,	giving out your boundless waters,
ir viendo que una gota	watching a drop fall
caía sobre un corazón quemado	on a burned-out heart
y desde sus cenizas revivía.	and see it revived from its ashes.
Pero	But
no me bastó tampoco.	that didn't suffice me either.

Tanto anduve contigo
que te perdí el respeto.
Dejé de verte como
náyade vaporosa,
te puse a trabajar de lavandera,
a vender pan en las panaderías,
a hilar con las sencillas tejedoras,
a golpear hierros en la metalurgia.

Y seguiste conmigo
andando por el mundo,
pero tú ya no eras
la florida
estatua de mi infancia.
Hablabas
ahora
con voz férrea.
Tus manos
fueron duras como piedras.
Tu corazón
fue un abundante
manantial de campanas,
elaboraste pan a manos llenas,
me ayudaste
a no caer de bruces,
me buscaste
compañía,
no una mujer,
no un hombre,
sino miles, millones.
Juntos, Poesía,
fuimos
al combate, a la huelga,
al desfile, a los puertos,
a la mina,
y me reí cuando saliste

We had walked together so long
that I lost respect for you.
I no longer saw you
as a diaphanous nymph,
I put you to work as laundress,
selling bread in bakeries,
spinning with simple weavers,
smiting irons in the smithy.

And you continued by my side
roaming through the world,
but you were no longer
the ornate
statue of my infancy.
Now
you spoke
with steely voice.
Your hands
became hard as rocks.
Your heart
a flowing
fountain of bells,
you kneaded bread with hands full of dough,
you kept me from
falling flat on my face,
you sought out
company for me,
not one woman,
nor one man,
but thousands, millions.
Together, Poetry,
we went
to combat, to strikes,
to parades and ports,
to the mines,
and I laughed when you emerged,

con la frente manchada de carbón
o coronada de aserrín fragante
de los aserraderos.
Ya no dormíamos en los caminos.
Nos esperaban grupos
de obreros con camisas
recién lavadas y banderas rojas.

Y tú, Poesía,
antes tan desdichadamente tímida,
a la cabeza
fuiste
y todos
se acostumbraron a tu vestidura
de estrella cuotidiana,
porque aunque algún relámpago delató tu
familia
cumpliste tu tarea,
tu paso entre los pasos de los hombres.
Yo te pedí que fueras
utilitaria y útil,
como metal o harina,
dispuesta a ser arado,
herramienta,
pan y vino,
dispuesta, Poesía,
a luchar cuerpo a cuerpo
y a caer desangrándote.

Y ahora,
Poesía,
gracias, esposa,
hermana o madre
o novia,
gracias, ola marina,
azahar y bandera,
motor de música,

your forehead smudged with coaldust,
or crowned with aromatic sawdust
from the sawmills.
We no longer slept along the roads.
Groups of workers
awaited us with freshly laundered
shirts and red flags.

And you, Poetry,
before so unhappily timid,
went
to the head,
and everyone got used to your clothing
of daily star,
for though some lightning bolt betrayed
your family,
you complied with your task,
your step among men's footsteps.
I asked you to be
utilitarian and useful,
like metal or flour,
ready to be plow,
tool,
bread and wine,
ready, Poetry,
to fight body to body
and fall shedding your blood.

And now,
Poetry,
thanks, wife,
sister, mother,
or sweetheart,
thanks, sea wave,
orange blossom and banner,
motor of music,

largo pétalo de oro,
campana submarina,
granero
inextinguible,
gracias,
tierra de cada uno
de mis días,
vapor celeste y sangre
de mis años,
porque me acompañaste
desde la más enrarecida altura
hasta la simple mesa
de los pobres,
porque pusiste en mi alma
sabor ferruginoso
y luego frío,
porque me levantaste
hasta la altura insigne
de los hombres comunes,
Poesía,
porque contigo
mientras me fui gastando
tú continuaste
desarrollando tu frescura firme,
tu ímpetu cristalino,
como si el tiempo
que poco a poco me convierte en tierra
fuera a dejar corriendo eternamente
las aguas de mi canto.

long golden petal,
submarine bell,
unending
granary,
thanks
earth for each one of my days,
heavenly mist and blood
of my years,
because you accompanied me
from the rarest heights
to the poor folks'
simple table,
because you placed in my soul
the taste of iron
and chilling fire,
because you raised me
to the famous heights
of ordinary men,
Poetry,
because with you,
while I squandered myself,
you kept on
evolving in your firm freshness,
your limpid momentum,
as if time
which little by little is turning me into
earth
were to stop the flow forever
of the waters of my song.

148 / ODE TO THE POPULAR POETS

Oda a los poetas populares

TRANSLATED BY ILAN STAVANS

Poetas naturales de la tierra,
escondidos en surcos,
cantando en las esquinas,
ciegos de callejón, oh trovadores
de las praderas y los almacenes,
si al agua
comprendiéramos
tal vez como vosotros hablaría,
si las piedras
dijeran su lamento
o su silencio,
con vuestra voz, hermanos,
hablarían.
Numerosos
sois, como las raíces.
En el antiguo corazón
del pueblo
habéis nacido
y de allí viene
vuestra voz sencilla.
Tenéis la jerarquía
del silencioso cántaro de greda
perdido en los rincones,
de pronto canta
cuando se desborda
y es sencillo
su canto,
es sólo tierra y agua.

Natural poets of the earth,
hidden in furrows,
singing in corners,
alley blinds, troubadours
of prairies and stores,
if we understood
what water is
perhaps I would speak like you,
if the stones
would deliver their lament
or their silence,
brothers, they would speak
with your voice.
You are
numerous, like the roots.
You were born
in the people's
ancient heart
and your simple voice
comes from there.
You have the hierarchy
of the silent clay pitcher
lost in obscure corners,
which suddenly sings
as it finds itself overwhelmed,
and it's a simple
song,
only earth and water.

Así quiero que canten
mis poemas,
que lleven
tierra y agua,
fertilidad y canto,
a todo el mundo.
Por eso,
poetas
de mi pueblo,
saludo
la antigua luz que sale
de la tierra.
El eterno
hilo en que se juntaron
pueblo
y
poesía,
nunca
se cortó
este profundo
hilo de piedra,
viene
desde tan lejos
como
la memoria
del hombre.
Vio
con los ojos ciegos
de los vates
nacer la tumultuosa
primavera,
la sociedad humana,
el primer beso,
y en la guerra
cantó sobre la sangre,
allí estaba mi hermano

I want my poems
to sing,
to carry
earth and water,
fertility and song
into the entire world.
That's why,
poets of my people,
I salute
the ancient light emerging
from the earth.
The eternal
thread
by which
people
and poetry were joined,
never
was this profound
thread of stone
cut,
it comes
from as far away
as
the memory
of man.
The spring
saw,
with blind eyes,
bards
born in tumultuous
seasons,
human society,
the first kiss,
and war
sang over the blood,
my red-bearded

barba roja,
cabeza ensangrentada
y ojos ciegos,
con su lira,
allí estaba
cantando
entre los muertos,
Homero
se llamaba
o Pastor Pérez,
o Reinaldo Donoso.
Sus endechas
eran allí y ahora
un vuelo blanco,
una paloma,
eran la paz, la rama
del árbol del aceite,
y la continuidad de la hermosura.
Más tarde
los absorbió la calle,
la campiña,
los encontré cantando
entre las reses,
en la celebración
del desafío,
relatando las penas
de los pobres,
llevando las noticias
de las inundaciones,
detallando las ruinas
del incendio
o la noche nefanda
de los asesinatos.

Ellos,
los poetas

brother was present,
his head bloodied
and his eyes blinded,
with his lyre,
singing
right there
among the dead.
Homer
was his name,
or Pastor Pérez,
or Reinaldo Donoso.
Their verses
were there and now
a white flight,
a dove,
were the peace, the branch
of the tree of oil,
and the continuity of beauty.
A bit later
they were absorbed by the street,
the countryside,
I found them singing
among the cattle,
in celebration
of defiance,
recounting the sorrows
of the poor,
carrying news
of inundations,
detailing the ruins
from fire
or the heinous night
of the assassins.

They,
the poets

de mi pueblo,	of my people,
errantes,	wanderers,
pobres entre los pobres,	poor among the poor,
sostuvieron	retained
sobre sus canciones	a smile
la sonrisa,	through their songs,
criticaron con sorna	criticized the exploiters
a los explotadores,	with mockery,
contaron la miseria	chronicled the miner's
del minero	misery
y el destino implacable	and the soldier's
del soldado.	implacable fate.
Ellos,	They,
los poetas	the poets
del pueblo,	of the people,
con guitarra harapienta	with a ragged guitar
y ojos conocedores	and eyes knowledgeable
de la vida,	of life,
sostuvieron	sustained
en su canto	through their song
una rosa	a rose,
y la mostraron en los callejones	displaying it in alleys
para que se supiera	so it would be known
que la vida	that life
no será siempre triste.	isn't always sad.
Payadores, poetas	Muleteers, humble, proud
humildemente altivos,	poets,
a través	through
de la historia	history
y sus reveses,	and its reversals,
a través	through
de la paz y de la guerra,	peace and war,
de la noche y la aurora,	night and dawn,
sois vosotros	you have been
los depositarios,	depositories,
los tejedores	weavers

de la poesía,	of poetry,
y ahora	and now
aquí en mi patria	here in my homeland
está el tesoro,	is the treasure,
el cristal de Castilla,	the crystal of Castile,
la soledad de Chile,	the solitude of Chile,
la pícara inocencia,	the sly innocence,
y la guitarra contra el infortunio,	and the guitar against misfortune,
la mano solidaria	the solitary hand
en el camino,	on the road,
la palabra	the word
repetida en el canto	repeated in the song
y transmitida,	and transmitted,
la voz de piedra y agua	the voice of stone and water
entre raíces,	amid roots,
la rapsodia del viento,	the rhapsody of wind,
la voz que no requiere librerías,	the voice without need of bookstores,
todo lo que debemos aprender	all we the proud
los orgullosos:	need to learn:
con la verdad del pueblo	with the people's truth
la eternidad del canto.	the eternal song.

149 / ODE TO POVERTY

Oda a la pobreza

TRANSLATED BY ILAN STAVANS

Cuando nací,
pobreza,
me seguiste,
me mirabas
a través
de las tablas podridas
por el profundo invierno.
De pronto
eran tus ojos
los que miraban desde los agujeros.
Las goteras,
de noche,
repetían
tu nombre y apellido
o a veces
el salero quebrado,
el traje roto,
los zapatos abiertos,
me advertían.
Allí estaban
acechándome
tus dientes de carcoma,
tus ojos de pantano,
tu lengua gris
que corta
la ropa, la madera,
los huesos y la sangre,

When I was born,
poverty,
you chased me,
you looked at me
through
the wood rotted
by the abysmal winter.
Suddenly
it was your eyes
looking through keyholes.
Water, leaking
at night,
repeated
your first and last names,
or sometimes
I was admonished
by the useless salt shaker,
the ragged suit,
the worn-out shoes.
There they were,
threatening me,
your woodworm teeth,
swamp eyes,
colorless tongue,
cutting
through clothes, timber,
bones and blood.

allí estabas
buscándome,
siguiéndome
desde mi nacimiento
por las calles.

Cuando alquilé una pieza
pequeña, en los suburbios,
sentada en una silla
me esperabas,
o al descorrer las sábanas
en un hotel oscuro,
adolescente,
no encontré la fragancia
de la rosa desnuda,
sino el silbido frío
de tu boca.
Pobreza,
me seguiste
por los cuarteles y los hospitales,
por la paz y la guerra.
Cuando enfermé tocaron
a la puerta:
no era el doctor, entraba
otra vez la pobreza.
Te vi sacar mis muebles
a la calle:
los hombres
los dejaban caer como pedradas.
Tú, con amor horrible,
de un montón de abandono
en medio de la calle y de la lluvia
ibas haciendo
un trono desdentado
y mirando a los pobres
recogías

There you were,
probing,
trailing me
since my birth
on the streets.

When I rented a small
flat in the suburbs,
you waited for me
seated on a chair,
or when I, an adolescent,
unfolded
the blankets of a dark hotel,
I didn't come across
the aroma of a naked rose
but, instead, your mouth's
cold whistle.
Poverty,
you chased me
through military quarters and hospitals,
at war and in peace.
When I got sick, someone
knocked at the door:
it wasn't the doctor, you
were pursuing me again.
I saw you dispose of my furniture
on the street,
men let it fall
like bedrock.
You, with terrorizing love,
with a pile of abandon,
patiently built
a ruined throne
in the rain, half-way down the street,
and appraising the poor,
you stole my last plate,

mi último plato haciéndolo diadema.
Ahora,
pobreza,
yo te sigo.
Como fuiste implacable,
soy implacable.
Junto
a cada pobre
me encontrarás cantando,
bajo
cada sábana
de hospital imposible
encontrarás mi canto.
Te sigo,
pobreza,
te vigilo,
te cerco,
te disparo,
te aíslo,
te cerceno las uñas,
te rompo
los dientes que te quedan.
Estoy
en todas partes:
en el océano con los pescadores,
en la mina
los hombres
al limpiarse la frente,
secarse el sudor negro,
encuentran
mis poemas.
Yo salgo cada día
con la obrera textil.
Tengo las manos blancas
de dar el pan en las panaderías.
Donde vayas,

turning it into a hairband.
So now,
poverty,
I'm the one following you.
Since you were implacable,
I'm implacable.
You'll find me singing
near
every poor person,
under
every impossible
hospital sheet
you'll find my song.
I follow you now,
poverty,
I spy on you,
I besiege you,
I fire at you,
I round you up,
I chop your nails,
I smash
your surviving teeth.
I'm
everywhere now:
on the ocean along with fishermen,
in the mine
with men
undusting their heads,
drying the black sweat,
people find
my poems.
Every day I walk beside
the factory worker.
My hands are white
from handing out bread in bakeries.
Wherever you go,

pobreza,
mi canto
está cantando,
mi vida
está viviendo,
mi sangre
está luchando.
Derrotaré
tus pálidas banderas
en donde se levanten.
Otros poetas
antaño te llamaron
santa,
veneraron tu capa,
se alimentaron de humo
y desaparecieron.
Yo
te desafío,
con duros versos te golpeo el rostro,
te embarco y te destierro.
Yo con otros,
con otros, muchos otros,
te vamos expulsando
de la tierra a la luna
para que allí te quedes
fría y encarcelada
mirando con un ojo
el pan y los racimos
que cubrirán la tierra
de mañana.

poverty,
my song
will be singing,
living,
my blood
will be fighting.
I shall defeat
your colorless flags
wherever they are raised.
Other poets
of bygone years
called you
a saint,
praised your cape,
were fed with smoke
and disappeared soon after.
I
defy you,
I round you up and deport you,
slapping your face with harsh verses.
And, along with others,
with others, with many others,
I help propel you
from the earth to the moon
so that you stay there,
cold and imprisoned,
your eye looking at
the bread and grapes
meant to cover the earth
of tomorrow.

150 / ODE TO THE PRESENT

Oda al presente

TRANSLATED BY ILAN STAVANS

Este	This
presente	present tense,
liso	flat
como una tabla,	like a table,
fresco,	fresh,
esta hora,	this hour,
este día	this day,
limpio	clean
como una copa nueva	like a new cup
—del pasado	—of the past
no hay una	there is not a
telaraña—,	spiderweb—,
tocamos	we touch
con los dedos	the present
el presente,	with our fingers,
cortamos	we cut
su medida,	its measure,
dirigimos	we direct
su brote,	its emergence,
está viviente,	it is alive,
vivo,	living,
nada tiene	it has nothing
de ayer irremediable,	of the irremediable yesterday,
de pasado perdido,	of the lost past,
es nuestra	it is our
criatura,	creature,
está creciendo	it is growing

en este
momento, está llevando
arena, está comiendo
en nuestras manos,
cógelo,
que no resbale,
que no se pierda en sueños
ni palabras,
agárralo,
sujétalo
y ordénalo
hasta que te obedezca,
hazlo camino,
campana,
máquina,
beso, libro,
caricia,
corta su deliciosa
fragancia de madera
y de ella
hazte una silla,
trenza
su respaldo,
pruébala,
o bien
escalera!

Sí,
escalera,
sube
en el presente,
peldaño
tras peldaño,
firmes
los pies en la madera
del presente,

this
very moment, it is carrying
sand, it is eating
from our hands,
grab it,
let it not slip away,
let it not lose its dreams
and words,
grab it,
hold it,
and order it
until it obeys you,
turn it into path,
bell,
machine,
kiss, book,
caress,
cut its delicious
fragrance of wood
and, from it,
make a chair for yourself,
braid
its back,
try it,
or rather
a staircase!

Yes,
staircase,
climb
into the present,
step
by step,
firm
its feet on the wood
of the present,

hacia arriba,
hacia arriba,
no muy alto,
tan sólo
hasta que puedas
reparar
las goteras
del techo,
no muy alto,
no te vayas al cielo,
alcanza
las manzanas,
no las nubes,
ésas
déjalas
ir por el cielo, irse
hacia el pasado.
Tú
eres
tu presente,
tu manzana:
tómala
de tu árbol,
levántala
en tu
mano,
brilla
como una estrella,
tócala,
híncale el diente y ándate
silbando en el camino.

upward,
upward,
not too high,
at least
until you're able
to repair
the roof
leaks,
not too high,
don't go to heaven,
reach for
the apples,
not the clouds,
leave
those
to travel for the sky, heading
toward the past.
You
are
your present,
your apple:
take it
from your tree,
pick it up
with
your hand,
it shines
like a star,
touch it,
bite it and move on
whistling on the road.

151 / ODE TO RAIN

Oda a la lluvia

TRANSLATED BY KEN KRABBENHOFT

Volvió la lluvia.
No volvió del cielo
o del oeste.
Ha vuelto de mi infancia.
Se abrió la noche, un trueno
la conmovió, el sonido
barrió las soledades,
y entonces,
llegó la lluvia,
regresó la lluvia
de mi infancia,
primero
en una ráfaga
colérica,
luego
como la cola
mojada
de un planeta,
la lluvia
tic tac mil veces tic
tac mil
veces un trineo,
un espacioso golpe
de pétalos oscuros
en la noche,
de pronto
intensa

The rain returned.
It didn't come from the sky
or out of the West:
it came straight from my childhood.
Night split open, a peal of thunder
rattled, the racket
swept every lonely corner,
and then
the rain came,
rain returning
from my childhood,
first
a raging
gust,
then
a planet's
soggy
tail.
The rain
goes ticktock, a thousand ticks
a thousand
tocks, a sleigh
or an ample burst
of dark petals
in the night,
suddenly
intense,

acribillando	riddling
con agujas	the leaves
el follaje,	with needles;
otra veces	other times it's
un manto	a stormy
tempestuoso	cloak
cayendo	drifting down
en el silencio,	in silence.
la lluvia,	Rain,
mar de arriba,	sea of the upper air,
rosa fresca,	fresh,
desnuda,	naked rose,
voz del cielo,	voice of the sky,
violín negro,	black violin,
hermosura,	sheer beauty:
desde niño	I have loved you
te amo,	since childhood
no porque seas buena,	not for your goodness
sino por tu belleza.	but for your beauty.
Caminé	I trudged along
con los zapatos rotos	in my ruined shoes
mientras los hilos	while threads
del cielo desbocado	of streaming sky
se destrenzaban sobre	unraveled over
mi cabeza,	my head,
me traían	bringing
a mí y a las raíces	a message
las comunicaciones	from on high,
de la altura,	to me and to roots,
el oxígeno húmedo,	humid oxygen,
la libertad del bosque.	freedom of the forest.
Conozco	I know
tus desmanes,	how mischievous you can be,
el agujero	the hole
en el tejado	in the roof
cayendo	dripping

su gotario
en las habitaciones
de los pobres:
allí desenmascaras
tu belleza,
eres hostil
como una
celestial
armadura,
como un puñal de vidrio,
transparente,
allí
te conocí de veras.
Sin embargo,
enamorado
tuyo
seguí
siendo,
en la noche
cerrando la mirada
esperé que cayeras
sobre el mundo,
esperé que cantaras
sólo para mi oído,
porque mi corazón guardaba toda
germinación terrestre
y en él se precipitan los metales
y se levanta el trigo.
Amarte, sin embargo
me dejó en la boca
gusto amargo,
sabor amargo de remordimiento.
Anoche solamente
aquí en Santiago
las poblaciones
de la Nueva Legua

measured drops
on poor peoples'
rooms.
That's when you rip off the mask
of beauty,
when you're as mean
as
heavenly
armor
or a dagger of transparent
glass.
That's where
I really came to know you.
But
I was
still
yours
in love,
in the night,
shutting my eyes tight,
I hoped you would fall
on the world.
I hoped you would sing
for my ears alone,
because my heart cradled
the earth's sprouting,
in my heart metals merge,
wheat springs out of my heart.
But loving you still
left a bitter taste
in my mouth,
the bitter aftertaste of regret.
Just last night,
here in Santiago,
houses
in Nueva Legua

se desmoronaron,
las viviendas
callampas,
hacinados
fragmentos de ignominia,
al peso de tu paso
se cayeron,
los niños
lloraban en el barro
y allí días y días
en las camas mojadas,
sillas rotas,
las mujeres,
el fuego, las cocinas,
mientras tú, lluvia negra,
enemiga,
continuabas cayendo
sobre nuestras desgracias.
Yo creo
que algún día,
que inscribiremos en el calendario,
tendrán techo seguro,
techo firme,
los hombres en su sueño,
todos
los dormidos,
y cuando en la noche
la lluvia
regrese
de mi infancia
cantará en los oídos
de otros niños
y alegre
será el canto
de la lluvia en el mundo,
también trabajadora,

collapsed,
fragile
mushrooms,
heaps
of humiliation.
Because of your heavy footsteps
they fell,
children
cried in the mire
and day after day
in rain-soaked beds,
on shattered chairs,
the women,
bonfires for kitchens
while you, black rain,
enemy rain,
kept on falling
on our misery.
I believe
that some day—
a day we will mark on calendars—
they will live under sound roofs,
dry roofs,
men with their dreams,
everyone
who sleeps,
and when in the middle of the night
the rain
returns
from my childhood,
it will sing
for other children to hear,
and the song
of rain falling on the world
will be joyous.
It will be industrious, too,

proletaria,
ocupadísima
fertilizando montes
y praderas,
dando fuerza a los ríos,
engalanando
el desmayado arroyo
perdido en la montaña,
trabajando
en el hielo
de los huracanados
ventisqueros,
corriendo sobre el lomo
de la ganadería,
dando valor al germen
primaveral del trigo,
lavando las almendras
escondidas,
trabajando
con fuerza
y con delicadeza fugitiva,
con manos y con hilos
en las preparaciones de la tierra.

Lluvia
de ayer,
oh triste
lluvia
de Lonoche y Temuco,
canta,
canta,
canta sobre los techos
y las hojas,
canta en el viento frío,
canta en mi corazón, en mi confianza,
en mi techo, en mis venas,

and proletarian,
absorbed
in fertilizing mountains
and plains,
revitalizing rivers,
festooning
collapsed gullies
forgotten in the hills,
hard at work
in the ice
of gale-force
winds,
dancing on the backs
of cattle,
fortifying spring seeds
of wheat,
bathing secretive
almond trees,
working
at full steam
and with elusive subtlety,
all hands and threads,
on earth's preparations.

Rain
from yesterday,
O sad
rain
of Loncoche and Temuco,
sing,
sing,
sing on rooftops
and in leaves,
sing in freezing winds,
sing in my heart, in my trust,
on my roof, in my veins,

en mi vida,
ya no te tengo miedo,
resbala
hacia la tierra
cantando con tu canto
y con mi canto,
porque los dos tenemos
trabajo en las semillas
y compartimos
el deber cantando.

sing in my whole life.
I'm no longer scared of you:
go on, slide down
toward the earth
singing your song
and mine.
We've got to get to work
with these seeds.
We'll share
our duties singing.

152 / ODE TO RAMÓN GÓMEZ DE LA SERNA

Oda a Ramón Gómez de la Serna

TRANSLATED BY ILAN STAVANS

Ramón	Ramón
está escondido,	is hiding,
vive en su gruta	he lives in his grotto
como un oso de azúcar.	like a sugar bear.
Sale sólo de noche	He leaves only at night
y trepa por las ramas	and climbs the city
de la ciudad, recoge	branches, picks up
castañas tricolores,	tricolor chestnuts,
piñones erizados,	spiky pine nuts,
clavos de olor, peinetas de tormenta,	nails made of smells, dress combs of storm,
azafranados abanicos muertos,	dead, saffronlike fans,
ojos perdidos en las bocacalles,	eyes lost in side streets,
y vuelve con su saco	and returns with his sack
hasta su madriguera trasandina	to his trans-Andean den
alfombrada con largas cabelleras	carpeted with long heads of hair
y orejas celestiales.	and heavenly ears.
Vuelve lleno de miedo	He returns filled with fear
al golpe de la puerta,	to the sound of doors closing,
al ímpetu	to the special
espacial	impetus
de los aviones,	of airplanes,
al frío que se cuela	to the cold trickling
desde España,	from Spain,
a las enredaderas, a los hombres,	to creepers, to men,
a las banderas, a la ingeniería.	to flags, to engineering.
Tiene miedo de todo.	He is afraid of everything.

Allí en su cueva
reunió los alimentos
migratorios
y se nutre
de claridad sombría
y de naranjas.
De pronto
sale un fulgor, un rayo
de su faro
y el haz ultravioleta
que encerraba
su frente
nos ilumina el diámetro y la fiesta,
nos muestra el calendario
con Viernes más profundos,
con Jueves como el mar vociferante,
todo repleto, todo
maduro con sus orbes,
porque el revelador del universo
Ramón se llama y cuando
sopla en su flor de losa, en su trompeta,
acuden manantiales,
muestra el silencio sus categorías.

There, in his cave,
he has gathered the migrating
food
and is nurtured
by somber clarity
and oranges.
Suddenly,
a gleam of light goes out, a thunderbolt
from his lighthouse
and the ultraviolet beam,
imprisoning
his forehead,
illuminates for us the diameter and the feast,
shows us the calendar
with even deeper Fridays,
and Thursdays like a shouting sea,
all full, all
mature like his worlds,
because Ramón is the name
of the revealer of the universe and when
the flower of his paving stone blows, in his
trumpets,
springs converge,
and silence displays its categories.

Oh rey Ramón,
monarca
mental,
director
ditirámbico
de la interrogadora poesía,
pastor de las parábolas
secretas, autor
del alba y su
desamparado
cataclismo,

Oh king Ramón,
mental
monarch,
dithyrambic
director
of interrogated poetry,
shepherd of secret
parables, author
of daybreak and its
helpless
cataclysm,

poeta
presuroso
y espacioso,
con tantos sin embargos,
con tantos ojos ciegos,
porque
viéndolo todo
Ramón se irrita
y se desaparece,
se confunde en la bruma
del calamar lunario
y el que todo lo dice
y puede
saludar lo que va y lo que viene,
de pronto
se inclina hacia anteayer, de un cabezazo
contra el sol de la historia,
y de ese encuentro salen chispas negras
sin la electricidad de su insurgencia.

Escribo en Isla Negra,
construyo
carta y canto.
El día estaba roto
como la antigua estatua
de una diosa marina
recién sacada de su lecho frío
con lágrimas y légamo,
y junto al movimiento
descubridor
del mar y sus arenas,
recordé los trabajos
del Poeta,
la insistencia radiante de su espuma,
el venidero viento de sus olas.

profuse
and spacious
poet,
with many nothwithstandings,
with many blind eyes,
because,
looking at everything,
Ramón gets irritated
and disappears,
vanishes into the mist
of the lunar squid,
and he who tells it all,
and is able
to greet what comes and goes,
suddenly
bends over the day before yesterday,
bangs its head
against the sun of history,
and from that encounter black sparks
emerge
without the electricity of his insurgence.

I write in Isla Negra,
I build
letter and song.
The day was broken
like the ancient statue
of a sea goddess
newly drawn from her cold bed
with tears and slime,
and near the discovering
movement
of the sea and its sands,
I remembered the Poet's
labors,
the radiant insistence of his foam,
the waves' coming wind.

Y a Ramón
dediqué
mis himnos matinales,
la culebra
de mi caligrafía,
para cuando
salga
de su prolija torre de carpincho
reciba la serena
magnitud de una ráfaga de Chile
y que le brille al mago el cucurucho
y se derramen todas sus estrellas.

And I dedicated
to Ramón
my morning hymns,
the snake
of my calligraphy,
so when
he comes out
of his extensive tower of mysteries
he receives the serene
magnitude of a gleam of light from Chile,
and let the magician's pointed hat shine
and all his stars spill over.

153 / ODE TO A RED TRUCK LOADED WITH BARRELS

Oda a un camión colorado cargado con toneles

TRANSLATED BY GEORGE D. SCHADE

En impreciso
vapor, aroma o agua,
sumergió
los cabellos del día:
errante olor,
campana
o corazón de humo,
todo
fue envuelto
en ese deshabitado hangar,
todo
confundió sus colores.

Amigo, no se asuste.

Era sólo
el otoño
cerca de Melipilla,
en los caminos,
y las hojas
postreras,
como un escalofrío
de violines,
se despedían
de los altos árboles.

An indefinable
steam, smell or water
immersed
the hairs of day:
stray odor,
bell
or heart of smoke,
all
was shrouded
in that deserted truck shed,
all colors blending
in confusion.

Friend, don't be afraid.

It was just
autumn
on the roads
near Melipilla,
and the last
leaves,
like a shudder
of violins,
were saying good-bye
to the tall trees.

No pasa nada. Espere.

Las casas, los tejados,
las tapias
de cal y barro, el cielo,
eran
una sola amenaza:
eran un libro
largo
con personajes
sumamente tristes.

Esperemos. Espere.

Entonces
como un toro
atravesó el otoño
un camión colorado
cargado con toneles.
Surgió de tanta niebla
y tanto vago cielo,
rojo, repleto
como una
granada,
alegre como el fuego,
despeñando su rostro
de incendio, su cabeza
de león fugitivo.

Instantáneo, iracundo,
preciso y turbulento,
trepidante y ardiente
pasó
como una estrella colorada.
Yo apenas
pude

Nothing happens. Wait.

The houses, the roofs,
the walls of
lime and mud, the sky
were
all a single threat:
they were a long
book
with very
sad characters.

Let's wait. Wait.

Then
like a bull
a red truck
loaded with barrels
streaked across the autumn,
emerging from so much mist
and blurry sky,
red, stuffed
full as a
pomegranate,
happy as a flame,
hurtling its fiery
face, its fleeting
lion's head.

Instantaneous, wrathful,
precise and raging,
shaking aflame
it passed
like a bright red star.
I could
scarcely

ver
esa sandía
de acero, fuego y oro,
el coro
musical
de los toneles:
toda esa
simetría
colorada
fue
sólo
un
grito,
un
estremecimiento
en el otoño
pero
todo cambió:
los árboles, la inmóvil
soledad, el cielo
y sus metales moribundos
volvieron a existir.

Así fue como el fuego
de un vehículo
que corría anhelante
con su carga
fue
para mí
como si desde el frío de la muerte
un meteoro
surgiera y me golpeara
mostrándome
en su esplendor colérico
la vida.

see
that watermelon
of steel, fire and gold,
the musical
chorus
of the barrels:
all that
red
symmetry
was
just
a
cry,
a
quiver
in autumn
but
everything changed:
the trees, the still
loneliness, the sky
and its dying metals
came alive once again.

So it was that fiery
vehicle
racing along panting
with its cargo
was
for me
as if a meteor
had burst and struck me
from the chill of death,
showing me
in its angry splendor
life.

Sólo
un camión
cargado
con toneles,
desbocado, cruzando
los caminos,
cerca de Melipilla, en una
mañana,
acumuló
en mi pecho
desbordante
alegría
y energía:
me devolvió el amor y el movimiento.
Y derrotó
como una llamarada
el desmayo del mundo.

Just
a runaway truck
loaded
with barrels,
crossing
the roads,
near Melipilla, on a
morning,
heaped
my chest with
overflowing
joy
and energy:
bringing me again love and movement,
and defeating
like a blaze
the world's in a swoon

154 / ODE TO RESTLESSNESS

Oda a la intranquilidad

TRANSLATED BY KEN KRABBENHOFT

Madre intranquilidad, bebí en tus senos
electrizada leche,
acción severa!
No me enseñó la luna
el movimiento.
Es la intranquilidad la que sostiene
el estático vuelo
de la nave,
la sacudida del motor decide
la suavidad del ala
y la miel dormiría en la corola
sin la inquietud insigne de la abeja.
Yo no quiero escaparme
a soledad ninguna.
Yo no quiero
que mis palabras aten a los hombres.
Yo no quiero
mar sin marea, poesía
sin hombre,
pintura
deshabitada, música
sin viento!
Intranquila es la noche
y su hermosura,
todo palpita bajo
sus banderas

Restless mother, from your breasts I
sucked
electrified milk,
harsh lessons!
It wasn't the moon that taught me
how to move:
restlessness is what fuels
the ship's
static flight,
the engine's vibration sets
the smoothness of the wing,
and if it weren't for the bee's singular
ambition,
honey would lay dormant in flowers.
I have no wish to run away
to some solitary place.
I don't want
my words to tie anybody down.
I have no yearning
for a sea without its tide or poetry
without people,
for unpopulated
paintings or music
without wind!
The night is restless,
as is its beauty:
everything throbs beneath
its flags,

y el sol
es encendido movimiento,
ráfaga de alegría!
Se pudren en la charca
las estrellas,
y canta en la cascada
la pureza!
La razón intranquila
inauguró los mares,
y del desorden hizo
nacer el edificio.
No es inmutable
la ciudad, ni tu vida
adquirió la materia de la muerte.
Viajero, ven conmigo.
Daremos
magnitud a los dones de la tierra.
Cambiaremos la espiga.
Llevaremos la luz al más remoto
corazón castigado.
Yo creo
que bajo la intranquila primavera
la claridad
del fruto
se consume,
se extiende
el desarrollo del aroma,
combate el movimiento con la muerte.
Y así llega a tu boca la dulzura
de los frutos gloriosos,
la victoria
de la luz intranquila
que levanta los labios de la tierra.

and the sun
is burning movement,
a gust of joy!
The stars are rotting
in puddles,
and perfection sings
in the waterfall.
Restless reason
inaugurated the seas
and made buildings
rise out of chaos.
Cities are not
unchanging, and your life
has not acquired the raw material of death.
Traveler, come with me:
we will give
grandeur to the earth's blessings.
We will transform crops,
we will deliver light to the remotest
chastised heart.
I believe
that beneath restless spring
the fruit's
brightness
is devoured,
maturing scents
unfold,
battling movement with death.
This is how the sweetness of those glorious
fruits
reaches your mouth,
the triumph
of a restless light
that raises its lips from earth.

155 / ODE TO RÍO DE JANEIRO

Oda a Río de Janeiro

TRANSLATED BY ILAN STAVANS

Río de Janeiro, el agua	Río de Janeiro, water
es tu bandera,	is your flag,
agita tus colores,	it shakes your colors,
sopla y suena en el viento,	blows and sounds in the wind,
ciudad,	city,
náyade negra,	black water nymph,
de claridad sin fin,	your fabric
de hirviente sombra,	is made of endless clarity,
de piedra con espuma	boiling shadow,
es tu tejido,	stones covered in foam,
el lúcido balance	the lucid balance
de tu hamaca marina,	of your sea hammock,
el azul movimiento	the blue movement
de tus pies arenosos,	of your sandy feet,
el encendido ramo	the ignited bouquet
de tus ojos.	of your eyes.
Río, Río de Janeiro,	Río, Río de Janeiro,
los gigantes	giants
salpicaron tu estatua	sprinkled your statue
con puntos de pimienta,	with pepper tips,
dejaron	they left
en tu boca	in your mouth
lomos de mar, aletas	loins of sea
turbadoramente tibias,	disturbingly tepid flippers,
promontorios	headlands
de la fertilidad, tetas del agua,	of fertility, breasts of water,
declives de granito,	slopes of granite,

labios de oro,	lips of gold,
y entre la piedra rota	and amid the broken stone
el sol marino	the marine sun
iluminando	illuminating
espumas estrelladas.	the starry foam.
Oh Belleza,	Oh Beauty
oh ciudadela	Oh fortress
de piel fosforescente,	of fluorescent skin,
granada	grenade
de carne azul, oh diosa	of blue meat, oh goddess
tatuada en sucesivas	tattooed in successive
olas de ágata negra,	waves of black agate,
de tu desnuda estatua	from your naked statue
sale un aroma de jazmín mojado	an aroma of wet jasmine emerges
por el sudor, un ácido	through the sweat, an acid
relente	dew
de cafetales y de fruterías	of coffee plantations and fruit stands
y poco a poco bajo tu diadema,	and little by little under your headband,
entre la duplicada maravilla	between the duplicated marvel
de tus senos,	of your breasts,
entre cúpula y cúpula	between cupola and cupola
de tu naturaleza	of your nature
asoma el diente de la desventura,	the tooth of misfortune peeps out,
la cancerosa cola	the cancerous tail
de la miseria humana,	of human misery,
en los cerros leprosos	in the leprous hills
el racimo inclemente	the inclement bunch
de las vidas,	of lives,
luciérnaga terrible,	menacing firefly
esmeralda	emerald
extraída	extracted
de la sangre,	from blood,
tu pueblo hacia los límites	your people reach
de la selva se extiende	to the confines of the jungle
y un rumor oprimido,	and an oppressed rumor,

pasos y sordas voces,
migraciones de hambrientos,
oscuros pies con sangre,
tu pueblo,
más allá de los ríos,
en la densa
amazonia,
olvidado,
en el norte
de espinas,
olvidado
con sed en las mesetas,
olvidado,
en los puertos, mordido
por la fiebre,
olvidado,
en la puerta
de la casa de donde lo expulsaron,
pidiéndote
una sola mirada,
y olvidado.

En otras tierras,
reinos, naciones,
islas,
la ciudad capital,
la coronada,
fue colmena
de trabajos humanos,
muestra de la desdicha
y del acierto,
hígado de la pobre monarquía,
cocina de la pálida república.
Tú eres el cegador
escaparate
de una sombría noche,

steps and deft voices,
migrations of hungry,
dark feet with blood,
your people,
beyond the rivers,
in the dense
Amazon forest,
forgotten,
in the northern region
of thorns,
forgotten
with thirst in the plateaus,
forgotten,
in the ports, bitten
by fever,
forgotten,
at the door
of the house from which it was expelled,
asking
for a single glance,
and forgotten.

In other lands,
kingdoms, nations,
islands,
the capital city
the crowned one
was a beehive
of human labor,
sample of unhappiness
and dexterity,
liver of poor monarchies,
kitchen of the pallid republic.
You are the blinding
display window
of a shady night,

la garganta
cubierta
de aguas marinas
y oro
de un cuerpo
abandonado,
eres
la puerta
delirante
de una casa vacía,
eres
el antiguo pecado,
la salamandra
cruel,
intacta
en el brasero
de los largos dolores de tu pueblo,
eres
Sodoma,
sí,
Sodoma
deslumbrante,
con un fondo sombrío
de terciopelo verde,
rodeada
de crespa sombra, de aguas
ilimitadas, duermes
en los brazos
de la desconocida
primavera
de un planeta salvaje.
Río, Río de Janeiro,
cuántas cosas
debo decirte. Nombres
que no olvido,
amores

the throat
of an abandoned
body
covered
in ocean water
and gold,
you are
the delirious
door
of an empty house,
you are
the old sin,
the cruel
salamander,
untouched
in the brazier
of the sustained pains of your people,
you are
Sodom,
yes,
Sodom
dazzling,
in a shady background
of green velvet,
surrounded
by a curled shadow, by unlimited
waters, you sleep
in the arms
of the unknown
springtime
of a savage planet.
Río, Río de Janeiro,
how much
I need to tell you. Names
I don't forget,
affairs

que maduran su perfume,
citas contigo, cuando
de tu pueblo
una ola
agregue a tu diadema
la ternura,
cuando
a tu bandera de aguas
asciendan las estrellas
del hombre,
no del mar,
no del cielo,
cuando
en el esplendor
de tu aureola
yo vea
al negro, al blanco, al hijo
de tu tierra y de tu sangre,
elevados
hasta la dignidad de tus hermosura,
iguales en tu luz resplandeciente,
propietarios
humildes y orgullosos
del espacio y de la alegría,
entonces, Río de Janeiro,
cuando
alguna vez
para todos tus hijos,
no sólo para algunos,
des tu sonrisa, espuma
de náyade morena,
entonces
yo seré tu poeta,
llegaré con mi lira
a cantar en tu aroma
y dormiré en tu cinta

with maturing perfume,
appointments with you, when
from your people
a wave
adds tenderness
to your hair band,
when
to your flag of waters
the stars of man
ascend,
not from the sea,
not from the sky,
when
in the splendor
of your halo
I see
a black man, a white man, the child
of your soil and your blood,
elevated
to the dignity of your beauty,
equal in your resplendent light,
humble and proud
owners
of space and happiness,
then, Río de Janeiro,
when
one day
for all your children,
not only a few,
you give your smile, water-nymph
mulatto foam,
then
I will be your poet,
I will arrive with my lyre
to sing in your aroma
and will sleep in your platinum

de platino,
en tu arena
incomparable,
en la frescura azul del abanico
que abrirás en mi sueño
como las alas de una
gigantesca
mariposa marina.

ribbon,
in your incomparable
sand,
in the fresh blue of the fan
you will open in my dream
like the wings of a
gigantic
sea butterfly.

156 / ODE TO THE ROAD

Oda al camino

TRANSLATED BY ILAN STAVANS

En el invierno azul	In the blue winter
con mi caballo	with my horse
al paso al paso	step by step
sin saber	unknowingly
recorro	I cross
la curva del planeta,	the planet's curve,
las arenas	the sand
bordadas	embroidered
por una cinta mágica	by a magic ribbon
de espuma,	of foam,
caminos	roads
resguardados	sheltered
por acacias, por boldos	by acacia trees, by dusty
polvorientos,	herbal tea,
lomas, cerros hostiles,	hillocks, hostile hills,
matorrales	thickets
envueltos	enwrapped
por el nombre del invierno.	in the name of winter.
Ay viajero!	Ay traveler!
No vas y no regresas:	You don't go and don't return:
eres	you are
en los caminos,	made of roads,
existes	you exist
en la niebla.	in fog.
Viajero	Traveler
dirigido	guided

no a un punto, no a una cita,
sino sólo
al aroma
de la tierra,
sino sólo al invierno
en los caminos.

Por eso
lentamente
voy
cruzando el silencio
y parece
que nadie
me acompaña.

No es cierto.

Las soledades cierran
sus ojos
y sus bocas
sólo
al transitorio, al fugaz, al dormido.
Yo voy despierto.
Y
como
una nave en el mar
abre
las aguas
y seres invisibles
acuden y se apartan,
así
detrás del aire,
se mueven
y reúnen
las invisibles vidas
de la tierra, las hojas

neither to a particular point, nor to an
appointment,
but only
to the aroma
of the earth,
but only to the winter
of the roads.

That's why
I will
slowly
cross the silence
and it appears
as if no one
is with you.

It isn't true.

Solitude closes
its eyes
and mouths
only
to those in passing, in flight, sleeping.
I am awake.
And
like
a ship at sea
it opens
the waters
and invisible beings
gather around and depart,
thus
behind the air,
the invisible lives
of the earth
move,
the leaves

suspiran en la niebla,
el viento
oculta
su desdichado rostro
y llora
sobre
la punta, de los pinos.
Llueve,
y cada gota cae
sobre una pequeñita
vasija de la tierra:
hay una copa de cristal que espera
cada gota de lluvia.

Andar alguna vez
sólo
por eso! Vivir
la temblorosa
pulsación del camino
con las respiraciones sumergidas
del campo en el invierno:
caminar para ser, sin otro
rumbo
que la propia vida,
y como, junto al árbol,
la multitud
del viento
trajo zarzas, semillas,
lianas, enredaderas,
así, junto a tus pasos,
va creciendo la tierra.

Ah viajero,
no es niebla,
ni silencio,
ni muerte,

sigh in the fog,
the wind
hides
its wretched face
and cries
above
the pines' tips.
It rains,
and each drop falls
over a tiny
vessel of the earth:
a crystal cup awaits
each raindrop.

So it's sometimes
necessary
to walk alone! To live
the road's
shaking
with the sunken breath
of the field in winter:
to walk in order to be, without
any direction
other than life itself,
and how, near the tree,
the multitude
of wind
brought blackberry bushes, seeds,
lianas, bindweeds,
thus, along with your steps,
the earth keeps growing.

Ah traveler,
it's neither the fog,
nor silence,
nor death,

lo que viaja contigo,
sino
tú mismo con tus muchas vidas.

Así es como, a caballo,
cruzando
colinas y praderas,
en invierno,
una vez más me equivoqué:
creía
caminar por los caminos:
no era verdad,
porque
a través de mi alma
fui viajero
y regresé
cuando no tuve
ya secretos
para la tierra
y
ella
los repetía con su idioma.

En cada hoja está mi nombre escrito.

La piedra es mi familia.

De una manera o de otra
hablamos o callamos
con la tierra.

that travels with you,
but
you yourself with your many lives.

That's how, on horseback,
crossing
hills and meadows,
in winter,
once again I was wrong:
I thought
I was walking the roads:
it isn't true,
because
in my soul
I was a traveler
and returned
when I no longer had
any secrets
for the earth
and
the earth
repeated them in her language.

In each leaf my name is written.

The stone is my family.

One way or another,
we speak or not
with the earth.

157 / ODE TO THE ROOSTER

Oda al gallo

TRANSLATED BY STEPHEN MITCHELL

Vi un gallo
de plumaje
castellano:
de tela negra y blanca
cortaron
su camisa,
sus pantalones cortos
y las plumas arqueadas
de su cola.
Sus patas enfundadas
en botas amarillas
dejaban
brillar los espolones
desafiantes
y arriba
la soberbia
cabeza
coronada
de sangre
mantenía
toda aquella apostura:
la estatua
del orgullo.

Nunca
sobre
la tierra

I saw a rooster
with Castilian
plumage:
from black and white cloth
his shirt
had been cut,
and his knee-breeches,
and the arched feathers
of his tail.
His feet, sheathed
in yellow boots,
revealed
the glitter of his defiant
spurs,
and on top
the lordly
head,
crowned
with blood,
maintained
that demeanor:
a statue
of pride.

Never
on
earth

vi tal seguridad,
tal gallardía:
era
como si el fuego
enarbolara
la precisión final
de su hermosura:
dos oscuros
destellos
de azabache
eran
apenas
los desdeñosos ojos
del gallo
que caminaba como
si danzara
pisando casi sin tocar la tierra.

Pero apenas
un grano
de maíz, un fragmento
de pan vieron sus ojos,
los levantó en el pico
como un joyero
eleva
con dedos delicados un diamante,
luego
llamó con guturales oratorias
a sus gallinas
y desde lo alto les dejó caer
el alimento.

Presidente no he visto
con galones y estrellas
adornado
como este

had I seen such confidence,
such valor:
it was
as if fire
had hoisted
the final precision
of its beauty:
two dark
flashes
of jet
were
the disdainful eyes
of the rooster
who walked as
if he were dancing,
almost without touching the ground.

But the moment
his eyes saw
a grain
of corn or a crumb
of bread,
he lifted it in his beak
as a jeweler's
delicate fingers hold up
a diamond,
then
with a guttural oration he called
his hens
and from on high let the food
fall.

Never have I seen a president
with gold braid and stars
adorned
like this

gallo	rooster
repartiendo	parceling out
trigo,	wheat,
ni he visto	nor have I seen
inaccesible	a tenor
tenor	unapproachable
como este puro	as this pure
protagonista de oro	protagonist of gold
que desde	who from
el trono	the central
central de su universo	throne of his universe
protegió a las mujeres	protected the women
de su tribu	of his tribe
sin dejarse en la boca	keeping nothing in his mouth
sino orgullo,	but pride,
mirando a todos lados,	looking in all directions,
buscando	searching for
el alimento	the food
de la tierra	of the earth
sólo	only
para su ávida	for his insatiable
familia,	family,
dirigiendo los pasos	walking toward
al sol, a las vertientes,	the sun, toward the slopes,
a otro grano	toward another grain
de trigo.	of wheat.
Tu dignidad de torre,	Your dignity like a tower's,
de guerrero	like a benign
benigno,	warrior's,
tu himno	your hymn
hacia las alturas	lifted
levantado,	to the heights,
tu rápido	your quick
amor, rapto	love, rapture
de sombras emplumadas,	of feathered shadows,

celebro,	I celebrate,
gallo	black and
negro	white
y blanco,	rooster,
erguido,	strutting
resumen	epitome
de la viril integridad campestre,	of virile honor,
padre	father
del huevo frágil, paladín	of the fragile egg, paladin
de la aurora,	of the dawn,
ave de la soberbia,	bird of pride,
ave sin nido,	bird without a nest,
que al hombre	who bestows his sacrifice
destinó su sacrificio	upon mankind
sin someter	without compromising
su estirpe,	his lineage
ni derrumbar su canto.	or ruining his song.
No necesita vuelo	Your nobility
tu apostura,	doesn't need flight,
mariscal del amor	field marshal of love
y meteoro	and meteor
a tantas excelencias	devoted
entregado,	to so many excellences
que si	that if
esta	this
oda	ode
cae	falls
al gallinero	into the yard
la picarás con displicencia suma	you will peck it with supreme aloofness
y la repartirás a tus gallinas.	and parcel it out to your hens.

158 / ODE TO THE ROSE

Oda a la rosa

TRANSLATED BY ILAN STAVANS

A la rosa,	To the rose,
a esta rosa,	this rose,
a la única,	the one rose,
a esta gallarda, abierta,	this gallant, unfurnished,
adulta rosa,	adult rose,
a su profundidad de terciopelo,	to its depths of velvet,
al estallido de su seno rojo.	its outburst of red breast.
Creían,	They thought,
sí,	yes,
creían	they thought
que renunciaba a ti,	I had given up on you,
que no te canto,	that I don't sing you,
que no eres mía, rosa,	that you are not mine, rose,
sino ajena,	but someone else's,
que yo	that I
voy por el mundo	go around the world
sin mirarte,	ignoring you,
preocupado	concerned
sólo	only
del hombre	with man
y su conflicto.	and his conflicts.
No es verdad, rosa,	It is not true, rose:
te amo.	I love you.
Adolescente	As a teenager,
preferí las espigas,	I preferred brambles,
las granadas,	pomegranates,
preferí ásperas flores	I preferred rugged bouquets

de matorral, silvestres
azucenas.
Por elegante
desprecié tu erguida
plenitud,
el raso matinal de tu corpiño,
la indolente insolencia
de tu agonía, cuando
dejas caer un pétalo
y con los otros
continúas ardiendo
hasta que se esparció todo el tesoro.
Me perteneces,
rosa,
como todo
lo que hay sobre la tierra,
y no puede
el poeta
cerrar los ojos
a tu copa encendida,
cerrar el corazón a tu fragancia.
Rosa, eres dura:
he visto
caer la nieve en mi jardín:
el hielo
paralizó la vida,
los grandes árboles
quebraron sus ramajes,
solo,
rosal,
sobreviviste,
terco,
desnudo, allí en el frío,
parecido a la tierra,
pariente
del labrador, del barro,

of bush flowers, wild
lilies.
As a young dandy,
I disdained your upright
abundance,
the satin of your morning body,
the indolent insolence
of your agony as
you allow a petal to fall,
and, along with others,
go on burning
until all your treasure is scattered.
You belong to me,
rose,
like everything
on earth;
and the poet
can't
close his eyes
to your chalice of fire,
can't close his heart to your fragrance.
Rose, you are hard:
I have seen
snow fall on my garden:
ice
paralyzes life,
great trees
lose their branches;
you alone,
rosebush,
survived,
stubborn,
naked, there in the cold,
like the earth,
kin
to the peasant, to clay,

de la escarcha,
y más tarde
puntual, el nacimiento
de una rosa,
el crecimiento de una llamarada.

Rosa obrera,
trabajas
tu perfume,
elaboras
tu estallido escarlata o tu blancura,
todo el invierno
buscas en la tierra,
excavas
minerales,
minera,
sacas fuego
del fondo
y luego
te abres,
esplendor de la luz, labio del fuego,
lámpara de hermosura.

A mí
me perteneces,
a mí y a todos,
aunque
apenas
tengamos
tiempo para mirarte,
vida para
dedicar a tus llamas
los cuidados,
rosa
eres nuestra,
vienes

to frost,
and, later,
the punctual birth
of a rose,
a first-flame flowing.

Rose of toil.
You labor to spread
your perfume,
you elaborate
your scarlet burst or whiteness,
in winter
you search the earth,
you excavate
minerals,
miner,
you bring up fire
from below
and then
you open,
splendor of light, lip of fire,
lamp of beauty.

You belong
to me,
to me and to everyone,
though
we barely
have
time to admire you,
or life to
dedicate
to the cultivation of your flames;
rose,
you are ours,
you come

del tiempo consumido
y avanzas,
sales de los jardines
al futuro.
Caminas
el camino
del hombre,
inquebrantable y victoriosa eres
un pequeño
capullo de bandera.
Bajo tu resistente y delicado
pabellón de fragancia
la grave tierra derrotó a la muerte
y la victoria fue tu llamarada.

from bygone times
and advance,
you emerge from the gardens,
into the future.
You walk
the road
of man,
indestructible, victorious,
the source
that one day will turn into a flag.
Under your resistance, delicate
pavilion of fragrance,
the grave earth defeated death
and victory was your flowing.

159 / ODE TO SADNESS

Oda a la tristeza

TRANSLATED BY ILAN STAVANS

Tristeza, escarabajo
de siete patas rotas,
huevo de telaraña,
rata descalabrada,
esqueleto de perra:
Aquí no entras.
No pasas.
Ándate.
Vuelve
al Sur con tu paraguas,
vuelve
al Norte con tus dientes de culebra.
Aquí vive un poeta.
La tristeza no puede
entrar por estas puertas.
Por las ventanas
entra el aire del mundo,
las rojas rosas nuevas,
las banderas bordadas
del pueblo y sus victorias.
No puedes.
Aquí no entras.
Sacude
tus alas de murciélago,
yo pisaré las plumas
que caen de tu manto,
yo barreré los trozos

Sadness, beetle
of seven shattered feet,
spider's egg,
wounded rat,
bitch's skeleton:
you aren't allowed here.
Stop.
Go away.
Go back
to the south with your umbrella,
go back
to the north with your serpent fangs.
A poet lives here.
Sadness cannot
come through these doors.
The wind of the world
enters through the windows,
the new red roses,
the people's
embroidered flags and their victories.
You can't.
There's no room.
Rumble
your bat wings,
I shall step on the plumes
falling from your mantle,
I shall sweep the remains

de tu cadáver hacia
las cuatro puntas del viento,
yo te torceré el cuello,
te coseré los ojos,
cortaré tu mortaja
y enterraré tus huesos roedores
bajo la primavera de un manzano.

of your corpse
to the wind's four corners,
I shall wring your neck,
sew your eyes,
tailor your shroud
and bury your rodent bones
under the spring of an apple tree.

160 / ODE TO SALT

Oda a la sal

TRANSLATED BY PHILIP LEVINE

Esta sal
del salero
yo la vi en los salares.
Sé que
no
van a creerme,
pero
canta,
canta la sal, la piel
de los salares,
canta
con una boca ahogada
por la tierra.
Me estremecí en aquellas
soledades
cuando escuché
la voz
de
la sal
en el desierto.
Cerca de Antofagasta
toda
la pampa salitrosa
suena:
es una
voz
quebrada,
un lastimero
canto.

In the salt mines
I saw the salt
in this shaker.
I know you won't believe me,
but there
it sings,
the salt sings, the skin
of the salt mines
sings
with a mouth choking
on dirt.
Alone
when I heard
the voice
of salt,
I trembled
in the empty
desert.
Near Antofagasta
the whole
salted plain
shouts out
in its
cracked
voice
a pitiful
song.

Luego en sus cavidades
la sal gema, montaña
de una luz enterrada,
catedral transparente,
cristal del mar, olvido
de las olas.
Y luego en cada mesa
de ese mundo,
sal,
tu substancia
ágil
espolvoreando
la luz vital
sobre
los alimentos.
Preservadora
de las antiguas
bodegas del navío,
descubridora
fuiste
en el océano,
materia
adelantada
en los desconocidos, entreabiertos
senderos de la espuma.
Polvo del mar, la lengua
de ti recibe un beso
de la noche marina:
el gusto funde en cada
sazonado manjar tu oceanía
y así la mínima,
la minúscula
ola del salero
nos enseña
no sólo su doméstica blancura,
sino el sabor central del infinito.

Then in its caverns
jewels of rock salt, a mountain
of light buried under earth,
transparent cathedral,
crystal of the sea, oblivion
of the waves.
And now on each table
of the world
your agile
essence,
salt,
spreading
a vital luster
on
our food.
Preserver
of the ancient
stores in the holds
of ships, you were
the explorer
of the seas,
matter
foretold
in the secret, half-open
trails of foam.
Dust of water, the tongue
receives through you a kiss
from the marine night:
taste melds
your oceanity
into each rich morsel
and thus the least
wave
of the saltshaker
teaches us
not merely domestic purity
but also the essential flavor of the infinite.

161 / ODE TO SAND

Oda a la arena

TRANSLATED BY GEORGE D. SCHADE

Arena pura, cómo	Pure sand, how did you
se acumuló, impalpable,	accumulate, impalpable,
tu grano dividido	your divided grain
y cinturón del mar, copa del mundo,	and sea belt, cup of the world,
pétalo planetario,	planetary petal?
fuiste reuniendo frente al alarido	Were you gathering by the scream
de olas y aves salvajes	of the waves and the wild birds
tu anillo eterno y tu unidad oscura?	your eternal ring and dark unity?
Arena, madre	Sand, you are
eres	mother
del océano,	of the ocean,
él en tu piedra innumerable	which in your innumerable rocks
depositó el racimo de la especie,	deposited the seed of the species,
hiriendo	wounding
con sus gritos seminales	your nature with its green
de toro verde tu naturaleza.	bull's seminal roars.
Desnudo sobre	Naked on
tu fragmentaria piel	your fragmentary skin
siento	I feel
tu beso, tu susurro	your kiss, your murmur
recorriéndome	running over me,
más ceñidos que el agua,	tighter than water,
el aire, el tiempo,	air and time,
plegándose	folding
a las líneas de mi cuerpo,	into the lines of my body,
volviéndome a formar	forming me again,

y cuando	and when
sigo errando	I continue roving
por la playa marina	along the sea beach
el hueco de mi ser queda un instante	the impress of my being stays for an instant
en tu memoria, arena,	in your memory, sand,
hasta que aire,	until air,
ola	wave
o noche	or night
borren mi peso gris en tu dominio.	erase my grey stamp in your domain.
Sílice demolida,	Demolished silica,
mármol disperso, aro	scattered marble, crumbling
desgranado,	hoop,
polen	pollen
de la profundidad,	from the sea depths,
polvo marino,	marine dust,
te elevas	you rise
en las dunas	in the silvery
plateadas	dunes
como	like
gargantas	the throat
de paloma,	of a dove,
te extiendes	you extend
en el desierto,	in the desert,
arena	sand
de la luna,	of the moon,
sin límite,	limitless,
circular y brillante	circular and brilliant
como un anillo,	like a ring,
muerta,	dead,
sólo silencio	only silence
hasta que el viento silba	until the wind whistles
y aterrador acude	and terrifyingly appears,
sacudiendo	shaking
la piedra demolida,	the pulverized stone,
la sábana	the sheet
de sal y soledad,	of salt and solitude,

y entonces
la enfurecida arena
suena como un castillo
atravesado
por una racha de violines,
por una tumultuosa
velocidad de espada en movimiento.

Caes
hasta que el hombre
te recoge
en su pala
y a la mezcla
del edificio
serenamente acudes
regresando
a la piedra,
a la forma,
construyendo
una
morada
reunida de nuevo
para servir
la voluntad del hombre.

and then
the sand, enraged,
sounds like a castle
crossed
by a squall of violins,
by the tumultuous velocity
of a sword in movement.

You fall
until man
gathers you
up with his spade
and in the building
mixture
serenely you appear,
returning
to stone,
to form,
building
a
dwelling
joined together again
to serve
the will of man.

162 / ODE TO SAN DIEGO STREET

Oda a la calle San Diego

TRANSLATED BY ILAN STAVANS

Por la calle
San Diego
el aire de Santiago
viaja al Sur majestuoso.

No viaja en tren el aire.

Va paso a paso
mirando
primero las ventanas,
luego los ríos,
más tarde los volcanes.

Pero,
largamente,
en la esquina
de la calle Alameda
mira un café pequeño
que parece
un autobús
cargado de viajeros.
Luego viene
un negocio
de sellos, timbres, placas.
Aquí se puede
comprar en letras blancas
y fondo azul bruñido

Along
San Diego Street
the Santiago air
travels majestically south.

The air doesn't travel by train.

It goes step by step
looking
first at the windows,
then at the rivers,
later at the volcanoes.

But,
copiously,
in the corner
of Alameda Street,
it looks at a small café
resembling
a bus
full of travelers.
Then comes
a business
of stamps, seals, plates.
Here one can
buy, in white letters
and polished blue ink,

el título temible de «Dentista».
Me deslumbra esta tienda.
Y las que siguen tienen
ese arrebato
de lo que quiso ser
tan sólo transitorio
y se quedó formado
para siempre.
Más lejos
venden
lo imaginario, lo inimaginable,
útiles espantosos,
incógnitos bragueros,
endurecidas
flores de ortopedia,
piernas
que piden cuerpos,
gomas enlazadoras
como brazos
de bestias submarinas.

Paso mirando puertas.
Atravieso
cortinas,
compro pequeñas
cosas
inservibles.

Soy el cronista errante
de la calle San Diego.

En el número 134,
la librería Araya.
El antiguo librero
es una piedra,
parece el presidente

the pretentious title of "Dentist."
I'm dazzled by this store.
And the next ones display
the pomposity
of what wanted to be
only transitory
and became forever
fixed.
Farther away,
what's imagined, what's imaginable
is on sale,
horrible materials,
unknown trusses,
hardened
orthopedic flowers,
legs
begging for bodies,
linking prophylactics
like arms
of submarine beasts.

I pass, looking at doors.
I go through
cantinas,
buy useless
little
things.

I'm the wandering chronicler
of San Diego Street.

In number 134,
the Araya Bookstore.
The old bookseller
is a stone,
he resembles the president

de una república
desmantelada,
de una bodega verde,
de una nación lluviosa.
Los libros
se acumulan. Terribles
páginas que amedrentan
al cazador de leones.
Hay geografías
de cuatrocientos tomos:
en los primeros
hay luna llena, jazmines de archipiélagos:
los últimos volúmenes
son sólo soledades:
reinos de nieve, susurrantes renos.

En el siguiente número
de la calle
venden pobres juguetes,
y desde puertas próximas
la carne asada
inunda
las narices
de la crepuscular ciudadanía.
En el hotel que sigue
las parejas
entran con cuentagotas:
es tarde
y el negocio
se apresura:
el amor busca plumas
clandestinas.
Más allá venden catres
de bronce deslumbrante,
camas descomunales
construidas

of some dismantled
republic,
of a green bodega,
of a rainy nation.
Books
accumulate. Frightening
pages discouraging
the lion hunter.
There are geographies
of four hundred volumes:
in the early ones
there is a full moon, jasmine in
archipelagoes:
the last volumes
are only about loneliness:
kingdoms of snow, whispering reindeer.

At the street's
next number
poor toys are sold,
and from nearby doors
roasted beef
inundates
the nostrils
of the crepuscular citizenry.
In the hotel that follows
couples
enter in dribs and drabs:
it is late
and the business
is in a hurry:
love seeks clandestine
pens.
Over there, cots of dazzling bronze
are sold,
massive beds
built

tal vez
en astilleros.
Son como
eternos barcos amarillos:
deben salir de viaje,
llenarse
con nacimientos y agonías.
Toda la calle espera
la ola del amor y su marea.
En la ventana
que sigue hay un violín
roto,
pero encrespado en su dulzura
de sol abandonado.
Habita esa ventana
incomprendido
por los zapatos que se acumularon
sobre él y las botellas
vacías
que adornan su reposo.

Ven
por la transmigratoria
calle
San Diego
de Santiago de Chile,
en este año:
olor a gas, a sombra,
olor a lluvia seca.
Al paso
de los obreros que se desgranaron
de los agonizantes autobuses
suenan
todos los tangos en todas las radios
en el mismo minuto.

perhaps
in shipyards.
They're like
eternal yellow boats:
they must go on vacation,
be filled
with births and agonies.
The entire street awaits
the wave of love and its tide.
In the following
window there is a broken
violin,
but curled up in its sweetness
of abandoned sun.
It inhabits that window
misunderstood
by the shoes accumulating
on top of it and the empty
bottles
adorning its repose.

Come
this year
through the transmigrating
San Diego
Street
in Santiago, Chile:
the smell of gas, of shadow,
the smell of dry rain.
At the footsteps
of workers spilled out
of agonizing buses
one can hear
all the tangos on every radio
at the same time.

Busca conmigo
una copa gigante,
con bandera,
honor y monumento
del vino y de la patria cristalina.

Mitin relámpago.

Gritan
cuatrocientos obreros
y estudiantes:

Salarios!

El cobre para Chile!
Pan y Paz!

Qué escándalo!

Se cierran
los negocios,
se oye
un disparo,
surgen de todas partes
las banderas.

La calle
corre ahora
hacia arriba,
hacia mañana:
una ola
venida
del fondo
de mi pueblo
en este río
popular

Come look with me
for a giant cup,
with a flag,
honor and monument
of wine and the crystalline homeland.

Quick street march.

Four hundred workers
and students
scream:

Wages!

The copper belongs to Chile!
Bread and peace!

What a scandal!

Businesses
close,
a gunshot
is heard,
from everywhere
flags emerge.

The street
now runs
upward,
toward tomorrow:
a wave
coming
from the depths
of my people
in this popular
river

recibió sus afluentes
de toda la extensión del
territorio.

De noche, la calle
San Diego
sigue por la ciudad, la luz la llena.
Luego,
el silencio
desliza en ella su navío.

Algunos pasos más: una campana
que despierta.
Es el día que llega
ruidoso, en autobús desvencijado,
cobrando su tarifa matutina
por ver el cielo azul
sólo un minuto, apenas un minuto
antes de que las tiendas,
los sonidos,
nos traguen y trituren
en el largo intestino
de la calle.

receiving its tributaries
from everywhere
in the land.

By night, San Antonio
Street
goes on through the city, light filling it.
Then,
silence
slides its ship through.

A few steps farther: a wakening
bell.
The day arrives
noisily, a battered bus,
charging a morning rate
to see the blue sky
for a single minute, barely a minute
before the stores,
the sounds,
devour and crush us
in the long bowels
of the street.

163 / ODE TO THE SAW

Oda al serrucho

TRANSLATED BY GEORGE D. SCHADE

Entre las nobles
herramientas,
el esbelto
martillo,
la hoz recién cortada de la luna,
el biselado, recio
formón, la generosa
pala,
eres, serrucho,
el pez, el pez
maligno,
el tiburón de aciaga dentadura.

Sin embargo, la hilera
de tus
mínimos dientes
cortan cantando
el sol
en la madera,
la miel del pino, la acidez
metálica del roble.
Alegremente
cortas
y cantando
el aserrín esparce tus proezas
que el viento mueve y que la lluvia hostiga.

Among the noble
tools,
the slender
hammer,
the sickle just sliced from the moon,
the beveled strong
chisel, the generous
shovel,
you are, saw,
fish, malignant
fish, the shark with fatal dentures.

Nonetheless, the row
of your
minimal teeth
cut singing
the sun
in the wood,
the pine honey, the metallic
acidity of the oak.
Joyfully
you cut away,
and singing,
the sawdust scatters your prowess,
moved by the wind and lashed by the rain.

No asumiste apostura	You don't assume a jauntiness
como la del insólito martillo	like the incredible hammer,
que decoró con dos plumas de gallo	its head of steel
su cabeza de acero,	decorated with two rooster feathers,
sino que	but
como un pez	like a fish
de la profunda	from the profound
plenitud submarina,	submarine plenitude,
luego de tu tarea natatoria	after your natatorial task,
te inmovilizas y desapareces	you are immobilized and disappear
como en el lecho oscuro del océano.	as in the dark bed of the ocean.
Serrucho, pez amigo	Saw, fish friend
que canta,	that sings,
no devoras	you don't devour
el manjar que cortó tu dentadura,	the tasty food cut by your teeth,
sino que lo derramas	but scatter it
en migas de madera.	in crumbs of wood.
Serrucho azul, delgado	Blue saw, slim
trabajador, cantando	worker, singing
cortaste	you cut
para mí	for me
las tablas del ropero,	the boards of my clothes closet,
para todos	frames
marcos	for everyone,
para que en ellos	so the painting
fulgure la pintura	may flash in them
o penetre a la casa	or the river of light may
el río de la luz por la ventana.	penetrate the house through the window.
Por toda la tierra	All over the earth
con sus ríos	with its rivers
y sus navegaciones,	and navigations,
por los	through the
puertos,	ports,

en las embarcaciones del océano,
en lo alto
de aldeas suspendidas
en la nieve,
aún
lejos, más lejos:
en
el
secreto
de los institutos,
en la casa florida
de la amante,
y también
en el patio abandonado
donde murió un Ignacio, un Saturnino,
así como
en las profundas herrerías,
en todas partes
un serrucho
vigila,
un serrucho
delgado, con sus
pequeños dientes
de pescado casero y su vestido
de mar, de mina azul, de florete olvidado.

Así, serrucho,
quiero
aserrar
las cosas amarillas de este mundo,
cortar,
maderas puras,
cortezas de la tierra y de la vida,
encinas, robles, sándalos
sagrados,
otoño

at ocean embarkations,
in the heights
of villages suspended
in the snow,
even
farther, much farther:
in
the
secrets
of the institutes,
in the lover's
house full of flowers,
and also
in the abandoned patio
where an Ignatius or Saturnine died,
likewise,
in the deep set back blacksmith shops,
everywhere,
a saw
keeps watch,
a slim
saw, with its
tiny teeth
of domestic fish and its sea
dress, of blue mine and forgotten foil.

So, saw,
I want
to saw
the yellow things of this world,
to cut
pure woods,
bark from earth and life,
oaks, live oaks, sacred
sandalwood,
autumn

en largas leguas extendido.
Yo quiero
tu escondida
utilidad, tu fuerza
y tu frescura,
la segura modestia
de tu dentado acero,
tu lámina de luna!

Me despido
de ti,
benéfico
serrucho,
astral
y submarino,
diciéndote
que
me quedaría
siempre con tu metálica victoria
en los aserraderos,
violín del bosque, pájaro
del aserrín, tenaz
tiburón de la madera!

spread out over long leagues.
I want
your hidden
utility, your force
and freshness,
the sure modesty
of your toothed steel,
your blade of moon!

I bid
you good-bye,
beneficent
saw,
astral
and submarine,
telling you
that
I would stay forever
with your metal victory in the sawmills,
forest violin, sawdust
bird, tenacious
wood shark!

164 / ODE TO THE SEA

Oda al mar

TRANSLATED BY GEORGE D. SCHADE

Aquí en la isla
el mar
y cuánto mar
se sale de sí mismo
a cada rato,
dice que sí, que no,
que no, que no, que no,
dice que sí, en azul,
en espuma, en galope,
dice que no, que no.
No puede estarse quieto,
me llamo mar, repite
pegando en una piedra
sin lograr convencerla,
entonces
con siete lenguas verdes
de siete perros verdes,
de siete tigres verdes,
de siete mares verdes,
la recorre, la besa,
la humedece
y se golpea el pecho
repitiendo su nombre.
Oh mar, así te llamas,
oh camarada océano,
no pierdas tiempo y agua,
no te sacudas tanto,

Here on the island
the sea—
and how much sea—
can't contain itself,
at every moment,
says yes, then no,
says no, no, no,
says yes, in blue,
in foam, at a gallop,
says no, and no.
It can't stay still,
my name's sea, it repeats,
smashing on a rock
unable to convince it,
then,
with seven green tongues
of seven green hounds,
of seven green tigers,
of seven green seas,
it goes all over,
kissing and soaking the rock,
beating its breast,
repeating its name.
Oh, sea, that's your name,
oh ocean comrade,
don't waste time and water,
don't shake yourself so much,

ayúdanos,
somos los pequeñitos
pescadores,
los hombres de la orilla,
tenemos frío y hambre,
eres nuestro enemigo,
no golpees tan fuerte,
no grites de ese modo,
abre tu caja verde
y déjanos a todos
en las manos
tu regalo de plata:
el pez de cada día.

Aquí en cada casa
lo queremos
y aunque sea de plata,
de cristal o de luna,
nació para las pobres
cocinas de la tierra.
No lo guardes,
avaro,
corriendo frío como
relámpago mojado
debajo de tus olas.
Ven, ahora,
ábrete
y déjalo
cerca de nuestras manos,
ayúdanos, océano,
padre verde y profundo,
a terminar un día
la pobreza terrestre.
Déjanos
cosechar la infinita
plantación de tus vidas,

help us out,
we're the tiny little
fishermen,
the men on shore,
we're cold and hungry,
you are the enemy,
don't hit so hard,
don't roar like that,
open your green box
and leave us all
in our hands
your silver present:
our daily fish.

Here in every house
we want it,
though it may be of silver,
of crystal or moon,
it was born for the poor
kitchens of the world.
Don't hold on to it,
miser,
rushing cold as
wet lightning
under your waves.
Come, now,
open up
and leave it
near our hands,
help us, ocean,
deep green father
to some day end
poverty on this earth.
Let us
harvest the infinite
plantations of your lives,

tus trigos y tus uvas,
tus bueyes, tus metales,
el esplendor mojado
y el fruto sumergido.

your wheat and grapes,
your oxen and metals,
the moist splendor
and submerged fruit.

Padre mar, ya sabemos
cómo te llamas, todas
las gaviotas reparten
tu nombre en las arenas:
ahora, pórtate bien,
no sacudas tus crines,
no amenaces a nadie,
no rompas contra el cielo
tu bella dentadura,
déjate por un rato
de gloriosas historias,
danos a cada hombre,
a cada
mujer y a cada niño,
un pez grande o pequeño
cada día.
Sal por todas las calles
del mundo
a repartir pescado
y entonces
grita,
grita
para que te oigan todos
los pobres que trabajan
y digan,
asomando a la boca
de la mina:
«Ahí viene el viejo mar
repartiendo pescado».
Y volverán abajo,
a las tinieblas,

Father sea, now we know
what you're called, all
the seagulls shrill
your name across the sands:
now, behave yourself,
don't toss your mane,
don't threaten anyone,
don't break your lovely
set of teeth against the sky,
forget your glorious
history for a moment,
give each man,
each
woman and child,
a big or small fish
every day.
Go forth on every street
in the world
to dole out fish,
and then
shout,
shout
so all the working
poor can hear you,
and say,
appearing at the mouth
of the mine:
"Here comes the old sea
doling out fish."
And they'll go back down
into the darkness,

sonriendo, y por las calles
y los bosques
sonreirán los hombres
y la tierra
con sonrisa marina.

Pero
si no lo quieres,
si no te da la gana,
espérate,
espéranos,
lo vamos a pensar,
vamos en primer término
a arreglar los asuntos
humanos,
los más grandes primero,
todos los otros después,
y entonces
entraremos en ti,
cortaremos las olas
con cuchillo de fuego,
en un caballo eléctrico
saltaremos la espuma,
cantando
nos hundiremos
hasta tocar el fondo
de tus entrañas,
un hilo atómico
guardará tu cintura,
plantaremos
en tu jardín profundo
plantas
de cemento y acero,
te amarraremos
pies y manos,
los hombres por tu piel

smiling, and in the streets
and forests
men and the earth
will smile
with a marine smile.

But
if you don't want to,
if you don't feel like it,
wait,
wait for us,
we'll think it over,
first we're going to
fix human
concerns,
the biggest first,
all the others later on,
and then
we'll enter you,
we'll cut the waves
with a fiery knife,
on an electric horse
we'll leap over the foam,
singing
we'll sink down
until we touch the bottom
of your entrails,
an atomic thread
will guard your waist,
we'll plant
in the depths of your garden
plants
of cement and steel,
we'll tie you
hand and foot,
men will pass by

pasearán escupiendo,	spitting on your skin,
sacándote racimos,	yanking out your fruit clusters,
construyéndote arneses,	building you harnesses,
montándote y domándote,	mounting and taming you,
dominándote el alma.	controlling your soul.
Pero eso será cuando	But that will be when
los hombres	we men
hayamos arreglado	have fixed
nuestro problema,	our problem,
el grande,	the big one,
el gran problema.	the big problem.
Todo lo arreglaremos	We'll fix it all
poco a poco:	little by little:
te obligaremos, mar,	we'll force you, sea,
te obligaremos, tierra,	we'll force you, earth,
a hacer milagros,	to perform miracles,
porque en nosotros mismos,	because in ourselves,
en la lucha,	in the struggle,
está el pez, está el pan,	lie the fish, the bread,
está el milagro.	the miracle.

165 / ODE TO THE SEA GULL

Oda a la gaviota

TRANSLATED BY MARGARET SAYERS PEDEN

A la gaviota
sobre
los pinaros
de la costa,
en el viento
la sílaba
silbante de mi oda.

Navega,
barca lúcida,
bandera de dos alas,
en mi verso,
cuerpo de plata,
sube
tu insignia atravesada
en la camisa
del firmamento frío,
oh voladora,
suave
serenata de vuelo,
flecha de nieve, nave
tranquila en la tormenta transparente
elevas tu equilibrio
mientras
el ronco viento barre
las praderas del cielo.

To the sea gull
high above
the pine woods
of the coast,
on the wind
the sibilant
syllable of my ode.

Sail,
bright boat,
winged banner,
in my verse,
stitch,
body of silver,
your emblem
across the shirt
of the icy firmament,
oh, aviator,
gentle
serenade of flight,
snow arrow, serene
ship in the transparent storm,
steady, you soar
while
the hoarse wind sweeps
the meadows of the sky.

Después del largo viaje,
tú, magnolia emplumada,
triángulo sostenido
por el aire en la altura,
con lentitud regresas
a tu forma
cerrando
tu plateada vestidura,
ovalando tu nítido tesoro,
volviendo a ser
botón blanco del vuelo,
germen
redondo,
huevo de la hermosura.

Otro poeta
aquí
terminaría
su victoriosa oda.
Yo no puedo
permitirme
sólo
el lujo blanco
de la inútil espuma.
Perdóname,
gaviota,
soy
poeta
realista,
fotógrafo del cielo.
Comes,
comes,
comes,
no hay
nada que no devores,

After your long voyage,
feathered magnolia,
triangle borne
aloft on the air,
slowly you regain
your form,
arranging
your silvery robes, shaping
your bright treasure in an oval,
again a
white bud of flight,
a round
seed,
egg of beauty.

Another
poet
would end here
his triumphant ode.
I cannot
limit myself
to
the luxurious whiteness
of useless froth.
Forgive me,
sea gull,
I am
a realist
poet,
photographer of the sky.
You eat,
and eat,
and eat,
there is nothing
you don't devour,

sobre el agua del puerto
ladras
como perro de pobre,
corres
detrás del último
pedazo de intestino
de pescado,
picoteas
a tus hermanas blancas,
robas
la despreciable presa,
el desarmado cúmulo
de basura marina,
acechas los
tomates
decaídos,
las descartadas
sobras de la caleta.
Pero
todo
lo transformas
en ala limpia,
en blanca geometría,
en la estática línea de tu vuelo.

Por eso,
ancla nevada,
voladora,
te celebro completa:
con tu voracidad abrumadora,
con tu grito en la lluvia
o tu descanso
de copo desprendido
a la tormenta,
con tu paz o tu vuelo,

on the waters of the bay
you bark
like a beggar's dog,
you pursue
the last
scrap of
fish gut,
you peck
at your white sisters,
you steal
your despicable prize,
a rotting clump
of floating garbage,
you stalk
decayed
tomatoes,
the discarded
rubbish of the cove.
But
in you
it is transformed
into clean wing,
white geometry,
the ecstatic line of flight.

That is why,
snowy anchor,
aviator,
I celebrate you as you are:
your insatiable voraciousness,
your screech in the rain,
or at rest
a snowflake blown
from the storm,
at peace or in flight,

gaviota,
te consagro
mi palabra terrestre,
torpe ensayo de vuelo,
a ver si tú desgranas
tu semilla de pájaro en mi oda.

sea gull,
I consecrate to you
my earthbound words,
my clumsy attempt at flight;
let's see whether you scatter
your birdseed in my ode.

166 / ODE TO SEA RAIN

Oda a la lluvia marina

TRANSLATED BY ILAN STAVANS

El ave grande cruza
entre agua y agua,
el cielo
se deshoja,
llueve
sobre el océano de Chile.
Dura
como roca ondulada
el agua madre
mueve
su barriga
y como desde un pino
en movimiento
caen agujas verdes
desde el cielo.
Llueve
de mar a mar,
desde los archipiélagos
hasta las osamentas amarillas
del litoral peruano,
llueve,
y es como flecha el agua
sin flechero,
la transparencia
oblicua
de los hilos,
el agua dulce

The great bird crosses
from water to water,
the sky
is stripped of its leaves,
it rains
over the ocean in Chile.
Hard
like a wavy rock
the mother water
moves
its belly
and as if from a pine
in movement
green needles fall
from the sky.
It rains
from sea to sea,
from the archipelagos
all the way to the yellow skeleton
of the Peruvian coast,
it rains,
and it is like an arrow of water
without an archer,
the oblique
transparency
of the threads,
sweet water

sobre el agua amarga.
En
el azul mojado,
ceniciento,
baila el albatros
en el aire puro,
nave orgullosa, clave
de la ecuación marina.
Y agitando
las plumas
en la lluvia,
la nevada paloma estercolaria,
la golondrina antártica,
el pájaro playero,
cruzan las soledades,
mientras
las olas y la espuma
combatiendo
rechazan y reciben
la inundación
celeste.

Aguacero
marino,
por tus hebras
fue bruñido y lavado
como un navío
el mundo:
la partida
se prepara en la costa,
chorros
de fuerza transparente
limpiaron la estructura,
brilló, brilló la proa
de madera
en la lluvia:

over sour.
In
the wet blue,
ashen,
the albatross dances
in fresh air,
proud vessel, code
of a marine equation.
And agitating
its feathers
in the rain,
the snowy debris-hunting pigeon,
the Antarctic swallow,
the beach bird,
crisscross their solitudes
while
battling
waves and foam
reject and receive
the celestial
inundation.

Sea
shower,
the world
was polished and washed
like a boat
through your filaments:
the departure
is ready on the coast,
spurts
of translucent strength
cleaned the structure,
the wooden prow
shone, shone
in the rain:

el hombre,
entre
océano
y cielo,
terso, en la luz del agua,
terminó su aspereza,
como un beso en su frente
se deshojó
la lluvia
y una racha
del mar,
una ola aguda
como un erizo de cristal salado
lo retiró del sueño
y bautizó con sal su desafío.

Aguas, en esta hora
de soledad terrestre,
activas aguas puras,
parecidas
a la verdad, eternas,
gracias
por la lección y el movimiento,
por la sal tempestuosa
y por el ritmo frío,
porque el pino del cielo
se deshoja
cristalino, en mi frente,
porque de nuevo existo,
canto, creo,
firme, recién lavado
por la lluvia marina.

man,
between
ocean
and sky,
terse, in the water light,
finished his roughness,
like a kiss on his forehead
the rain
stripped itself
and a spell
of sea,
an acute wave
like a hedgehog of salty glass
retired him from the dream
and baptized his challenge with salt.

Waters, with this hour
of earthly solitude,
pure active waters,
resembling
truth, eternal,
thank you
for the lesson and the movement,
for the tempestuous salt
and the cold rhythm,
because the pine from the sky
crystalline
strips itself on my forehead,
because I exist again,
I sing, I believe,
firm, newly washed
by sea rain.

167 / ODE TO THE SEASHORE CACTUS

Oda al cactus de la costa

TRANSLATED BY GEORGE D. SCHADE

Pequeña	Little
masa pura	pure mass
de espinas estrelladas,	of star-shaped thorns,
cactus de las arenas,	cactus of the sands,
enemigo,	enemy,
el poeta	the poet
saluda	salutes
tu salud erizada:	your prickly health:
en invierno	in winter
te he visto:	I've seen you:
la bruma carcomiendo	the fog eating away
el roquerío,	the rock formations,
los truenos	the thundering
del oleaje	waves
caían	fall
contra Chile,	against Chile,
la sal tumbando estatuas,	the salt knocking down statues,
el espacio	space
ocupado	occupied
por las arrolladoras	by the sweeping
plumas de la tormenta,	plumes of the storm,
y tú,	and you,
pequeño	little
héroe	spiny
erizado,	hero,
tranquilo	tranquil
entre dos piedras,	between two stones,

inmóvil,
sin ojos y sin hojas,
sin nidos y sin nervios,
duro, con tus raíces
minerales
como argollas terrestres
metidas
en el hierro del planeta,
y encima
una cabeza,
una minúscula
y espinosa cabeza
inmóvil,
firme, pura,
sola en la trepidante oceanía,
en el huracanado territorio.

Más tarde agosto llega,
la primavera duerme
confundida en el frío
del hemisferio negro,
todo en la costa tiene
sabor negro,
las olas
se repiten
como pianos,
el cielo
es una nave
derribada, enlutada,
el mundo es un naufragio,
y entonces
te escogió la primavera
para volver
a ver
la luz sobre la tierra
y asoman

immobile,
eyeless and leafless,
without nests or nerves,
tough, with your mineral
roots
like earthly rings
stuck
in the iron of the planet,
and above
a head,
a minuscule
thorny head,
immobile,
firm, pure,
alone in the vibrating expanse of ocean,
in the tempestuous territory.

Later August arrives,
spring slumbers,
confounded in the cold
of the black hemisphere,
everything on the coast has
a black flavor,
the waves
repeat themselves
like pianos,
the sky
is a demolished
ship, dressed in mourning,
the world is a shipwreck,
and then
spring chose you
to see
again
light on earth,
and two drops of blood

dos gotas de la sangre
de su parto
en dos de tus espinas solitarias,
y nace
allí
entre piedras,
entre tus alfileres,
nace
de nuevo
la marina
primavera,
la celeste y terrestre
primavera.

Allí, de todo
lo que existe, fragante,
aéreo, consumado,
lo que tiembla en las hojas
del limonero o entre
los aromas dormidos
de la imperial magnolia,
de todo lo que espera
su llegada,
tú, cactus de las arenas,
pequeño bruto inmóvil,
solitario,
tú fuiste el elegido
y pronto
antes de que otra flor te desafiara
los botones
de sangre
de tus sagrados dedos
se hicieron flor rosada,
pétalos milagrosos.

appear
at its birth
in two of your solitary thorns,
and there
is born
among the stones,
among your pins,
the marine
spring
is born
again,
celestial and terrestrial
spring.

There, of all
that exists, fragrant,
airy, consummate,
what trembles in the leaves
of the lemon tree or among
the dormant redolence
of the imperial magnolia,
of all that waits for
its arrival,
you, cactus of the sands,
tiny immobile brute,
solitary,
you were the chosen one,
and soon
before any other flower could challenge you,
the blood-red
buds
of your sacred fingers
turned into pink flowers,
miraculous petals.

Así es la historia,
y ésta
es la moral
de mi poema:
donde
estés, donde vivas,
en la última
soledad de este mundo,
en el azote
de la furia terrestre,
en el rincón
de las humillaciones,
hermano,
hermana,
espera,
trabaja
firme
con tu pequeño ser y tus raíces.

Un día
para ti,
para todos,
saldrá
desde tu corazón un rayo rojo,
florecerás también una mañana:
no te ha olvidado, hermano,
hermana,
no te ha olvidado,
no,
la primavera:
yo te lo digo,
yo te lo aseguro,
porque el cactus terrible,
el erizado
hijo de las arenas,

That's the story,
and this
is the moral
of my poem:
wherever
you are, wherever you live,
in the uttermost
solitude of this world,
in the whip
of earthly fury,
in the corner
of humiliations,
brother,
sister,
wait,
work
hard
with your small being and your roots.

One day,
for you,
for all,
a red ray will emerge
from your heart,
you too will flower some morning;
no,
spring
has not forgotten you, brother,
nor forgotten you,
sister,
I tell you,
I assure you,
for the terrible cactus,
the spiny
son of the sands,

conversando	conversing
conmigo	with me,
me encargó este mensaje	charged me with this message
para tu corazón desconsolado.	for your disconsolate heart.
Y ahora	And now
te lo digo	I tell you
y me lo digo:	and tell myself:
hermano, hermana,	brother, sister,
espera,	wait,
estoy seguro:	I'm sure:
No nos olvidará la primavera.	spring will not forget us.

168 / ODE TO SEAWEEDS

Oda a las algas del océano

TRANSLATED BY MARGARET SAYERS PEDEN

No conocéis tal vez
las desgranadas
vertientes
del océano.
En mi patria
es la luz
de cada día.
Vivimos
en el filo
de la ola,
en el olor del mar,
en su estrellado vino.

A veces
las altas
olas
traen
en la palma
de una
gran mano verde
un tejido
tembloroso:
la tela
inacabable
de las algas.
Son
los enlutados

You may not know
the spilling beads
of the slopes
of the ocean.
In my homeland,
ocean is the light
of each new day.
We live
on the edge
of the wave,
with the smell of the sea,
with its starry wine.

At times
the high
waves
bear
in the palm
of a
great green hand
a quivering
web:
the never-finished
cloth
of seaweeds.
They are
the mourning

guantes
del océano,
manos
de ahogados,
ropa
funeraria,
pero
cuando
en lo alto
del muro de la ola,
en la campana
del mar,
se transparentan,
brillan
como
collares
de las islas,
dilatan
sus rosarios
y la suave turgencia
naval de sus pezones
se balancea
al peso
del aire que las toca!

Oh despojos
del gran
torso marino
nunca desenterrado,
cabellera
del cielo submarino,
barba de los planetas
que rodaron
ardiendo
en el océano.
Flotando sobre

gloves
of the ocean,
hands
of the drowned,
widow's
weeds,
but
when
on the crest
of a wall of waves,
in the bell
of the sea,
light gleams through them,
they shine
like
necklaces
of the islands,
bestow
their rosaries,
and the gentle nautical
swell of their nipples
sways
beneath the touch
of the caressing air!

Oh, plunder
from the great
torso of the sea,
never unearthed,
comet
of an underwater sky,
beard of planets
that orbited
blazing
in the ocean.
Floating on

la noche y la marea,	the night and the tide,
tendidas	riding
como balsas	like rafts
de pura	of gelatinous
perla y goma,	pearls,
sacudidas	shaken
por un pez, por el sol, por el latido	by a fish, the sun, the throb
de una sola sirena,	of a single siren,
de pronto	suddenly
en una	with a
carcajada de furia,	bellow of fury,
el mar	the sea spreads its spoils
entre las piedras	among the rocks
del litoral las deja	of the shore
como jirones	like dark
pardos	tatters
de bandera,	of a flag,
como flores caídas de la nave.	like flowers fallen from a ship.
Y allí	And there
tus manos, tus pupilas	your hands, your eyes,
descubrirán	will discover
un húmedo universo de frescura,	a moist universe of coolness,
la transparencia del	the transparency of
racimo	the fruit
de las viñas sumergidas,	of submerged vines,
una gota	a drop
del tálamo	from a marine
marino,	bridal couch,
del ancho lecho azul	the wide blue bed
condecorado	encrusted
con escudos de oro,	with coins of gold,
mejillones minúsculos,	minuscule mussels,
verdes protozoarios.	green protozoa.
Anaranjadas, oxidadas formas	Orange, rusted spatulate
de espátula, de huevo,	shapes, eggs

de palmera,
abanicos
errantes
golpeados
por el
inacabable
movimiento
del corazón
marino,
islas de los sargazos
que hasta mi puerta
llegan
con el despojo
de
los arcoiris,
dejadme
llevar en mi cuello, en mi cabeza,
los pámpanos mojados
del océano,
la cabellera muerta
de la ola.

of date palms,
drifting
fans
flailed
by the
eternal
flux
of a marine
heart,
islands of sargasso
that reach
my door
with the plunder
of
the rainbow,
let me
wear around my neck, on my head,
the wet vine tendrils
of the ocean,
the spent comet
of the wave.

169 / ODE TO A SECRET LOVE

Oda al secreto amor

TRANSLATED BY KEN KRABBENHOFT

Tú sabes	They've guessed
que adivinan	our secret,
el misterio:	you know.
me ven,	They see me,
nos ven,	they see us,
y nada	and nothing
se ha dicho,	has been said—
ni tus ojos,	neither your eyes
ni tu voz, ni tu pelo,	nor your voice, neither your hair
ni tu amor han hablado,	nor your love have said a word—
y lo saben	but suddenly
de pronto,	they know,
sin saberlo	they know without even knowing
lo saben:	they know.
me despido y camino	I wave goodbye and set off
hacia otro lado	in another direction,
y saben	and they know
que me esperas.	you're waiting for me.
Alegre	Joyfully
vivo	I live
y canto	and sing
y sueño,	and dream,
seguro	sure
de mí mismo,	of myself.
y conocen	They are aware,
de algún modo	somehow,
que tú eres mi alegría.	that you are my joy.

Ven
a través del pantalón oscuro
las llaves
de tu puerta,
las llaves
del papel, de la luna
en los jazmines,
del canto en la cascada.
Tú, sin abrir la boca,
desbocada,
tú, cerrando los ojos,
cristalina,
tú, custodiando
entre las hojas negras
una paloma roja,
el vuelo
de un escondido corazón,
y entonces
una sílaba,
una gota
del cielo,
un sonido
suave de sombra y polen
en la oreja,
y todos
lo saben,
amor mío,
circula
entre los hombres,
en las librerías,
junto
a las mujeres,
cerca
del mercado
rueda
el anillo

They see
through my heavy trousers
the keys
to your door,
the keys
to writing paper, to moonlight
among jasmines,
to the song that sings in the waterfall.
And you without opening your mouth
speaking,
you crystal-clear
closing your eyes
or nursing
a red dove
nestled in black leaves,
the flight
of a hidden heart
and then
a syllable,
a drop
from heaven,
in one's ear
the soft
sound of shade and pollen,
and everybody
knows it,
my love:
it makes the rounds
of men
in bookstores
and women
as well,
and close by
the marketplace,
whirling,
the ring

de nuestro
secreto
amor
secreto.

Déjalo
que se vaya
rodando
por las calles,
que asuste
a los retratos,
a los muros,
que vaya y vuelva
y salga
con las nuevas
legumbres del mercado,
tiene
tierra,
raíces,
y arriba
una amapola:
tu boca:
una amapola.
Todo
nuestro secreto,
nuestra clave,
palabra
oculta,
sombra,
murmullo,
eso
que alguien
dijo
cuando no estábamos presentes,
es sólo una amapola,
una amapola.

of our
secret
secret
love.

Let it
go
rolling
through the streets,
let it take
portraits
and walls by surprise,
let it come and go
and pop up
with fresh
greens in the market.
It has
soil
and roots
and a poppy
on top,
your mouth
a poppy.
Our
entire secret,
our key,
our hidden
word,
our shadow or
whisper,
comments
someone
made
when we weren't around—
it's just a poppy,
a poppy.

Amor,
amor,
amor,
oh flor secreta,
llama
invisible,
clara
quemadura!

Love
love
love—
O secret flower,
invisible
flame,
bright scar
from the burning brand!

170 / ODE TO SEPTEMBER

Oda a septiembre

TRANSLATED BY ILAN STAVANS

Mes de banderas,	Month of flags,
mes seco, mes	dry month, wet
mojado,	month,
con quince días verdes,	with fifteen green days,
con quince días rojos,	with fifteen red days,
a medio cuerpo	from inside you
te sale humo	smoke
del techo,	emerges,
después	then
abres de golpe las ventanas,	you suddenly open the windows,
mes en que sale al sol	month in which the sun comes out
la flor de invierno	the winter flower
y moja una vez más	and wets
su pequeña	its small
corola temeraria,	fearful corolla once again,
mes cruzado por mil	month crossed by a thousand
flechas de lluvia	arrows of rain
y por mil	and a thousand
lanzas de sol quemante,	spears of burning sun,
septiembre,	September,
para que bailes,	for you to dance,
la tierra	the earth
pone bajo tus pies	lays under your feet
la hierba festival	the festival of grass
de sus alfombras,	like a carpet,
y en tu cabeza	and in your head
un arcoiris loco,	a crazy rainbow,

una cinta celeste
de guitarra.

Baila, septiembre, baila
con los pies de la patria,
canta, septiembre, canta
con la voz
de los pobres:
otros
meses
son largos
y desnudos,
otros
son amarillos,
otros van a caballo hacia la guerra,
tú, septiembre,
eres un viento, un rapto,
una nave de vino.

Baila
en las calles,
baila
con mi pueblo,
baila con Chile, con
la primavera,
corónate
de pámpanos copiosos
y de pescado frito.
Saca del arca
tus
banderas
desgreñadas,
saca de tu suburbio
una camisa,
de tu mina
enlutada

the celestial strip
of a guitar.

Dance, September, dance
with your feet in the homeland,
sing, September, sing
with the voice
of the poor:
other
months
are long
and naked,
others
are yellow,
others go to war on a horse,
you, September,
are a wind, a rapture,
a ship of wine.

Dance
in the streets,
dance
with my people,
dance with Chile, with
spring,
crown yourself
with copious tendrils
and fried fish.
Bring out from the ark
your
disheveled
flags,
bring out of your suburb
a shirt,
of your mourning
mine

un par
de rosas,
de tu abandono
una canción florida,
de tu pecho que lucha
una guitarra,
y lo demás
el sol,
el cielo puro
de la primavera,
la patria lo adelanta
para que algo
te suene en los bolsillos:
la esperanza.

a pair
of roses,
of your abandonment
the florid song,
of your fighting chest
a guitar,
and the rest
is sun,
the open sky
of spring,
the homeland advances it
so something
rumbles in your pockets:
hope.

171 / ODE TO A SHIP IN A BOTTLE

Oda al buque en la botella

TRANSLATED BY MARGARET SAYERS PEDEN

Nunca navegó	No one ever
nadie	sailed
como en tu barco:	as your ship sails;
el día	transparent
transparente	day
no tuvo	never saw
embarcación ninguna	a vessel
como	like that
ese mínimo	tiny
pétalo	petal
de vidrio	of glass
que aprisionó	imprisoned
tu forma	in your clasp
de rocío,	of dew,
botella,	bottle,
en cuyo	your winds
viento	fill
va el velero,	its sails,
botella,	bottle,
sí,	yes,
o viviente	substance of
travesía,	sea voyage,
esencia	essence
del trayecto,	of trajectory,
cápsula	capsule
del amor sobre las olas,	of love upon the waves,
obra	work
de las sirenas!	of sirens!

Yo sé que
en tu garganta
delicada
entraron
pequeñitos
carpinteros
que volaban
en una abeja, moscas que traían
en su lomo
herramientas,
clavos, tablas,
cordeles
diminutos,
y así en una botella
el perfecto navío
fue creciendo:
el casco fue la nuez de su hermosura,
como alfileres elevó sus palos.

Entonces
a
sus
pe-
que-
ñí-
simas
islas
regresó el astillero
y para navegar
en la botella
entró
cantando
la minúscula, azul
marinería.

Así, botella,
adentro

I know that
through your delicate
throat
passed
tiny
carpenters
on the backs
of bees, that flies
hauled in
tools,
nails, boards,
the finest strands
of rope;
and thus, within a bottle,
the perfect ship
took form:
the hull was the kernel of its beauty,
the masts rose thin as pins.

Then
to
their
in-
fini-
tes-
imal
islands
the shipbuilders returned,
and to sail the ship
inside the bottle
came,
singing,
a miniature crew
in blue.

And so, bottle,
within

de tu
mar, de tu cielo,
se levantó
un navío
pequeño, sí,
minúsculo
para el inmenso mar que lo esperaba:

la verdad
es que nadie
lo construyó
y no navegará sino en los sueños.

your
sea and sky
was raised
a ship,
tiny, no,
minuscule
compared to the enormous waiting sea.

But the truth is,
no one
built it,
and only in dreams will it sail.

172 / ODE TO THE SIMPLE MAN

Oda al hombre sencillo

TRANSLATED BY ILAN STAVANS

*Voy a contarte en secreto
quién soy yo,
así, en voz alta,
me dirás quién eres,
quiero saber quién eres,
cuánto ganas,
en qué taller trabajas,
en qué mina,
en qué farmacia,
tengo una obligación terrible
y es saberlo,
saberlo todo,
día y noche saber
cómo te llamas,
ése es mi oficio,
conocer una vida
no es bastante
ni conocer todas las vidas
es necesario,
verás,
hay que desentrañar,
rascar a fondo
y como en una tela
las líneas ocultaron,
con el color, la trama
del tejido,
yo borro los colores*

I will tell you in secret
who I am,
just like that, for everyone to hear,
you will tell me who you are,
I want to know who you are,
how much you carn,
in what shop you work,
in what mine,
in what pharmacy,
I have a terrible obligation
and it is to know,
to know it all,
night and day, to know
what your name is,
that is my job:
to know a life
is not enough,
nor is it necessary
to know all lives.
You see,
one needs to unravel,
scratch beyond the surface,
and the way in a piece of cloth
the plaids get obscured
by the color, the quality
of texture,
I go beyond colors

y busco hasta encontrar
el tejido profundo,
así también encuentro
la unidad de los hombres,
y en el pan
busco
más allá de la forma:
me gusta el pan, lo muerdo,
y entonces
veo el trigo,
los trigales tempranos,
la verde forma de la primavera,
las raíces, el agua,
por eso
más allá del pan,
veo la tierra,
la unidad de la tierra,
el agua,
el hombre,
y así todo lo pruebo
buscándote
en todo,
ando, nado, navego
hasta encontrarte,
y entonces te pregunto
cómo te llamas,
calle y número,
para que tú recibas
mis cartas,
para que yo te diga
quién soy y cuánto gano,
dónde vivo,
y cómo era mi padre.
Ves tú qué simple soy,
qué simple eres,
no se trata

and search until I find
the deeper tone,
thus I also come across
the unity of men
and I look
in bread
for something beyond its shape:
I like bread, I bite it,
and then
I appreciate wheat
the early wheat fields,
the green shape of spring,
the roots, water.
That is how,
beyond bread,
I see the earth,
the unity of our earth,
water,
man,
and so, I try everything
looking for you
in everything:
I walk, swim, sail
till I find you;
and then I ask you
what your name is,
street and number,
so you can receive
my letters,
so I can tell you
who I am and how much I earn,
where I live,
and how my father did.
You see how simple I am,
how simple you are.
There is nothing

de nada complicado,
yo trabajo contigo,
tú vives, vas y vienes
de un lado a otro,
es muy sencillo:
eres la vida,
eres tan transparente
como el agua,
y así soy yo,
mi obligación es ésa:
ser transparente,
cada día
me educo,
cada día me peino
pensando como piensas,
y ando
como tú andas,
como, como tú comes,
tengo en mis brazos a mi amor
como a tu novia tú,
y entonces
cuando esto está probado,
cuando somos iguales
escribo,
escribo con tu vida y con la mía,
con tu amor y los míos,
con todos tus dolores
y entonces
ya somos diferentes
porque, mi mano en tu hombro,
como viejos amigos
te digo en las orejas:
no sufras,
ya llega el día,
ven,
ven conmigo,

complicated about it.
I work with you.
You live, you come and go
from one place to another,
it is very simple:
you are life,
you are as transparent
as water,
and I am too,
that is my duty:
to be transparent.
Each day
I educate myself,
each day I comb my hair
thinking how you think;
and I walk
the way you walk,
eat the way you eat,
I have my love in my arms
like you your bride;
and then
when this is all clear,
when we are the same
I write:
I write with your life and with mine,
with your love and mine,
with all your pains;
and then
we become different
because, my hand on your shoulder,
like old friends
I tell you in your ear:
don't suffer,
the day has come,
come,
come with me,

ven
con todos
los que a ti se parecen,
los más sencillos,
ven,
no sufras,
ven conmigo,
porque aunque no lo sepas,
eso yo sí lo sé:
yo sé hacia dónde vamos,
y es ésta la palabra:
no sufras
porque ganaremos,
ganaremos nosotros,
los más sencillos,
ganaremos,
aunque tú no lo creas,
ganaremos.

come
with everyone
who are alike,
the simplest,
come,
don't suffer,
come with me,
because though you may not know it,
I do know it:
I know where we are going,
and this is the word:
don't suffer,
because we will win,
we will win,
we who are the simplest,
we will win,
even if you don't believe it,
we will win.

173 / ODE TO SIMPLICITY

Oda a la sencillez

TRANSLATED BY ILAN STAVANS

Sencillez, te pregunto,
me acompañaste siempre?
O te vuelvo a encontrar
en mi silla, sentada?
Ahora
no quieren aceptarme
contigo,
me miran de reojo,
se preguntan quién es
la pelirroja.
El mundo,
mientras nos encontrábamos
y nos reconocíamos,
se llenaba de tontos
tenebrosos,
de hijos de fruta tan repletos
de palabras
como los diccionarios,
tan llenos de viento
como una tripa que nos quiere hacer
una mala jugada
y ahora que llegamos
después de tantos viajes
desentonamos
en la poesía.
Sencillez, qué terrible lo que nos pasa:

Simplicity, I ask you:
were you always with me?
Or am I finding you again
on the chair, seated?
Now
they don't want to accept me
along with you,
they look at me with suspicion,
they ask me who
the red-haired one is.
The world,
while we were finding
and recognizing each other,
was filling up with gloomy
idiots,
with children of fruit as full
of words
as dictionaries,
so full of wind
like gut wanting to play a
trick on us
and, now that we're back
after so many trips,
our poetry
is out of tune.
Simplicity, how terrible what's
happening to us:

no quieren recibirnos
en los salones,
los cafés están llenos
de los más exquisitos
pederastas,
y tú y yo nos miramos,
no nos quieren.
Entonces
nos vamos
a la arena,
a los bosques,
de noche
la oscuridad es nueva,
arden recién lavadas
las estrellas, el cielo
es un campo de trébol
turgente, sacudido
por su sangre
sombría.
En la mañana
vamos
a la panadería,
tibio está el pan como un seno,
huele
el mundo a esta frescura
de pan recién salido.
Romero, Ruiz, Nemesio,
Rojas, Manuel Antonio,
panaderos.
Qué parecidos son
el pan y el panadero,
qué sencilla es la tierra
en la mañana,
más tarde es más sencilla,
y en la noche
es transparente.

they don't want to greet us
in the classrooms,
the cafés are full
of the most exquisite
child molesters,
and you and I look at each other,
we aren't wanted.
Then
we leave
for the sand,
for the forests,
at night
darkness is new,
the new-washed stars
shine, the sky
is a field of tumid
clover, shaken
by its somber
blood.
In the morning
we go
to the bakery,
the bread is lukewarm, like a breast,
the world
smells of this freshness
of newly baked bread.
Romero, Ruíz, Nemesio,
Rojas, Manuel Antonio,
bakers.
How alike are
bread and baker,
how simple is the earth
in the morning,
later is even simpler,
and at night
it is transparent.

Por eso	That's why
busco	I look
nombres	for names
entre la hierba.	in the grass.
Cómo te llamas?	What is your name?
le pregunto	I ask
a una corola	a corolla
que de pronto	that, suddenly
pegada al suelo entre las piedras pobres	stuck to the soil amid poor stones,
ardió como un relámpago.	burned like lightning.
Y así, sencillez, vamos	And thus, simplicity, we start
conociendo	becoming acquainted
los escondidos seres, el secreto	with the hidden beings, the secret
valor de otros metales,	valve of other metals,
mirando la hermosura de las hojas,	looking at the beauty of the leaves,
conversando con hombres y mujeres	conversing with men and women
que por sólo ser eso	who are remarkable only because
son insignes,	they are who they are.
y de todo,	And you enrapture me
de todos,	with everything
sencillez, me enamoras.	and everyone, simplicity.
Me voy contigo,	I go with you,
me entrego a tu torrente	surrendering to the torrent
de agua clara.	of clear water.
Y protestan entonces:	And, therefore, they protest:
Quién es ésa	Who is she
que anda con el poeta?	who is with the poet?
Por cierto	We certainly
que no queremos nada	don't want anything to do
con esa provinciana.	with that country girl.
Pero si es aire, es ella	But if it's air, it's she
el cielo que respiro.	the air I breathe.
Yo no la conocía o recordaba.	I didn't know or remember her.
Si me vieron	If they saw me
antes	before
andar con misteriosas	walking with mysterious

odaliscas,
fueron sólo deslices
tenebrosos.
Ahora,
amor mío,
agua,
ternura,
luz luminosa o sombra
transparente,
sencillez,
vas conmigo ayudándome a nacer,
enseñándome
otra vez a cantar,
verdad, virtud, vertiente,
victoria cristalina.

odalisques,
they were but gloomy
slips.
Now,
my love,
water,
tenderness,
luminous light and translucent
shadow,
simplicity,
are at my side, helping me to be born,
teaching me
to sing again,
truth, virtue, waterfall,
crystalline victory.

174 / ODE TO A SINGLE SEA

Oda a un solo mar

TRANSLATED BY ILAN STAVANS

Es vertical el día
como una lanza azul. Entro en el agua.

Es el agua del Asia,
el mar de China.

No reconozco sierras ni horizontes,
sin embargo este mar, esta ola viene
de tierra americana: esta marea,
este abismo, esta sal,
son una cinta pura de infinito
que enlaza dos estrellas:
los volcanes lejanos
de mi patria,
la agricultura diáfana de China.

Qué sereno sería
si yo te navegara,
si mi cuerpo o mi nave
condujera
a través de las olas y la luna,
mar doblemente mío,
hasta llegar donde me está esperando
mi casa junto al manantial marino.

Qué azul, qué transmigrante,
qué dorado sería

The day is vertical
like the blue spear. I enter the water.

It is the water from Asia,
the sea of China.

I know neither sierras nor horizons,
nonetheless this sea, this wave comes
from American soil: this tide,
this abyss, this salt,
are a simple infinite ribbon
that ties two stars:
the distant volcanoes
of my country,
the diaphanous agriculture of China.

How serene it would be
if I could navigate you,
if my body or my vessel
conducted
through the waves and moon,
sea twice mine,
until reaching where my house
near the sea well awaits me.

How blue, how transmigrating,
how gold it would be

si caminara el mar con pies desnudos,
si el mar, mi propio mar, me transporta.

Vería el vuelo
de las hambrientas aves oceánicas,
contaría tortugas,
resbalaría sobre los pescados,
y en el gran instituto
de la aurora
mi corazón mojado
como un marisco se deslizaría.

Hasta que tú, sirena,
junto a mí, transparente
nadadora,
con sal de mar mezclaras
tus amorosos besos
y saliéramos juntos del océano
a comprar pan y despertar la leña.
Un sueño, sí, pero
qué es el mar sino sueño?

Ven a soñar, nadando,
el mar de China y Chile,
ven a nadar el sueño,
ven a soñar el agua que nos une.
Amor o mar o sueño,
hicimos juntos esta travesía,
de tierra a tierra un solo mar soñando,
de mar a mar un solo sueño verde.

if I could walk the sea with naked feet,
if the sea, my own sea, could carry me.

I would see the flight
of the hungry oceanic birds,
would count turtles,
would slide over the fish,
and in the great institute
of daybreak
my wet heart
like a shellfish would slip away.

Until you, mermaid,
near me, translucent
swimmer,
would mix
your amorous kisses with sea salt
and we would leave the ocean together
to buy bread and wake the firewood.
A dream, yes, but what is
the sea if not a dream?

Swimming, come to dream
the sea of China and Chile,
come to swim the dream,
come to dream the water uniting us.
Love or sea or dream,
together we made this voyage,
from land to land a single dreaming sea,
from sea to sea a single green dream.

175 / ODE TO A SLEEPING HOUSE

Oda a la casa dormida

TRANSLATED BY MARGARET SAYERS PEDEN

Hacia adentro, en Brasil, por altas sierras
y desbocados ríos,
de noche, a plena luna . . .
Las cigarras
llenaban
tierra y cielo
con su telegrafía
crepitante.
Ocupada la noche
por la redonda
estatua
de la luna
y la tierra
incubando
cosas ciegas,
llenándose
de bosques,
de agua negra,
de insectos victoriosos.

Far away, in Brazil, across high sierras
and flooding rivers, one night
in the light of the full moon . . .
Cicadas
filled
earth and sky
with crackling
telegraphy.
Night busied herself
with the round
statues
of the moon
and earth,
with hatching
sightless creatures,
creating
forests,
ebony water,
triumphant insects.

Oh espacio
de la noche
en que no somos:
praderas
en que sólo
fuimos un movimiento en el camino,
algo que corre

Oh, the land
of nights
we have never lived:
meadows where
we were a flicker
of movement on the road,
something running,

y corre	running,
por la sombra.	through the shadow . . .
Entramos	We entered
en	the
la	sleeping
casa nocturna,	house,
ancha, blanca, entreabierta,	spacious, white, the door ajar,
rodeada,	an island
como una isla,	encircled
por la profundidad de los follajes	by impenetrable foliage
y por las olas	and the bright
claras	waves
de la luna.	of the moon.
Nuestros zapatos por las escaleras	Our shoes on the stair steps
despertaban	awakened
otros antiguos	other ancient
pasos,	footsteps,
el agua	water
golpeando	dripping
el lavatorio	in the basin
quería	had a story
decir algo.	to tell.
Apenas	We turned out the lights
se apagaron las luces	and immediately
las sábanas	the quivering
se unieron palpitando	sheets
a nuestros sueños.	merged into our dreams.
Todo	Everything
giró	whirled
en el centro	in the center
de la casa en tinieblas	of the shadowy house,
despertada de súbito	abruptly awakened
por brutales	by brutish
viajeros.	latecomers.

Alrededor
cigarras,
extensa luna,
sombra,
espacio, soledad
llena de seres,
y silencio
sonoro . . .

sonoro . . .

apagó sus ojos,
cerró todas
sus alas
y dormimos.

All around,
cicadas,
moonlight,
shadow,
space, a solitude
filled with presences
and sonorous
silence . . .

Then the house
shut its eyes,
folded its many
wings,
and we slept.

176 / ODE TO THE SMELL OF FIREWOOD

Oda al olor de la leña

TRANSLATED BY MARK STRAND

Tarde, con las estrellas
abiertas en el frío
abrí la puerta.
El mar
galopaba
en la noche.

Como una mano
de la casa oscura
salió el aroma
intenso
de la leña guardada.

Visible era el aroma
como
si el árbol
estuviera vivo.
Como si todavía palpitara.

Visible
como una vestidura.

Visible
como una rama rota.

Anduve
adentro

It was late.
I opened the door
and the stars
were shining
in the cold.
And the sea
was galloping
in the night.

The intense
aroma
of firewood
slipped from the house
like a hand.

As if the tree
still lived,
still breathed,
the aroma was visible.

Visible
as a dress.

Visible
as a broken branch.

I walked
around

de la casa
rodeado
por aquella balsámica
oscuridad.
Afuera
las puntas
del cielo cintilaban
como piedras magnéticas
y el olor de la leña
me tocaba
el corazón
como unos dedos,
como un jazmín,
como algunos recuerdos.

No era el olor agudo
de los pinos,
no,
no era
la ruptura en la piel
del eucaliptus,
no eran
tampoco
los perfumes verdes
de la viña,
sino
algo más secreto,
porque aquella fragancia
una sola,
una sola
vez existía,
y allí, de todo lo que vi en el mundo,
en mi propia
casa, de noche, junto al mar de invierno,
allí estaba esperándome
el olor

in the house
enveloped
by the fragrant
dark.
Outside
the sky's
sharp points
sparkled
like magnetic stones,
and the odor of firewood
touched
my heart
like fingers,
like jasmine,
like certain memories.

It was not the piercing
odor of pine,
no,
nor of the torn bark
of eucalyptus,
neither
was it
the green perfume
of the vineyard,
but something more secret,
because that fragrance
existed
just once,
just once,
and there, with all that I have seen in the world,
in my own
house at night
by the winter sea,
there waiting for me

de la rosa más profunda,
el corazón cortado de la tierra,
algo
que me invadió como una ola
desprendida
del tiempo
y se perdió en mí mismo
cuando yo abrí la puerta
de la noche.

the odor
of the deepest rose,
the wounded heart of the earth,
something
that entered me like a wave
cut loose from time
and was lost within myself
when I opened the door
in the night.

177 / ODE TO SOAP

Oda al jabón

TRANSLATED BY GEORGE D. SCHADE

Acercando	Putting
el	a bar of
jabón	soap
hasta mi cara	up to my face,
su cándida fragancia	its candid fragrance
me enajena:	intoxicates me:
No sé	I don't know
de dónde vienes,	where you come from,
aroma,	aroma,
de la provincia	are you from
vienes?	the provinces?
De mi prima?	From my cousin?
De la ropa en la artesa	From the clothes in the wash basin
entre las manos	among the hands
estrelladas de frío?	chapped by the cold?
De las lilas	From those
aquéllas,	lilacs,
ay, de aquéllas?	oh, from those?
De los ojos	From the eyes
de María campestre?	of the country girl María?
De las ciruelas verdes	From the green plums
en la rama?	on the branch?
De la cancha de fútbol	From the soccer field
y del baño	and the bath
bajo los	under the
temblorosos	tremulous
sauces?	willows?

Hueles a enramada,
a dulce amor o a torta
de onomástico? Hueles
a corazón mojado?

Qué me traes,
jabón,
a las narices
de pronto,
en la mañana,
antes de entrar al agua
matutina
y salir por las calles
entre hombres abrumados
por sus mercaderías?
Qué olor de pueblo
lejos,
qué flor
de enaguas,
miel de muchachas silvestres?
O tal vez
es el viejo
olvidado
olor del almacén
de ultramarinos
y abarrotes,
los blancos lienzos fuertes
entre las manos de los campesinos,
el espesor
feliz
de la chancaca,
o en el aparador de la casa
de mis tíos
un clavel rojo
como un rayo rojo,
como una flecha roja?

Do you smell of a bower of branches?
Sweet love or a birthday
cake? Do you smell
of a tearful heart?

What do you bring,
soap,
to my nostrils,
suddenly,
in the morning
before washing up
early in the day
and going out on the streets
among men weighed down
by their merchandise?
What odor of faraway
village?
What flower
of petticoats?
Honey of woodland girls?
Or maybe
it's the old
forgotten
smell of grocery
and dry goods stores,
sturdy white linens
in the farmers' hands,
the sweet
thickness
of a slab of brown sugar,
or on the sideboard in my
aunt and uncle's house,
a red carnation,
like a red ray
or a red arrow?

Es eso
tu agudo
olor
a tienda
barata, a colonia
inolvidable, de peluquería,
a la provincia pura,
al agua limpia?
Eso
eres,
jabón, delicia pura,
aroma transitorio
que resbala
y naufraga como un
pescado ciego
en la profundidad de la bañera.

Is that
your sharp
odor
of cheap store, unforgettable
cologne in barbershops,
of the pure provinces,
of clean water?
That's what
you are,
soap, pure delight,
fleeting smell
that slips
and sinks like a
blind fish
in the depths of the bathtub.

178 / ODE TO SOLIDARITY

Oda a la solidaridad

TRANSLATED BY ILAN STAVANS

Y allí qué hicieron?	And what did they do there?
Sabes?	Do you know?
Estás de acuerdo?	Do you agree?
Quiénes?	Who?
Algo pasa y es tu culpa.	Something happens and it's your fault.
Pero tú no sabrás.	But you won't know.
Ahora	I'm telling you
yo te advierto.	now.
No puedes	You can't
dejar así las cosas.	leave things that way.
Dónde	Where's
tienes el corazón?	your heart?
Tú tienes boca.	You can speak.
Me estás mirando	You're looking at me
de manera extraña.	strangely.
Parece	It seems
que de repente	as if suddenly
sabes	you know
que te falta una mano,	you're missing a hand,
los dos ojos,	both eyes,
la lengua,	your tongue,
o la esperanza.	your hope.
Pero	But
es posible, Pedro	is it possible, Pedro,
o Juan o Diego,	Juan, Diego,
que perdieras	is it possible you lost

algo
tan necesario
sin que te dieras cuenta?
Caminabas
dormido?
Qué comías?
No miraste
los ojos de las gentes?
No entraste
a un tren, a una barraca,
a una cocina,
no notaste la luz
enmascarada,
no has visto que las manos
del que va y viene
no sólo son sus manos:
es alguien
y algo que te buscaba?

A ti, no mires
a otro lado,
porque
no llamo a tu vecino,
a ti
te estoy hablando.
Los otros me dijeron:
«Búscalo,
estamos solos».
Las hojas
recién nacidas de la primavera
preguntaron:
«Qué hace Pedro?»
Yo no supe, no pude
contestar
y luego
el pan de cada día

something
so essential
without realizing it?
Were you
sleepwalking?
What were you eating?
Didn't you look
into people's eyes?
Didn't you come into
a train, a barracks,
a kitchen,
didn't you see the masked
light,
have you not seen that the hands
of him who comes and goes
aren't his hands only:
that he's someone
or something looking for you?

You, don't look
the other way
because
I'm not calling your neighbor,
I'm talking
to you.
Others told me:
"Look for him,
we're alone."
The leaves of springtime,
just born,
asked:
"What's Pedro doing?"
I didn't know, cannot
answer,
and then
the daily bread,

y el cielo con estrellas	the starry sky,
todo	everything
pregunta	asks:
dónde vive	Where does
Juan,	Juan live?
y	Has
si Diego	Diego
se ha perdido	gotten lost?
y ellos,	And they,
ellos	they
allí solos	alone
y cada día	are there,
solos,	every day,
entre	between
silencio	silence
y muro	and a wall,
mientras	while
que tú,	you
que yo,	and I
fumamos.	smoke.
Humo,	Smoke,
círculos, arabescos,	circles of smoke, arabesques,
anillos	rips
de humo	of smoke
y humo,	and smoke
anillos de humo y humo,	rings of smoke and smoke—
son las vidas?	are these their lives?
No es cierto.	It isn't true.
No te escapes.	Don't escape.
Ahora	Now
me ayudarás. Un dedo,	you'll help me. A finger,
una palabra,	a word,
un signo	a sign
tuyo	from you,
y cuando	and when
dedos, signos, palabras	fingers, signs, words

caminen y trabajen
algo
aparecerá en el aire inmóvil,
un
solidario sonido en la ventana,
una
estrella en la terrible paz nocturna,
entonces
tú dormirás tranquilo,
tú vivirás tranquilo:
serás parte
del sonido que acude a la ventana,
de la luz que rompió la soledad.

walk and work,
something
will appear in the motionless air,
a
solidarity will sound in the window,
a
star in the appalling nocturnal peace;
then
you will sleep peacefully,
you will live in peace:
you will be part
of the sound that comes from the window,
of the light dismantling loneliness.

179 / ODE TO SOLITUDE

Oda a la soledad

TRANSLATED BY KEN KRABBENHOFT

Oh soledad, hermosa
palabra, hierbas
silvestres
brotan entre tus sílabas!
Pero eres sólo pálida
palabra, oro
falso,
moneda traidora!
Yo describí la soledad con letras
de la literatura,
le puse la corbata
sacada de los libros,
la camisa
del sueño,
pero
sólo la conocí cuando fui solo.
Bestia no vi ninguna
como aquélla:
a la araña peluda
se parece
y a la mosca
de los estercoleros,
pero en sus patas de camello tiene
ventosas de serpiente submarina,
tiene una pestilencia de bodega
en donde se pudrieron por los siglos
pardos cueros de focas y ratones.

O solitude, beautiful
word: crab-
grass
grows between your syllables!
But you are only a pale
word, fool's
gold
and counterfeit coin!
I painted solitude in literary
strokes,
dressed it in a tie
I had copied from a book,
and the shirt
of sleep.
But
I first really saw it when I was by myself.
I'd never seen an animal
quite like it:
it looks like
a hairy spider
or the flies
that hover over dung,
and its camel paws have
suckers like a deep-sea snake.
It stinks like a warehouse piled high
with brown hides of rats and seals
that have been rotting forever.

Soledad, ya no quiero	Solitude, I want you
que sigas	to stop
mintiendo por la boca de los libros.	lying through the mouths of books.
Llega el joven poeta tenebroso	Consider the brooding young poet:
y para seducir	he's looking for a black marble slab
así a la soñolienta señorita	to seduce
se busca mármol negro y te levanta	the sleeping señorita; in your honor he erects
una pequeña estatua	a simple statue
que olvidará	that he'll forget
en la mañana de su matrimonio.	the morning of his wedding.
Pero	But
a media luz de la primera vida	in the half-light of those early years
de niños la encontramos	we boys stumble across her
y la creemos una diosa negra	and take her for a black goddess
traída de las islas,	shipped from distant islands.
jugamos con su torso y le ofrendamos	We play with her torso and pledge
la reverencia pura de la infancia.	the perfect reverence of childhood.
No es verdad	As for the creativity
la soledad creadora.	of solitude: it's a lie.
No está sola	Seeds don't live
la semilla en la tierra.	singly underneath the soil:
Multitudes de gérmenes mantienen	it takes hordes of them to insure
el profundo concierto de las vidas	the deep harmony of our lives,
y el agua es sólo madre transparente	and water is but the transparent mother
de un invisible coro sumergido.	of invisible submarine choirs.
Soledad de la tierra	The desert
es el desierto. Y estéril	is the earth's solitude, and mankind's
es como él	solitude
la soledad	is sterile
del hombre. Las mismas	like the desert. The same
horas, noches y días,	hours, nights and days
toda la tierra envuelven	wrap the whole planet
con su manto	in their cloak—
pero no dejan nada en el desierto.	but they leave nothing in the desert.
La soledad no recibe semillas.	Solitude does not accept seeds.

No es sólo su belleza
el barco en el océano:
su vuelo de paloma sobre el agua
es el producto
de una maravillosa compañía
de fuego y fogoneros,
de estrella y navegantes,
de brazos y banderas congregados,
de comunes amores y destinos.

La música
buscó para expresarse
la firmeza coral del oratorio
y escrita fue
no sólo por un hombre
sino por una línea
de ascendientes sonoros.

Y esta palabra
que aquí dejo en la rama suspendida,
esta canción que busca
ninguna soledad sino tu boca
para que la repitas
la escribe el aire junto a mí, las vidas
que antes que yo vivieron,
y tú que lees mi oda
contra tu soledad la has dirigido
y así tus propias manos la escribieron
sin conocerme, con las manos mías.

A ship on the sea
isn't the only image of its beauty.
It flies over the water like a dove,
end product
of wondrous collaborations
between fires and stokers,
navigators and stars,
men's arms and flags in congregation,
shared loves and destinies.

In its search for self-expression
music sought out
the choir's coral hardness.
It was written
not by a single man
but by a whole score
of musical relations.

And this word
which I pose here suspended on a branch,
this song that yearns
solely for the solitude of your lips
to repeat it—
the air inscribes it at my side, lives
that were lived long before me.
And you, who are reading my ode:
you've used it against your own solitude.
We've never met, and yet it's your hands
that wrote these lines, with mine.

180 / ODE TO THE SOUTHERN CROSS

Oda a la Cruz del Sur

TRANSLATED BY MARGARET SAYERS PEDEN

Hoy 14 de abril,
viento
en la costa,
noche
y viento,
noche
sombría
y viento,
se conmovió la sombra,
se enarboló el ciprés
de las estrellas,
las hojas de la noche
volcaron
polvo muerto
en el espacio
y todo quedó limpio
y tembloroso.

Árbol
de espadas
frías
fue la sombra
estrellada,
copa
del
universo,
cosecha

Today, April 14,
wind
along the coast,
night
and wind,
somber
night
and wind,
the shadows were stirred,
a starry cypress
appeared in the sky,
the leaves of night
shook
dead dust
into space,
everything was clean
and quivering.

The spangled
shadow
was a tree
of icy
swords,
the crown
of the
universe,
harvest

de
platino,
todo
ardía
en las altas
soledades
marinas,
en Isla Negra
andando
del brazo
de mi amada,
y ella
entonces
levantó un brazo apenas
sumergido
en la sombra
y como un rayo de ámbar
dirigido
desde la tierra al cielo
me mostró
cuatro estrellas:
la Cruz del Sur inmóvil
sobre nuestras cabezas.

En un instante
se apagaron todos
los ojos
de la noche
y sólo vi clavadas
al cielo solitario
cuatro rosas azules,
cuatro piedras heladas,
y le dije,
tomando
mi lira
de poeta

of
platinum,
everything
blazed
in the high
solitudes
above the sea;
in Isla Negra
I walked
arm in arm
with my beloved,
and then
she
raised an arm
barely visible
in the shadow
and like a ray of amber
beaming
from earth to sky
she pointed out
four stars:
the motionless Southern Cross
above our heads.

In an instant
all the eyes
of the night
were closed
and I saw only
four blue roses,
four frozen gems
studding the solitary sky.
And I said to them,
taking up
my poet's
lyre,

frente al viento
oceánico, entre las dentelladas
de la ola:
Cruz
del Sur, olvidado
navío
de mi patria,
prendedor
sobre el pecho
de la noche turgente,
constelación marina,
luz
de las casas pobres,
lámpara errante, rombo
de lluvia y terciopelo,
tijera de la altura,
mariposa,
posa tus cuatro labios
en mi frente
y llévame
en tu nocturno
sueño
y travesía
a las islas del cielo,
a las vertientes
del agua de la noche,
a la roca
magnética,
madre de las estrellas,
al tumulto
del sol, al viejo carro
de la aurora
cubierto de limones.

Y no me respondió
la Cruz del Sur:

facing the oceanic
wind, between the nibbles
of the wave:
Cross
of the South, forgotten
ship
of my homeland,
brooch
upon the swelling
breast of night,
constellation of the sea,
light
for humble houses,
drifting lamp, rhombus
of rain and velvet,
scissors of space,
butterfly,
rest your four lips
upon my forehead
and transport me
in your nocturnal
dream,
in your voyage
to the islands of the sky,
to the springs
of night's water,
to the magnetic
pole,
mother of the stars,
to the convulsion
of the sun, to the ancient
lemon-bedecked
chariot of the dawn.

The Southern Cross
did not reply:

siguió, siguió viajando
barrida
por el viento.
Dejé la lira entonces
a un lado,
en el camino,
y abracé a mi amada
y al acercar mis ojos
a sus ojos,
vi en ellos,
en su cielo,
cuatro puntas
de diamante encendido.

La noche y su navío
en su amor
palpitaban
y besé una por una
sus estrellas.

swept
by the winds
it traveled on.
So I left my lyre
by the side
of the road
and embraced my beloved,
and as I looked into her
eyes
I saw in them,
in their sky,
four points
of brilliant diamond.

The night and its ship
pulsed
with love
and one by one I kissed
their stars.

181 / ODE TO THE SPOON

Oda a la cuchara

TRANSLATED BY KEN KRABBENHOFT

Cuchara,	Spoon,
cuenca	scoop
de	formed
las más antigua	by man's
mano del hombre,	most ancient hand,
aún	in your design
se ve en tu forma	of metal or of wood
de metal o madera	we still see
el molde	the shape
de la palma	of the first
primitiva,	palm
en donde	to which
el agua	water
trasladó	imparted
frescura	coolness
y la sangre	and savage
salvaje	blood,
palpitación	the throb
de fuego y cacería.	of bonfires and the hunt.
Cuchara	Little
pequeñita,	spoon
en la	in an
mano	infant's
del niño	tiny hand,
levantas	you raise
a su boca	to his mouth

el más
antiguo
beso
de la tierra,
la herencia silenciosa
de las primeras aguas que cantaron
en labios que después
cubrió la arena.

El hombre
agregó
al hueco desprendido
de su mano
un brazo imaginario
de madera
y
salió
la cuchara
por el mundo
cada
vez
más
perfecta,
acostumbrada
a pasar
desde el plato a unos labios clavelinos
o a volar
desde
la pobre sopa
a la olvidada boca del hambriento.

Sí,
cuchara,
trepaste
con el hombre
las montañas,

the earth's
most
ancient
kiss,
silent heritage
of the first water to sing
on lips that later lay
buried beneath the sand.

To this hollow space,
detached from the palm of our hand,
someone
added
a make-believe wooden
arm,
and
spoons
started turning up
all over the world
in ever
more
perfect
form,
spoons made for
moving
between bowl and ruby-red lips
or flying
from thin soups
to hungry men's careless mouths.

Yes,
spoon:
at mankind's side
you have climbed
mountains,

descendiste los ríos,
llenaste
embarcaciones y ciudades,
castillos cocinas,
pero
el difícil camino
de tu vida
es juntarte
con el plato del pobre
y con su boca.

Por eso el tiempo
de la nueva vida
que
luchando y cantando
proponemos
será un advenimiento de soperas,
una panoplia pura
de cucharas,
y en un mundo
sin hambre
iluminando todos los rincones,
todos los platos puestos en la mesa,
felices flores,
un vapor oceánico de sopa
y un total movimiento de cucharas.

swept down rivers,
populated
ships and cities,
castles and kitchens:
but
the hard part
of your life's journey
is to plunge
into the poor man's plate,
and into his mouth.

And so the coming
of the new life
that,
fighting and singing,
we preach
will be a coming of soup bowls,
a perfect panoply
of spoons.
An ocean of steam rising from pots
in a world
without hunger,
and a total mobilization of spoons,
will shed light where once was darkness,
shining on plates spread all over the table
like contented flowers.

182 / ODE TO SPRING

Oda a la primavera

TRANSLATED BY KEN KRABBENHOFT

Primavera	Fearsome
temible,	spring,
rosa	zany
loca,	rose,
llegarás,	you will arrive
llegas	unnoticed—
imperceptible,	here you come now—
apenas	the merest
un temblor de ala, un beso	flit of a wing, a kiss
de niebla con jazmines,	of jasmine-scented mist.
el sombrero	Hats
lo sabe,	can feel it,
los caballos,	and horses.
el viento	The wind
trae una carta verde	delivers a green letter
que los árboles leen	for all the trees to read
y comienzan	and the leaves
las hojas	take
a mirar con un ojo,	a first peek,
a ver de nuevo el mundo,	a fresh look at things.
se convencen,	They're sure:
todo está preparado,	everything is ready—
el viejo sol supremo,	the ancient, uncontestable sun,
el agua que habla,	and talking water,
todo,	everything.
y entonces	Now
salen todas las faldas	skirts of foliage

del follaje,
la esmeraldina,
loca
primavera,
luz desencadenada,
yegua verde,
todo
se multiplica,
todo
busca
palpando
una materia
que repita su forma,
el germen nueve
pequeños pies sagrados,
el hombre
ciñe
el amor de su amada,
y la tierra se llena
de frescura,
de pétalos que caen
como harina,
                    la tierra
brilla recién pintada
mostrando
su fragancia
en sus heridas,
los besos de los labios de claveles,
la marea escarlata de la rosa.
Ya está bueno!
Ahora,
primavera,
dime para qué sirves
y a quién sirves.
Dime si el olvidado
en su caverna

spread all at once,
spring dressed in emerald green,
zany
spring,
unfettered sunlight,
green mare.
The whole world
stretches,
the whole world
reaches out
groping for
substance
in which to repeat its form.
Seeds shuffle
their tiny sacred feet,
men
squeeze
the love in their beloveds,
and the earth is filled
with newness,
with petals falling
like sifting flour,
                    the earth
shines freshly painted,
exposing
its fragrance
in open wounds,
kisses from the lips of carnations,
roses in scarlet tides.
This is how it should be!
Now,
spring,
tell me your purpose,
and who's your master.
And that man shut away
in a cave—

recibió tu visita,
si el abogado pobre
en su oficina
vio florecer tus pétalos
sobre la sucia alfombra,
si el minero
de las minas de mi patria
no conoció
más que la primavera negra
del carbón
o el viento envenenado
del azufre!

Primavera,
muchacha,
te esperaba!
Toma esta escoba y barre
el mundo!
Limpia
con este trapo
las fronteras,
sopla
los techos de los hombres,
escarba
el oro
acumulado
y reparte
los bienes
escondidos,
ayúdame
cuando
ya
el
hombre
esté libre
de miseria,

did you pay him a call?
Did the poor lawyer
huddled in his office
see your petals blossom
on his dusty carpet?
Did the miner
in the mineshaft back home
know nothing
beyond a spring blackened
with coal
and poisoned by a sulfurous
wind?

Spring,
my girl,
I've been waiting for you!
Here, take this broom, sweep
the world clean!
Take this cloth
and scour
the farthest places,
blow
on mankind's rooftops,
blast open
those deposits
of ore,
share with us
all that hidden
wealth.
Lend me a hand
when
mankind
is
finally
free
from poverty,

polvo,
harapos,
deudas,
llagas,
dolores,
cuando
con tus transformadoras manos de hada
y las manos del pueblo,
cuando sobre la tierra
el fuego y el amor
toquen tus bailarines
pies de nácar,
cuando
tú, primavera,
entres
a todas
las casas de los hombres,
te amaré sin pecado,
desordenada dalia,
acacia loca,
amada,
contigo, con tu aroma,
con tu abundancia, sin remordimiento,
con tu desnuda nieve
abrasadora,
con tus más desbocados manantiales,
sin descartar la dicha
de otros hombres,
con la miel misteriosa
de las abejas diurnas,
sin que los negros tengan
que vivir apartados
de los blancos,
oh primavera
de la noche sin pobres,
sin pobreza,

dust,
and rags,
free from debts,
sores,
and pain,
when
your elfin hands and the hands
of the people make magic,
when on this earth
fire and love
caress your leaping
pearly feet,
when
you, spring,
come into
the houses
of all mankind.
It will be no sin to love you,
deranged dahlia,
crazed acacia—
my beloved,
to stand by your side, your scent
and your abundance, without regret to love
your naked
burning snow
and your gushing
(never excluding
the happiness of other men),
and the mysterious honey
brewed by bees that work all day,
without black people kept
separate
from whites.
O spring
of poor people's nights:
free of poverty,

primavera
fragante,
llegarás,
llegas,
te veo
venir por el camino:
ésta es mi casa,
entra,
tardabas,
era hora,
qué bueno es florecer,
qué trabajo
tan bello:
qué activa
obrera eres,
primavera,
tejedora,
labriega,
ordeñadora,
múltiple abeja,
máquina
transparente,
molino de cigarras,
entra
en todas las casas,
adelante,
trabajaremos juntos
en la futura y pura
fecundidad florida.

fragrant
spring:
you will arrive,
as you are now arriving.
I see you
coming up the road.
Yes, this is my house.
Come in.
You've been detained,
I know, you're late—
but how good it is to bloom,
what wonderful
labor!
You're a hard
worker,
spring,
with your weaving
and sweating in the fields,
and milking the cows.
You're a bee multiplied,
a machine
invisible,
a cicada mill.
Come in,
come into all our houses,
come on in.
We'll work together
in the perfect, flowering
abundance to come.

183 / ODE TO THE SPUD

Oda a la papa

TRANSLATED BY ILAN STAVANS

Papa	Spud
te llamas,	they call you,
papa	spud
y no patata,	and not potato;
no naciste con barba,	you weren't born with a beard,
no eres castellana:	you're not from Castile:
eres oscura	you're dark
como	like
nuestra piel,	our skin;
somos americanos,	we're Americans,
papa,	spud,
somos indios.	we're Indians.
Profunda	You are deep
y suave eres,	and soft,
pulpa pura, purísima	pure pulp, purest
rosa blanca	buried
enterrada,	white rose,
floreces	you flowering
allá adentro	there inside
en la tierra,	the soil,
en tu lluviosa	in your rainy
tierra	original
originaria,	earth,
en las islas mojadas	in the damp islands
de Chile tempestuoso,	of stormy Chile,
en Chiloé marino,	in seaside Chiloé,

en medio de la esmeralda que abre
su luz verde
sobre el austral océano.

Papa,
materia
dulce,
almendra
de la tierra,
la madre
allí
no tuvo
metal muerto,
allí en la oscura
suavidad de las islas
no dispuso
el cobre y sus volcanes
sumergidos,
ni la crueldad azul
del manganeso,
sino que con su mano,
como en un nido
en la humedad más suave,
colocó tus redomas,
y cuando
el trueno
de la guerra
negra,
España
inquisidora,
negra como águila de sepultura,
buscó el oro salvaje
en la matriz
quemante
de la Araucanía,

amid the emerald spreading
its green light
over the southern ocean.

Spud,
sweet
matter,
almond
of the earth,
the mother
there
had no dead
metal,
in the dark
softness of the islands
she didn't offer
copper and the buried
volcanoes with
the blue cruelty
of manganese;
instead, with her hand,
in a nest,
in the softest dampness,
she deposited your balloons,
and when
the thunder
of the black
war,
when inquisitorial
Spain,
black like a death-dealing eagle,
searched for savage gold
in the burning
matrix
of Araucanía,

sus uñas
codiciosas
fueron exterminadas,
sus capitanes,
muertos,
pero cuando a las piedras de Castilla
regresaron
los pobres capitanes derrotados,
levantaron en las manos sangrientas
no una copa de oro,
sino la papa
de Chiloé marino.

Honrada eres
como
una mano
que trabaja en la tierra,
familiar
eres
como
una gallina,
compacta como un queso
que la tierra elabora
en sus ubres
nutricias,
enemiga del hambre,
en todas
las naciones
se enterró tu bandera
vencedora
y pronto allí,
en el frío o en la costa
quemada,
apareció
tu flor

its greedy
nails
were exterminated,
its captains
killed;
and when the defeated, pitiable captains
returned
to their Castilian cliffs,
in their bloody hands they held
not a golden chalice,
just a spud
from marine Chiloé.

You are honest
like
a hand
working the land,
you are
familiar
like
a hen,
compact like a cheese
produced by the soil
in its nourishing
udders,
enemy of hunger,
your flag was buried,
victorious,
in every
nation,
and soon, right there,
in the cold or on the burning
coast,
your
anonymous flower

anónima	appeared,
anunciando la espesa	announcing the thick,
y suave	soft
natalidad de tus raíces.	nativity of your roots.
Universal delicia,	Universal delight,
no esperabas	you did not expect
mi canto	my song
porque eres sorda	because you are deaf
y ciega	and blind
y enterrada.	and underground.
Apenas	You barely
si hablas en el infierno	talk in the hell
del aceite	of oil,
o cantas	or sing
en las freidurías	in the ports'
de los puertos,	frying pans,
cerca de las guitarras,	near the guitars:
silenciosa,	silent one,
harina de la noche	flour of the underground
subterránea,	night,
tesoro interminable	unending treasure
de los pueblos.	of the people.

184 / ODE TO A STAG'S BIRTH

Oda al nacimiento de un ciervo

TRANSLATED BY ILAN STAVANS

Se recostó la cierva
detrás
de la alambrada.
Sus ojos eran
dos oscuras almendras.
El gran ciervo velaba
y a mediodía
su corona de cuernos
brillaba
como
un altar encendido.

Sangre y agua,
una bolsa turgente,
palpitante,
y en ella
un nuevo ciervo
inerme, informe.

Allí quedó en sus turbias
envolturas
sobre el pasto manchado.
La cierva los lamía
con su lengua de plata.
No podía moverse,
pero
de aquel confuso,

The doe lay down
behind
the wire fence.
Her eyes were
two dark almonds.
The grand stag kept vigil
and at midnight
his crown of antlers
shone
like
a lighted altar.

Blood and water,
a tumescent bag,
vibrating,
and in it
a new stag
defenseless, unformed.

He lay there in his muddy
wrappings
on the stained grass.
The doe licked him
with her silver tongue.
He couldn't move,
but
in that blurred,

vaporoso envoltorio,
sucio, mojado, inerte,
fue asomando
la forma,
el hociquillo agudo
de la real
estirpe,
los ojos más ovales
de la tierra,
las finas
piernas,
flechas
naturales del bosque.
Lo lamía la cierva
sin cesar, lo limpiaba
de oscuridad, y limpio
lo entregaba a la vida.

Así se levantó,
frágil, pero perfecto,
y comenzó a moverse,
a dirigirse, a ser,
a descubrir las aguas en el monte.
Miró el mundo radiante.

El cielo sobre
su pequeña cabeza
era como una uva
transparente,
y se pegó a las ubres de la cierva
estremeciéndose como si recibiera
sacudidas de luz del firmamento.

vaporous wrapping,
dirty, wet, lifeless,
he began to take
shape,
the sharp little snout,
of royal
stock,
the oval eyes more rounded
than the earth,
the fine
legs,
natural
arrows of the forest.
The doe licked him
incessantly, cleaning him
of darkness, and delivered him
clean to life.

So he stood up,
fragile, yet perfect,
and began to move,
to find direction, to be,
to discover the water in the mountain.
He admired the radiant world.

The sky over
his small head
was like a grape,
transparent,
and he tied himself to the doe's udders,
shivering as if receiving
bolts of light from the firmament.

185 / ODE TO A STAMP ALBUM

Oda al libro de estampas

TRANSLATED BY MARGARET SAYERS PEDEN

Libro de estampas puras!	Album of perfect stamps!
Mariposas,	Butterflies,
navíos,	ships,
formas del mar, corolas,	sea shapes, corollas,
torres que se inclinaron,	leaning towers,
ojos oscuros, húmedos,	dark eyes, moist and
redondos como uvas,	round as grapes,
libro	album
liso	smooth
como	as
un	a
pez	slippery
resbaloso,	fish,
libro	with thousands
de mil	of glistening
escamas,	scales,
cada página	each page
corre	a
como	racing
un corcel	charger
buscando	in search of
lejanas cosas, flores	distant pleasures, forgotten
olvidadas!	flowers!
Otras páginas son	Other pages are
hogueras o claveles,	bonfires or carnations,

rojas ramas de piedras	red clusters of stones
encendidas	set afire
por el rubí secreto	by a secret ruby,
o nos revelan	some display
la nieve,	the snow,
las palomas	the doves
de Noruega,	of Norway,
la arquitectura clara del rocío.	the architectural clarity of the dew.
Cómo pudieron	How was it possible
unirse	to bring
en tu papel	to paper
tantas bellezas,	such beauty,
tantas	so many
expediciones	expeditions
infinitas?	into infinity?
Cómo	How
llegó	possible
a fulgurar en ti	to capture
la inaccesible	the ineffable
luz	glow
de	of
la mariposa	the Sambuca
sambucaria	butterfly
con sus fosforescentes	and its phosphorescent
poblaciones de orugas,	caterpillar colonies,
y al mismo	and,
tiempo	as well,
aquella	that
dulce	gentle
locomotora	locomotive
que cruza las praderas	puffing through pastures
como un	like an
pequeño	iron
toro	bull,

ardiente	small
y duro,	but fiery,
y tantas	and that
plantas del sol lejano,	fauna from a distant sun,
elegantes	elegant
avispas,	wasps,
serpientes submarinas,	sea serpents,
increíbles	incredible
camellos?	camels?
Mundo de los milagros!	World of miracles!
Espiral	Insatiable
insaciable	spiral,
o cabellera	comet's tail
de todos	of all earth's
los caminos,	highways,
diccionario	dictionary
del viento,	of the wind,
libro	star-struck album
lleno de adoraciones estrelladas	bulging
de magnánimas	with noble
frutas y regiones,	fruits and territories,
tesorero	treasure-keeper
embarcado	sailing
en su tesoro,	on its treasure,
granada	garnet
desgranada,	pomegranate,
libro	nomadic
errante!	stamp album!

186 / ODE TO A STAR

Oda a una estrella

TRANSLATED BY ILAN STAVANS

Asomando a la noche	Looking at the night
en la terraza	from the terrace
de un rascacielos altísimo y amargo	of a very high and sour skyscraper,
pude tocar la bóveda nocturna	I could touch the nocturnal vault
y en un acto de amor extraordinario	and, in an extraordinary act of love,
me apoderé de una celeste estrella.	I took control of a celestial star.
Negra estaba la noche	Black was the night
y yo me deslizaba	and I traversed
por la calle	the street
con la estrella robada en el bolsillo.	with the stolen star in my pocket.
De cristal tembloroso	It resembled
parecía	trembling glass
y era	and appeared
de pronto	suddenly
como si llevara	as if I were carrying
un paquete de hielo	a package of ice
o una espada de arcángel en el cinto.	or an archangel's spear in my belt.
La guardé	Fearing,
temeroso	I hid it
debajo de la cama	under the bed
para que no la descubriera nadie,	so no one would find it,
pero su luz	but its light
atravesó	first
primero	crossed
la lana del colchón,	the wool of the mattress,

luego
las tejas,
el techo de mi casa.

Incómodos
se hicieron
para mí
los más privados menesteres.

Siempre con esa luz
de astral acetileno
que palpitaba como si quisiera
regresar a la noche,
yo no podía
preocuparme de todos
mis deberes
y así fue que olvidé pagar mis cuentas
y me quedé sin pan ni provisiones.

Mientras tanto, en la calle,
se amotinaban
transeúntes, mundanos
vendedores
atraídos sin duda
por el fulgor insólito
que veían salir de mi ventana.

Entonces
recogí
otra vez mi estrella,
con cuidado
la envolví en mi pañuelo
y enmascarado entre la muchedumbre
pude pasar sin ser reconocido.
Me dirigí al oeste,

then
the tiles,
the roof of my house.

The most
private errands
became uncomfortable
for me.

Always with that light
of astral acetylene
palpitating as if it wanted
to return to the night,
I could not
attend to all
my duties
and thus I forgot to pay my bills
and found myself without bread and provisions.

Meanwhile, on the street,
passersby gathered
in mutiny, mundane
vendors
no doubt attracted
by the cursed flash of light
they saw coming from my window.

Then
I again picked up my star,
carefully
wrapped it in a kerchief,
and masked amid the crowds
I managed to pass by without being recognized.
I walked west,

al río Verde,
que allí bajo los sauces
es sereno.

Tomé la estrella de la noche fría
y suavemente
la eché sobre las aguas.

Y no me sorprendió
que se alejara
como un pez insoluble
moviendo
en la noche del río
su cuerpo de diamante.

to the Green River,
which there, under the willows,
is serene.

I took the star of the cold night
and softly
threw it on the water.

And I was not surprised
when it departed
like an indissoluble fish,
moving
its diamond body
in the night of the river.

187 / ODE TO THE STARS

Oda a las estrellas

TRANSLATED BY ILAN STAVANS

Serenas piedras puras
de la noche, cubiertas
de soledad, vacías
para el hombre,
agujeros
horadados
en el diamante negro,
flechas
del terciopelo
tembloroso,
cereal
de platino
espolvoreado
en la sombra,
y bueno,
basta!
Ahora
qué uso,
de qué manera,
cómo y cuándo
serviréis para algo?
Estoy cansado,
estamos,
de tanta
inútil
y magnánima
hermosura.

Restful stones of purity
in the night, covered
with solitude, hollow
from man's perspective,
silkworm
holes
in the black diamond,
arrows
of trembling
velvet,
cereal
of fine platinum
dusted
in shadow,
and well,
enough!
What is your purpose
now,
how, when,
and in what way
will you be useful?
I'm tired,
we all are,
of such
uselessness,
such magnanimous
beauty.

Sois las más primorosas
doncellas
de los setenta cielos,
con zapatos de raso,
con ojos de diamante,
muchachas
que no saben
cocinar,
ni manejar tractores,
estatuas
de lejano
corazón,
hasta cuándo?

Queremos
que
estéis
llenas de racimos,
radiantes,
pero embarazadas,
magnéticas,
sí,
pero queremos una
llena como un tonel
de milenario vino,
otra
que sea
usina
cargada
de relojes,
otra
con olor a camello,
a buey, a vaca,
otra
repleta
de pescados,

You're the most gorgeous
maidens
of the seven mighty heavens,
you with your humble shoes,
your eyes like diamonds,
girls
unable
to cook,
or drive tractors,
statues
with distant
hearts,
until when?

We want you
to
be
filled with grapes,
radiant
yet pregnant,
magnetic,
yes,
but we want one of you
to be plentiful like a barrel
of ancestral wine,
we want another
to be
a power plant
endowed
with clocks,
yet another
to smell like camel,
ox, cow,
and one more
to be full
of fish,

otra
con los ladrillos que se necesitan
en la tierra
para construir casas a las viudas
de los obreros muertos,
otra
estrella
con panes,
si es posible
con mantequilla en medio.
No te olvides, poeta,
me gritan,
de una estrella
con corderos,
de otra
con ensaladas,
con colchones,
de una con mobiliario,
otra con libros!

Estrellas:
no por eso
me creáis
tonto,
insistiendo,
como en las oficinas,
con
vagas
peticiones.
Escuchadme:
la tierra
es nuestra estrella.
Primero
la fecundaremos
hasta que esté colmada
como un canasto verde

and still one more
to have the bricks we need
in our land
to build houses for the widows
of dead workers,
another
star
to offer bread,
and if possible
to butter it.
Don't forget all this, poet,
I hear myself being told
from a star
with lambs,
another
with salads,
with mattresses,
another with furniture,
and yet one more with books!

Stars:
don't think
I'm
a fool,
insisting,
as in an office,
a harangue
of vague
petitions.
Listen:
the earth
is our star.
First
we shall inseminate it
until it's full,
like a green basket

con los dones
que
le sacaremos
y entonces,
arriba!
A las otras estrellas!
Al aire!
Al sol!
Al viento!
A la espléndida costa
de los nuevos espacios
llegaremos,
a la remota estrella,
con una pala
y un profundo libro,
con corazones simples,
descartada
la antigua astronomía
vendrá la agricultura
de los astros,
ordeñaremos
los senos de la estrella,
y en la noche
mugirá en la distancia
de los cielos
nuestra ganadería.
Inútiles
estrellas,
cada noche
de mi creciente vida
más hermosas
me parecéis, más altas:
contempladlas
a través de la fría transparencia
de la noche de Chile.
A medida

with the gifts
we
intend to harvest
and then,
onward!
To the stars!
To the air!
To the sun!
To the wind!
We shall arrive
on the splendid coast
of unexplored space,
a remote star,
with a shovel
and a meaningful book,
with a simple heart,
and the old agricultural ways
shall be replaced
by a new
cultivation of the galaxy,
we shall milk
the breasts of stars,
and at night
our livestock, at a distance,
will bellow
to the skies.
Useless
stars,
every night
of my maturing life
you show up
more beautiful, taller:
you shine
through the cold transparency
of the Chilean night,
as my years

que mis años crecen
duermo más con vosotras
o vigilo
bajo vuestra
belleza
innumerable,
por eso
en esta intimidad
de los
amores,
dejadme a mí,
polígamo
del espacioso tálamo
nocturno,
dejadme
levantar
a la más alta altura
mi mano de poeta
y dejar
a la sombra constelada,
a las remotas, a las temblorosas
estrellas,
una advertencia, un golpe
en sus glaciales
puertas,
una ráfaga
de semillas humanas,
una carta, una oda
que anticipe
en el cielo
la terrestre
invasión
progenitora.

pass by,
I sleep among you longer
and witness
your
infinite
fairness,
that is why
in the intimacy
of
love,
let me,
a polygamous lover
of the spacious
nighttime
bedroom, allow me
to rise
to the highest place
my poet's hand
so I can leave for
the orchestrated shadow,
the remote, the trembling
stars,
a warning, a smack
in their glacial
doors,
a flash
of human seeds,
a letter, an ode
anticipating,
in the sky,
the inseminating
earthbound
invasion.

188 / ODE TO THE STONE

Oda a la piedra

TRANSLATED BY GEORGE D. SCHADE

América elevada	America, lofty
por la piedra	in its Andean
andina:	stone:
de piedra libre	of free stone
y	and
solitario viento	solitary wind
fuiste,	you were,
torre oscura	a dark tower
del mundo,	of the world,
desconocida madre	unknown mother
de los ríos,	of rivers,
hasta que desató el picapedrero	until the stonecutter chipped away,
su cintura morena	loosening your dark waist,
y las antiguas manos	and ancient hands
cortaron piedra	cut stone
como	as if
si cortaran luna,	they were cutting the moon,
granito espolvoreado	granite scattered
por las olas,	by the waves,
sílice trabajada por el viento.	silica wrought by the wind.
Plutónico	Plutonic
esqueleto	skeleton
de aquel	of that
mundo,	world,
cumbres ferruginosas,	mountain peaks shot with iron,
alturas de diamante,	diamond heights,

todo	all
el	the
anillo	ring
de la	of the
furia	icy
helada,	fury,
allá arriba durmiendo	sleeping there above
entre sábana y sábana	between sheet and sheet
de nieve,	of snow,
entre soplo y silbido	between gust and whistle
de huracanes.	of hurricanes.
Arriba	Above
cielo	heaven
y piedra,	and stone,
lomos grises,	gray backs,
nuestra	our
terrible	terrible
herencia encarnizada,	hard-fought inheritance,
trenzas,	flowing tresses,
molinos,	windmills,
torres,	towers,
palomas y banderas	doves and flags
de piedra verde,	of green stone,
de	of
agua endurecida,	hardened water,
de rígidas	of rigid
catástrofes,	catastrophes,
piedra nevada,	snowcapped stone,
cielo nevado	snowclad sky,
y nieve.	and snow.
La piedra fue la proa,	Stone was the prow,
se adelantó al latido de la tierra,	before the earth's heartbeat,
el ancho continente	the wide American
americano	continent

avanzó a cada lado
del granito,
los ríos
en la cuenca
de la roca
nacieron.
Las águilas oscuras
y los pájaros de oro
soltaron sus destellos,
cavaron
un duro nido abierto
a picotazos
en la nave de piedra.
Polvo y arena frescos
cayeron
como plumas
sobre
las playas del planeta
y la humedad
fue un beso.
El beso de la vida
venidera
fue colmando la copa
de la tierra.
Creció el maíz y derramó su especie.
Los mayas estudiaron sus estrellas.
Celestes edificios
hoy
en el polvo abiertos
como antiguas
granadas
cuyos granos
cayeron,
cuyos viejos destellos de amaranto
en la tierra profunda se gastaron.
Casas talladas en

advanced on each side
of the granite,
the rivers
were born
in the watershed
of the rock.
The dark eagles
and golden birds
let loose their flashes,
dug
a hard open nest,
pecking
at the ship of stone.
Fresh dust and sand
fell
like feathers
over
the planet's beaches,
and the humidity
was a kiss.
The kiss of life
to come
was filling the earth's
cup.
Corn grew and spread its species.
The Mayas studied their stars.
Celestial buildings
today
in the dust open
like ancient
pomegranates
whose seeds
dropped,
whose old amarynth glitters
wore away deep down in the earth.
Houses carved

piedra peruana,	in Peruvian stone,
dispuestas en el filo	laid out along the edge
de las cumbres	of the peaks
como hachas de la noche	like nocturnal hatchets
o nidos de obsidiana,	or obsidian nests,
casa desmoronadas en que aún	crumbled houses in which the rock is still
la roca es una estrella	a divided
dividida,	star,
un fulgor que palpita	a flash throbbing
sobre la destrucción de su sarcófago.	over the destruction of its sarcophagus.
Constelas	You glitter
todo	all over
nuestro	our
territorio,	territory,
luz	light
de la piedra,	of stone,
estrella vertebrada,	vertebrate star,
frente de nieve en donde	front of snow buffeted
golpea el aire andino.	by the Andean wind.
América,	America,
boca	mouth
de piedra muda,	of mute stone,
aún hablas con tu lengua perdida,	you still speak with your lost tongue,
aún hablarás, solemne,	you still will speak, solemnly,
con nueva	with a new
voz	voice
de piedra.	of stone.

189 / ODE TO THE STORM

Oda a la tormenta

TRANSLATED BY NATHANIEL TARN

Anoche
vino
ella,
rabiosa,
azul, color de noche,
roja, color de vino,
la tempestad
trajo
su cabellera de agua,
ojos de frío fuego,
anoche quiso
dormir sobre la tierra.
Llegó de pronto
recién desenrollada
desde su astro furioso,
desde su cueva celeste,
quería dormir
y preparó su cama,
barrió selvas, caminos,
barrió montes,
lavó piedras de océano,
y entonces
como si fueran plumas
removió los pinares
para hacerse su cama.
Sacó relámpagos
de su saco de fuego,

Last night
she
came,
livid,
night-blue,
wine-red:
the tempest
with her
hair of water,
eyes of cold fire—
last night she wanted
to sleep on earth.
She came all of a sudden
newly unleashed
out of her furious planet,
her cavern in the sky;
she longed for sleep
and made her bed:
sweeping jungles and highways,
sweeping mountains,
washing ocean stones,
and then
as if they were feathers,
ravaging pine trees
to make her bed.
She shook the lightning
from her quiver of fire,

dejó caer los truenos
como grandes barriles.
De pronto
fue silencio:
una hoja
iba sola en el aire,
como un violín volante,
entonces,
antes
de que llegara al suelo,
tempestad, en tus manos
la tomaste,
pusiste todo el viento
a soplar su bocina,
la noche entera
a andar con sus caballos,
todo el hielo a silbar,
los árboles
salvajes
a expresar la desdicha
de los encadenados,
la tierra
a gemir como madre
pariendo,
de un solo soplo
escondiste
el rumor de la hierba
o las estrellas,
rompiste
como un lienzo
el silencio inactivo,
se llenó el mundo
de orquesta y furia y fuego,
y cuando los relámpagos
caían como cabellos
de tu frente fosfórica,

dropped thunderclaps
like great barrels.
All of a sudden
there was silence:
a single leaf
gliding on air
like a flying violin—
then,
before
it touched the earth,
you took it
in your hands, great storm,
put all the winds to work
blowing their horns,
set the whole night
galloping with its horses,
all the ice whistling,
the wild
trees
groaning in misery
like prisoners,
the earth
moaning, a woman
giving birth,
in a single blow
you blotted out
the noise of grass
or stars,
tore
the numbed silence
like a handkerchief—
the world filled
with sound, fury and fire,
and when the lightning flashes
fell like hair
from your shining forehead,

caían como espadas
de tu cintura guerrera,
y cuando ya creíamos
que terminaba el mundo,
entonces,
lluvia,
lluvia,
sólo
lluvia,
toda la tierra, todo
el cielo
reposaban,
la noche
se desangró cayendo
sobre el sueño del hombre,
sólo lluvia,
agua
del tiempo y del cielo:
nada había caído,
sino una rama rota,
un nido abandonado.

Con tus dedos
de música,
con tu fragor de infierno,
con tu fuego
de volcanes nocturnos,
jugaste
levantando una hoja,
diste fuerza a los ríos,
enseñaste
a ser hombres
a los hombres,
a temer a los débiles,
a llorar a los dulces,
a estremecerse

fell like swords
from your warrior's belt,
and when we were about to think
that the world was ending,
then,
rain,
rain,
only
rain,
all earth, all
sky,
at rest,
the night
fell, bleeding to death
on human sleep,
nothing but rain,
water
of time and sky:
nothing had fallen
except a broken branch,
an empty nest.

With your musical
fingers,
with your hell-roar,
your fire
of volcanoes at night,
you played
at lifting a leaf,
gave strength to rivers,
taught
men
to be men,
the weak to fear,
the tender to cry,
the windows

a las ventanas,
pero
cuando
ibas a destruirnos, cuando
como cuchilla
bajaba del cielo la furia,
cuando temblaba
toda la luz y la sombra
y se mordían los pinos
aullando
junto al mar en tinieblas,
tú, delicada
tempestad, novia mía,
furiosa,
no nos hiciste daño:
regresaste
a tu estrella
y lluvia,
lluvia verde,
lluvia llena
de sueños y de gérmenes,
lluvia
preparadora
de cosechas,
lluvia que lava el mundo,
lo enjuga
y lo recrea,
lluvia para nosotros
y para las semillas,
lluvia
para el olvido
de los muertos
y para
nuestro pan de mañana,
eso sólo
dejaste,

to rattle—
but
when
you prepared to destroy us, when
like a dagger
fury fell from the sky,
when all the light
and shadow trembled
and the pines devoured
themselves howling
on the edge of the midnight sea,
you, delicate storm,
my betrothed,
wild as you were,
did us no wrong:
but returned
to your star
and rain,
green rain,
rain full
of dreams and seeds,
mother
of harvests
rain,
world-washing rain,
draining it,
making it new,
rain for us men
and for the seeds,
rain
for the forgetting
of the dead
and for
tomorrow's bread—
only the rain
you left behind,

agua y música,	water and music,
por eso,	for this,
tempestad,	I love you,
te amo,	storm,
cuenta conmigo,	reckon with me,
vuelve,	come back,
despiértame,	wake me up,
ilumíname,	illuminate me,
muéstrame tu camino	show me your path
para que a ti se junte y cante con tu canto	so that the chosen voice,
la decidida voz	the stormy voice of a man,
tempestuosa de un hombre.	may join and sing your song with you.

190 / ODE TO THE STORMS OF CÓRDOBA

Oda a las tormentas de Córdoba

TRANSLATED BY ILAN STAVANS

El pleno mediodía	The plain, resplendent
refulgente	noon
es una	is
espada de oro,	a golden spear.
de pronto	Suddenly,
cae un trueno	thunder rumbles
como una	like a
piedra	rock
sobre un tambor de cuero rojo,	over red drumhead,
se raja el aire	the air is rent
como	like
una bandera,	a flag,
se agujerea el cielo	the sky is pierced
y toda su agua verde	and all its green water
se desploma	pours down
sobre la tierra tierra	over the soil soil
tierra tierra	soil soil
tachonada	studded
por las ganaderías.	with livestock.
Ruidosa es la aventura	Clamorous is the adventure
del agua desbocada	of the disgorged
en las alturas:	water from above:
parece que corrieran	it looks as if horses
caballos en el cielo,	are galloping across the sky,
caen montañas blancas,	white mountains fall,
caen sillas, sillones	chairs fall, armchairs,
y entonces	and then

las centellas	the lightning
arden, huyen, estallan,	blazes, leaps, flashes,
el campo tiembla a cada	the field trembles with
latigazo celeste,	each celestial lash,
el rayo	thunderbolts
quema	brand
solitarios	solitary
árboles	trees
con fósforo de infierno	with phosphorus from hell
mientras	while
el agua	water
convertida en granizo	turned into hail
derriba muros, mata	knocks down walls, kills
gallineros,	hen coops,
corre asustada la perdiz, se esconde	the partridge runs frightened, the ovenbird
en su recámara el hornero,	hides in its chamber,
la víbora atraviesa	the snake slithers
como lento relámpago	like slow lightning,
el páramo buscando	a hawk, seeking
un agujero, cae	a hole,
un halcón	falls
golpeado	battered
por la piedra celeste	by celestial pebbles
y ahora	and now
el viento de la sierra,	the wind of the mountains,
gigantesco,	gigantic,
rabioso,	rabid,
corre	runs unleashed
por la llanura	across
desatado.	the plain.
Es un	It is
gigantesco demente	a gigantic madman
que se escapó de un cuento	who has escaped from some tale
y con brazos en cruz	and with arms outstretched
atraviesa, gritando, las aldeas:	goes through the villages blustering:
el viento loco	the mad wind

ataca
los duros algarrobos,
rompe
la cabellera
de los dulces sauces,
suena
como
una
catarata
verde,
que arrastrara
barricas y follajes,
carretas de cristal, camas de plomo.
De pronto,
vertical
regresa
el día
puro,
azul es su madeja,
redonda la medalla
del sol encarnizado,
no se mueve
una hoja,
las cigarras
zumban como sopranos,
el cartero
de Totoral reparte
palomas de papel en bicicleta,
alguien sube
a un caballo,
un toro muge,
es verano,
aquí, señores,
no ha
pasado
nada.

assaults
the hard carob trees,
breaks
the hair
of the gentle willows,
sounds
like
a
green
waterfall,
dragging
kegs and foliage,
crystal carts, leaden bedsteads
Suddenly
the vertical
clear
day
returns,
its hair is blue
its medallion
of bitter-red sun round.
Not a leaf
stirs,
cicadas
buzz like sopranos,
the postman
from Totoral, on his bicycle,
delivers paper doves,
someone rides
a horse,
the bull bellows,
it is summer,
here, señores,
nothing
has
happened.

191 / ODE TO SUMMER

Oda al verano

TRANSLATED BY MARGARET SAYERS PEDEN

Verano, violín rojo,	Summer, red violin,
nube clara,	bright cloud,
un zumbido	a buzzing
de sierra	of saw
o de cigarra	and cicada
te precede,	precedes you,
el cielo	your sky
abovedado,	is vaulted,
liso, luciente como	smooth and shining as
un ojo,	an eye,
y bajo su mirada,	and beneath its gaze,
verano,	summer,
pez del cielo	fish of the
infinito,	infinite sky,
élitro lisonjero,	pleasing elytron,
perezoso	lazy,
letargo,	lethargic,
barriguita	rounded bee's
de abeja,	belly,
sol	fiendish
endiablado,	sun,
sol terrible y paterno,	terrible, paternal sun,
sudoroso	sweaty as a
como un buey trabajando,	laboring ox,
sol seco	parched sun
en la cabeza	pounding on your head
como un inesperado	like an unexpected

garrotazo,
sol de la sed
andando
por la arena,
verano,
mar desierto,
el minero
de azufre
se llena
de sudor amarillo,
el aviador
recorre
rayo a rayo
el sol celeste,
sudor
negro
resbala
de la frente
a los ojos
en la mina
de Lota,
el minero
se restriega
la frente
negra,
arden
las sementeras,
cruje
el trigo,
insectos
azules
buscan
sombra,
tocan
la frescura,
sumergen

clubbing,
thirsty sun
trudging
across the sand,
summer,
desert sea.
The sulfur
miner
drips
yellow sweat;
ray by ray
the pilot
flies
the celestial sun;
black
sweat
slides
down a forehead
into eyes
in the mine
at Lota,
the miner
wipes
his black
forehead,
sowed fields
blazc,
wheat
rustles,
blue
insects
seek
shade,
touch
coolness,
dip

la cabeza	their heads
en un diamante.	in a diamond.
Oh verano	Abundant
abundante,	summer,
carro	wagon
de	of
manzanas	ripe
maduras,	apples,
boca	strawberry
de fresa	mouth
en la verdura, labios	in the greenness, lips
de ciruela salvaje,	of wild plums,
caminos	roads
de suave polvo	of soft dust
encima	layered
del polvo,	on dust,
mediodía,	midday,
tambor	red
de cobre rojo,	copper drum,
y en la tarde	and in the afternoon
descansa	the fire
el fuego,	relents,
el aire	the air
hace bailar	makes clover
el trébol, entra	dance, invades
en la usina desierta,	the desert furnace,
sube	a cool
una estrella	star
fresca	rises
por el cielo	in the somber
sombrío,	sky,
crepita	in the crackling
sin quemarse	though unscorched
la noche	summer
del verano.	night.

192 / ODE TO THE SUN

Oda al sol

TRANSLATED BY ILAN STAVANS

No conocía el sol.
Viví en invierno.
Era
en los montes australes.
Las aguas
invasoras
sostenían
la tierra,
el firmamento era
un pálido paraguas
desbordado,
una medusa
océanica
de cabellera
verde.
Llovía
sobre el techo,
sobre las hojas negras
de la noche,
bajaba
agua celeste
desde los desdentados
ventisqueros.
Después crucé los climas.
Y en el desierto,
redondo, arriba, solo,
el sol de fuego

I didn't know the sun.
I lived in winter.
It was
in the hills of Patagonia.
The invading
waters
supported
the earth,
the firmament was
a pale, overwhelmed
umbrella,
an oceanic
jellyfish
with a green
head of hair.
It was raining
on the roof,
over the black leaves
of the night,
celestial water
descended
from the toothless
snowdrifts.
Afterward, I moved climates.
And in the desert,
rounded, above, alone,
the sun was on fire,

con sus deslumbradoras
crines rojas,
el león en su círculo
de espadas,
la flor central
del cielo.

Oh sol,
cristal paterno,
horario
y poderío,
progenitor planeta,
gigante
rosa rubia
siempre
hirviendo de fuego,
siempre
consumiéndote
encendido,
cocina
cenital,
párpado
puro,
colérico y tranquilo,
fogón y fogonero,
sol,
yo quiero
mirarte
con los viejos
ojos de América:
guanaco
huracanado,
cabeza
de maíz,
corazón amarillo,
lunar de oro,

with its dazzling
red manes,
a lion in his circle
of spears,
the central flower
in the sky.

Oh sun,
fatherly crystal,
schedule
and authority,
planet progenitor,
giant
blond rose,
always
boiling with fire,
always
being consumed
in ignition,
zenith
kitchen,
pristine
eyelid,
furious and tranquil,
stove and stoker.
Sun,
I want
to look at you
with America's
ancient eyes,
hurricane-driven
guanaco,
head
of maize,
yellow heart,
golden mole,

cuerpo quemante,	burning body,
zanahoria ardiente,	scalding carrot.
hermosa	Your gaze
es tu mirada,	is beautiful.
apenas	No sooner
tocas	do you touch
la rama	the branch
nace	than spring
la primavera,	arrives,
apenas,	amber tail.
cola de ámbar,	No sooner
tocas	do you touch
los trigales	the wheat fields
y se derrama el trigo	than wheat spills over
repitiendo	repeating
tu forma,	your form,
pan,	bread.
pan del cielo,	Bread of heaven,
horno sagrado,	sacred oven,
tú no fuiste	you were no
estrella blanca,	white star.
hielo,	Ice,
diamante congelado	frozen diamond
en la mirada	in the glance
de la noche:	of night:
fuiste	you were
energía,	energy,
diurno,	day quality,
fuerte fecundador, potro celeste,	forceful inseminator, celestial colt,
seminal semillero	seminal seedbed
y bajo	and under
tu palpitante pulso	your palpitating pulse,
la semilla	the seed
creció,	grew,
la tierra	earth
desnudó su forma verde	undressed its green form

y nosotros	and we
levantamos	raised
las uvas	the grapes
y la tierra	and the earth
en una copa	in a blazing
ardiendo:	cup:
te heredamos:	we inherited you:
somos	we are
hijos	children
del sol y de la tierra.	of the sun and the earth.
Los hombres	We, the men
de América	of America,
así fuimos creados,	were thus created,
en nuestra sangre	in our blood
tierra y sol circulan	circulating earth and sun,
como imanes nutricios,	like nutritious magnets.
y te reverenciamos,	And we revere you,
esfera tutelar, rosa de fósforo,	tutelary sphere, rose of phosphorus,
volador	flying
volcán del cielo,	volcano of heaven,
padre de cordilleras,	father of cordilleras,
tigre germinador,	germinating tiger,
patriarca de oro,	patriarch of gold,
anillo	cracking
crepitante,	ring,
germen total, incubador profundo,	total germ, profound incubator,
gallo del universo.	rooster of the universe.

193 / ODE TO THE TABLE

Oda a la mesa

TRANSLATED BY KEN KRABBENHOFT

Sobre las cuatro patas de la mesa	I work out my odes
desarrollo mis odas,	on a four-legged table,
despliego el pan, el vino	laying before me bread and wine
y el asado	and roast meat
(la nave negra	(that black boat
de los sueños),	of our dreams).
o dispongo tijeras, tazas, clavos,	Sometimes I set out scissors, cups and nails,
claveles y martillos.	hammers and carnations.
La mesa fiel	Tables are trustworthy:
sostiene	titanic quadrupeds,
sueño y vida,	they sustain
titánico cuadrúpedo.	our hopes and our daily life.
Es	The rich man's table,
la encaracolada	scrolled and shining,
y refulgente	is
mesa del rico un fabuloso buque	a fabulous ship
cargado con racimos.	bearing bunches of fruit.
Es hermosa la mesa de la gula,	Gluttony's table is a wonder,
rebosante de góticas langostas,	piled high with gothic lobsters,
y hay una mesa	and there is also a lonesome
sola, en el comedor de nuestra tía	table in our aunt's dining room,
en verano. Corrieron	in summer. They've closed
las cortinas	the curtains,
y un solo rayo agudo del estío	and a single ray of summer light
penetra como espada	strikes like a sword

a saludar sobre la mesa oscura
la transparente paz de la ciruelas.
Y hay una mesa lejos, mesa pobre,
donde están preparando
una corona
para
el minero muerto,
y sube de la mesa el frío aroma
del último dolor desbaratado.
Y cerca está la mesa
de aquella alcoba umbría
que hace arder el amor con sus incendios.
Un guante de mujer quedó temblando
allí, como la cáscara del fuego.

El mundo
es una mesa
rodeada por la miel y por el humo,
cubierta de manzanas o de sangre.
La mesa preparada
y ya sabemos cuando
nos llamaron:
si nos llaman a guerra o a comida
y hay que elegir campana,
hay que saber ahora
cómo nos vestiremos
para sentarnos
en la larga mesa,
si nos pondremos pantalones de odio
o camisa de amor recién lavada:
pero hay que hacerlo pronto,
están llamando:
muchachas y muchachos,
a la mesa!

upon this table sitting in the dark
and greets the plums' transparent peace.
And there is a faraway table, a humble table,
where they're weaving
a wreath
for
a dead miner.
That table gives off the chilling odor
of a man's wasted pain.
There's a table
in a shadowy room nearby
that love sets ablaze with its flames.
A woman's glove was left behind there,
trembling like a husk of fire.

The world
is a table
engulfed in honey and smoke,
smothered by apples and blood.
The table is already set,
and we know the truth
as soon as we are called:
whether we're called to war or to dinner
we will have to choose sides,
have to know
how we'll dress
to sit
at the long table,
whether we'll wear the pants of hate
or the shirt of love, freshly laundered.
Its time to decide,
they're calling:
boys and girls,
let's eat!

194 / ODE TO THINGS

Oda a las cosas

TRANSLATED BY ILAN STAVANS

Amo las cosas loca,	I love crazy things,
locamente.	crazily.
Me gustan las tenazas,	I enjoy tongs,
las tijeras,	scissors.
adoro	I adore
las tazas,	cups,
las argollas,	rings,
las soperas,	soup spoons,
sin hablar, por supuesto,	not to mention, of course,
del sombrero.	the hat.
Amo	I love
todas las cosas,	all things,
no sólo	not only
las supremas,	the grand ones
sino	but
las	the
infinita-	infinite-
mente	ly
chicas,	small,
el dedal,	the thimble,
las espuelas,	spurs,
los platos,	plates,
los floreros.	flower vases.
Ay, alma mía,	Ay, soul of mine,
hermoso	the planet

es el planeta,
lleno
de pipas
por la mano
conducidas
en el humo,
de llaves,
de saleros,
en fin,
todo
lo que se hizo
por la mano del hombre, toda cosa:
las curvas del zapato,
el tejido,
el nuevo nacimiento
del oro
sin la sangre,
los anteojos,
los clavos,
las escobas,
los relojes, las brújulas,
las monedas, la suave
suavidad de las sillas.

Ay cuántas
cosas
puras
ha construido
el hombre:
de lana,
de madera,
de cristal,
de cordeles,
mesas
maravillosas,
navíos, escaleras.

is gorgeous,
full
of pipes
taken
by hand
amid the smoke,
of key rings,
salt shakers,
in short,
everything
made
by the hand of man, all things:
the curves of a shoe,
fabric,
the new birth
of gold
without blood,
eyeglasses,
nails,
brooms,
clocks, compasses,
coins, the soft
softness of chairs.

Ay, how many
pristine
things
man
has built:
of wool,
wood,
glass,
ropes,
marvelous
tables,
ships, staircases.

Amo	I love
todas	all
las cosas,	things,
no porque sean	not because they
ardientes	blaze
o fragantes,	or are fragrant,
sino porque	but because
no sé,	I don't know,
porque	because
este océano es el tuyo,	this ocean is yours,
es el mío:	is mine:
los botones,	buttons,
las ruedas,	wheels,
los pequeños	small
tesoros	forgotten
olvidados,	treasures,
los abanicos en	feathered fans
cuyos plumajes	on whose feathers
desvaneció el amor	love spread
sus azahares,	its orange blossoms,
las copas, los cuchillos,	cups, knives,
las tijeras,	scissors,
todo tiene	everything rests
en el mango, en el contorno,	on the handle, in the contour,
la huella	the trace
de unos dedos,	of fingers,
de una remota mano	a remote hand
perdida	lost
en lo más olvidado del olvido.	in the most forgotten of oblivions.
Yo voy por casas,	I wander through
calles,	houses,
ascensores,	elevators,
tocando cosas,	touching things,
divisando objetos	spotting objects
que en secreto ambiciono:	I secretly covet:

uno porque repica,
otro porque
es tan suave
como la suavidad de una cadera,
otro por su color de agua profunda,
otro por su espesor de terciopelo.

Oh río
irrevocable
de las cosas,
no se dirá
que sólo
amé
los peces,
o las plantas de selva y de pradera,
que no sólo
amé
lo que salta, sube, sobrevive, suspira.
No es verdad:
muchas cosas
me lo dijeron todo.
No sólo me tocaron
o las tocó mi mano,
sino que acompañaron
de tal modo
mi existencia
que conmigo existieron
y fueron para mí tan existentes
que vivieron conmigo media vida
y morirán conmigo media muerte.

one because it chimes,
another because
it is as soft
as the softness of a hip,
another for its color of deep water,
another for the thickness of its velvet.

Oh irrevocable
river
of things,
it should not be said
that I loved
only
fish,
or the jungle plants and the prairie,
that I not only
loved
what jumps, ascends, survives, sighs.
It isn't true:
many things
told me everything.
They not only touched me
or were touched by my hand,
but they accompanied
my existence
to such an extent
that they lived with me
and were so full of life for me
that they lived with me half a life
and would live with me for half a death.

195 / ODE TO THE THIRD DAY

Oda al tercer día

TRANSLATED BY ILAN STAVANS

Eres el lunes, jueves,
llegarás o pasaste.
Agosto en medio
de su red escarlata
de pronto te levanta,
o junio,
junio,
cuando menos pensábamos
un pétalo
con llamas
surge
en medio
de la semana fría,
un pez rojo recorre
como un escalofrío,
de repente,
el invierno,
y comienzan las flores
a vestirse,
a llenarse de luna,
a caminar por la calle,
a embarcarse
en el viento,
es un día
cualquiera,
color de muro,
pero

You are Monday, Thursday,
you will come or go.
August, amid
its red scarlet
suddenly wakes up,
or June,
June,
before we know it,
a petal
with flames
emerges
in the middle
of a cold week,
a red fish wanders
like a shiver.
Suddenly,
winter is here,
flowers begin
to dress up,
to be filled by the moon,
to walk on the street,
to board
the wind.
It's an average
day,
the color of a wall,
but

algo sube a la cima	something arises from the top
de un minuto, oriflama	of a minute, a banner,
o sal silvestre,	wild salt,
oro de abeja sube a las banderas,	bee gold ascending to the flags.
miel escarlata desarrolla el viento,	The wind develops scarlet honey.
es un día sin nombre,	It's a nameless day,
pero	but,
con patas de oro	with feet of gold,
camina en la semana,	it advances during the week.
el polen se le pega	Pollen sticks to
en el bigote,	its mustache,
la argamasa celeste	the celestial mortar
se adelanta en sus ojos,	penetrates its eyes,
y bailamos	and we dance,
contentos,	happily,
cantamos persiguiendo	we sing while pursuing
las flores del cerezo,	flowers in the cherry tree,
levantamos la copa	we raise the cup
enamorados,	in love,
saludamos la hora	greeting
que se acerca, el minuto	the approaching hour, the minute
que transcurrió,	gone by,
que nace	born
o que fermenta.	and fermenting—
Diosa del día,	goddess of the day,
amapola	unconscious
inconsciente,	poppy flower,
rosa descabellada,	hairless rose,
súbita primavera,	sudden spring.
jueves,	Thursday,
rayo escondido en medio	hidden ray amid
de la ropa,	the clothing,
te amo,	I love you,
soy	I'm
tu novio.	your groom.
Comprendo, pasajera,	I understand, passenger,

pasajero
que pasas: debemos
despedirnos,
pero una gota
de esplendor,
una uva
de sol imaginario
llegó a la sangre ciega
de cada día,
y guardaremos
este destello rojo
de fuego y ambrosía,
guardaremos
este día insurgente
ardiendo
inolvidable
con su llama
en medio del polvo y del tiempo.

passerby
passing: we must
say goodbye,
only a drop
of splendor,
a grape
of imaginary sun
reaches the blind blood
of each day,
and we will keep
this red sparkle
of fire and ambrosia for us.
We will keep
this insurgent day
burning,
unforgettable,
its flame
amid dust and time.

196 / ODE TO THE THREAD

Oda al hilo

TRANSLATED BY MARGARET SAYERS PEDEN

Éste es el hilo
de la poesía.
Los hechos como ovejas
van cargados
de lana
negra
o blanca.
Llámalos y vendrán
prodigiosos rebaños,
héroes y minerales,
la rosa del amor,
la voz del fuego,
todo vendrá a tu lado.
Tienes a tu merced
una montaña,
si te pones
a cruzarla a caballo
te crecerá la barba,
dormirás en el suelo,
tendrás hambre
y en la montaña todo
será sombra.
No lo puedes hacer,
tienes que hilarla,
levanta un hilo,
súbelo:
interminable y puro

This is the thread
of poetry.
Events, like sheep,
wear wooly
coats of
black
or white.
Call, and wondrous
flocks will come,
heroes and minerals,
the rose of love,
the voice of fire,
all will come to your side.
You have at your call
a mountain.
If you set out
to cross it on horseback
your beard will grow,
you will sleep on the ground,
you will know hunger,
and on the mountain
all will be shadow.
You can't do it that way.
You must spin it,
fly a thread
and climb it.
Infinite and pure,

de tantos sitios sale,
de la nieve,
del hombre,
es duro porque todos
los metales lo hicieron,
es frágil porque el humo
lo dibujó temblando,
así es el hilo
de la poesía.
No tienes
que enredarlo de nuevo,
volverlo a confundir
con el tiempo y la tierra.
Al contrario,
es tu cuerda,
colócalo en tu cítara
y hablará con la boca
de los montes sonoros,
trénzalo
y será enredadera
de navío,
desarróllalo,
cárgalo de mensajes,
electrízalo,
entrégalo
al viento, a la intemperie,
que de nuevo, ordenado,
en un a larga línea
envuelva al mundo,
o bien, enhébralo,
fino, fino,
sin descuidar el manto
de las hadas.

Necesitamos mantas
para todo el invierno.

it comes from many sources,
from snow,
from man;
it is strong because
it was made from ores;
it is fragile because it was
traced by trembling smoke;
the thread of poetry
is like that.
You don't have to
tangle it again,
to return it
to time and the earth.
On the contrary,
it is your cord,
string it on your zither
and you will speak with the mouth
of mighty mountains,
braid it,
and it will be the rigging
of a ship,
unwind it,
hang it with messages,
electrify it,
expose it
to wind and weather,
so that, straight again,
in one long line it will wind
around the world,
or thread it,
fine, oh so fine,
remembering the fairies'
gowns.

We need blankets
to warm us through the winter.

Ahí vienen
los campesinos,
traen
para el poeta
una gallina, sólo
una pobre gallina.
Qué vas a darles tú,
qué vas a darles?
Ahora,
ahora,
el hilo,
el hilo
que se irá haciendo ropa
para los que no tienen
sino harapos,
redes
para los pescadores,
camisas
de color
escarlata
para los fogoneros
y una bandera
para todos.
Entre los hombres,
entre sus dolores
pesados como piedras,
entre sus victorias
aladas como abejas,
allí está el hilo
en medio
de lo que está pasando
y lo que viene,
abajo
entre carbones,
arriba
en la miseria,

Here come people
from the farms,
they are bringing
a hen
for the poet, one
small hen.
And what will you give them,
you, what will you give?
Now!
Now,
the thread,
the thread
that will become cloth
for those who have
only rags,
nets
for fishermen,
brilliant
scarlet
shirts
for stokers,
and a flag
for each and every one.
Through men,
through their pain
heavy as stone,
through their victories
winged like bees,
goes the thread,
through the middle
of everything that's happening
and all that is to come,
below the earth,
through coal;
above,
through misery,

con los hombres,
contigo,
con tu pueblo,
el hilo,
el hilo
de la poesía.
No se trata
de consideraciones:
son órdenes,
te ordeno,
con la cítara al brazo,
acompáñame.
Hay muchos
oídos esperando,
hay
un terrible
corazón enterrado,
es nuestra
familia, nuestro pueblo.
Al hilo!
Al hilo!
A sacarlo
de la montaña oscura!
A transmitir relámpagos!
A escribir la bandera!
Así es el hilo
de la poesía,
simple, sagrado, eléctrico,
fragante y necesario
y no termina en nuestras pobres manos:
lo revive la luz de cada día.

with men,
with you,
with your people,
the thread,
the thread
of poetry.
This isn't a matter
for deliberation:
it's an order,
I order you,
with your zither under your arm,
come with me.
Many ears
are waiting,
an awesome
heart
lies buried,
it is our
family, our people.
The thread!
The thread!
Draw it
from the dark mountain!
To transmit lightning!
To compose the flag!
That is the thread
of poetry,
simple, sacred, electric,
fragrant and necessary,
and it doesn't end in our humble hands:
it is revived by the light of each new day.

197 / ODE TO TIME

Oda al tiempo

TRANSLATED BY JANE HIRSHFIELD

Dentro de ti tu edad
creciendo,
dentro de mí mi edad
andando.
El tiempo es decidido,
no suena su campana,
se acrecienta, camina,
por dentro de nosotros,
aparece
como un agua profunda
en la mirada
y junto a las castañas
quemadas de tus ojos
una brizna, la huella
de un minúsculo río,
una estrellita seca
ascendiendo a tu boca.
Sube el tiempo
sus hilos
a tu pelo,
pero en mi corazón
como una madreselva
es tu fragancia,
viviente como el fuego.
Es bello
como lo que vivimos
envejecer viviendo.

Inside your body, your age
is growing,
inside my body, my age
places foot after wandering foot.
Time is unwavering,
it never rings its bell for time out,
it increases, it journeys,
it shows up within us
like water that deepens
within our own watching,
until next to the chestnut burning
that is your eyes
a slender grass blade arrives,
and the trace of a tiny river,
and a small dry star
ascends to your lips.
Then time raises
its threads in your hair,
and still in my heart
your fragrance of honeysuckle
lives like a fire.
It is beautiful,
how, as we live,
we grow old in the living.
Each day
was a transparent stone,
each night for us was a rose of blackness,

Cada día
fue piedra transparente,
cada noche
para nosotros fue una rosa negra,
y este surco en tu rostro o en el mío
son piedra o flor,
recuerdo de un relámpago.
Mis ojos se han gastado en tu hermosura,
pero tú eres mis ojos.
Yo fatigué tal vez bajo mis besos
tu pecho duplicado,
pero todos han visto en mi alegría
tu resplandor secreto.
Amor, qué importa
que el tiempo,
el mismo que elevó como dos llamas
o espigas paralelas
mi cuerpo y tu dulzura,
mañana los mantenga
o los desgrane
y con sus mismos dedos invisibles
borre la identidad que nos separa
dándonos la victoria
de un solo ser final bajo la tierra.

and this crease that has come to your face,
to mine,
is its stone or its flower,
the souvenir and memory of a bolt of
lightning.
My eyes were consumed
by your loveliness,
but you have become my eyes.
I exhausted your twin breasts
under my kisses it seems,
but all have viewed in my joy
their secret splendor.
Love, it doesn't' matter
if time
(that same time that lifted
my body and your softness
as if they were two rising flames
or two stalks of wheat growing side by side)
tomorrow keeps them aloft and living
or mills them away—
the same invisible fingers
erasing the very existence that kept us apart
will give us our victory,
of being a single being under the earth.

198 / ODE TO THE TIME TO COME

Oda al tiempo venidero

TRANSLATED BY ILAN STAVANS

Tiempo, me llamas. Antes	Time, you call me. You were
eras	pure space
espacio puro,	before,
ancha pradera.	open meadow.
Hoy hilo o gota	Today you are
eres,	thread or drop,
luz delgada	slender light
que corre como liebre hacia las zarzas	running like a hare toward thickets
de la cóncava noche.	of concave night.
Pero,	But
ahora	now
me dices, tiempo, aquello	you tell me, time, what
que ayer no me dijiste:	you didn't tell me yesterday:
tus pasos apresura,	hurry up, get going,
tu corazón reposa,	rest your heart,
desarrolla tu canto.	develop your song.
El mismo soy. No soy? Quién, en el cauce	I am the same, am I not? Who, by the
de las aguas que corren	path of its running waters,
identifica el río?	identifies the river?
Sólo sé que allí mismo,	All I know is right there,
en una sola	my heart pounds
puerta	on a single
mi corazón golpea,	door,

desde ayer, desde lejos,
desde entonces,
desde mi nacimiento.

Allí
donde responde
el eco oscuro
del mar
que canta y canto
y que
conozco
sólo
por un ciego silbido,
por un rayo
en las olas,
por sus anchas espumas en la noche.

Así, pues, tiempo, en vano
me has medido,
en vano transcurriste
adelantando
caminos al errante.

Junto a una sola puerta
pasé toda la noche,
solitario, cantando.

Y ahora
que tu luz se adelgaza
como animal que corre
perdiéndose en la sombra
me dices,
al oído,
lo que no me enseñaste
y supe siempre.

since yesterday, since long ago,
since then,
since my birth.

There
where the sea's
obscure echo
responds
by singing, and I sing,
and
this I only
know
through a blind whistle,
by the lighting
on the waves,
by its thick froth in the night.

And so, time, in vain
you have measured me,
in vain you have passed by
a step ahead
of this wanderer.

Near a single door
I spent the whole night,
alone, singing.

And now
that your light shrinks
like a speeding animal,
fading into the shadow,
tell me,
to my ear,
what you taught me
and I knew forever.

199 / ODE TO THE TOMATO

Oda al tomate

TRANSLATED BY STEPHEN MITCHELL

La calle
se llenó de tomates,
mediodía,
verano,
la luz
se parte
en dos
mitades
de tomate,
corre
por las calles
el jugo.
En diciembre
se desata
el tomate,
invade
las cocinas,
entra por los almuerzos,
se sienta
reposado
en los aparadores,
entre los vasos,
las mantequilleras,
los saleros azules.
Tiene
luz propia,
majestad benigna.

The street
filled with tomatoes,
midday,
summer,
the light
splits
in two
halves
of tomato,
the juice
runs
through the streets.
In June
the tomato
cuts loose,
invades
the kitchens,
takes over lunches,
sits down
comfortably
on sideboards,
among the glasses,
the butter dishes,
the blue saltshakers.
It has
its own light,
a benign majesty.

Debemos, por desgracia,
asesinarlo:
se hunde
el cuchillo
en su pulpa viviente,
es una roja
víscera,
un sol
fresco,
profundo,
inagotable,
llena las ensaladas
de Chile,
se casa alegremente
con la clara cebolla,
y para celebrarlo
se deja
caer
aceite,
hijo
esencial de olivo,
sobre sus hemisferios entreabiertos,
agrega
la pimienta
su fragancia,
la sal su magnetismo:
son las bodas
del día,
el perejil
levanta
banderines,
las papas
hierven vigorosamente,
el asado
golpea
con su aroma

Unfortunately, we have to
assassinate it:
the knife
plunges
into its living flesh,
it is a red
viscera,
a cool,
deep,
inexhaustible
sun
fills the salads
of Chile,
is cheerfully married
to the clear onion,
and to celebrate,
oil
lets itself
fall,
son and essence
of the olive tree,
onto the half-open hemispheres,
pepper
adds
its fragrance,
salt, its magnetism:
it is the day's
wedding,
parsley
raises
little flags,
potatoes
vigorously boil,
with its aroma
the steak
pounds

en la puerta,
es hora!
vamos!
y sobre
la mesa, en la cintura
del verano,
el tomate,
astro de tierra,
estrella
repetida
y fecunda,
nos muestra
sus circunvoluciones,
sus canales,
la insigne plenitud
y la abundancia
sin hueso,
sin coraza,
sin escamas ni espinas,
nos entrega
el regalo
de su color fogoso
y la totalidad de su frescura.

on the door,
it's time!
let's go!
and on
the table, in the belt
of summer,
the tomato,
luminary of earth,
repeated
and fertile
star,
shows us
its convolutions,
its canals,
the illustrious plenitude
and the abundance
without pit,
without husk,
without scales or thorns,
it hands us
the gift
of its fiery color
and the totality of its coolness.

200 / ODE TO THE TOOTH OF THE SPERM WHALE

Oda al diente de cachalote

TRANSLATED BY ILAN STAVANS

Del mar vino algún día
rezumando
existencia,
sangre, sal, sombra verde,
ola quc ensangrentó la cacería,
espuma acuchillada
por la erótica forma
de su dueño:
baile
de los
oscuros,
tensos,
monasteriales
cachalotes
en el sur del océano
de Chile.
Alta
mar
y marea,
latitudes
del más lejano
frío:
el aire
es una
copa

From the sea it came one day
oozing
existence,
blood, salt, green shadow,
wave imbuing the hunt with blood,
foam stabbed
by the erotic form
of its owner:
dance
from the
depths,
tense,
monastic
sperm whales
in the southern ocean
of Chile.
High
sea
and tide,
latitudes
of the most distant
cold:
the air
is a
cup

de
claridad helada
por
donde
corren
las alas
del albatros
como skíes del cielo.

Abajo
el mar
es una
torre
desmoronada y construida,
una paila en que hierven
grandes olas de plomo,
algas que sobre
el lomo de las aguas
resbalan
como escalofríos.
De pronto sobrevienen
la boca
de la vida
y de la muerte:
la bóveda
del semisumergido
cachalote,
el cráneo
de las profundidades,
la cúpula
que sobre
la ola eleva
su dentellada,
todo
su
aserradero submarino.

of
iced clarity
through
which
run
the wings of
the albatross
like skies of sky.

Below
the sea
is a
tower
dismantled and constructed,
a frying pan in which
great waves of lead boil,
algae which on
the spine of water
slide
like shivers.
Suddenly,
the mouth
of life
and death arrive:
the vault
of the semisubmerged
sperm whale,
the cranium
of the deep,
its cupola
elevating
its tooth line
over the wave,
its
entire
submarine sawmill.

Se encienden, centellean
las ascuas de marfil,
el agua
inunda
aquella atroz sonrisa,
mar y muerte navegan
junto
al navío negro que entreabre
como una catedral su dentadura.
Y cuando ya la cola
enfurecida
cayó como palmera
sobre el agua,
el animal
salido del abismo
recibió
la centella
del hombre pequeñito
(el arpón
dirigido
por la mano mojada
del chileno).

Cuando
regresó
de los
mares,
de su sangriento día,
el marinero
en uno
de los dientes
de la bestia
grabó con su cuchillo
dos retratos: una
mujer y un hombre
despidiéndose,

The ivory embers
are illuminated, sparkle,
water
inundates
that atrocious smile,
sea and death sail
near
the black boat half-opening
like a cathedral its teeth.
And when the furious
tail
fell down like a palm tree
over the water,
the animal
from the abyss
received
the flashing bolt
from the tiny man
(the harpoon
targeted
by the Chilean's
wet hand).

When
it came back
from the
seas,
in its bloody day,
the mariner,
in one
of the beast's
teeth,
engraved, with his knife,
two portraits: a
woman and a man
saying goodbye,

un navegante
por el amor
herido,
una novia en la proa
de la ausencia.

Cuántas
veces tocó mi corazón, mi mano,
aquella
luna
de miel
marina
dibujada
en el diente.
Cómo amé
la corola
del
doloroso
amor
escrita
en marfil
de ballena
carnicera,
de cachalote loco.

Suave
línea
del
beso
fugitivo,
pincel
de flor marina
tatuada
en el hocico
de la ola,
en la fauce terrible

a sailor
injured
by love,
a bride in the prow
of absence.

How frequently
it touched my heart, my hand,
that
seaside
honeymoon
drawn
on the tooth.
How much I loved
the corolla
of
the painful
love
written
on a butcher
whale's
ivory,
a crazy sperm whale.

Soft
line
of
furtive
kiss,
brush
of marine flower
tattooed
in the muzzle
of the wave,
in the terrible faucet

del océano,	of the ocean,
en el alfanje	in the unchained
desencadenado	scimitar
desde	from
las tinieblas:	darkness:
allí	there
estampado	the song
el canto	of
del	wandering love
amor errante,	is stamped,
la despedida	the farewell
de los azahares,	of the
la niebla,	orange blossoms
la luz	of fog,
de aquel	the light
amanecer	of that wet
mojado	sunrise
por tempestuosas lágrimas	by tempestuous tears
de aurora ballenera.	of whaling aurora.
Oh amor,	Oh love,
allí	there,
a los labios	on the lips
del mar,	of the sea,
condicionado	conditioned
a	to
un	a
diente	tooth
de la ola,	of the wave,
con el	with the
rumor	rumor
de	of
un	a
pétalo	generic
genérico	petal
(susurro de ala rota	(whisper of a broken wing

entre el intenso
olor
de los jazmines),
(amor
de hotel
entrecerrado, oscuro,
con hiedras amarradas
al ocaso),
(y un beso
duro como
piedra que asalta),
luego
entre boca y boca
el mar
eterno,
el archipiélago,
el collar de las
islas
y las naves
cercadas
por el frío,
esperando
el animal azul
de las profundidades
australianas
del océano,
el animal nacido
del diluvio
con su ferretería
de zafiros.

Ahora aquí descansa
sobre mi mesa y frente
a las aguas de marzo.
Ya vuelve
al regazo arenoso de la costa,

amid
the intense smell
of jasmine),
(love
from a locked-up
hotel, dark,
with tied-up ivy
at the end),
(and a harsh
kiss like
an assaulting stone),
then
from mouth to mouth
the eternal
sea,
the archipelago,
the necklace of
the islands
and the vessels
surrounded
by the river,
waiting
for the blue animal
of the ocean's
Australian
depths,
the animal
born in the deluge
with its hardware store
of sapphire.

Now it rests here
on my table and before
the March waters.
It's coming back
to the sandy lap of the coast,

el vapor del otoño, la lámpara
perdida,
el corazón de niebla.
Y el diente de la bestia,
tatuado por los dedos delicados
del amor,
es la mínima nave
de marfil que regresa.
Ya las vidas
del hombre y sus amores,
su arpón sangriento, todo
lo que fue carne y sal, aroma y oro
para el desconocido marinero
en el mar de la muerte se hizo polvo.
Y sólo de su vida
quedó el dibujo
hecho
por el amor
en el diente terrible
y el mar, el mar
latiendo,
igual que ayer, abriendo
su abanico de hierro,
desatando y atando
la rosa sumergida
de su espuma,
el desafío
de su vaivén eterno.

the vapor of autumn, the lost
lamp,
the heart of fog.
And the beast's tooth,
tattooed by the delicate fingers
of love,
is the minuscule
returning ivory vessel.
Already the lives
of man and his affairs,
the bloody harpoon, everything
that was flesh and salt, aroma and gold
became dust for the unknown sailor
in the sea of death.
And from his life
only the picture
remains,
made for love
on the terrible tooth
and the sea, the pulsating
sea,
like yesterday, opening
its iron fan,
untying and tying
the submerged rose
of its foam,
a challenge
of its eternal fluctuation.

201 / ODE TO A TRAIN IN CHINA

Oda a un tren en China

TRANSLATED BY ILAN STAVANS

La tierra va rodando,	The earth rolls around,
el tren rodando,	the train rolls,
sólo el cielo está quieto.	only the sky is still.
Llanuras y banderas,	Evenness and flags,
maíz, maíz de cabellera verde,	corn, corn with green hair,
de cuando en cuando una bandera roja,	from time to time a red flag,
flor fugaz, amapola del camino.	fleeting flower, road poppy.
El tren cruza corriendo	The train crosses speedily
hacia Tsing Tao,	toward Qingdao,
voy hacia el mar, hacia mi mar, el mismo,	I'm on my way to the sea, toward my sea, the same,
el mismo convertido en misteriosa	the same one turned into mysterious
arena y sal que no conoce mi alma.	sand and salt unacquainted with my soul.
El aire inmóvil recubierto	The motionless air, once again covered
por escamosas nubes, por vapores	by scaly clouds, by vapor
de lluvia gris, por silenciosas cintas	of gray rain, by silent ribbons
que circundan y cubren	circulating and covering
la claridad, la soledad del cielo.	the clarity, the solitude of the sky.
Oh viaje de mi vida,	Oh journey of my life,
una vez más plena luz,	plain light once again,
en plena proporción y poesía	I go as the train rolls around
voy con el tren rodando,	in plain proportion and poetry,
como ayer en la infancia más lluviosa	like yesterday in the rainiest childhood
voy con el tren aprendiendo la tierra	I go as the train rolls capturing the earth
hacia donde el océano me llama.	going where the ocean calls me.

202 / ODE TO TRAINS OF THE SOUTH

Oda a los trenes del Sur

TRANSLATED BY GEORGE D. SCHADE

Trenes del Sur, pequeños
entre
los volcanes,
deslizando
vagones
sobre
riele
mojados
por la lluvia vitalicia
entre montañas
crespas
y pesadumbre
de palos quemados.

Oh
frontera
de bosques goteantes,
de anchos helechos, de agua,
de coronas.
Oh territorio
fresco
recién salido del lago,
del río,
del mar o de la lluvia
con el pelo mojado,
con la cintura llena
de lianas portentosas,

Trains of the South, midgets
among
the volcanoes,
cars
sliding
over
wet-slick
rails
from the lifelong rains,
among undulating
mountains
and sorrowing
for the charred tree stumps.

Oh
frontier
of dripping forests,
vast ferns, water,
and wreaths.
Oh fresh
territory,
newly emerged from lake,
and river,
sea or rain,
with sopping hair,
waist girdled by
prodigious vines,

y entonces	and then
en el medio	in the midst
de las vegetaciones,	of all the greenery,
en la raya	parting
de la multiplicada cabellera,	the heavy head of hair,
un penacho perdido,	a lost streamer,
el plumero	plume
de una locomotora fugitiva	of a fleeting locomotive,
con un tren arrastrando	with a train dragging
cosas vagas	vague things
en la solemnidad aplastadora	through the shattering solemnity
de la naturaleza,	of nature,
lanzando	voicing
un grito	a cry
de ansia,	of anxiety,
de humo,	smoke,
como un escalofrío	like a hot-and-cold chill
en el paisaje!	on the landscape!
Así	So
desde sus olas	from their waves
los trigales	the wheatfields
con el tren pasajero	converse
conversan como	with the passing train
si fuera	as if it were
sombra, cascada o ave	shadow, waterfall, or bird
de aquellas latitudes,	of those latitudes,
y el tren	and the train
su chisperío	spits out
de carbón abrasado	its sparks
reparte	of burning coal,
con oscura	with the dark
malignidad	malice
de diablo	of the devil,
y sigue,	and continues on,
sigue,	and on,

sigue,
trepa el alto viaducto
del río Malleco
como subiendo
por una guitarra
y canta
en las alturas
del equilibrio azul
de la ferretería,
silba el vibrante tren
del fin del mundo
como
si
se despidiera
y se fuera a caer donde
termina
el espacio terrestre,
se fuera a despeñar entre las islas
finales del océano.

Yo voy contigo,
tren, trepidante
tren
de la frontera:
voy a Renaico,
espérame,
tengo que comprar lana en Collipulli,
espérame, que tengo
que descender en Quepe,
el Loncoche, en Osorno,
buscar piñones, telas
recién tejidas, con olor
a oveja y lluvia . . .
Corre,
tren, oruga, susurro,
animalito longitudinal,

and on,
climbing the high viaduct
of the River Malleco
like mounting
a guitar,
singing
on the heights
of the balancing blue
steelwork,
the vibrant train whistles
at the end of the world
just
as if
it were saying good-bye
and going to fall where
earthly space
ends,
and plunge down among the last
islands of the sea.

I'm going with you,
train, rattling
frontier
train:
I'm going to Renaico,
wait, for me,
I have to buy wool in Collipulli,
wait, for I have
to get off in Quepe,
Loncoche and Osorno,
to look for pine nuts, new
woven fabrics, smelling
of sheep and rain . . .
Run
train, caterpillar, murmur,
longitudinal little animal,

entre las hojas
frías
y la tierra fragante,
corre
con
taciturnos
hombres de negra manta,
con monturas,
con silenciosos sacos
de papas de las islas,
con la madera
del alerce rojo,
del oloroso coigue,
del roble sempiterno.

Oh tren
explorador
de soledades,
cuando vuelves
al hangar de Santiago,
a las colmenas
del hombre y su cruzado poderío,
duermes tal vez
por una noche triste
un sueño sin perfume,
sin nieves, sin raíces,
sin islas que te esperan en la lluvia,
inmóvil
entre anónimos
vagones.

Pero
yo, entre un océano
de trenes,
en el cielo
de las locomotoras,

among the cold
leaves
and the fragrant earth,
run
accompanied by
taciturn
men in black mantles
on horseback,
with silent sacks
of potatoes from the islands,
with the wood
of red larch,
of fragrant beech,
of eternal oak.

Oh train,
explorer
of lonely places,
when you return
to the Santiago yards,
to the beehives
of men and their criss-crossed domain,
perhaps you'll sleep
for one sad night
a dream without perfume,
snow or roots,
or islands waiting for you in the rain,
motionless
among anonymous
railroad cars.

But
I, in an ocean
of trains,
in a sky full
of locomotives,

te reconocería
por
cierto aire
de lejos, por tus ruedas
mojadas allá lejos,
y por tu traspasado
corazón que conoce
la indecible, salvaje,
lluviosa,
azul fragancia!

would recognize you,
by
a certain air
from afar, by your wheels
wettened there far away,
and by your grieving
heart that knows
the unspeakable, savage,
rain-drenched
blue fragrance!

203 / ODE TO TWO AUTUMNS

Oda al doble otoño

TRANSLATED BY MARGARET SAYERS PEDEN

Está viviendo el mar mientras la tierra	The sea is alive while the earth
no tiene movimiento:	lies dormant:
el grave otoño	the somber autumn
de la costa	of the coast
cubre	colors
con su muerte	with its death
la luz inmóvil	the still light
de la tierra,	over the land,
pero	but
el mar errante, el mar	the roving sea, the sea
sigue viviendo.	is alive.
No hay	There is not
una	one
sola	single
gota	drop
de	of
sueño,	sleep,
muerte	death
o	or
noche	night
en su	in its
combate:	combat:
todas	all
las máquinas	the machinery
del agua, las azules	of the water, its blue
calderas,	vats,

las crepitantes fábricas
del viento
coronando
las olas
con
sus violentas flores,
todo
vivo
como
las vísceras
del toro,
como
el fuego
en la música,
como
el acto
de la unión amorosa.

Siempre fueron oscuros
los
trabajos
del otoño
en la tierra:
inmóviles
raíces, semillas
sumergidas
en el tiempo
y arriba
sólo
la corola del frío,
un vago
aroma de hojas
disolviéndose
en
oro:
nada.

the roaring factories
of the wind
crowning
the waves
with
violent blossoms,
all is
vital
as
the viscera
of the bull,
as
the fire
of music,
as
the act
of consummated love.

Forever dark have been
the
labors
of autumn
in the earth;
stilled
roots, seeds
buried
in time,
and above,
only
the corolla of the cold,
the vague
aroma of leaves
disintegrating
into
gold:
nothingness.

Un hacha	An ax
en el bosque	in the forest
rompe	shatters
un tronco de cristales,	a crystal trunk,
luego	then
cae	evening
la tarde	falls
y la tierra	and the land
pone sobre su rostro	covers her face with
una máscara	a mask of
negra.	black.
Pero	But
el mar	the sea
no descansa, no duerme, no se ha muerto.	never rests, or sleeps, it never dies.
Crece en la noche	Night's belly
su barriga	swells,
que combaron	warped
las estrellas	by moist stars
mojadas, como trigo en el alba,	like wheat in the dawn
crece,	it swells,
palpita	throbs,
y llora	and weeps
como un niño	like a lost
perdido	child,
que sólo con el golpe	and only with the heat
de la aurora,	of dawn's drum
como un tambor, despierta,	does it awaken,
gigantesco,	gigantic,
y se mueve.	and begin to stir.
Todas sus manos mueve,	All its hands move into action,
su incesante organismo,	its restless organism,
su dentadura extensa,	its long rows of teeth,
sus negocios	its transactions
de sal, de sol, de plata,	of salt, sun, silver,
todo	everything is

lo mueve, lo remueve
con sus arrasadores
manantiales,
con el combate
de su movimiento,
mientras
transcurre
el triste
otoño
de la tierra.

moved and stirred
by its irresistible
currents,
by the furor
of its motion,
while
on the land
the mournful
autumn
reigns.

204 / ODE TO TYPOGRAPHY

Oda a la tipografía

TRANSLATED BY CARLOS LOZANO

Letras largas, severas,	Letters, long, severe,
verticales,	vertical,
hechas	made
de línea	of pure
pura,	line,
erguidas	erect
como el mástil	like a ship's
del navío	mast
en medio	in the middle
de la página	of the page
llena	filled
de confusión y turbulencia,	with confusion and turbulence;
Bodonis	algebraic
algebraicos,	Bodoni,
letras	complete
cabales,	letters,
finas	lean
como lebreles,	as greyhounds,
sometidas	subject
al rectángulo blanco	to the white rectangle
de la geometría,	of Geometry;
vocales	Elzevirian
elzeviras	vowels
acuñadas	cast
en el menudo acero	in the minute steel
del taller junto al agua,	of the printshop by the water,
en Flandes, en el norte	in Flanders, in the North
acanalado,	of the canals,

cifras
del ancla,
caracteres de Aldus,
firmes como
la estatura
marina
de Venecia
en cuyas aguas madres,
como vela
inclinada,
navega la cursiva
curvando el alfabeto:
el aire
de los descubridores
oceánicos
agachó
para siempre el perfil de la escritura.

Desde
las manos medioevales
avanzó hasta tus ojos
esta
N
este 8
doble
esta
J
esta
R
de rey y de rocío.
Allí
se trabajaron
como si fueran
dientes, uñas,
metálicos martillos
del idioma.
Golpearon cada letra,

ciphers
of the anchor;
Aldine characters
firm as
the marine
stature
of Venice,
in whose mother waters,
like a leaning
sail,
navigates the cursive
curving the alphabet:
the air
of the oceanic
discovers
bent down
forever the profile of writing.

From
medieval hands
to your eyes advanced
this
N,
this double
8,
this
J,
this
R
of regal and rain.
There
they were shaped
like
teeth, nails,
metallic hammers
of language.
They beat each letter,

la erigieron,
pequeña estatua negra
en la blancura,
pétalo
o pie estrellado
del pensamiento que tomaba forma
de caudaloso río
y que al mar de los pueblos navegaba
con todo
el alfabeto
iluminando
la desembocadura.
El corazón, los ojos
de los hombres
se llenaron de letras,
de mensajes,
de palabras,
y el viento pasajero
o permanente
levantó libros
locos
o sagrados.
Debajo
de las nuevas pirámides escritas
la letra
estaba viva,
el alfabeto ardiendo,
las vocales,
las consonantes como
flores curvas.
Los ojos
del papel, los que miraron
a los hombres
buscando
sus regalos,
su historia, sus amores,

erected it,
a small black statue
on the whiteness,
a petal
or a starry foot
of thought taking the form
of a swollen river,
rushing to a sea of people
with all
the alphabet
illuminating
the outlet.
The hearts, the eyes
of men
became filled with letters,
messages,
words,
and the passing or permanent
wind
raised mad
or sacred
books.
Beneath
the newly written pyramids
the letter
was alive,
the alphabet burning,
the vowels,
the consonants like
curved flowers.
The paper's
eyes, which looked
at men
seeking
their gifts,
their history, their loves;

extendiendo	extending
el tesoro	the accumulated
acumulado,	treasure;
esparciendo de pronto	spreading suddenly
la lentitud de la sabiduría	the slowness of wisdom
sobre la mesa	over the printer's word
como una baraja,	like a deck of cards;
todo	all
el humus	the secret
secreto	humus
de los siglos,	of the ages,
el canto, la memoria,	song, memories,
la revuelta,	revolt,
la parábola ciega,	blind parable,
de pronto	suddenly
fueron	were
fecundidad,	fecundity,
granero,	granary,
letras,	letters,
letras	letters
que caminaron	that travelled
y encendieron,	and kindled,
letras	letters
que navegaron	that sailed
y vencieron,	and conquered,
letras	letters
que despertaron	that awakened
y subieron,	and climbed,
letras	letters
que libertaron,	that liberated,
letras	letters
en forma de paloma	dove-shaped
que volaron,	that flew,
letras	letters
rojas sobre la nieve,	scarlet in the snow;

puntuaciones,
caminos,
edificios
de letras
y Villon y Berceo,
trovadores
de la memoria
apenas
escrita sobre el cuero
como sobre el tambor
de la batalla,
llegaron
a la espaciosa nave
de los libros,
a la tipografía
navegante.

Pero
la letra
no fue sólo belleza,
sino vida,
fue paz para el soldado,
bajó a las soledades
de la mina
y el minero
leyó
el volante duro
y clandestino,
lo ocultó en los repliegues
del secreto
corazón
y arriba,
sobre la tierra,
fue otro
y otra
fue su palabra.

punctuation,
roads,
buildings
of letters,
and Villon and Berceo,
troubadours
of memory
faintly
written on leather
as on battle
drum,
arrived
at the spacious nave
of books,
at the sailing
typography.

Yet
the letter
was not beauty alone,
but life,
peace for the soldier;
it went down to the solitudes
of the mine,
and the miner
read
the hard and
clandestine leaflet,
hid it in the folds
of the secret
heart
and above,
on earth,
he was different
and different
was his word.

La letra
fue la madre
de las nuevas banderas,
las letras
procrearon
las estrellas
terrestres
y el canto, el himno ardiente
que reúne
a los pueblos,
de
una
letra
agregada
a otra
letra
y a otra,
de pueblo a pueblo fue sobrellevando
su autoridad sonora
y creció en la garganta de los hombres
hasta imponer la claridad del canto.

The letter
was the mother
of the new banners;
the letters
begot
the terrestrial
stars
and the song, the ardent hymn
that unites
peoples;
from
one
letter
added
to another
letter
and another,
from people to people went bearing
its sonorous authority,
and welling in the throats of men
it imposed the clarity of the song.

Pero,
tipografía,
déjame
celebrarte
en la pureza
de tus
puros perfiles,
en al redoma
de la letra
O,
en el fresco
florero
de la
Y

But,
typography,
let me
celebrate you
in the purity
of your
pure profiles,
in the retort
of the letter
O,
in the fresh
flower vase
of the
Greek

griega,
en la
Q
de Quevedo
(cómo puede pasar
mi poesía
frente a esa letra
sin sentir el antiguo escalofrío
del sabio moribundo?),
a la azucena
multi
multiplicada
de la

V
de victoria,
en la
E
escalonada
para subir al cielo,
en la
Z
con su rostro de rayo,
en la P
anaranjada.

Amor,
amo
las letras
de tu pelo,
la
U
de tu mirada,
las
S
de tu talle.

Y,
in the
Q
of Quevedo
(how can my poetry
pass
before that letter
and not feel the ancient shudder
of the dying sage?),
in the lily
multiplied
of the

V
of victory,
in the
E
echeloned
to climb to heaven,
in the
Z
with its thunderbolt face,
in the orange shaped
P.

Love,
I love
the letters
of your hair,
the
U
of your glance,
the
S
of your figure.

En las hojas
de la joven primavera
relumbra el alfabeto
diamantino,
las esmeraldas
escriben tu nombre
con iniciales frescas de rocío.
Mi amor,
tu cabellera
profunda
como selva o diccionario
me cubre
con su totalidad
de idioma
rojo.
En todo,
en la estela
del gusano
se lee,
en la rosa se lee,
las raíces
están llenas de letras
retorcidas
por la humedad del bosque
y en el cielo
de Isla Negra, en la noche,
leo,
leo
en
el firmamento frío
de la costa,
intenso,
diáfano de hermosura,
desplegado,
con estrellas capitales
y minúsculas

In the leaves
of the young springtime
sparkles the diamantine
alphabet;
emeralds
write your name
with the fresh initials of dew.
My love,
your hair
profound
as jungle or dictionary
covers me
with its totality
of red
language.
In everything,
in the wake
of the worm,
one reads,
in the rose, one reads,
the roots
are filled with letters
twisted
by the dampness of the forest
and in the heavens
of the Black Isle, in the night,
I read,
read
in
the cold firmament
of the coast,
intense,
diaphanous with beauty
unfurled,
with capital
and lower case stars

y exclamaciones
de diamante helado,
leo, leo
en la noche de Chile
austral, perdido
en las celestes soledades
del cielo,
como en un libro
leo
todas
las aventuras
y en la hierba
leo,
leo
la verde, la arenosa
tipografía
de la tierra agreste,
leo
los navíos, los rostros
y las manos,
leo
tu corazón
en donde
viven
entrelazados
la inicial
provinciana
de tu nombre
y
el arrecife
de mis apellidos.
Leo
tu frente,
leo
tu cabellera

and exclamations
of frozen diamond;
I read, read
in the night of austral
Chile, lost
in the celestial solitudes
of heaven,
as in a book
I read
all
the adventures
and in the grass
I read,
read
the green, the sandy
typography
of the rustic earth,
I read
the ships, the faces
and the hands,
I read
your heart
where
live
entwined
the provincial
initial
of your name
and
the
reef
of my surnames.
I read
your forehead,
I read
your hair

y en el jazmín
las letras
escondidas
elevan
la incesante
primavera
hasta que yo descifro
la enterrada
puntuación
de la amapola
y la letra
escarlata
del estío:
son las exactas flores de mi canto.
Pero,
cuando
despliega
sus rosales
la escritura,
la letra
su esencial
jardinería,
cuando lees
las viejas y las nuevas
palabras, las verdades
y las exploraciones,
te pido
un pensamiento
para el que las ordena
y las levanta,
para el que para
el tipo,
para el linotipista
con su lámpara
como un piloto
sobre

and in the jasmine
the hidden
letters
elevate
the unceasing
springtime
until I decipher
the buried
punctuation
of the poppy
and the scarlet
letter
of summer:
they are the exact flowers of my song.
But,
when
writing
unfolds
its roses,
and the letter
its essential
gardening,
when you read
the old and the new
words, the truths
and the explorations,
I beg
a thought
for the one who orders
and raises them,
for the one who sets
type,
for the linotypist
and his lamp
like a pilot
over

las olas del lenguaje	the waves of language
ordenando	ordering
los vientos y la espuma,	winds and foam,
la sombra y las estrellas	shadow and stars
en el libro:	in the book:
el hombre	man
y el acero	and steel
una vez más reunidos	once more united
contra el ala nocturna	against the nocturnal wing
del misterio,	of mystery,
navegando,	sailing,
horadando,	perforating,
componiendo.	composing.
Tipografía,	Typography,
soy	I am
sólo un poeta	only a poet
y eres	and you are
el florido	the flowery
juego de la razón,	play of reason,
el movimiento	the movement
de los alfiles	of the chess bishops
de la inteligencia.	of intelligence.
No descansas	You rest
de noche	neither night
ni de invierno,	nor winter,
circulas	you circulate
en las venas	in the veins
de nuestra	of our
anatomía	anatomy
y si duermes	and if you sleep,
volando	flying
durante	during
alguna noche o huelga	some night or strike
o fatiga o ruptura	or fatigue or break
de linotipia	of linotype,

bajas de nuevo al libro
o al periódico
como nube
de pájaros al nido.
Regresas
al sistema,
al orden
inapelable
de la inteligencia.

Letras,
seguid cayendo
como precisa lluvia
en mi camino.
Letras de todo
lo que vive
y muere,
letras de luz, de luna,
de silencio,
de agua,
os amo,
y en vosotras
recojo
no sólo el pensamiento
y el combate,
sino vuestros vestidos,
sentidos
y sonidos:
A
de gloriosa avena,
T
de trigo y de torre
y
M
como tu nombre
de manzana.

you go down anew to the book
or newspaper
like a cloud
of birds to their nest.
You return
to the system,
to the unappealable
order
of intelligence.

Letters,
continue to fall
like precise rain
along my way.
Oh, letters of all
that lives
and dies,
letters of light, of moon,
of silence,
of water,
I love you,
and in you
I gather
not only thought
and combat,
but your dress,
senses,
and sounds:
A
of glorious avena,
T
of trigo and tower,
and
M
like your name
of manzana.

205 / ODE TO VALPARAÍSO

Oda a Valparaíso

TRANSLATED BY MARGARET SAYERS PEDEN

Valparaíso,	Valparaíso,
qué disparate	what a clown
eres,	you are,
qué loco,	what a madman,
puerto loco,	crazy port,
qué cabeza	what a head
con cerros,	lumped with hills,
desgreñada,	tousled hair,
no acabas	always
de peinarte,	combing,
nunca	never
tuviste	time
tiempo de vestirte,	to put your clothes on,
siempre	life
te sorprendió	always takes you
la vida,	by surprise,
te despertó la muerte,	death has caught you
en camisa,	in your shirtsleeves,
en largos calzoncillos	in long, polka-dotted
con flecos de colores,	drawers,
desnudo	caught you naked
con un nombre	with only a hat
tatuado en la barriga,	and a name
y con sombrero,	tattooed on your belly,
te agarró el terremoto,	when the earthquake grabbed you
corriste	you ran in all directions,
enloquecido,	crazed,

te quebraste las uñas,
se movieron
las aguas y las piedras,
las veredas,
el mar,
la noche,
tú dormías
en tierra,
cansado
de tus navegaciones,
y la tierra,
furiosa,
levantó su oleaje
más tempestuoso
que el vendaval marino,
el polvo
te cubría
los ojos,
las llamas
quemaban tus zapatos,
las sólidas
casas de los banqueros
trepidaban
como heridas ballenas,
mientras arriba
las casas de los pobres
saltaban
al vacío
como aves
prisioneras
que probando las alas
se desploman.

Pronto,
Valparaíso,
marinero,

you tore your fingernails,
water and rock
shook,
sidewalks,
sea, and
night,
you slept
on the ground,
exhausted
from your wild gyrations,
and earth,
infuriated,
launched new waves
wilder than
the wildest storm at sea,
dust
covered
your eyelids,
flames
scorched your shoes,
the solid
houses of the bankers
heaved and pitched
like wounded whales,
while above,
the houses of the poor
leapt
into the void
like captive
birds
that, trying their wings,
plummet to the ground.

Soon,
Valparaíso,
hardy sailor,

te olvidas	you brush away
de las lágrimas,	your tears,
vuelves	you hang the houses
a colgar tus moradas,	on your hills again,
a pintar puertas	paint your doors
verdes,	green,
ventanas	your windows
amarillas,	yellow,
todo	your rubble
lo transformas en nave,	becomes a ship,
eres	the refurbished
la remendada proa	prow
de un pequeño,	of a small but
valeroso	courageous
navío.	craft.
La tempestad corona	The storm crowns
con espuma	your humming cords
tus cordeles que cantan	with sea foam,
y la luz del océano	the ocean light
hace temblar camisas	trembles on shirts
y banderas	and flags, you sway,
en tu vacilación indestructible.	but you are indestructible.
Estrella	You are
oscura	from afar
eres	a dark
de lejos,	star,
en la altura de la costa	your light shines
resplandeces	high in the hills of the coast
y pronto	and suddenly
entregas	you reveal
tu escondido fuego,	your hidden fire,
el vaivén	the coming and going
de tus sordos callejones,	in your muted alleyways,
el desenfado	the confidence of
de tu movimiento,	your milling activity,

la claridad
de tu marinería.
Aquí termino, es esta
oda,
Valparaíso,
tan pequeña
como una camiseta
desvalida,
colgando
en tus ventanas harapientas,
meciéndose
en el viento
del océano,
impregnándose
de todos
los dolores
de tu suelo,
recibiendo
el rocío
de los mares, el beso
del ancho mar colérico
que con toda su fuerza
golpeándose en tu piedra
no pudo
derribarte,
porque en tu pecho austral
están tatuadas
la lucha,
la esperanza,
la solidaridad
y la alegría
como anclas
que resisten
las olas de la tierra.

the glory
of your ships and sailors.
Here, Valparaíso,
I end
this ode,
as insignificant
as a tattered
undershirt
hanging in one of
your ragged windows,
flapping
in the ocean
breeze,
absorbing
all
the sorrows
of your soil,
welcoming
the sea dew,
the kiss
of the vast, irate sea that
pounding with all its might
against your rocks
could not
destroy you,
because on your austral chest
are tattooed
struggle,
hope,
solidarity,
and joy,
anchors
that withstand
the shock waves of the earth.

206 / ODE TO A VILLAGE MOVIE THEATER

Oda a un cine de pueblo

TRANSLATED BY MARGARET SAYERS PEDEN

Amor mío,	Come, my love,
vamos	let's go to the movies
al cine del pueblito.	in the village.
La noche transparente	Transparent night
gira	turns
como un molino	like a silent
mudo, elaborando	mill, grinding out
estrellas.	stars.
Tú y yo entramos	We enter the
al cine	tiny theater, you and I,
del pueblo, lleno de niños	a ferment of children
y aroma de manzanas.	and the strong smell of apples.
Son las antiguas cintas,	Old movies
los	are
sueños ya gastados.	secondhand dreams.
La pantalla ya tiene	The screen is the color
color de piedra o lluvias.	of stone, or rain.
La bella prisionera	The beautiful victim
del villano	of the villain
tiene ojos de laguna	has eyes like pools
y voz de cisne,	and a voice like a swan;
corren	the fleetest
los más vertiginosos	horses in the world
caballos	career
de la tierra.	at breakneck speed.

Los vaqueros
perforan
con sus tiros
la peligrosa luna
de Arizona.
Con el alma
en un hilo
atravesamos
estos
ciclones
de violencia,
la formidable
lucha
de los espadachines en la torre,
certeros como avispas,
la avalancha emplumada
de los indios
abriendo su abanico en la pradera.

Muchos
de los muchachos
del pueblo
se han dormido,
fatigados del día en la farmacia,
cansados de fregar en las cocinas.

Nosotros
no, amor mío.
No vamos a perdernos
este sueño
tampoco:
mientras
estemos
vivos
haremos nuestra

Cowboys
make
Swiss cheese of
the dangerous Arizona
moon.
Our hearts
in our mouths,
we thread our way
through
these
cyclones
of violence,
the death-defying
duel of the swordsmen in the tower,
unerring as wasps,
the feathered avalanche
of Indians,
a spreading fan on the prairie.

Many of the
village
boys and girls
have fallen asleep,
tired after a day in the shop,
weary of scrubbing kitchens.

Not we,
my love,
we'll not lose
even this one
dream;
as long
as we
live
we will claim

toda	every minute
la vida verdadera,	of reality,
pero también	but claim
los sueños:	dreams as well:
todos	we
los sueños	will dream
soñaremos.	all the dreams.

207 / ODE TO A VIOLIN IN CALIFORNIA

Oda al violín de California

TRANSLATED BY KEN KRABBENHOFT

Como piedra en la costa
de California, un día
caí, desamparado:
la mañana era un látigo amarillo,
la tarde era una ráfaga
y llegaba la noche
como una copa limpia
colmada por estrellas y frescura.

Oh firmamento
grávido, tembloroso
pecho de estatua azul
sobre los arrabales mexicanos,
y allí en la costa
con
aquella tristeza transeúnte,
con una soledad de palo seco,
consumido y quemado,
tirado en el vaivén
de la marea
a la siniestra sal de California.

Entonces, en la noche
subió la voz
de un violín
flaco
y pobre:

One day I fell like a stone
upon the California
coast, on my own and out of luck.
Morning came, a yellow whiplash,
and evening a gust of wind.
Night came
like an immaculate bowl
overflowing with stars and newness.

O pregnant
sky, blue sculpture's
breast trembling
above Mexico's borders,
and on the shore
alone there with
only the wayfarer's sadness,
a withered stick all alone,
wrung out and blistered,
washed up
on California's sinister salt shore
by the tide's whim.

Suddenly the voice of a violin,
thin
and hungry,
floated
on the evening air

era como un aullido
de perro vagabundo
que me lloraba y me buscaba,
era
la compañía,
el hombre que aullaba,
era otra soledad sobre la arena.

like a stray dog's
howling.
It mourned for me, it sought me out:
it was
my companion,
it was mankind howling,
it was someone else's loneliness upon the sand.

Busqué el violín nocturno
calle por calle negra,
casa por casa oxidada,
estrella por estrella:
se perdía,
callaba,
y era de pronto un surtidor,
un fuego
de Bengala en la noche salobre,
era una red de fósforo sonoro,
una espiral de dimensión sonora,
y yo por calle y calle
buscando
el hilo
del violín oscuro,
la raíz sumergida en el silencio
hasta que en una
puerta
de taberna
el hombre estaba con su
violín pobre.

I sought that violin in the night.
I searched street by pitch-black street,
went house by weathered house,
star by star.
It faded
and fell silent
then suddenly surged,
a flare
in the brackish night.
It was a pattern of incendiary sound,
a spiral of musical contours,
and I went on searching
street by street
for the dark violin's
lifeline,
the source submerged in silence.
Finally, there
he was,
at the entrance to a bar:
a man and his
hungry violin.

Ya el último borracho
tambaleaba
hacia los dormitorios del navío,
las mesas ultrajadas
despedían las copas:
tampoco allí

The last drunk
weaved homeward
to a bunk on board a ship,
and violated tables
shrugged off empty glasses.
Nobody was left waiting,

esperaba nada a nadie:
el vino había partido,
la cerveza dormía,
y en la puerta
el violín con su raído
compañero,
volando,
volando
sobre la noche sola,
con una sola escala
de plata y de lamento,
con una sola red que sacaba
del cielo
fuego errante, cometas, trovadores,
y yo semidormido,
tragado por la boca
del estuario
toqué el violín, las cuerdas
madres de aquellos solitarios
llantos,
la madera gastada
por tantos dedos sumergidos,
reconocí la suavidad, el tacto
del instrumento puro, construido,
aquel violín de pobre
era familia,
era pariente mío,
no sólo por sonoro,
no sólo porque pudo levantar
su aullido
entre hostiles estrellas,
sino porque aprendió
desde su nacimiento
a acompañar perdidos,
a cantar para errantes.

and nobody was on the way.
The wine had left for home,
the beer was sound asleep,
and in the doorway
soared
the violin with its ragged
companion,
it soared
over the lonely night,
on a solitary scale
sounding of silver and complaint,
a single theme that wrung
from the sky
wandering fire, comets, and troubadors,
and I played my violin
half asleep,
held fast in the estuary's
mouth, the strings
giving birth to those desolate
cries,
the wood worn smooth
by the plunging of many fingers.
I honored the smoothness, the feel
of a perfect instrument, perfectly assembled.
That hungry man's violin
was like family to me,
like kin,
and not just because of its sound,
not just because it raised
its howling
to the angry stars,
no: because it had grown up
learning
how to befriend lost souls
and sing songs to wandering strangers.

208 / ODE TO THE VOYAGER ALBATROSS

Oda a un albatros viajero

TRANSLATED BY MARGARET SAYERS PEDEN

Un gran albatros
gris
murió aquel día.
Aquí cayó
en las húmedas
arenas.
En este
mes
opaco, en
este día
de otoño plateado
y lloviznero,
parecido
a una red
con peces fríos
y agua
de mar.
Aquí
cayó
muriendo
el ave magna.

Era
en
la muerte
como una cruz negra.
De punta a punta de ala

A great gray
albatross
died the other day.
Here's where it fell
upon the wet
sands.
In this
gloomy
month, on
a silvery,
drizzly
autumn
day
like a web
of cold fish
and seawater.
This
is where
it fell
dying,
the *magna avis*.

It
was
in death
a cross of black.
The wings spanned

tres metros de plumaje	three feathered meters,
y la cabeza curva	the head curved
como un gancho	like a hook,
con los ojos ciclónicos	the cyclonic eyes were
cerrados.	tightly sealed.
Desde Nueva Zelandia	From New Zealand
cruzó todo el océano	it had crossed an ocean
hasta	to die
morir en Chile.	in Chile.
Por qué? Por qué? Qué sal,	Why? Why? What salt,
qué ola, qué viento	what wave, what wind could
buscó en el mar?	it have sought in the sea?
Qué levantó su fuerza	Why pit its strength
contra todo	against all
el espacio?	space?
Por qué su poderío	Why test
se probó en las más duras	its powers in the harshest
soledades?	solitudes?
O fue su meta	Or was its goal
la magnética rosa	the magnet
de una estrella?	of a star?
Nadie	No one
podrá saberlo, ni decirlo.	will ever know, or tell.
El océano en este	No island breaks
ancho sendero	this broad
no tiene	expanse
isla ninguna,	of ocean,
y el albatros errante	and the albatross, tracing
en la interplanetaria	a parabola
parábola	of victorious flight
del victorioso vuelo	between planets,
no encontró sino días,	encountered only days,
noches, agua,	nights, water,

soledades,
espacio.

Él, con sus alas, era
la energía,
la dirección, los ojos
que vencieron
sol y sombra:
el ave
resbalaba en el cielo
hacia
la más
lejana
tierra
desconocida.

Pájaro extenso, inmóvil
parecías
volando
entre los continentes
sobre mares perdidos,
un solo
temblor de ala,
un ágil
golpe de campana y pluma:
así cambiaba apenas
tu majestad el rumbo
y triunfante seguías
fiel en el implacable,
desierto
derrotero.

Hermoso eras girando
apenas
entre la ola y el aire,
sumergiendo la punta

solitude, and
space.

In flight, the bird was
energy,
direction, eyes
conquering
sun and shadow,
as it
slipped
through the skies
toward
the farthest
unknown
land.

Far-ranging bird, aloft
you seemed
suspended
between continents
over lost seas,
a flick
of a wing,
a bell clap
of feathers:
majestically, you changed
your course a fraction
and, triumphant and true,
continued on your implacable,
lonely
route.

How beautiful you were,
wheeling
between wave and air,
trailing the tip

de tu ala en el océano
o sentádote en medio
de la extensión marina
con las alas cerradas como un cofre
de secretas alhajas,
balanceado
por las
solitarias
espumas
como una profecía
muda
en el movimiento de los salmos.

Ave albatros, perdón,
dije, en silencio,
cuando lo vi extendido,
agarrotado
en la arena, después
de la inmensa
travesía.
Héroe, le dije, nadie
levantará sobre la tierra
en una
plaza de pueblo
tu arrobadora
estatua,
nadie.
Allí tendrán en medio
de los tristes laureles
oficiales
al hombre de bigotes
con levita o espada,
al que mató
en la guerra
a la aldeana,
al que con un solo

of a wing in the sea
or resting in the vast
oceanic expanse,
wings closed like a coffer
of secret jewels,
rocked
on the
lonely
foam
like a mute
prophecy
in the movement of the psalms.

I'm sorry, albatross,
I thought
when I saw you lying
rigid
on the sand after
your intrepid
crossing.
Hero, I said, no one
will erect
on the soil
of some public plaza
your inspiring
statue,
no one.
Instead, amid
somber official laurels
will be installed
a mustached man
in frock coat or with sword,
a man who killed
a peasant woman
in the war,
a man who with a single

obús sangriento
hizo polvo
una escuela
de muchachas,
al que usurpó
las tierras
de los indios,
o al cazador
de palomas, al
exterminador
de cisnes negros.

Sí,
no esperes,
dije
al rey del viento,
al ave de los mares,
no esperes
un túmulo
erigido
a tu proeza,
y mientras
tétricos ciudadanos
congregados en torno a tus despojos
te arrancaban
una pluma, es decir,
un pétalo, un mensaje
huracanado,
yo me alejé
para que,
por lo menos,
tu recuerdo,
sin piedra, sin estatua,
en estos versos vuele
por vez postrera contra
la distancia
y quede así cerca del mar tu vuelo.

bloody shell
demolished
a school for
little girls,
a man who usurped
the Indians'
lands,
a hunter
of doves,
exterminator
of black swans.

Oh
no,
I said
to the king of the wind,
the bird of the seas,
don't expect
them to erect
a monument
to your feats;
and while
melancholy spectators
gathered around your remains,
plucking
a feather,
a petal, a message
from a hurricane,
I walked away,
so that,
at least,
your memory,
without a stone, without a statue,
might on these lines fly
for that last time into
space
and your flight near to the sea.

Oh, capitán oscuro,
derrotado en mi patria,
ojalá que tus alas
orgullosas
sigan volando sobre
la ola final, la ola de la muerte.

Oh, dark captain,
defeated in my country,
may your proud
wings
still soar above
the final wave, the wave of death.

209 / ODE TO WALT WHITMAN

Oda a Walt Whitman

TRANSLATED BY ILAN STAVANS

Yo no recuerdo
a qué edad,
ni dónde,
si en el gran Sur mojado
o en la costa
temible, bajo el breve
grito de las gaviotas,
toqué una mano y era
la mano de Walt Whitman:
pisé la tierra
con los pies desnudos,
anduve sobre el pasto,
sobre el firme rocío
de Walt Whitman.

Durante
mi juventud
toda
me acompañó esa mano,
ese rocío,
su firmeza de pino patriarca, su extensión
de pradera,
y su misión de paz circulatoria.

Sin
desdeñar
los dones
de la tierra,

I don't remember
at what age,
or where,
in the great wet south
or on the fearsome
coast, under the brief
scream of seagulls,
I touched a hand and it was
Walt Whitman's hand:
I stepped on soil
with bare feet,
I walked on grass,
on Walt Whitman's
firm dew.

During
my whole
youth,
that hand accompanied me,
its dew,
the firmness of its patriarchal pine, its
broadness of prairies,
its mission of circulatory peace.

Without
rejecting
the earth's
gifts,

la copiosa
curva del capitel,
ni la inicial
purpúrea
de la sabiduría,
tú
me enseñaste
a ser americano,
levantaste
mis ojos
a los libros,
hacia
el tesoro
de los cereales:
ancho,
en la claridad
de las llanuras,
me hiciste ver
el alto
monte
tutelar. Del eco
subterráneo,
para mí
recogiste
todo,
todo lo que nacía,
cosechaste
galopando en la alfalfa,
cortando para mí las amapolas,
visitando
los ríos,
acudiendo en la tarde
a las cocinas.

Pero no sólo
tierra
sacó a la luz

the spire's
copious curve,
or the initial
purple
wisdom,
you
taught me
how to be an American.
You lifted
my eyes
to books,
toward
the treasure
of grain:
wide,
in the clarity
of plains,
you made me
see the soaring,
tutelary mountain.
From the subterranean
echo,
you collected
everything
for me,
everything born
you harvested
galloping in the alfalfa,
gathering poppies for me,
visiting
rivers,
appearing in kitchens
in the afternoon.

Not only did
your shovel
bring earth

tu pala;	to light:
desenterraste	you unearthed
al hombre,	man
y el	and the
esclavo	humiliated
humillado	slave,
contigo, balanceando	maligned like you, balancing
la negra dignidad de su estatura,	the black dignity of his height,
caminó conquistando	walking in the conquest
la alegría.	of happiness.
Al fogonero,	To the stoker,
abajo,	in the engine room
en la caldera,	below,
mandaste	you sent
un canastito	a little basket
de frutillas,	filled with fruit.
a todas las esquinas de tu pueblo	To all corners of your land,
un verso	your verse
tuyo llegó de visita	traveled for a visit;
y era como un trozo	it was like a piece
de cuerpo limpio	of clean body,
el verso que llegaba,	your migrating verse,
como	like
tu propia barba pescadora	your own fisherman's beard
o el solemne camino de tus piernas de acacia.	or the solemn road of your acacia legs.
Pasó entre los soldados	Your bard's silhouette
tu silueta	passed among the soldiers,
de bardo, de enfermero,	the nurse,
de cuidador nocturno	the night watchman
que conoce	who knows
el sonido	the sound
de la respiración en la agonía	of agony's dying breath
y espera con la aurora	and waits with daybreak
el silencioso	for the quiet
regreso	return
de la vida.	of life.

Buen panadero!
Primo hermano mayor
de mis raíces,
cúpula
de araucaria,
hace
ya
cien
años
que sobre el pasto tuyo
y sus germinaciones,
el viento
pasa
sin gastar tus ojos.

Nuevos
y crueles años en tu patria:
persecuciones,
lágrimas,
prisiones,
armas envenenadas
y guerras iracundas,
no han aplastado
la hierba de tu libro,
el manantial vital
de su frescura.
Y, ay!
los
que asesinaron
a Lincoln
ahora
se acuestan en su cama,
derribaron
su sitial
de olorosa madera
y erigieron un trono
por desventura y sangre
salpicado.

Good baker!
My older cousin
of the same lineage,
cupola
of araucaria pine,
it's
a hundred
years
already
since wind
blew
over your grass
without
diminishing your eyes.

New
and cruel years in your homeland:
persecutions,
tears,
prisons,
poisoned weapons
and furious wars
haven't smashed
the grass of your book,
the vital well
of your freshness.
And, ay!
those
who killed
Lincoln
now
lie in his bed.
They brought down
his seat of honor,
made of fragrant wood,
instead raising a throne
sprinkled with
misbegotten blood.

Pero
canta en
las estaciones
suburbanas
tu voz,
en
los
desembarcaderos
vespertinos
chapotea
como
un agua oscura
tu palabra,
tu pueblo
blanco
y negro,
pueblo
de pobres,
pueblo simple
como
todos
los pueblos,
no olvida
tu campana:
se congrega cantando
bajo
la magnitud
de tu espaciosa vida:
entre los pueblos con tu amor camina
acariciando
el desarrollo puro
de la fraternidad sobre la tierra.

But
your voice
sings
in
the
suburban
stations,
your word
dabbles
in the afternoon
ports like
dark water,
your people,
black
and white,
in poverty,
your people,
like
all people,
won't forget
your bell:
they
congregate
singing
under
the magnitude
of your spacious life:
your love walks
among them,
caressing
the clean growth
of humankind on earth.

210 / ODE TO THE WALTZ OVER THE WAVES

Oda al vals sobre las olas

TRANSLATED BY ILAN STAVANS

Viejo vals, estás vivo
latiendo
suavemente
no a la manera
de un
corazón enterrado,
sino como el olor
de una planta profunda,
tal vez como el aroma
del olvido.

No conozco
los
signos
de la música,
ni sus libros sagrados,
soy un
pobre poeta
de las calles
y sólo
vivo y muero
cuando
de los sonidos enlutados
emerge sobre un mar de madreselva
la miel
antigua,
el baile coronado
por un ramo celeste de palmeras.

Old waltz, you're alive
gently
beating
not like
a
buried heart,
but like the smell
of a deep plant,
perhaps like the aroma
of forgetfulness.

I don't know
the
signs
of music
or its sacred books,
I'm a
poor poet
of the street
and I only
live and die
when
from the mourning sounds
the ancient
honey
emerges over a honeysuckle sea,
the dance crowned
with a celestial branch of palm trees.

Oh, por las enramadas,
en la arena
de aquella costa, bajo
aquella luna,
bailar contigo el vals
de las espumas
apretando tu talle
y a la sombra
del cielo y su navío
besar sobre tus párpados tus ojos
despertando
el rocío
dormido en el jazmín fosforescente!

Oh, vals de labios puros
entreabiertos
al vaivén
amoroso
de las olas,
oh corazón
antiguo
levantado
en la nave
de la música,
oh vals
hecho
de humo,
de palomas,
de nada,
que vives
sin embargo
como una cuerda fina,
indestructible,
trenzada con
recuerdos
imprecisos,

Oh, through the canopy,
in the sand
of that coast, under
that moon,
to dance the waltz
of the foam with you
pressing your waist
and under the shadow
of the sky and its ship
to kiss over your eyelids your eyes
awakening
the dew
sleeping in phosphorescent jasmine!

Oh, waltz of pure lips
half-opened
to the amorous
swaying
of the waves,
oh ancient
heart
raised
from the craft
of music,
oh waltz
made
of smoke,
of doves,
of nothing,
living
nevertheless
like a fine string,
indestructible,
plaited with
imprecise
memories,

con soledad, con tierra,
con jardines!

Bailar contigo, amor,
a la fragante
luz
de aquella luna,
de aquella antigua
luna,
besar, besar tu frente
mientras rueda
aquella
música
sobre las olas!

with solitude, with earth,
with gardens!

To dance with you, my love,
under the fragrant
light
of that moon,
of that old
moon,
to kiss, kiss your forehead
while that
music
rolls
over the waves!

211 / ODE TO A WATCH AT NIGHT

Oda a un reloj en la noche

TRANSLATED BY W. S. MERWIN

En la noche, en tu mano
brilló como luciérnaga
mi reloj.
Oí
su cuerda:
como un susurro seco
salía
de tu mano invisible.
Tu mano entones
volvió a mi pecho oscuro
a recoger mi sueño y su latido.

El reloj
siguió cortando el tiempo
con su pequeña sierra.
Como en un bosque
caen
fragmentos de madera,
mínimas gotas, trozos
de ramajes o nidos,
sin que cambie el silencio,
sin que la fresca oscuridad termine,
así
siguió el reloj cortando
desde tu mano invisible,
tiempo, tiempo,
y cayeron

At night, in your hand
my watch shone
like a firefly.
I heard
its ticking:
like a dry rustling
coming
from your invisible hand.
Then your hand
went back to my dark breast
to gather my sleep and its beat.

The watch
went on cutting time
with its little saw.
As in a forest
fragments
of wood fell,
little drops, pieces
of branches or nests
without silence changing,
without the cool darkness ending,
so
the watch went on cutting
from its invisible hand
time, time,
and minutes

minutos como hojas,
fibras de tiempo roto,
pequeñas plumas negras.

Como en el bosque
olíamos raíces,
el agua en algún sitio desprendía
una gotera gruesa
como uva mojada.
Un pequeño molino
molía noche,
la sombra susurraba
cayendo de tu mano
y llenaba la tierra.
Polvo,
tierra, distancia
molía y molía
mi reloj en la noche,
desde tu mano.

Yo puse
mi brazo
bajo tu cuello invisible,
bajo su peso tibio
y en mi mano
cayó el tiempo,
la noche,
pequeños ruidos
de madera y de bosque,
de noche dividida,
de fragmentos de sombra,
de agua que cae y cae:
entonces
cayó el sueño
desde el reloj y desde
tus dos manos dormidas,

fell like leaves,
fibres of broken time,
little black feathers.

As in the forest
we smelled roots,
the water somewhere released
a fat plopping
as of wet grapes.
A little mill
milled night,
the shadow whispered
falling from your hand
and filled the earth.
Dust,
earth, distance,
my watch in the night
ground and ground
from your hand.

I placed
my arm
under your invisible neck,
under its warm weight,
and in my hand
time fell,
the night,
little noises
of wood and of forest,
of divided night,
of fragments of shadow,
of water that falls and falls:
then
sleep fell
from the watch and from
both your sleeping hands,

cayó como agua oscura
de los bosques,
del reloj
a tu cuerpo,
de ti hacia los países,
agua oscura,
tiempo que cae
y corre
adentro de nosotros.

Y así fue aquella noche,
sombra y espacio, tierra
y tiempo,
algo que corre y cae
y pasa.

Y así todas las noches
van por la tierra,
no dejan sino un vago
aroma negro,
cae una hoja,
una gota
en la tierra
apaga su sonido,
duerme el bosque, las aguas,
las praderas,
las campanas,
los ojos.

Te oigo y respiras,
amor mío,
dormimos.

it fell like a dark water
from the forests,
from the watch
to your body,
out of you it made the nations,
dark water,
time that falls
and runs
inside us.

And that was the way it was that night,
shadow and space, earth
and time,
something that runs and falls
and passes.

And that is the way all the nights
go over the earth,
leaving nothing but a vague
black odour, a leaf falls,
a drop
on the earth,
its sound stops,
the forest sleeps, the waters,
the meadows,
the fields,
the eyes.

I hear you and breathe,
my love,
we sleep.

212 / ODE TO THE WATERFALL

Oda a la cascada

TRANSLATED BY ILAN STAVANS

De pronto, un día	Early one day,
me levanté temprano	I suddenly woke up
y te di una cascada.	and gave you a waterfall.
De todo	Of everything
lo que existe	that is
sobre la tierra,	on earth,
piedras	stones,
edificios,	buildings,
claveles,	carnations,
de todo	of everything
lo que vuela en el aire,	sailing the air,
nubes,	clouds,
pájaros,	birds,
de todo	everything
lo que existe	existing
bajo la tierra,	underground,
minerales,	minerals,
muertos,	the dead,
no hay	there is
nada tan fugitivo,	nothing so fugitive,
nada que cante	nothing that sings
como una cascada.	like a waterfall.
Ahí la tienes:	There it is:
ruge	it roars
como leona blanca,	like a white lioness,
brilla	shines

como la flor del fósforo,	like the phosphorescent flower,
sueña	dreams
con cada uno de tus sueños,	with each of your dreams,
canta	sings
en mi canto	in my song,
dándome	giving me
pasajera platería.	a fleeting silver set.
Pero	Yet
trabaja	it works as well,
y mueve	churning
la rueda	the mill
de un molino	wheel,
y no sólo	and not only
es herido crisantemo,	does it become a wounded chrysanthemum,
sino realizadora	it produces
de la harina,	flour too:
madre del pan que comes	mother of the bread we eat
cada día.	daily.
Nunca	What I've given you
te pesará lo que te he dado	will never weigh on you
porque siempre	because
fue tuyo	it was
lo que te di, la flor o la madera,	always yours, flower and wood,
la palabra o el muro	word and wall,
que sostienen	sustaining
todo el amor errante que reposa	all the errant love that stays,
ardiendo en nuestras manos,	burning in our hands;
pero de cuanto	yet of all
te di,	I've given you,
te doy,	I now add,
te entrego,	I will deliver you
será esta	this
secreta	secret
voz	water
del agua	voice,

la que un día	which one day
dirá en su idioma cuanto	will say, in its own language, whatever
tú y yo callamos,	you and I concealed:
contará nuestros besos	it will count our kisses
a la tierra,	to the earth,
a la harina,	the flour;
seguirá	it will keep on
moliendo	grinding
trigo,	wheat,
noche,	night,
silencio,	silence,
palabras,	words,
cuentos,	stories,
canto.	song.

213 / ODE TO WATERING

Oda para regar

TRANSLATED BY ILAN STAVANS

Sobre la tierra, sobre los pesares,
agua desde tu mano
para el riego
y parece que caen
arqueándose
otras aguas,
no las de la ciudad para las bocas,
para las ollas, sino que
regando
la manguera
trae aguas escondidas
del oculto, del fresco
corazón enramado de la tierra.

De allí
sale este hilo,
se desarrolla en agua,
se multiplica en gotas,
se dirige a la sed de las lechugas.

Del polvo y de las plantas
un nuevo aroma
crece
con el agua.
Es un olor mojado
de astro verde,
es la resurrección de la frescura,

Over the earth, over grief,
water from your hand
for watering
and it seems as if
other water
falls in arcs,
not in cities for mouths,
for pots, but,
while watering,
the hose
brings hidden waters
from the hidden fresh
heart spiraling up from the earth.

From there,
this trickle emerges,
evolving into water,
multiplied in drops,
aired out toward the lettuces' thirst.

From dust and plants,
a new aroma
grows
with the water.
It's the wet scent
of a green star,
it's the resurrection of freshness,

la fragancia perdida
del corazón remoto
huérfano de los bosques,
y crece el agua
como
la música en tus manos:
con fuerza cristalina
construyes una lanza
transparente
que ataca, empapa y mueve
su comunicación con las raíces.

La acción del agua silba,
chisporrotea, canta,
desenreda
secretas fibras, sube
y cae como copa
desbordada,
limpia las hojas hasta
que parecen campanas
en la lluvia,
atormenta los viajes
del insecto,
deja caer sobre la cabecita
de un ave sorprendida
un chaparrón de plata,
y vuela
y baja
hasta que tu jardín o tu sembrado,
el rayo de tus rosas
o la piel genital de la magnolia,
agradecen
el don
recto
del agua
y tú, con tu manguera,

lost fragrance
of a lost heart
orphaned among the trees,
and water grows
like
music in your hands:
with crystalline force,
you build a spear,
translucent:
it attacks, soaks, and moves
in communication with the roots.

Water's action whistles,
splutters, sings,
untangles
secret fibers, vises,
falls like an overflowing
cup,
cleaning the leaves till
they look like bells
in the rain,
it torments the insect's
journeys,
prompts a silver downpour
over the tiny head
of a stunned bird,
it takes off
and lands
until your garden or your planted field,
the ray of your roses,
or the magnolia's genital skin
give thanks
for the upright
gift
of water,
and you, with your hose,

rodeado
por las emanaciones de tu huerto,
por la humedad del suelo, coronado
como el rey de una isla
por la lluvia,
dominador de todos
los elementos,
sabes,
al guardar la manguera,
y enrollarla
como una
purísima serpiente,
sabes que por sobre ti, sobre tus ramas
de roble polvoriento,
agua de riego, aroma,
cayó mojando tu alma:
y agradeces el riego que te diste.

surrounded
by the emanations of your garden,
by the wetness of the soil,
king of the island
crowned by the rain,
master of all
elements,
you know,
while you put your hose away,
winding it,
like the purest of snakes,
you know that over you, over your branches
of dusty oak,
water for crops and aroma
descended to fill your soul:
and you give thanks to the watering
that you have given yourself.

214 / ODE TO THE WATERMELON

Oda a la sandía

TRANSLATED BY ILAN STAVANS

El árbol del verano
intenso,
invulnerable,
es todo cielo azul,
sol amarillo,
cansancio a goterones,
es una espada
sobre los caminos,
un zapato quemado
en las ciudades:
la claridad, el mundo
nos agobian,
nos pegan
en los ojos
con polvareda,
con súbitos golpes de oro,
nos acosan
los pies
con espinitas,
con piedras calurosas,
y la boca
sufre
más que todos los dedos:
tienen sed
la garganta,
la dentadura,
los labios y la lengua:

The tree of summer,
intense,
invulnerable,
is all blue sky,
yellow sun,
exhaustion dripping.
It's a sword
above the roads,
a burned shoe
in the cities:
clarity and the world
overwhelm us,
hit us
in the eye
with dust,
with sudden blows of gold;
they harass
our feet
with thorns,
with heated stones,
and the mouth
suffers
more than all the toes:
the throat
is thirsty,
the teeth,
the lips and tongue:

queremos
beber las cataratas,
la noche azul,
el polo,
y entonces
cruza el cielo
el más fresco de todos
los planetas,
la redonda, suprema
y celestial sandía.

Es la fruta del árbol de la sed.
Es la ballena verde del verano.

El universo seco
de pronto
tachonado
por este firmamento de frescura
deja caer
la fruta
rebosante:
se abren sus hemisferios
mostrando una bandera
verde, blanca, escarlata,
que se disuelve
en cascada, en azúcar,
en delicia!

Cofre del agua, plácida
reina
de la frutería,
bodega
de la profundidad, luna
terrestre!
Oh pura,
en tu abundancia

we want
to drink waterfalls,
the blue night,
the pole,
and just then
the coolest of all
planets
crosses the sky,
the rounded, supreme
and celestial watermelon.

It's the fruit from the tree of thirst.
It's the green whale of summer.

The dry universe,
suddenly
marked
by this firmament of
coolness,
allows the fruit
to drop:
its hemispheres open,
showing a flag
—green, white, scarlet—
dissolving itself
in cascades, sugar,
delight!

Water coffer,
placid fruit
queen,
warehouse
of depth,
earthly moon!
Oh, purity
incarnate,

se deshacen rubíes
y uno
quisiera
morderte
hundiendo
en ti
la cara,
el pelo,
el alma!
Te divisamos
en la sed
como
mina o montaña
de espléndido alimento,
pero
te conviertes
entre la dentadura y el deseo
en sólo
fresca luz
que se deslíe,
en manantial
que nos tocó
cantando.
Y así
no pesas
en la siesta
abrasadora,
no pesas,
sólo
pasas
y tu gran corazón de brasa fría
se convirtió en el agua
de una gota.

rubies fall apart
in your abundance.
We would like
to bite you,
sinking
the face,
the hair,
the soul
into you!
Thirsty,
we see you
like
a mine or mountain
of splendid food,
but
you transform
between our teeth and desire
into
fresh light
that unleashes us,
becoming
a spring
that touches us,
singing.
And then,
you're weightless
in the all-embracing
siesta,
only
passing by,
and your great heart of cold coal
is transformed into water
contained in a single drop.

215 / ODE TO THE WATERS OF THE PORT

Oda a las aguas de puerto

TRANSLATED BY ILAN STAVANS

Nada del mar flota en los puertos	Nothing from the sea but broken drawers
sino cajones rotos,	float on the port,
desvalidos sombreros	destitute hats
y fruta fallecida.	and dead fruit.
Desde arriba	From above
las grandes aves negras	large black birds
inmóviles, aguardan.	wait, motionless.
El mar se ha resignado	The sea is now resigned
a la inmundicia,	to filthiness,
las huellas digitales del aceite	the tactile footprints of oil
se quedaron impresas en el agua	remain printed on the water
como	as if
si alguien hubiera andado	someone had wandered around
sobre las olas	the waves
con pies oleaginosos,	with oleaginous feet,
la espuma	the foam
se olvidó de su origen:	had forgotten its origins:
ya no es sopa de diosa	it no longer is a goddess soup
ni jabón de Afrodita,	nor Aphrodite soap;
es la orilla enlutada	it's a cook's
de una cocinería	disposable shore,
con flotantes, oscuros,	with floating, obscure,
derrotados repollos.	defeated cabbage.
Las altas aves negras	High above,
de sutiles	the tall black birds
alas como puñales	of subtle

esperan
en la altura,
pausadas, ya sin vuelo,
clavadas
a una nube,
independientes
y secretas
como
litúrgicas tijeras,
y el mar que se olvidó de su marina,
el espacio del agua
que desertó
y se hizo
puerto,
sigue solemnemente examinado
por un comité frío
de alas negras
que vuela sin volar,
clavado al cielo
blindado, indiferente,
mientras el agua sucia balancea
la herencia vil caída de las naves.

wings like daggers
await,
pausing, with no more flight,
nailed
onto a cloud,
independent
and secret,
like
liturgical scissors,
and the sea forgot its marine life,
it deserted
the space of water,
becoming
a port,
continuing to be solemnly examined
by a cold committee
of dark algae
flying without flying,
nailed to the sky,
encased, indifferent,
while the filthy water balances
the vile legacy descending from the boats.

216 / ODE TO THE WAVE

Oda a la ola

TRANSLATED BY ILAN STAVANS

Otra vez a la ola	Once more my verse goes
va mi verso.	toward the wave.
No puedo	I can't
dejar mil veces mil,	stop singing
mil veces, ola,	to you, wave, a thousand times a thousand,
de cantarte,	a thousand times,
oh novia fugitiva del océano,	oh fugitive bride of the ocean,
delgada	slim
venus	green
verde	Venus
levantas	you raise
tu campana	your bell
y en lo alto	and topple
derribas	lilies
azucenas.	at the top.
Oh	Oh
lámina	incessant
incesante	sheet
sacudida	shaken
por	by
la	the
soledad	loneliness
del viento,	of the wind,
erigida como una	erect like a
estatua	see-through

transparente	statue
mil veces mil	a thousand times a thousand
cristalizada, cristalina,	crystallized, crystalline,
y luego	and then
toda la sal al suelo:	all the salt thrown to the ground:
el movimiento	movement
se convierte	turns you
en espuma	into foam
y de la espuma el mar	and the sea foam
se reconstruye	is turgidly reconstructed
y de nuevo resurge la turgencia.	and redone again.
Otras veces,	On other occasions,
caballo,	horse,
yegua pura,	pure mare,
ciclónica	cyclonic
y alada,	and winged,
con las crines	with the horsehair
ardiendo de blancura	burning in whiteness
en la ira del aire	in the ire of the air
en movimiento,	in movement,
resbalas, saltas, corres	you slip, jump, run,
conduciendo el trineo	driving the sled
de la nieve marina.	of the sea's snow.
Ola, ola, ola,	Wave, wave, wave,
mil veces mil	a thousand times a thousand
vencida, mil	defeated, a thousand
veces mil erecta	times a thousand erected
y derramada:	and spilled:
viva	alive
la ola,	wave,
mil veces siempreviva	a thousand times immortal,
la ola.	wave.

217 / ODE TO THE WHEAT OF INDIGENOUS PEOPLE

Oda al trigo de los indios

TRANSLATED BY ILAN STAVANS

Lejos	I was born
nací,	far away,
más lejos	farther away
de donde tú naciste.	than you were born.
Yo nací	I was born
lejos,	far away,
lejos,	far away,
en la	in the
mojada	wet
y	and
roja	red
Araucanía,	Araucanía
y	and
en	in
el verano	the red
rojo	summer
de mi infancia	of my childhood,
se movía la tierra:	the earth moved:
un peñasco,	a large rock,
un árbol espinoso,	a thorny tree,
una quebrada:	a gorge:
era un indio,	I was an Indian,

un indio
que venía
en su caballo.

Fui a los cerros, crucé,
las desembocaduras,
los abruptos, heridos
territorios,
los lagos
encendidos
bajo
sus diademas nevadas,
mi tierra
verde y roja,
sonora
y pura
como
una campana,
tierra,
tierra,
canelos,
un perfume
indecible
de raíces
tan profundo
como
si la tierra
fuera una sola rosa
humedecida.

Y entonces
más arriba
estaba el trigo,
el trigo de los indios,
el último, el menguado,

an Indian
who, riding his horse,
arrived.

I went to the hills, crossed,
the river's mouths,
the abrupt, injured
territories,
the lit
lakes
under
their snowy hairbands,
my land
green and red
resonant
and pure
like
a bell,
land,
land,
cinnamon tree,
unspeakable
perfume
made of roots
as deep
as
if the land
were a single, moistened
rose.

And then
higher up,
was the wheat,
the Indians' wheat,
the remaining, diminished,

el harapiento
oro
de la pobre Araucanía.
Vi llegar los caciques,
dura cara,
ralos bigotes,
ponchos
menoscabados,
y no me sonreían
porque
para el último rey
soy extranjero.
Era
la cosecha del trigo.
Paja
seca
volaba,
la trilladora
ardía
y las pobres espigas
desgranaban
el último,
el hambriento,
el raído
oro
del pan
de la pobre Araucanía.

Las indias,
sentadas
como cántaros
de greda,
miraban desde
el tiempo,
desde el agua,
remotas.

ragged
gold
of poor Araucanía.
I saw caciques arrive,
hard faces,
sparse mustaches,
overused
ponchos,
and they didn't smile at me,
because
I'm a foreigner
to the last king.
It was
wheat harvest.
Dry
straw
flew around,
the threshing machine
boiled hot
and the poor spikes
spouted
the last,
hungry
scraped
gold
from the bread
of poor Araucanía.

The Indian women,
sitting
with clay
pitchers,
looked
remotely
from time immemorial,
from water.

A veces
en el círculo
del trigo
un grito
o una
quemante carcajada
eran como dos piedras
que caían
en el agua.
Los sacos
se llenaban
de cereal, de pronto
la trilladora
detenía
su jadeo
y los indios
sentados
como sacos
de tierra
y los sacos
de trigo
como espectros
de la antigua Araucanía,
testigo
de la pobreza, mudos,
vigilantes,
y arriba
el cielo
duro,
la piedra azul del cielo,
y abajo
tierra pobre y lluviosa,
trigo pobre
y los sacos:
los espectros
de mi patria.

Sometimes
in the circle
of wheat
a scream
or
burning laugh
were like two stones
falling
on water.
The sacks
were filled
with cereal, suddenly
the threshing machine
stopped
the panting
and the Indians
seated
like sacks
of earth
and the sacks
of wheat
like ghosts
of ancient Araucanía,
a witness
to poverty, mute,
watchful,
and above
the harsh
sky,
the blue stone of the sky,
and below
poor and rainy land,
poor wheat
and the sacks:
the ghosts
of my homeland.

Recuerdo
aquellas tierras
saqueadas
por jueces
y ladrones,
la cosecha,
los indios
del verano
con menos tierra y trigo
en cada estío,
mirando
la terrible
trilladora,
el desgranado
pan de las sementeras,
allí arriba,
en mi tierra,
en la montaña,
y
abajo
los feudales,
sus abogados y su policía,
matándolos
con papeles,
arrinconándolos
con sentencias, providencias,
exhortos,
los curas
aconsejándoles el cielo
con mejores terrenos
para el trigo.

Aquella zona verde
y roja,
nieve, arboledas,
aquella tierra con

I remember
those lands
ransacked
by judges
and thieves,
the harvest,
the Indians
of summer
each autumn
with less land and less wheat,
looking
at the terrible
threshing machine,
the threshed
bread of the sown land,
there above,
in my land,
in the mountain
and,
below,
the feudal lords,
their lawyers and police,
killing them
with papers,
cornering them
with judgments, commands,
request letters,
the priests
recommending afterlife
with better soil
for planting wheat.

That green and red
zone,
snow, woods,
that land with

ramos de avellano,	branches from hazel trees,
que son	which are
como los brazos de una estrella,	like the arms of a star,
fue	was
mi cuna, mi razón,	my cradle, my reason,
mi nacimiento,	my birth,
y ahora	and now
les pregunto:	I ask them:
a quién le doy el trigo,	whom shall I give the wheat to,
a quién le dejo	whom shall I leave with
el oro,	the gold,
de quiénes	the land belongs
es la tierra?	to whom?
Araucanos,	Araucanos,
padres	fathers
de la nación,	of the nation,
amigos enemigos	enemy friends
del español Ercilla:	of the Spaniard Ercilla:
otro	another
poeta	poet
viene	arrives
cantando:	with his song:
ya nunca más	the war
la guerra,	no more,
sino el trigo,	but the wheat,
ya nunca más la sangre,	the blood no more,
sino el último	but the last
pan de sus hermanos,	bread of his brothers,
la última	the last
cosecha	harvest
para	for
su pobre	the poor
pueblo.	people.
Otro	Another
poeta	poet

llega
ahora
a defender
la espiga
y sube
por los cerros
espinosos,
cruza
los lagos acostados
bajo el fuego
de los viejos volcanes
y se sienta
entre
sacos
silenciosos
esperando
la luz
de la batalla,
reclamando en su canto
la justicia,
pidiendo patria
para sus hermanos,
reconquistando
el trigo
de los indios.

now
arrives
to defend
the spike of wheat
and climbs
the thorny
hills,
crosses
the reclining lakes
under the fire
of the ancient volcanoes
and sits down
amid
silent
sacks
waiting
for the light
of battle,
reclaiming justice
in his song,
asking for a homeland
for his brothers,
reconquering
the wheat
of the indigenous people.

218 / ODE TO WINE

Oda al vino

TRANSLATED BY ILAN STAVANS

Vino color de día,	Wine the color of day,
vino color de noche,	wine the color of night,
vino con pies de púrpura	wine with your feet of purple
o sangre de topacio,	or topaz blood,
vino,	wine,
estrellado hijo	starry child
de la tierra,	of earth,
vino, liso	wine, smooth
como una espada de oro,	like a golden sword,
suave	soft,
como un desordenado terciopelo,	like disorderly velvet,
vino encaracolado	spiral-seashelled
y suspendido,	and floating wine,
amoroso,	amorous,
marino,	marine,
nunca has cabido en una copa,	you've never been contained in a goblet,
en un canto, en un hombre,	a song, a man,
coral, gregario eres,	you are choral, gregarious,
y cuando menos, mutuo.	and, at least, mutual.
A veces	Sometimes
te nutres de recuerdos	you feed on mortal
mortales,	memories,
en tu ola	your wave
vamos de tumba en tumba,	carries us from tomb to tomb,
picapedrero de sepulcro helado,	stonecutter of frozen sepulcher,
y lloramos	and we weep
lágrimas transitorias,	transient tears,

pero
tu hermoso
traje de primavera
es diferente,
el corazón sube a las ramas,
el viento mueve el día,
nada queda
dentro de tu alma inmóvil.
El vino
mueve la primavera,
crece como una planta la alegría,
caen muros,
peñascos,
se cierran los abismos,
nace el canto.
Oh tú, jarra de vino, en el desierto
con la sabrosa que amo,
dijo el viejo poeta.
Que el cántaro de vino
al beso del amor sume su beso.

Amor mío, de pronto
tu cadera
es la curva colmada
de la copa,
tu pecho es el racimo,
la luz del alcohol tu cabellera,
las uvas tus pezones,
tu ombligo sella puro
estampado en tu vientre de vasija,
y tu amor la cascada
de vino inextinguible,
la claridad que cae en mis sentidos,
el esplendor terrestre de la vida.

but
your gorgeous
spring dress
is different,
the heart rises through the branches,
the wind provokes the day,
nothing remains
inside your motionless soul.
Wine
stirs the spring,
grows like a plant of joy,
walls fall,
boulders,
abysses close up,
as song is born.
Oh you, jug of wine, in the desert
with the luscious woman I love,
said the old poet.
Let the wine pitcher
add its kiss to the kiss of love.

My love, suddenly
your side
is the full curve
of the goblet,
your breast is the cluster,
your hair light of alcohol,
your nipples grapes,
your navel pure seal
stamped on the vessel of your belly,
and your love a cascade
of inextinguishable wine,
clarity falling on my senses,
earthly splendor of life.

Pero no sólo amor,
beso quemante
o corazón quemado
eres, vino de vida,
sino
amistad de los seres, transparencia,
coro de disciplina,
abundancia de flores.
Amo sobre una mesa,
cuando se habla,
la luz de una botella
de inteligente vino.
Que lo beban,
que recuerden en cada
gota de oro
o copa de topacio
o cuchara de púrpura
que trabajó el otoño
hasta llenar de vino las vasijas
y aprenda el hombre oscuro,
en el ceremonial de su negocio,
a recordar la tierra y sus deberes,
a propagar el cántico del fruto.

Besides, you, wine of life,
are more than love,
burning kiss,
or burned heart,
but
friendship of beings, translucency,
chorus of discipline,
abundance of flowers.
I like on your table,
as people talk,
the light of a bottle
of intelligent wine.
Let them drink it,
let them remember in each
drop of gold
or topaz cup
or spoon of purple
that autumn labored
to fill the vessels with wine,
and in the ceremony of his trade
let the somber man remember
to thank the earth and his duties,
to propagate the canticle of fruit.

219 / ODE TO THE WINGS OF SEPTEMBER

Oda a las alas de septiembre

TRANSLATED BY ILAN STAVANS

He visto entrar a todos los tejados
las tijeras del cielo:
van y vienen y cortan transparencia:
nadie se quedará sin golondrinas.

Aquí era todo
ropa, el aire espeso
como frazada y un vapor de sal
nos empapó el otoño
y nos acurrucó contra la leña.

Es en la costa de Valparaíso,
hacia el sur de la Planta Ballenera:
allí todo el invierno se sostuvo
intransferible con su cielo amargo.

Hasta que hoy al salir
volaba el vuelo,
no paré mientes al principio, anduve
aún entumido, con dolor de frío,
y allí estaba volando,
allí volvía
la primavera a repartir el cielo.

Golondrinas de agosto y de la costa,
tajantes, disparadas
en el primer azul,

I have beheld the scissors of the sky
descending on every roof:
they fly off and on while offering transparency:
no one shall be deprived of swallows.

Everything is cloth
here, the thick air
with a blanket and salty vapor
soaks us with autumn,
huddling us against the wood.

It is on the coast of Valparaíso,
south of Planta Ballenera:
the whole winter was on hold there,
static in its bitter sky.

Until today, as I left
on a rush,
I didn't notice at first stop; I walked,
numbly even, the cold causing me pain.
And there it was, flying,
spring was back,
reimagining the sky.

The swallows of August, on the coast,
decisive, shoot
a primal azure,

saetas del aroma:
de pronto respiré las acrobacias
y comprendí que aquello
era la luz que volvía a la tierra,
las proezas del polen en el vuelo,
y la velocidad volvió a mi sangre.
Volví a ser piedra de la primavera.

Buenos días, señoras golondrinas
o señoritas o alas o tijeras,
buenos días al vuelo del cielo
que volvió a mi tejado:
he comprendido al fin
que las primeras flores
son plumas de septiembre.

arrows of aroma:
I suddenly breathed their acrobatics
and realized it was the light
coming back to earth,
the adventurous pollen on its flight.
Speed returned to my blood.
I once again became stone in spring.

Good morning, she-sparrows
and señoritas and waves and scissors;
good morning to the flight of the sky
coming back to my roof:
I have finally understood
that the first flowers blooming
are the plumes of September.

220 / ODE TO WINTER

Oda al invierno

TRANSLATED BY ILAN STAVANS

Invierno, hay algo	Winter, there is something
entre nosotros,	between us,
cerros bajo la lluvia,	hills under the rain,
galopes	galloping
en el viento,	in the wind,
ventanas	windows
donde se acumuló tu vestidura,	where your clothes accumulated,
tu camisa de fierro,	your iron shirt,
tu pantalón mojado,	your wet pants,
tu cinturón de cuero transparente.	your belt of translucent leather.
Invierno,	Winter,
para otros	for us
eres bruma	you are mist
en los malecones,	at the jetty,
clámide clamorosa,	clamorous cape,
rosa blanca,	white rose,
corola de la nieve,	snow corolla,
para mí, invierno,	for me, winter,
eres	you are
un caballo,	a horse,
niebla te sube del hocico,	fog ascends from your muzzle,
gotas de lluvia caen	raindrops fall
de tu cola,	on your tail,
electrizadas ráfagas	electrified bursts
son tus crines,	are your manes,
galopas	you gallop
interminablemente	endlessly

salpicando de lodo
al transeúnte,
miramos
y has pasado,
no te vemos la cara,
no sabemos
si son de agua de mar
o cordillera
tus ojos, has pasado
como la cabellera
de un relámpago,
no quedó indemne un árbol,
las hojas
se reunieron
en la tierra,
los nidos
quedaron como harapos
en la altura,
mientras tú galopabas
en la luz moribunda del planeta.

Pero eres frío, invierno;
y tus racimos
de nieve negra y agua
en el tejado
atraviesan
las casas
como agujas,
hieren
como cuchillos oxidados.
Nada
te detiene.
Comienzan
los ataques de tos, salen los niños
con zapatos mojados,
en las camas la fiebre

splashing with mud
the passerby,
we look
and you're gone,
we don't see your face,
we don't know
if your eyes are made
of seawater
or cordillera, you've passed
like the head of hair
of lightning,
the tree was not unharmed,
the leaves
gathered
on the ground,
the nests
were left up high
like tatters,
while you were galloping
in the planet's moribund light.

But you are cold, winter;
and your piles
of black snow and water
on the roof
cross
the houses
like needles,
they injure
like rusty knives.
Nothing
stops you.
Cough attacks
begin, children go out
with wet shoes,
fever in beds

es como	is like
la vela de un navío	the sail of a ship
navegando a la muerte,	sailing toward death,
la ciudad de los pobres	the city of the poor
que se quema,	that burns,
la mina	the slippery
resbalosa,	mine,
el combate del viento.	the wind's combat.
Desde entonces,	Since then,
invierno, yo conozco	winter, I know
tu agujereada ropa	your pierced cloths
y el silbato	and the whistle
de tu bocina entre las araucarias	of your horn amid the araucarias
cuando clamas	when you clamor
y lloras,	and cry,
racha en la lluvia loca,	spell of crazy rain,
trueno desenrollado	uncurled thunder
o corazón de nieve.	and heart of snow.
El hombre	The man
se agigantó en la arena,	became a giant on the sand,
se cubrió de intemperie,	protected himself with the outdoors
la sal y el sol vistieron	salt and the sun dressed up
con seda salpicada	with splattered silk
el cuerpo de la nueva nadadora.	the body of a new female swimmer.
Pero	But
cuando viene el invierno	when the winter arrives
el hombre	the man
se hace un pequeño ovillo	makes himself a small clew
que camina	moving
con mortuorio paraguas,	like a funeral umbrella,
se cubre	he covers himself
de alas impermeables,	with waterproof wings,
se humedece	he becomes humid
y se ablanda	and soft

como una miga, acude
a las iglesias,
o lee tonterías enlutadas.
Mientras tanto,
arriba,
entre los robles,
en la cabeza de los ventisqueros,
en la costa,
tú reinas
con tu espada,
con tu violín helado,
con las plumas que caen
de tu pecho indomable.

Algún día
nos reconoceremos,
cuando
la magnitud
de tu belleza
no caiga
sobre el hombre,
cuando
ya no perfores
el techo
de mi hermano,
cuando
pueda acudir a la más alta
blancura de tu espacio
sin que puedas morderme,
pasaré saludando
tu monarquía desencadenada.
Me sacaré el sombrero
bajo la misma lluvia
de mi infancia
porque estaré seguro
de tus aguas:

like a crumb, attends
church,
and reads mourning trifles.
Meanwhile,
above,
amid the oak trees,
at the head of the snowdrifts,
on the coast,
you reign
with your spear,
with your frozen violin,
with the falling plumes
of your indomitable chest.

Someday
we'll recognize each other,
when
the magnitude
of your beauty
won't fall
over man,
when
you will no longer penetrate
my brother's
roof,
when
I will be able to reach
your tallest space of whiteness
without you biting me,
I will pass by while greeting
your unchained monarchy.
I will tip my hat
under the same rain
of my childhood
because I will be sure
of your waters:

ellas lavan el mundo,
se llevan los papeles,
trituran la pequeña
suciedad de los días,
lavan,
lavan tus aguas
el rostro de la tierra
y bajan hasta el fondo
donde
la primavera
duerme.
Tú la estremeces, hieres
sus piernas transparentes,
la despiertas, la mojas,
comienza a trabajar,
barre las hojas muertas,
reúne su fragante
mercancía,
sube las escaleras
de los árboles
y de pronto la vemos
en la altura
con su nuevo vestido
y sus antiguos ojos
verdes.

they wash the world,
take away the papers,
crush the days'
small dirtiness,
wash,
wash your waters
the face of the earth
and descend to the bottom
where
spring
sleeps.
You shake her, injure
her translucent legs,
awake her, wet her,
she starts laboring,
sweeps the dead leaves,
collects their fragrant
merchandise,
climbs the staircase
of the trees
and suddenly we see her
up high
with a new dress
and her old green
eyes.

221 / ODE IN WINTER TO THE MAPOCHO RIVER

Oda de invierno al río Mapocho

TRANSLATED BY JACK SCHMITT

Oh, sí, nieve imprecisa,
oh, sí, temblando en plena flor de nieve,
párpado boreal, pequeño rayo helado
quién, quién te llamó hacia el ceniciento valle,
quién, quién te arrastró desde el pico del águila
hasta donde tus aguas puras tocan
los terribles harapos de mi patria?
Río, por que conduces
agua fría y secreta,
agua que el alba dura de las piedras
guardó en su catedral inaccesible,
hasta los pies heridos de mi pueblo?
Vuelve, vuelve a tu copa de nieve, río amargo,
vuelve, vuelve a tu copa de espaciosas escarchas,
sumerge tu plateada raíz en tu secreto origen
o despéñate y rómpete en otro mar sin lágrimas!
Río Mapocho, cuando la noche llega
y como negra estatua echada

O, yes, imprecise snow,
O, yes, trembling in full snowy blossom,
boreal eyelid, little frozen ray,
who, who called you to the ashen valley,
who, who dragged you from the eagle's beak
down to where your pure waters touch
my country's terrible tatters?
River, why do you convey
cold secret water,
water that the stones' hard dawn
preserved in its inaccessible cathedral,
to the wounded feet of my people?
Return, return to your chalice of snow, bitter river,
return, return to your chalice of spacious frost,
submerge your silvery root in your secret source
or plunge and burst in another tearless sea!
Mapocho River, when night falls
and, like a black recumbent statue,

duerme bajo tus puentes con un racimo negro
de cabezas golpeadas por el frío y el hambre
como por dos inmensas águilas, oh río,
oh duro río parido por la nieve,
por qué no te levantas como inmenso fantasma
o como nueva cruz de estrellas para los
olvidados?
No, tu brusca ceniza corre ahora
junto al sollozo echado al agua negra,
junto a la manga rota que el viento endurecido
hace temblar debajo de las hojas de hierro.
Río Mapocho, adónde llevas
plumas de hielo para siempre heridas,
siempre junto a tu cárdena ribera
la flor salvaje nacerá mordida por los piojos
y tu lengua de frío rasgará las mejillas
de mi patria desnuda?
Oh, que no sea,
oh, que no sea, y que una gota de tu espuma
negra
salte del légamo a la flor del fuego
y precipite la semilla del hombre!

sleeps under your bridges with a black
cluster
of heads smitten by cold and hunger
like two immense eagles, O river,
O harsh river born of the snow,
why don't you rise like an immense
phantom
or a new cross of stars for the forsaken?
No, your brusque ash now runs
beside the sob cast into the black water,
beside the torn sleeve that the cruel wind
makes shiver beneath the iron leaves.
Mapocho River, where do you carry
plumes of ice forever wounded,
will the wildflower blossom forever
bitten by lice beside your purple banks,
with your cold tongue rasping
my naked country's cheeks?
O, let it not be so,
O, let it not be so, and let a drop of your
black foam
leap from the loam to the flower of fire
and precipitate mankind's seed!

222 / ODE TO A WOMAN GARDENING

Oda a la jardinera

TRANSLATED BY MARGARET SAYERS PEDEN

Sí, yo sabía que tus manos eran
el alhelí florido, la azucena
de plata:
algo que ver tenías
con el suelo,
con el florecimiento de la tierra,
pero
cuando
te vi cavar, cavar,
apartar piedrecitas
y manejar raíces
supe de pronto,
agricultora mía,
que
no sólo
tus manos
sino tu corazón
eran de tierra,
que allí
estabas
haciendo
cosas tuyas,
tocando
puertas
húmedas
por donde
circulan

Yes, I knew that your hands were
the sweet dianthus, the silvery
lily:
knew that you were allied
with the soil,
with the flowering of the earth,
but
when
I saw you digging, digging,
removing rocks
and coping with roots,
I knew at once,
my little farmer,
that
not only
your hands
but your heart
were of the earth,
that there
you were
working
your wonders,
touching
moist
doors
where
seeds

las
semillas.

Así, pues,
de una a otra
planta
recién
plantada,
con el rostro
manchado
por un beso
del barro,
ibas
y regresabas
floreciendo,
ibas
y de tu mano
el tallo
de la alstromeria
elevó su elegancia solitaria,
el jazmín
aderezó
la niebla de tu frente
con estrellas de aroma y de rocío.
Todo
de ti crecía
penetrando
en la tierra
y haciéndose
inmediata
luz verde,
follaje y poderío.
Tú le comunicabas
tus semillas,
amada mía,
jardinera roja:

come
and go.

So, from
one
newly planted
plant
to another,
your face
stained
with an earthy
kiss,
you went
back and forth
flowering,
and
from your hand
the stalk
of the amaryllis
raised its solitary elegance,
the jasmine
adorned
the mist of your brow
with stars of aroma and dew.
Everything
grew from you,
penetrating
the earth,
immediately
becoming
green light,
foliage and strength.
You communicated your seeds
to the earth,
my beloved
auburn-haired gardener:

tu mano	your hand
se tuteaba	spoke lovingly
con la tierra	to the earth,
y era instantáneo	and bright budding
el claro crecimiento.	was instantaneous.
Amor, así también	Love, so too
tu mano	your hand
de agua,	of water,
tu corazón de tierra,	your heart of earth,
dieron	lent
fertilidad	fertility
y fuerza a mis canciones.	and force to my songs.
Tocas	You touch
mi pecho	my chest
mientras duermo	while I sleep
y los árboles brotan	and trees bud
de mi sueño.	from my dream.
Despierto, abro los ojos,	Awake, I open my eyes,
y has plantado	and you have planted
dentro de mí	in me
asombradas estrellas	astonished stars
que suben	that soar
con mi canto.	with my song.
Es así, jardinera:	It is true, gardener:
nuestro amor	our love
es	is
terrestre:	earthly:
tu boca es planta de la luz, corola,	your mouth is the plant of light, corolla,
mi corazón trabaja en las raíces.	my heart toils among the roots.

223 / ODE TO WOOD

Oda a la madera

TRANSLATED BY MARGARET SAYERS PEDEN

Ay, de cuanto conozco
y reconozco
entre todas las cosas
es la madera
mi mejor amiga.
Yo llevo por el mundo
en mi cuerpo, en mi ropa,
aroma
de aserradero,
olor de tabla roja.
Mi pecho, mis sentidos
se impregnaron
en mi infancia
de árboles que caían
de grandes bosques llenos
de construcción futura.
Yo escuché cuando azotan
el gigantesco
alerce,
el laurel alto de cuarenta metros.
El hacha y la cintura
del hachero minúsculo
de pronto picotean
su columna arrogante,
el hombre vence y cae
la columna de aroma,
tiembla la tierra, un trueno

Oh, of all I know
and know well,
of all things,
wood
is my best friend.
I wear through the world
on my body, in my clothing,
the scent
of the sawmill,
the odor of red wood.
My heart, my senses,
were saturated
in my childhood
with the smell of trees
that fell in great forests
filled with future buildings.
I heard when they scourged
the gigantic
larch,
the forty-meter laurel.
The ax and the wedge
of the tiny woodsman
begin to bite into
the haughty column;
man conquers and the
aromatic column falls,
the earth trembles, mute

sordo, un sollozo negro
de raíces, y entonces
una ola
de olores forestales
inundó mis sentidos.
Fue en mi infancia, fue sobre
la húmeda tierra, lejos
en las selvas del Sur,
en los fragantes, verdes
archipiélagos,
conmigo
fueron naciendo vigas,
durmientes
espesos como el hierro,
tablas
delgadas y sonoras.
La sierra rechinaba
cantando
sus amores de acero,
aullaba el hilo agudo,
el lamento metálico
de la sierra cortando
el pan del bosque
como madre en el parto,
y daba a luz en medio
de la luz
y la selva
desgarrando la entraña
de la naturaleza,
pariendo
castillos de madera,
viviendas para el hombre,
escuelas, ataúdes,
mesas y mangos de hacha.
Todo
allí en el bosque

thunder, a black sob
of roots, and then
a wave
of forest odors
flooded my senses.
It was in my childhood, on
distant, damp earth
in the forests of the south,
in fragrant green
archipelagoes;
I saw
roof beams born,
railroad ties
dense as iron,
slim and resonant
boards.
The saw squealed,
singing
of its steely love,
the keen band whined,
the metallic lament
of the saw cutting
the loaf of the forest,
a mother in birth throes
giving birth in the midst
of the light
of the woods,
ripping open the womb
of nature,
producing
castles of wood,
houses for man,
schools, coffins,
tables and ax handles.
Everything
in the forest

dormía bajo las hojas mojadas
cuando
un hombre
comienza
torciendo la cintura
y levantando el hacha
a picotear la pura
solemnidad del árbol
y éste
cae,
trueno y fragancia caen
para que nazca de ellos
la construcción, la forma,
el edificio,
de las manos del hombre.
Te conozco, te amo,
te vi nacer, madera.
Por eso
si te toco
me respondes
como un cuerpo querido,
me muestras
tus ojos y tus fibras,
tus nudos, tus lunares,
tus vetas
como inmóviles ríos.
Yo sé
lo que ellos
cantaron
con la voz del viento,
escucho
la noche tempestuosa,
el galope
del caballo en la selva,
te toco y te abres

lies sleeping
beneath moist leaves,
then
a man
begins
driving in the wedge
and hefting the ax
to hack at the pure
solemnity of the tree,
and the tree
falls,
thunder and fragrance fall
so that from them will be born
structures, forms,
buildings,
from the hands of the man.
I know you, I love you,
I saw you born, wood.
That's why
when I touch you
you respond
like a lover,
you show me
your eyes and your grain,
your knots, your blemishes,
your veins
like frozen rivers.
I know
the song
they sang
on the voice of the wind,
I hear
a stormy night,
the galloping
of a horse through deep woods,
I touch you and you open

como una rosa seca
que sólo para mí resucitara
dándome
el aroma y el fuego
que parecían muertos.
Debajo
de la pintura sórdida
adivino tus poros,
ahogada me llamas
y te escucho,
siento
sacudirse
los árboles
que asombraron mi infancia,
veo
salir de ti,
como un vuelo de océano
y palomas,
las alas de los libros,
el papel
de mañana
para el hombre,
el papel puro para el hombre puro
que existirá mañana
y que hoy está naciendo
con un ruido de sierra,
con un desgarramiento
de luz, sonido y sangre.
Es el aserradero
del tiempo,
cae
la selva oscura, oscuro
nace
el hombre,
caen las hojas negras
y nos oprime el trueno,

like a faded rose
that revives for me alone,
offering
an aroma and fire
that had seemed dead.
Beneath
sordid paint
I divine your pores,
choked, you call to me
and I hear you,
I feel
the shuddering
of trees that shaded
and amazed my childhood,
I see
emerge from you
like a soaring wave
or dove
wings of books,
tomorrow's
paper
for man,
pure paper for the pure man
who will live tomorrow
and who today is being born
to the sound of a saw,
to a tearing
of light, sound, and blood.
In the sawmill
of time
dark forests fall,
dark
is born
man,
black leaves fall,
and thunder threatens,

hablan al mismo tiempo
la muerte y la vida,
como un violín se eleva
el canto o el lamento
de la sierra en el bosque,
y así nace y comienza
a recorrer el mundo
la madera,
hasta ser constructora silenciosa
cortada y perforada por el hierro,
hasta sufrir y proteger
construyendo
la vivienda
en donde cada día
se encontrarán el hombre, la mujer
y la vida.

death and life
speak at once
and like a violin rises
the song, the lament,
of the saw in the forest,
and so wood is born
and begins to travel the
world,
until becoming a silent builder
cut and pierced by steel,
until it suffers and protects,
building
the dwelling
where every day
man, wife, and life
will come together.

224 / ODE TO THE YELLOW BIRD

Oda al pájaro sofré

TRANSLATED BY W. S. MERWIN

Te enterré en el jardín:	I buried you in the garden:
una fosa	a grave
minúscula	minute
como una mano abierta,	as an open hand,
tierra	southern
austral,	earth,
tierra fría	cold earth
fue cubriendo	went in covering
tu plumaje,	your plumage,
los rayos amarillos,	the yellow flashes,
los relámpagos negros	the black lightnings
de tu cuerpo apagado.	of your extinguished body.
Del Matto Grosso,	From the Matto Grosso,
de la fértil Goiania,	from fertile Goiania
te enviaron	they sent you,
encerrado.	shut in.
No podías.	You couldn't stand it.
Te fuiste.	You went.
En la jaula	In the cage
con las pequeñas	with the small
patas tiesas,	feet stiff
como agarradas	as though clutching
a una rama invisible,	an invisible branch,
muerto,	dead,
un pobre atado	a poor bunch
de plumas	of extinguished
extinguidas,	feathers

lejos
de los fuegos natales,
de la madre
espesura,
en tierra fría,
lejos.
Ave
purísima,
te conocí viviente,
eléctrico,
agitado,
rumoroso,
una flecha
fragante
era tu cuerpo,
por mi brazo y mis hombros
anduviste
independiente, indómito,
negro de piedra negra
y polen amarillo.
Oh salvaje
hermosura,
la dirección erguida
de tus pasos,
en tus ojos
la chispa
del desafío, pero
así
como una flor es desafiante,
con la entereza
de una terrestre integridad, colmado
como un racimo, inquieto
como un descubridor,
seguro
de su débil arrogancia.

far
from the natal fires,
from the mother thicket,
far
in the cold earth.
Bird
most pure,
I knew you alive,
electric,
excited,
murmurous,
a fragrant
arrow
your body was,
over my arm and my shoulders
you walked
independent, untamed,
blackness of black stone
and pollen yellow.
Oh savage
beauty,
the unbending direction
of your steps,
in your eyes
the spark
of defiance, but
as
a flower is defiant,
with the completeness
of a terrestrial integrity, overflowing
like a flowering branch, restless
as a discoverer,
sure
of your frail arrogance.

Hice mal, al otoño
que comienza
en mi patria,
a las hojas
que ahora desfallecen
y se caen,
al viento Sur, galvánico,
a los árboles duros, a las hojas
que tú no conocías,
te traje,
hice viajar tu orgullo
a otro sol ceniciento
lejos del tuyo
quemante
como cítara escarlata,
y cuando
al aeródromo metálico
tu jaula
descendió,
ya no tenías
la majestad del viento,
ya estabas despojado
de la luz cenital que te cubría,
ya eras
una pluma de la muerte,
y luego,
en mi casa,
fue tu mirada última
a mi rostro, el reproche
de tu mirada indomable.
Entonces,
con las alas cerradas,
regresaste
a tu cielo,
al corazón extenso,

Suffering, to the autumn
as it is beginning
in my country,
to the leaves
that are fading now
and falling,
to the galvanic wind of the South,
to the hard trees, to the leaves
that you did not know,
they brought you,
they made your pride travel
to an ashen sun
other
far from yours
that burns
like a scarlet zither,
and when
your cage
came down
on the metallic aerodrome,
you had already lost
the majesty of the wind,
were already despoiled
of the light from the zenith that had covered you,
already
you were a feather of death,
and then
in my house
your final look
at my face, the reproach
of your untamable regard.
Afterward
with closed wings
you went back
to your sky,
to the spacious heart,

al fuego verde,
a la tierra encendida,
a las vertientes,
a las enredaderas,
a las frutas,
al aire, a las estrellas,
al sonido secreto
de los desconocidos manantiales,
a la humedad
de las fecundaciones en la selva,
regresaste
a tu origen,
al fulgor amarillo,
al pecho oscuro,
a la tierra y al cielo de tu patria.

to the green fire,
to the slopes,
to the trailing vines,
to the fruits,
to the air, to the stars,
to the secret sound
of the unknown springs,
to the moisture
of the conceivings in the forest,
you went back
to your origin,
to the yellow flame,
to the dark breast,
to the earth and sky of your country.

225 / ODE TO YOUR HANDS

Oda a tus manos

TRANSLATED BY ILAN STAVANS

Yo en un mercado	I, in a market
o en un mar de manos	or in a sea of hands,
las tuyas	would recognize
reconocería	yours
como dos aves blancas,	like two white birds,
diferentes	different
entre todas las aves:	from all the birds:
vuelan entre las manos,	they fly among the hands,
migratorias,	migratory,
navegan en el aire,	navigate on the air,
transparentes,	translucent,
pero	but
vuelven	they come back
a tu costado,	to your side,
a mi costado,	to my side,
se repliegan, dormidas, en mi pecho.	they fold in, asleep, on my chest.
Diáfanas son delgadas	They are transparent, slim
y desnudas,	and naked,
lúcidas como	lucid like
una cristalería,	glassware,
y andan	and walk
como	like
abanicos	spritsails
en el aire,	in the air,
como plumas del cielo.	like feathers from heaven.

Al pan también y al agua se parecen,
al trigo, a los países de la luna,
al perfil de la almendra, al pez salvaje
que palpita plateado
en el camino
de los manantiales.
Tus manos van y vienen
trabajando,
lejos, suenan
tocando tenedores,
hacen fuego y de pronto chapotean
en el agua
negra de la cocina,
picotean la máquina aclarando
el matorral de mi caligrafía,
claven en las paredes,
lavan ropa
y vuelven otra vez a su blancura.

Por algo
se dispuso en la tierra
que durmiera y volara
sobre mi corazón
este milagro.

They're like bread and water,
wheat, countries of the moon,
the profile of an almond, the savage fish
palpitating, silvery,
on the road
to the springs.
Your hands, when working,
come and go,
far away, they sound
like tuning forks,
make fire and suddenly splash about
in the black
kitchen water,
peck the typing machine clearing out
the thicket of my calligraphy,
nail on the wall,
wash clothes
and return again to their whiteness.

For some reason,
it was deemed necessary on earth
that this miracle
would sleep and fly
over my heart.

EPILOGUE / THE HOUSE OF ODES

Epílogo: La casa de las odas

TRANSLATED BY ILAN STAVANS

Escribiendo
estas
odas
en este
año mil
novecientos
cincuenta y cinco,
desplegando y tañendo
mi lira obligatoria y rumorosa,
sé lo que soy
y adónde va mi canto.

Comprendo
que el comprador de mitos
y misterios
entre
en mi casa de odas,
hecha
con adobe y madera,
y odie
los utensilios,
los retratos
de padre y madre y patria
en las paredes,
la sencillez
del pan
y del salero.
Pero es así la casa de mis odas.

Writing
these
odes
in this
year one thousand
ninc hundred
fifty-five,
unfolding and strumming
my obligatory and rumor-driven lyre,
I know what I am
and where my song goes.

I realize
the myth and mystery
buyer
might enter
my house of odes,
built
of adobe and wood,
and hate
the utensils,
the portraits
on the wall
of father and mother and country,
the simplicity
of bread
and saltshaker.
But that's how the house of my odes is built.

Yo destroné la negra monarquía
la cabellera inútil de los sueños,
pisé la cola
del reptil mental,
y dispuse las cosas
—agua y fuego—
de acuerdo con el hombre y con la tierra.
Quiero que todo
tenga
empuñadura,
que todo sea
taza o herramienta.
Quiero que por la puerta de mis odas
entre la gente a la ferretería.

Yo trabajo
cortando
tablas frescas,
acumulando miel
en las barricas,
disponiendo
herraduras, arneses,
tenedores;
que entre aquí todo el mundo,
que pregunte,
que pida lo que quiera.

Yo soy del Sur, chileno,
navegante
que volvió
de los mares.

No me quedé en las islas,
coronado.

No me quedé sentado
en ningún sueño.

I dethroned the black monarchy,
the useless hair of dreams,
I stepped on the tail
of the mental reptile
and organized things
—water and fire—
according to man and earth.
I want everything
to have
a handle,
everything to be
cup or tool.
I want people to enter the hardware store
through the door of my odes.

I work
by cutting
fresh boards,
accumulating honey
in kegs,
arranging
horseshoes, armor,
forks:
let everyone come in,
let them ask,
let them request whatever they want.

I am the south, Chilean,
navigator
who returned
from the seas.

I didn't stay crowned
in the islands.

I didn't stay seated
in any dream.

Regresé a trabajar sencillamente
con todos los demás
y para todos.

Para que todos vivan
en ella
hago mi casa
con odas
transparentes.

I simply came back to work
along with everyone else
and for everyone.

So that everyone may live
in it
I make my house
with see-through
odes.

Notes on Neruda's Odes

Neruda identified the odes he wrote by using the word *oda* in their titles. He attached two poems to this production, "The Invisible Man" and "The House of Odes," which he perceived to be introductions to it. The vast majority of Neruda's odes were written during one of his periods of most prolific output, between 1952 and 1957, when he was in his late forties and early fifties, living in Chile with Matilde Urrutia, whom he had met in 1946 and who became his third wife in 1966. Many of the odes describe his life in his house at Isla Negra. There are also odes to places in Santiago and Valparaíso. Alone and with Matilde, Neruda constantly traveled abroad during this period, visiting Brazil, China, Sweden, and Venezuela, among other countries.

In Spanish, the odes were collected in nine volumes first released in four different countries. The following is the full bibliographical information: *Residencia en la tierra* (Santiago: Nascimento, 1933, 176 pages); *Tercera residencia* (Buenos Aires: Editorial Losada, 1947, 111 pages); *Canto general* (Mexico: Talleres Gráficos de la Nación, 1950, 567 pages); *Los versos del Capitán*, published anonymously (Naples, Italy: Imprenta L'Arte Tipografica, 1952, 184 pages); *Odas elementales* (Buenos Aires: Editorial Losada, 1954, 254 pages); *Nuevas odas elementales* (Buenos Aires: Editorial Losada, 1956, 184 pages); *Tercer libro de las odas* (Buenos Aires: Editorial Losada, 1957, 207 pages); *Navegaciones y regresos* (Buenos Aires: Editorial Losada, 1959, 146 pages); and *Plenos poderes* (Buenos Aires: Editorial Losada, 1962, 88 pages). Neruda organized the content in alphabetical order only in four of them: *Odas elementales*, *Nuevas odas elementales*, *Tercer libro de las odas*, and *Navegaciones y regresos*.

For this volume, I used as my ur-text the four volumes of *Obras Completas*, edited by Hernán Loyola, with the advice of Saúl Yurkievich (Barcelona: Galaxia Guttenberg/Círculo de Lectores, 1999). This is considered to be the most authoritative edition of Neruda's oeuvre. For the preparation of the notes, I consulted a handful of critical editions in Spanish, which I found useful for the scholarly apparatus below: *Residencia en la tierra*, edited by Hernán Loyola (Madrid: Cátedra, 1987), *Odas elementales*, edited by Jaime Concha (Madrid: Cátedra, 1997), and *Canto general*, edited by Enrico Mario Santí (Madrid: Cátedra, 1998). And I perused the following three scholarly monographs: Amado Alonso's *Poesía y estilo de Pablo Neruda* (Buenos Aires: Losada, 1940), Alan Sicard's *El pensamiento poético de Pablo Neruda* (Madrid: Gredos, 1981), and David G. Anderson's *On Elevating the Commonplace: A Structural Analysis of the "Odes" of Pablo Neruda* (Valencia, Spain: Albatros Hispanófila Ediciones, 1987).

Neruda's odes in English are featured in the volumes listed below, assorted by date of publication. (I have not included chapbooks in this list; instead, I have made reference to them in pertinent notes.)

Residence on Earth, and Other Poems, translated by Angel Flores. Norfolk, Conn.: New Directions, 1946.

The Elementary Odes of Pablo Neruda, translated by Carlos Lozano. New York: Las Americas, 1961.

A New Decade: 1958–1967, edited by Ben Belitt, translated by Ben Belitt and Alastair Reid. New York: Grove, 1969.

Selected Poems, edited by Nathaniel Tarn, translated by Anthony Kerrigan, Alastair Reid, and Nathaniel Tarn. New York: Delacorte, 1972.

Neruda and Vallejo: Selected Poems, edited by Robert Bly, translated by Robert Bly, John Knoepfle, and James Wright. Boston: Beacon Press, 1971.

The Captain's Verses, translated by Donald D. Walsh. New York: New Directions, 1972.

Residence on Earth, translated by Donald D. Walsh. New York: New Directions, 1973.

Five Decades: A Selection (1925–1970), edited and translated by Ben Belitt. New York: Grove, 1974.

Pablo Neruda: A Basic Anthology, selected by Robert Pring-Mill. Oxford: Dolphin Books, 1975.

Fully Empowered, translated by Alastair Reid. New York: Farrar, Straus and Giroux, 1975.

Selected Odes by Pablo Neruda, translated by Margaret Sayers Peden. Berkeley: University of California Press, 1990; reprinted as *Elemental Odes*. London: Libris, 1991.

Canto General, translated by Jack Schmitt. Berkeley: University of California Press, 1991.

Ode to Common Things, selected and illustrated by Ferris Cook, translated by Ken Krabbenhoft. Boston: Little, Brown, 1994.

Odes to Opposites, selected and illustrated by Ferris Cook, translated by Ken Krabbenhoft. Boston: Little, Brown, 1995.

Neruda's Garden: An Anthology of Odes, translated by María Jacketti. Pittsburgh: Latin American Literary Review Press, 1995.

Fifty Odes, translated by George D. Schade. Austin: Host Publications, 1996.

Full Woman, Fleshly Apple, Hot Moon: Selected Poems of Pablo Neruda, translated by Stephen Mitchell. New York: HarperFlamingo, 1997.

The Poetry of Pablo Neruda, edited by Ilan Stavans. New York: Farrar, Straus and Giroux, 2003.

The Essential Neruda, edited by Mark Eisner. San Francisco: City Lights, 2004.

I Explain a Few Things: Selected Bilingual Poems, edited by Ilan Stavans. New York: Farrar, Straus and Giroux, 2007.

The following spare critical annotations offer context to the composition of the odes. Unlike the poems in *Residence on Earth* and *Canto General*, which have given place to profuse commentary, for the most part the information in these cases is limited because Neruda sought to include everything he wanted readers to know, which was often the bare essentials, in the poems themselves. Still, basic facts are available in the form of date of composition, the place of publication of the Spanish original, the volume in which they were collected, and their English translator, which I have included. If and when appropriate, I have connected some themes in the odes to Neruda's life, politics, and literature, and relevant historical references are established. For the sake of simplicity, I use this nomenclature of abbreviations:

Residencia en la tierra [RT]
Tercera residencia [TR]
Canto general [CG]
Los versos del Capitán [VC]
Odas elementales [OE]
Nuevas odas elementales [NOE]
Tercer libro de las odas [TLO]
Navegaciones y regresos [NR]
Plenos poderes [PP]

Prologue: "The Invisible Man" (Prólogo: "El hombre invisible"), translated by Ilan Stavans. Composed in Europe, perhaps Italy, 11/28/52. Not an ode per se, at least not according to its title, Neruda used it as the introduction to *Odas elementales*. As in "The House of Odes," he employed italics to emphasize the uniqueness of the poem.

1. "Ode to an Abandoned House" ("Oda a la casa abandonada") [TLO], translated by Margaret Sayers Peden. Composed in 1956.

2. "Ode to Acario Cotapos" ("Oda a Acario Cotapos") [PP], translated by Ilan Stavans. Acario Cotapos (1889–1969): Chilean music composer and a friend of Neruda and the other major Chilean poet of the time, Vicente Huidobro, he lived in the United States, France, and Spain.

3. "Ode to Age" ("Oda a la edad") [TLO], translated by Ilan Stavans.

4. "Ode to an Aged Poet" ("Oda al viejo poeta") [TLO], translated by Margaret Sayers Peden. Composed in 1956.

5. "Ode to Air" ("Oda al aire") [OE], translated by Ilan Stavans. Composed 11/30/52 in Neruda's home in Isla Negra, after he returned from Europe to Chile via Argentina.

6. "Ode to the Americas" ("Oda a las Américas") [OE], translated by Margaret Sayers Peden. Composed 12/7/53. The ode is a critique of the foreign policy of the government of the United States toward progressive regimes in Latin America such as those of Jacobo Árbenz Guzmán (1945–51) and Juan José Arévalo (1951–54) in Guatemala and in favor of right-wing dictators such as Fulgencio Batista, who assumed power in Cuba in a coup d'état in 1952. There is a special edition that includes three odes (this, "Oda al libro," and "Oda a la luz"): *Odas/al libro/a las Américas/a la luz* (Caracas: Edición de la Asociación de Escritores Venezolanos, 1959). See also "Ode to Guatemala."

7. "Ode to the Anchor" ("Oda al ancla") [NR], translated by Ilan Stavans. This ode is a celebration of the large anchor resting on the beachfront at Neruda's home in Isla Negra. He acquired the anchor in 1954.

8. "Ode to the Andean Cordillera" ("Oda a la cordillera andina") [NOE], translated by Ilan Stavans.

9. "Ode to Ángel Cruchaga" ("Oda a Ángel Cruchaga") [OE], translated by Ilan Stavans. Composed 7/31/53. Ángel Cruchaga Santa María (1893–1964): Chilean writer; he received the National Prize in Literature in 1948. This ode was published as part of the prologue to *Pequeña antología de Angel Cruchaga Santa María* (Santiago: Talleres de la Escuela Nacional de Artes Plásticas, 1953). In the prologue, Neruda writes: "Like a tolling of black bells, with a prophetic, diametrical trembling and sound, the words of this magus cut across the solitudes of Chile, absorb from the atmosphere various qualities of superstition and rain . . . Like rings of atmosphere at the coming of an autumn dawn, the poems of Ángel come to one frozen in an icy clarity with a certain extraterrestrial or sublunar quivering, clad, as it were, in the skin of the stars. Like the nebulous coffer of embroideries and almost-abstract jewels, still dazzling bright, that produce an unhealthy sadness, they seem to adapt immediately to what one has seen and felt before, to the ancient and the bitter, to darkly sensitive roots that pierce the soul, leaving there all their dolorous needs and painful oblivion."

10. "Ode to the Apple" ("Oda a la manzana") [TLO], translated by Ilan Stavans. Composed in 1956.

11. "Ode to the Araucanian Araucaria" ("Oda a la araucaria araucana") [NOE], translated by Ilan Stavans. Arauco refers simultaneously to the city and municipality of Arauco, Chile. Araucanian Araucaria: evergreen tree that grows 130 feet tall and 7 feet in diameter, native to southern Chile, western Argentina, and southern Brazil. See also "Ode to the Erosion in Malleco Province."

12. "Ode to the Artichoke" ("Oda a la alcachofa") [OE], translated by Ilan Stavans. Composed 4/16/54.

13. "Ode to the Atom" ("Oda al átomo") [OE], translated by Margaret Sayers Peden. Composed at the end of 1954. In this ode Neruda celebrates the spirit of science and technology of the modern age, championing in particular the scientific desire "to rectify errors" that in his view was exemplified by the Soviet Union. See also "Ode to Energy."

14. "Ode to Autumn" ("Oda al otoño") [OE], translated by Ilan Stavans.

15. "Ode to the Azure Flower" ("Oda a la flor azul") [OE], translated by Ilan Stavans. As suggested in the poem, composed in November 1953.

16. "Ode to the Bad Blind Man" ("Oda al mal ciego") [NR], translated by Ilan Stavans.

17. "Ode to Barbed Wire" ("Oda al alambre de púa") [NOE], translated by Ilan Stavans.

18. "Ode to a Beautiful Nude" ("Oda a la bella desnuda") [NOE], translated by Nathaniel Tarn.

19. "Ode to the Bed" ("Oda a la cama") [NR], translated by Ilan Stavans.

20. "Ode to Bees" ("Oda a la abeja") [TLO], translated by Margaret Sayers Peden.

21. "Ode to Bicycles" ("Oda a la bicicleta") [TLO], translated by Margaret Sayers Peden. Composed in 1956.

22. "Ode to Bird Migration" ("Oda a la migración de los pájaros") [TLO], translated by Ilan Stavans. This and the next two odes exemplify Neruda's passion for the birds of his country, also evident in the book *Arte de pájaros* (Art of Birds, 1966).

23. "Ode to the Birds of Chile" ("Oda a las aves de Chile") [OE], translated by Margaret Sayers Peden.

24. "Ode to Bird-Watching" ("Oda a mirar pájaros") [OE], translated by Ilan Stavans.

25. "Ode to a Black Pantheress" ("Oda a la pantera negra") [TLO], translated by Margaret Sayers Peden. Composed 1955 in the small village of Totoral, near El Quisco, Chile.

26. "Ode to the Book I" ("Oda al libro I") [OE], translated by Edward Hirsch. There is a special edition that includes three odes (this, "Oda a las Américas," and "Oda a la luz"): *Odas/al libro/a las Américas/a la luz* (Caracas: Edición de la Asociación de Escritores Venezolanos, 1959).

27. "Ode to the Book II" ("Oda al libro II") [OE], translated by Edward Hirsch.

28. "Ode to a Bouquet of Violets" ("Oda a un ramo de violetas") [TLO], translated by Ilan Stavans. Composed in 1956.

29. "Ode to a Box of Tea" ("Oda a la caja de té") [TLO], translated by Ken Krabbenhoft. Composed in 1955.

30. "Ode to Bread" ("Oda al pan") [OE], translated by Ken Krabbenhoft.

31. "Ode to Broken Things" ("Oda a las cosas rotas") [NR], translated by Ilan Stavans.

32. "Ode to the Building" ("Oda al edificio") [OE], translated by Ilan Stavans.

33. "Ode and Burgeonings" ("Oda y germinaciones") [VC], translated by Donald D. Walsh.

34. "Ode to the Butterfly" ("Oda a la mariposa") [TLO], translated by Ilan Stavans.

35. "Ode to the Carnation" ("Oda al alhelí") [TLO], translated by Ilan Stavans. Composed in 1956.

36. "Ode to the Cat" ("Oda al gato") [NR], translated by Ken Krabbenhoft.

37. "Ode to César Vallejo" ("Oda a César Vallejo"), translated by Ilan Stavans. César Vallejo (1892–1938): Peruvian poet of Catholic faith and communitarian affinities and a friend of Neruda, wrote about his cross-ethnic background and Catholic faith, as well as poverty and oppression. His books include *Los heraldos negros* (The Black Heralds) and *España, aparta de mí este cáliz* (Spain, Take This Chalice from Me). Vallejo's last poetic period concentrated on the Spanish Civil War. He was expelled from Spain and died in Paris. In *Para nacer he nacido* (1978, English 1983), Neruda includes an obituary to Vallejo (published in *Aurora*, Santiago, 8/1/38), in which he describes him thus: "Old warrior of hope, old friend. Is it possible? And what can we do in this world to be worthy of your silent, enduring work, of your private, essential growth? In recent years, brother, your body, your soul, longed for American soil but the flames of Spain held you in France, where no one was more alien. Because you were the American specter—Indian-American, as you preferred to say—of our martyred America, a specter mature in its liberty and its passions. There was something of a mine about you, of a lunar excavation, something earthily profound."

38. "Ode to the Chair" ("Oda a la silla") [NR], translated by Ken Krabbenhoft.

39. "Ode to a Chestnut on the Ground" ("Oda a una castaña en el suelo") [OE], translated by Stephen Mitchell.

40. "Ode to Clarity" ("Oda a la claridad") [OE], translated by Ilan Stavans.

41. "Ode to Clothes" ("Oda al traje") [OE], translated by W. S. Merwin.

42. "Ode to Clouds" ("Oda a las nubes") [TLO], translated by Ken Krabbenhoft.

43. "Ode to the Coastal Flowers" ("Oda a las flores de la costa") [NOE], translated by Ilan Stavans.

44. "Ode to the Color Green" ("Oda al color verde") [TLO], translated by Ilan Stavans. Composed in 1956.

45. "Ode to Conger Chowder" ("Oda al caldillo de congrio") [OE], translated by Margaret Sayers Peden.

46. "Ode to Copper" ("Oda al cobre") [OE], translated by Ilan Stavans.

47. "Ode to a Couple" ("Oda a la pareja") [OE], translated by Margaret Sayers Peden.

48. "Ode to the Cranium" ("Oda al cráneo") [NOE], translated by Margaret Sayers Peden.

49. "Ode to Criticism" ("Oda a la crítica") [OE], translated by Margaret Sayers Peden.

50. "Ode to Criticism II" ("Oda a la crítica II") [NOE], translated by Ilan Stavans.

51. "Ode to a Day of Victories: Seventh of November" ("Oda a un día de victorias: Siete de noviembre") [TR], translated by Donald D. Walsh. This ode is part of the third installment of *Residencia en la tierra*, known as *Tercera Residencia*, written between 1934 and 1945. Donald D. Walsh's translation was published under the title "Seventh of November: Ode to a Day of Victories"; for unifying purposes, I have inverted the title and subtitle.

52. "Ode to a Dead Carob Tree" ("Oda al algarrobo muerto") [TLO], translated by Margaret Sayers Peden. Composed 1/19/56, in Totoral, Córdoba Province, Argentina. See also "Ode to the Storms of Córdoba."

53. "Ode to the Dead Millionaire" ("Oda a un millonario muerto") [TLO], translated by Ilan Stavans.

54. "Ode to the Dictionary" ("Oda al diccionario") [NOE], translated by Ilan Stavans.

55. "Ode to the Displaced Cactus" ("Oda al cactus desplazado") [TLO], translated by Ilan Stavans. Composed in 1956.

56. "Ode to the Diver" ("Oda al buzo") [TLO], translated by Ilan Stavans.

57. "Ode to the Dog" ("Oda al perro") [NR], translated by George D. Schade.

58. "Ode to Don Jorge Manrique" ("Oda a don Jorge Manrique") [NOE], translated by Ilan Stavans. Manrique (circa 1440–1479): Spanish poet who wrote in the tradition of courtly love, known for his work *Coplas a la muerte de su padre* (Stanzas on the Death of His Father). In *Memoirs* (1974, English 1977), Neruda celebrates the durability of Manrique in the work of contemporary Spanish poets such as Rafael Alberti.

59. "Ode to the Earth" ("Oda a la tierra") [OE], translated by Margaret Sayers Peden.

60. "Ode to the Earth II" ("Oda a la tierra II") [NR], translated by Ilan Stavans.

61. "Ode to the Elephant" ("Oda al elefante") [NR], translated by Ilan Stavans. The imagery in this ode is from Neruda's time as Chile's cultural attaché in Sri Lanka, where he wrote *Residence on Earth*. In *Passions and Impressions* (1978, English 1983), edited by Matilde Urrutia and Miguel Otero Silva, Neruda includes an essay titled "The Jungle of Ceylon," where he describes the country's fauna. See "Ode Before the Island of Ceylon."

62. "Ode to Enchanted Light" ("Oda a la luz encantada") [TLO], translated by Mark Strand.

63. "Ode to Energy" ("Oda a la energía") [OE], translated by Ken Krabbenhoft. In this and the "Ode to the Atom," Neruda showcases his view of the advances and handicaps of modernity.

64. "Ode to Envy" ("Oda a la envidia") [OE], translated by Ken Krabbenhoft.

65. "Ode to the Erosion in Malleco Province" ("Oda a la erosión en la provincia de Malleco") [NOE], translated by Ilan Stavans. Malleco Province: one of two provinces in the southern Chilean region of Araucanía.

66. "Odes for Everyone" ("Odas de todo el mundo") [TLO], translated by Margaret Sayers Peden.

67. "Ode to the Eye" ("Oda al ojo") [NOE], translated by Ilan Stavans.

68. "Ode to a Fallen Bell" ("Oda a la campana caída") [NR], translated by George D. Schade.

69. "Ode to Federico García Lorca" ("Oda a Federico García Lorca") [RT], translated by Angel Flores. Federico García Lorca (1898–1936): Spanish poet and playwright from Andalucía killed by the fascists before the Spanish Civil War, he is the author of *Romancero gitano* (Gypsy Romancer, 1928) and *Bodas de sangre* (Blood

Wedding, 1932). This ode is part of the second installment of *Residencia en la tierra*, written between 1933 and 1935.

70. "Ode to the Fertility of the Soil" ("Oda a la fertilidad de la tierra") [OE], translated by Ilan Stavans.

71. "Ode to a Few Yellow Flowers" ("Oda a unas flores amarillas") [TLO], translated by Ilan Stavans.

72. "Ode to Fire" ("Oda al fuego") [OE], translated by Ken Krabbenhoft.

73. "Ode to Firefoot" ("Oda a Pies de Fuego") [NOE], translated by Margaret Sayers Peden.

74. "Ode to the Firewood Car" ("Oda al carro de la leña") [TLO], translated by Ilan Stavans.

75. "Ode to the First Day of the Year" ("Oda al primer día del año") [TLO], translated by Ilan Stavans.

76. "Ode to the Fishing Boat" ("Oda al barco pesquero") [TLO], translated by Ilan Stavans. Composed in 1956.

77. "Ode to the Flower" ("Oda a la flor") [OE], translated by Ilan Stavans.

78. "Ode to the Flowers of Datitla" ("Oda a las flores de Datitla") [TLO], translated by Ilan Stavans. There is a special chapbook edition in Spanish: *Oda a las flores de Datitla* (Santiago: Sintesys, 2002). In 1952, on his way back from Europe, Neruda, along with his lover and future third wife, Matilde Urrutia, took a ship to Montevideo, Uruguay, from where he planned to travel to Chile. On the ship he met Alberto Mantaras, a Uruguayan architect and filmmaker. Mantaras offered them his weekend home in Atlantida, a resort on the Costa de Oro, some twenty-eight miles from Montevideo. Neruda's political beliefs had made him persona non grata in Chile. Matilde continued to Buenos Aires while Neruda discussed the return to his homeland with members of Chile's Communist Party. In the end, Matilde returned to Uruguay, and she and Neruda spent a brief time in Atlantida, which he cryptically nicknamed Datitla because he was still married to Delia del Carril and didn't want her to suspect he was having an affair there. For a while the house served as a museum. It closed in 2008 and was placed on the market as a rental.

79. "Ode to the Fortunate Voyage" ("Oda al viaje venturoso") [TLO], translated by Ilan Stavans. Composed in 1957 after Neruda traveled to Finland and the Soviet Union, returning home with a stop in Uruguay.

80. "Ode to French Fries" ("Oda a las papas fritas") [NR], translated by Ilan Stavans.

81. "Ode to the Gentle Bricklayer" ("Oda al albañil tranquilo") [TLO], translated by Margaret Sayers Peden. Composed in 1956.

82. "Ode to the Globe" ("Oda al globo terráqueo") [TLO], translated by Ilan Stavans.

83. "Ode to the Good Blind Man" ("Oda al buen ciego") [NR], translated by Ilan Stavans.

84. "Ode to Gratitude" ("Oda a las gracias") [NR], translated by Ilan Stavans.

85. "Ode to the Great Wall in the Fog" ("Oda a la gran muralla de la niebla") [NR], translated by Ilan Stavans. Neruda visited the Great Wall of China in 1955. The same year, he visited the Soviet Union and other Communist countries of the Soviet Bloc.

86. "Ode to Guatemala" ("Oda a Guatemala") [OE], translated by Ilan Stavans. Composed in 1954 after the CIA-orchestrated coup d'état in Guatemala in which the democratically elected military figure Jacobo Árbenz Guzmán (1945–51) was replaced by the dictator Juan José Arévalo (1951–54). Amatitlán: town that is a popular destination on the banks of Lake Amatitlán, in the country's Guatemala Department. Dulce River: located within the Izabal Department.

87. "Ode to the Guitar" ("Oda a la guitarra") [NR], translated by Ilan Stavans.

88. "Ode to Happiness" ("Oda a la alegría") [OE], translated by Ilan Stavans.

89. "Ode to the Happy Day ("Oda al día feliz") [OE], translated by Ilan Stavans. Composed 1/10/53 in Atlantida, the resort on Uruguay's Costa de Oro. See the note to "Ode to the Flower."

90. "Ode to a Hare-Boy" ("Oda al niño de la liebre") [NOE], translated by Paul Muldoon.

91. "Ode to Her Scent" ("Oda a su aroma") [NOE], translated by Ilan Stavans.

92. "Ode to Hope" ("Oda a la esperanza") [OE], translated by Ilan Stavans. Composed 12/29/53, exactly a year after "Ode to Sadness."

93. "Ode to the Horse" ("Oda al caballo") [NR], translated by Ilan Stavans.

94. "Ode to the Hummingbird" ("Oda al picaflor") [NOE], translated by Margaret Sayers Peden.

95. "Ode to the Inconsequential Day" ("Oda al día inconsecuente") [NOE], translated by Ilan Stavans.

96. "Ode to Ironing" ("Oda para planchar") [PP], translated by Ilan Stavans.

97. "Ode Before the Island of Ceylon" ("Oda frente a la isla de Ceylán") [NR], translated by Ilan Stavans. Ceylon (Sri Lanka): Neruda held a diplomatic position

there in 1929. His first post was in Rangoon, Burma, in 1927. He also served in Singapore, Argentina, and Spain. See also "Ode to the Elephant."

98. "Ode to Jean Arthur Rimbaud" ("Oda a Jean Arthur Rimbaud") [NOE], translated by Ilan Stavans. Jean Arthur Rimbaud (1854–91): French poet of the Decadent Movement, author of *Une Saison en Enfer* (A Season in Hell). In *Memoirs* (1974, English 1977), Neruda writes of reading Rimbaud in Ceylon along with Quevedo and Proust. He also describes him as "embittered, perpetually wandering . . ."

99. "Ode to Juan Tarrea" ("Oda a Juan Tarrea") [NOE], translated by Ilan Stavans. Rubén Darío (1867–1916): Nicaraguan poet and leader of the literary movement known as Modernismo. He is the author of *Prosas profanas* (Profane Prose) and *Cantos de vida y esperanza* (Songs of Life and Hope). César Vallejo (1892–1938): see "Ode to César Vallejo."

100. "Ode to a Laboratory Technician" ("Oda al laboratorista") [OE], translated by Margaret Sayers Peden.

101. "Ode with a Lament" ("Oda con un lamento") [RT], translated by Donald D. Walsh. This ode is part of the second installment of *Residencia en la tierra*, written between 1933 and 1935.

102. "Ode to a Large Tuna in the Market" ("Oda a un gran atún en el mercado") [TLO], translated by Margaret Sayers Peden. Composed in 1956.

103. "Ode to the Last Voyage of *La Bretona*" ("Oda al último viaje de 'La Bretona'") [NR], translated by Ilan Stavans.

104. "Ode to Laziness" ("Oda a la pereza") [OE], translated by William Carlos Williams.

105. "Ode to the Lemon" ("Oda al limón") [TLO], translated by Stephen Mitchell. Composed in 1956.

106. "Ode to Lenin" ("Oda a Lenin") [NR], translated by Ilan Stavans. Composed in Moscow during the fortieth anniversary of the Soviet Revolution. Vladimir Lenin (1870–1924): Russian revolutionary, political theorist, and creator of the Soviet Communist Party. Neruda received the Stalin Peace Prize in December 1953. Intriguingly, the ode doesn't showcase Lenin as a warrior, as a popular leader. Instead, it presents him in a restive mode as he is fishing in a lake. V. Uliánov: Lenin's full name was Vladimir Ilyich Ulyanov Lenin. Lake Lakhta, a.k.a. Lake Razliv: located in the Primorsky District of Leningrad, now Saint Petersburg.

107. "Ode to Leningrad" ("Oda a Leningrado") [OE], translated by Ilan Stavans. Leningrad: name of the city of Saint Petersburg between 1924 and 1991. Neruda vis-

ited the Soviet Union in 1955. *Netochka Nezvanova*: unfinished novel by Fyodor Dostoyevsky, the first completed section of which was published in 1849. Nevsky Avenue: main street in Leningrad.

108. "Ode to Life" ("Oda a la vida") [OE], translated by Ilan Stavans.

109. "Ode to the Liver" ("Oda al hígado") [NOE], translated by George D. Schade.

110. "Ode to the Lizard" ("Oda a la lagartija") [NOE], translated by Margaret Sayers Peden.

111. "Ode to Love" ("Oda al amor") [OE], translated by Ilan Stavans. Composed 10/19/53. The object of love is Matilde Urruria, with whom Neruda had an affair in Chile in 1945–46, and whom he reencountered in Mexico in 1949 and subsequently married. *The Captain's Verses* is also inspired by her.

112. "Ode to the Magnolia" ("Oda a la magnolia") [TLO], translated by Ilan Stavans.

113. "Ode to Maize" ("Oda al maíz") [TLO], translated by Margaret Sayers Peden. Composed in 1956.

114. "Ode to the Malvenida" ("Oda a la malvenida") [OE], translated by Ilan Stavans.

115. "Ode to Marine Light" ("Oda a la luz marina") [TLO], translated by Ilan Stavans. Composed in 1956.

116. "Ode to Marine Space" ("Oda al espacio marino") [NOE], translated by Ilan Stavans.

117. "Ode to a *Mirabilis Jalapa*: The Night-Blooming Four O'Clock" ("Oda a don Diego de la Noche") [NOE], translated by Margaret Sayers Peden.

118. "Ode to the Month of August" ("Oda al mes de agosto") [TLO], translated by Ilan Stavans.

119. "Ode to the Moon" ("Oda a la luna") [NOE], translated by Ilan Stavans.

120. "Ode to the Moon of the Sea" ("Oda a la luna del mar") [NOE], translated by Margaret Sayers Peden.

121. "Ode to a Morning in Brazil" ("Oda a una mañana del Brasil") [NR], translated by Ken Krabbenhoft. In 1955, Neruda gave readings in Brazil and Uruguay. He also spent time in Argentina. See also "Ode to Río de Janeiro."

122. "Ode to a Morning in Stockholm" ("Oda a una mañana en Stokholmo") [NR], translated by Ken Krabbenhoft. Composed twelve years before Neruda received the Nobel Prize in Literature. Here and elsewhere he refuses to Hispanicize the spelling he used to refer to the Swedish capital city.

123. "Ode to the Murmur" ("Oda al murmullo") [OE], translated by Ilan Stavans.

124. "Ode to the Myrrh Tree" ("Oda al aromo") [TLO], translated by Ilan Stavans. Composed in 1956.

125. "Ode About My Sorrows" ("Oda de mis pesares") [TLO], translated by Ken Krabbenhoft.

126. "Ode to the Names of Venezuela" ("Oda a los nombres de Venezuela") [NR], translated by Ilan Stavans. In 1959, Neruda spent five months traveling through Venezuela, where he was hailed as Latin America's most important poet. Years before, an editor friend, the Venezuelan writer Miguel Otero Silva, asked him to write a weekly ode for a column in the Venezuelan newspaper *El Nacional*. See the introduction to this volume.

127. "Ode to Night" ("Oda a la noche") [OE], translated by Ilan Stavans.

128. "Ode to a Nocturnal Washerwoman" ("Oda a una lavandera nocturna") [NOE], translated by Ilan Stavans. In *Passions and Impressions* (1978, English 1983), edited by Matilde Urrutia and Miguel Otero Silva, Neruda includes a speech of the same title delivered before a woman's congress held in Santiago's Caupolican Theater, in which he states: "I, a poet of our times, saw in that washerwoman not a ritual but a sorrowful reality, the lives of millions of women of our enormous, forsaken America. The same candles, at the same hour, winter or summer, might also be lighting the harsh duties of a mother in Ecuador, Bolivia, or Venezuela. From the Orinoco to Patagonia, from the sumptuous volcanoes that were nature's gift to us, to the gigantic thorny cactus of the Mexican plateau, the washerwoman, that nocturnal woman washing clothes while her children slept, was for me the dark heroine of our people. I never met her, and perhaps she never knew I watched her from the darkness of my home." Also in *Passions and Impressions*, the translator, Margaret Sayers Peden, includes an English rendition of the ode, which Neruda read at the end of the speech.

129. "Ode with Nostalgia for Chile" ("Oda con nostalgias de Chile") [TLO], translated by Ilan Stavans. Composed in 1956.

130. "Ode to Numbers" ("Oda a los números") [OE], translated by Margaret Sayers Peden.

131. "Ode to an Offended Picaro" ("Oda al pícaro ofendido") [TLO], translated by Margaret Sayers Peden. Composed in 1956.

132. "Ode to Oil" ("Oda al aceite") [NOE], translated by Margaret Sayers Peden.

133. "Ode to the Old Mapocho Station, in Santiago, Chile" ("Oda a la vieja Estación Mapocho, en Santiago de Chile") [TLO], translated by Ilan Stavans. Mapocho Station: built at the beginning of the twentieth century, this railway station in Santiago

connected the city with the nation's northern regions as well as with Valparaíso and Buenos Aires.

134. "Ode to the Onion" ("Oda a la cebolla") [OE], translated by Stephen Mitchell. Composed 12/31/53. Hernán Loyola suggests the possible inspiration of the cooking of the New Year's dinner.

135. "Ode to the Orange" ("Oda a la naranja") [TLO], translated by Ken Krabbenhoft. Composed in 1956.

136. "Ode to a Pair of Scissors" ("Oda a las tijeras") [TLO], translated by Ilan Stavans. Composed in 1956.

137. "Ode to a Pair of Socks" ("Oda a los calcetines") [NOE], translated by Mark Strand. Maura Mori is Maruja Vargas, wife of Neruda's friend the painter Camilo Mori.

138. "Ode to the Past" ("Oda al pasado") [OE], translated by Margaret Sayers Peden.

139. "Ode to Paul Robeson" ("Oda a Paul Robeson") [NOE], translated by Ilan Stavans. Paul Robeson (1898–1976): American black singer and actor known for his activism during the civil rights era.

140. "Ode to Peace and Quiet" ("Oda a la tranquilidad") [OE], translated by Ken Krabbenhoft.

141. "Ode to the People's Army" ("Oda solar al ejército del pueblo") [TR], translated by Richard Schaaf. This ode is part of the third installment of *Residencia en la tierra*, known as *Tercera Residencia*, written between 1934 and 1945. It belongs to section IV of *España en el corazón: Himnos a las glorias del pueblo en guerra* (1936–137). The original title of Schaaf's rendition is "Solar Ode to the People's Army."

142. "Ode to the Petrified Forest" ("Oda al bosque de las Petras") [TLO], translated by Ilan Stavans. Composed in 1956.

143. "Ode to the Pharmacy" ("Oda a la farmacia") [NOE], translated by Ilan Stavans.

144. "Ode to the Piano" ("Oda al piano") [NR], translated by George D. Schade.

145. "Ode to the Plate" ("Oda al plato") [NR], translated by Ilan Stavans.

146. "Ode to the Plum" ("Oda a la ciruela") [TLO], translated by Ilan Stavans. Composed in 1956.

147. "Ode to Poetry" ("Oda a la poesía") [OE], translated by George D. Schade. First published in *Letras del Ecuador* (Quito), September–October 1953.

148. "Ode to the Popular Poets" ("Oda a los poetas populares") [OE], translated

by Ilan Stavans. Written to be read at the Congreso Nacional de Poetas y Cantores Populares, held in Santiago April 15–18, 1954. In 1957, Neruda was made president of the Society of Chilean Writers.

149. "Ode to Poverty" ("Oda a la pobreza") [OE], translated by Ilan Stavans.

150. "Ode to the Present" ("Oda al presente") [NOE], translated by Ilan Stavans.

151. "Ode to Rain" ("Oda a la lluvia") [OE], translated by Ken Krabbenhoft.

152. "Ode to Ramón Gómez de la Serna" ("Oda a Ramón Gómez de la Serna") [NR], translated by Ilan Stavans. Ramón Gómez de la Serna (1888–1963): avant-garde Spanish writer and dramatist, he was a mentor to the Argentinian intellectual Jorge Luis Borges and the influential Spanish filmmaker Luis Buñuel.

153. "Ode to a Red Truck Loaded with Barrels" ("Oda a un camión colorado cargado con toneles") [TLO], translated by George D. Schade. Composed in 1956.

154. "Ode to Restlessness" ("Oda a la intranquilidad") [OE], translated by Ken Krabbenhoft.

155. "Ode to Río de Janeiro" ("Oda a Río de Janeiro") [OE], translated by Ilan Stavans. Neruda gave readings in Brazil in 1955. See also "Ode to a Morning in Brazil."

156. "Ode to the Road" ("Oda al camino") [TLO], translated by Ilan Stavans. Composed in 1956.

157. "Ode to the Rooster" ("Oda al gallo") [TLO], translated by Stephen Mitchell.

158. "Ode to the Rose" ("Oda a la rosa") [NOE], translated by Ilan Stavans.

159. "Ode to Sadness" ("Oda a la tristeza") [OE], translated by Ilan Stavans. Composed 12/29/52 between Recife and Río de Janeiro, "at an altitude of 3,500 meters," while flying in an airplane. In fact, the manuscript was crafted on the plane's menu. The content is an expression of the anxiety Neruda felt as his reencounter with Matilde Urrutia was about to take place and the possible sadness he would experience should an obstacle impede it. First published 1/18/53 in *Diario de Noticias* (Río de Janeiro).

160. "Ode to Salt" ("Oda a la sal") [TLO], translated by Philip Levine. Composed in 1956.

161. "Ode to Sand" ("Oda a la arena") [NOE], translated by George D. Schade.

162. "Ode to San Diego Street" ("Oda a la calle San Diego") [TLO], translated by Ilan Stavans. This ode celebrates a favorite central destination in Santiago, at one side of the Universidad de Chile, a street replete with bookstores, restaurants, and attractive stores.

163. "Ode to the Saw" ("Oda al serrucho") [TLO], translated by George D. Schade. Composed in 1956.

164. "Ode to the Sea" ("Oda al mar") [OE], translated by George D. Schade. Composed 11/28/1952 in Isla Negra, it was the first ode written by Neruda upon his return from Europe to Chile.

165. "Ode to the Sea Gull" ("Oda a la gaviota") [NOE], translated by Margaret Sayers Peden.

166. "Ode to Sea Rain" ("Oda a la lluvia marina") [NOE], translated by Ilan Stavans.

167. "Ode to the Seashore Cactus" ("Oda al cactus de la costa") [NOE], translated by George D. Schade.

168. "Ode to Seaweeds" ("Oda a las algas del océano") [TLO], translated by Margaret Sayers Peden. Composed in 1956.

169. "Ode to a Secret Love" ("Oda al secreto amor") [NOE], translated by Ken Krabbenhoft.

170. "Ode to September" ("Oda a septiembre") [NOE], translated by Ilan Stavans.

171. "Ode to a Ship in a Bottle" ("Oda al buque en la botella") [TLO], translated by Margaret Sayers Peden.

172. "Ode to the Simple Man" ("Oda al hombre sencillo") [OE], translated by Ilan Stavans. First published 10/16/52.

173. "Ode to Simplicity" ("Oda a la sencillez") [OE], translated by Ilan Stavans.

174. "Ode to a Single Sea" ("Oda a un solo mar") [NR], translated by Ilan Stavans.

175. "Ode to a Sleeping House" ("Oda a la casa dormida") [TLO], translated by Margaret Sayers Peden.

176. "Ode to the Smell of Firewood" ("Oda al olor de la leña") [NOE], translated by Mark Strand.

177. "Ode to Soap" ("Oda al jabón") [NOE], translated by George D. Schade.

178. "Ode to Solidarity" ("Oda a la solidaridad") [NOE], translated by Ilan Stavans.

179. "Ode to Solitude" ("Oda a la soledad") [OE], translated by Ken Krabbenhoft.

180. "Ode to the Southern Cross" ("Oda a la Cruz del Sur") [NOE], translated by Margaret Sayers Peden.

181. "Ode to the Spoon" ("Oda a la cuchara") [TLO], translated by Ken Krabbenhoft.

182. "Ode to Spring" ("Oda a la primavera") [OE], translated by Ken Krabbenhoft.

183. "Ode to the Spud" ("Oda a la papa") [NOE], translated by Ilan Stavans.

184. "Ode to a Stag's Birth" ("Oda al nacimiento de un ciervo") [TLO], translated by Ilan Stavans.

185. "Ode to a Stamp Album" ("Oda al libro de estampas") [TLO], translated by Margaret Sayers Peden.

186. "Ode to a Star" ("Oda a una estrella") [TLO], translated by Ilan Stavans.

187. "Ode to the Stars" ("Oda a las estrellas") [NOE], translated by Ilan Stavans.

188. "Ode to the Stone" ("Oda a la piedra") [TLO], translated by George D. Schade. Composed in 1956.

189. "Ode to the Storm" ("Oda a la tormenta") [OE], translated by Nathaniel Tarn.

190. "Ode to the Storms of Córdoba" ("Oda a las tormentas de Córdoba") [TLO], translated by Ilan Stavans. In 1957, Neruda was arrested in Buenos Aires and spent a day and a half in the National Penitentiary. The Chilean consul obtained his release. Totoral: department in Córdoba Province, Argentina. See also "Ode to a Dead Carob Tree."

191. "Ode to Summer" ("Oda al verano") [OE], translated by Margaret Sayers Peden.

192. "Ode to the Sun" ("Oda al sol") [NOE], translated by Ilan Stavans.

193. "Ode to the Table" ("Oda a la mesa") [NR], translated by Ken Krabbenhoft.

194. "Ode to Things" ("Oda a las cosas") [NR], translated by Ilan Stavans.

195. "Ode to the Third Day" ("Oda al tercer día") [OE], translated by Ilan Stavans.

196. "Ode to the Thread" ("Oda al hilo") [OE], translated by Margaret Sayers Peden.

197. "Ode to Time" ("Oda al tiempo") [OE], translated by Jane Hirshfield.

198. "Ode to the Time to Come" ("Oda al tiempo venidero") [TLO], translated by Ilan Stavans.

199. "Ode to the Tomato" ("Oda al tomate") [OE], translated by Stephen Mitchell.

200. "Ode to the Tooth of the Sperm Whale" ("Oda al diente de cachalote") [TLO], translated by Ilan Stavans. Composed in 1956.

201. "Ode to a Train in China" ("Oda a un tren en China") [NR], translated by Ilan Stavans. Qingdao, a.k.a. Tsingtao: city in the eastern Shandong Province, China.

202. "Ode to the Trains of the South" ("Oda a los trenes del Sur") [NR], translated by George D. Schade. In English, this ode has also appeared in a chapbook: *Ode to the Southern Trains*, translated by Don Olsen (Marshall, Minn.: Ox Head Press, 1983).

203. "Ode to Two Autumns" ("Oda al doble otoño") [TLO], translated by Margaret Sayers Peden. Composed in 1956.

204. "Ode to Typography" ("Oda a la tipografía") [NOE], translated by Carlos Lozano. There is a special edition: *Oda a la tipografía* (Santiago: Nascimento, 1956). And, in English in independent volumes, the ode has appeared in the following books: *Oda a la tipografía/Ode to Typography*, translated by Carlos Lozano (Toronto: Aliquando Press, 1977), *Ode to Typography*, translated by Enrique Sacerio-Garí (Torrance, Calif.: Labyrinth Editions, 1970), and *Oda a la tipografía/Ode to Typography*, translated by Stephen Kessler, with six aquatints by Joseph Goldyne (Berkeley: Peter Koch, 1998).

205. "Ode to Valparaíso" ("Oda a Valparaíso") [OE], translated by Margaret Sayers Peden. Valparaíso: Chilean seaport and the nation's third-largest city.

206. "Ode to a Village Movie Theater" ("Oda a un cine de pueblo") [TLO], translated by Margaret Sayers Peden. Composed in 1956.

207. "Ode to a Violin in California" ("Oda al violín de California") [NR], translated by Ken Krabbenhoft. The ode appears to refer to Neruda's experience during his first stay in Mexico (1940–43).

208. "Ode to the Voyager Albatross" ("Oda a un albatros viajero") [TLO], translated by Margaret Sayers Peden. Composed in 1956.

209. "Ode to Walt Whitman" ("Oda a Walt Whitman") [NOE], translated by Ilan Stavans. Walt Whitman (1819–92): populist American poet of the Civil War, author of *Leaves of Grass*. Neruda strongly identified with him, dreaming of becoming the Whitman of Latin America. In *Memoirs* (1973, English 1977), Neruda writes: "I was barely fifteen when I discovered Walt Whitman, my primary creditor. I stand here among you today still owing this marvelous debt that has helped me live. To negotiate this debt is to begin by making it public, by proclaiming myself the humble servant of the poet who measured the earth with long, slow strides, pausing everywhere to love and to examine, to learn, to teach, and to admire. That man, that lyric moralist, chose a difficult road; he was a torrential and didactic bard. These two qualities seem antithetical, more appropriate for a caudillo than for a writer. But what really matters is that the professor's chair, teaching, the apprenticeship of life held no fear for Walt Whitman, and he accepted the responsibility of teaching with candor and eloquence. Clearly, he feared neither morality nor immorality, nor did he attempt to define the boundaries between pure and impure poetry. He is the first absolute poet, and it was his intention not only to sing but to impart his vast vision of the relationship of men and of nations. In this sense, his obvious nationalism is part of an organic universality.

He considers himself indebted to happiness and sorrow, to advanced cultures and primitive societies."

210. "Ode to the Waltz over the Waves" ("Oda al vals sobre las olas") [TLO], translated by Ilan Stavans.

211. "Ode to a Watch at Night" ("Oda a un reloj en la noche") [OE], translated by W. S. Merwin. Composed in Europe, perhaps Italy, 7/19/52.

212. "Ode to the Waterfall" ("Oda a la cascada") [NOE], translated by Ilan Stavans. One of Neruda's three houses in Chile, La Chascona, was near a small waterfall.

213. "Ode to Watering" ("Oda para regar") [TLO], translated by Ilan Stavans.

214. "Ode to the Watermelon" ("Oda a la sandía") [NR], translated by Ilan Stavans.

215. "Ode to the Waters of the Port" ("Oda a las aguas de puerto") [NR], translated by Ilan Stavans.

216. "Ode to the Wave" ("Oda a la ola") [TLO], translated by Ilan Stavans. Composed in 1956.

217. "Ode to the Wheat of Indigenous People" ("Oda al trigo de los indios") [NOE], translated by Ilan Stavans. Alonso de Ercilla y Zúñiga (1533–94): Spanish nobleman, soldier, and poet, author of the epic poem *La Araucana*.

218. "Ode to Wine" ("Oda al vino") [OE], translated by Ilan Stavans.

219. "Ode to the Wings of September" ("Oda a las alas de septiembre") [NR], translated by Ilan Stavans.

220. "Ode to Winter" ("Oda al invierno") [OE], translated by Ilan Stavans.

221. "Ode in Winter to the Mapocho River" ("Oda de invierno al río Mapocho") [CG], translated by Jack Schmitt. First published in *Revista de las Españas* (July–August 1938). Mapocho River: flowing west from the Andes, it passed Chile's capital, Santiago. In Mapuche, the name means "water that penetrates the land." This ode is part of section VII of *Canto General*, subtitled "Canto General de Chile." Jack Schmitt's translation was published under the title "Winter Ode to the Mapocho River"; I have changed it here (with permission) for unifying purposes.

222. "Ode to a Woman Gardening" ("Oda a la jardinera") [TLO], translated by Margaret Sayers Peden. Composed in 1956.

223. "Ode to Wood" ("Oda a la Madera") [OE], translated by Margaret Sayers Peden. First published 6/21/53, in the Buenos Aires newspaper *La Prensa*.

224. "Ode to the Yellow Bird" ("Oda al pájaro sofré") [OE], translated by W. S. Merwin.

225. "Ode to Your Hands" ("Oda a tus manos") [NOE], translated by Ilan Stavans. This ode mimics Neruda's poem "Your Hands" in *The Captain's Verses*.

Epilogue: "The House of Odes" (Epílogo: "La casa de las odas") [NOE], translated by Ilan Stavans. Composed in 1955. Not an ode by title, Neruda used it as prologue to *Nuevas odas elementales*. As in "The Invisible Man," he employed italics to emphasize the uniqueness of the poem.

Acknowledgments

My wholehearted gratitude to Jonathan Galassi, whose support over the years has led me to extraordinary revelations. The Pablo Neruda Foundation endorsed the project of collecting and retranslating Neruda's odes and gave generous permission to reprint the Spanish originals. In Chile, I thank my friends Felipe Agüero, Fabia Fuenzalida, Cecilia García Huidobro, Rafael Gumucio, Iván Jaksić, Sergio Missana, Nicanor Parra, Rodrigo Rojas, Patricio Tapia, and Raúl Zurita. In the United States, my thanks go to Margaret Sayers Peden, Aileen El-Kadi, Martín Espada, John Felstiner, Matthew Glassman, Casey Kitrell, Stacy Klein, James Maraniss, María Negroni, Carol Purington, Susan Todd, Carlos Uriona, and Richard Wilbur. I also appreciate the support of Laszlo Erdelyi, Juan Carlos Marset, and Martín Felipe Yriart.

I thank Amado Alonso, David G. Anderson, Jaime Concha, Hernán Loyola, Enrico Marío Santí, and Alan Sicard for their scholarly work. After years of abandoning him, I reencountered Neruda as the result of a serendipitous invitation to read him in public. The invitation came from Jesse Lytle, to whom I owe more than is describable in words. My students in the Pablo Neruda course were an extraordinary source of ideas. Gracias to Jesse Coleman, Miranda Popkey, and Erika Seidman at Farrar, Straus and Giroux, as well as to my student assistants Derek García, Federico Sucre, and Irina Troconis, and, also at Amherst College, to Roberta Helinski and Elizabeth Eddy.

Likewise, I offer a sincere gracias to all the translators of Neruda's odes, of which this volume features eighteen. Translation is the journey a text undertakes from one language to another. Translators are the enablers, the conduits of this journey. I am grateful for permission to reprint their translations.

Index of Spanish Titles

Index of First Lines

Permissions Acknowledgments

Grateful acknowledgment is made for permission to reprint the following poems by Pablo Neruda:

"Ode to an Abandoned House," "Ode to an Aged Poet," "Ode to the Americas," "Ode to the Atom," "Ode to Bees," "Ode to Bicycles," "Ode to the Birds of Chile," "Ode to a Black Pantheress," "Ode to Conger Chowder," "Ode to a Couple," "Ode to the Cranium," "Ode to Criticism," "Ode to a Dead Carob Tree," "Ode to the Earth," "Odes for Everyone," "Ode to Firefoot," "Ode to the Gentle Bricklayer," "Ode to the Hummingbird," "Ode to a Laboratory Technician," "Ode to a Large Tuna in the Market," "Ode to the Lizard," "Ode to Maize," "Ode to a *Mirabilis Jalapa*: The Night-Blooming Four O'Clock," "Ode to the Moon of the Sea," "Ode to Numbers," "Ode to an Offended Picaro," "Ode to Oil," "Ode to the Past," "Ode to the Sea Gull," "Ode to Seaweeds," "Ode to a Ship in a Bottle," "Ode to a Sleeping House," "Ode to the Southern Cross," "Ode to a Stamp Album," "Ode to Summer," "Ode to the Thread," "Ode to Two Autumns," "Ode to Valparaíso," "Ode to a Village Movie Theater," "Ode to the Voyager Albatross," "Ode to a Woman Gardening," and "Ode to Wood," from *Selected Odes of Pablo Neruda*, selected and translated by Margaret Sayers Peden. Copyright © 1990 by The Regents of the University of California. Reprinted by permission of the University of California Press.

"Ode to a Beautiful Nude," "Ode to the Clothes," "Ode to the Storm," "Ode to a Watch at Night," and "Ode to the Yellow Bird," from *Selected Poems* by Pablo Neruda. Copyright © 1970 by Anthony Kerrigan, W. S. Merwin, Alastair Reid, and Nathaniel Tarn. Published by Jonathan Cape. Reprinted with permission.

"Ode to the Book I," "Ode to the Book II," "Ode to Enchanted Light," "Ode to a Hare-Boy," "Ode to a Pair of Socks," "Ode to Salt," "Ode to the Smell of Firewood," and "Ode to Time," from *The Poetry of Pablo Neruda* by Pablo Neruda, edited by Ilan Stavans, translated by several translators. Copyright © 2003 by Pablo Neruda and Fundación Pablo Neruda. Introduction and notes copyright © 2003 Pablo Neruda. Reprinted by permission of Farrar, Straus and Giroux, LLC.

"Ode to a Box of Tea," "Ode to Bread," "Ode to the Cat," "Ode to the Chair," "Ode to My Grief," "Ode to the Orange," "Ode to Peace and Quiet," "Ode to Restlessness," "Ode to the Spoon," "Ode to the Table," and "Ode to a Violin in California," from *Odes to Common Things* by Pablo Neruda, translated by Ken Krabbenhoft, selected and illustrated by Ferris Cook. Odes (Spanish) copyright © 1994 by Pablo Neruda and Fundación Pablo Neruda. Odes (English translation) copyright © 1994 by Ken Krabbenhoft. Illustrations and compilation copyright © 1994 by Ferris Cook. Reprinted by permission of Bullfinch. All rights reserved.

"Ode and Burgeonings," from *The Captain's Verses* by Pablo Neruda, translated by Donald D. Walsh. Copyright © 1972 by Pablo Neruda and Donald D. Walsh. Reprinted by permission of New Directions Publishing Corp.

"Ode to César Vallejo," "Ode to the Elephant," "Ode to the Eye," and "Ode to Walt Whitman," from *I Explain a Few Things: Selected Poems* by Pablo Neruda, translated and edited by Ilan Stavans. Copyright © 2007 by Pablo Neruda and Fundación Pablo Neruda. Reprinted by permission of Farrar, Straus and Giroux, LLC.

"Ode to a Chestnut on the Ground," "Ode to the Lemon," "Ode to the Onion," "Ode to the Rooster," and "Ode to the Tomato," from *Full Woman, Fleshy Apple, Hot Moon: Selected Poetry of Pablo Neruda*, translated by Stephen Mitchell. Translation copyright © 1997 by Stephen Mitchell. Reprinted by permission of HarperCollins Publishers.

"Ode to Clouds," "Ode to Energy," "Ode to Envy," "Ode to Fire," "Ode to a Morning in Brazil," "Ode to a Morning in Stockholm," "Ode to Rain," "Ode to a Secret Love," "Ode to Solitude," and "Ode to Spring," from *Odes to Opposites* by Pablo Neruda, translated by Ken Krabbenhoft, selected and illustrated by Ferris Cook. Odes (Spanish) copyright © 1995 by Pablo Neruda and Fundación Pablo Neruda. Odes (English translation) copyright © 1995 by Ken Krabbenhoft. Illustrations and compilation copyright © 1995 by Ferris Cook. Reprinted by permission of Bullfinch. All rights reserved.

"Ode to a Day of Victories: Seventh of November" (originally published as "7th of November: Ode to a Day of Victories") and "Ode with a Lament," from *Residence on Earth* by Pablo Neruda, translated by Donald D. Walsh. Copyright © 1973 by Pablo Neruda and Donald D. Walsh. Reprinted by permission of New Directions Publishing Corp.

"Ode to the Dog," "Ode to the Fallen Bell," "Ode to the Liver," "Ode to the Piano," "Ode to Poetry," "Ode to a Red Truck Loaded with Barrels," "Ode to Sand," "Ode to the Saw," "Ode to the Sea," "Ode to the Seashore Cactus," "Ode to Soap," "Ode to the Stone," and "Ode to Trains of the South," from *Fifty Odes* by Pablo Neruda, translated by George D. Schade. Copyright © 1996 by Host Publications, Inc.

"Ode to Federico García Lorca," from *Residence on Earth* by Pablo Neruda, translated by Angel Flores. Copyright © 1946 by Pablo Neruda and Angel Flores. Reprinted by permission of New Directions Publishing Corp.

"Ode to Laziness," translated by William Carlos Williams, from *By Word of Mouth: Poems from the Spanish, 1916–1959*, compiled and edited by Jonathan Cohen. Copyright © 2011 by Fundación Pablo Neruda, translation copyright © 1954 by William Carlos Williams. Reprinted by permission of New Directions Publishing Corp.

"Ode to the People's Army" (originally published as "Solar Ode to the People's Army"), from *Spain in the Heart: Hymn to the Glories of the People at War (1936–1937)*, translated by Richard Schaaf, Azul Editions, 2006.

"Ode to Typography," translated by Carlos Lozano, *Chicago Review*, vol. 17, no. 1 (1964): 10–20.

"Ode in Winter to the Mapocho River" (originally published as "Winter Ode to the Mapocho River"), from *Canto General* by Pablo Neruda, translated by Jack Schmitt. Copyright © Fundación Pablo Neruda. Copyright © 1991 by The Regents of the University of California. Reprinted by permission of the University of California Press.

A NOTE ABOUT THE AUTHOR

PABLO NERUDA (1904–1973) was born in Parral, in central Chile. His father was a railway worker and his mother, who died when Neruda was a child, was a schoolteacher. He was educated at the Instituto Pedagógico in Santiago and at the University of Chile. Neruda is among the most widely translated poets in the world. His celebrated collections include *Twenty Love Poems and a Song of Despair*, *Residence on Earth*, *Canto General*, *The Captain's Verses*, *One Hundred Love Sonnets*, and *Fully Empowered*. He is also the author of two nonfiction works, *Memoirs* and *Passions and Impressions*. Neruda was the recipient of many honors during his lifetime, including the World Peace Prize in 1950, which he shared with Paul Robeson and Pablo Picasso, as well as the Nobel Prize in Literature in 1971. He died in 1973, at sixty-nine, in Santiago.

A NOTE ABOUT THE EDITOR

ILAN STAVANS is the Lewis-Sebring Professor in Latin American and Latino Culture at Amherst College. He is the award-winning author of numerous books, including *The Hispanic Condition* (1995), *On Borrowed Words* (2001), and *Love and Language* (2005), and the editor of *The Poetry of Pablo Neruda* (2003). The translator of Juan Rulfo, he is also the general editor of *The Norton Anthology of Latino Literature* (2011). His work, translated into a dozen languages, has been adapted for theater and film. He is the recipient of Chile's Presidential Medal.